PRAIS

"Le Brun des Marettes's *Lit*… of information about customs, architecture, clothing, piety, liturgy, social life in early modern Europe. This modern edition was prepared with loving attention to detail and good taste. It exudes the fascination of solemn liturgy. It is an antidote for ignorance and neglect, a treasure trove of information and competent commentary for deepening our understanding of the West's liturgical tradition."
— **P. ALKUIN SCHACHENMAYR**, O.Cist., Professor of Church History, Benedict XVI Philosophical-Theological University, Heilgenkreuz

"It is high time to re-evaluate the complex phenomenon of Neo-Gallicanism and to study its representatives with genuine interest. But the bloom of liturgical studies in the last two centuries owes so much to Solesmes that it is hard to rehabilitate that earlier wave of liturgical enthusiasm profoundly denounced by Dom Guéranger. True, Neo-Gallican compilers relentlessly subverted the textual heritage of the Roman service books. But they also had a passion for ceremonial: the non-verbal aspects of worship such as church furnishing, vestments, musical performance, processions, the topography and choreography of sacred spaces. Le Brun des Marettes and his contemporaries were an early modern sort of ethnologists, combining thorough philology with fieldwork. Their liturgical travelogues open up an unexpected fountain of information: a world of cathedrals, parishes, and monasteries, throbbing with life in ancien régime France. If we let them take us by the hand, we will discover a bewildering mixture of medieval survival, baroque pomposity, and enlightened antiquarianism. Read with due criticism, they shed light on undocumented aspects of ancient rituals and allow us to understand a forgotten period and its intellectual protagonists in their own right."
— **MIKLÓS ISTVÁN FÖLDVÁRY**, Head of the Research Group of Liturgical History, ELTE Eötvös Loránd University, Budapest

"Liturgical life after Trent has all too often been portrayed as one of lifeless submission to centralised Roman rubricism. Not so — at least in France — as this volume makes perfectly clear. Le Brun immerses us in the colourful landscape of pre-Revolution Catholic worship which, in spite of many differences in local detail, displays a living liturgical and cultural integrity that is utterly enviable in our own highly compartmentalised and fragmented set of secular subcultures. The riches offered in this careful translation, eruditely edited, are a testament to the power and vitality of traditional Catholic worship in a particular and quite different period of history from our own. So too, the opinions of its author underline the possibility of its critical appraisal, then and now. *Liturgical Travels Through France* will be instructive for students of many disciplines, just as it will be for those today who seek to impose liturgical uniformity on Western liturgical tradition even though its history, as related herein, bears witness to the wisdom and value of its rich historical diversity."

—**DOM ALCUIN REID**, OSB, author, *The Organic Development of the Liturgy*

"Originally intended as a kind of ecclesiastical *Michelin Guide*, Le Brun's travelogue through the churches of France now serves as a liturgical time machine. While one may not always find oneself in sympathy with the author's judgments, the spirited, imaginary debates a reader can have with Le Brun make for delightful company along this literary pilgrimage."

—**URBAN HANNON**, author of *Thomistic Mystagogy*

"In our age of information saturation, it is astonishing how little access the English speaker has to data about the worship practices of our Catholic ancestors. Filling this lacuna is a fresh translation of Le Brun's eighteenth-century classic. Readers will be surprised by how much authentic liturgical diversity existed during a time of alleged Tridentine ossification."

—**MICHAEL P. FOLEY**, Baylor University, Waco, Texas

LITURGICAL TRAVELS THROUGH FRANCE

OS JUSTI STUDIES
in
LITURGICAL HISTORY AND REFORM
General Editor
MATTHEW HAZELL

1
LE BRUN DES MARETTES
Liturgical Travels Through France

2
GUÉRANGER
Liturgical Institutions

LITURGICAL TRAVELS THROUGH FRANCE

OR

Researches made in various Cities of the Realm

By the Sieur DE MOLÉON,
Containing many Particularities touching
the Rites and Uses of the Churches:
With Discoveries in ecclesiastical and pagan Antiquity
by
JEAN-BAPTISTE LE BRUN DES MARETTES

Edited and translated by
GERHARD EGER
and
ZACHARY THOMAS

with a foreword by
FR. CLAUDE BARTHE

OS JUSTI PRESS

Copyright © 2025 Gerhard Eger and Zachary Thomas
All rights reserved.

No part of this book may be reproduced, stored in a retrieval system, or transmitted in any form, or by any means, electronic, mechanical, photocopying, or otherwise, without the prior written permission of the publisher, except by a reviewer, who may quote brief passages in a review.

Os Justi Press
P.O. Box 21814
Lincoln, NE 68542
www.osjustipress.com
Send inquiries to
info@osjustipress.com

ISBN 978-1-965303-27-6 (paperback)
ISBN 978-1-965303-28-3 (hardcover)
ISBN 978-1-965303-29-0 (ebook)

Book design by Michael Schrauzer
Cover: Charles Wild,
Choir of the Cathedral of Amiens (1823);
etching, aquatint, hand-colored.
Courtesy of The British Museum;
used with permission.

To Marcel Pérès,
whose love for ecclesiastical chant
has inspired a generation

CONTENTS

Table of Plates. XIII
Foreword XV
Introduction. XXXV
Translators' Preface LIV

LITURGICAL TRAVELS THROUGH FRANCE 1
Approbations 2
Author's Preface. 3
Vienne 7
    Church of Saint-Sévère · 7; Church of Saint-André-le-Bas · 8; The Table ronde · 8; Notre-Dame-de-la-Vie · 8; Cloisters of Saint-Maurice · 8; The Salle des Clementines · 30; Church of St-Pierre of Vienne · 30
Lyon 32
    The Pyramide at the Porte d'Avignon · 32; Church of Saint-Just of Lyon · 54; Church of Saint-Irenée of Lyon · 54; Aqueducts, the Amphitheater, and the Arena · 54; Abbey of Saint-Pierre of Lyon · 55; Collegiate Church of Saint-Paul · 55; Church of Saint-Laurent and Asylum of Lyon · 57
Clermont 57
Bordeaux 59
Poitiers 59
Nantes. 60
Angers 60
    The Office on Solemn Days · 64; Maundy Thursday · 71; Good Friday · 73; Holy Saturday · 73; Easter · 74; St. Mark's Day · 75; Rogation Processions · 75; Abbey of Saint-Nicolas · 77; Abbey of Le Ronceray · 77; Collegiate Church of Saint-Julien · 79; Collegiate Church of Saint-Maurille · 80; Collegiate Church of Saint-Pierre · 81
Doué 82
    The Amphitheater of Doué · 82; The Arena · 82
Fontevraud 83
Marmoutier. 86
Tours 87
    Cathedral of Saint-Gatien · 87; Saint-Martin of Tours · 90

SAINT-CYRAN. 102

BOURGES 104
    Cathedral of Saint-Étienne

NEVERS. 107
    Cathedral of Saint-Cyr

LIMOGES 108

MÂCON 108
    Cathedral of Saint-Vincent

CLUNY 109
    Chapel of Saint-Pierre-le-Vieux·111; The Lavatory Stone·111

CHALON-SUR-SAÔNE 113
    The Cathedral

BESANÇON 113

DIJON. 114
    Church of Saint-Étienne·114; Church of Saint-Michel·114; The Carthusians·115; Church of Saint-Seine·115

AUXERRE 115
    Cathedral of Saint-Étienne

SENS 118
    Cathedral of Saint-Étienne

REIMS 128
    Cathedral of Notre-Dame

LAON. 129

MEAUX 132

SAINT-MAUR-DES-FOSSÉS. 132

ÉTAMPES 132

ORLÉANS 133
    Cathedral of Sainte-Croix·133; Extract of Principal Items Contained in a Three-Hundred-Year-Old Manuscript Breviary of Orléans·142; Extract of Principal Items in the Ritual of Orléans of 1581·146; Royal and Collegiate Church of Saint-Aignan·149; Saint-Euverte·155; Saint-Pierre-en-Pont, Saint-Pierre-Puellier, Saint-Pierre-Lentin, and Saint-Pierre-en-Sentelée·156

JARGEAU 158

ABBEY OF SAINT-MESMIN 160

CLÉRY 160

BLOIS. 161
HUISSEAU. 161
LE MANS 161
    Cathedral of Saint-Julien
LA TRAPPE 164
CHARTRES 165
    Notre-Dame of Chartres
GALLARDON 170
VAUX-DE-CERNAY. 170
PORT-ROYAL 171
PARIS. 178
    Notre-Dame of Paris · 178; *Saint-Germain-des-Prés* · 186; *Abbey of Saint-Victor* · 187; *The Carmelites of the Place Maubert* · 187; *Saint-Étienne-du-Mont* · 188; *Sainte-Geneviève* · 188; *Val-de-Grâce* · 188; *The Sorbonne* · 188; *Collège de Cluny* · 188; *Hôtel de Cluny* · 189; *Church of the Sépulcre* · 189; *Hôpital de la Salpêtrière* · 189; *The Palace and the Sainte-Chapelle* · 190

ABBEY OF SAINT-DENIS 190
ABBEY OF MAUBUISSON 191
CHURCH OF THE DEUX-AMANTS 191
ROUEN 192
    Clameur de haro · 192; *Cathedral of Notre-Dame* · 193; *Public Penance Observed in Rouen* · 232; *Extract from a memorandum by M. François de la Fosse, Grand Penitentiary of the church of Rouen, 1673* · 232; *Ash Wednesday Ceremony for the Imposition of Public Penance* · 233; *The Public Reconciliation Ceremony on Absolution Thursday* · 234; *Processions in Rouen* · 235; *Procession for the Release of a Prisoner on the Day of Our Lord's Ascension* · 241; *Procession on the Day of Corpus Christi* · 242; *Exposition of the Blessed Sacrament for the King* · 243; *General Procession after Vespers on Assumption Day, 15 August* · 244; *Sermons in the Cathedral* · 245; *Archiepiscopal Sermons* · 246; *Reception of the Archbishop of Rouen, Primate of Normandy, Upon His First Entrance or Taking Possession* · 246; *Dignitaries of the Chapter of Rouen* · 247; *Ceremonies Observed During the Offices* · 248; *High Mass* · 249; *General Chapter of the Cathedral* · 255; *Funerals, Obits, and the Thirty Canonesses of the Church of Rouen* · 257; *Archbishops of Rouen and Illustrious Persons* · 258; *The Cathedral Sacristy, Fountain, and Hebdomadary's Chamber* · 259; *The Belfry, Great Portal, Towers, Parvis, and Fountain of Rouen Cathedral* · 261; *Exterior of*

Rouen Cathedral · 262; Hôtel-Dieu of Rouen · 265; Saint-Ouen · 265; Saint-Amand · 265; Saint-Lô · 266; Notre-Dame-de-la-Ronde · 276; Saint-Georges · 277; The Filles-Dieu · 277; Saint-Vincent · 278; Saint-André · 278; Saint-Étienne-des-Tonneliers · 278; Saint-Candé-le-Vieux · 279; The Vieille Tour where the Prisoner Lifts the Feretory · 280; Saint-Maclou · 280; Saint-Godard · 281; Saint-Laurent · 282; Saint-Gervais · 282; Saint-Sauveur · 282; Saint-Herbland · 282; The Prône and Administration of Baptism · 282; Marriage and Agapes in the Churches of Rouen · 283; Some Practices of the Church of Rouen · 285; Extreme Unction. Bread and Silver Distributed at Funerals · 285

PLATES. 287

APPENDIX 1: A Short Presentation of the Cathedral Chapters of the Ancien Régime by François Hou 343

APPENDIX 2: A Brief History of Christian Altars and Sanctuaries by Shawn Tribe 353

BIBLIOGRAPHY 364

INDICES 381
SUBJECTS AND PROPER NAMES 381
LITURGICAL BOOKS 392
CATHEDRALS, CHURCHES, AND MONASTERIES 394

TABLE OF PLATES

PLATE 1: Depiction of the choir of Notre-Dame of Paris in the High Middle Ages
PLATE 2: Frontispiece of Pierre Le Brun's *Explication littérale, historique et dogmatique des prières et cérémonies de la Messe* (1718)
PLATE 3: The Tour de Pilate
PLATE 4: Marble altars with recessed tables
PLATE 5: The Pyramide near the Porte d'Avignon and the altar in the apse of St-Jean of Lyon
PLATE 6: View of the cathedral of St-Jean of Lyon
PLATE 7: The astronomical clock of St-Jean of Lyon
PLATE 8: Part of the rood screen of the cathedral of Lyon
PLATE 9: The *râtelier* of St-Jean of Lyon
PLATE 10: Canon of Lyon in summer habit and the amphitheater of Lyon
PLATE 11: Types of surplices
PLATE 12: Canon of Lyon in winter habit
PLATE 13: Pontifical Mass in St-Jean of Lyon
PLATE 14: View of the apse during the Creed at a pontifical Mass in St-Jean of Lyon
PLATE 15: View of the main entrance of St-Maurice of Angers
PLATE 16: Choir and altar of the cathedral of Angers before 1699
PLATE 17: View of the altar of the cathedral of Angers before 1699
PLATE 18: A sailor's cape and hood, a tonsured cleric with an almuce, a folded chasuble, and maniples
PLATE 19: View of Notre-Dame of Le Ronceray
PLATE 20: An ash urn and a choir chandelier
PLATE 21: The amphitheater of Doué and a choir chandelier
PLATE 22: The arena of Doué
PLATE 23: View of the abbey of Marmoutier
PLATE 24: Hat of the country women of the Mâconnais and a lavatory stone for the dead
PLATE 25: Exterior view of the chevet of the abbey of Cluny
PLATE 26: A breviary miniature depicting a clerical choir
PLATE 27: The rood screen of the cathedral of Reims
PLATE 28: St. Gregory's Mass, as depicted in the 1519 missal of Orléans
PLATE 29: The main altars of the cathedrals of Paris and Arras in the Middle Ages
PLATE 30: Forms of medieval suspended pyxes
PLATE 31: An offertory procession in the cathedral of Auxerre
PLATE 32: View of the Cistercian abbey of St-Mesmin

PLATE 33: The cathedral of St-Julien of Le Mans
PLATE 34: The choir of the abbey of La Trappe
PLATE 35: A bed of ashes and the choir faldstool of the bishop of Chartres
PLATE 36: Three views of the abbey of Port-Royal-des-Champs
PLATE 37: Nun with a maniple and a canon regular of Deux-Amants
PLATE 38: Carthusian nun in ceremonial habit
PLATE 39: The high altar of Notre-Dame of Paris, 1703
PLATE 40: The elevation during Mass at Notre-Dame of Paris
PLATE 41: Canon of the Congregation of France in summer habit
PLATE 42: Canon of the Congregation of France in winter habit
PLATE 43: *The Mass of Canon Antoine de La Porte*, Jean-France de Jouvenet
PLATE 44: View of the abbey of St-Germain-des-Prés
PLATE 45: The summer habit of the canons of St-Victor
PLATE 46: Order of procession with the relics of St. Genevieve
PLATE 47: *Monjoies* on the road between Paris and St-Denis
PLATE 48: Depiction of the choir of the abbey of St-Denis in the High Middle Ages
PLATE 49: *Aumussons* and almuces
PLATE 50: Dominicans performing the *prostratio super formas*
PLATE 51: The procession of the gargoyles in Rouen
PLATE 52: The offertory procession, *Chronique de Normandie*
PLATE 53: View of the entrance of the Benedictine abbey of St-Amand
PLATE 54: The former habit of the canons regular of St-Lô
PLATE 55: A Fille-Dieu of Rouen

FOREWORD

ONE cannot be too grateful to the translators of this edition of the *Voyages liturgiques de France* (Paris, 1718).[1] They rightly believe that this publication will be a discovery for the English-speaking scholarly public and hope that it will stimulate research in the Anglophone world concerning the liturgical and ecclesiastical culture of the seventeenth and eighteenth centuries, which have been garnering increasing scholarly interest.

Jean-Baptiste Le Brun des Marettes, also known as Sieur de Moléon, was born in Rouen in 1651 and died in Orléans in 1731.[2] Though his life merits elaboration in a full-length biography, such has yet to be written, and so we must content ourselves with a brief sketch drawn from early-modern sources.[3] His father, Bonaventure Le Brun, was a printer and bookseller in Rouen; today he might be called a publisher. Jean-Baptiste also plied this trade, and like his father lived in close association with the abbey of Port-Royal, the great Jansenist stronghold. In fact he came from a militant Jansenist family. His father was sentenced to the galleys for publishing books favorable to the controversial abbey. The notice devoted to Jean-Baptiste in the Jansenist weekly *Nouvelles ecclésiastiques* on 17 April 1731 indicates that he was "a student of Port-Royal."[4] In all probability he was supported, along with his mother and brother Bonaventure (later a printer in Rouen like his father), by a network of Jansenist patrons who enabled him to receive an excellent education at the Petites Écoles de Port-Royal, which turned out such famous pupils as Jean Racine. These Petites Écoles continued to operate discreetly even after the closing of the Granges de Port-Royal in 1660, thanks to these powerful patrons. The notes of affection in Jean-Baptiste's descriptions of important Jansenist sites in the *Liturgical Travels Through France* are very telling.[5]

---

[1] The complete original title is *Voyages Liturgiques ou Recherches faites en diverses villes du royaume par le Sieur de Moléon, contenant plusieurs particularitez touchant les rits & les usages des Églises: avec des découvertes sur l'antiquité ecclésiastique & payenne* ("Liturgical travels through France, or Researches made in various cities of the realm, by the Sieur de Moléon, containing many particularities touching the rites and usages of the churches: with discoveries in ecclesiastical and pagan antiquity").

[2] Moléon may be the name of a family property. Les Marettes is a *lieu-dit* north of Rouen.

[3] For the most recent biographical sketch, see Le Brun des Marettes, *Lettres inédites de Lebrun Desmarettes à Baluze*, ed. Joseph Nouaillac (Crauffon, 1905). Older sources include the Jansenist publication of Pierre Guilbert, *Mémoires historiques et chronologiques sur l'Abbaye de Port-Royal des Champs. Depuis de la paix de l'Église en 1668, jusqu'à la mort des dernières Religieuses et Amis de ce Monastère* (Utrecht, 1756), 7:502–6; and the work of Melchior Du Lac, *La liturgie Romaine et les liturgies françaises* (Le Mans, 1849).

[4] "D'Orléans, le 4 avril," *Nouvelles ecclésiastiques*, 17 April 1731, 79.

[5] On the abbey of St-Cyran-en-Brenne, whose commendatory abbot was Jean Duvergier de Hauranne, a friend of Cornelius Jansen, Le Brun remarks: "These monks of St. Benedict belong to no congregation or reform; rather, one can truly say that they are the most

An excellent Latin scholar, his publications are marked by an expertise in Patristics and a keen interest in liturgy. His scholarly work was inaugurated with his revised edition of the ordinal of John of Avranches (Rouen, 1679) — the base text for the liturgical use of his native diocese — originally published in 1642 by three canons of Rouen, which he enriched with copious notes. The book was issued anonymously in a gesture of humility common to Jansenist writers of the time.[6] Its rich annotations were des Marettes's first foray into the realm of comparative liturgy and its success within his literary circles likely inspired the more wide-ranging work of the *Travels*.

In addition, he published a Life of St. Paulinus and an edition of his selected works (Paris, 1685), a Life of St. Prosper as an introduction to the complete works of St. Prosper of Aquitaine which he edited with Luc-Urbain Mangeant (1711) and, together with Nicolas Letourneux, a fellow native of Rouen and official confessor of Port-Royal, a *Concordia librorum Regum et Paralipomenon* (1682). He also took part in the drafting and publication of the new breviaries of Orléans and Nevers, as discussed below. After his death were edited his translation of the works of Lactantius (1748) and his correspondence with the learned patrologist, historian, and canonist, Étienne Baluze (1827, repr. 1905), who belonged to the same liturgical "party."

The *Nouvelles ecclésiastiques* indicate that he was an acolyte, in other words a cleric in minor orders, and Le Brun speaks of performing liturgical functions in Paris.[7] He may have received this minor order in Rouen or Orléans, since he was close to Jacques-Nicolas Colbert (1655–1707), archbishop of Rouen, son of the state minister Jean-Baptiste Colbert, and to Cardinal Pierre-Armand du Cambout de Coislin (1636–1706), bishop of Orléans, who was manifestly inclined to Jansenism, but beloved by the king because of his remarkable piety and life of penance.

After the death of his protector, Cardinal de Coislin, Le Brun des Marettes's association with the Jansenists led to his imprisonment from 1707 to 1712, his brother Bonaventure having already been placed under arrest previously. He was released after signing the Formulary rejecting Jansenist ideas, but retracted his statement in 1717, when pressure on the Jansenists was relaxed in the early days of the regency of Philip II, duke of Orléans. At the time he alleged that he had signed under duress after being deprived of water for several days during a heatwave. He thus became a sort of martyr for the cause. His release enabled him finally to publish the *Travels*. While

---

reformed, for they follow the Rule of St. Benedict to the letter, nay, to the last iota"; and about the erstwhile abbey of Port-Royal: the church's "simplicity and cleanliness inspire respect and devotion"; "the woodwork of the sanctuary and parquet floor is very clean"; "the nuns' habits are coarse"; "the abbey receives girls without a dowry"; etc.
[6] See Charles Magnin, review of *Drames liturgiques du moyen âge*, by M. E. de Coussemaker, article 2, *Journal des savants* (September 1860): 530n3.
[7] See p. 180.

leading a scholarly life, he earned a living by running a boarding school in Orléans for about fifteen boys. He died in this city on 19 March 1731, during a period of renewed anti-Jansenist rigor. The *Nouvelles ecclésiastiques* tell us that, to avoid the refusal of the last rites by the parish priest, "he dragged himself to church on Palm Sunday and received holy communion there the day before his death."[8]

FROM TRENT TO THE FRENCH REVOLUTION: A ROMAN LITURGY IN THE FRENCH STYLE

The French liturgy described in Le Brun des Marettes's *Liturgical Travels Through France*, a Roman liturgy with many particular local expressions, had developed over the course of the two centuries between the twin blows of the Protestant Reformation, with its ensuing period of wars and destruction ended by the Edict of Nantes promulgated by Henry IV in 1598, and the French Revolution, whose program of religious destruction was inaugurated by the promulgation of the Civil Constitution of the Clergy in 1790.[9]

During the early modern period, the Roman liturgy "in the French style" no longer enjoyed the serene atmosphere of the Middle Ages, when everything was taken for granted. It was by force of circumstance a Counter-Reformation liturgy. It had to be explained, described, and defended. In France in particular, the bishops set in motion a program of reconstruction that aimed to preserve local traditions while conforming more or less to the Tridentine liturgical books and legislation, and the result was a loss of some of its peculiar features. Faced with the imperative to Romanize their customs according to the new Roman editions,[10] bishops had to choose between embracing the ultramontane books *tout court*, or receiving them with adaptations, or composing new books that conserved French usages but introduced modifications in a spirit of enlightened criticism.

The disciplinary decree of the Council of Trent, *De observandis et evitandis in celebratione missae*, reveals the abuses that had crept into the celebration through ignorance and poor training, or due to the upheavals caused by the Protestant Reformation. The dogmatic decrees of the twenty-second session of the council (17 September 1562) and the decree "On the Catalogue

---

[8] Pierre Guilbert, *Mémoires historiques et chronologiques sur l'abbaye de Port-Royal des Champs* (Utrecht, 1756), 7:505. This edifying episode of his last communion is plausible, but 18 March fell on the second Sunday of Lent in 1731.

[9] For brief introductions in English, see James F. White, *Roman Catholic Worship: Trent to Today* (Liturgical Press, 2003), 31–32, 39–40 and Ellen F. Weaver, "The Neo-Gallican Liturgies Revisited," *Studia liturgica* 16, no. 3–4 (1986): 54–72.

[10] It would be more accurate to speak of "further Romanization," since the Tridentine reforms were preceded by a wide diffusion of the curial rite brought about especially by the Franciscans in the thirteenth century, and before that by the reforms of the Carolingian era. The nineteenth-century wave of ultramontanism, and the campaigns waged against the neo-Gallican rites by Dom Prosper Guéranger's *Institutions liturgiques*, published between 1840 and 1851, led to the definitive victory of the Roman books.

of Books, the Catechism, the Breviary, and the Missal" of the twenty-fifth session form the touchstone for the Council of Trent's codification of the liturgy. The council fathers entrusted the pope with the task of publishing the most perfect possible edition of the Roman liturgical books, which by this point in history meant the ones used by the Roman Curia. It was on the basis of these books that the council solemnly reaffirmed and defined the sacrificial value of the Mass, the legitimacy of the rites used to celebrate it, and the dignity of the Roman Canon. In other words, they were an indispensable source for the conciliar decrees, and were republished by order of that council in order to carry forward the reform of doctrine and morals envisioned by the council fathers. They were thus to acquire greater dignity, authority, and extension in the Latin Church than ever before.[11]

The council was followed by the promulgation of six principal liturgical books:

>   1568: The *Roman Breviary* (St. Pius V)
>   1570: The *Roman Missal* (St. Pius V)
>   1584: The *Roman Martyrology* (Gregory XIII[12])
>   1595: The *Roman Pontifical* (Clement VIII)
>   1600: The *Ceremonial of Bishops* (Clement VIII)
>   1614: The *Roman Ritual* (Paul V)

The bulls which promulgated the breviary (*Quod a nobis*) and missal (*Quo primum*) show clearly that the pope did not wish to compose new liturgical books, but rather to unify the form of celebration of the Latin rite based on the books then in use in Rome. Concretely that meant proposing to or imposing on the whole Latin church (at least in the case of the breviary and missal) the books of the papal chapel, edited according to the best manuscripts and printed sources. Those secular and religious churches which could boast a liturgical use more than two hundred years old were exempt from the obligation to adopt the new books.

Even though most existing diocesan books could claim more than two hundred years of antiquity, and so take advantage of the exemption, in the decades that followed 1568 a significant part of the Latin world, already quite Romanized, adopted the Roman books. In certain places, in the face of stiff resistance from cathedral chapters, attempts were made to preserve local uses, especially pontifical rites, by harmonizing them with Roman custom.[13]

The publication of Roman books as exemplary models resulted in a

---

[11] On the Tridentine reforms, see Uwe Michael Lang, *The Roman Mass: From Early Christian Origins to Tridentine Reform* (Cambridge University Press, 2022), 343–90, and Michael Fiedrowicz, *The Traditional Mass: History, Form, and Theology of the Classical Roman Rite* (Angelico Press, 2020), 24–37.

[12] Who also reformed the kalendar, replacing the Julian with the Gregorian.

[13] For a general study of the continuity of diocesan uses after Trent, see Miklós István Földváry, *USUARIUM: A Guide to the Study of Latin Liturgical Uses in the Middle Ages and the Early Modern Period* (Budapest, 2023; privately published study).

theological consolidation,[14] but also led to the abandonment of numerous customs and texts proper to the various churches and religious orders. This effacement of local particularities must not be exaggerated, however. The loss was much less than that which occurred during the ultramontanist phase of the late nineteenth and early twentieth century.[15] Thus, it took time for the Roman *Ceremonial of Bishops* to replace cathedral customaries and ceremonies, and the nature of the early modern world ensured the survival of innumerable uses which cathedral and collegiate chapters, parish churches, and religious communities passed on through living memory. Particularly noteworthy were the processions (see PLATES 46, 51), which played a significant role in the weekly and annual liturgy all over Europe right up to the secularization of the post-revolutionary age. These processions served as the stage par excellence for particular customs, with not only each cathedral but each parish church, religious house, and chapel keeping its own ritual for processions, ostentions of relics, and local pilgrimages.[16]

The attire of the clergy, which one must keep in mind was extremely numerous, also varied to some extent from one place to another for canons of various ranks, clerics, cantors, choristers, beadles, and other officials. Furthermore, this dress changed with the season and circumstances. Additionally, local saints were always honored with particular Masses and Offices, and with hymns and sequences that were cherished and piously handed down or composed anew, for we must remember that divine worship continued to be enriched in the sixteenth and seventeenth centuries by the composition of new Latin liturgical pieces, and indeed entire Masses and Offices. It was not uncommon, for example, for superiors of religious congregations to compose Masses or Offices for the use of their religious communities, as Cardinal Pierre de Bérulle did for the Congregation of the Oratory of Jesus.[17] The various efforts of liturgical reform collectively termed "neo-Gallican" by Dom Henri Leclercq, which took place in France in the last third of the seventeenth century and all throughout the eighteenth, were not entirely unprecedented, even if the more ideological interventions of "enlightened" Jansenist or Gallican liturgists could elicit passionate reactions, to say nothing of the people's natural resistance to the disruption of deeply ingrained habits.

---

[14] The post-Tridentine Roman editions emphasize that these books contain the Roman *lex orandi*, free of any error.

[15] The complete Romanization of the liturgy in the dioceses of France between 1839 and 1875, spearheaded by the impetuous Dom Guéranger, was uncompromising, going beyond even the intentions of its most fervent promoter, who had wished to preserve certain ancient and venerable Gallican elements. But on the mixed results of the early modern reforms, see Miklós István Földváry, "Continuity and Discontinuity in Local Liturgical Uses," *Ephemerides Liturgicae* 137 (2023): 23–26.

[16] On these customs, see the collected essays in *Les cérémonies extraordinaires du catholicisme baroque*, ed. Bernard Dompnier (Presses universitaires Blaise-Pascal, 2009).

[17] Cardinal de Bérulle wrote a Mass and Office for the feast of Jesus (28 January) and its octave, the patronal celebration of this congregation he himself founded. See Pierre de Bérulle, *L'office de Jésus* (Paris, 1673).

Indeed, the French bishops undertook to revise their diocesan liturgical books, especially rituals and missals and breviaries.[18] The books of this early stage are a mix of neo-Gallican innovation, Romanization, and the restoration of medieval elements. Their aim was to conserve or rehabilitate venerable local uses and texts in order to extol the particular customs of the Gallican Church, and also to pass them through the sieve of criticism as regards their history and meaning. So, for example, it was thought more appropriate to place the holy water font outside the church to allow for a rite of purification before entering the sacred place. Likewise, it was considered preferable for the altar to remain bare outside of the celebration, without cloths, crucifix, and candles, as in more ancient times, etc. It is crucial to emphasize that this critical approach, despite superficial similarities, must be sharply distinguished from efforts to adapt the liturgy to the modern world that took place in the aftermath of the Second Vatican Council.

Two of these new books caused quite a stir: the missals of Meaux and of Troyes. The missal of Meaux, published in 1709 by Cardinal de Bissy — a staunch champion of the bull *Unigenitus*, cast like a Jovian bolt against the Jansenist propositions of Pasquier Quesnel — and prepared by François Ledieu, a former secretary of Bossuet, introduced the novelty of the saying of the Canon aloud, and its rubrics invited those assisting to respond "Amen" at various points in the Eucharistic prayer.[19] Going even further, the missal of Troyes, published in 1736 by the militant Gallican and pro-Jansenist Jacques-Bénigne Bossuet, nephew of the great Bossuet, reduced feasts of Our Lady to a minimum, prescribed the Canon, Secret, and the several iterations of *Domine non sum dignus* to be said "in a clear voice," and ordered the altar to remain bare of any accoutrements besides a crucifix. The publication of the missal of Troyes ignited a major, heated controversy, headed by the chapter, who protested the suppression of the cathedral's proper rites and essentially accused the Gallican bishop of assaulting ancient French liturgical customs. Royal intervention forced the bishop to abandon the most radical changes.

Nevertheless, these books closely resembled the Tridentine books: the prayers of the ordinary, especially the offertory and Canon, were identical, and so, in most respects, was the temporal cycle. But they made substantial

---

[18] For inventories of printed books, see Robert Amiet, ed., *Missels et bréviaires imprimés* (Éditions du Centre national de la recherche scientifique, 1990); Andrew Pettegree and Malcolm Walsby, eds., *French Books III & IV*, 2 vols (Brill, 2012); Louis Desgraves et al., eds., *Répertoire bibliographique des livres imprimés en France au XVIIe siècle*, 32 vols (V. Koerner, 1968–2017); Jean-Baptiste Molin and Annik Aussedat-Minvielle, eds., *Répertoire des rituels et processionnaux imprimés conservés en France* (Éditions du Centre national de la recherche scientifique, 1984). One should also browse the Universal Short Title Catalogue and the *Usuarium* database.

[19] Trent, as mentioned above, anathematized those who condemned saying the Canon in silence (a practice attested from the ninth century), although this does not mean that the creators of the missal of Meaux fell under the anathema.

modifications to the sanctoral cycle: the commons of saints, Masses for the Dead, and votive Masses. They rigorously applied the principle of the primacy of the temporal over the sanctoral cycle, suppressed several octaves, and made it so that all the antiphons, verses, and short chapters of the Office, as well as the Introits, Offertories, and Communions of the missal were taken from Scripture, and purged the sanctoral of anything that smacked of pious fable. For example, they dispensed with the thesis of the apostolic origins of the churches of France and their supposed foundation in the first or second century, which historical criticism had pushed back to the third. Le Brun des Marettes, who participated in the drafting and edition of the new breviaries of Orléans (1693) and Nevers (1727),[20] is wholly within this antiquarian yet modern and critical approach to safeguarding French customs.

It would be particularly interesting to open a debate on the connections between, on the one hand, the liturgical reform movement of the seventeenth and eighteenth centuries, together with the Catholic Enlightenment more broadly (Josephinism, the Synod of Pistoia, and the initiatives discussed within the Constitutional Church during the French Revolution), and, on the other hand, the Liturgical Movement of the twentieth century and the liturgical "reform," or rather, revolution, that followed Vatican II. There are indeed manifest similarities between these two movements; for instance, the desire to say the Canon aloud; the elimination of non-scriptural texts in the proper chants of the Mass; the tendency to downplay elements deemed too redolent of popular piety; the preference for the simple altar of antiquity, without retable, candles, or furnishings; the simple bishop's chair in the center of the apse; and interest in ceremonial concelebration. However, there are also many differences. The strict rigorism of the composers of the neo-Gallican books and the decrees of Pistoia clearly situate them in a different world from that of the architects of the post-conciliar liturgy, who purged the missal of references to sin and penance and eliminated the discipline of fasting.[21] For the former, permission to use the vernacular was limited to the ritual of the sacraments and was meant to facilitate the assimilation of the "new Catholics" (that is, the Protestant converts who entered the Church after the revocation of the Edict of Nantes) rather than to create ecumenical bridges between Catholicism and Calvinism.[22] At the very least, the passion for the ancient

---

[20] Typically for a neo-Gallican production, this breviary removed the Office of St. Andochius, putatively one of the first evangelizers of Gaul in the apostolic age (see Vincent Petit, *Église et nation. La question liturgique en France au XIXe siècle* [Presses universitaires de Rennes, 2010]).

[21] See Lauren Pristas, *Collects of the Roman Missals: A Comparative Study of the Sundays in Proper Seasons Before and after the Second Vatican Council* (Bloomsbury, 2013).

[22] Annibale Bugnini, "Le 'Variationes' ad alcuni testi della Settimana Santa," *L'Osservatore Romano*, 19 March 1965, where he reports that the *Consilium* was moved by the "desire

customs of French cathedrals and churches which animated des Marettes and his associates stands in stark contrast to the desire to create a liturgy "for our times" that characterized the Bugninian reformers.[23]

All this activity took place in the midst of a vibrant intellectual ferment: religious history benefited from the critical tools that the humanism of the sixteenth century had cultivated, and from the considerable improvements in clerical formation that followed upon the establishment of seminaries after the Council of Trent, which resulted in a more uniformly educated clergy.[24] It must also be noted that apart from this reforming-conservationist movement, the distant ancestor of the Liturgical Movement and some of the reforms that followed Vatican II, local ecclesiastical authorities regularly republished their own liturgical books. Hence Le Brun des Marettes speaks in passing of these regular reeditions, as for example the breviary of the collegiate church of St-Martin of Tours in 1635. With the aid of the printing press, these editions became more frequent, introducing small modifications or precisions here and there, just as the successive typical editions of the Tridentine missal would do.

The French Revolution came as a massive cultural and cultic earthquake that shattered the liturgical edifice of the church of France: worship was restricted then forbidden, the clergy wracked with division then drastically reduced, seminaries and convents closed, chapters ruined, treasuries and libraries pillaged. The concordat of 1801 between Pius VII and Napoleon reestablished Catholic worship and redrew the map of the French church, suppressing many dioceses and a great number of cathedral and collegiate chapters. The order of canons, who had for so long regulated and preserved the liturgical life of the French church,[25] were reduced to a body of diocesan priests who were given the title of "canon" as a mere honor, usually to crown their careers.[26]

A powerful ultramontane movement then arose, manifesting itself in every domain: moral theology witnessed the relaxation of sacramental

---

to ease in any way the road to union of the separated brethren, removing every stone that could even remotely constitute an obstacle or reason for discomfort."

[23] In a recent monograph, Shaun Blanchard has argued to the contrary, stressing the continuities between the liturgical and ecclesiological program of Pistoia and the decrees of Vatican II (see *The Synod of Pistoia and Vatican II: Jansenism and the Struggle for Catholic Reform* [Oxford University Press, 2019]). Besides managing to prove that many aspects of the post-Vatican II liturgical reforms were condemned in advance by Pius VI, the comparisons he makes are often anachronistic. It would be even more anachronistic to compare this reform to the programs of Lediceu, de Vert, or Le Brun des Marettes.

[24] The authoritative study of the learned culture of the Gallican Church is Bruno Neveu, *Érudition et religion aux XVIIe et XVIIIe siècles* (Bibliothèque Albin Michel, 1994).

[25] See the references to the work of Christophe Maillard, p. xxxiv, n. 56.

[26] See the several publications of François Hou on these subjects, especially *Chapitres et société en Révolution: les chanoines en France de l'Ancien Régime à la monarchie de Juillet* (Presses universitaires de Rennes, 2023).

discipline,[27] popular piety saw the great development of devotion to the Sacred Heart, and liturgy was likewise affected. Dom Prosper Guéranger (1805–1875), abbot of Solesmes and restorer of Benedictine life in France, emerged as the most outstanding figure of the liturgical life of the nineteenth century, becoming the most effective advocate for adoption of the Roman books. In 1840, the several volumes of his *Institutions liturgiques* began to appear, in which he denounced the "anti-liturgical heresy" promoted by the Jansenist-influenced French books of the preceding two centuries. Pressure to adopt the Roman books became irresistible, the diocese of Orléans being the last to embrace them in 1875, under Bishop Dupanloup. But along with the innovations of the early modern period, the ancient usages of the cathedrals of France were also rejected nearly everywhere. A few sequences, a number of Prefaces and proper Masses of the sanctoral cycle were kept under the guise of "diocesan propers" conceded by the Sacred Congregation of Rites and inserted as supplements in missals and, in the case of proper saints' Offices, in breviaries.

This movement was carried into the next century by a purist restoration of ecclesiastical chant, made less "rustic" and brought in line with contemporary musical taste. The great artisans of this reform were the disciples of Dom Guéranger: Doms Paul Jausions (1834–1870), Joseph Pothier (1835–1923), and André Mocquereau (1849–1930). They would impose a uniform tempo, a higher vocal range that suited upper tenor voices, and a singing style at once elegant and very different from the Baroque manner of the parish and cathedral cantors of the Ancien Régime.[28] Despite it all, clear vestiges of the older manner of singing survived until the end of the twentieth century, such as the French pronunciation of Latin or the performance style of parish cantors.[29] Le Brun de Marettes's descriptions of the eighteenth century, its worship environment, its rules of precedence especially in the chapters, its ecclesiastical dress, and its endlessly varied customs, remind us of a past that is both tantalizingly recent and at the same time forever lost.

There is growing interest among historians and musicologists throughout Europe in retrieving these local liturgical uses that partially survived the

---

[27] Moving away from strict discipline that, for example, led confessors to impose a waiting period on penitents before granting them absolution, in order to assess the sincerity of their firm purpose of amendment.

[28] On the parish cantors, especially those of the countryside, who lost their posts in the course of these changes, see Xavier Bisaro, *Chanter toujours. Plain-chant et religion villageoise dans la France moderne (XVIe-XIXe siècle)* (Presses universitaires de Rennes, 2020).

[29] Like liturgical uses, Latin pronunciation varied by country, region, and even town. It took decades after St. Pius X standardized the Italian pronunciation of ecclesiastical Latin for regional variants to largely disappear. English readers may be familiar with "Oxford pronunciation," which is a relic of the traditional English pronunciation of Latin. With regard to parish cantors, they sang in a full-throated, operatic style, in a baritone range rather than the tenor range advocated by Solesmes.

Council of Trent into the nineteenth century. One thinks of the musician and musicologist László Dobszay (1935–2011), who along with the Schola Hungarica has led a unique effort to rediscover the sacred music traditions specific to Hungary, notably by unearthing the ancient rite of Esztergom, the *ritus Strigoniensis*, whose liturgical books have been published under the direction of Professor Balázs Déri, director of the Department of Latin Studies at the University of Budapest (ELTE). Likewise, scholarly activity around the rite of Sarum has increased since the publication of the apostolic constitution *Anglicanorum coetibus* in 2009, which allowed for the creation of specific ordinariates for reintegrating Anglicans into the Catholic Church.[30] This variant of the Roman rite was used across most of the British isles, and is so called after the diocese of Salisbury, or Sarum. It was formed after the Norman conquest through a synthesis between English uses and the rite used in Rouen at the time. Many of its particularities (e.g., the use of the rood screen and loft, riddles around the altar, a pyx suspended over the altar, acolytes vested in tunicles like subdeacons, cantors in copes, seven deacons and seven subdeacons on Maundy Thursday, kissing of the Gospel book by the clergy, the solemn episcopal benediction after the *Pater noster* and before communion) hark back to rites common in French cathedrals until the Revolution. Likewise, German scholars have begun to take a special interest in the liturgies of the Holy Roman Empire, Belgium, and the Netherlands.[31]

LITURGICAL SCHOLARSHIP IN THE EIGHTEENTH CENTURY

One might say that in the seventeenth century a "liturgical anxiety"—to borrow the words of Henri Bremond in his *Histoire littéraire du sentiment religieux en France*—beset a number of spiritual authors who belong to what he calls the French School of spirituality, influenced by Cardinal de Bérulle, Charles de Condren, and Jean-Jacques Olier, among others. After the great unrest of the Protestant Reformation, an urgent need was felt to instruct pastors who could teach the people about the mysteries of divine worship and the Holy Sacrifice of the Mass. This apologetic angle also affected historical scholarship. Toward the end of the seventeenth century and during the first part of the eighteenth, a slew of scholarly works was published on the history of the liturgy, all of them in one way or another showing an interest in local tradition.

André Bocquillot, a canon of Avallon and ardent Jansenist, authored a number of works, including a *Traité historique de la liturgie sacrée, ou*

---

[30] For example, the Gregorian Institute of Canada, based at McMaster's University, has published numerous volumes of critical editions and English translations of Sarum liturgical books, many of them available as PDFs on their website: https://hmcwordpress.humanities.mcmaster.ca/renwick/.
[31] See the works of Andreas Odenthal, Arnold Angenendt, and Martin Klöckener, to name a few.

de la messe (Paris, 1701).³² Jean Grancolas, a professor at the Sorbonne, wrote several historical works on Christian worship, such as the *Traité de la Messe et de l'Office divin* (Paris, 1713). Dom Jean Mabillon (1632–1707), a Benedictine monk of the abbey of St-Germain-des-Prés and luminary of the learned Congregation of St-Maur, dedicated a special study to the French liturgy in his *De liturgia Gallicana* of 1685. These works applied the methods of critical scholarship to the history of the liturgy, and made great strides in the understanding of the sources. But the advent of the critical method also called into question the mystical interpretation of worship which had flourished in the Middle Ages.³³ When reading the *Liturgical Travels Through France*, one must keep in mind that authors writing about divine worship at the time were divided between:

(1) Those who took no interest whatsoever in critical history and continued unperturbed the traditional allegorical exegesis of the Fathers, especially the medieval writers who followed Amalar of Metz (d. 850).³⁴ They brought a modern inflection to this tradition by integrating the exegesis that had flourished in the medieval *expositiones Missae* with the literature of spirituality. This approach legitimized the traditional method of exegesis but also deprived it of the scientific aim which it could have rightfully claimed, since symbolic interpretation is a part of the history of liturgy and the evolution of rites. Authors such as Claude Villette, with his *Les raisons de l'office et des cérémonies qui se font dans l'Église catholique, apostolique et romaine* (1611), and François Van der Burch, archbishop of Cambrai, with his *Brevis elucidatio totius Missae* (1639), continued in the tradition of the *expositiones missae*. But the most celebrated work of mystical exegesis of the liturgy was that of Jean-Jacques Olier—pastor of St-Sulpice in Paris and principal founder, in France, following the Council of Trent, of major seminaries for the formation of candidates for the priesthood—with his 1657 work *Explication des cérémonies de la grand'messe de paroisse selon l'usage romain* (the original title Olier gave to his manuscript was *L'esprit des cérémonies*).³⁵ However, this exegetical stream was lost in the sand after

---

³² Des Marettes mentions this work with approbation on p. 219, n. 85.
³³ On the history and method of allegorical interpretation of the liturgy, see Claude Barthe, introduction to *A Forest of Symbols: The Traditional Mass and Its Meaning*, trans. David J. Critchley (Angelico Press, 2023), 1–18; Mary M. Schaefer, "Latin Mass Commentaries from the Ninth through the Twelfth Centuries: Chronology and Theology" in *Fountain of Life*, ed. Gerard Austin (The Pastoral Press, 1991), 35–49; and Roger Reynolds, "Liturgy, Treatises on" in *Dictionary of the Middle Ages*, ed. Joseph R. Strayer (Charles Scribner's Sons, 1986), 7:624–33.
³⁴ See Amalar of Metz, *On the Liturgy*, ed. and trans. Eric Knibbs, 2 vols., Dumbarton Oaks Medieval Library 35 and 36 (Harvard University Press, 2014) and *Amalarii Episcopi opera liturgica omnia*, ed. Jean Michel Hanssens, Studi e testi 138–140 (Biblioteca Apostolica Vaticana, 1948–1950).
³⁵ Jean-Jacques Olier, *The Mystical Meaning of the Ceremonies of the Mass*, trans. David J. Critchley (Angelico Press, 2024). Martin Sonnet's *Caeremoniale Parisiense ad usum omnium ecclesiarum collegiatarum, parochialium et aliarum urbis et dioecesis Parisiensis*

the dispute between Bossuet and Fénelon ended in the Quietists' defeat, which led to an eclipse of mystical literature in general.[36]

(2) Those who, on the contrary, despised the "Gothic" style of commentary found in the *expositiones Missae* and preached instead an entirely naturalistic — not to say utilitarian — interpretation. They had among other concerns the aim of encouraging the integration of the "newly converted," namely the Protestants who entered the Church after the revocation of the Edict of Nantes. Such converts, in their judgment, would bridle at abstruse allegories. The most eminent representative of this current was Dom Claude de Vert, vicar general of Cluny, whose *Explication simple, littérale et historique des cérémonies de l'Église pour les nouveaux convertis* (Paris, 1709–1713) set out to demonstrate that all the ceremonies of the Church have a simple and natural origin, rendering an appeal to allegory unnecessary. Le Brun des Marettes, who assures us that Dom de Vert "was without question one of France's most accomplished scholars of the Church's rites and customs,"[37] shared this perspective, as did all Jansenists, para-Jansenists, and militant Gallicans.

The quintessential example of the controversy over the rational explanation of the liturgy is the use of candles, which from the anti-allegorical point of view are purely and simply for giving light. They saw nothing more than poetry in the mystical exegesis that the candle wax is a representation of the most pure Body of Christ, its flammable wick a symbol of his holy soul, and its flame the radiance of his divinity. In the anti-allegorists' defense, they lived at a time without electricity, when numerous candles were an absolute necessity, as Le Brun des Marettes is fond of pointing out every time he mentions the candle carried to the pulpit before the subdeacon or lector or the candles of the many-branched chandelier that was lit near the cantors' eagle (the great pulpit formed like a soaring eagle), without which they could not carry out their duties.[38]

(Paris, 1662) is prefaced by a treatise on the mystical meanings of the Mass and the sacred vestments.

[36] The French rigorist current was anti-mystical in every sense of the term, distrusting mysticism in spirituality (see, for instance, Pierre Nicole's 1679 *Traité de l'oraison*) as well as liturgy (as demonstrated by the case of Dom Claude de Vert). The Quietism defended by Fénelon was in many ways the zenith of the mystical tendency, and many Jansenists, such as Nicole, joined Bossuet in his opposition to it. As a result, the condemnation of Fénelon in 1699 represented a defeat for mysticism even beyond the confines of the Quietist controversy.

[37] See p. 59. A contemporary reviewer of the *Travels* remarks apropos of Le Brun des Marettes's sympathy for de Vert: "He will often give a brief remark about the literal reasons for the ceremonies he describes, and without undertaking to defend M. De Vert explicitly against some of the criticisms that have been made of his work, we find that he nearly always accords with the latter, even in those conjectures which more recent authors have deemed less sound." See "Article I," *L'Europe savante* 5, no. 2 (October 1718): 165–66.

[38] He makes this point repeatedly throughout the book. To take one example, at St-Étienne of Bourges, from the Gospel to the *Pater noster* the candle-bearers used to withdraw, since the celebrant knew the Canon by heart and had no need of light (p. 106).

(3) Finally, there was a sort of third party which valued the scientific method highly but still acknowledged the importance of liturgical symbolism. Critical responses to Dom de Vert were mounted by Jean-Joseph Languet de Gergy in *Du véritable esprit de l'Église dans l'usage de ses cérémonies* (Paris, 1715), and especially by Pierre Le Brun in his *Explication littérale, historique et dogmatique des prières et des cérémonies de la Messe* (Paris, 1716).[39] Le Brun, who was without a doubt the most outstanding French liturgical historian of the eighteenth century, renowned for his rigorous and precise approach, belonged to the Oratory, a congregation often suspected of Jansenism. He was himself a rigorist in the French way, but did not hesitate to call liturgists like de Vert to account for their manipulations of liturgical history.

Supporters of both de Vert and Le Brun, however, were animated by the same interest in liturgical history and the same affection for the idiosyncrasies of the church of France. A whole series of erudite clergy and religious scholars diligently investigated and collected the liturgical usages of the cathedrals and collegiate and pilgrimage churches, which the diffusion of Roman books—and especially their paradoxical adoption by the royal chapel, whose Vincentian chaplains were some of the staunchest Romanists—threatened to relegate to oblivion.[40]

The Maurist Dom Edmond Martène (1654–1739), a student and collaborator of Mabillon, was one of these collectors. Among his many works, he published a *De antiquis ecclesiae ritibus* (Rouen, 1700) and a *Tractatus de antiqua ecclesiae disciplina in divinis officiis celebrandis* (Lyon, 1706). Above all, along with Dom Ursin Durand, another Benedictine of the Congregation of St-Maur, he was the author of the *Voyage littéraire de deux religieux bénédictins de la congrégation de St-Maur*, published partially in 1717 and fully in 1724. Notably, it included description of "many usages of the cathedral churches and monasteries relating to the discipline and history of the churches of the Gauls."[41] The two monks had been sent to scour the archives of France and Belgium in search of materials for a revised edition of the *Gallia Christiana*, a detailed dictionary of all the dioceses and monasteries of France with biographical lists of bishops, abbots, and abbesses, directed by Dom Denis de Ste-Marthe of the same Benedictine congregation. The work is largely a travelogue, describing the buildings they encountered, discussing their history, and delighting in quoting epitaphs or revealing unique rituals discovered within books.

---

[39] An English translation of this work by Harry B. Oesman has begun to be published, in a projected 4 or 5 volumes. The first has been released: *The Mass: A Literal, Historical, and Dogmatic Explanation of Its Prayers and Ceremonies* (Ubi Caritas Press, 2024).
[40] On the use of the royal chapel, see Alexandre Maral, *La chapelle royale de Versailles sous Louis XIV. Cérémonial, liturgie et musique* (Éditions Mardaga, 2010).
[41] See Daniel-Odon Hurel, "Le *Voyage littéraire* de dom Edmond Martène et de dom Ursin Durand (Paris, 1717 et 1724), édition critique. Érudition mauriste et regard sur la vie religieuse en France, aux Pays-Bas et en Allemagne au début du XVIIIe siècle" (PhD diss., University of Tours, 1991).

But the most ambitious researches into the rites of the Gallican Church were assuredly those of the aforementioned Pierre Le Brun (1661–1729). Le Brun did not travel, but rather dispatched a circular letter of 111 questions to various churches. Though the responses were never published in their raw form, he collected them before and during the composition of his *Explication littérale historique et dogmatique des prières et des cérémonies de la Messe*. The results first appeared as one volume in 1716, expanded to three volumes ten years later. It also included fifteen *Dissertations historiques et dogmatiques sur les liturgies de toutes les églises du monde chrétien*.[42] Xavier Bisaro (1972–2018), the greatest historian and musicologist of early-modern French liturgy, taken from us too soon, dedicated a whole book precisely to Le Brun's research, its difficulties, and even its failures: *Le passé présent. Une enquête liturgique dans la France du début du XVIIIᵉ siècle* (Cerf, 2012).

Chronologically situated between Le Brun's researches and the *Voyage littéraire* of the two monks of St-Maur, Le Brun des Marettes's *Liturgical Travels Through France* offers the most immediately instructive insights into divine worship in early eighteenth-century France. The author has, it is true, interwoven personal remarks and numerous digressions about rites formerly practiced which he thinks ought to be restored, to such an extent that careful reading is sometimes required to discern whether he is discussing contemporary practices or those of the past that should be revived. Even so, one is still plunged, as it were, directly into the *passé présent* or "ever-present past," to use Xavier Bisaro's expression.

A ROADMAP OF THE *TRAVELS*

Since we are dealing with a historical document, one must, of course, read the *Liturgical Travels Through France* with a properly critical eye. Le Brun des Marettes describes rituals he had himself practiced in Rouen and Orléans, or had seen with his own eyes during his stays in Paris and other places. He also reports first-hand testimonies and the contents of books he consulted — both with and without attribution — which was typical in the travel literature of the time and does not detract from the value of this particular work. Le Brun des Marettes spoke with canons and other clergy, took

---

[42] The most famous of these dissertations is the fifteenth, "On the custom of reciting part of the Mass in silence in all the churches of the world," where he confutes the pretensions of Jansenist liturgists who would have the Canon recited aloud, the assistants respond "Amen" to the prayers of the Canon and even to the narrative of institution, and communicants say "Amen" as a sort of profession of faith during the formula for the distribution of communion: *Corpus Domini nostri Jesu Christi — Amen — custodiat animam tuam ad vitam aeternam. Amen.* See Édouard de Moreau, "Récitation du canon de la messe à voix basse. Étude historique," *Nouvelle revue théologique* 51, no. 2 (1924): 65–94. Le Brun shows that it was Nicolas Letourneux who surreptitiously introduced this Amen into a missal for the use of the faithful in 1681. Des Marettes is, of course, favorable to the Amen during the distribution of communion: at Notre-Dame of Paris, "those who receive communion from the priest respond *Amen*, as in Orléans, after the words *Corpus Domini nostri Jesu Christi*, following the ancient custom of the Greek and Latin churches."

part in the Offices, consulted the books they showed him, gathered what they had to say about former usages, and noted the particularities of ceremonies, processions, pontifical Masses, and canonical Offices in Vienne, Lyon, Angers, Doué, Fontevrault, Marmoutier, Tours, St-Cyran, Nevers, Limoges, Mâcon, Cluny, Dijon, etc. Notably, the description of the usages of Rouen, a church dear to his heart, occupies a significant portion of his account.

We will content ourselves with the mention of a few points amidst the abundance of information one may harvest from perusing the *Liturgical Travels Through France*, in order to concretely demonstrate their remarkable interest.

In several places, Le Brun des Marettes speaks of the riddel curtains around the altar that were opened at the moment of the consecration or, conversely, closed from the beginning of the Preface until the *Pater noster*. Liturgical specialists are all too familiar with the mysteries shrouding these famous curtains. They balk at connecting them to the Eastern iconostasis, which is more closely related to the rood screen closing off the choir, or the Lenten veil that used to be lowered in front of the sanctuary. Moreover, these curtains were placed most of the time not in front of the altar but to its right and left sides, as depicted in iconography (see PLATES 16, 29, 31). They delimited the altar of sacrifice rather than concealing it.[43] Another hypothesis proposes that these curtains functioned like the drapes that hang from an honorary daïs, such as one covering a throne, or like a high-ranking figure's bed curtains, opened during visits.

On many occasions, our traveler describes with evident delight another distinct Gallican characteristic: it was still common for the Blessed Sacrament to be kept not in a Borromean tabernacle fixed on the altar, but in a suspended Eucharistic vessel called a pyx or ciborium, which hung on a chain from a crosier-head fixture above the altar (see PLATES 29, 30, 39). This ciborium could be covered with a veil in the form of a tent, a *tabernaculum*, with four sides and surmounted, as in the collegiate church of St-Julien in Angers, by a dove. The hanging pyx itself often took the form of a dove in the Middle Ages and at the beginning of the eighteenth century proper Eucharistic doves were still to be found. It was this arrangement of a suspended ciborium that Philippe de Champaigne represented in his painting *The Vision of St. Juliana*, now housed at the Barber Institute in Birmingham. The ciborium is covered in this case with a veil made of the same red fabric as the two riddles, one closed and the other open to permit our view of the altar.

Another Gallican practice worth noting is the use of the tunicle by numerous subdeacons or acolytes. At Vienne, for example, there were

---

[43] See, despite the fact that his theological remarks are unconvincing, Paul Nourrigeon, "Voiler l'autel," in *Le rideau, le voile et le dévoilement du Proche-Orient ancien à l'Occident médiéval*, ed. Lucien-Jean Bord, Vincent Debiais, and Éric Palazzo (Geuthner, 2019), 91–100.

subdeacon candle-bearers and subdeacon thurifers. One recalls too that at the abbey of Ste-Croix in Poitiers, the nuns in alb and maniple — *horresco referens!* — served as acolytes at the high Mass.[44]

A foe of allegory, Le Brun des Marettes explains that the choirboys of Cluny wore a maniple — originally a handkerchief — for the simple reason that "one had to hold one's kerchief in the hand or on the arm to use as needed." He also tells us that the cantors of Le Puy-en-Velay carried a rod rather than a staff, just so they could strike anyone who chattered instead of singing. This led him to suppose that the disciplinary function of the cope-bearers is perhaps the origin of the familiar cantor's staff. Of course, our conservationist-innovator is careful to point out every case when according to ancient custom candles are not placed on the altar until the time for Mass. After all, in the *Ordo Romanus* I, the pope's seven acolytes put down their candles on the ground after the entrance procession (see PLATES 13, 31, 43).[45]

The *Travels* also give us indications about liturgical colors, which varied greatly. Red was used in Bourges during the two weeks of Passiontide, and in Paris for All Saints because of the great number of martyrs, as well as for the feast of Corpus Christi. This may have been the case in Rome as well, which would explain why the riddels of the altar baldachin are red. Ash gray was worn in Paris on Sundays in Lent.

The types of vestments and the manner of wearing them could also be unique. In Lyon, Vienne, Mâcon, and other places, some clerics wore the miter (as in some Italian cathedral chapters) in place of the *bonnet*, the equivalent of the Roman biretta.

Of the innumerable processions, the one attached to the aspersion before Sunday high Mass enjoyed particular importance. It could traverse various places, even venturing into the nearby streets, the cathedral cloister, the tombs of deceased canons, and relics. In reality, there were as many aspersion rites as there were cathedrals and even churches.

There was also variation regarding the place where the ministers said the prayers of confession (today generally called the prayers at the foot of the altar): as they traversed the choir toward the altar, at the tomb of St. Martin at the collegiate church of Tours, and sometimes partly in the sacristy with the *Confiteor* said later at the foot of the altar.

At Cluny, the ministers communed under two species on Sundays and feasts, drinking the Precious Blood with a fistula (just like the pope at a papal Mass or the king during his coronation at Reims) at a small altar called, as in the East, the *prothesis*, where the deacon had carried the chalice.

At St-Jean in Lyon, at certain specific moments, they kissed the celebrant on the shoulder — *ad scapulas* — an early medieval or perhaps late-antique use.

---

[44] But see p. 59, n. 1.
[45] *Ordo Romanus* 1.52, in Michel Andrieu, ed., *Les* Ordines Romani *du haut moyen âge* (Spicilegium sacrum Lovaniense, 1948), 2:84.

As at papal Masses, the Epistle and Gospel were sometimes chanted in both Latin and Greek at St-Denis, and on the most solemn days the whole Mass was sometimes chanted entirely in Greek.

The Gospel procession could take on impressive proportions reminiscent of the Byzantine Little Entrance. So in Paris following the crucifix flanked by acolytes walked six vested deacons and six vested subdeacons known as *induts* (*indutum*, vestment; *induti*, vested) or *revêtus*, that is, canons dressed in the vestments of their canonical order.[46]

The rood screen[47] was often still a feature of French churches at the time of Le Brun des Marettes (see PLATES 1, 13, 16, 27, 48). Only between the very end of the seventeenth century and the Revolution did French cathedrals begin to be rearranged in the "Roman style." Most rood screens disappeared, to be replaced by tall grilles or two-part screens open in the center, each side having a pulpit for Office readings and the chanting of the Epistle and Gospel, and against which were two altars for the celebration of parish Masses.[48] The Gospel was often chanted from the screen by the deacon facing north. In Rouen, the subdeacon, after giving the open book to the celebrant to kiss, brought it closed to be kissed by certain members of the clergy.

At St-Maurice in Vienne (and in other places such as Lyon), communion at a pontifical Mass was preceded by the ancient Gallican and Ambrosian invitatory *Venite populi* and, for the canons, the archbishop's kiss of peace.[49]

Le Brun des Marettes notes that at Clermont, when a burial was celebrated in the afternoon and therefore without Mass (the Eucharistic fast before the relaxations of Pius XII forbade even the drinking of water after midnight, and so made late Masses impossible), it was replaced by a "dry Mass," i.e., one lacking a consecration. Despite being considered an abuse, dry Masses continued to be celebrated in certain places until the mid-twentieth century. Perhaps one could describe the ceremony celebrated on Maundy Thursday in Angers to recall the Last Supper, where the clergy gathered around a table at the episcopal palace to drink two glasses of white

---

[46] Just as cardinals are divided into three orders of cardinal deacons, cardinal priests, and cardinal bishops, canons could be divided into canon-subdeacons, canon-deacons, and canon-priests and dignities of the chapter, each one wearing the uniform of his order: respectively the tunicle, dalmatic, chasuble, or cope.

[47] The rood screen or *jubé* in French was a high wood or stone barrier, pierced with grilles, separating the choir from the nave. On the loft or walkway on top of it stood several pulpits from which Office and Mass readings were chanted. The name *jubé* is the French pronunciation of the Latin word *jube*, the first word of the reader's request for the presider to bless him: *Jube domne benedicere*. For a spirited and erudite defense of the *jubés* at the time they fell into disfavor, see Jean-Baptiste Thiers, "Dissertation des jubés des églises," in *Dissertations ecclésiastiques* (Paris, 1688).

[48] See Mathieu Lours, *L'autre temps des cathédrales. Du concile de Trente à la Révolution française* (Picard, 2010).

[49] It is likely that the traditional practice of kissing the bishop's hand before receiving the host, which in the twentieth century became a kiss of his ring due to the indulgence attached to this gesture, is a vestige of the kiss of peace preceding communion.

and one of red wine and to listen to a Latin discourse on the institution of the Eucharist, as a dry Mass. Or, rather, a well-lubricated one.

In Paris, during the offertory at high Mass, the subdeacon put the paten into a large silver basin covered by a veil, which was held up in front of the altar by the *spé*, the dean of the choirboys (see PLATES 2, 40). Then the subdeacon took it back and brought it to the altar during the *Pater noster*, giving it to the deacon at the words *panem nostrum*. One can add further details given by Pierre Le Brun: the cleric holding the basin was vested in a special cope called a *soc*, which he wore backwards, with two slots for his arms;[50] in Grenoble, the paten was left on the altar still wrapped in the chalice veil.[51]

To end our survey, we must mention the *Liturgical Travels Through France*'s references to concelebration.[52] It is important to note that, up to the Revolution, at least certain cathedrals of France—Chartres, Blois, Reims, Sens, Paris, Lyon, Toul, and Bourges—had retained the custom of concelebration on Maundy Thursday. The practice seems to have been imported into Frankish territory from Rome during the Carolingian age, but Rome abandoned it around the twelfth century. At the Mass, all of the vested canon-priests (*induts*), or six of them, or even just two, came to join the bishop at the altar and celebrated with him from the offertory onward. This took place exclusively on Maundy Thursday, probably due to the fact that on that day the *induts* joined him for the blessing of the holy chrism and the oil of catechumens. This custom disappeared with the definitive adoption of the Roman books in the nineteenth century, except in Lyon, where the *induts* participating in the consecration of the holy oils continued to concelebrate Mass this way until the reform of Paul VI. The *Liturgical Travels Through France* states that on Maundy Thursday at the cathedral of Orléans, six canons celebrated with the bishop with the following peculiarity, which sparked intense discussion under Pius XII: only the bishop pronounced the words of consecration, after which he gave the six canons communion from the small hosts.[53] In Chartres, on

---

[50] See Sonnet, *Caeremoniale Parisiense* 1.31.6, III. This book explains the Roman rite, which Paris adopted after the Council of Trent while keeping a great number of local usages. The *soc* can be seen in PLATES 2 and 40.
[51] See Pierre Le Brun, *Explication*, 324.
[52] On the history and theology of concelebration in the West, see Joseph de Sainte-Marie, *The Holy Eucharist—The World's Salvation: Studies on the Holy Sacrifice of the Mass, its Celebration, and its Concelebration* (Gracewing, 2015).
[53] The debate centered on whether such "ceremonial concelebration," where the concelebrants did not pronounce the words of consecration, could be considered "sacramental concelebration." Theologians such as Bernard Botte and Karl Rahner argued in favor of its validity, whereas others, including Jean Michel Hanssens and Alfons Raes, opposed this view. Pius XII sought to end the controversy in his allocution to the 1956 International Congress of Pastoral Liturgy held in Assisi by declaring that pronouncing the words of consecration was indeed necessary for sacramental concelebration (see *The Assisi Papers: Proceedings of the First International Congress of Pastoral Liturgy, Assisi-Rome, September*

the other hand, the six priest-archdeacons who celebrated with the bishop communed under two species from the same host and the same chalice. In Sens, two canon-priests concelebrated with the bishop, performing the same ceremonies and pronouncing the same words as him, even the words of consecration, but communing under the species of bread with a small host, while kneeling "as in priestly ordinations."

Le Brun des Marettes believed that the priests and *curés* assisting the bishop on other occasions than Maundy Thursday once enjoyed the same privilege. The idea is not unreasonable, since the pope's concelebration with the cardinal-priests took place in antiquity at Easter, Pentecost, Sts. Peter and Paul, and Christmas.[54] In Sens, Angers, and Troyes, thirteen cardinal-priests assisted the bishop, while in Orléans there were twelve, vested in chasubles. The six priests assisting the bishop on Christmas in Vienne (along with seven deacons, seven subdeacons, and seven candle-bearers, two of them subdeacons) may once have had the same function, as also the seven priests who joined the bishop (also along with seven deacons, seven subdeacons, and seven candle-bearers) in Lyon on Christmas, Easter, and Pentecost.

This form of concelebration during the pontifical Mass of Maundy Thursday seems a suitable illustration of the fact that several peculiarities of French liturgy that seem to us most "Gallican" might actually be witnesses to the state of the Romano-Frankish liturgy in the Carolingian era. In other words, Gallicanism led French cathedrals to remain, in this instance, more Roman than Rome.

❖ ❖ ❖

In the final analysis, one can say that the efflorescence of liturgical studies and practice during the seventeenth and eighteenth centuries, exemplified by numerous clerics and scholars including Le Brun des Marettes, as anti-Roman as it may sometimes have appeared in its rhetoric, actually shared the apologetic agenda that motivated the Tridentine Counter-Reformation's liturgical project: to consolidate the Catholic liturgy, to promote its worthy celebration, and to defend its antiquity. Furthermore, the effort to document ritual practices through travelers' accounts, first-hand testimonies, and especially the composition of ceremonials was part of a general movement to commit custom to writing.[55]

The liturgical customs and uses of the French church were gravely threatened not only by the Roman books, but also by the new

---

18–22, 1956 [Liturgical Press, 1957], 229). The Holy Office formally issued a dogmatic statement to this effect on 23 May 1957 (*Acta Apostolicae Sedis* 49 [1957]: 370). For a summary of the controversy, see Bernard Xibaut, "La concélébration dans le Mouvement liturgique et dans l'œuvre du Concile," *La Maison-Dieu* 224 (2000): 7–27.
[54] *Ordo Romanus* 3.1 and 4.52, in Andrieu, *Les Ordines Romani*, 2:131 and 163.
[55] See Cécile Davy-Rigaux, Bernard Dompnier, and Daniel-Odon Hurel, eds., *Les cérémoniaux catholiques en France à l'époque moderne. Une littérature de codification des rites liturgiques* (Brepols, 2009).

neo-Gallican books which, in their desire to return to the traditions of the primitive Church, sought to rationalize and purify them of any features that smelled too much of the Middle Ages. The publication of these books led, willy nilly, to the unification of the liturgy within dioceses and the realm a whole, especially in the wake of the successful missal (1736) and breviary (1738) of Archbishop Vintimille, adopted by nearly half the dioceses in France. Although threatened, local uses remained very much alive, as the cathedral and collegiate chapters defended their particularisms tooth and nail.[56]

After reading the *Liturgical Travels Through France*, one is left pondering what Le Brun des Marettes's true sentiments were after all. His close ties to the conservationist-cum-reformers of the Gallican church's liturgy are incontestable, but he is also viscerally attached to its "archaisms." Ultimately a satisfactory answer to this question requires a more detailed study, notably one that takes into account his personal correspondence. At any rate, for the particularities of the rich and diversified Roman liturgy in the French style, reinvigorated and contested in his day and destined to perish forever in the cataclysm of the Revolution, Le Brun des Marettes remains one of our most valuable witnesses.

Fr. Claude Barthe

---

[56] See Christophe Maillard, "Les chanoines et la défense des traditions cérémonielles au XVIIIe siècle," in *Les langages du culte aux XVIIe et XVIIIe siècles*, ed. Bernard Dompnier (Presses universitaires Blaise-Pascal, 2020), 97–109 and Christophe Maillard, "La fête de Saint-Martin d'hiver à Saint-Martin de Tours au XVIIIe siècle. Le maintien d'une liturgie particulière dans le plus illustre chapitre collégial de France," in *Les cérémonies extraordinaires du catholicisme baroque*, ed. Dompnier, 525–44.

INTRODUCTION

THE liturgical culture of France between the Council of Trent and the Revolution has seen a renewal of research since Dom Prosper Guéranger's *Institutions liturgiques*.[1] Yet despite burgeoning interest in early-modern Catholicism, many primary sources for this rich field are underexplored.[2] Jean-Baptiste Le Brun des Marettes's *Liturgical Travels Through France* is one such source. Published in 1718, it provides a sweeping panorama of the bustling centers of worship—cathedrals, monasteries, parishes, and city streets—that were the focal points of the church in France, often furnishing details of religious practice, civic life, and folk religion for which no other record has survived. Besides its obvious interest for liturgical historians,[3] it also affords a valuable resource for students of cultural and early-modern mentalities, as well as for anyone who asks questions such as: What did it mean for a Frenchman to go to church circa 1700 and what could he have seen, heard, smelled, sung, and felt there? What rituals framed the lives of Frenchmen of all estates in the Grand Siècle? For historians of music and drama, the author's remarks on liturgical drama and musical practice provide food for reflection on the performance landscape of Ancien Régime France, illuminating a world where worship was not merely a matter of devotion but an all-encompassing sensory and civic experience.

---

[1] In addition to the recent works by Xavier Bisaro, Claude Barthe, Alexandre Marale, and Miklós István Földváry cited in the foreword, see general overviews by Henri Leclercq, "Liturgies néo-gallicanes," in *Dictionnaire d'archéologie chrétienne et de liturgie*, ed. Ferdinand Cabrol and Henri Leclercq, vol. 9.2 (Letouzey et Ané, 1907), 1636–729 and Hélène Bricout and Gilles Drouin, "Liturgie in Frankreich in der nachtridentinischen Epoche," in *Geschichte der Liturgie in den Kirchen des Westens: Rituelle Entwicklungen, theologische Konzepte und kulturelle Kontexte*, ed. Jürgen Bärsch and Benedikt Kranemann, vol. 2, *Moderne und Gegenwart* (Aschendorff, 2018), 7–50; and on the intersection of music and politics, the study by Peter Bennett, *Music and Power in the Court of Louis XIII: Sounding the Liturgy in Early Modern France* (Cambridge University Press, 2021).

[2] Historiography has used many labels for this period of Catholic history: "Counter Reformation" (ca. 1555–1648) refers to efforts to reinvigorate Catholic doctrine and practice in the face of Protestant critique; "Catholic Reformation" to broader movements of renewal that were often but not necessarily tied to the Council of Trent, and "Catholic reform," referring to more localized efforts to improve the quality of religious life (e.g., Barbara B. Diefendorf, *Planting the Cross: Catholic Reform and Renewal in Sixteenth- and Seventeenth-Century France* [Oxford University Press, 2019]). John O'Malley advocates for the more capacious term "early modern Catholicism." For discussion, see O'Malley, *Trent and All That* (Oxford University Press, 2009). Recent scholarship has also spoken of the Catholic Enlightenment, i.e., the ecclesiastical reform movement that sought to defend Catholic Christianity by appeal to modern terminology and the core values of the Enlightenment process. See, for example, Ulrich Lehner, *The Catholic Enlightenment* (Oxford University Press, 2016).

[3] He was prized, for example, by Joseph Jungmann, *The Mass of the Roman Rite*, trans. Francis Brunner, 2 vols. (Benziger, 1951/1955).

Le Brun des Marettes's text also offers a case study in how Catholics of reforming, Jansenist, and Enlightened sympathies interacted with, criticized, and transformed the ritual culture of their time. Far more than a cabinet of curiosities or an innocent travelogue, the *Liturgical Travels* conceals, behind a façade of impartial reporting, an elaborate argument for the renewal of ecclesial society according to the canons of antiquity, albeit an antiquity as filtered through the lens of a dawning Enlightenment. His book plunges us into the midst of a French church simultaneously proud and insecure about its ritual patrimony and the wealthy clerical estate that sustained it, caught in the crossfires of Protestant and Enlightened critique, and contending with ever-increasing papal intervention. As a minor érudit and partisan of the Jansenist bastion of Port-Royal who sympathized with the new critical methods of the age, des Marettes belonged to a far-flung network of scholars and reformers, lay and ecclesiastic, and many vital channels of contemporary controversy flow through his deceptively simple pages. This book is his archive and workshop.

Le Brun des Marettes's *Liturgical Travels* is a vital source for scholarship on the *longue durée* roots of twentieth-century liturgical reforms. The book is a product of the movement for liturgical change and renewal that dominated the church of France and beyond during the century before the French Revolution. It was a period of flourishing *ressourcement* in the fields of Scripture and patristics as well as liturgy in the wake of the Council of Trent,[4] when groundbreaking historical scholarship—especially the work of Giuseppe Maria Tomasi, Cardinal Giovanni Bona, and Maurists like Jean Mabillon and Edmond Martène—led to a critical reexamination of ritual texts and practices. Under Louis XIV, as national pride swelled, a French church that had once shown greater willingness to conform to the post-Tridentine Roman books increasingly asserted the legitimacy of diocesan and other local rites. The revocation of the Edict of Nantes, too, compelled churchmen to adapt catechetical and sacramental practice to the competing needs of both cradle Catholics and Protestant converts. This confluence of factors spurred most French dioceses to adopt new liturgical books, known today as the "neo-Gallican" rites. Some clerics pursued even more radical innovations, crowned by the revolutionary Synod of Pistoia (1786), whose liturgical decrees were rejected by both pope and populace.[5] Historians of twentieth-century liturgical reforms have eagerly sought precedents in this earlier era of

---

[4] On the milieu of the érudits, see the classic study by Bruno Neveu, *Érudition et religion aux XVIIe et XVIIIe siècles* (Bibliothèque Albin Michel, 1994), and on post-Tridentine reforming trends, Fr. Barthe's foreword.

[5] This synod called for a radical simplification of liturgical ceremonies and church furnishings, a reduction of processions, the celebration of all rites in the vernacular and aloud, and a curtailing of devotions to the Blessed Virgin and the saints. For a translation of the pertinent Pistoian documents, see *Jansenism: An International Anthology*, ed. Shaun Blanchard and Richard T. Yoder (Catholic University of America Press, 2024), 316–33.

upheaval.⁶ Le Brun des Marettes's book provides a window into its formative stage, one which presents a challenge to facile narratives of liturgical history.

For our own moment, Le Brun des Marettes's work and career helpfully illustrate the delicate interplay between liturgical tradition and reform. Both traditionalists and progressives may be tempted—they would not be the first—to wield his work in support of a free-for-all approach, suggesting that if a certain practice was done in the past, it should be embraced today. Des Marettes himself may not be innocent of this kind of antiquarianism. Whatever his flaws as a historian or reformer, for readers today it remains true that knowledge of the French rites he describes can inform and enrich our understanding of the broader Latin tradition, offering pathways through the impasse of either positivist, post-Tridentine rubrical centralism or unmoored presentism.

In every age, the Church faces the difficult question of how to balance a legitimate respect for the authority of ancient local customs anchored in real piety while also reforming or correcting such customs in harmony with the practice of the universal Church. Here Le Brun des Marettes can help. His careful—albeit not always impartial—attention to and respect for historical sources, his zeal for local tradition, and his concern for the integrity of ritual forms richly expressive of Christian doctrine and piety have much to teach scholars and churchmen today.

Ultimately, we hope that readers will discover in these pages inspiring portrayals of the liturgical culture of Christendom across some of its most brilliant ages: a triumphant, public, and colorful religion sustained by cathedrals and monasteries with their pontifical Masses, long and stately processions, and the fascinating diversity in the unity that once flourished within the Latin rite in old Christendom. A first-hand experience—if only a literary and vicarious one—of the formally integral and culturally integrated celebration of Latin rites in an era of incontestable splendor and fulsome development can enrich one's understanding of the nature and potential of ritual prayer. It is also a necessary support for the informed discussion and indeed scholarly critique of later reforms that is the duty of our present moment.⁷

---

⁶ Recent examples in Anglophone literature include Shaun Blanchard, *The Synod of Pistoia and Vatican II: Jansenism and the Struggle for Catholic Reform* (Oxford University Press, 2020) and Keith Pecklers, "The Jansenist Critique and the Liturgical Reforms of the Seventeenth and Eighteenth Centuries," *Ecclesia orans* 20 (2003): 325–39.

⁷ Following Cardinal Joseph Ratzinger's call to rediscover the nature of the liturgical rite, Fr. Franck Quoëx has argued: "Faced with the general anti-ritualism of modernity and with a certain liturgical minimalism that continues to look upon rite and symbol with suspicion, it is urgent to propose a rediscovery of the liturgy in all the riches of its anthropological, historical, theological, and spiritual dimensions" (*Liturgical Theology in Thomas Aquinas: Sacrifice and Salvation History*, trans. Zachary Thomas [Catholic University of America Press, 2024], 261).

LE BRUN DES MARETTES:
ROUENNAIS ÉRUDIT AND FRIEND OF PORT-ROYAL

Our author is little known today—partly due to his own efforts to conceal his authorship—and only one attempt has been made to go beyond the generalities of the nineteenth-century French biographical dictionaries.[8] Based on a close reading of the *Travels*, we are able to offer further precisions of Le Brun des Marettes's identity, authorship, and aims. This introduction therefore complements Fr. Claude Barthe's broader presentation of this historical period, and supplies a preliminary answer to his call for a study of the author's liturgical views.

Le Brun des Marettes began his study of French rites in his native city of Rouen, working like his father with the network of reformers and scholars around the cathedral chapter and its library. His first work in the field of liturgy was an edition of John of Avranches's *Liber de officiis ecclesiasticis*, an ordinal which had codified the practices of the church of Rouen in the eleventh century. Published in 1679 by his father Bonaventure,[9] it followed the earlier 1642 edition put out by three canons of Rouen: Georges Ridel, Jacques Malet, and Jean Le Prévost. The latter was in charge, from 1637 until his death, of the capitular library,[10] a collection that was widely admired, not least by Le Brun des Marettes himself.[11]

Le Prévost (1600–1648) also played a key role in the correction of Rouen's liturgical books under Archbishop François de Harlay.[12] His principles and concerns are reflected in the notes he appended to his edition of John of Avranches's ordinal. Des Marettes, whose admiration for Le Prévost is evident,[13] builds on the canon's approach in his 1679 edition, adding his own notes to the main text as well as transcriptions of manuscripts relating to the use of Rouen. For these manuscripts he was indebted to the library of another Rouennais scholar, Émery Bigot (1626–1689). This

---

[8] Namely, André Fouré, "Jean-Baptiste Le Brun des Marettes. Visiteur janséniste de la Cathédrale de Rouen à la fin du XVIIe siècle," *Précis analytique des travaux de l'Académie des sciences, belles-lettres et arts de Rouen* (1967): 71–97.

[9] The edition was published anonymously, but Le Brun des Marettes's authorship is proven by Canon Jacques-Accurse Auvray's testimony at the beginning of the *Liturgical Travels*. It was reprinted by Jacques-Paul Migne in the *Patrologia Latina* (hereafter PL) 147:15B–264C.

[10] He was the first to hold this office after the chapter library—largely destroyed by Huguenot depredations—was restored thanks to the canon-archdeacon Pierre Acarie's 1634 bequest of over 40,000 books and an annual rent of 600 pounds for its maintenance. The most extensive account of Le Prévost's life, including his liturgical work mentioned below, is found in Charles de Beaurepaire, "Notice sur le chanoine Jean Le Prevost, bibliothécaire du chapitre de Rouen, 1600–1648," *Revue catholique de Normandie* 7 (1897): 181–204.

[11] See p. 194.

[12] Uncle of the homonymous Parisian bishop who undertook a revision of the Parisian liturgical books. The elder de Harlay's revisions were much more conservative than the radical reforms promulgated by his nephew.

[13] See p. 260.

learned bibliophile, who stood "at the very center of a firmly established, smoothly functioning network of mutual assistance and scholarly information which linked the countries of western Europe," must have put his younger compatriot in touch with the wide world of érudits,[14] including his friends Luc d'Achéry, Charles Du Fresne (sieur Du Cange), and Étienne Baluze. Another Rouen native with whom des Marettes worked closely was Nicolas Letourneux or Le Tourneux (1640–1686), official confessor of Port-Royal-des-Champs and among the vanguard of liturgical reformers in the late seventeenth century. Letourneux was a key influence on the earliest neo-Gallican books, namely the 1680 breviary and 1685 missal of Paris promulgated by Archbishop François de Harlay de Champvallon, and the 1686 breviary of Cluny, which set the tone for the books that would proliferate in the subsequent century. Moreover, he penned several volumes intended to facilitate lay participation in the liturgy, the most notorious of which was the thirteen-volume commentary and translation of the Mass and liturgical year, *L'année chrétienne* (1677–1701). His translation of the Tridentine Roman breviary appeared posthumously in 1688.[15] Des Marettes collaborated with Letourneux on a *Concordia librorum Regum et Paralipomenon*, published anonymously in 1682 and reprinted in 1691.

Others of Le Brun des Marettes's contacts are named in the *Travels*, several in such a way as to imply friendship. Many were associated with Port-Royal and also reformers of liturgical books.[16] We know that he was in correspondence with Claude Châtelain or Chastelain (1639–1712), a canon of Notre-Dame of Paris who helped revise Parisian liturgical books under Bishop de Harlay. He consulted his former teacher Louis

---

[14] See Leonard E. Doucette, *Émery Bigot: Seventeenth-Century French Humanist* (University of Toronto Press, 1970), Preface.

[15] *L'année chrétienne* was condemned by Pope Innocent XII and placed on the Index of Prohibited Books in 1695, and the translation of the breviary—which, according to Guéranger, Letourneux merely edited (*Institutions*, 2:24)—was censured by the diocesan *officialis* or *officiel* (the judicial vicar in modern usage) of Paris in 1688. The latter sentence spurred the prominent Jansenist theologian Antoine Arnauld to pen a *Défense des versions de l'Écriture sainte, des offices de l'Église, et des ouvrages des Pères* (Cologne, 1688), which defended the translation of the breviary in particular. Other figures linked to Port-Royal also produced controversial translations of liturgical and Biblical texts at this time, but the activity was taken up by non-Jansenists as well, including Jesuits. For more details, see Bernard Chédozeau, "Les grandes étapes de la publication de la Bible catholique en français du concile de Trente au XVIIIe siècle," in *Le Grand Siècle et la Bible*, ed. Jean-Robert Armogathe, Bible de tous les temps 6 (Beauchesne, 1989), 341–60, and Louis Cognet, "Spirituality in Seventeenth-Century France: Christian Life," in *The History of the Church*, vol. 6, *The Church in the Age of Absolutism and Enlightenment*, ed. Hubert Jedin and John Dolan, trans. Gunther J. Holst (Crossroad, 1981), 84–88.

[16] For a study of the so-called "neo-Gallican" liturgies in relation to Jansenism and Port-Royal, see Ellen Weaver, "The Neo-Gallican Liturgies Revisited," *Studia Liturgica* 16 (1986), 54–72. She points out that scarcely a single personality involved in liturgical revision at this time was not tied in some way to Port-Royal. Labeling this network "Jansenist," however, is not accurate. Rather, they were united by a common vision of the Catholic Reformation (61–62).

Sébastien Le Nain de Tillemont (1637–1698); this distinguished historian was closely associated with the intellectual circle of Port-Royal, where he served as priest from 1676 to 1679.[17] A canon and subdean of the church of St-Martin of Tours, one M. Bourrault or Boureau, a Jansenist sympathizer, lent him an ordinary and notes for his description of that church.[18] The patrologist, historian, and canonist Étienne Baluze gave him his personal papers.[19] Jean-Claude de la Poype de Vertrieu (1655–1732), once count-canon of Lyon and then bishop of Poitiers, also supplied him with information.[20] If he praises other leading figures, such as the Maurist monks and Jean-Baptiste Santeuil (1630–1697), a canon of St-Victor whose Latin hymns were published in the new Cluniac and Parisian breviaries,[21] he is more cautious when calling out his opponents, never naming them. Rather, he derides the mystical explanations of unknown Lyonese "rubricists" and attacks the views of the Barnabite Bartholomew Gavantus (1569–1638)—a consultor to the Sacred Congregation of Rites, whose monumental *Thesaurus sacrorum rituum* defended mystical interpretations—under the epithet of "new rubricists."[22]

By far the most formative influence on our author's approach to liturgical studies, however, was the "apostle of naturalism," Dom Claude de Vert.[23] The first volume of his magnum opus, the *Explication simple, littérale et historique des cérémonies de l'Église pour les nouveaux convertis*, was published posthumously in 1709, once the bulk of the *Travels* had already been written, yet des Marettes shows an intimate familiarity with de Vert's views, including at least one almost verbatim borrowing.[24] De Vert had begun to develop his system of liturgical exegesis, prizing "natural" explanations for ritual actions over allegorical ones, during a visit to Rome around 1662, and his perspectives were already widely known by 1690, when the Cluniac penned an open letter to the Huguenot minister Pierre Jurieu, who had used de Vert's approach to attack Catholic liturgy. In 1694 de Vert published a *Dissertation sur les mots de Messe et de Communion*, whose positions des Marettes often echoes. The reasons for the parallels between the *Travels* and the *Explication* are less easily explained. De Vert read a draft of the *Travels* in 1698, whence he may have gleaned information for his own

---

[17] See p. 80. On Tillemont's life and literary activities, see Ronald T. Ridley, "On Knowing Sébastien Le Nain de Tillemont: For the Tercentenary of His *Histoire*," *Ancient Society* 23 (1992): 233–95.
[18] See p. 101.
[19] See p. 139, n. 17. Their entire correspondence has been published by Joseph Nouaillac, *Lettres inédites de Lebrun Desmarettes à Baluze* (Crauffon, 1905).
[20] See p. 51.
[21] See pp. 186 and 187. Le Brun des Marettes had recourse to several of the Maurist Dom Mabillon's works, and corresponded with him, according to Fouré, "Jean-Baptiste Le Brun des Marettes," 77.
[22] See pp. 207 and 255.
[23] Guéranger, *Institutes*, 2:197. De Vert's views are described by Fr. Barthe in the foreword.
[24] See pp. 37–38.

work. Nevertheless, it is also possible that des Marettes had himself read drafts of the *Explication*, or corresponded with de Vert, since he credits the Cluniac for several observations.[25]

Le Brun des Marettes put his studies to use in reforming a series of liturgical books before and after publishing his *Travels*. In 1692, Archbishop Colbert named des Marettes to the commission tasked with preparing a new breviary for Rouen. The result, which reworked the Sunday Offices and replaced the ancient texts of responsories and antiphons of saints' feasts with passages of strictly scriptural origin, just as the Cluny breviary had done, was rejected by the canons of Rouen.[26] Des Marettes's efforts met better fortune in Orléans, where he composed a breviary at the instance of the bishop, Cardinal de Coislin. Promulgated in 1693, it also replaced non-scriptural texts — known as "ecclesiastical compositions" — with scriptural ones,[27] and ancient hymns with those of Santeuil. Finally, he also compiled a breviary for Nevers, issued in 1727. The Nivernais bishop Charles Fontaine des Montées de Prémery, in whose reign it was issued, claims in a preface to have sought to "restore the ancient integrity of the Divine Offices," while simultaneously replacing old ecclesiastical texts with novel scriptural ones.[28]

While maintaining a low profile, Le Brun des Marettes was integrated into a wide network of scholars and eminent churchmen who mutually assisted one another's researches and liturgical reforms. Firmly rooted in Rouen, Orléans, and the Port-Royal circle, he corresponded with notable monastics and cathedral canons of the realm, enjoyed the protection of powerful bishops, and left his mark on the early neo-Gallican movement.

THE *LITURGICAL TRAVELS*: A DRAMATIC GENESIS

Le Brun des Marettes's *Liturgical Travels* was first published under the pseudonym Sieur de Moléon by Florentin Delaulne in Paris in 1718.[29] The preface indicates, however, that most of the work had been written ten years earlier, with some portions dating back a further eight or ten

---

[25] See p. 59.
[26] Fouré, "Jean-Baptiste Le Brun des Marettes," 81.
[27] Cardinal de Coislin wrote in the preface, "We deemed that nothing should be inserted into the antiphons, nor in the versicles and responsories, that is not drawn from the Scriptures, so that in all these God himself may address us, or supply the words wherewith we may address him," and goes on to defend this decision (*Breviarium Aurelianense, Pars aestiva* [Orléans, 1693], 4).
[28] *Breviarium insignis ecclesiae Nivernensis, Pars verna* (Orléans, 1727), Preface.
[29] Le Brun des Marettes's preface to his edition of John of Avranches's *Liber de officiis ecclesiasticis* explains his penchant for publishing his works anonymously, quoting Salvian of Marseille's epistle to Salonius (PL 147:23B–24B). In summary, he refrained from using his own name to avoid worldly glory and human praise, and lest the authority of his writings be called into question given his own reputation. The latter reason seems especially pertinent in the case of the *Liturgical Travels*, published when Le Brun des Marettes's name was tarnished by his Jansenist associations.

years. The initial draft appears to have been already completed by 1697, as Jacques-Accurse Auvray (1633–1710), canon-penitentiary of Rouen, wrote an approbation in that year, later printed in the book's front matter. Auvray further urged des Marettes to write a chapter on Rouen, drawing on his edition of John of Avranches. This final chapter was likely composed in the same year, for it reproduces the Rouen Paschal table from 1697. At this point some controversy must have arisen over the book's discussion of pagan antiquities, since both de Vert's 1698 approbatory review and des Marettes's preface address the matter.

Then almost twenty years passed. Des Marettes alleged the press of business to explain his failure to publish the book earlier.[30] Nevertheless, it seems certain that the crackdown on Jansenism during the latter years of Louis XIV's reign caused his position to deteriorate and made further publicity unwise. The policy of "respectful silence" the Jansenists had adopted vis-à-vis Pope Alexander VII's 1665 formulary of submission became untenable when, at the king's request in 1705, Clement XI demanded open assent to the condemnations of Jansenist propositions. When the community of Port-Royal refused to accept the formulary, the pope suppressed their abbey. In 1709, the king's men forcibly removed the nuns and, two years later, destroyed most of the abbey's buildings. Des Marettes himself declined to sign the formulary, and soon lost his principal episcopal supporters, Cardinal de Coislin (d. 1706) and Archbishop Jacques-Nicolas Colbert of Rouen (d. 1707). Perhaps at this point he made a last-ditch effort to bring out the work: why else did he request a favorable review of the *Travels* from Canon Châtelain in 1706? But on 18 November 1707, on account of his recalcitrance on the matter of the formulary, and de Coislin's successor's enmity towards his predecessor's favorites, a commissary and six officers dragged him away from his home to the Bastille, where he remained imprisoned for five years. Many of his papers were seized and never returned, leaving him unable to finish and publish his annotated edition of Usuard's martyrology and other works, including perhaps a life of St. Jerome.[31] Nevertheless, Le Brun des Marettes did manage to preserve the draft of his *Travels*.

---

[30] See p. 5.
[31] Charles-Hugues Le Febvre de Saint-Marc and Claude-Pierre Goujet, *Supplément au nécrologe de l'abbaïe de Notre-Dame de Port-Royal des Champs* (n.p., 1735), 1:491, and Olivier Pinault, *Histoire abrégé de la dernière persécution de Port-Royal* (n.p., 1750), 1:331. Saint-Marc and Goujet state that the notes on Usuard eventually fell into the hands of the Jesuit Jean-Baptiste Du Sollier, who included them in his 1714 edition of the martyrology with no mention of their true authorship. Saint-Marc and Goujet wryly remark that Du Sollier "was graciously pleased to do M. des Marettes's notes the honor of associating them with his own. The public, which is indebted to him for this favor, would only have wished that he had carried his generosity so far as to apprising it thereof." Le Brun des Marettes's vanished work on St. Jerome is mentioned in Claude-Pierre Goujet, *Supplément au grand dictionnaire historique, généalogique, &c., de M. Louis Moréri* (Paris, 1735), 1:199.

Having signed the formulary, he was released in October 1712, and continued to make numerous additions to the manuscript. Some—such as a reference to the 1703 Parisian ceremonial[32]—were inserted tacitly; others, such as the curt footnotes registering the destruction of the abbey of Port-Royal-des-Champs, more explicitly. Further expansions, including an entire chapter on Laon, appear in a section entitled *Supplément* following the chapter on Rouen. After the index, Le Brun des Marettes made a few final corrections in a section headed *Omissions et fautes à corregir*. Finally, after the Sun King's death, the regency of Philip II, duke of Orléans, brought a relaxation of persecution, and on 25 June 1717, Delaulne secured the *approbation et privilège du roi* necessary for publication. Appended to the published *Travels* was a forty-five-page booklet entitled *Questions sur la liturgie de l'église d'Orient*, which contains the questions our author posed to the Syrian priest Philippe Guailan, with his answers.[33] Following Le Brun des Marettes's death, the *Liturgical Travels* and *Questions* were reprinted in 1757 in Paris by Nicolas-Martin Tilliard in an identical edition.

HISTORICAL RECORD, PILGRIMAGE ACCOUNT, OR REFORMIST TRACT?

Le Brun des Marettes's study of local rites is by no means an objective or comprehensive description, nor is it devoid of polemical intent, hidden and overt. He is a careful curator of the facts he presents—and, more important, leaves out. At times it is difficult to judge whether he is describing the past or present; that ambiguity may be part of his purpose, to create a tangible link with an "ever-present past," to borrow Xavier Bisaro's expression.[34] Freely mixing eyewitness accounts of contemporary ceremonies with reports of the contents of older books, he conjures for each diocese or religious house a sort of classic, ideal image, a kaleidoscopic view of its history that preserves only its best colors. Arguably his aim was to furnish an elaborate apology and scholarly sourcebook for the reforms that he and his circle were then introducing in their revision of diocesan rites throughout France, evoking French liturgies as yet uncorrupted by bad taste, ignorance, and impiety. As a travel account with a pious purpose, one may even describe the *Liturgical Travels* as pilgrimage literature, a quest to uncover and restore connection with a sacred past.

---

[32] See p. 57.
[33] The first page (437) states the questions were submitted to Guailan on 22, 23, and 24 March 1704, and describes him as a "Syrian priest, monk of St. Basil, and archdeacon of Antioch, formerly a schismatic, and for the past thirty years a Roman Catholic, persecuted by the Eastern schismatics of Damascus, and imprisoned for two years in a dungeon for having brought two bishops, six priests, and two hundred persons back into the communion of the Catholic, Apostolic, and Roman Church." Nothing further is known about this figure.
[34] Xavier Bisaro, *Le passé présent. Une enquête liturgique dans la France du début du XVIIIᵉ siècle*, Histoire religieuse de la France 38 (Cerf, 2012).

The *Travels* were written in piecemeal fashion, as Le Brun des Marettes admits at the beginning of the work. Whether by accident or design, his views are, therefore, scattered about the work as a number of "talking points," some of which are listed in his preface, and which gradually emerge as the work's leitmotifs. At times he freely signals his approval or distaste — with expressions like "this is perfectly natural," "this is the right way," or else "I will not amuse myself by recounting," "I pass over a number of things . . . that are neither beautiful nor useful," etc. In most cases, however, he will fully develop his perspectives on any particular subject only in a single chapter, so that one has to read the work through to the end in order to reconstruct his opinions. Moreover, given his predilection for antiquity, it is reasonable to assume that he prefers the more ancient practices he describes, but he does not always state so expressly, much less call for their restoration beyond the place in question. His nearly hundred-page index, which lists well-nigh every detail of ceremony, text, or material culture noted in the work, serves not only as a guide to the text's scattered remarks but also as a précis of his opinions on the topics discussed.

This reticence was good policy. He wrote during a fraught time, when liturgical preferences or even notes of merely historical interest could be interpreted as a sign of theological allegiance to Jansenism; indeed such views were the object of interrogation during his imprisonment.[35] As a result, in certain chapters he appears to conceal information that might have fueled anti-Jansenist animosity. His chapter on Port-Royal, in particular, is relatively laconic about the liturgical customs of the star-struck abbey, which were of keen interest, however, to his inquisitors at the Bastille.[36] At the same time, he openly praises the abbey of St-Cyran-en-Brenne, suppressed and destroyed for its Jansenist ties in 1712.

To aid readers in reconstructing des Marettes's worldview, we have compiled a list of the themes — architectural, disciplinary, ceremonial, etc. — that he returns to again and again, referring readers to the index to track down the relevant texts, and the footnotes for further study. While a

---

[35] The Jesuit Dominique de Colonia included Dom de Vert's *Explication* in his catalogue of Jansenist works for claiming that the Canon and Secrets were once said out loud, even though the Cluniac did not extend this matter of supposed historical fact into a prescription (*Bibliothèque Janseniste* [Brussels, 1739], 1:189). It is true that the Jansenist *curé* of Asnières near Paris, Jacques Jubé, adopted the custom of saying the Secret and Canon aloud, together with other practices des Marettes would have favored, such as the priest not reading any of the parts sung by one of the ministers or by the choir. The 1709 neo-Gallican missal of Meaux implied the Canon was to be said out loud, although the fierce opposition this aroused prevented its being put into practice.

[36] In the course of his interrogations, des Marettes insisted that Port-Royal followed the missal of Paris, as he does again in the *Travels* (pp. 174–75), but also admitted that their chaplain, Guillaume Marignier, heard the Epistle sitting and read the Secrets aloud, neither of which is mentioned in the book (Fouré, "Jean-Baptiste Le Brun des Marettes," 78). Elsewhere in the text, des Marettes does defend the practice of the celebrant listening to the readings as they are chanted by someone else.

more thorough examination of his œuvre is surely to be desired, the views exposed and gathered here in summary do give us a clear impression of how deeply des Marettes is implicated in de Vert's rationalist school, as the 1718 reviewer in *L'Europe savante* recognized immediately.[37] It may also surprise readers to notice how many of these ideas were embraced by the Liturgical Movement and eventually made their way into the rite of Paul VI.

Liturgical Art and Architecture

Des Marettes exhibits a general hostility to the artistic and architectural developments of the late-medieval and Tridentine periods, with their "trifling ornamentation" and lack of taste for "antiquity," lavishing his attention instead on earlier arrangements. For example, our author believes that:

- The bishop's throne should be simple and stand behind the altar in the apse, visible from the nave and not obscured by a retable (see PLATES 5, 13, 14). Nearly all churches in his day had moved the bishop's chair to the north or south side, with the exception of Lyon.
- Until the time for Mass, altars should be bare, without cloths, candles, reliquaries, or retable. Such items should be brought up during the procession or set out before Mass by the sacristan.
- Since the altar is a table, its cloths ought to resemble tablecloths falling around evenly on all sides.
- The frontals or veils hung in front, to his mind originally meant to protect the reliquary cases housed under the altar, are nonsensical except on sepulcher-altars, and besides do not allow for the preferred tablecloth-style covering.
- The retable is an innovation that breaks up visibility in the sanctuary and forces unfortunate rearrangements in ceremonies and in layout, such as moving the episcopal chair from the center of the apse.
- Holy water stoups, because they are a replacement for the fountains in the porticos of ancient basilicas meant for Christians to wash themselves in before entering a church, should be outside the front doors, and only used upon entering, not upon exiting, which people only do out of habit because they have forgotten the original meaning.
- The tabernacle should not be fixed on the altar as prescribed by the 1614 Roman ritual, because this shows a complete lack of "taste for antiquity." He prefers suspended pyxes or small aumbries built into pillars or walls.
- Early Christians said Masses in the Roman catacombs to avoid persecution, and the crypt-chapels of many churches have their origin in this practice. Further, the use of candles at Mass goes back to these primitive days when they were required to give light underground, and have no mystical meaning.

---

[37] "Article I," *L'Europe savante* 5, no. 2 (October 1718): 165–66.

Discipline of the Eucharist

Le Brun des Marettes is impatient with restricting communion at most Masses to the celebrating priest, and interested in relics of practices of more frequent communion by clerics and religious. However, he never advocates for more frequent communion by the laity. He believes that:

- Hosts should be consumed at the Mass for which they are consecrated, and subsequently reserved only for Viaticum, which was the primitive practice.
- Communion of the clergy under two species is desirable, as well as communion of the priest and his ministers from the same host.
- Mass in the presence of the Blessed Sacrament, and frequent exposition in general, is an inappropriate modern innovation.
- At the elevation and at exposition of the Blessed Sacrament, silent adoration is most fitting, without song or ceremony.
- All should receive communion on Good Friday, or at least the altar ministers.
- Extreme Unction before Viaticum is more ancient, even if contrary to the order prescribed by the 1614 Roman ritual.

Discipline of the Other Sacraments and Rituals

Des Marettes favors the restoration of penitential disciplines such as fasting, abstinence, and public penance during Lent. Regarding the other sacraments, several ancient practices catch his attention:

- Baptism should take place near the church door.
- He shows interest in and provides documentation for the practice of giving communion and Confirmation to infants immediately after their baptism.
- Exorcisms should not be said when the ceremonies of baptism are supplied; this was a much-debated issue given the recent mass conversion of Huguenots.
- He finds the renewal of baptismal vows by the young girls at the Hôpital de la Salpêtrière in Paris a "very beautiful and timely" practice, and wishes it were implemented in parish churches.
- He frequently commends the practice of expulsion and reconciliation of penitents during Lent.
- He notes with interest the custom of blessing the nuptial bed.
- Abstinence used to include milkmeats as well, and indults for their consumption still had to be granted each year.
- Saturday abstinence is novel and still not followed in many places (Spain), or is mitigated (not after Christmas in Orléans).

Death and Funerals

He reports pious funeral customs especially as they express solidarity between the classes and a humble awareness of the gravity of death and judgment. For example, he often describes:

- Placing the moribund on ashes and washing their bodies after death;
- Accompanying bodies to the cemetery and giving money to the poor on their anniversaries;
- Funerals and foundations that include almsgiving;
- Burying the poor in the church's cemeteries for free.
- He believes that the custom of burying priests and bishops in churches facing west, and laymen facing east, is a recent and therefore deplorable custom.
- Funeral Masses should always be said in the presence of the body.

Vestments

Regarding vestments, des Marettes is keen to promote de Vert's rational, evolutionary accounts of their origin and development as older forms of everyday clothing with practical, not mystical, meanings.

- The maniple was originally a handkerchief to wipe the nose or face, and acolytes used to have them too (at Cluny for example).
- The cope was originally a mere hood, then evolved into a cape with a pointed hood, which was finally reduced to a semi-circular flap in back.
- The ornamental batons carried in processions or used at Mass were originally used to lean on, or as walking sticks, or to control the crowd, or by the cantor to control the singers.
- Clergy should pray bareheaded in church, so he pays special attention to the use of clerical headwear (birettas, camails, etc).
- The almuce was originally a head covering; only with time did it come to be generally carried over the arm.
- Chasubles used to be conical and ample, covering the whole body.

Divine Office: Practice and Ceremonial

In the *Travels*, des Marettes shows less interest in reforms of the Divine Office, but he is content to apply de Vert's principles to explain the origin of ceremonies.[38]

- The hours should be sung separately at their proper times, according to the ancient custom, not anticipated or grouped together for convenience.
- During Lent, Vespers should not be said in the early afternoon in order to anticipate dinner, but at the same time as the rest of the year.
- Evening Tenebrae during Lent is an irrational mistake; moreover, the extinguishing of candles at this ceremony is common to Matins and Lauds all year, and so requires no mystical explanation on this occasion.
- The nocturns of Matins were originally celebrated separately.
- The medieval liturgical dramas, like the *pastourelles* and *Quem quaeritis* plays, "have been wisely abolished, for they are not to the taste of our century."

---

[38] Curiously, he makes no mention of the two most prominent changes he introduced into the breviaries of Orléans and Nevers—features common to all the neo-Gallican books—namely, the reordering of the psalms in the canonical hours and the principle that the texts of all antiphons, responsories, and versicles should be scriptural.

Mass Ceremonial

When it comes to the Mass, Le Brun des Marettes thoroughly applies de Vert's rationalism to explain the origin of ceremonies. He also shows a concern for hygiene and cleanliness.

• He favors the full pre-Mass procession with water blessing, sprinkling of the people, and visitation of the chapter house; in his day it had been reduced in most places to a sprinkling of the choir.

• The Tridentine rite's prayers at the foot of the altar were a preparation for Mass better said in the sacristy or on the way to the altar.

• He disdains the tropes he finds in medieval missals.

• The whole *Gloria* and *Credo* should be sung by both sides of the choir, not in alternation.

• Ablutions that involve drinking water or wine used to rinse the fingers are unsanitary.

• "Doubling" of readings by the priest is a late and regrettable development; this includes all the sung propers, not just Epistle and Gospel.

• The *Per quam haec omnia* prayer is a blessing of grapes, rather than a prayer over the Eucharistic gifts: an important matter of controversy in his day.

• The kiss of peace is more ancient than the pax-brede and a more fitting expression of communion, although it had nearly vanished in France by his time.

• He is proud of the pontifical blessing after the *Agnus Dei*, a Gallican feature that was being restored by some bishops in his day.

• The last Gospel is a modern innovation, which he is content to point out has not caught on in many places in France.

• He is delighted by the use of assistant priests, the *curés-cardinaux*, at pontifical Masses on major feasts, because of their antiquity and their uniqueness to France, and possibly because of the priestly collegiality the practice shows.

• The eating of blessed bread by the congregation after Mass is a vestige of the ancient Christian love feast or agape.

• The meaning of the term *submissa voce*, together with what parts of the Mass were to be said silently, was being fiercely disputed by liturgists at the time, and des Marettes gathers evidence and stakes out his own opinion.

• He is fond of de Vert's treatise on ritual gestures (see *Explication*, volume 2), in every case explaining gestures in the Mass and Office (e.g., raising the voice or hands, signs of the cross, bows, etc.) as physical effects of liturgical texts (*Sursum corda*, *Supplices*, etc).

The Liturgical Year

• There should be no octaves or feasts during Lent or Advent.

• He points out that laity take home the new fire blessed at the Easter Vigil, and in general stresses the practical origins of this practice.

- He loves stations and processions of all kinds (Rogations, Lenten stations, etc.), but mentions few devotions to saints or the Blessed Virgin Mary.
- Use of the common Preface for Sundays of Lent is more ancient and logical, since these days are not fasting days.
- There should be no fasting on the vigil of Pentecost, because it is part of Eastertide.
- Private Masses should not be said on Holy Saturday, despite contemporary custom to the contrary.

Clerical Discipline and Religious Life
- Clerics should be willing to serve in any liturgical role, even those "beneath" their level of ordination (e.g., a deacon acting as a candle-bearer); defense of the lower orders was a personal matter for des Marettes, who remained a minor cleric his whole life.
- Choirboys serving at the altar should have their heads shorn.
- He is interested in the consecration of nuns and their veils by bishops.
- Full-length prostration on the ground is the true, ancient form of humiliation, not the more modern forms of kneeling or bowing.
- Cathedral chapters were once corporate bodies that lived and ate in common and in fraternity with their bishop; he points out vestiges of this common life wherever he finds it.
- Likewise, he lavishes praise on communities that observe an exemplary asceticism, especially the monks of the Benedictine abbey of Saint-Cyran-en-Brenne, where one of the foremost French Jansenists, Jean Duvergier de Hauranne, was once commendatory abbot.
- He often notes the presence of the parish church (or vestiges thereof) in a side chapel of the cathedral. There may be a veiled note of critique here of canons' lack of pastoral responsibilities.[39]
- He is convinced that the *potus caritatis* of Maundy Thursday is a vestige of the paleo-Christian love feast or agape, and shows great interest in it.
- He admires the ancient custom of singing the Office from memory, particularly commending the chapters of Lyon and Rouen for maintaining this discipline.

Even this cursory glance at Le Brun des Marettes's views permits us to establish several points. First, he was definitely a partisan of Dom Claude de Vert's rationalist school, which was described in the foreword. But he was also sympathetic to several tenets upheld by the Jansenists and other reformers: one notes the pronounced moral rigorism and the allergy to elements of Baroque piety. He also shared his generation's enthusiasm

---

[39] See p. 347.

for the fresh discoveries in liturgical antiquities recently brought to light by authors like the Maurist fathers and a general preference for what was regarded as ancient purity, free of "Gothic" contamination.

Instead of hastily resorting to worn-out labels, however, it will be more helpful to reframe the conversation. It is evident that receptions of this period of liturgical history have hitherto been highly tendentious. At the outset, Dom Guéranger lambasted writers in the school of Dom de Vert and the early neo-Gallican reformers as the vanguard of an "anti-liturgical heresy,"[40] whose termitic influence undermined the church in France and even set the stage for the French Revolution. More recent scholarship, on the other hand, has turned this condemnation on its head, lionizing the Jansenists and neo-Gallicans as brave visionaries whose ideas foreshadowed the Liturgical Movement of the twentieth century and the new rites that claimed its paternity. Any motivated reading of the period with a priori polemical intent, however, is destined to fail to do it justice. It deserves to be studied on its own terms.

To achieve a more balanced approach, the term "Jansenist," often applied indiscriminately to figures of this period, requires more rigorous scrutiny. Earlier broad-brush and pejorative portrayals of Jansenism have recently given way to more positive appraisals, seeing it as "an alternative stream of Tridentine Reform" or "a Reformation that failed,"[41] and acknowledging its complexity.[42] Unfortunately, the term is still applied disparagingly as well as inaccurately to many who had no direct interest in Cornelius Jansen's theological claims. Ellen Weaver's division of Jansenism into monastic, theological, moral, and erudite streams is a useful step toward sorting out the motivations that drew people to the movement.[43] Jansenist leaders, it is true, took an interest in the liturgy from the start. Antoine Arnauld wrote several treatises on pastoral practice during his exile in the Netherlands, and was involved in the redaction of the 1664 ritual of Alet, which drew criticism for its Jansenist tinge. Port-Royalists, such as our author's friend Nicolas Letourneux, tended to encourage reverence in the ceremonies, the translation of liturgical texts, and lay understanding of both.[44] Later Jansenist figures, such as the parish priest Jacques Jubé (1674–1745), went in a more radical direction, reciting the Canon out loud, for example. But in most cases these reformers shared

---

[40] For Guéranger's definition of this concept, see his *Institutions*, 2:397–407.
[41] See Blanchard and Yoder, *Jansenism*, 5 and Ellen Weaver, *The Inner History of a Reformation That Failed: The Monastery of Port-Royal (1647–1684)* (Princeton University Press, 1973).
[42] For an up-to-date bibliography and an international selection of Jansenist texts, see Blanchard and Yoder, *Jansenism*.
[43] See Weaver, "Neo-Gallican Liturgies."
[44] See, for example, Weaver, "Neo-Gallican Liturgies," and Weaver, "Liturgy for the Laity: The Jansenist Case for Popular Participation in Worship in the Seventeenth and Eighteenth Centuries," *Studia liturgica* 19 (1989), 47–59.

the ultimate goals of the Tridentine Counter-Reformation, and indeed, interest in liturgy was common to Catholic reform movements far beyond Jansenist circles. Although, as Weaver has pointed out, most of the men involved in the revision of books in this period had ties to Port-Royal, the true extent of theological Jansenism in the neo-Gallican reforms has to be studied on a case-by-case basis.

One must also be wary of the breezy enthusiasm with which some authors have compared the neo-Gallican movement to the programs of Pistoia or Paul VI. Le Brun des Marettes's voice was one in a diverse chorus of transalpine post-Tridentine reformers whose melodies were cut off abruptly by the Revolution and occluded after Vatican I.[45] Whether the Liturgical Movement and the discussions during and after Vatican II were truly in harmony with this chorus is less clear. Despite obvious overlap in particulars—such as the location and decoration of the altar, communion under both species, or a general distaste for the medieval period—Le Brun des Marettes's views on liturgical reform differ from twentieth-century programs in important respects. Notably, his interest in lay participation, or in what would later be called "pastoral liturgy," is minimal. Although he does describe laymen's enthusiastic participation in the ritual life of their cities, his focus is on the choral Office, that monumental edifice of the Mass and liturgical hours that was the supreme expression of the common life of canons and monks. For him, the integrity of religious life is intimately tied to proper ceremonial splendor. It was the role of the cathedral to set the tone for worship, and for the parishes to strive to imitate it as their resources allowed. In this respect, des Marettes is more akin to earlier reformers and liturgical commentators like Radulph of Rivo—who concerned himself exclusively with excellence in the canonical liturgy—rather than to the Liturgical Movement.[46]

Still less does the *Travels* suggest that there is any unhealthy separation between the people and the ministers. Nowhere does Le Brun des Marettes intimate that rood screens, the silent Canon, or the Latin language are barriers to participation. Some in his generation did indeed want the laity to take a more active role in the ceremonies—encouraging them to sing the ordinary along with the priest, printing vernacular missals, removing rood screens, and having the silent parts said aloud, etc.—but such ambitions are not apparent in the *Travels*. Des Marettes's observation regarding laymen bespeak a fascination with antiquity rather than

---

[45] On Catholic ecclesiological perspectives before Vatican I, see Francis Oakley, *The Conciliarist Tradition: Constitutionalism in the Catholic Church 1300–1870* (Oxford University Press, 2003) and John O'Malley, *Vatican I: The Council and the Making of the Ultramontane Church* (Belknap Press of Harvard University Press, 2018).
[46] Radulph of Rivo, *De canonum observantia*, ed. and trans. Gerhard Eger and Zachary Thomas, *On the Observance of Canons*, Brepols Library of Christian Sources 16 (Brepols, 2025).

anything akin to the pastoral Weltanschauung of the twentieth century.

Further, Le Brun des Marettes's classicism does not envisage a return to a maximally primitive, apostolic Christianity along the lines of Pistoia or the architects of the post-Vatican II liturgy. For Le Brun des Marettes, de Vert, and the composers of neo-Gallican books contemporary with them, the enormous choral Offices of France's cathedrals, collegiate churches, and monasteries, which had developed across late antiquity and the Middle Ages, were the undisputed norm for Catholic liturgy. They may have rejected a bevy of particular innovations, but they did not seek "noble simplicity" as a matter of principle. Rather, Le Brun des Marettes and de Vert show a highly developed ritual sense. Their taste seeks out the integral forms of liturgical life in the Latin tradition: the Sunday sprinkling rite of the church and common places, survivals of ancient baptismal rituals in the Easter Vigil, the full episcopal liturgy concelebrated with local clergy, and the processions, stations, and other rituals of urban religion that assimilated French towns to the liturgical fabric of the Rome of St. Gregory the Great. If Le Brun des Marettes discovers these rites currently in use, he praises them; if he finds them observed in centuries past, he lavishes his attention on the older state of affairs. He lauds the restoration of previous forms, and curtly reports their lapse within his own lifetime.[47] In each case, the picture he limns, based on both contemporary practices and ceremonies drawn from ancient sources, is an idealized vision of liturgical life at its zenith, when the chapters were observant, the people wholeheartedly participating, and the liturgy fully integrated into urban life.

In these and other ways, this generation of Catholic reformers stand in stark contrast to the tendencies of the radical Enlightenment, and their distance from the later Liturgical Movement is even greater. The destruction wrought by waves of modern revolutions upon the sacred landscape of western Europe resulted in the near-total extinction of the sung choral liturgy in cathedral chapters, monasteries, and collegiate churches. Even the most valiant attempts to restore liturgical observance in the wake of this maelstrom—one thinks of Guéranger's work at Solesmes—resulted in mere echoes of the grandeur of Ancien Régime ceremony. As a result, the participants of the twentieth-century Liturgical Movement were formed in a period in which much civic, martial, and religious ceremony had evaporated. In response and as a partial concession to post-World War II bourgeois culture and an ascendant Marxism, many reformers focused their attention instead on ritual simplicity and ecumenical reconciliation, de-emphasized the sacrificial priesthood in favor of lay involvement in the

---

[47] See, e.g., p. 145, where he praises his patron Cardinal de Coislin for restoring the episcopal blessing, or, contrariwise, p. 278, where he notes that Notre-Dame-de-la-Ronde abandoned the offertory procession at funeral Masses.

Mass, and discarded the redemptive witness of the evangelical counsels in favor of a warmer attitude toward the secular order: decisive factors in the creation of the modern rite of Paul VI. Needless to say, the appetite for a "pre-Constantinian," "de-Hellenized" Christianity and the primitivist art forms that marked the mid-twentieth century could not be further removed from Le Brun des Marettes's taste for the public religion of antiquity and his admiration for fine craftsmanship, just as the love of fasting and penance that was part and parcel of his generation's concept of Christian antiquity found no place in the post-conciliar reception of the early Church.

Rather than relying upon ready-made labels and comparisons that do not respect the integrity of historical epochs, it is more instructive to see Le Brun des Marettes's work as a product of his own time and as an expression of his own personal taste, deeply formed by his experiences at Port-Royal and his friendship with Letourneux, but just as equally by figures such as Mabillon and de Vert who had no relation to Port-Royal or Jansenism at all but belonged to the broader currents of early-modern liturgical antiquarianism, Catholic reform, and rationalizing trends. Des Marettes's personal "taste"—the first word of his preface, a watchword of de Vert, and a major theme of his century—is a decisive factor in his account. His quest for "the most pure and ancient antiquity" in the cities and provinces of France was intended to please the fancies of that century of Italian journeys and Versailles's Apollonian king. The same taste led him to admire the enduring ceremonial inheritance of late antiquity as much as the vestiges of Roman baths and funeral urns. The classic ideals he sketches for each of the cities he visits present us with his own vision of reform: an image of an ecclesial society reborn.

Edinburgh
Feast of St. Benedict
2025

TRANSLATORS' PREFACE

THIS volume offers a complete translation of Jean-Baptiste Le Brun des Marettes's *Liturgical Travels Through France*, including the original plates, preface, and approbations. We strove to preserve the tenor of the author's style, "off-putting [...] heavy [...] dense and poorly composed" though it may be.[1] Des Marettes used square brackets to mark passages that digress somewhat from the main thrust of his remarks, but since this practice is alien to modern conventions and might distract the reader, we have chosen not to retain them. We have also silently incorporated the emendations and additions printed after the text. The names of churches are kept in French, but the names of chapels are put into English. Terms without a ready English equivalent, such as *aumusson*, remain in French, as do peculiarly regional terms, such as *marguillier* and *clergeon*. We have opted for modern orthography of toponyms, providing des Marettes's spelling in parentheses only if they are of interest. Latin quotations appear as in the original, except for the use of ligatures and diacritical marks, with translations in footnotes. These translations are our own except for scriptural passages, for which we have used the Douay-Rheims edition.

The footnotes trace the ritual books, scholarly sources, and learned correspondents on which Le Brun des Marettes relied in crafting his accounts, and they occasionally offer anecdotes that help to bring the period to life. The edition, therefore, permits an assessment of our author's fidelity as an historian as well as a granular picture of the network of Catholic reformers active at the turn of the eighteenth century. The length of the *Table de matières* prohibits reproducing it in full, although careful students of the text may wish to consult it. In its place, we have assembled a set of three indices: one of subjects, another of churches mentioned in the work, and a third listing all liturgical books cited, whether by Le Brun des Marettes—including those we were unable to identify—or by the editors and other contributors.

To supply further insight into the period, a foreword by Fr. Barthe discusses the ritual life of seventeenth-century France and contemporary schools of thought about its reform. In appendix 1, François Hou presents the personnel, structure, and activities of the early modern French cathedral chapters responsible for the custody, financing, and deployment of the daily round of worship which Le Brun des Marettes describes. Finally, in appendix 2, Shawn Tribe describes the sanctuaries in which the ceremonies took place, in light of their historical development and their contemporary critique by enlightened reformers.

---

[1] See Fouré, "Jean-Baptiste Le Brun des Marettes," 81.

Translators' Preface

This project was begun under the spell of Dom Prosper Guéranger's charming prose and irresistible love for the Latin liturgical tradition. Subsequent visits and pilgrimages to France have confirmed our affection for a country that still retains some of the ancient charm that belonged to the Church's Eldest Daughter. Several friends made along the way deserve our gratitude for their contribution to this translation. We would like to thank the Frenchmen who lent their expertise to help resolve knotty problems of translation: Philippe Guy; Laurent Ferri, curator at the Division of Rare and Manuscript Collections at Cornell University; Henri Adam de Villiers of the Schola Sainte-Cécile; and Bruno de Labriolle of the École Grégorienne.

We are especially obliged to Fr. Claude Barthe, François Hou, and Shawn Tribe, whose learned contributions have enriched the work. Moreover, Fr. Jean-Pierre Herman and Fr. Ambrose Bennett deserve our thanks for casting an attentive eye on the drafts of the manuscript, as does Matthew Hall for his thoughtful comments on the introduction. We extend our gratitude to Richard Yoder as well for his insight on the history of Port-Royal-des-Champs.

Much of the research for this volume would have been difficult or impossible without the very useful Usuarium database, directed by Miklós István Földváry, whose cheerful and unrelenting assistance have made him an exemplary colleague. His studies on medieval ritual diversity have also profoundly informed our own approach to liturgical research. We are grateful, too, to Régis Garand at the Archives départementales de la Seine-Maritime, who kindly answered inquiries on the publication history of the *Liturgical Travels*, and to the staff of the British Museum and the Bibliothèque nationale de France for providing us with several stunning and little-known images for this volume.

Finally, we would be remiss to conclude without expressing our appreciation for the readers of the Canticum Salomonis weblog, who saw the first fruits of our translation efforts and whose interest therein was a fillip to their full harvest, now made available thanks to Os Justi Press and Peter Kwasniewski, for whose assistance we are obliged.

VOYAGES
LITURGIQUES DE FRANCE,
OU
RECHERCHES
FAITES EN DIVERSES VILLES
DU ROYAUME,

Par le Sieur DE MOLEON.
Contenant plusieurs particularitez touchant
les Rits & les Usages des Eglises:
Avec des Découvertes sur l'Antiquité
Ecclesiastique & Payenne.

A PARIS,
Chez FLORENTIN DELAULNE, Libraire,
rue Saint-Jacques, à l'Empereur.

M. DCCXVIII.
Avec Approbation & Privilege du Roy.

LITURGICAL TRAVELS THROUGH FRANCE

OR

Researches made in various Cities of the Realm

By the Sieur DE MOLÉON,

Containing many Particularities touching
the Rites and Uses of the Churches:

With Discoveries in ecclesiastical and pagan Antiquity

APPROBATIONS

BY order of my Lord the Chancellor, I have read a manuscript entitled *Liturgical Travels Through France*. This work contains a great number of curious observations, which seem to me most useful for understanding the ceremonies of the Church. At Paris, 7 June 1717.

Jean-Antoine PASTEL

❖ ❖ ❖

Approbations of M. Châtelain, canon of Notre-Dame of Paris and delegate for the revision of Church books; of M. de Vert, and of M. Auvray.

M. Châtelain, canon of the cathedral of Notre-Dame of Paris, having read this book, gave the following testimony in writing: "There are excellent things to be learned from this work. At Paris, 18 February 1706."

Claude CHÂTELAIN, canon of the church of Paris

M. de Vert, treasurer and vicar general of Cluny, having read this book, gave the following testimony in writing: "This work cannot fail to be most useful to the Church and to give great pleasure to those who love and know something about these matters. I am not among those who find fault with the profane erudition woven into the work; on the contrary, it appears entirely appropriate. But I digress; I cannot exhort you enough to offer your *Travels* to the public. At Abbeville, 8 September 1698."

Claude DE VERT

M. Auvray, canon penitentiary of the cathedral of Rouen, and doctor of theology in the faculty of Paris: "The work on the rites of France's churches that you are urged to offer to the public can bring nothing but use and advantage. No one desires more heartily than I to see it in print. One can hope that you will not overlook those of the church of Rouen, which you know so well, of that church which is your mother, from which you have your spiritual birth. Given your edition of John of Avranches, how could you not be well-informed about them? At Rouen, 18 April 1697."

Jacques-Accurse AUVRAY

AUTHOR'S PREFACE

MY enduring taste for the rites and ancient customs of the churches of France has led me to undertake many journeys through the provinces of France. I have visited the majority of the most well-known churches and cathedrals, and believe that in the course of these journeys I have made some discoveries in ecclesiastical and pagan antiquities that may be of some use to the public and especially to the Church. My principal care has been to note the various rites and particular practices of the churches I have visited. I am persuaded that they will be received with some amount of pleasure, and that those who travel to the same places, if they desire to stop to hear high Mass or Vespers in the cathedral churches, will be more edified by the ceremonies that take place there for being informed about them in advance. Additionally, they will have learned the literal reasons for the practices and ceremonies of the Church, and the spirit of her prayers.

As for the rest, the reader will find in these *Travels* a description of the underground crypts that served as Christendom's first churches; ancient altars, the rood screens and veils that surrounded them; the origin and use of veils, lamps, candles, and chandeliers. He will also find canon-priests, archdeacons and other dignitaries, who even today chant the Mass at the altar together with the bishop and receive communion with him under the two species; the twelve *curés-cardinaux* of many churches in France, and where the word "cardinal" comes from; the various habits of the canons, chaplains, cantors, clerks, and choir boys; the almuces they wear on their head, shoulders, and arms; their *aumussons*, miters, small miters, calottes, round birettas, and square birettas; the four different kinds of surplice, albs, tunics, and chasubles; kerchiefs and maniples attached to the right arm of nuns and choir boys, or held between their fingers, and the reason why; the origin of the habit and hood of monks, and the veil of the nuns still consecrated specially by the bishop; details about nuns' reception of the sacred host, such as their solemn communion during the octave of their consecration, and about new priests who take communion for forty days after their ordination; the origin of the cloths of the communion table, the kiss of peace, and communion under two species that is still practiced in several churches; Confirmation given by the bishop to newly-baptized infants, holy communion from the chalice given to the same infants on the day of their Baptism, and to other children brought by their mothers and wet-nurses; the scrutiny or examination of catechumens; the four kinds of bows and four kinds of prostrations in practice today among ecclesiastics and religious men and women; the severity exercised in Lyon and Rouen against canons and cantors who are not present for their functions during the Office, or who sin against good morals; the various sorts of inclinations, reverences, and genuflexions, and the reverence similar to a woman's curtsy that cardinals make when greeting the pope in chapel, by foreign ambassadors greeting the king, by canons and other ecclesiastics of many churches, and by all choir boys of all the churches of France; the practice of public penance in the principal churches; of ashes, vergers, and the sackcloth exposed in the church on Ash Wednesday; the bed of ashes on which dying clerics, monks, and laymen expire; of lavatory stones to wash the dead before their burial, and more, along with the most significant ancient customs, rites, practices, and ceremonies of the Gallican church that I have observed in various places: the origin of the collation on fasting days; dry Masses and Masses of the presanctified; agapes still practiced in churches today; bread baked for the poor and distributed to the poor during funerals and burials; houses, lands, and vineyards given to the Church to provide the bread and wine necessary for the sacrifice of the altar; bread and wine offered at Masses for the Dead and carried to the altar; charters of donations made to churches and monasteries and placed on the altar; serfs or slaves of both sexes given to the church; the manumission and enfranchisement of these serfs; prisoners freed by bishops; the oath of fidelity and obedience sworn by suffragan bishops to their metropolitans, and by abbots and abbesses to the diocesan bishop; religious men and women who are still subject to the diocesan bishop and who sing the Office of the diocese; public processions at which religious once assisted with the clergy and monks, in which rods, sticks, and clubs were carried, and where many canons and other clerics still walk barefoot; the processions held before Mass and Vespers on major feasts to conduct the bishop from the episcopal palace to his church; Sunday processions before the high Mass to sprinkle the altars, the church, the clergy and people, the dorter, the infirmary, the cemetery, the cloister, the well, the refectory, and to bless the table; the proclamation of Easter on the day of Epiphany; descriptions of the most important churches and monasteries along with their unique customs; the most beautiful mausolea of the realm, ancient caskets, tombs, and sepulchers of Christians and pagans; urns where the ashes of cremated pagans were placed; amphitheaters, arenas, grottos, aqueducts, and public baths, pyramids, asyla, ancient inscriptions both pagan and Christian, and the neighborhoods and places of the towns, churches, and palaces where all of these are found, of which the reader will find a number of engravings in this work.

It may perhaps be accounted a fault that I have mixed profane antiquity with ecclesiastical. But one may easily be comforted, if one wishes, by drawing some utility and instruction from it. Was not the Church built on the ruins of paganism? And what danger could there be in showing that the pagans adored false divinities and placed all their glory in haughty edifices, in statues and inscriptions, in order to immortalize their name and memory? That they spent their time in games, spectacles, and other public entertainments that were sometimes horrifying? Indeed among these frightful diversions there were athletic combats, gladiators and ferocious beasts, in which the martyrs were sometimes cast to be devoured in the arenas of the amphitheaters. Is it so terrible that I have noted what I have seen, and described it in passing, in addition to pyramids, urns, and other things of this nature? All of this will help us better understand how much more spiritual and excellent our religion is than that of the pagans, and how necessary it was that the apostles and their successors worked to reduce the pride of these sages of the world under the yoke of the Gospel and to the humble maxims of the crucified Jesus.

In my descriptions of cities I have not sought to amuse myself by recounting the old fables about their foundation and etymology, and I think that they will not be sorely missed, because in all such things there is almost nothing verifiable. But I have reported a few interesting things about them, and about their privileges and prerogatives.

The style of these *Travels* is simple, natural, and without affectation, as befits a traveler, and as concise as possible. I have tried to wed utility and pleasure, so that every reader may find something pleasing. I have noted in each place that which is most curious and most worthy of observation, and I have put the names of cities, countries, and rivers in Latin for the benefit of men of letters. They will find them listed in alphabetical order at the end of the book. I have also added an index of the main subjects, for the convenience of all.

Since most of these journeys were made ten years ago, and some of them even eight or ten years before that, I beg the reader to regard them as a product of their time, and not to accuse me of falsehood if he perceives that some changes have taken place in the meantime, since I cannot guarantee that things have remained the same. The many works with which I have been charged, and certain other businesses that have arisen, have prevented me from publishing them sooner.

VIENNE

VIENNE in the Dauphiné, *Vienna Allobrogum* in Latin, was a Roman colony, and holds the distinction of being one of the oldest cities in Gaul, boasting a rich collection of antiquities. It is built in the form of a semicircle on the slopes of three mountains along the banks of the rivers Rhône (*ad Rhodanum*) and Gère (*ad Jairam*).

Vienne was not only a Roman colony but in all likelihood the seat of the praetorian prefect of the Gauls. It is listed before Lyon in the *Notitia* of the Western Empire[1] and in the letter written by the two churches of Vienne and Lyon to the churches of Asia and Phrygia about their first martyrs, as Eusebius reports in his *Ecclesiastical History*.[2]

The Romans greatly enjoyed Vienne, as evidenced by what is left of their monuments. The magnificent array of ruins, including fortresses, amphitheaters, aqueducts, baths, grottos, pyramids, and ancient inscriptions, serve as enduring testaments to its original glory. The modern city is nearly buried by ruins of the old; there is, indeed, no other city in France where so many monuments of antiquity are preserved.

Near the Porte de Lyon (see PLATE 3), there is a tower dubbed the Tour de Pilate, because, according to popular tradition, Pilate ended his days there. The veracity of this tale, however, is not certain. Although it is true that Ado, archbishop of Vienne, recounts in his chronicle that Pilate was exiled to Vienne and ended his days there, taking his own life out of despair, one would wish for a more ancient source on the matter than a ninth-century writer.[3]

Church of Saint-Sévère

Beyond this tower, on the left stands the church of St-Sévère. It preserves stone tombs and epitaphs that seem to be of very ancient origin.

According to his epitaph, albeit not contemporary, set on the pavement in front of the high altar, with two others nearby, the eponymous Saint Severus was a priest of Vienne in antiquity who had this church built and is buried therein.

The church preserves the epitaphs of many pagans, who were usually buried on the verges of main roads.

Inside a chapel beyond the main altar to the left there is an ancient Greek epitaph of a Christian lady who died during the consulship of Valentinian and Anatolius (the year 440) and was buried on the day of the Parasceve, or

---

[1] *Notitia dignitatum*, ed. Otto Seeck (Berlin, 1876), 105. This was a document of the late Roman Empire that details its administrative organization.
[2] Eusebius of Caesarea, *Ecclesiastical History* 5.1.1, ed. Gustave Bardy, *Histoire ecclésiastique*, Sources chrétiennes 41 (Cerf, 1955), 6.
[3] Ado of Vienne, *Chronicon*, *Aetas sexta* (PL 123:77C).

Good Friday, in the hope of resurrection with Jesus Christ. The presence of this epitaph shows that some Greek families settled in Vienne, and that at that time the Greek language was not yet entirely unknown.

In a chapel near the one just mentioned, there is an epitaph where the name "Epagathus" appears twice. This might refer to a member of the family of Saint Epagathus of Vienne, who was called "advocate of the early Christians"[4] and suffered martyrdom in Lyon together with Saint Blandina and her companions.

Church of Saint-André-le-Bas

The abbey church of St-André-le-Bas is beautifully built. Two marble columns of striking height and breadth support the choir vault. The church contains many ancient epitaphs, such as one near the belfry, which reports that a certain King Conrad, finding the church in dilapidated state, undertook its restoration and established therein a community of monks or endowed it generously.[5] This Conrad was king of Burgundy and Arles in the tenth century, and one of the most pious princes of his age.

The Table ronde

Near this monastery, on the other side of the street, there is an ancient asylum called the Table ronde ("round table"), apparently because there used to be one there. All that remains of it today are four pillars standing upright over a platform. Those who sought refuge here could not be seized, nor could goods deposited here be confiscated.

Notre-Dame-de-la-Vie

A bit further on, in the middle of a square, stands a church called Notre-Dame-de-la-Vie ("Our Lady of Life"). It is said to be the location of the old praetorium, where justice was administered. One can still see very tall Corinthian columns supporting the square roof of the church. In front of the altar lies the tomb of Jean Faber or Le Fèvre, archbishop of Tarsus.

Next to this church is the place where justice is administered along with the *conciergerie*,[6] whose prisons are very beautiful, if such a thing can be said about prisons.

A five-hundred-year-old ordinary of the church of Vienne states that the nuns of the monastery of Ste-Colombe used to assist at the Rogation processions with the clergy of the cathedral.

Cloisters of Saint-Maurice

At the entrance to what are called the cloisters of St-Maurice there is a gate that leads to the Porte d'Avignon. On the gate of these cloisters

---

[4] Eusebius of Caesarea, *Ecclesiastical History* 5.1.10, ed. Bardy, 8.
[5] *Corpus des inscriptions de la France médiévale* 15, no. 78.
[6] *Conciergeries* were prisons run by a Parlement.

there is a very ancient pagan inscription, engraved on a large stone in the coarse characters that used be called uncials:

> DD. FLAMINICA VIENNAE
> TEGULAS AENEAS AURATAS,
> CUM CARPUSCULIS ET
> VESTITURIS BASIUM, ET SIGNA
> CASTORIS ET POLLUCIS CUM EQUIS,
> ET SIGNA HERCULIS ET MERCURI.
> D. S. D.[7]

This inscription shows that Castor and Pollux, as well as Hercules and Mercury, used to be venerated in Vienne as gods, and that they had not only priests called *flamines*, but also priestesses called *flaminicae*. One of the latter consecrated this inscription to the memory of these four children of Jupiter.[8]

The main portal of the cathedral of St-Maurice of Vienne is very beautiful. It is flanked by two smaller portals on each side, and adorned by two tall towers that also serve as belfries.

The church is very beautiful inside, well-lit, large, and entirely whitewashed, with azure vaults. It is a sign of its eminence that this church used always to be referred to as "holy"—*Sancta Viennensis Ecclesia*—and as "the most ancient church in Gaul", and that thirty-seven or thirty-eight of its archbishops are recognized as saints.

There is nothing on top of the high altar except a small retable between one and one and a half feet tall. The altar table is slightly recessed (see PLATE 4).[9]

There are chapels all along the walls of the church. One is dedicated to the Holy Ghost and is also known as the Chapelle tabernière on account of a vineyard that was given to the chapel for the purpose of supplying the sacristy with wine for the Holy Sacrifice. Several other churches in France have received certain lands, vineyards, or houses as alms to provide bread and wine, the matter for the Sacrifice of our altars.[10]

---

[7] "By decree of the decurions, the *flaminica* of Vienne gave the gilded brazen tiles with the antefixes and decorations of its pedestals, the statues of Castor and Pollux with their horses, as well as those of Hercules and Mercury. At her own expense" (*Corpus Inscriptionum Latinarum* 12.1904, *Inscriptiones Latinae Selectae* 3400, *Inscriptions latines de Narbonnaise* Vienne 88).

[8] Author's note: Pollux, however, was not strictly speaking the son of Jupiter: he was actually the son of Leda, whom Jupiter loved, and of Tyndareus her husband.

[9] Altars with a recessed center, many of which are still extant, were meant to contain the Precious Blood in the event of its spilling.

[10] This explanation for the chapel's sobriquet comes from Nicolas Chorier, *Histoire sur les antiquitez de la ville de Vienne*, 2nd ed. (Vienne, 1673), 199, who adds that the wine produced by the attached vineyard was placed in a vessel set atop a table in this chapel, such that every priest who went to say Mass in this church could serve himself, so that the appellation *tabernière* arose from the Latin *taberna* or *tabernarius* ("tavern," "taverner"). But Alfred de Terrebasse, *Inscriptions antiques et du Moyen Âge de Vienne*

In the pavement of the church, near the middle of the nave towards the main portal, one can see the remains of a chapel that St. Ado, archbishop of Vienne, had built in honor of Our Lord's Holy Sepulcher.[11] When the chapel was moved to the small cloister, its former place was marked on the pavement with these words engraved onto several stones:

Hic
erat Capella
sancti Sepulchri.[12]

Abutting the left side of the church is a cloister enclosing a small cemetery with the small chapel of the Sepulcher at the center. Based on several epitaphs dating to the mid-thirteenth century, it appears that the canons and other clerics of this church were still leading a common life at that time, and in the corner of the cloister there are even the remains of a refectory, a dorter, and two epitaphs, among others, that, mention a *generali refectione* ("common meal") and a *Conventu istius ecclesiae* ("convent of this church"). Another epitaph is of a very different sort: it refers to a canon named Berlio, who in 1252 set up a chantry or obit for the souls of those he had defrauded or robbed, *pro remedio animarum illorum quos in aliquo defraudaverat, quod fiet in festo Mortuorum.*[13]

The cloister's second gallery, on the eastern side, houses three large chapels. The first was initially dedicated to the Holy Machabees, and later to St. Maurice. It is decorated with quite beautiful old paintings. One of the most remarkable shows a procession of the entire cathedral clergy with their habits and vestments. The canons are wearing an almuce over their chasubles,[14] as they do in Rouen during winter, and the precentor, the

---

en Dauphiné (Vienne, 1875), 2:339–41, suspects that "Chorier wrote these lines either mistakenly or in jest," explaining that the chapel was thus called because it was founded by Pierre Tabernier, and that no vineyard was attached thereto. He laments that Le Brun des Marettes propagated Chorier's fanciful account, although it is true that lands and vineyards were often granted to churches to provide bread and wine for the Sacrifice, and the cathedral of Vienne had two such foundations.

[11] On the construction and symbolism of Sepulcher imitations in Western Europe, see Geneviève Bresc-Bautier, "Les imitations du Saint-Sépulcre de Jérusalem (IXe–XVe siècles). Archéologie d'une dévotion," *Revue d'histoire de la spiritualité* 50 (1974): 319–42, and Robert Ousterhout, "*Loca Sancta* and the architectural response to pilgrimage," in *The Blessings of Pilgrimage*, ed. Robert Ousterhout (University of Illinois Press, 1990), 108–24.

[12] "Here once stood the Chapel of the Holy Sepulcher."

[13] "In satisfaction for the souls of those he had in any way defrauded, to be held on All Souls."

[14] The almuce or amess (Latin *almutium* or *almutia*) was a hooded cape of varying length, usually of fur or fur-lined, used as choir dress. As birettas became more popular, the almuce's hood stopped being used, and moreover during the summer it began to be worn over the arm, a custom which in some places came to be extended year-round, as Le Brun des Marettes notes throughout this work. By the seventeenth century, a lighter kind of shoulder cape, the mozzetta, was gaining popularity over the almuce; for instance, Pope Paul V had the canons of Annecy replace the almuce with the mozzetta, which the canons of Lyon themselves decided to do in 1748. For

cantor,[15] the *capiscol* or scholastic,[16] and the choirmaster[17] are depicted with long staves like a pilgrim might use as a sign of being dignitaries or officers.

After this chapel, in the middle of this gallery, stands the chapel of St. John the Baptist, which used to be a baptistery where catechumens and infants were baptized. In the old ordinary of Vienne it is called the "Chapel of the patriarchs, prophets, and St. John the Baptist."[18] One must take note of this name in order to properly understand what is mentioned later on in this ordinary. Queen Ermengarda, wife of King Rudolph, was buried there, as stated in an inscription that is scarcely legible today.[19]

Further along and near the door leading to the archbishop's palace stands yet another chapel, dedicated to Our Lady. At its entry lies the tomb of Queen Matilda, wife of King Conrad, of whom we spoke on page 8.

This is her epitaph:

> VI. Kl. Decemb. ob. Magtildis uxor Regis Conradi, qui obiit xiv. Kl. Novem. et dedit S. Mauritio villam Lusiniacum CUM SERVIS ET ANCILLIS, & omnibus appendiciis; et dicta Regina dedit thuribulum magnum totum aureum, & Crucem auream, et dedit coronam lampadarum totam argenteam ante domini sepulcrum: quae Regina jacet intus parietem ante Capellam B. Mariae Virginis.[20]

It is clear, therefore, that there were still slaves of both sexes in tenth-century Gaul, and that those who gifted lands to the Church or to monasteries sometimes also gifted slaves.[21]

---

an extensive discussion of the almuce's shape and manner of use throughout seventeenth-century France, with illustrative engravings, see de Vert, *Explication*, 2:257–65.
[15] In the Vienne, the two cantors, the first of which was sometimes called precentor, were dignitaries who ranked after the dean in precedence and were high-ranking dignitaries in charge of intoning or pre-intoning the psalms, antiphons, and responsories on greater feasts. See Ulysse Chevalier, *Étude historique sur la constitution de l'église métropolitaine et primatiale de Vienne* (H. Martin, 1922), 1:32–33.
[16] In Vienne, the *capiscol* (in Latin *scholasticus, caput scholae, cabiscolus, scabiscolus, capiscolus* or *scapiscolus*), was a dignitary in charge of teaching chant and overseeing its execution, as well as admitting *clergeons*. He was almost always a canon. See Chevalier, *Étude historique*, 34–36.
[17] The choirmaster (*maître du chœur*) was a minor dignitary, subject to the dean and *capiscol*, in charge of the instruction of the *clergeons*. Together with the *capiscol*, he was also in charge of assigning priests, deacons, subdeacons, and clerks to the celebration of the Offices of each week. See Chevalier, *Étude historique*, 36–37.
[18] The cathedral ordinary in question was written around 1240 and acquired by Le Brun des Marettes in Vienne in 1686 with the intent of publishing it. The same manuscript was later edited by Ulysse Chevalier, *Ordinaire de l'église cathédrale de Vienne* (A. Picard, 1923). The manuscript styles this chapel an *ecclesia*, see 24 and 50.
[19] *Corpus des inscriptions de la France médiévale* 15, no. 3.
[20] "On 16 November died Matilda, wife of King Conrad, who died on 19 October and gave to St-Maurice the estate of Luzinay with its slaves male and female and all its dependencies. The said queen gave a large thurible of solid gold, and a golden cross, and a chandelier of solid gold [to hang] before the Lord's sepulcher. The queen lies within the wall before the chapel of the Blessed Virgin Mary" (*Corpus des inscriptions de la France médiévale* 15, no. 2).
[21] For a general history of ecclesiastical slavery, the reader may consult Mary E. Sommar, *The Slaves of the Churches: A History* (Oxford University Press, 2020).

In the cathedral, the Blessed Sacrament is reserved within the rood screen at the foot of the great rood, *sub titulo Crucis,* along the inner wall of the choir, and a lamp hangs in front of it. Behind it, against the outside of the screen, there is a parish altar[22] where the Mass of the vigil[23] is sung after Prime (formerly after Sext) on days when a vigil coincides with a saint's feast.

On ordinary days, the archbishop's throne is situated after the last choir stall on the east end, as in Rouen. It is very simple, raised two or three feet above the canons' seats, with a similar stall, and partially covered with a small wooden pediment, without a canopy above.

The choir is a recent construction of very tall and beautiful woodwork. It has only two rows of stalls. The cantors who are priests sit in the upper row with the canons and do not wear the almuce. The others occupy the second row, except for ten clerks and choirboys or *clergeons* who have not even the ledge of a seat to lean on, but remain standing throughout the whole Office.

The boys wear a black cassock and are tonsured like all minimally regular ecclesiastics. Their surplices, like those of the canons and cantors, are extremely short, with a lace trim around the neck and a frog fastener rather like those of round shoulder capes or Brandenburg coats. Its sleeves are closed like those of the canons of Lyon.[24]

The style of their chant blends elements from Lyon and Rouen. They once wore the almuce over their shoulders, as in Lyon, as one can see in a chapel next to the choir, where a canon from a century ago is seen wearing it in this way. They only started wearing the almuce over their arm after the wars.

I am not entirely sure when they placed nine lecterns in their choir, but it is certain that they once chanted from memory. In 1524 the lower choir held rehearsals called *recordations* ("memorizations") every Saturday.[25]

They never chant minor hours back to back. They say Prime at eight in the morning, Terce at nine before high Mass, followed by Sext, None (which is not sung on major feasts) at two in the afternoon, and Vespers at three. The new breviary of Vienne recommends this practice.[26] It used to

---

[22] Cathedrals often had a parish altar under the vaults of the rood screen, called the altar of the Holy Cross due to its location under the great rood.

[23] The Mass of a vigil was typically celebrated after None, breaking the day's fast (hence its name *messe du jeûne*); a feast was always celebrated after Terce. When the two coincided, moving the Vigil Mass after Prime, as here, preserves the tradition of breaking the fast with communion on fast days, while allowing conventual Mass after Terce to be of the saint.

[24] Ancient surplices had open sleeves similar to those of English choirmasters or Roman dalmatics. But in this case they are not open.

[25] These sessions were meant for the junior members of the choir, who had not yet learned all the chants by heart.

[26] See *Breviarium sanctae Viennensis ecclesiae* (Paris, 1678), where the archbishop writes in his dedicatory letter, "Following the ancient custom, celebrate the hours of the Office at distinct times, not all together hurriedly and hastily."

be forbidden to say hours of the Divine Office back to back, as we shall see at the end of this account, and the spirit of the primitive Church was to say the major and minor hours at intervals of three hours or thereabouts. The three nocturns were said separately during the night, Lauds at dawn, Prime at sunrise, Terce at nine, Sext at midday (the hour is even called *Meridies* in the ordinaries of Lyon and Soissons), None at two or three in the afternoon, Vespers at five or six as the Collège de Cluny in Paris still does, and finally Compline immediately before going to bed, as most religious still do.

On major feasts, at St-Maurice of Vienne Compline is chanted only by the sacristan and two or three chaplains who assist him. The choir does not attend.

On Thursday at Vespers they do not repeat *Quoniam in aeternum misericordia ejus* after each verse of psalm 135.

At all the Offices, after the celebrant has chanted the *Deus in adjutorium meum intende*, all respond with *Domine ad adjuvandum me festina* and *Gloria Patri* at a lower fifth up to the *Alleluia*, which is sung at a higher note and serves as the antiphon for the minor hours, since there is never a hymn except at Compline, as in Lyon and everywhere else in France on the last three days of Holy Week and during the Easter Octave.

At choir Masses the celebrant, deacon, and subdeacon never wear the almuce to the altar. On solemn days, all three wear miters, and the thurifer, who is also a subdeacon, wears an alb and tunicle. The two *clergeons* carrying the candles wear albs.

The deacon and subdeacon approach the altar and say the confession with the priest, after which the subdeacon and the thurifer for the most part stand at the Epistle side of the altar, two paces away from it, facing the priest.[27] The deacon stands behind the priest, either to his side or in the center of the altar, at a distance of five or six paces. He only approaches him when necessary.

The candle-bearers do almost everything as in Lyon.

After the Gospel, during the *Credo*, the subdeacon brings the open Gospel book to the canons to be kissed, just as he brought it to the celebrant.

After the celebrant has incensed the *oblata* and the altar, he incenses around the whole altar himself (which the deacon does in Lyon and Rouen), while the deacon lifts his chasuble from the back with both hands. The priest begins this incensation in the center of the altar, then moves to the Gospel side, then goes around the back and returns by the Epistle side. Then he is incensed by the deacon.

The subdeacon receives the paten and goes to the east end of the choir until the *Sanctus*. At the *Sanctus* he goes behind the altar until the *Nobis quoque peccatoribus*, when he walks behind the deacon and gives him the paten. The deacon presents it to the priest or archbishop.

---

[27] A "pace" (*pas*) was a unit of measurement corresponding to about two English feet.

When there are several subdeacons, they follow the officiating subdeacon in all his movements.

During the *Pater*, the priest elevates the host and chalice at *in coelo* and kisses both at *in terra*, as in Lyon, in conformity with the literal sense of the prayer.

Everything else is done mostly the same as at Lyon, except that the deacon faces north to sing the *Ite, missa est*. Once the priest has given the blessing and recited the Gospel *In principio*, he returns with the other ministers in the same order they came.

On major feasts when the archbishop celebrates Mass, he is assisted by six priests, seven deacons, and seven subdeacons — the pious and illustrious current archbishop re-established this custom on Pentecost day 1697 — and formerly seven candle-bearers who are no longer seen except on Easter day. The six assistant priests walk in front of the canon-deacon and -subdeacon, as the six assistant deacons walk in front of the main subdeacon, even though he is a canon. As in Lyon, the archbishop sits on his throne which is at the back and center of the apse.

I think it will edify the reader to know about some of the most ancient customs that were formerly observed in this famous church, drawn from an ordinary written 450 years ago.[28] In this ordinary there is no mention of the feast of the Trinity, Corpus Christi, St. Bernard, King St. Louis of France, All Souls on 2 November, nor of the Conception of the Blessed Virgin Mary. These details allow us to estimate the date the age of the manuscript, as does its script, which contains characters and symbols in use about five hundred years ago.

Solemn feasts are marked with the words *cantores* and *baudes*. *Cantores* refers to the precentor and the cantor who lead the choir. *Baudes* refers to the great bells, the largest of which is called *bauda*.[29]

On Sunday, the priest, bareheaded and wearing a cope, blessed water in a stoup as in Lyon, and then sprinkled the altars. He performed the rest of the aspersion as it is still done today, during the procession before Mass, wearing his biretta. Hence it is clear that the Sunday procession before Mass was originally meant to accompany the aspersion of the various places: the church, cloisters, refectory, dorter, kitchen, and the assistants,

---

[28] Perhaps the same mentioned above on p. 11, n. 18.

[29] *Cantores* and *Cantores et baudes* were the terms used in Vienne to designate the second-highest and highest ranking feasts respectively. In both classes of feast, the two cantors intoned or pre-intoned the chants; the *Te Deum*, *Gloria*, and *Ite, missa est, alleluia, alleluia* were said; the *Benedictus* and *Magnificat* antiphons were repeated; *Benedicamus Domino, alleluia* was said at the end of Vespers; the Invitatory at Matins was repeated; the Introit of the Mass was said thrice; and there was an Alleluia in place of the chapter at second Vespers. On *Cantores et baudes* feasts, the *bauda* was rung as well, three times on twenty-one feasts, and four times on eight feasts: Christmas, St. John the Evangelist, Easter, the Dedication, Pentecost, the Assumption, St. Maurice, and All Saints (see Chevalier, *Étude historique*, 158–59, 164).

as we will see again later on. In fact, at Vienne they call it the "aspersion" rather than the "procession," saying "sound the aspersion," or "go to the aspersion."[30] The old ordinary states that the whole church was sprinkled, as well as all the clergy as they left the choir, the cloisters, the refectory, in front of which they said *Oremus dilectissimi*,[31] as well as the other side of the cloister where the infirmary apparently stood, judging from the collect *Omnipotens sempiterne Deus moestorum*.[32]

Today they still hold several stations while singing responsories. This gives the celebrant time to sprinkle everything, the station's sole purpose being to wait for him, and the responsory's to give the choir something to do. The ordinary indicates that the deacon carried the cross and the subdeacon the stoup, which should make lesser clerics who think these duties beneath them blush with shame.

There is a rubric that we must not forget to mention. It states that the procession should be done in this way every Sunday, unless the reliquary with the head of St. Maurice is exposed on the altar, in which case there should be no procession in the cloister—doubtless so as not to leave the church where the relic of the holy Patron is exposed. We can deduce from this that on the Sunday within the octave of Corpus Christi (or on a patronal feast) when the Body of Christ, the Holy of Holies, is exposed on the altar, the procession should not leave the church.

On all ferias of Advent and from Septuagesima to Easter, they sang the hymn *Christe qui lux es et dies* at Compline.[33]

They triumphed the great O antiphons, i.e., they repeated them after every verse of the *Magnificat*, as they still do in Lyon and Rouen, where they sing them three times in the course of the *Magnificat* and *Benedictus* on triple or solemn feasts.

They used to hold a station at a certain church on every Sunday of Advent and on its Ember days.[34]

Candle-bearers were often subdeacons, as stated in many places in the

---

[30] In many places, including Paris (*Caeremoniale Parisiense*, 1662, 585–89), the blessing of the water and the aspersion of the choir and people preceded the Sunday procession to the regular places, which were not sprinkled. Le Brun des Marettes laments, both here and elsewhere, the omission of the sprinkling of these places, which was the procession's original purpose.
[31] A processional antiphon: *Oremus, dilectissimi nobis, Deum patrem omnipotentem ut cunctis mundum purget erroribus, morbos auferat, famem depellat, aperiat carceres, vincula dissolvat. peregrinantibus reditum, infirmantibus sanitatem, navigantibus portum salutis indulgeat, et pacem tribuat in diebus nostris, insurgentesque repellat inimicos, et de manu inferni liberet nos propter nomen suum, alleluia* (Cantus ID 004190).
[32] *Omnipotens sempiterne Deus, maestorum consolatio, laborantium fortitudo, perveniant ad te preces de quacumque tribulatione clamantium, ut omnes sibi in necessitatibus suis misericordiam tuam gaudeant adfuisse* (CO 3852, Corpus Christianorum Series Latina 160, 6:70).
[33] Cantus ID 830070.
[34] An imitation of the ancient Roman custom. Vienne also held stations on certain feast days; see Chevalier, *Étude historique*, 216–24.

ordinary; this was the case on Ember Saturday of Advent and on Christmas, among other times. On solemn feasts, it was even two priests in copes who carried the candles before the bishop. These lesser functions used to be seen in a different light than they are today. Subdeacons, deacons, and even priests considered it an honor to do what even the lowest-ranking clerics deem beneath them today. The only reason for this is pride, or lack of understanding of how important these ministries are.[35]

On solemn feasts the archbishop incensed the altar during the third, sixth, and ninth responsories, as well as during the *Te Deum*. After the *Gloria Patri*, they repeated the response once again from the beginning up to the verse to give him time to finish the incensation.

At Christmas Matins the first six lessons were chanted by canons, the seventh by an archdeacon, the eighth by the dean, and the ninth by the archbishop while two priests in copes held two candles in front of him.

During the ninth responsory the archdeacon put on more beautiful vestments in the sacristy. Two subdeacons in albs carried candles before him, a third subdeacon in tunicle carried the thurible, and a fourth subdeacon also in tunicle carried the Gospel book. Thus all five went to the rood loft where the archdeacon sang the Genealogy *cum cantu*.[36]

The archbishop said the midnight Mass with two subdeacons bearing candles, one subdeacon thurifer, one canon-subdeacon, and an archdeacon. Before Mass they held a station at the Lady chapel. At the beginning of Lauds, they did not say the priestly versicle[37] nor the *Deus in adjutorium*. Rather, Lauds was embedded within the Mass, right after the Communion with the antiphon *Natus est nobis*[38] and the psalms, during which the celebrant sat down. They did not say a chapter or versicle, but after

---

[35] Le Brun des Marettes does not think highly of clerics who refuse to perform the functions of ecclesiastical grades beneath them. If he marvels at the two candle-bearing priests here, it is because, along with prostrations, community life, communing with the bishop, and other forms of clerical fraternity, it testifies in his mind to a clergy less riven by the social divisions of the Ancien Régime, on which see pp. 353–54. A 1718 review of the *Travels* published in *L'Europe savante* objects to this passage, alleging that the use of higher ministers for lower functions came about because of the vanity of bishops who wanted to surround themselves with ministers of high rank and that it is much more in accord with sound discipline for ministers to perform the functions appropriate to their rank; see *L'Europe savante* 5.2 (1718): 179–180. Le Brun des Marettes himself chose to remain an acolyte throughout his life, despite the opportunity for priestly ordination and a proposal from Bishop Colbert of Rouen make him a canon in his diocese; see Fouré, "Jean-Baptiste Le Brun des Marettes," 73–74.

[36] The singing of the Genealogy of Jesus Christ according to St. Matthew (1:1–16) at the end of Christmas Matins was a common custom throughout Latin dioceses. It was usually sung to a special mode 4 melody (*cum cantu*), although the degree of ornamentation varied widely. The 1784 Vienne missal, pp. 23–26, prints a version sung in that church. For a study of the melodies used for the Genealogy, see Anna Vildera, "Formulari processionali per il canto del vangelo *Liber generationis*," *De musica disserenda* 9, no. 1–2 (2013): 139–55.

[37] A versicle intoned by the celebrant at the very beginning of Lauds.

[38] Cantus ID 003857.

the *Benedictus* and its antiphon, the celebrant returned to the altar to say the Postcommunion, and the deacon said *Benedicamus Domino, alleluia, alleluia*. The same rite is observed today. An archdeacon always serves as deacon when the archbishop officiates, and the four archdeacons each have assigned feasts when they must serve as deacon to the archbishop. As solemn as the midnight Mass on Christmas was, the Mass after Terce was even more solemn.

At dawn they held a station at the chapel of St. Anastasia in imitation of Rome. This Roman practice probably explains why there is a commemoration of St. Anastasia in the Mass. The dean officiated, the deacon was a simple canon, and at the end he said *Ite, missa est, alleluia*.

The archbishop also celebrated the high Mass after Terce with six assistant priests, seven deacons including an archdeacon, seven subdeacons, and seven candle-bearers, five of whom were subdeacons and the two other *clergeons*.

The archbishop put on his pontifical vestments in the chapterhouse during Terce. The six assistant priests, seven deacons, seven subdeacons, and seven candle-bearers vested either behind the altar or in the sacristy. The upper choir all wore silk copes during the Mass, before which they all went in procession to escort the bishop from the chapterhouse, in this order: first the seven candle-bearers, then a subdeacon carrying the thurible and the canon-subdeacon carrying the Gospel book with a gold cover, with the six assistant subdeacons; then the archdeacon carrying the golden cross followed by six other deacons and six assistant priests; and then the cantors, who, having received the archbishop's blessing, re-entered the choir and began the Introit of the Mass and the psalm verse. The rest of the procession with its multitude of ministers entered into the choir with the archbishop at the *Gloria Patri*. All removed their miters and hoods or almuces—*capellis et mitris remotis*—in the middle of the choir. The archbishop first bowed to the altar, then to the right side of the choir, then the left, and was likewise saluted by the two choirs. Then he walked forward in front of the altar and there said the *Confiteor* with his ministers. Some of the candles were set on the altar, and some at the front and back of the choir.

The archbishop ascended the altar and incensed it, assisted by the archdeacon. Then, turning his back to the altar and supported by two deacons, he gave the kiss of peace to the deacons, assistant priests, and his chaplain, who was vested in a cope. Then the archbishop went to his throne, a marble chair elevated on four steps behind the altar against the wall in the center of the apse, where he still sits today. Thus he can be seen by the clergy and the people, as in Lyon.

Next they sang the *Kyrie eleison* with the trope *Te Christe*, which has since been suppressed. The *Gloria in excelsis* was sung in three choirs, the bishop and his assistants comprising one. As still today in Lyon, the

Gradual and Alleluia were sung *per rotulos* with two *clergeons* holding up the tablets with the music.[39]

After the oration *Concede*,[40] two major canon-priests chanted the praises or acclamations *Christus vincit, Christus regnat, Christus imperat*, which is still done today here and in Rouen. Before returning to their places in choir, these priests received the archbishop's blessing, just like those who sang the Epistle, Gradual, and Alleluia.

The Offertory was sung with several verses, as it is still done at Lyon and formerly at Rouen.

The six assistant priests recited the Canon with the bishop and made the same gestures as he, as noted in the 1524 cathedral ordinary: *Suburbani signa faciant durante Missa ad modum Episcopi; et sic in omnibus aliis majoribus Festivitatibus.*

As in Lyon, immediately after the *Agnus Dei*, the cantors standing before the altar sang the *Venite populi* to invite the clergy and people to the holy table to participate in the Holy Eucharist.[41] The archbishop gave the kiss of peace to all members of the upper choir, namely the major canons and the perpetuals, as they stood around the altar, while the lower choir stood in front of the *râtelier*.[42] Those who wished to receive communion remained there, while the others returned to the choir. They sang the following praises after the Communion antiphon:

> Hunc diem, multos annos, istam sedem Deus conservet. Summum pontificem Apostolicae sedis Deus conservet. Episcopum nostrum Deus conservet. Populum Christianum Deus conservet. Feliciter, feliciter, feliciter. Tempora bona habeant. Multos annos Christus in eis regnet: in ipso semper vivant. Amen.[43]

---

[39] "In ancient churches, or rather in churches that have preserved their ancient liturgy, after the Epistle the choirboys put down their candles at the foot of the *râtelier* (a large seven-branched candelabrum), went to the altar to take silver tablets, on which the Gradual and Alleluia are written upon pages of vellum and present them to a canon and three perpetuals who placed themselves in the first high chairs of the right side of the crucifix on the Epistle side. Then they left their places to four others to whom they left the tablets to chant the Alleluia and verse. This whole ceremonial is called *cantare per rotulos*. The precentor held the first place on the Epistle side and the cantor occupied the first on the Gospel side, each of them with their silver rods next to them" (Jacques-Paul Migne, *Troisième et dernière encyclopédie théologique* [Paris, 1856], 15:1680).

[40] CO 778 (Corpus Christianorum Series Latina 160, 1:382).

[41] Cantus ID a00294. This piece is a remnant of the ancient Gallican rite, where it was sung to invite the people to communion. On its origins and historical extent, see André Mocquereau, ed., *Le codex 903 de la Bibliothèque nationale de Paris (XIᵉ siècle). Graduel de Saint-Yrieix*, Paléographie musicale 13 (Société Saint Jean Évangeliste, 1925), 30–32, 33–35.

[42] Author's note: "The *râtelier* was a large, seven-branched brass candelabrum. There is also one in St-Jean of Lyon," p. 34. According to Chevalier, the *rastrum* mentioned in the ordinary held twenty-four candles (*Ordinaire*, xvii).

[43] "On this day, may God save this see for many years. May God save the supreme pontiff of the Apostolic see. May God save our bishop. May God save the Christian people. Happily, happily, happily. May they have prosperous times. May Christ reign in them for

This kept the clergy and people occupied during the communion.

All of this is still practiced at Vienne on Christmas, Easter, and Pentecost, except that the seven candles are only carried on Easter.

The purpose of the Sunday procession before high Mass was to sprinkle the ordinary places with holy water. Similarly, the purpose of processions before high Mass on solemn feasts was solely to escort the bishop. The full Sunday procession is still done in Vienne, with other churches doing it in full or in part.

The number of Sundays to occur between Epiphany and Septuagesima, and between Pentecost and Advent, was announced at the yearly synod.

Wednesdays and Fridays had proper Epistles and Gospels at Mass.

On all Sundays from Septuagesima to Easter there was a procession or station at a church in the city.

On Ash Wednesday there were also stations.

The ashes were blessed after None. Then the archbishop (or in his absence the abbot of St-Pierre of Vienne) and his chaplain, vested in black silk copes, came into the choir, taking the place of the dean, along with the deacon and subdeacon who carried the ashes. The archbishop or the abbot distributed the ashes to all the clergy, who had to have their tonsures newly shaven, in the same way as the Sunday aspersion; they advanced through the nave two by two singing the penitential psalms. As in Rouen, it is not stated that the archbishop either took or received the ashes. The archbishop then prostrated himself before the pulpit. Afterwards, he invited the public penitents to approach and recited the usual orations, after which he expelled them from the church singing the responsory *In sudore vultus tui vesceris pane tuo*, the words that were said unto Adam when he was expelled from earthly paradise.[44] The archbishop closed the doors of the church after them, and delivered a sermon to the people, after which a procession took place.

On the first Monday of Lent, they commenced the reading of the *Dialogues* of St. Gregory before Compline, as they used to do at Rouen not a hundred years ago, and as is still done in Reims and other neighboring churches. It was the duty of the subdeacon to perform the incensations, as in Lyon, and at each hour they kissed the ground, as in Rouen where each one kisses his seat before beginning each hour.

During the whole of Lent, before the collect they say *Flectamus genua*, and after a brief interval, *Levate*: *et facto brevi intervallo, Levate*.

On all days of Lent before Compline they said the Office of the Dead

---

many years. May they live in him forever." On the lauds or praises offered to kings and bishops during the liturgy throughout the Middle Ages, see the classic study by Ernst Kantorowicz, *Laudes Regiae: A Study in Liturgical Acclamations and Mediaeval Ruler Worship*, University of California Publications in History 33 (University of California Press, 1946; repr. 1958).

[44] "In the sweat of thy face shalt thou eat thy bread." Cantus ID 006937.

and then went to the chapterhouse for a reading from the *Dialogues* of St. Gregory, after which they went to the refectory to drink some wine prepared by the refectorians. They called this the *potus caritatis*. Therefore, they did not take any collation with this drink at the time of this ordinary; this was a later development.

In the ordinary of Vienne, as in its most recent missal, the Wednesday of the fourth week of Lent is called *Feria quarta in scrutiniis*. They still perform the scrutinies today in this church, even though all those to be baptized are children, with the subdeacon reciting the Creed for each child before the priest as a profession of faith. For good reason, the Gradual of this Mass is *Venite filii*, "Come, ye children."[45] The ceremonies are too long to record here in French. They can be found in Latin in the ordinary we hope to make available to the public.[46]

They said the *Te Deum laudamus* on Palm Sunday, as in Lyon and among the Benedictines on the Sundays of Advent and Lent, and indeed there seems no good reason for omitting it.

The archbishop (or in his absence the abbot of St-Pierre) blessed the palms vested in alb, amice, stole, and green silk cope. The cross was uncovered in the procession and they did not say the *Attollite portas*.

At Mass on Holy Wednesday they said all the solemn intercessions as on Good Friday, and still do so today.

On Maundy Thursday after None the archbishop — vested in alb, amice, stole, and silk cope with his miter and crosier — went to the doors of the church to admit the public penitents who awaited permission to enter. Then he delivered a sermon, at the end of which he said three times: *Venite filii*, "Come, ye children." He said the verse *Accedite*, "Approach ye," and let in the penitents. Immediately thereafter the seven penitential psalms were said, during which the archbishop and penitents lay prostrate before the pulpit. Then the archbishop said the prayers, versicles, and orations, and gave them the pardon and indulgence. Today there is no more trace of this public penitence except the seven penitential psalms, along with this rubric in the supplement to the missal: *Feria V in Ecclesia Primatiali ante Missam fit Officium Catechumenorum et Reconciliatio poenitentium, et ideo dicuntur septem Psalmi poenitentiales*.[47] They still hold the Office of the Catechumens.

The blessing of the oil of the sick was done before the *Per quem haec omnia Domine* and the blessing of the oil of catechumens and chrism after the *Pax Domini*. Vespers was inserted into the Mass and ended with the Postcommunion.

---

[45] Cantus ID g01162.
[46] See Chevalier, *Ordinaire*, 32–33.
[47] "On Thursday in the primatial church, the Office of the catechumens and reconciliation of penitents is held before Mass, and hence the seven penitential psalms are said" (*Supplementum Missalis Romani ad usum ecclesiarum dioecesis Viennensis* [Lyon, 1680], 20).

To this day, after the Mass, the deacon carries the Blessed Sacrament to the place prepared for it, and brings it back the next day to the high altar for the Mass *ex praesanctificatis*, as in Chartres.

The archbishop, his ministers, and the clergy were barefoot for the Maundy. The archbishop and the dean washed the canons' feet, poured water over their hands, then gave them unleavened bread and wine blessed by the prelate.

On Good Friday, the archbishop vested in a black silk cope and his ministers only in albs said the *Confiteor* in the sacristy, then came out entirely barefoot (this is still the case today), prostrated themselves before the altar, and spent some time in prayer. Rising, the reading of the two prophecies began, and the chanting of the two tracts. Then an archdeacon chanted the Passion according to St. John. The whole rest of the Office is nearly the same as in the old ordinary of Rouen written 450 years ago. Afterwards they returned barefoot to the sacristy.

After communion, the celebrant said (and still says) in a loud voice *In nomine Patris, et Filii, et Spiritus sancti*. The response was *Et cum spiritu tuo*. This is still the case in the missal of 1519,[48] but the response today is *Amen*. Then the cantors, standing before the altar, begin a responsory with its verse and then repeat the response to the verse while the archbishop performs the incensation. From ancient times up to the present in Vienne, this constitutes the whole of Vespers for this day.

On Holy Saturday the archbishop, vested in a silk cope, and the archdeacon, vested in a white dalmatic, preceded by candle-bearers, a subdeacon, and the twelve assistant parish priests,[49] and the choirmaster went to the chapel of Our Lady in the cloister to admit the infants to be baptized, and the archdeacon said: *Orate Electi, flectite genua. Levate. Complete orationem vestram, et dicite Amen.*[50] Then they made the sign of the cross on their foreheads. The archbishop asked each infant's name, then said the exorcism *Nec te lateat, Satana*. Then the archdeacon said *Catechumeni recedant. Si qui Catechumeni, exeant foras.*[51] After the catechumens left, the archdeacon, having received the archbishop's blessing, went with the subdeacon in front of the altar to bless the Paschal candle. Meanwhile, the lower choir stood and the upper choir sat until the deacon said *Dominus vobiscum*.

During the blessing of the candle, the *capiscol*, vested in a silk cope,

---

[48] *Missale ad vsum sancte Viennensis ecclesie* (Lyon, 1519), fol. 92r.
[49] Called *suburbani* in the ordinary, these were parish priests of various churches in Vienne or chaplains who held benefices in the city or its environs. They were obliged to assist at Mass in the cathedral on certain feasts. See Chevalier, *Étude historique*, 197–99. This institution imitated the six cardinal-bishops of the suburbicarian dioceses around Rome, and was also found in other dioceses of France—including Sens (p. 123), Angers (p. 72), Troyes, Soissons, and medieval Paris—where they were called *prêtres*- or *curés-cardinaux*. On the origin of the cardinals, see p. 123, n. 13.
[50] "Pray, chosen ones. Kneel. Rise. Finish your prayer, and say, Amen."
[51] "Catechumens, begone. If any are catechumens, go outside."

blessed the incense and fire and then carried the grains of incense to the archdeacon, helping him insert them into the holes of the candle at the proper time. Then the archdeacon lit the Paschal candle with the new fire. Some of the faithful take flames from this blessed fire back to their homes, as in Lyon and Rouen. Then a lector mounted the rood loft to read the prophecies, which were intermixed with orations and Tracts, as they are today. According to the 1519 missal of Vienne, each of the twelve parish priests chanted one oration after each of the twelve prophecies.[52] Today only two priests sing them in alternation.

When they began the Tract *Cantemus Domino*,[53] the choirmaster took a priest and his choirboys with him (and perhaps the rest of the cantors too) and went to the baptismal font in the chapel of St. John the Baptist in the cloister, where they chanted the litany, repeating each verse three times. This is called the *litania terna* — the origin of the ninefold *Kyrie eleison* at Mass — in which each group of three was sung by the cantor and the two choirs in alternation. After the litany, everyone returned to the choir.

After the prophecies, Tracts, and orations were finished, they called up those who were to be baptized. They placed the boys on the right side and the girls on the left and said the prayers for catechumens over them. In the procession to the baptismal font, the parish priest of St-Jean walked with the assistant priests carrying the vase of holy chrism, while the cantors sang the second litany and the two choirs responded. After it was finished, the archbishop blessed the font conjointly with the twelve parish priests, as they do today in Troyes; that is, they made the blessings in the form of the cross and the aspirations with the bishop, and held their hands up like him, albeit without touching either the water or the candle, as is marked in the 1524 ordinary of the cathedral of Vienne.

The reason these parish priests assisted at the blessing of the font at the vigils of Easter and Pentecost is that they brought with them all their parishioners' children to be baptized in the cathedral. For in ancient times the only baptismal font in a city was the cathedral's, as is still the case today in Florence, Pisa, Parma, Padua, and elsewhere. The bishop put holy chrism in the water in the form of a cross. After the usual examinations regarding the faith of the creed and other things, the priest baptized each of the children with three immersions, plunging him three times in the water (*sub trina mersione*) while invoking the holy Trinity, saying, *Et ego te baptizo in nomine Patris*, then plunging the infant once into the water, then *et Filii*, and plunging him for a second time, and *et Spiritus Sancti*, and plunging him in for the third time. Taking the child from the font, the priest took a bit of holy chrism with his thumb and made a sign of the cross

---

[52] The missal assigns each oration to a specific parish priest (fols. 96v, 97v, 98v, 99r, 100r, 100v, 101r, 101v, 102v).

[53] Cantus ID g02371.

on the top of his head saying the prayer *Deus omnipotens*. Then the priest clothed him in a white robe in the form of an alb, saying the usual words *Accipe vestem candidam* ("Receive this robe, white and without blemish, which thou must carry before the tribunal of Our Lord Jesus Christ if thou wishest to attain eternal life.") Terrible words on which Christians would do well to reflect, and pastors teach as part of the obligations of baptism, for ignorance of these obligations is at the source of the wicked life most Christians lead.

After this, according to the ordinary, if the bishop was present, he also administered the sacrament of Confirmation to the children: *Si episcopus adest, statim confirmari oportet infantulum.*[54] Then the procession returned to choir as two priests chanted the third litany, which was repeated seven times.

The archbishop went to prepare for the Mass, and as he went to the altar the deacon said (and still says) in a loud voice: *Accendite*,[55] as the canons still do in Lyon, and used to do in Rouen not a century ago, and as is also still done in Angers on major feasts. Then all the candles were lit and the *Kyrie eleison* began. The whole rest of the Mass and Vespers were celebrated just as everywhere else, except that at the end, instead of *Ite, missa est*, the deacon said, on account of Vespers, *Benedicamus Domino* without alleluia.

I was very surprised not to find in this Mass mention of the communion of the newly baptized, which, as Rosweyde in his notes on St. Paulinus[56] and Cardinal Bona in *De rebus liturgicis*, book 2, chapter 19, prove,[57] used to be given not only to adults but also to newborn infants. It is found in the ancient *Ordo Romanus*, chapter *De sabbato sancto*,[58] and was still practiced in France in the twelfth century in the time of Hugh of St. Victor, who in his first book *De caeremoniis, sacramentis, officiis et observationibus ecclesiasticis*, chapter 20, speaking of a newly baptized, states that the priest dipped the end of his finger in the blood of Christ and in this way gave the sacrament of the Eucharist to the newly baptized infant who has learned by nature to suck: *Pueris recens natis idem sacramentum in specie sanguinis est ministrandum digito sacerdotis, quia tales naturaliter sugere*

---

[54] Chevalier, *Ordinaire*, 36.
[55] In the *Ordo Romanus* 1.40–41, this is the word said by the subdeacon to indicate that the pope is ready to leave the sacristy and begin the stational Mass: "Once this has been announced, the subdeacon, fourth of the schola, follows. He stands before the pontiff until the pontiff signals to him that they should chant. The subdeacon nods assent and forthwith goes out before the sacristy doors and says, 'Light up!' When they have lit, the subdeacon-*sequens* holding a golden thurible puts incense in it standing outside the door so that he may walk before the pontiff" (*Les* Ordines Romani *du haut moyen âge*, ed. Michel Andrieu, 5 vols [Spicilegium sacrum Lovaniense, 1957–1961], 2:80).
[56] Heribert Rosweyde, ed., *Divi Paulini episcopi Nolani Opera* (Antwerp, 1622), 760.
[57] Giovanni Bona, *Rerum Liturgicarum libri duo* 2.19 (Rome, 1671), 451–55.
[58] *Ordo Romanus antiquus*, ed. Melchior Hittorp, *De divinis catholicae Ecclesiae officiis et mysteriis* (Paris, 1624), 75–76; *Ordo Romanus* 50.30.1, ed. Andrieu, 5:261–64.

possunt.[59] On this question, see St. Augustine in his treatise to Boniface against the Pelagian heresy, book 1, chapter 22,[60] and his letter to Vitalis;[61] St. Ambrose, *Liber de initiandis*, chapter 8;[62] and St. Paulinus, letter 32.[63] Everyone knows that in the African church the deacon gave both species to infants in their mothers' arms,[64] something the Greeks still do today.

This practice of giving communion to newly baptized infants is attested, not only in the twelfth century, but in Beauvais less than three hundred years ago, as we see in the ordinaries of this church that date from that time. This is the origin of the current custom of carrying the newly baptized infants to the high altar, which is done in the whole diocese of Rouen and in many others.

On Easter, as the last bell for Matins rang, the two candle-bearers were sent to escort the archbishop, who came to the Sepulcher vested in a white cope and said the *Confiteor*. After saying this prayer, he kissed the Sepulcher and the altars. Then, preceded by the two candles, he went to kiss the dean and entered the choir. Standing with the cantors, he said, *Resurrexit Dominus*, and the cantor responded, *Et apparuit Petro*. Then the archbishop gave the kiss of peace to the two cantors. All the other ecclesiastics did the same thing. This kiss of peace during the *Resurrexit Dominus* on Easter day is still practiced not only in Vienne, but also in the famous collegiate church of the canons of St-Vulfran of Abbeville. It is found in the ancient *Ordo Romanus*, in the chapter *In vigilia sancti Paschae in nocte*.[65] Less than a century ago it was still done in Rouen. Today in the Eastern Church the clergy and people greet one another from Easter to Ascension exclusively by saying Χριστός ἀνέστη, "Christ is risen."

On Easter the whole Office was done, as still today, with the same number of assistant priests, ministers, and candle-bearers as on Christmas, and they also chanted neums with every antiphon.[66] There are only three or four peculiarities which I will describe.

After Lauds, the archbishop or the dean, dressed in priestly vestments,

---

[59] "Newborn babes are to be given the same sacrament in the species of blood by the priest's finger, for they can naturally suck" (PL 177:392C). This treatise was more likely written by Robert Paululus.

[60] St. Augustine, *Contra duas epistulas Pelagianorum* 1.22 (PL 44:570), ed. Karl F. Urba and Joseph Zycha, Corpus Scriptorum Ecclesiasticorum Latinorum 60 (Hoelder-Pichler-Tempsky, 1913), 457–58.

[61] St. Augustine, *Epistula* 217.5 (PL 33:984–85), ed. Alois Goldbacher, Corpus Scriptorum Ecclesiasticorum Latinorum 57 (Hoelder-Pichler-Tempsky, 1911), 415.

[62] St. Ambrose, *De mysteriis* 8 (PL 16:403B), ed. Otto Faller, Corpus Scriptorum Ecclesiasticorum Latinorum 73 (Hoelder-Pichler-Tempsky, 1955), 107.

[63] St. Paulinus of Nola, *Epistula* 32.5, ed. Jean-Baptiste Le Brun des Marettes (Paris, 1685), 1:202; ed. Wilhelm von Hartel, Corpus Scriptorum Ecclesiasticorum Latinorum 29 (Vienna, 1894), 280.

[64] St. Cyprian, *De lapsis* 25, ed. Maurice Bénevot, Corpus Christianorum Series Latina 3 (Brepols, 1972), 235.

[65] *Ordo Romanus antiquus*, ed. Hittorp, 84E; *Ordo Romanus* 50.30.1, ed. Andrieu, 5:297.

[66] Neums were melismas sung at the end of antiphons or responsories.

blessed water and sprinkled the altars and the people, while the subdeacon carried the stoup. Then they returned to the sacristy and went to sing a high Mass at the altar of the Sepulcher.

After Terce, the Lord Archbishop donned his pontifical vestments for Mass before the Sepulcher, and his six assistant priests, seven deacons, seven subdeacons, and seven candle-bearers did so behind the altar or in the sacristy. Then they went in procession to the chapel of the Sepulcher to escort the bishop in the same order as on Christmas day. Thereafter the dean, having received the archbishop's blessing, went with the other canons through the middle of the choir behind the altar, where they chanted *O mors*, repeating it after the verse.[67] Then they returned to the Sepulcher. There the candle-bearers said the antiphon *Ite, nuntiate* in a loud voice.[68] When this was finished, all turned toward the Sepulcher. At that point the cantors, with their back to the Sepulcher, sang, *Quem quaeritis?* Two canons responded, *Jesum Nazarenum.* The cantors: *Non est hic, surrexit.* The two canons chanted *Alleluia, Resurrexit Dominus*[69] as they returned to choir where, when the procession arrived, the cantors immediately began the Introit *Resurrexi*[70] in a low voice, as in Lyon. This is indicated in the old ordinary by the term *voce submissa*. As they chanted the *Gloria Patri* in a higher voice, the archbishop entered in full pomp with all his ministers, and said the Mass with all the same ceremonies as on Christmas, with Lauds and the *Venite populi* at communion. The Mass ended with *Ite, missa est, alleluia*.

Throughout the whole day, except during Mass, the archbishop was vested in a cope over his alb with stole and maniple, and at all the minor hours as well as after Mass he was conducted by two candle-bearers back to his residence, with his miter on his head and his crosier in hand. He even dined that day in his pontifical vestments.

At the stroke of Vespers the archbishop, so vested, went from his residence into the cloister (as still done today on major feasts) preceded by two candle-bearers. These immediately went to the choir to fetch the deacon-crucifer, who was vested in cope and came with the candle-bearers and all the clergy and cantors in copes, with miters atop their heads and staves in hand, to lead the archbishop in procession into to the church.

Vespers was done very much as in Rouen:[71] they chanted the psalm *Laudate pueri* while going to the font, and the psalm *In exitu* on their return.[72] The two *Benedicamus* of Vespers and the procession were sung

---

[67] Cantus ID 004045.
[68] Cantus ID 003462.
[69] Cantus ID 001352.
[70] Cantus ID g01007.
[71] These stational Vespers were still in the propers of many twentieth-century French dioceses and the tradition is still kept in some places. They all have in common the procession to the font before the psalm *In exitu*, which is sung processionally, farced with alleluias.
[72] Psalms 112 and 113 respectively.

with two alleluias, after which the archbishop gave the blessing, saying *Sit nomen Domini benedictum*.

On Easter Monday they held the station at St-Pierre. The archbishop sang Mass with five deacons and five subdeacons. Between the sequence *Victimae*[73] and the Gospel there was a sermon for the people, and then the archbishop gave the indulgence. As the bells rang for Vespers the clergy assembled at the archbishop's residence, where tables were set with honey, wine, and other provisions. At the final stroke everyone proceeded to the chapel of Our Lady, and then they went to the church as on the previous day.

On Saturday and Sunday *in albis* they continued to perform the procession to the baptismal font, but they chanted a responsory with an oration in place of the psalms said on the other days.

On the three Rogation days, the clergy and the whole people assembled at the cathedral after Terce. The clergy of St-Sévère, the nuns of Ste-Colombe, the nuns of St-André-le-Haut, the monks of St-André-le-Bas, and the monks of St-Pierre all attended. When they entered the church of St-Maurice, all the bells were rung.

The archbishop, standing in the dean's place—or the dean if he were a priest, or else the hebdomadary—sprinkled the whole clergy, monks, and nuns as they left the choir two by two. A deacon carried the banner, two canons of the lower choir carried two crosses, the subdeacon-hebdomadary a third cross, the deacon-hebdomadary the Gospel book, and a clerk the tablets on which the litany was written. Those who carried the crosses were, as in Lyon and Bec and still today in Milan, barefoot, and their heads covered with ashes. The celebrant wears a chasuble in this procession even today. As soon as the procession arrived at the stational church, a priest and two deacons prostrated themselves before the altar until the end of the litany. They held six or seven stations each day. The canons, monks, and nuns took turns singing the litany. We shall see nuns assisting at these processions elsewhere too.

On Ascension day after Terce, the clergy, vested in copes, with the archbishop—or, in his absence, with the abbot of St-Pierre—held a procession in which they carried all the reliquaries. It went down by the steps of the main portal and entered through the door of the cloister. After they were all arranged in the nave of the church, the archbishop, wearing his pontifical vestments—or, in his absence, the abbot of St-Pierre—went to the altar of the Sepulcher preceded by two *clergeons* bearing candles, three subdeacons also carrying candles, a fourth subdeacon thurifer, the major subdeacon carrying the Gospel book, the archdeacon carrying the golden cross, followed by the other deacons, and lastly himself. Then the cantors, with their backs turned to the Sepulcher said, *Quem creditis?* Two or three canons responded, *Christum qui surrexit.* The cantors: *Jam ascendit.* The

---

[73] Cantus ID ah54007.

canons: *Alleluia*. As they were singing this, the procession re-entered the choir and the archbishop began the Mass with the same ceremonies as on Easter, but without assistant priests and without the *Venite populi*.

There was a peculiarity about this feast. After the Offertory with its verses there was a procession into the almonry. First went the stoup-bearer, the two candle-bearers, and the thurifer, chanting the responsory *Christus resurgens* with its verse.[74] There they blessed the food saying *Edent pauperes*, sprinkling water on it and incensing it. Then there was a sermon. Afterwards, Mass was said in the usual way.

On the vigil of Pentecost they held the same baptismal ceremonies as on Holy Saturday. Six vested priests assisted at the baptisms, but not at Mass. Today they no longer say the *Accendite* before the start of Mass. Before the Postcommunion they said Vespers with the psalm *Laudate Dominum omnes gentes*[75] and the *Magnificat* with each of their antiphons, imitating the rite of Holy Saturday, and Vespers ended with the Postcommunion. This is still done today.

On Pentecost day, the old ordinary indicates all the same practices and ceremonies as on Easter day, except the Office of the Sepulcher. Before Vespers and before Mass there was a *Processio ad introducendum archiepiscopum* as on Christmas;[76] the *Venite populi* for the Eucharist was sung as on Easter and Christmas; and the same rite of Vespers was used as on Easter, singing the psalm *Laudate pueri* during the procession to the font and *In exitu* on the way back. The same was done on Monday, Tuesday, Wednesday, Thursday, and Friday. And indeed the rites ought to be identical, for the Saturdays before Easter and Pentecost were devoted to solemn baptism of the catechumens, and during the week after Vespers the newly baptized were taken in procession to the baptismal font where they had been regenerated, and the priest said a prayer over them. Note that the prayer *ad fontes* is especially for them.

After the octave of Pentecost they read not only the books of Kings, but also Paralipomenon, as formerly in Rouen.

After Vespers on Christmas and the feasts of St. Stephen and St. John they held solemn processions for the deacons, priests, and choirboys, as formerly in Rouen. The following morning at Mass there were solemnities for them.[77] The choirboys elected a boy-bishop who presided over the whole Office except the Mass.

---

[74] Cantus ID 600355.
[75] Psalm 116.
[76] Chevalier, *Ordinaire*, 69.
[77] The Masses of all three feasts were celebrated by the archbishop, who delivered a sermon to the people with a blessing and indulgence. Moreover, on St. John all priests wore silk copes. The deacons and priests led the hours of the Office on the first two feasts respectively, as did the boy bishop on the third, but none had a special role in their day's Mass. See Chevalier, *Ordinaire*, 83–86.

On Holy Innocents, the *Te Deum, Gloria in excelsis,* and Alleluia before the Gospel are still sung in Vienne, as in Lyon. Elsewhere they are not said because formerly Christians fasted on this day *more Quadragesimali.*

On Candlemas, after Prime, the archbishop or abbot of St-Pierre, vested in an appareled alb, amice, stole, maniple, and white cope with his miter and crosier, preceded by his ministers, went to the altar to bless the candles which he sprinkled and incensed. The sacristans distributed candles to the clergy, who lit them and then held a procession in the cloister.

On St. Mark's day there is no mention of the Major Litany or any procession, and these are still not observed in Vienne, just as they are not in Lyon.[78]

On 2 June, the feast of St. Blandina and her companion martyrs, a great solemnity was held in Vienne, called the *Fête des Miracles* (Feast of Miracles). There were great festivities held on boats upon the Rhône. The clergy of the church of St-Sevère, of the cathedral, the monks, and the nuns of St-André-le-Haut all went in procession to the church of Ste-Blandine, preceded by two crosses and followed by all the people. There they said the Mass of the holy martyrs. After the Epistle they chanted the Gradual, then read the martyrs' acts in the manner of an Epistle, taken from book 5, chapter 1 of Eusebius's *Ecclesiastical History* of Eusebius with the title *Lectio Libri Ecclesiasticae Historiae.*[79] They still do this today. This is worthy of note, because it reflects a practice mentioned by St. Gregory of Tours, namely that the acts of the martyrs were recited not only during the Divine Office, but sometimes even at Mass. After this reading of the Acts they sang the Alleluia and Prose, and then the deacon read the Gospel.

There were three different Masses of St. John the Baptist counting that of the vigil.[80] The second was said after Lauds, and the third after Terce.

On 30 June, instead of *Commemoratio S. Pauli* one finds *Celebratio,* like the term *Celebritas* used in Lyon.

On 1 August, the account of the martyrdom of the Machabees was read after the Epistle at the conventual Mass, as is still done today.

On 8 August, the feast of St. Severus, priest of Vienne, the cathedral

---

[78] The Major Rogation on St. Mark's day was a Roman custom, whereas in Gaul they held the Rogations, later called "lesser," on the three days before the Ascension. Indeed, it was St. Mamertus, archbishop of Vienne, who instituted this latter custom. Eventually most French dioceses adopted the Major Rogation as well.

[79] See *Missale ad vsum sancte Viennensis ecclesie* (Lyon, 1519), fol. 209r-v. This lesson is actually taken from Ado's Martyrology, which quotes from Rufinus of Aquileia's translation of Eusebius's *Ecclesiastical History* 5.1.59–61, and goes on to list the names of the martyrs and the discovery of their relics, which had been cast into the Rhône. It concludes with the note that "from ancient tradition, [the citizens of Lyon] call this the day of miracles" (PL 123:278C–279B).

[80] The custom arose in the Carolingian period to celebrate a dawn Mass on the feast of St. John the Baptist in addition to the usual day Mass found in the oldest sacramentaries.

clergy went at night in procession to the church of St-Sévère: *in ipsa nocte statio ad sanctum Severum*.[81]

The day of St. Maurice was like Christmas. After first Vespers the monks of St-André-le-Bas went to the cathedral to chant Matins, and then the monks of St-Pierre did the same. After Prime, processions went to the cathedral, and when they arrived all the bells rang. The archbishop, vested in chasuble and pallium, incensed the altar at the beginning of Mass and then went to sit at his throne of white marble behind the high altar. After the Prose the archbishop gave a sermon to the people and granted an indulgence.

In other sources we find that in the diocese of Vienne until 1100 Lent began on the Monday after Quinquagesima—which they currently call, by corruption, *Lundi gras*—and not on Ash Wednesday, as is done now.[82] Perhaps this is why some communities abstain from meat on these two days.

Formerly no one in Vienne could be married between Rogations and Trinity.

In the missal of Vienne one finds the blessing of nuts at *Per quem haec omnia* on 25 July and of raisins on 6 August.

If a canon quits his canonry, he can no longer assist at the cathedral as an honorary member. However, if the canon who quits had been a choirboy, he retains the right to continue to assist if he were a canon because he was nurtured and brought up *in gremio Ecclesiae*. Even if he were later given a second canonry, he resumes his old place, always retaining the right to assist and keep his rank.

In Vienne, if a pauper asks, at the moment of death, to be buried in the little cemetery of the cathedral cloister, and he dies as a true Christian fortified by the sacraments, he is buried there in the following manner. All the bells of the cathedral are rung, just as they would be for a canon. All the canons, the whole rest of their clergy, and even the archbishop when he is in the city go, preceded by the cross and silver candlesticks, to take the body and bury it with as much ceremony as if the man had been a canon, except the things that are proper to priests alone. In the second week after Easter many Masses are said for these poor departed in the chapel of the Sepulcher. This is an example of extraordinary piety and charity toward the poor, and we shall see something like it elsewhere.

The Wednesday after the fourth Sunday of Lent is called the *Feria quarta in scrutiniis*, and they still hold the examination of the catechumens in the cathedral on that day. On Maundy Thursday they hold the Office of the Catechumens.

---

[81] Chevalier, *Ordinaire*, 115.
[82] William Durand confirms that in his time the Lenten fast began on the Monday after Quinquagesima in the Provence; see *Rationale diuinorum officiorum* 6.28.4, ed. Anselme Davril and Timothy Thibodeau, Corpus Christianorum Continuatio Mediaeualis 140A (Brepols, 1998), 249.

On Holy Saturday, the faithful bring the new blessed fire back to their homes.

Quasi modo Sunday is here called *Dominica in Albis depositis*.

Feasts of nine lessons have twelve when they fall on a Sunday, because the eighth and the ninth lessons are read as one, and for the ninth they read the Gospel of the Sunday and the three lessons of its homily, which are read as one. Likewise, on many feasts of three lessons one finds five of them, even during Eastertide, because quite often they say the two or three lessons of the Gospel as one. Their breviary still has very long lessons, but this gives rise to no complaints in Vienne, no more than it does in Lyon.

On solemn feasts the Necrology is not read after Prime and the customary prayers for the dead are not said. In their place they say a versicle that is appropriate to the mystery or the feast.

On the first Monday of Lent and on the vigil of Christmas in the primatial church of Vienne, before conventual Mass, they pardon canons who have broken the chapter's statutes.

At the three Christmas Masses, in addition to the Epistle they also chant a prophetic reading, following the ancient practice of the Gallican church.[83] This was also done in Rouen and Orléans not 150 years ago, but in Vienne the Prophecy is read after the Epistle.

During Advent and from Septuagesima to Easter they use black vestments outside of feasts.

On Palm Sunday they use green, and white for the Masses of Maundy Thursday and Holy Saturday.

The Salle des Clementines

Next to the archbishop palace's palace stands the Salle des Clementines ("Hall of the Clementines"), because of the name of the decrees that were passed at the Council of Vienne under Clement V, which was held there. This hall has undergone quite the change of fortunes: nowadays it is used as a hayloft for an inn.

Church of St-Pierre of Vienne

Along the banks of the Rhône is the church of St-Pierre, formerly a celebrated abbey of the order of St. Benedict, which, it is said, housed over five hundred monks. Today it is a collegiate church of canons, boasting not only a dean and a *capiscol*, like the cathedral, but also an abbot.

The church of St-Pierre and its grounds are full of inscriptions and epitaphs of illustrious Christians and pagans. This should come as no surprise, for the latter used to be buried along the highways outside of cities and this church lies along the main road to Avignon. In this church are also buried

---

[83] Isaias 9:2, 6–7 at the cockcrow Mass; 61:1–3, 62:11–12 at the dawn Mass; and 52:6–10 at the day Mass.

the abbots of the old monastery and several illustrious archbishops of Vienne, including St. Mamertus, who instituted the Rogations before Ascension; St. Ado, who authored a martyrology and a chronicle; the learned St. Alcimus Avitus; St. Hesychius; St. Domninus; and the Blessed Burchard.

Only archbishops of Vienne and abbots of St-Pierre are buried in this church. The canons are instead interred in the chapel of St. Barbara outside this church.

In the portico of the church of St-Pierre is buried Willa, wife of Hugh, count of Vienne and Arles, king of Burgundy, and emperor of Italy; a certain illustrious Girard, called "father of the city of Vienne," who died in 1050;[84] and Abbot William, who died in 1224.[85] These burials testify to the degree of reverence this church once enjoyed.

The nave of the church is beautifully built and sustained by a double row of columns. On both sides of the entry of the nave, there are pagan epitaphs and inscriptions.

Near the high altar, on the left side, lies the tomb of the holy abbot Leonianus who, according to the epitaph, lived as a recluse in Vienne for over forty years and attracted several monks to himself by his sanctity. He also set up a monastery of sixty nuns in Vienne. He is believed to be the first abbot of St-Pierre, and Ado states that he was also the founder of the nunnery of St-André-le-Haut.[86]

Facing the right side of the altar is the epitaph of St. Mamertus, archbishop of Vienne. It is unremarkable except for these words: *Hic triduanum solennibus Letaniis indixit jejunium ante diem qua celebramus Domini Ascensum.*[87]

The surface of the high altar's table is slightly recessed, like that of the high altar in St-Maurice of Vienne and the churches of St-Jean and St-Étienne in Lyon.

Behind the high altar at the center of the back wall of the apse there is, just as in the cathedral church of St-Maurice, a beautiful stone pulpit resembling white marble at the top of three steps, with this passage taken from St. Gregory's *Regula pastoralis*: *Desinat locum docendi suscipere, qui nescit docere.*[88] A terrible sentence for ignorant pastors! And yet one scarcely sees them refuse positions on that account, still less renounce them.

The vault of the choir is supported by two tall columns made of a Open Rremarkably beautiful stone I have not been able to identify. The vault itself is covered with ancient frescos.

---

[84] *Corpus des inscriptions de la France médiévale* 15, no. 57.
[85] See Augustine Allmer and Alfred de Terrebasse, eds., *Inscriptions antiques et du moyen âge de Vienne en Dauphiné* (Vienne, 1875), 5:303–4.
[86] *Corpus des inscriptions de la France médiévale* 15, no. 130.
[87] "He instituted a three day fast and a solemn litany before the day on which we celebrate Our Lord's Ascension" (*Corpus des inscriptions de la France médiévale* 15, no. 129).
[88] "Let he who knows not how to teach renounce his teaching post." The passage is actually from St. Isidore, *Sentences* 3.35.1b, ed. Pierre Cazier, Corpus Christianorum Series Latina 111 (Brepols, 1998), 275.

The Pyramide at the Porte d'Avignon

Outside the gate called the Porte d'Avignon, four or five hundred paces away from the city, there is a very ancient obelisk, called the Pyramide, set upon a square vault supported by four thick pillars, each set on a pedestal. They are flanked by two slightly raised square pilasters, forming an arcade with cornices on each side. This base structure is between twenty and twenty-five feet high. Although the center of the vault is flat, it is nonetheless able to bear the square pyramid, which is another twenty-four or twenty-five feet high, with an imperfect apex. The whole is made up of very hard, large, and thick stones without any cement, and there is no inscription. It lies in the middle of a field along a small stream, about eighty paces from the main road. See Fig. 1 (PLATE 5).

Looking down from this vantage-point, all along the city walls one sees in both directions, above the cathedral and the episcopal palace, the ancient remains of amphitheaters, baths, and aqueducts on the slopes of the hills.

Today this area is called Romêtang or Romestang, from the Latin *Romanorum stagnum*, since the Romans built a water reservoir here. Only the ruins are left of a structure that must have been erected at very great expense.

The almshouse is contiguous to the archiepiscopal palace, connected by a large door that provides easy access for an archbishop so devoted to charity towards the poor as the illustrious prelate who currently rules the church of Vienne.[89]

---

[89] Armand de Montmorin (r. 1694–1713).

LYON

LYON, *Lugdunum* in Latin, used to be called *Augusta Sequanorum*, meaning something like "the chief city of the Burgundians." Lying on the banks of the Rhône and the Saône, *ad Rhodanum et Ararim*, it is one of the largest and most celebrated cities in France.

Church of Saint-Jean of Lyon

There is a fountain in the parvis in front of the church (PLATE 6).[1]

The vaults of the nave and choir are of equal height, but the vault above the altar, which ends in the shell-shaped apse, is some twenty-five feet lower. There is a gallery that runs around the whole church, and one aisle on each side as well as another aisle for the chapels. The eastern end of the church terminates in the apse.

---

[1] The evolution of the holy water stoup from a larger fountain or pool in the parvis of ancient churches was discussed notably by Claude de Vert, *Dissertation sur les mots de Messe et de Communion* (Paris, 1694), 439–43. The objection to having them inside was that they were meant for washing before entering the holy place; see pp. 264–65.

The crossing does not run between the nave and choir, nor between the choir and sanctuary, but right over the choir and in line with its easternmost arcades.

In the crossing on the Gospel side near the sacristy is the famous clock,[2] about which we must say a few words (see PLATE 7). Atop its dome sits a cock that beats its wings, lifts its tail, and crows, just like a living cock, just before the hour is rung. Immediately after, the angels atop the dome's frieze play the hymn of St. John the Baptist, *Ut queant laxis*,[3] on the bells. While this music is playing, an angel opens the door to a room and hails the Blessed Virgin; then a panel of this room opens up and the Holy Spirit descends upon her, and the Eternal Father above gives his blessing to signify that after the Virgin's consent the mystery of the Incarnation has been accomplished. Then the Spirit returns to Heaven, the panel closes, and the angel leaves and closes the door. Once the chiming is finished, the hour sounds.

Further down the clock is a niche in which, at midnight each day, a different figure appears. On Sundays it is Christ risen, and below him the word *Dominica*. On Monday, Death personified, and below it *Feria secunda*. On Tuesday, St. John the Baptist, and below him *Feria tertia*. On Wednesday St. Stephen, and below him *Feria quarta*. On Thursday, Christ holding a host above a chalice, and below him *Feria quinta*. On Friday, an infant embracing a cross, and below it *Feria sexta*. On Saturday the Blessed Virgin, and below her the word *Sabbatum*.

Below this niche is a large astrolabe that represents all the movements of the heavens: of the sun with the hour of sunrise and sunset, the degree of the zodiac sign it is crossing, the length of days and nights, the length of morning and evening twilight; and the phases of the moon: waxing, full, waning, and the quarters. The alidade that traverses the entire astrolabe marks the twenty-four hours of the day, as well as the current month and day.

Under the astrolabe, at eye level, a sixty-six year kalendar marks the years since the birth of Our Lord, the golden number, the epact, the Dominical letter, and the movable feasts. It all changes instantly on the last day of the year at midnight, or so I am told.

It also has a perpetual almanac that marks the day of the month, the kalends, nones, ides, etc.

On its right side, facing the choir, it has a dial with a needle of very curious craftsmanship. The needle moves in an ellipse, marking the sixty minutes and quarter-hours, following the edge of the ellipse without ever going beyond or away from it.

The choir behind the canons' seats is covered with marble.

---

[2] For more details on this curious device, see Antoine Grand, "Notice historique et descriptive sur l'horloge astronomique de la cathédrale de Lyon," in *Mémoires de la Société littéraire, historique et archéologique de Lyon, années 1898 à 1902* (Louis Brun, 1903), 81–98.
[3] Cantus ID 008406.

The marble rood screen is quite beautiful (PLATE 8). The Matins lessons are chanted from its loft on feast days, as is the Gospel of the Mass on Sundays, doubles, vigils, Ember days, and during Advent and Lent.

The Epistle is chanted in choir by the subdeacon, bareheaded and seated on the misericord in the third stall of the top row on the right side near the great rood. On ferias it is read in the middle of the choir *quasi in semitono Evangelii*.[4]

There is no pulpit, cantors' bench, or eagle lectern in the choir of this church, save the lectern placed there for the Matins lessons on ferial days, because they chant everything, even the short chapters, by heart; if the officiant does not know these by heart, he has them written on a piece of paper or small breviary hidden in the sleeves of his surplice. They chant two and sometimes three notes on the last stressed syllable of the mediant of psalms in the second, third, fourth, fifth, seventh, and eighth tones.[5]

The dean's stall is located where the episcopal throne usually stands in cathedrals, separated from the others by a small door used to exit the choir for a procession or station at a chapel on that side; such stations are very common in Lyon. When the Lord Archbishop assists at the Office, the dean cedes his seat to him and takes the archdeacon's.

In the middle, between the choir and sanctuary, stands a seven-branched candelabrum called a *râtelier*, in Latin *rastrum* or *rastellarium* (PLATE 9).[6] It consists of two six-foot brass columns supporting a brass beam decorated with small cornices and moldings. The beam is fitted with seven brass bobèches for the seven candles, which are lit on doubles of the first and second class. See Fig. 2 (PLATE 9).

In addition to the *râtelier*, there are three silver crown chandeliers over the rood loft, each holding three candles, and several more candles at Matins, which are extinguished towards the end of Lauds because day has broken by then. Other churches also extinguish candles at the end of Lauds during the Holy Triduum, so there is no mystery about those days in particular.[7]

The high altar, which is about five feet wide, is enclosed in a fairly light brass balustrade, two or two and a half feet tall, that ends flush with the back of the altar (see Fig. 3, PLATE 5). The altar, whose marble table is

---

[4] That is, about a half-tone lower than the Gospel is sung.
[5] In the psalm tones used in Paris and elsewhere at the time, the note of the last stressed syllable of the mediant rose by just one tone above the reciting tone. In the use of Lyon, the last stressed syllable had more notes in the tones listed.
[6] The presence of a candelabrum, or of seven independent candles, is a very ancient feature of Christian worship preserved to this day in most rites. The *râtelier* of Lyon was destroyed by decision of the chapter in 1749, because it had an "archaic Jewish appearance," even though the seven branches were traditionally interpreted as representing the seven churches mentioned in the Apocalypse rather than the menorah. See Jean Marie H. Forest, *L'école cathédrale de Lyon* (Paris, 1885), 74, and Archdale King, *Liturgies of the Primatial Sees* (Longmans, Green and Co., 1957), 22.
[7] For instance, the Carthusians, Cistercians, Carmelites, Paris, and St-Martin in Tours. See de Vert, *Explication*, 4:427–8.

slightly recessed, is very simple, its only decoration being an antependium in front and a dossal over the retable above.[8] This retable has two crucifixes, one on each side. Scaliger says there were none there in his day. I watched them change the two wooden crucifixes for brass ones on 25 June 1696.[9] A single candlestick and candle is placed next to each crucifix. These two candlesticks are removed when others are put on the altar on the most solemn feasts of the year. Even the retable is removed when the archbishop celebrates Mass on Maundy Thursday, Easter, Pentecost, and Christmas, so that he may be seen from his episcopal throne, which is simple and raised on four steps in the center of the apse's back wall.[10] A large stone ledge, running along the apse wall on either side of this throne, about as high as the altar, is used to seat the numerous officiants who assist the archbishop when he celebrates Mass, namely six priests, seven deacons, the crucifer, the crosier-bearer, and the chaplains. In Greek it is called the *synthronos*, and in Latin *concessus*. There are also seven subdeacons and seven candle-bearers who do not, however, sit with the others. See the figure of the altar and apse with the episcopal throne, see Fig. 3 (PLATE 5).

On days when the archbishop officiates, before Matins, high Mass, and Vespers the count-canons[11] in surplice, preceded by two candle-bearers, go to the archiepiscopal palace to escort him. The bishop wears a cope, as do his crucifer, crosier-bearer, and chaplains. The count-canons escort him back to his residence in the same way, and no other crucifixes are carried but his.[12]

The priest celebrant always sits on the Epistle side next to the end of the semicircular stone ledge we just mentioned. There is a lectern next to

---

[8] In this arrangement, originating in the Middle Ages, a cloth of matching pattern was set up on the retable on the back edge of the altar surface.
[9] Although an undocumented hypothesis explained these two crucifixes as a vestige of the union of the Latin and Greek churches in the Council of Lyon in 1274 when the processions of the Latins and the Greeks each left their crucifix by the sides of the high altar, it seems more likely that one crucifix represents the archbishop, and another the chapter, ever wary of episcopal encroachments on their privileges. See Denys Buenner, *L'ancienne liturgie romaine. Le rite lyonnais* (Emmanuel Vitte, 1934), 134, 139–40.
[10] This retable was removed permanently by Archbishop Claude de Saint-Georges (r. 1693–1714).
[11] The long dispute between the archbishop of Lyon and the count of Forez over the temporal jurisdiction of Lyon ended in 1173, when Guy II of Forez abandoned his claim to the title "count of Lyon" and recognized the archbishop's power over the city. Guy's son Renaud, who became archbishop of Lyon in 1193, granted each of the canons of the cathedral chapter the title "canon." When Lyon was incorporated into the Kingdom of France in 1312, King Philip the Fair confirmed the canons' right to continue to use this title, which was purely honorific. Fully prebended canons of the cathedral of Lyon were therefore often referred to as "count-canons," as Le Brun des Marettes does throughout this chapter.
[12] On the canons' symbolic assertion of their jurisdiction over the cathedral through the placement of their own crucifix, see n. 9 above. The bishops of Lyon were forced to take an oath on accession all but denying them any authority over the choir and cloister. Further, they were not allowed to wear episcopal regalia when visiting any of the canons' churches, but had to dress as one of the canons, in a red cape, or black with red border. See Buenner, *L'ancienne liturgie*, 132–35.

him for reading the Epistle. He can bare or cover his head as he wishes, except when he reads the Gospel, for of everything chanted by the choir he reads only the Introit and the Communion at the altar.[13] On doubles half of the assistant priests sit to his right, and next to them the canon-deacon wearing a miter and half of the other assistant deacons. The other assistant priests and deacons sit on the opposite side facing them. The subdeacons never sit with them, but rather, they stand behind the altar, facing each other during the Epistle, Gradual, and Alleluia, and if the Prose is long, they go to sit in choir with the candle-bearers.

Behind the high altar and the brass balustrade there is a smaller contiguous altar dedicated to St. Speratus—the titular altar of the perpetuals, the semi-prebended incorporated beneficers and titulars of St-Jean of Lyon[14]—where a Mass, low or sung, is said daily.

Between this altar and the apse is a very large space, in the midst of which the officiant's cope is placed on a kind of lectern, and next to it a large brazier for the thurible's embers.

The thurible is hung on the rightmost pillar of the *râtelier* at the beginning of Vespers, and the boat is placed on the middle of the altar. The thurifer, who must be a subdeacon, vested in alb and rabat[15] without amice, goes behind the altar to take off the surplice he wears over his alb, picking up the thurible on his way. Even if he is a count, he helps the officiant put on his cope while the sacristan-clerk, who opened the doors of the

---

[13] The custom of the celebrant at high Mass reciting the parts sung by the choir or read by the ministers, is difficult to trace, but it seems to have developed gradually from the twelfth century. The mid-thirteenth-century Franciscan ordinal attributed to Haymo of Faversham has the celebrant read the Introit, *Kyrie*, Epistle, intercalary chants, and *Sanctus*, but the fourteenth-century ceremonial of the papal court of Avignon (Mabillon's *Ordo Romanus* 14) states only that the pontiff reads the Introit and ordinary, not the other sung propers or readings. Even Haymo's ordinal has the celebrant read the Epistle and subsequent chants while seated, and the rubrics of the Tridentine Missal are one of the earliest to require that the texts be recited at the altar in the manner of a low Mass. For an overview of this development, see Andrew J. M. Irving, "On the Counting of Mass Books," *Archiv für Liturgiewissenschaft* 57 (2015): 31–33, and, despite its grossly tendentious tone and dubious conclusions, Lambert Beauduin, "Messe basse ou messe solennelle?" *Les questions liturgiques et paroissiales* 5 (1919–1920): 90–97. De Vert, *Explication*, 4:59–67 and 122–32, criticizes this practice as an unwarranted intrusion of low Mass ceremonial into the high Mass—a belief echoed by Le Brun des Marettes on pp. 186–87—and some neo-Gallican reformers sought to do away with it. In Paris, it was decided in 1701 that the celebrant should sit after the collect and listen to the readings and chants (see p. 57, n. 84), and the 1736 missal of Troyes eliminated the duplication of readings entirely, although two years later the bishop restored the practice as part of his measures to quell the uproar the novel missal had aroused.

[14] The twenty semi-prebendaries of the cathedral chapter of Lyon were known as "perpetuals" (*perpétuels*), because they were strictly bound to assist at the celebration of the Offices day and night and to sing them by memory, being prohibited from using books. They said Mass at the altar of St. Speratus, since the high altar was reserved for the archbishop and count-canons.

[15] A type of clerical garment that appeared in the seventeenth century and consisted of two black white-fringed oblong pieces of cloth fixed to the collar, draping over the front.

balustrade on both sides after the last psalm, puts coals in the thurible.[16]

On solemn feasts the archbishop, archpriest,[17] or dean and their ministers go to the treasury on the right side of the crossing to vest for Mass.

When the archbishop celebrates high Mass on Easter, Pentecost, and Christmas, he has with him, besides his crucifer, crosier-bearer, and chaplains, six assistant priests commonly known as *les symmuses*, in Latin the *symmistae*, that is, concelebrants,[18] as well as seven deacons, seven subdeacons, and seven candle-bearers. One of the seven deacons is a count-canon who sings the Gospel, and one of the seven subdeacons is a count-canon who sings the Epistle. In the bishop's absence, the archpriest celebrates Mass rather than the dean, with the same number of assistants, except for the crucifer and crosier-bearer.

The seven candle-bearers are chosen from the twenty-four choirboys, twelve of whom are brought up *in gremio et sumptibus Ecclesiae*,[19] while the twelve others hold the right to succeed them. Their hair is cut short, but not entirely shaved. Their choir habit consists of a surplice over a red cassock, but they wear albs when serving.

Over their cassocks, the canons wear a surplice (*surplis*), or *soupelis* as it used to be pronounced, from the Latin *superpellicium*—which is written *subpellicium* or *suppellicium* in old manuscripts—*quasi sub pellibus*,[20] because the surplice is indeed worn under the fur almuce. The surplice has long closed sleeves,[21] such as nearly all clerics used to wear, and the canons of Lyon call it the *froc*. In winter, they wear one without sleeves or with narrow sleeves like those of an alb, and they called it a *frochon*, the diminutive of *froc*. Over this surplice or *froc* they wear a very large almuce that rests on their shoulders, reaches down to the waist, and wraps back around the front where it is pinned in place by a hook and small chain. The hood of the almuce—which they never pull over their heads, wearing a biretta instead—stays behind the neck, as shown in Fig. 4 (PLATES 10 and 11).

Proof that the hood of the almuce used to be drawn over the head is found in the chapel next to the clock, on a stained glass window that shows

---

[16] On clerics performing duties below their station, see p. 16, n. 35.

[17] Although the archpriest (*grand-prêtre*) was not counted among the eight dignitaries of the chapter of Lyon, this canon was one of its foremost members, and his role was to officiate as needed in place of the archbishop. See Jean Beyssac, "Les grands prêtres de l'église de Lyon," in *Mémoires de la Société littéraire, historique et archéologique de Lyon, années 1898 à 1902* (Louis Brun, 1903), 137–56.

[18] The Jesuit Dominique de Colonia, in his *Histoire littéraire de la ville de Lyon* (Lyon, 1730), 2:68, writes that the popular term for these assistant priests was actually *six muses*, but he agrees with Le Brun des Marettes that its origin must be the Latin *symmistae*. These were purely ceremonial concelebrants, since they did not pronounce the words of consecration with the bishop. See King, *Liturgies*, 75.

[19] "In the bosom of the Church and at her expense"

[20] "As if to say 'under the pelts.'"

[21] That is, the sleeves were closed underneath, unlike the "split and trailing" sleeves Le Brun des Marettes says were used in Paris and the province of Sens (see p. 63).

a count-canon named Bernard de Montiou in a red robe, wearing a surplice that reaches down to the middle of the leg, and the almuce over his head. This image is believed to date from the sixteenth century.[22]

The ancient canons regular of Deux-Amants in the diocese of Rouen also used to wear the almuce on the head before they were replaced by the reformed Congregation of Ste-Geneviève.

I have said that the canons of Lyon wear the biretta, but that does not include the lower-formers, even if they are count-canons,[23] who, like the other clerks and the choirboys (also called *clergeons*), still follow the ancient custom and do not wear it. They travel to and from the church bareheaded, showing that in former times they always prayed bareheaded inside the church, as the Apostle says (1 Cor. 11:4). We find proof of this in the Gregorian Sacramentary, p. 38 in Hugues Ménard's edition: *Nullus clericus in ecclesia stat operto capite, nisi habeat infirmitatem, ullo tempore*.[24]

Obviously, the ample almuce of the canons of Lyon is extremely uncomfortable in hot weather, and so it is not worn between Pentecost and Michaelmas. When the weather turns excessively hot before Pentecost, the canons remove their almuces sooner, after discussing the matter in chapter. Discomfort in hot weather is also the reason that canons elsewhere have taken to wearing the almuce over the arm rather than on the head, just as in the past fifty years we have seen the fashion arise among laymen of wearing one's coat over the shoulders or left arm in summer. Nevertheless, we shall also see other places where the almuce is worn over the shoulders or even on the head.[25]

The canons of Lyon begin wearing the almuce again on Michaelmas, when the cold begins to make itself felt. From Matins of the first Sunday of Advent until Easter they wear over their *froc*, a black cape with red fringe and a long train (PLATE 12),[26] which they let loose when crossing the choir or performing some function. Over this cape they wear a hood, large and pointed at the bottom, called the camail, under which they have a sort of furred skullcap that covers their entire head down to the forehead.

---

[22] This description is nearly identical to the one given by de Vert, *Explication*, 2:261. This stained glass is no longer extant, and the count-canon's name might be garbled; see Louis Morel de Voleine, "Du costume des chanoines de Lyon," *Revue du Lyonnais* 3 (1877): 233–34.
[23] Deacons- and subdeacons-canon sat in the lower form.
[24] "Let no cleric in church stand with his head covered at any time, unless he be ill." This admonition appears in a rubric before the title *Feria II intra Quadragesimam* in some later sacramentaries based on the Gregorian, such as the tenth-century one from Corbie that Dom Ménard used for his edition (PL 78:58D). The rubric is, however, absent from the authentic Gregorian Sacramentary; see Jean Deshusses, ed., *Le sacramentaire grégorien*, Spicilegium Friburgense 16 (Éditions Universitaires Fribourg Suisse, 1992), 1:135.
[25] In the abbey of St-Victor in Paris (p. 187) and formerly in Vienne and at the church of Deux-Amants in Paris (p. 191). For a longer discussion of the historical use of the almuce, see de Vert, *Explication*, 2:257–65.
[26] This winter cape was known as *domino*. See Forest, *L'école cathédrale*, 80.

The canons perpetual wear an almuce not unlike that of the count-canons, and in choir they sit with them in the upper form. In winter, under their camail, instead of the canons' furred skullcap, they wear a biretta which they never remove during the Office, not even at the elevation of the host. This biretta probably developed from the large calotte still worn by the choirboys in winter.

The canons—both counts and perpetuals—as well as the choirboys reverence the altar when they arrive at their places by bending their knees like a woman's curtsy and like choirboys in cathedral churches, with their hands and even their birettas hidden under the sleeves of their surplice or *froc*, as is expressly ordained by the old ordinal of this church.[27] Ambassadors perform a similar reverence when they greet the king of France, and the cardinals when they greet the pope on entering his chapel.

There is no organ or *musique* in the cathedral of St-Jean of Lyon.[28]

On Sundays before high Mass, water is blessed at the font in the nave by the main door. The priest wears a cope and miter, while the ministers stand around him in alb and maniple. The deacon, wearing an alb, stole, and miter, holds the salt in a scallop shell; the subdeacon, wearing an alb with maniple and miter, holds the cross; an acolyte holds the book. The versicle *Adjutorium* is said in a low voice, and the exorcisms and orations are said out loud. They return to the choir singing the *Asperges me* with the psalm *Miserere*. The celebrant sprinkles the altar, the processional cross, the ministers, and the clerics. Then the deacon goes to sprinkle the altars around the choir as well as the people he encounters on the way. Thereafter they go into the cloister in silence, and the celebrant sprinkles the fountain in the middle of the yard, *in pratello*—as is done in countless monasteries—and says the appropriate oration. He then enters the refectory, where he blesses the bread and wine on the choirboys' table as well as the fire and cooking pot, as the choir awaits him at the south corner of the cloister singing. Returning to choir, they hold a station in the nave, during which an acolyte sprinkles the nave chapels and the people on the way until he reaches the sacristy, where he leaves the holy water stoup.

It must be noted here that instead of the world *pietatis tuae* RORE found in modern missals in the last oration of the blessing of water on Sundays, one reads *pietatis tuae* MORE, that is, "by thine accustomed loving-kindness," in the 1530 missal of Lyon,[29] a thirteenth century manuscript missal of Auxerre,[30]

---

[27] The fourteenth-century ordinal of St-Just enjoins that "hands are not to appear outside the *froc*, nor books, if held in hand," but does not mention the biretta, although it does say that clerics should enter choir and make a reverence *remotis capuciis*; see the edition in Joseph Roux, *La liturgie de la Sainte Église de Lyon d'après les monuments* (Lyon, 1864), 73 and 71 respectively.
[28] On the *musique*, see p. 350.
[29] *Missale secundum ritum ecclesie Lugdunensis* (Lyon, 1530), fol. 198v.
[30] Paris, Bibliothèque nationale, Lat. 17316, fol. 206v.

the 1504 missal of Orléans, and those of Rouen of 1516, Vienne of 1519,[31] Paris of 1557, and in the rituals of Paris of 1526, Orléans of 1581,[32] Chartres of 1604, and the Ambrosian of Milan of 1687.[33] This makes much more sense than "by the dew of thy loving-kindness," and is the authentic reading.[34] The ritual of Milan also notes that the priest breathes over the salt while he says *Exorcizo te, creatura salis*, and likewise over the water saying, *Exorcizo te, creatura aquae.*[35]

The celebrant, deacon, and subdeacon also wear their miters at the blessing of the font on Holy Saturday and the vigil of Pentecost.

It is the choirboys' duty to bring out the altar cloths immediately before high Mass.

The major canons always act as deacon and subdeacon at the high altar;[36] they would rather do without than have others fill these roles. Note that these gentlemen do not regard these functions as beneath them.

All clerics, including the count-canons, always rise and turn towards the altar at the *Gloria Patri*, even at the minor hours, and they always chant the words *Patri et Filio et Spiritui* straight through in the reciting tone, in the Mass as well as the other Offices.

On doubles of the first class, the dean is assisted at Mass by two perpetual priests wearing chasubles who stand facing the altar, one at each side; by three deacons, of whom one is a count-canon wearing his miter, and the two others are without miter; and three subdeacons, one of whom is likewise mitered.

The choir first sings the Introit in a low tone, and then raises it by two or three pitches at the *Gloria Patri* to signal to the celebrants and the ministers that it is time to leave the vestry. Then all depart: two candle-bearers in albs walk out first after the mace-bearing verger; then follow two lower-form subdeacons; then the subdeacon count-canon wearing his miter, even in the presence of the Blessed Sacrament exposed on the altar. They go to the gate at the east end of choir and all together incline their heads toward the altar. Then the two candle-bearers set down their candles *in plano* at the east end by the third stall on each side. The three subdeacons immediately go to take their places at the west end of the choir in the second row of stalls near the

---

[31] *Missale ad vsum sancte Viennensis ecclesie* (Lyon, 1519), "Modus exorcizandi aquam benedictam."

[32] *Manuale continens modum sacramenta ecclesiastica secundum usum insignis ecclesie Aurelianensis* (Paris, 1581), 2v.

[33] *Rituale sacramentorum ad usum Mediolanensis ecclesiae* (Milan, 1687), 273.

[34] On this point, see de Vert, *Explication*, 1:180, note b, who states that he is the first to notice this manifest copyist's or printer's error, which slipped into the liturgical books "in the past hundred years." The oldest manuscripts of the Aniane supplement to the Gregorian Sacramentary (formerly attributed to Alcuin) confirm the reading *more* (ed. Deshusses, 1:474). The neo-Gallican missals of Laon (1702) and Meaux (1709) restored the authentic text, according to Pierre Le Brun, *Explication littérale, historique et dogmatique des prières et cérémonies de la Messe* (Paris, 1716), 1:78n4.

[35] *Rituale…Mediolanensis ecclesiae* (Milan, 1687), 271.

[36] In many places this role had devolved upon the semi-prebended canons. See pp. 349–50.

great rood, the subdeacon count-canon in the first place at the right-hand side, one subdeacon by his side in the second place, and the other on the other side in the first place. They all make a reverence upon arriving at their places.

Meanwhile, the celebrant goes up to the altar with the deacon-canon to his right (this is the sole occasion where the deacon seems to be in some way above the assistant priests, who always remain by the corners of the altar) followed by a vested priest and deacon, and similarly to his left a priest and a deacon. They say the *Confiteor* to one another on a long board called the *grand ais*, two paces away from the altar balustrade (PLATE 13).

The celebrant then enters the sanctuary with the two priests. He kisses the center of the altar and each of the priests kisses his corner. Thereafter the deacon-count goes up to the Gospel corner of the altar to kiss it, then returns to his place, passing behind the altar, at the aforesaid board together with the vested deacons, all at an equal distance from one another.

The candle-bearers immediately go to the west end of the stalls near the great rood behind the subdeacons and face one another until the beginning of the *Gloria in excelsis*, which is sung in its entirety by the two choirs together. At that point the candle-bearers go get their candles and hold them raised at the west end of the choir near the subdeacons during the collects until the *Per Dominum*, when they take them to the *râtelier*.

The subdeacon-count leaves his place in choir after the last *Kyrie* and goes up to the gate at the east end of the choir, with his miter on his head and his hands joined with interlocking fingers. At this gate he greets the altar with a head bow and then goes to the *râtelier* where he removes his miter. He makes an inclination near the altar, or a reverence if the Blessed Sacrament is exposed, and goes to the corner of the altar to pick up the Epistle book, which he takes behind the altar.

After the subdeacon-count leaves his place in choir, the subdeacon who had been at his side takes the place he vacated, and if there is another deacon in the same choir, as on the feast of St. John the Baptist, he takes the second place in order to maintain symmetry with the subdeacons on the opposite side. They leave their places after the *suscipe deprecationem nostram* of the *Gloria in excelsis*, and, making the same inclinations and reverences as the subdeacon-count, join him behind the altar.

Every time the celebrant turns towards the people to say *Dominus vobiscum*, the deacons on the *grand ais* also turn and greet the people.

At the beginning of the collect, the subdeacon-canon goes bareheaded to the raised third stall of the first row at the east end of the choir on the right-hand side. He leans on the misericord[37] and reads the Epistle in a middling tone, more like speech than song.

---

[37] Author's note: The misericord is a wooden board the size of about two hands, on which the canons and cantors lean while they sing the psalms and hymns, and this position is considered equivalent to standing.

After the collect, the celebrant goes to sit together with his assistant priests and deacons, half on each side. The celebrant reads the Epistle and what follows on a small iron lectern by his side.

The two choirboys set their candles on the ground by the foot of the *râtelier* after the collect and go up to the altar to retrieve the silver tablets which are inset with a vellum leaf containing the Gradual and Alleluia. They present them to a canon and three perpetuals who had just taken their places at the first upper stalls of the right side near the great rood. They sing the Gradual leaning on their stalls, then yield their places and the tablets over to four others who sing the Alleluia and its verse, after which they return to their places in choir. They call this singing *per rotulos*.[38] The precentor stands at the first place on the Epistle side and the cantor at the first place on the Gospel side near the great rood, their silver staves by their side.

After the Epistle has been sung, the subdeacon-canon goes back, saluting the altar at the top of the choir, then passes the side of the altar and the celebrant without ceremony, and goes straight up to the deacon-count, who is seated after the assistant priests. He makes a reverence to him and hands over the book, which the deacon-count must use for the Gospel. Then the subdeacon-canon takes the celebrant's book to the Gospel side, passing behind the altar. Then he returns, passing behind the altar again, and takes his seat with the two or four assistant subdeacons as at the beginning of Mass, at the west end of the choir near the great rood. Towards the end of the Prose the subdeacons leave the west end of the choir and go behind the altar, where the canon-subdeacon picks up the cushion. An assistant deacon takes the thurible and boat to the celebrant, who puts in the incense and blesses it. The deacon-canon then bows before the celebrant and asks his blessing; then all go to the rood loft in this order: the mace-bearer, the two candle-bearers, the subdeacon-canon holding the cushion in front of his breast, one of the assistant deacons carrying the thurible, and finally the deacon-canon holding the book, which no one reverences in any manner on the way. They mount the rood loft, the subdeacon faces the deacon, and after the words *Sequentia sancti Evangelii secundum N.* the deacon and the entire choir turn to face the altar; the deacon and celebrant make a triple sign of the cross. The assistant deacon holding the thurible incenses the screen's great rood with three swings before the Gospel, and again with three swings afterwards. The book is not incensed.

While the rood is incensed after the Gospel, the celebrant returns to the altar and begins the Creed, which, like the *Gloria in excelsis*, is sung in its entirety by both sides of the choir together, as the Carthusians do,

---

[38] The vellum leaves were kept rolled up when not in use, and hence known as *rotuli* or *rôles*. See Forest, *L'école cathédrale*, 114. Such a roll was also used in the Rogation processions, containing the names of the saints invoked at the stations.

rather than in alternation as almost everywhere else.³⁹ It is quite proper to sing the profession of faith entirely, rather than partly.

During the Creed (PLATE 14), the two candle-bearers and the subdeacon-thurifer depart the loft first, followed by the subdeacon-canon holding the cushion with the Gospel book, which is closed and held down by the cushion's two tassels, and then the deacon-canon, who holds his hands together with fingers interlocking. At the gate at the east end of the choir, they reverence the altar with an inclination of the head or *a vobis*, as they call it. Then the candle-bearers set their candles on the ground by the *râtelier* and the thurifer, subdeacon, and deacon approach the altar and make a reverence. The thurifer goes behind the altar, the deacon to his place at the center of the *grand ais*, and the subdeacon to the Epistle corner to present the book to the celebrant, who kisses it. Then he takes the book to be kissed by the canons and perpetuals in the upper stalls only, saying to each, *Haec sunt verba sancti Evangelii*, and then making a reverence to each dignitary.

After the Creed and the *Oremus* of the offertory, the two candle-bearers wash the celebrant's hands for the first time. One of them holds the basin and cruet and the other what resembles a large table napkin. Meanwhile, the choir sings the Offertory with several verses taken from a psalm in measured plainchant.⁴⁰

At the altar corner the subdeacon-canon — or if he has not yet returned from the choir where he has taken the book to be kissed, another subdeacon in his place — presents the chalice and paten already prepared to the deacon-canon, who gives them to the celebrant without supporting the chalice. The celebrant offers them both together with a single oration, as do the Carthusians, Carmelites, and Dominicans.⁴¹ Then he puts the host on the corporal and covers the chalice with the corporal's other side like the Carthusians, whose rite is quite similar to that of Lyon. The 1504 missal of Orléans also says the host and chalice used to be offered *per unum*, and that the chalice was then covered with the corporal.

Thereafter the celebrant puts incense into the thurible and blesses it. He incenses the crucifix with three swings and then the entire altar in the manner usual in other churches. He hands the thurible to the deacon, who incenses him with two swings. Then the deacon incenses around the altar

---

³⁹ Cf. de Vert, *Explication*, 1:303, who writes that only the Carthusians and the cathedral of Paris preserve the ancient custom of singing these parts of the Mass in unison rather than in alternation, and that in former times the people also joined the choir in singing these parts.
⁴⁰ Measured plainchant (*plain-chant composé*), also known as "musical" or "figured" plainchant (*musical* or *figuré*), was a style of liturgical chant popular in France between the seventeenth and nineteenth century. It amended the faults that the taste of the day found in the traditional Gregorian repertoire by removing melismas, giving notes fixed rhythmic values, adding more accidentals (including sharps), and other revisions. Henri Du Mont's widely popular *Cinq messes en plain-chant* (Paris, 1669), for instance, are written in this style, as are the liturgical music books edited by Guillaume-Gabriel Nivers.
⁴¹ I.e., the *In spiritu humilitatis*.

from outside the balustrade. When passing the center, both in front and behind, he pauses to incense the altar with three swings, as the Carthusians do. Meanwhile, the two candle-bearers wash the celebrant's hands again as he says the *Lavabo*, as in other churches. Then the deacon-canon returns to his usual place at the *grand ais* outside the balustrade, making a reverence to the altar there with the other deacons.

The assistant priests stand close to the four corners of the altar until the end of the Mass.

When the subdeacon-canon returns from choir, he makes an inclination as he passes the east end of the choir and a reverence by the altar, and goes to get the chalice, which he gives to the deacon. If this had already been done, he joins the other subdeacons behind the altar.

At the *Sanctus*, this subdeacon-canon goes to take the paten, covers it with half his maniple, and goes back behind the altar. The two candle-bearers each take a torch and stand in front of the altar, outside the balustrade. The other young *clergeons* come together in mid-choir to sing the entire stanza *O salutaris Hostia* by themselves. This practice is quite new.[42]

When the priest is ready to consecrate, the subdeacon-canon goes to the side of the altar *ex parte Epistolae* to adore the Blessed Sacrament. The count-deacon enters the sanctuary, kneels in the middle of the footpace, and takes both sides of the chasuble in his hands, raising it at the elevations of the host and chalice. Then he returns to his place in front of the altar outside the balustrade, while the subdeacon goes back behind the altar.

The celebrant elevates the host and chalice at the words *sicut in coelo* and lowers them at *et in terra*, following the sense of the words, rather than raising them at *omnis honor et gloria* as in other places (in Langres the minor elevation is done at *panem nostrum*).[43] After having placed them back on the corporal, he makes a reverence. Once the choir has responded *sed libera nos a malo* the celebrant sings the *Libera nos, quaesumus Domine*—as in Milan— to a melody similar to that of the *Pater*. At the beginning of this prayer, the subdeacon-canon goes to the right side of the altar and raises the paten for the people to see, as a sign that communion is near. Immediately thereafter the deacon enters the sanctuary, takes the paten, and presents it to the celebrant at *intercedente beata*. At *da propitius pacem* the celebrant kisses it.

---

[42] On 15 June 1512, King Louis XII requested that the *O salutaris Hostia* be sung at the elevation of the host at high Masses throughout his realm to beg for victory against Pope Julius II, given the words *Bella premunt hostilia / da robur fer auxilium*. It ceased to be sung in 1517, after the end of that war, but later kings again requested the singing of this hymn at the elevation, and by the seventeenth century it was a regular part of the celebration of conventual Mass on the highest feasts; the *O salutaris* was even included between the *Sanctus* and *Benedictus* (sung after the elevations) in the ordinary in the 1662 *Graduale iuxta Missale Parisiense*, clx. In Lyon, the chapter confirmed the singing of the *O salutaris* at the canons' high Mass on 24 January 1657. See Forest, *L'école cathédrale*, 115.
[43] On the many and varied gestures that accompanied the words of the rite in French liturgies, see the extensive catalogue and sympathetic study by de Vert, *Explication* 1:144–302, and on these words in particular, see 1:160–62 and 262–64.

When the archbishop celebrates Mass on greater feasts, he gives the solemn blessing before the *Agnus Dei*.[44]

At the *Agnus Dei*, the deacon presents the pax-brede to the celebrant for him to kiss. Only the deacon kisses it afterwards. The priest says *Pax tecum* and the deacon responds *Et cum spiritu tuo*. A manuscript ordinal of the church of St-Paul of Lyon,[45] written some four hundred years ago, states that the deacon gave the kiss of peace to both cantors, and then all the clerics one to another, and finally all the faithful.[46]

After the deacon makes a reverence to the altar, he passes behind it and goes with the subdeacon, walking to his left, to the Gospel side. They stand behind the assistant priests outside the balustrade during the priest's communion, which he does *per unum*, that is, with a single prayer formula.

On solemn feasts, the Communion antiphon is followed by a psalm verse, then the antiphon is sung again, then the *Gloria Patri*, and the antiphon a third time, just like the Introit. Thus the singing of the Mass propers ends as it began.[47]

---

[44] These tripartite blessings before communion, reserved to the bishop, are already attested by St. Augustine (*Epistulae* 149.16 and 179.4, ed. Alois Goldbacher, Corpus Scriptorum Ecclesiasticorum Latinorum 44 [Vienna, 1884], 362–63 and 693) and remained a part of the Gallican and Mozarabic rites. See Jungmann, *The Mass*, 2:294–97. Pope St. Zachary appears to have condemned them in his 751 letter to St. Boniface (*Epistula* 13, MGH Epp. 3:371, PL 89:951D), writing, "With respect to the blessings the Gauls perform, as you know, brother, they are marred by many faults. For they do not do this according to apostolic tradition, but act through vainglory, bringing damnation upon themselves, as it is written, 'If any one preach to you a gospel, besides the gospel which you have received, let him be anathema' [Gal. 1:9]. You have embraced the rule of the Catholic tradition, most beloved brother; so preach to all and teach everyone what you have received from the holy Roman Church, which, by God's will, we serve." It has been suggested, however, that St. Zachary was referring to simoniacal offerings in exchange for ordination, and that Rome did have episcopal blessings that eventually became the *orationes super populum* reserved for Lent. In any case, the papal letter did nothing to subdue enthusiasm for these blessings in Gaul, since they are found in the eighth-century Gelasian sacramentaries and the supplement to the Gregorian Sacramentary, although the latter ones seem to betray a Mozarabic influence. Thus they continued to be said in France after the loss of the Gallican use; de Vert, *Explication*, 1:347, notes that at his time they persisted in Paris, Reims, Meaux, Soissons, Le Mans, Angers, Chartres, Blois, Lyon, Clermont-en-Auvergne, Autun, Sens, and Orléans. In the last two dioceses their use had only recently been restored. For a discussion and inventory of these prayers, see Edmond Moeller, ed., *Corpus benedictionum pontificalium*, 3 vols., Corpus Christianorum Series Latina 162 (Brepols, 1971–73), and King, *Liturgies*, 131–39.

[45] This fourteenth-century ordinal is lost, but can be reconstructed based on several notarized copies. See Pascal Collomb, "L'ordinaire liturgique perdu de la collégiale Saint-Paul de Lyon (fin XIVᵉ siècle)," L'Institut de recherche et d'histoire des textes, last modified 24 September 2015, https://irht.hypotheses.org/650.

[46] The embrace and kiss of the ministers and the members of choir at the *Agnus Dei* had by Le Brun des Marettes's time been replaced in most French religious houses and cathedrals by the use of the pax-brede. Further, the kiss was often restricted to the ministers. For a contemporary discussion, see de Vert, *Explication*, 3:357–63, who sees the kiss as an important expression of equality among the clergy. The fourteenth-century ordinal of St-Just of Lyon states that a priest from choir gave the kiss of peace to the other choir members while a deacon gave it to the laity (Roux, *La liturgie*, 85).

[47] For reasons described by de Vert, *Explication*, 3:410–11, by the late Middle Ages the

As soon as the priest has received communion, the subdeacon enters the sanctuary through the left side. He goes up to the altar, kisses the celebrant's shoulder, takes the book and cushion, and takes both behind the altar to the right side. Meanwhile, the deacon enters the sanctuary, goes up to the altar, takes the corporal, and folds it while the celebrant purifies the chalice. On semidoubles, simples, and ferias, once the celebrant has put the paten on the chalice, he gives it to the deacon inclined on its side, kissing its pommel. The deacon likewise kisses it and takes it to the small altar of St. Speratus behind the high altar. The chalice veil and pall are not used in Lyon, as in the Carthusian use. The candle-bearers, subdeacons, deacons, and priests return to the vestry, or *revétoire* as it is called at Lyon, in the same order they came out. No last Gospel is said at the altar.

The Blessed Sacrament is not reserved in the cathedral of St-Jean. It is only exposed on Corpus Christi and on the Nativity and Decollation of St. John the Baptist, from seven in the morning until six in the evening, when it is taken back to the church of Ste-Croix for reservation.

Between the cathedral and the church of Ste-Croix stands the church of St-Étienne, contiguous to both, so that one can go *ex templo in templum*. It is said that this church of St-Étienne, which is much smaller than the other two, used to be the cathedral, and that in the ninth century St. Remigius, archbishop of Lyon, gave this church a marble altar which is still used as the stone of the high altar. It is recessed on top like the marble lavatory stone in the chapterhouse, upon which the bodies of the canons used to be washed before burial. This lavatory stone is recessed about three inches, with a small hole on one side. We shall see other such stones elsewhere.[48]

These three contiguous churches—St-Jean, St-Étienne, and Ste-Croix— say the Office at the toll of the same bells, and at the same times, except that at St-Étienne Matins begin when the cathedral of St-Jean reaches the verse *Hodie si vocem ejus audieritis*, at which point he who sings the Invitatory raises his voice. The church of Ste-Croix likewise begins Matins once the church of St-Étienne reaches the verse *Hodie si vocem*, sung higher than the preceding verses. This is done so that if a canon has not made it to St-Jean in time for Matins, he may go to St-Étienne or Ste-Croix. By obtaining a certification of his attendance from the *magister* of St-Étienne or Ste-Croix, he can still receive his distribution as if he had assisted at St-Jean. This applies even during the period of his strict residence in order to gain the *gros fruits*.[49] If a canon finds himself in the vicinity of St-Just, St-Paul, or

---

Communion had been reduced to a single antiphon (except at the *Requiem* Mass), where once, like the Introit, it was sung with psalm verses.
[48] See pp. 111–12 and 262.
[49] On the structure of prebends and the payment of the *gros fruits*, see p. 349; Alice Dubois, *Le chapitre cathédral de Saint-Lambert à Liège au XVIIe siècle* (Faculté de philosophie et lettres de Liège, 1949), 133–136; and Olivier Charles, *Chanoines de Bretagne: Carrières et cultures d'une élite cléricale au siècle des Lumières* (Presses universitaires de Rennes, 2004), 170, who explains: "The *gros*, generally equal for all prebends [of a

St-Nizier, he can even assist at the Office in one of these collegiate churches in choir dress and receive his distribution from the cathedral as if he had attended at St-Jean itself. The canons of these three churches respectively have the same right and privilege. On the five or six highest feasts of the year they go as a group to assist at high Mass in the cathedral. Some of them remain until after the Gospel, that is, until the end of the Mass of the Catechumens, and others until the priest's communion.

On doubles of the first class, a single canon or perpetual sings the Invitatory, the psalm *Venite exultemus Domino*, and the verses of the responsories of Matins. On these days, the minor hours are not sung, nor Compline, except when additional time is needed to vest for a ceremony immediately following, such as Benediction of the Blessed Sacrament. Each one says these hours privately outside of choir.

At Lauds and Vespers, as in the church of Vienne, the choirboys intone the first two or three words of the antiphons such as to form a meaningful phrase. Perpetuals or canons, depending on the feast, intone the psalms.

At the *Magnificat*, the celebrant incenses the altar as at the offertory of the Mass. Then he steps outside the enclosure of the balustrade and incenses around the altar until he faces the sedilia where he sits during Mass. At that point, he goes behind the altar to remove his cope and returns to the end east of the choir to sit at one of the two places on his side, with his back turned towards the altar.

The subdeacon-thurifer incenses the screen's great rood, the dignitaries, and the choir, and then goes behind the altar to get the *collectarium*, or book of orations. He brings it to the celebrant, who is standing in mid-choir, having first made an inclination at the top of the choir with another canon (or perpetual, according to the feast) who had detached a candle from the *râtelier*. Both greet the celebrant with a reverence *conversi ad invicem*, and then the candle-bearer puts his right hand between the celebrant and his candle, to make all its light reflect on the book. At the end of the oration, they each kiss the priest's shoulder on their side (*ad scapulas*, as the ancient ordinals say) and, having made a reverence, they go behind the altar if there is no procession afterwards. If there is a procession, the *collectarium*-bearer goes to stand at the right by the ledge of the stalls. All the choirboys or *clergeons* form up in a peloton behind the celebrant and sing the *Benedicamus Domino*. After the choir replies *Deo gratias*, the procession sets out without crucifix or candles to hold a station *ad sanctum Stephanum*, or to the chapel of the Holy Cross, or some other chapel in their vast church.

---

chapter], is the core of the prebend, dispensed at the end of the capitular year. Almost always deducted from the net income of the chapter.... the distributions constitute the variable part of the prebend and reward the assiduity of the canons at the hours, masses, processions, foundations and chapters." The canons of Lyon had to reside for six months at the cathedral or else risk being deprived of the *gros fruits* and even, after three years of delinquency, of the prebend itself.

On fasting days at the preces, the bareheaded choirboys prostrate themselves in mid-choir behind the hebdomadary, who says the oration kneeling on a prie-dieu.

They do not chant the Passion to a special tone, but like any other Gospel, as also used to be the practice in Rouen.

Tenebrae are said at the usual time for Matins. The Lamentations are sung without *Aleph, Beth, Ghimel*, just as at Vienne, Orléans, Cluny, and other places.

Choirboys sing the prophecies on Holy Saturday holding a maniple in their left hand, that is, between their fingers. This was originally a handkerchief ready to be used as needed while reading these very long lessons.

On Corpus Christi and the feast of St. John the Baptist, after Benediction of the Blessed Sacrament, the celebrant, vested in cope, takes the Sacrament in procession back to the parish church of Ste-Croix. He is preceded by a subdeacon count-canon wearing his miter and tunicle orphreys over his alb,[50] the choirboys, and the entire clergy, and at his sides go two perpetuals holding the ends of the humeral veil with which the Lord Dean carries the monstrance. Behind him a chaplain carries the Lord Dean's miter, which the dean wears when the procession returns to the cathedral, walking in the same order and without singing anything. There is no deacon in this procession.

On days of general communion, five or six priests bring up several hosts in the offertory procession. The *Agnus Dei* is only sung once and the *Venite populi* is sung during communion.

On the three main feasts of the year, to wit Christmas, Easter, and Pentecost — when all the faithful must receive holy communion according to canon 18 of the Council of Agde,[51] a decree of the Council of Elvira in Spain,[52] and canon 50 of the third Council of Tours under Charlemagne[53] — after

---

[50] These orphreys consist of two bands of material of the appropriate liturgical color that fall over the shoulders on the back and front and reach down to the cincture. A similar band joins them together on both sides, and the cincture keeps it in place. They were also used in Lyon by the thurifer at solemn Vespers and Lauds, and by the crucifer and banner-bearer at processions when the officiant wore sacred vestments (see Buenner, *L'ancienne liturgie*, 325). Le Brun des Marettes believes they were remnants of the full tunicle, but Forest, *L'école cathédrale*, 95, disagrees, noting that old inventories describe appareled albs used by the thurifers. He argues that these apparels, originally sewn into the albs, later became the removable orphreys.

[51] Canon 18: "Laymen who do not receive communion on Christmas, Easter, and Pentecost, are not to be reputed as Catholics, nor accepted among Catholics." This council was held in September 506 (Charles Munier, ed., *Concilia Galliae (a. 314–a. 506)*, Corpus Christianorum Series Latina 148 [Brepols, 1963], 202).

[52] See D. 2 de cons. c. 21, Emil Friedberg, ed., *Corpus iuris canonici* (Akademische Druck- und Verlagsanstalt, 1959), 1:1320–21; but the attribution it to the early fourth-century Council of Elvira is not authentic: "Everyone must abstain from his own wife three, four, or seven days before holy communion, nor shall those who do not receive communion on Easter, Pentecost, and Christmas be numbered among Catholics."

[53] "That laymen should receive communion at least thrice a year, if not more often,

the *Agnus Dei* the cantors still today invite the faithful to communion by singing this antiphon, which one might call an invitatory *ad Eucharistiam*, and which is termed *Transitorium* in a 1669 missal of Milan:[54]

> Venite populi ad sacrum immortale mysterium et libamen agendum: cum timore et fide accedamus, manibus mundis poenitentiae munus communicemus; quoniam Agnus Dei propter nos Patri sacrificium propositum est. Ipsum solum adoremus, ipsum glorificemus cum Angelis clamantes, Alleluia.[55]

In an old 1530 missal of Lyon, the priest is not instructed to place his hands over the host and chalice at the words *Hanc igitur oblationem*,[56] nor is he so instructed in three missals from the churches of England and Scotland before their separation from the Catholic Church, nor in the writings of the ancient commentators of the Divine Offices, who rather say that the priest bends down *usque ad altare* when saying *Hanc igitur oblationem*.[57]

According to this missal, the *Agnus Dei* is only said once, and there is no *Domine non sum dignus*. The communion of the priest is, as is still the case today, done *per unum*, that is, under only one prayer, namely, *Corpus Domini nostri Jesu Christi et Sanguis ejusdem custodiat me et perducat in vitam aeternam. Amen.*[58]

The ablution prayer is: *Quod ore sumpsimus, Domine, pura mente capiamus, ut de corpore et de sanguine Domini nostri Jesu Christi fiat nobis remedium sempiternum in vitam aeternam. Amen.*[59] In place of *de corpore et de sanguine Domini* someone has written *de munere temporali*. As we shall see later, in all missals of Rouen printed in the sixteenth century one finds *de corpore et de sanguine Domini*.[60]

---

except those who are impeded by some grave sin." This council was held in May 813 (MGH Conc. 2.1:293).
[54] *Missale Ambrosianum* (Milan, 1669), "Rubricae generales," 32, 217, 270.
[55] "Come ye people to perform the holy and immortal mystery and sacrifice. Let us approach in fear and faith, with clean hands let us share in the gift of repentance, because the Lamb of God was offered in sacrifice to the Father for us. Him alone let us adore him, let us glorify crying aloud with the angels, alleluia."
[56] *Missale secundum ritum ecclesie Lugdunensis* (Lyon, 1530), fol. 73v.
[57] Cf. de Vert, *Explication*, 1:236–37, and also the allegorical explanations of Bernold of Constance, "When we say *Hanc igitur oblationem*, we bend down over the altar, in imitation of Christ's example, who humiliated himself for us unto death on the cross" (*Micrologus* 14, PL 151:986D), and Honorius Augustodunensis, "When the priest says *Hanc igitur oblationem*, he bends down over the altar, because Christ began his Passion there when, in obedience to the Father, he bent over the altar of the Cross for us" (*Gemma animae* 1.46, ed. and trans. Zachary Thomas and Gerhard Eger, *Jewel of the Soul*, Dumbarton Oaks Medieval Library 79–80 [Harvard University Press, 2023], 1:90–91).
[58] "May the Body of Our Lord Jesus Christ and his Blood keep me and lead me to eternal life. Amen" (*Missale secundum ritum ecclesie Lugdunensis*, fol. 75v).
[59] "What we have taken with our mouth, may we receive in our mind, that from the Body and Blood of Our Lord Jesus Christ it might become for us an everlasting remedy for eternal life" (*Missale secundum ritum ecclesie Lugdunensis*, fol. 76v).
[60] See p. 223.

The Office of the church of Lyon is very long, both the chant and the lessons, three of which are sometimes combined into one.

On the principal feasts and for the eight days before Christmas, including the vigil, the antiphons of the *Magnificat* and *Benedictus* are triumphed, that is, they are sung after each verse.

The *Alleluia* is sung until Lauds of Septuagesima Sunday, so that *Laus tibi Domine* is first sung at Prime. This *Alleluia* or *Laus tibi Domine* serves as the antiphon at the minor hours, as it does at Vienne. All the minor hours are said separately, Prime at seven in the morning, high Mass between Terce and Sext, None at two in the afternoon, and Vespers at three. All respond *eodem tenore* ("in the same tone") to all the versicles sung by the choirboys.

The *Te Deum* is sung on all Sundays of Advent and Lent, just as in monastic churches that follow the Rule of St. Benedict.

All Saints has no octave, nor does any feast that falls during Lent.

The Office *de Beata in Sabbato* is not said in the church of St-Jean of Lyon. It only began to be said in Paris in 1608.

On all ferias of Advent, Lent, vigils, and Ember days, the major preces are said at both major and minor hours.

In Lyon, as in Milan, Vespers only begins to be said *ante comestionem* ("before the meal"), with the additional Lenten preces and litany, on the first Monday of Lent. This is a vestige of the more ancient fasting custom, before four additional days were added to Lent around the ninth or tenth century.

In the St-Jean of Lyon, the *Magnificat* canticle is triumphed on 17 December and the six subsequent days, such that the O antiphon is said in three parts, interspersed between each verse. Each of the three is sung in alternation by one of the two sides of the choir after every verse until the verse *Deposuit*, after which the antiphon is sung in its entirety after the remaining verses of the canticle. The *Magnificat* is intoned and sung *submissa voce*, that is, more quietly than usual, doubtlessly in order to emphasize the verse *Sicut locutus est ad patres nostros, Abraham et semini ejus in saecula*, which is sung higher according to the following rubric of the most recent breviary of Lyon: In *choro submissa voce intonat Canticum* Magnificat; *et sic canitur usque ad versum* Sicut locutus est *exclusive*.[61] Further on it states: *Hic vox elevatur*: Sicut locutus est ad patres nostros.[62]

The *Magnificat* is triumphed on the Saturday before Septuagesima. On Septuagesima Sunday, the psalm *Coeli enarrant*[63] in the third nocturn is triumphed until the verse *Et erunt ut complaceant* exclusive, as well as the last psalm of Lauds, *Laudate Dominum de coelis*,[64] and the *Benedictus* canticle until the versicle *Illuminare*, after which the antiphon is sung in full. From the end of Lauds on this day until Holy Saturday the alleluia is not sung.

---

[61] Breviarium sanctae Lugdunensis ecclesiae, Pars hyemalis (Lyon, 1693), 224.
[62] Breviarium sanctae Lugdunensis ecclesiae, Pars hyemalis (Lyon, 1693), 225.
[63] Psalm 18.
[64] Psalm 150.

The *Te Deum laudamus* is sung every Sunday, even on Sundays of Lent and on Palm Sunday after the ninth lesson, which is the entire Passion of Our Lord according to St. Mark.

No feast, even that of the church's patron, has an octave if it falls in Lent.

In the cathedral, on ferias of Lent, beginning on Monday after the first Sunday, the bread and wine for the consecration are offered by the first priest on each side of the choir.

When there is a general communion, all the clerics who receive communion are given wine thereafter.

In Lyon the alleluia is still sung at the end of every verse of the fifth psalm of Lauds[65] on Septuagesima Sunday,[66] and it was sung on the first Sunday of Lent in the Gallican rite, as one can see in Dom Jean Mabillon's book on the subject.[67]

During Lent the deacon and subdeacon wear a chasuble of the same shape as the priest's.[68]

On feasts of nine lessons during Lent, they do not say Vespers until the afternoon.

On the mornings of Ash Wednesday and Good Friday, rods are laid out on a prie-dieu in the back of the nave near the main portal of the cathedral. According to a learned rubricist of this church,[69] the archbishop used them to hit the public penitents on the head. This was apparently done to show them what weapons they ought to use against themselves to expiate their sins. The same function is served by the ash imposed on their heads, as well as the hairshirt which still today in Rouen is carried by the deacon at the end of a cane during the procession *in expulsione poenitentium* ("to expel public penitents from the church"). William Durand of Mende explains this in *Rationale divinorum officiorum*: *Cinis et cilicium sunt arma poenitentium*.[70]

From Vespers of the Saturday before Passiontide until Vespers of Holy Saturday (except Palm Sunday), the chant is sung in a slightly lower tone than usual.

---

[65] Psalms 148–150.
[66] *Breviarium sanctae Lugdunensis ecclesiae, Pars hyemalis*, 455 and 497–98.
[67] Jean Mabillon, *De liturgia Gallicana* (Lyon, 1685), 124.
[68] In Rome in the early centuries, the chasuble was worn by the priest, deacon, and subdeacon. By the ninth century, their use by the latter two orders was restricted to penitential days, and by the twelfth this became the general custom in major churches and monasteries. Eventually, however, ministers in most churches came to wear the Lenten chasuble only in the clipped form of a *planeta plicata* or as a pre-cut *stola latior*, a broad stole. Le Brun des Marettes is saying that in Lyon they have kept the ancient custom of using full folded chasubles, not pre-cut ones. See Joseph Braun, *Die liturgischen Paramente in Gegenwart und Vergangenheit* (Herder, 1924), 103, 105.
[69] Jean-Claude de la Poype de Vertrieu, once count-canon of Lyon and bishop of Poitiers when this book was written.
[70] "Ash and hairshirts are the weapons of the penitents" (Durand, *Rationale* 7.35.40, ed. Davril and Thibodeau, 3:100). For more on the use of hairshirts on Ash Wednesday in France, see de Vert, *Explication*, 2:218–19.

On Holy Saturday, the faithful take the new blessed fire to their homes to light their hearth. The 1530 missal of Lyon states, *Extinguatur totus ignis existens in ecclesia et recipiatur ignis novus; et si aliquis voluerit portare ignem benedictum pro ponendo in foco suo vel alibi, prout ei bonum videbitur, honeste portet.*[71]

On the Easter and Pentecost Vigils, the *Accendite* at the lighting of the candles is sung by the two cantors before beginning the *Kyrie eleison* of the Mass.[72]

Neither Lyon nor Vienne have a Major Litany procession on St. Mark's day.

On the three Rogation processions, the celebrant, deacon, subdeacon, the choirboy carrying the litany roll,[73] the banner-bearers, and the crucifers of the cathedral and of the collegiate churches of canons walk barefoot. The celebrant carries a staff in his right hand for support, and wears a hood that covers his entire head.

Among the capitular statutes set down in 1251,[74] besides the obligation to reside in common, one finds:

That the revenues of the canonry of someone who resigns or dies are shared among the other canons.

That no one can possess two *personnats*.[75]

That all priests, canons and otherwise, shall sit in the higher row, and the deacons-canon likewise.

That no one shall be admitted to the choir who is not born of legitimate wedlock.

After the first bell for Matins until after high Mass, and after Sext (here called *hora meridiana*) and after the second bell for None until leaving after Compline, canons are not allowed to pass in front of the church if not in choir dress, nor to remain in the parvis or in other places around the church, except passing on horseback to go to the country. After the last bell for each hour or Office no canon is permitted to sit in front of the church or in front of the choir, and during the singing of an Office in choir, no canon is to remain sitting or standing in front of the church. After the Divine Office, when everybody leaves the church, those canons who did not assist must not appear standing or sitting in any manner in the church, nor in the neighboring places, nor at the windows of their houses. Likewise, those who do not assist at procession must not be visible to their brethren while the procession goes to or fro.

---

[71] "Let all the existing fire in the church be extinguished and replaced with new fire. If someone should wish to take blessed fire to put in his hearth or elsewhere, as he shall see fit, let him take it decently" (*Missale secundum ritum ecclesie Lugdunensis*, fol. 63v).
[72] See p. 23, n. 55.
[73] See p. 42, n. 38.
[74] These are published in Luc d'Achery, ed., *Spicilegium* (Paris, 1723), 1:718–19.
[75] A *personnat* (Latin *personatus*) was a position that ranked below a dignity but above a simple canon. By the eighteenth century, the only *personnat* in the cathedral of Lyon was the choirmaster.

From the moment night falls, none of the canons shall tarry in a layman's house or in front of its door. Neither shall he wander its streets, unless on horseback, and even then he must be accompanied.

That those who violate these regulations are not to be received until they have made satisfaction in choir and in the refectory.

That if someone leaves town on a feast day, he is not to enter the church or cloister nor shall he have any part of the distributions or in the refectory on that day.

That if on a feast day he is in town and does not attend Matins, not only is he barred from entering the cloister on that day, from going out in public, and even from showing himself at the windows of his residence, but he shall also lose his distribution, which shall be given to the almonry.

The honors and dignities of this church are called *obediences*, in Latin *obedientiae*.

That if one of the canons or others who sit in the higher stalls commits a punishable fault, he shall be punished by the deacon in the chapterhouse; if one of the lower choir, by the cantor or by the *magister* in the church's school.

When a count-canon or semi-prebendary assigned to sing the Invitatory or a lesson or responsory fails to show up in church, they wait for a minute or two in silence. Since in this church no one is allowed to take another's duty, all the clerics then rise and go behind the high altar to the apse where they finish the Office *recto tono*, even if it were Easter Sunday. This is called saying the remainder of the Office *à privat*.[76]

If this happens at high Mass, those in the higher stalls remain in choir, but those in the second and third rows, namely the cantors or lower-formers together with the little choirboys, go to sing the remainder of the Mass in a low tone in the apse behind the altar. The priest then sings the Preface and *Pater* in a low and very doleful tone.

---

[76] The peculiar Lyonese custom of finishing an Office *à privat* (also spelled *à privâ*) when a count-canon failed to fulfill his assigned function was often shocking to outsiders. In 1555, Théodore de Vichy de Champrond, the cathedral's dean, was sufficiently exercised about the matter to write a letter to the faculty of theology at the Sorbonne requesting their opinion about this and other cathedral usages he felt were of dubious propriety. The Sorbonne replied with a condemnation of the practice, insisting that "the Divine Office must be finished in choir, in the presence of all the canons and others whose presence is required, as if there had been no absence or error committed." Infuriated with this intrusion into their affairs and ever jealous of their ancient customs, the canons of Lyon not only reprimanded the dean, but wrote to the king himself to request that the Sorbonne's faculty of theology be made to revoke their censure and expunge it from their records. Two cardinals were assigned to investigate, and, after deliberations with the Parlement of Paris and various prelates of the realm, the representatives of the theology faculty agreed with them to duly retract their criticisms, asserting that they never intended to contest the chapter of Lyon's jurisdiction. Archbishop Antoine de Montazet, who imposed a novel neo-Gallican liturgy on his diocese despite the vehement protests of the counts-canon, also considered the use of finishing an Office *à privat* "bizarre" and "manifestly abusive." See Antoine-François Prost de Royer and Jean-François-Armand Riolz, "A-priva," in *Dictionnaire de jurisprudence et des arrêts* (Lyon, 1786), 5:777–78.

The truant is not only deprived of all distributions for fifteen days, but is also barred from entering the church in choir habit; in other words, he is placed under interdict. That is the punishment for those who fail to fulfill their duty in the Divine Offices in the church of St-Jean of Lyon.

Church of Saint-Just of Lyon

Discipline is even more rigorous at the collegiate church of the canons of St-Just, where they meticulously observe everything that is practiced at St-Jean of Lyon. In addition to the discipline we have already reported, if a canon or perpetual of St-Just intones an antiphon incorrectly, he is banished from the choir for the rest of that Office, and another begins the antiphon. Behold how those truly devoted to the worship of God behave, allowing no negligence in their work for fear of incurring the curse God pronounced through the mouth of his prophet.[77] It is the true way to hold every man to his duty.

Church of Saint-Irenée of Lyon

The crypt of the church of St-Irenée is very deep underground and dark. One enters it by going down a staircase that leads to two others branching off on either side of the church. The middle section is fairly spacious, and at the very end there are three altars built over the bodies of the holy saints, with Irenaeus in the middle, Epipodius on the right, and Alexander on the left. Everything about the place suggests that it was an underground crypt or large cellar where early Christians assembled for the Sacrifice and common prayer, and I have no doubt that it is one of the first churches where the earliest Christians of Lyon gathered. The ancient trough-shaped tombs in the cemetery and outside by the road above seem to me to confirm this hypothesis. There are two lamps in this crypt that burn continually night and day before the precious tombs and ashes of these holy martyrs.

Aqueducts, the Amphitheater, and the Arena

Two hundred paces further along on the same road, one can see just on the left the remains of the arcades of the magnificent aqueducts that used to supply water to the city.

On the right, beyond the Garden of the Friars Minim, lie the ruins of the amphitheater of Lyon. All that remains is the *cavea* of the amphitheater, designed in a semi-circle, which survives in its entirety. See Fig. 5 (PLATE 10).

Underneath the church, near the sacristy, was the arena, the spot where the early Christians used to be martyred. A crucifix has since been erected as a memorial, still today called the Croix des décollés, in Latin *Crux decollatorum* ("Cross of the Beheaded").

---

[77] See Jeremias 48:10 ("Cursed be he that doth the work of the Lord deceitfully"), often cited in statutes and liturgical books as a warning against clerical sloth.

Abbey of Saint-Pierre of Lyon

The abbey of the nuns of St-Pierre, with its church both old and splendid, is well worth a visit. The nuns' choir is set on a loft above, leaving the entire space of the church free for the laity, for whom it also serves as a parish church. These nuns used to assist at the general processions.

On both sides of the high altar there are two very ancient pagan inscriptions, which lead me to believe that this is the site of an ancient temple dedicated to some false divinity.

Collegiate Church of Saint-Paul

An ordinal of the collegiate church of St-Paul, written some four hundred years ago, contains all the practices of the cathedral of Lyon adapted to the particular customs of St-Paul.[78]

At that time they still exchanged the kiss of peace.

On the main feasts of the year the clergy of the church of St-Paul attended high Mass at the cathedral of St-Jean of Lyon.

The great O antiphons sung eight days before Christmas were triumphed, that is, they were sung solemnly and repeated after each verse of the *Magnificat*.

On all great feasts, *Completorium et Horae sub silentio*,[79] perhaps because they were too busy and the major Offices on these days were said with such solemnity that, if they had also sung the minor hours and Compline, they would have had scarcely one hour of respite in the entire day.

On the three greatest feasts of the year, namely Christmas, Easter, and Pentecost, in which all the faithful were bound to receive communion, as we have seen above, the cantors sang the *Venite populi* after the *Agnus Dei*, as they still do today. This chant was an invitation for laymen to come up to the holy table to receive the Holy Eucharist, which they did only after embracing one another *in osculo pacis*, by a holy kiss of peace.

On these great feasts the archbishop celebrated Mass with six other priests, seven deacons, seven subdeacons, and seven candle-bearers. This is still the case today, both when the Lord Archbishop celebrates or when his place is taken by a count-canon appointed by him to officiate on these three days, even though the Lord Dean outranks him.

Three different priests (one of whom was the Lord Archbishop) celebrated the three Masses of Christmas.

During Lent they used simple wooden candlesticks and the altar was dressed with simple white cloths (*pannis albis*) adorned with black crosses. Practically everywhere today on Good Friday, a day on which ancient

---

[78] See p. 45, n. 45.
[79] "Compline and the [minor] hours in silence."

practices have been preserved, a similar sheet is placed over the altar for the Mass of the Presanctified, including in Paris.[80]

At Tenebrae they only began to extinguish the candles at Lauds.

The first litany of Holy Saturday is called *ad incensum*, the second *ad descensum fontis*, and the third *ad Introitum* (*ecclesiae* or *chori* implied). Vespers on this day was composed of three antiphons and the three last psalms of Saturday Vespers, as they still are today.[81]

The first litany of Holy Saturday was sung on Rogation Monday, the second on Rogation Tuesday, and the third on Rogation Wednesday. In bad weather, these processions were transferred to the following Friday, Saturday, and Monday, as is still done today. On these three days all the clergy went in procession barefoot, as used to be done in the abbey of Bec in Rouen, and with their heads sprinkled with ashes, as still today in Milan, where these Rogations always take place in the week after Ascension, with fasting until Vespers on the first two days and blessing and imposition of ashes on the first day, while the *Recordare homo qui* is sung, as M. Châtelain has informed me.[82] Nowadays the procession is led by the celebrant, deacon, subdeacon, the choirboy carrying the roll with the music for the litany, the banner-bearer, the crucifer of the cathedral of St-Jean, and the crucifers of the other collegiate churches of canons, all of whom walk barefoot. This is particularly uncomfortable, because the cobblestones of Lyon are very small and narrow, no more than the gravel that the Rhône carries and pushes to the riverbank. In processions such as these and that of Corpus Christi that pass through town, eight-foot-long staves are carried *ad defendendam processionem*, as the ordinary of St-Paul states. Two or three are usually carried by each group of clergy. One of these staves is carried by the master of choirboys and the other by one of the eldest perpetuals: thus, they explain, the rank and order of the way of procession are maintained.

During the octaves of Pentecost and Easter, they hold a procession at Vespers to the church where the baptismal font is located. The church of St-Jean processes to the church of Ste-Croix, and the church of St-Paul to the church of St-Laurent.

---

[80] *Caeremoniale Parisiense* 13.7 (Paris, 1662), 358: ...*sacrista unam tantum tobaleam albam et mundam extendit super nudum altare*...

[81] Psalms 145, 146, and 147. All three antiphons were triple alleluias. See *Breviarium sanctae Lugdunensis ecclesiae, Pars verna*, 587.

[82] Claude Châtelain or Chastelain (1639–1712), a canon of Notre-Dame of Paris who took part in the neo-Gallican revision of the Parisian liturgical books under Bishop François de Harlay and with whom Le Brun des Marettes corresponded. His role in neo-Gallican reforms from the 1670s onward was such that one historian has called him the "prince and high priest of French liturgists"; see Philippe Bernard, "Liturgies chrétiennes en Occident (de l'Antiquité tardive à l'époque moderne)," *Annuaire de l'École pratique des hautes études (EPHE), Section des sciences religieuses* 131 (2024), 187–192. Châtelain's praise for the *Liturgical Travels Through France* is printed at the beginning of the work.

Church of Saint-Laurent and Asylum of Lyon

The illustrious John Charlier, also called John Gerson, chancellor of the University of Paris, is buried in a sepulcher in this parish church. He died in Lyon on his way back from the general Council of Constance.

The place where the right of asylum of Lyon used to be located is in the *quartier* of St-Nizier. There is a pyramid in the center and a fountain surrounded by an iron trellis. Upon one of the gates rises a square column with this inscription:

HAC ITUR AD SECURITATEM.[83]

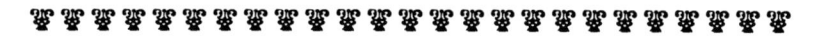

CLERMONT

CLERMONT in Auvergne was formerly called *Augustonemetum Arvernorum* in Latin, and is now known as *Clarus mons*.

In the church of Clermont, at high Mass the celebrant does not read the Epistle, Gradual, or Gospel, but listens to them instead. In the ceremonial of Paris, *aut legit, aut audit*, as in Lyon and among the Carthusians.[84]

The bells for the Mass of the faithful are sounded during the Prose, just like for the start of Mass.

Christmas Lauds is inserted into the midnight Mass after the priest's communion, as in Vienne, Paris, and Orléans. The *pastourelle* is still performed by five clerics and by a priest who concludes the ceremony. The psalm *Dominus regnavit*[85] is triumphed on this occasion, meaning that its verses are interwoven into each verse of the *Pastores dicite*. The rest of the text of the *pastourelle* is similar to what used to be said at Rouen, where all of these little *farces* or spiritual comedies have been abolished.[86] The faculty of theology of Paris itself exercised its zeal and authority to suppress them, so that they have been abolished in nearly all churches, at least as regards the play, but no thought was given to changing the texts

---

[83] "This way to safety."

[84] "He either reads or listens." The expression is found in the Carthusian ordinal: *Epistolam attente audit aut legit, cum Responsorio et Alleluia, vel Tractu* ("[The celebrant] attentively listens to or reads the Epistle, with the Gradual and Alleluia or Tract," *Ordinarium Cartusiense* 26.12 [Lyon, 1641], 245). In Paris, pursuant to a decision taken in 1701, during the Epistle and subsequent chants "all sit and listen, although the celebrant may read [the Epistle], if he should prefer" (*Caeremoniale Parisiense* 2.6 [Paris, 1703], 83). The earlier ceremonial of Martin Sonnet, however, clearly foresees the priest reading the Epistle, Gradual, Alleluia or Tract, and Gospel (*Caeremoniale Parisiense* 2.2.18, 139). On this change, see de Vert, *Explication*, 4:125–26.

[85] Psalm 92.

[86] On these *pastourelles* and the opposition they aroused in some quarters, see Bernard Dompnier, "Les 'petites farces ou comédies spirituelles' de Noël. Des traditions liturgiques contestées entre XVIIe et XVIIIe siècle," *Siècles* 21 (2005): 55–72.

themselves, which are still used as Lauds antiphons in most churches.[87]

Also on Christmas night, after the ninth responsory, a deacon vested in a dalmatic reads the Genealogy of Our Lord Jesus Christ according to St. Matthew from the rood loft.[88] Likewise, on the night of Epiphany, after the ninth responsory he reads the Genealogy according to St. Luke,[89] after which the Lord Cantor announces the date of Easter from the loft, facing south. The breviary states: *Qua finita Cantor in eodem loco dicit: Audiat dilectio vestra, Fratres carissimi, quod Pascha praesentis anni die N. mensis Martii (vel Aprilis) expectamus venturum.*[90]

When the bishop celebrates Mass on solemn feasts, he gives the blessing before the *Agnus Dei.*[91]

One custom peculiar to this diocese is that when a corpse is buried in the afternoon because it cannot be left until the following day without causing too much infection, a "dry" Mass, that is, a Mass without consecration, is said at the funeral. This shows that no one should be buried before a Mass is said for the deceased *corpore praesente*, as most rituals still now prescribe.[92]

In Clermont and the whole of Auvergne—Saint-Martin of Tours, Riom, and Brioude—as well as in the entire Premonstratensian order and at Ste-Croix-de-la-Bretonnerie, all kneel at the words *Descendit de coelis. Et incarnatus est*, and do not rise until *Et resurrexit*. Thus the two words *descendit* and *resurrexit* determine when they kneel and rise. Similarly in Palaiseau in the diocese of Paris they all rise at the words *Surrexit Christus spes mea* in the Prose *Victimae*, because long ago when they understood Latin they were struck by the word *surrexit*. In Paris, at Vespers, they rise at *Scimus Christum surrexisse.*[93]

---

[87] A reference to the letter written on 12 March 1445 by the faculty of theology of the University of Paris to the bishops and chapters of the Kingdom of France, urging them to abolish the celebration of the "feast of fools" during the Christmas octave, and condemning paraliturgical plays (*ludi*) like the *pastourelle* as well. In its seventh conclusion they declare that clerics who don secular, buffoonish, or otherwise profane costume during the Divine Offices commit a mortal sin and ought to be gravely punished, and in its tenth conclusion they assert that clerics, especially priests, should not perform characters in plays in the sight of the people (PL 207:1175A, C).

[88] Matthew 1:1–16.

[89] Luke 3:21–4:1.

[90] "Once it is finished the cantor, standing in the same place, says: Hearken, loved ones and dearest brethren: we await the coming of Easter this year on the nth day of the month of March (or April)."

[91] See p. 45, n. 44.

[92] See, for instance, Pope Paul V's *Rituale Romanum*, "De exequiis" (Rome, 1614), 101: "That most ancient institution should be maintained as much as possible, namely that Mass be celebrated for the deceased in the presence of his body before it is committed to burial." This ritual was widely adopted in France during the reign of Louis XIII, including in Clermont; see Stéphane Gomis, *Les "enfants prêtres" des paroisses d'Auvergne, XVIe-XVIIIe siècles* (Presses universitaires Blaise-Pascal, 2006), 198–99. The *Rituale ad usum dioeceseos Claromontensis* promulgated in 1656 was based on the Roman book (*iuxta ritus Romani formam*).

[93] See de Vert, *Explication*, 3:125–28; and also 1:235 and 2:47.

BORDEAUX

THERE is nothing particular in all the Guyenne save in Bordeaux, its capital city, where there is a seminary with twenty-four young clerics, founded by an archbishop of Bordeaux in the thirteenth century. They wear a tawny cassock, which is the ancient black used at the time by ecclesiastics, black monks, and monks of Cluny, and still preserved by the choirboys of the abbey of Cluny.

I borrow this observation and several others from Dom Claude de Vert, treasurer and vicar general of Cluny, who was without question one of France's most accomplished scholars of the Church's rites and customs.[1]

---

[1] See the note in de Vert, *Explication*, 2:358–59.

POITIERS

POITIERS, an episcopal city on the river Clain, *ad Clanum fluvium*. In the cathedral of St-Pierre of Poitiers and the collegiate church of St-Hilaire, and likewise the Benedictine abbey of Savigny in the diocese of Lyon, one of the two choirboys goes from the altar with his candlestick to provide light to the subdeacon when he chants the Epistle. The other provides light for the deacon while he reads the Gospel. After the Gospel reading, they both return from the rood loft with the deacon and the subdeacon.

Formerly, at Ste-Croix of Poitiers the nuns served as acolytes at the high Mass, wearing an alb and maniple, and held a candle for the deacon during the Gospel. And their ordinal states: *In die Epiphaniae dum legitur novissima lectio, induitur diaconus dalmatica, et acolytha alba et amictu*.[1]

---

[1] "On the day of Epiphany, while the last lesson is read, the deacon puts on a dalmatic and the she-acolyte an alb and amice." The ordinal, which dates from the thirteenth century, has been lost, but this extract is preserved in a handwritten transcription made in 1740 by Dom Léonard Fonteneau today in Poitiers, Médiathèque, MS. 512, 172 and published by Dom Pierre de Monsabert in "Documents inédits pour servir à l'histoire de l'abbaye de Sainte-Croix de Poitiers," *Revue Mabillon* 9 (1913–1914): 388. It adds that the *acolyta*, thus vested, went up *super ianuas* while the last responsory was sung, and, her head covered by a hat and with thirteen lit candles (*habens capellum in capite cum 13 candelis accensis*), intoned the hymn *Nuntium vobis* (Cantus ID 830231) and then the *Te Deum*. Thereafter the deacon sang the Genealogy. Léo Fayolle, "L'aube était-elle portée par les moniales de Sainte-Croix au XIIIe siècle?" *Bulletins de la Société des antiquaires de l'Ouest* 9, series 3 (1933): 672–75 questions whether this text truly refers to an acolytess, pointing out that the rest of the text transcribed by Dom Fonteneau only uses the masculine *acolytus*, even though not only Le Brun des Marettes, but also de Vert and Du Cange interpreted this passage as referring to a female acolyte. Fayolle seems to overlook the fact that these three had access to the full

NANTES

NANTES on the Loire and Ardre, *Nannetes* and *Nannetae*, seat of the dukes of Brittany, whose impressive mausolea are found in the Carmelite church.

It has a university.

In the cathedral of St-Pierre, the Blessed Sacrament is located above the high altar in a stone turret. They celebrate the entire Office and all ceremonies in the modern Roman manner.[1]

When the feast of St. Mark falls during the octave of Easter, the people refrain from work for the feast, even though the Office is transferred after the octave. Nevertheless the procession is always held on 25 April, the day to which it is assigned, rather than on the transferred feast day, but without abstinence. The same practice is followed in Rouen and Beauvais. Likewise the blessing of candles is fixed to 2 February and not to the feast, as evidenced by the violet color used at the blessing and procession in most churches and even in Rome. See the rubric in the Roman missal for the day of the Purification.

Neither Nantes, Angers, Chartres, nor Amiens fast on the Saturday vigil of Pentecost because of the Paschal season, following the ancient custom, which these churches have preserved in this case.

In the parish church of St-Nicholas, above the high altar there is a stained-glass window of extraordinary size, highly esteemed and with good reason. It depicts fifty-six mysteries or miracles of Jesus Christ, whose face is the same in each depiction. He has reddish-blond hair, as several ancient painters have passed down through tradition. The entire work is painted in a very beautiful and lifelike style.

---

manuscript, of which Dom Fonteneau only copied some excerpts, not including the *acolyta*'s use of the maniple or her holding a candle for the deacon, which Le Brun des Marettes—whom Fayolle bizarrely labels a Jesuit—mentions here. Nevertheless, it must also be noted that the use of the form *acolyta* to refer to a male acolyte is attested.

[1] The cathedral chapter of St-Pierre adopted the Roman books gradually beginning in 1610. The rest of the diocese slowly imitated the chapter's example, but the use of Nantes continued to be celebrated in some places as late as 1750. See Nicolas Travers, *Histoire civile, politique et religieuse de la ville et du comté de Nantes* (Nantes, 1841), 3:166–67.

ANGERS

ANGERS on the river Mayenne, *Andegavum ad Meduanam* in Latin, has a university with four faculties and is famous for its quarries of slate, which is used to roof the houses of the whole town.

Cathedral of Saint-Maurice

Following an ancient usage which has persisted elsewhere on Good Friday, and until recently on Holy Saturday as well,[1] the altars in the chapels of this church (PLATE 15) are left entirely bare of accouterments: they are covered with cloths only just before a Mass is said on them. These cloths hang over the edges like tablecloths, and there are no antependia.[2]

In the middle of the choir (PLATE 16), near the bench for the cope-bearers, stands a brass eagle lectern where the lessons of Matins are chanted. At the east end of the choir is another copper lectern with two desks where the Invitatory is sung. In front of these lecterns, there is a large three-branched copper candlestick holding three candles. There is another candlestick between them, to which is attached a table listing the Offices or chantry duties for the week. In Angers it is called the *table des gagnages* ("table of earnings"), because of the emoluments accruing to those who assist at these Offices; elsewhere it is known as the *tableau des fondations* ("table of chantry endowments").

Before the high altar there is a tall marble column between twelve and fifteen feet high, upon which the Paschal candle stands all year long, although it is not lit after Pentecost.

The copes have a somewhat pointed hood,[3] and the chasubles are so ample they reach five feet in breadth, and at least as many in length, and are only slightly clipped at the arms. They also have two Epistle books and

---

[1] Traditionally private Masses were prohibited on Holy Saturday. By the seventeenth century, however, since the Easter Vigil had come to be said in the morning, some defended the practice of saying private Masses on Holy Saturday after the vigil had begun, meaning that the side altars had to be covered. See the question disputed in Zaccaria Pasqualigo, *De sacrificio nouae legis quaestiones theologicae morales juridicae*, q. 358 (Lyon, 1662), 1:384–86. For the rubrics for private Masses on Holy Saturday in Paris, see Sonnet, *Caeremoniale Parisiense* 3.14.4, 373.

[2] Le Brun des Marettes, de Vert, and others of their contemporaries disparaged the antependium or altar frontal as unnecessary and in bad taste. As Le Brun des Marettes implies here, the more natural arrangement is for the altar cloths to hang down over the edges on all sides in the manner of a dining table, and Jean-Baptiste Thiers suggested that this is indeed more ancient; see "Dissertation sur les principaux autels des églises," in *Dissertations ecclésiastiques* (Paris, 1688), 165. But this was impeded by the antependium, a decorative cloth originally either hung or sown onto the altar cloths but by the sixteenth century stretched over a wooden frame that was set against the front of the altar. On the origins of the antependium, see also p. 170 and de Vert, *Explication*, 2:297.

[3] The cope's hood used to have a conic shape. According to de Vert, *Explication*, 2:298–99, the origins of the cope lie in a simple pointed hood, which was later extended down to the shoulders, to the loins, to the knees, and finally all the way to the ground. This garment gave rise not only to the cope, but also to the scapular, the monastic cowl, the camail, and to various capes and cloaks worn by laymen. As clerics increasingly preferred to wear a separate headdress, the cope's hood became purely ornamental, and eventually lost its pointed form and acquired a rounded, shield-like shape. According to Joseph Braun, the transition from a practical to an ornamental hood took place between the tenth and thirteenth centuries, and the ornamental hood's change from a triangular shape to a shield between the fifteenth and sixteenth; see his discussion of the origins of this vestment in *Die liturgische Gewandung*, 307–9, and of the history of its hood, 318–21.

two Gospel books which are quite beautiful. The front of the altar and the retable are of gilded silver, and represent the entire life of Our Lady in relief figures. They are very beautiful, and for that reason antependia are never used. Before high Mass nothing is on the altar except a cross set on the gradine and the Epistle and Gospel books, one at each end with the two pax-bredes. The sanctuary is enclosed by a wooden rail (PLATE 17). There are no riddels on the sides, but the closed railing has the same effect as riddels.

In front of the altar stand four silver basins with four yellow candles.

The gilded silver reliquary of St. Maurilius, bishop of Angers, is set above the retable. It is remarkably large. Above it, without a canopy, hangs the holy pyx, and above that a large tester spreads over the entire altar. The reliquary is flanked on one side by a statue of Our Lady, and on the other by a statue of St. Maurice, patron of the church, and there are two candles on each side.

Behind the high altar there is another small altar at the back of the apse where the morrow Mass is usually said every day. On the Epistle side, between this small altar and the sacristy, there is a large, beautiful oval basin made of a rare and remarkable stone, four or five feet wide, where it is said that the children of the dukes of Anjou used to be baptized.

I will refrain from discussing the stone pitchers from the wedding at Cana, one of which they claim to possess.[4]

In the nave of the church, there are three old stone sarcophagi containing the remains of three people; note that they have not been buried in the ground.

On the left, against the wall, is a tomb elevated one foot above the ground, with a depiction of a bishop of Angers in white marble atop a black marble tombstone.

Facing it on the right side of the nave is a wooden sarcophagus with ornaments and plaques on top, partly set into the wall, and raised about three feet above the ground. Within it rests the body of Bishop Ulger, depicted in a miniature on top of the sarcophagus wearing a miter turned

---

[4] This relic was gifted to the cathedral chapter of Angers by René, duke of Anjou and claimant to the Kingdom of Naples, who purchased it from the convent of St-Paul in Marseille in 1449. He ordered that a special celebration be held in honor of the pitcher on the second Sunday of Epiphany. On that day, the relic-keeper (*garde-reliques*) filled the pitcher with wine during Prime and then exposed it for public veneration upon the credence on the Epistle side until Sext, while a candle burned in front of it. Before Mass, a major chaplain blessed the wine after blessing the water. Until 1666, after the aspersion two major chaplain carried the pitcher around the cloister in procession. In that year, the pitcher was broken and, although repaired, it was not carried in procession again. Instead, the relic-keeper filled a silver vase with the wine that had been blessed in the pitcher. During the procession before Mass, two coped chaplains bore lit torches and a major chaplain in cope and humeral veil carried the silver vase, his hands covered by the veil. All three had a flower wreath on their heads, symbolizing the bride and bridegroom of the wedding feast at Cana. This blessed wine was used at Mass, and after Sext, the relic-keeper distributed it among the multitudes of people who assisted at this celebration. See *Cérémonial de l'église d'Angers* (Angers, n.d.), 199–200, and de Farcy, *L'ancien trésor*, 112–15.

to the side and adorned with horns, a unique shape not found elsewhere. It bears an inscription which we print here all the more readily since the brothers de Sainte-Marthe neglected to include its fourth verse in pentameter in their *Gallia Christiana*:[5]

> Hic jacet Eulgerius teneris consuetus ab annis
> Lingua, mente, manu fructificare Deo.
> Hujus opus, multis prodesse, docere, monere;
> *Extirpare scelus, consolidare fidem;
> Flentem solari, nudum vestire, superbum
> Frangere, nec quemquam laedere, recta sequi.[6]

Near this tomb is the door to the cloister, on the right side of which, facing west, the large and beautiful refectory still stands. University professors hold their lectures and classes there. It is furnished with a rostrum and benches, and the large refectory table can still be seen. I am told one of the councils of Touraine was held here in 1448.[7]

The cloister encloses a courtyard with a well in the middle, as in St-Jean in Lyon.

The canons of Angers once wore purple cassocks on major feasts. The sleeves of their surplices are split and trailing, as in Paris and the rest of the province of Sens. The canons, even those in the lower form, and ten officers or cantor-priests wear the almuce over their arm, and these ten officers have their seats in the higher stalls. The four cantor-deacons and -subdeacons do not wear the almuce. On episcopal feasts, the dignitaries wear red robes over their surplices.

The ten choirboys wear a white cassock like the pope. When it is cold or when they go into town, they wear a robe over their white cassock that is red one year and purple the next, and so on in alternation. Their biretta is always purple. At the Office their heads are shorn and bare,[8]

---

[5] See *Gallia Christiana* (Paris, 1656) 2:135a.
[6] "Here lies Ulger, who from tender years used / By tongue, by mind, by hand to yield divine fruit. / He helped, taught, admonished many; / Rooted out crime, made the faith strong; / Consoled the weeping, clothed the naked, made / The proud yield, hurt no one, and walked in the right" (*Corpus des inscriptions de la France médiévale* 24, no. 4).
[7] A provincial council did indeed assemble in this refectory under John Bernard, archbishop of Tours, in July 1448. See its acts in Joseph Avril, *Les conciles de la province de Tours* (Éditions du Centre national de la recherche scientifique, 1987), 442–59.
[8] An anonymous eighteenth-century writer of an *Explication du bréviaire* now kept in Le Mans, Bibliothèque municipale, MS. A 372, explained, "Many think that choirboys' shorn heads and obligation to follow so many petty rules are vestiges of the monasticism several chapters used to profess.... The choirboys are therefore still treated a bit like novices. Moreover, their shorn heads, red habit..., and youth symbolize respectively detachment from the world, the fire of divine love, and the innocence requisite in chanting God's praises. Even so does the eagle in the choir where they oftimes chant show the need to soar to the heavens for this wholly angelic task" (cited in Bernard Girard, "Conflits, violences et transgressions dans les trois psallettes de la France de l'Ouest aux XVIIe et XVIIIe siècles," in *Maîtrises et chapelles aux XVIIe et XVIIIe siècles*, ed. Bernard Dompnier [Presses universitaires Blaise-Pascal, 2003], 94). See the shorn heads of the choirboys in PLATES 40, 43, and 46.

and they stand throughout. When they sing alone, whether a versicle or a responsory, they always stand at the east end of the choir, as in Rouen, at the end of a bench.

The canons of Angers have retained the custom of proclaiming their faults at the four general chapters, but they use only a general formula: "I admit, my lords, before God and before the Church, that I have committed many faults in choir. I submit to the correction that it shall please the chapter to impose."

All the canon-priests who live in the city have the right of keeping a domestic clerk in their homes, who has the right *ex officio* to enter the choir and to participate in the distribution of chantries like the other officers and chaplains.

The sacraments are administered to the canons and other ecclesiastics of the cathedral choir, wherever in the city they might dwell, by the *grand corbelier*.[9] He is the highest-ranking of the officers with this name, which comes from the Latin *corbicularius*, or, according to others, *cubicularius*.[10] In ancient times he carried out his functions alone. In Angers it is thought that he used to be the infirmarian or the sacristan.

The chapter buries all the canons and other ecclesiastics of the choir wherever they have died. Indeed, some ten or twelve years ago there was a canon whose ancestral burial ground belonged to a parish of Angers, and the chapter buried him there without the participation of the parish priest.

The Office on Solemn Days

When the Office is said solemnly, they light all the candles and ring all the great bells, which along with the musicians' choir (*musique*) are some of the best in France.[11]

The five cope-bearers leave the sacristy and go to the choir preceded by four vergers, except at Matins, when they don their copes at the main

---

[9] The *grand corbelier* was the principal officer, and considered the *curé* of the choir, hence his duty to administer the last sacraments to its members. He was also in charge of the burials of the officers, chaplains, *psalteurs*, and choirboys, and had the right to receive the breviaries left behind by deceased canons, officers, and chaplains. See Louis Michel Thorode, *Notice de la ville d'Angers* (Angers, 1897), 117n1.

[10] Also *corbillarius* or *corbaillarius*. Two explanations have been put forward for the name: that it arose from the baskets (*corbeilles*) on which they served loaves of bread to those in choir, or that it came from the white rochet they wore, which was called a *corbula*. There were four *corbeliers*, including the *grand corbelier*, and they were foremost of the fourteen officers of the chapter, who belonged to the lower form. See Thorode, *Notice*, 116.

[11] A *musique* was an ensemble of musicians and instrumentalists hired by a chapter, or even a parish, to perform non-Gregorian music in more solemn Offices. Its size and quality varied from place to place, but Angers's was large and renowned. The *musique* is often distinguished from the *psallette*, which was the cathedral's choir school, composed of choirboys and choristers directed by a *maître de musique*. On these diverse and understudied institutions, see the studies of Bernard Dompnier cited in Appendix A and Jean Poirier, *La maîtrise de la cathédrale d'Angers. Six cents ans d'histoire* (self-pub., 1983).

altar, and when the Lord Cantor, wearing a cope, exits the sacristy alone, entering the choir with his staff and *mitelle*, a round head covering. The latter is perhaps what was once called the crown (*couronne*).[12]

After first Vespers, at the beginning of Compline, a cleric goes up to the highest row of stalls and tells the canons which lessons or responsories they have to sing the next day at Matins.

The Lord Cantor and his two assistants intone the psalms and responsories. They sit in the first stalls of the second row during the whole Office, except when the Lord Cantor makes one or two circuits at the beginning of each Office. When they intone a psalm or responsory, they go to the cantors' bench, because although the beginning of the responsory is intoned by two of them, all three always begin it again, even when it has been correctly intoned in the first place.

The canons sing the lessons.

Those who chant the lessons and responsories wear copes, taking them from the little altar located behind the high altar.

At the *Te Deum*, the choirboys on each side move to the east end of the choir, turn towards the choristers or *psalteurs* of their side,[13] and sing the *Te Deum* all together, even when the feast is only a semidouble. No additional incensation is performed during the *Te Deum*, since the incensation of the third nocturn is still going on, for there is an incensation at the end of each nocturn, as in Orléans (in former times it took place during the prose with which each nocturn ended[14]), and also at the end of Lauds during the *Benedictus* and at Vespers during the *Magnificat*.

---

[12] On this puzzling allusion, see "Corona," in Du Cange, et al., *Glossarium mediae et infimae latinitatis*, ed. Léopold Favre (Niort, 1883–87), 2:575C, who cites the following passage from the 1407 statutes of the Sainte-Chapelle of Bourges: "Likewise that each and every member of the said college should wear honorable and decent crowns for the honor of the church, not like those of lawyers and laity, but like men of the Church, so that the difference between clergy and laity is apparent."

[13] The *psalteurs*—whose number in the Angers cathedral was eleven in the seventeenth century—were musicians, both clergymen and laymen, admitted into the lower choir by the chapter to sing and play instruments (for instance organ, serpent, bassoon, and clarinet) at the Offices. They were obliged to attend all the hours and to sing both plainchant and measured music, written as well as improvised. They were paid and unbeneficed. On the Angers *psalteurs*, see Poirier, *La maîtrise*, 57–87.

[14] From an early date, certain responsories on the most solemn feasts were often adorned with an additional melisma or neum (*pneuma*) near the end of the respond. If texts were added to these melismas, they were called *prosae* or *prosulae*. From the ninth until the thirteenth centuries, singing a neum or prose at the last responsory of each nocturn is an attested custom in several churches of the Loire Valley, including the cathedral of Angers; for more see Michel Huglo, "Du répons de l'Office avec prosule au répons organisé," in *Altes im Neuen. Festschrift Theodor Göllner zum 65. Geburtstag*, ed. Bernd Edelmann and Manfred Schmid (Hans Schneider, 1995), 25–36. In Sens, neums for the Vespers responsory on annual feasts survived into the eighteenth century (see *Processional de Sens* [Sens, 1756], cciii–ccvi). De Vert's suggestion (*Explication*, 3:108n10) that the neum or prose was meant to cover the incensation is likely wrong, since there are simpler ways of lengthening the responsory such as singing more slowly or repeating the whole response rather than only the second half. Moreover, in the Middle Ages responsories

The incensations are performed by two canons who each go to the altar to put on a cope. Both of them incense the high altar while kneeling *intra cancellos*, and then both kiss it. Then, standing, they incense the relics on their respective sides, and then the small altars *extra cancellos*, without kissing them. Then they incense the clergy and are finally incensed themselves. They remove their copes at the main altar. At Lauds and Vespers, the officiating canon dons a cope at the *Sicut erat* and, preceded by the two candle-bearers, goes to stand at the west end of the choir to the left of the Lord Cantor, and there says the oration, for in this church the cantor or whoever intones the chant stands on the right, the celebrant on the left.

On solemn days, Terce is chanted solemnly with five copes, but the officiant does not wear one, and says the oration from his usual place. Even in winter, when they wear the camail, he does not bare his head to sing the oration, but this is a very modern practice, and an abuse. When the choir are all in copes, he wears one as well for Terce and the procession. During Terce, the two minor deacons and the two minor subdeacons wear tunicles and stand below, *in plano*, in front of the choirboys, facing the side of the choir to which they belong.

On solemn days, even outside of Sundays, they perform the aspersion with holy water after Terce. The head cantor and his four assistants go stand between the choir and the altar. There, the cantor and two others intone *Sanctus Deus, Sanctus fortis*. While they sing this, one of the major chaplains (*maires-chapelains*) in cope sprinkles the altars and the members of the choir. The other major chaplain, who belongs to the side of choir that leads for the week, sings the collect or oration. This same major chaplain says the oration at the station in the nave after the procession when the bishop is not celebrating. In Latin, "major chaplain" is *major capellanus*.[15]

After the aspersion and oration, the cantors begin the processional responsory. The procession is done in this order: the two minor vergers; the two major vergers; a choirboy in cope carrying the holy water stoup and two others in tunicle carrying the candles; two deacons in dalmatics carrying two processional crosses if it is a *fetâge*,[16] otherwise a processional cross and a Gospel book; two other deacons carrying two other books; a *corbelier* in cope with a humeral veil carrying the relics of a saint; at his

---

other than the one concluding each nocturn sometimes had neums or proses as well, and there was never any incensation during the Vespers responsory, which sometimes was adorned with neums or proses as well. On these tropes, see David Hiley, *Western Plainchant: A Handbook* (Oxford University Press, 1993), 200–201, 204–8, and for further bibliography Thomas Forrest Kelly, "Modal Neums at Sens," in *Western Plainchant in the First Millenium: Studies in the Medieval Liturgy and its Music*, ed. Sean Gallagher et al. (Routledge, 2003), 449, note 2.

[15] There were four of these lower-form officers, and they received their name because they were particularly attached to service at the high altar (*majores capellani qui majori altari deserviunt et ideo majores nominati*). See Thorode, *Notice*, 118.

[16] On the *fêtages*, see below, p. 69, n. 21.

side two choirboys in tunicles holding two fuming thuribles; the two major chaplains in cope; the officiating canon and the succentor in copes; and the cantor by himself also wearing a cope, holding his staff in his hand and wearing a red biretta covered in silk. Then walk two-by-two the choirboys, the *psalteurs*, the clerics, the chaplains, the officers, the canons, and the bishop.

When they reach the nave, the coped cantors and the entire clergy line up in choir formation at the west end of the nave. The deacons and others, the *corbelier* carrying the relic, and the candle-bearers stand at the east end of the nave facing west.

The cantor (or the bishop, if he is celebrating) begins another responsory which is continued by the organ. The bishop, the cantor, the dignitaries, the canons, and the four assistants to the cantor go to kiss the relic and offer a coin. Then the choir finishes the responsory, and four canons (or six dignitaries, if it is a *fetâge*) advance toward the east end of the nave, and there, facing east, they sing the responsory's versicle. Then the oration is said, whereafter the *corbelier* gives a blessing with the relic in an audible voice.

If it is a *fetâge*, when the entire clergy have returned to the choir, before the start of the Mass, a small musical ensemble sings at the front of the choir: *Accendite faces lampadarum, eia! Psallite, fratres. Hora est: cantate Deo, eia, eia, eia!*[17]

At Mass there are three deacons and three subdeacons, namely the four in vestments whom we have already mentioned and two canons who are called the major deacon (*grand-diacre*) and major subdeacon (*grand-soûdiacre*). The celebrant and these latter two wear appareled amices and albs, and never lower the amice from their heads except from after the *Sanctus* until communion.

They go from the sacristy to the altar in this order: a deacon in dalmatic precedes the two thurifers and the two candle-bearers, carrying the cross. He is followed by two minor subdeacons and the other minor deacon, then the major subdeacon and major deacon, and finally the officiant, all

---

[17] "Light ye the torches, eia! Sing ye, brothers. It is time, sing to God, eia, eia, eia!" The ancient papal Mass began with the subdeacon's command to the acolytes and subdeacon *sequens* to light the tapers and incense (*Accendite!*); see p. 23, n. 55. In eighth-century Gaul, at the Easter vigil, this cry became linked with a series of tropes on the introit *Resurrexi*, such as *Quem quaeritis*, *Psallite*, and *Hora est: cantate Deo, eia!* sung at the moment when the people and clergy lit their candles in the church after the vigil as the Mass began (see O. B. Hardison, *Christian Rite and Christian Drama in the Middle Ages: Essays in the Origin and Early History of Modern Drama* [Johns Hopkins University Press, 1965, repr. 2019], 200–204.) It would appear that at Angers, these ancient tropes were detached from the Easter vigil and said at the Masses of several great feasts. At this point in the eighteenth century, however, they were performed by a musical ensemble. Le Brun des Marettes notes the survival of the *Accendite* in several places: sung by a deacon at Vienne in the pontifical Mass (p. 23), at Lyon by two choristers on the Easter and Pentecost Vigils (p. 52), and by a chorister at Tours (p. 96–97) and Auxerre on the same days (p. 118).

without almuce. If the bishop is celebrating, the major subdeacon and major deacon act as archdeacons.

When they have all arrived at the foot of the altar, they arrange themselves to the right and the left of the celebrant, three on each side, the cross remaining to the left of the priest. The major subdeacon, with his back to the altar, holds the Gospel book before the priest until the latter goes up to the altar. At that point, the subdeacon gives him the book to kiss.

The celebrant sits not only during the *Gloria in excelsis* and the *Credo*, but also during the Gradual and Alleluia, with the major deacon at his left and the subdeacon at the left of the major deacon. The minor deacons and subdeacons also sit across from them on the other side. They never wear the biretta when they are in the enclosure of the altar, even when they sit.

During the Alleluia, the Lord Cantor goes to the major deacon to intone the *Ante Evangelium*, which is usually the *Benedictus* antiphon.[18] Apparently it has replaced the sequences said in former times.[19]

The deacon says the *Munda* and receives the priest's blessing. The priest rises to give the blessing, staying at his place, and sits again thereafter. The two minor subdeacons and one of the minor deacons imitate this movement.

The major deacon begins the antiphon known as the *Ante Evangelium* and the organ continues it. Meanwhile, they go to the rood loft in this order: two thurifers perfume the way with incense on both sides, followed by the two candle-bearers. Then a minor deacon holding the cross, the major subdeacon holding the Epistle book, and the major deacon the Gospel book, go all three by the Epistle side and climb into the loft, where the major deacon incenses the Gospel book with three swings and then sings facing the choir, with the cross at his left, the subdeacon at his right, and the two candle-bearers at his sides.

After reading the Gospel, the deacon and his assistants leave the loft by the Gospel side, in the same order they came in, with the two thurifers incensing as before.

At the offertory, the canons join the offertory procession as they did at the station in the nave. The solemn incensations are done as at the *Kyrie*:

---

[18] The 1717 *Missale Andegavense* does not print the *Ante Evangelium* antiphons, instead noting in the *Rubricae generales* 4.8: "In the cathedral and collegiate churches, however, on Sundays and double feasts, at the choir Mass the choir solemnly sings the *Benedictus* antiphon or another taken from the Office of the day according the custom of each church. This antiphon is therefore called *Ante Evangelium*, and is intoned by the deacon at the altar, after the precentor has announced it to him." On medieval examples of the *Ante Evangelium*, see Anne Walters Robertson, "From Office to Mass: The Antiphons of Vespers and Lauds and the Antiphons before the Gospel in Northern France," in *The Divine Office in the Latin Middle Ages: Methodology and Source Studies, Regional Developments, Hagiography*, ed. Rebecca A. Baltzer and Margot E. Fassler (Oxford University Press, 2000), 300–23. See Durand, *Rationale* 4.24.1, ed. Davril and Thibodeau, 1:340–1.

[19] The *Missale Andegavense* of 1489 indeed supplies many sequences which do not appear in eighteenth-century books.

first of the altar by the celebrant, then of the choir by the major deacon and major subdeacon, who are themselves incensed by the two thurifers in the same place where the two canons were incensed at the *Benedictus* and *Magnificat*.[20] On the most solemn days, called *de fêtage*,[21] the Lord Cantor goes to the altar to present the water for the Mass, as was once done in Rouen,[22] and gives it to one of the minor deacons.

When the bishop celebrates on great feasts, he gives the solemn blessing immediately before the *Agnus Dei*.[23]

After the *Ite, missa est*, the celebrant gives the blessing and, still facing the clergy, immediately begins the *Deus in adjutorium* for Sext. He then goes to the corner of the altar to say the last Gospel.

On Saturdays after Vespers a station is held in the nave in front of the great rood.

On Sundays during Terce a major chaplain vested in alb, stole, maniple, and cope stands at the altar on the Epistle side with the two candle-bearers to bless in a low voice the water, placed in a vessel on the lowest step of the altar, while a coped choirboy at his right holds the cross.

After Terce, the coped succentor intones the antiphon *Asperges me* standing between the choir and the altar. All those who were in the higher stalls go down to the lower ones, and those who were in the lower stalls, except the junior canons, advance to the middle of the choir and there form a line on each side to be sprinkled with holy water.

Then they hold the procession: a choirboy carrying the stoup, then two others bearing candles, the deacon carrying the cross, at his side the subdeacon holding the Gospel book, a coped chaplain called the *garde-reliques* ("relic-keeper") holding a relic, and the rest. When the celebrant enters into the cloister where the chaplains and *psalteurs* are buried, he sprinkles only the pavement three times with the aspergillum, which is given to him by the choirboy who carries the stoup at the head of the procession.

Every time the celebrant, deacon, and subdeacon wear the alb, whether for a procession or another ceremony, they always wear the maniple.

Once the O antiphons begin in Advent, after Lauds in the morning until Christmas day exclusive, they sing *O Noël*, which is repeated twelve to fifteen times.[24]

---

[20] The two canons who performed the incensations at Vespers, Matins, and Lauds went to stand at the sides of the cantor to be incensed by the thurifers. See Lehoreau, *Cérémonial*, 56.

[21] The term *fêtage*, peculiar to Angers, originally referred to a banquet offered by the bishop on certain feasts to the canons, officers, *psalteurs*, choirboys, and even bell-ringers of the cathedral. Eventually the meal was replaced by a money payment. The term eventually became used to refer to the highest feasts, when these payments were to be made.

[22] The offering of water by the head cantor is an ancient feature of the Roman liturgy, mentioned in *Ordo Romanus* 1.80. See Andrieu, *Les Ordines Romani*, 2:93.

[23] On the Gallican episcopal blessing, see p. 45, n. 44.

[24] Absent from any medieval liturgical text, *Noël* seems to have been at first a spontaneous cry of popular acclamation used on solemn occasions such as royal entries, coronations,

On Christmas, Lauds in Angers are as in Orléans, except for two antiphons of the *pastourelle*,[25] one of which is said by the Lord Cantor and the other by the choirboys before the fifth antiphon of Lauds.

On every first Sunday of the month, there is a general procession in the morning after the Canon Theologian's sermon.[26] They go to one of the collegiate churches of Angers in alternation and the Mass is sung there *en musique*.[27] This is the order of procession: the Franciscans, the Augustinians, the Dominicans, the Carmelites, each following their own cross. Then come five crosses followed by five chapters, then the cross and chapter of the canons regular; two crosses and two royal chapters; and finally the cross and chapter of the cathedral.

During Lent, each chapter holds stational processions on Wednesdays and Fridays in different churches, one on each day. On the way to the church they sing penitential responsories. When they arrive, they kneel and sing a suffrage, versicles, a psalm, and collects or orations. Going back, they sing the litany which is begun by the last canon and a succentor.

At the end of Tenebrae, while the *Kyrie eleison* is sung without tropes except *Domine miserere*,[28] the choirboys go to the east end of the choir and lie fully prostrate until the end. This is a true prostration.[29]

---

and important noble births. This connection with royalty and nativities eventually let it find a place in the Christmas liturgy, such as in Paris where it was repeatedly sung by clerics during the elevation at the third Mass, as well as after Compline. See Cécile Davy-Rigaud, "La Fête de Noël dans le diocèse de Paris au XVIIème siècle," *Siècles* 21 (2005): 27–39 and Didier Lett and Nicolas Offenstadt, "Les pratiques du cri au Moyen Âge," in *Haro! Noël! Oyé! Pratiques du cri au Moyen Âge*, ed. Didier Lett and Nicolas Offenstadt (Éditions de la Sorbonne, 2003), 5–41. The chant of *Noël* to the tune of the *Conditor alme siderum* after Compline in use of Paris can be found in Martin Sonnet, *Directorium chori Parisiensis* (Paris, 1656), 104–7, which unconvincingly seeks to explain the ejaculation as a corruption of "Emmanuel."

[25] See p. 57–58.

[26] The Council of Trent ("Decretum secundum publicatum in eadem quinta sessione super lectione et praedicatione," in *Concilii Tridentini actorum pars altera acta post sessionem tertiam usque ad Concilium Bononiam translatum*, ed. Stephanus Ehses, Concilium Tridentinum diariorum, actorum, epistolarum, tractatuum nova collectio 4 [Herder, 1964], 241–3) established that every chapter was to have a resident theologian to deliver lectures on Sacred Scripture.

[27] A Mass in which plainchant is replaced by a polyphonic setting sung by the *musique* mentioned above.

[28] On the sometimes florid tropes of the Kyrie at the end of Tenebrae, see Pedro Romano Rocha, "Les 'tropes' ou versets de l'ancien office de Ténèbres," in *Mens concordet voci: pour Mgr A. G. Martimort à l'occasion de ses quarante années d'enseignement et des vingt ans de la Constitution 'Sacrosanctum Concilium'*, edited by Jacques Dutheil and Claude Dagens (Desclée, 1983), 691–702.

[29] In the preface our author promises to discuss four types of prostration. One of them is the full, face-down prostration mentioned here, which he considers to be the true, "ancient" prostration (see also pp. 48 and 216). Below he also notes the profound bow while kneeling made by the choirboys in Angers. Later, he mentions the *prostratio super formas* (in Fontevraud, p. 84 and Rouen, pp. 237 and 272). The fourth type is presumably kneeling on both knees, as in Rouen, where, he says, penitents "prostrate themselves on their knees."

Throughout the entire year, all kneel at the versicle *Te ergo quaesumus* of the *Te Deum laudamus*, as in Rouen.

At the three Gospel canticles, all of the canons and other clerics stand without leaning on their stalls.

Every time the *Confiteor* is said at Prime and Compline, the choirboys line up in front of the officiant or hebdomadary. They kneel and bow down so that their face almost touches the ground while they say the *Confiteor* and while the officiant says the *Misereatur* and *Indulgentiam*. This is also a sort of prostration: we shall later see two other types. If the bishop is present at Prime or Compline, he is the one who makes and receives the confession and gives absolution. Otherwise, the hebdomadary does so, not the dean.

Every day of the year, at the end of Compline, a choirboy carries the holy water stoup to the west end of the choir in the middle of the cope-bearers' bench. He presents the aspergillum to the *grand corbelier*, who, his back to the altar, sprinkles each of the canons and other clerics with holy water as they step out one by one. If the bishop is present, the *grand corbelier* hands him the aspergillum and the prelate sprinkles all the canons with holy water. Then the *grand corbelier* does the same for the rest of the clergy.

At Masses in Lent, on Sundays as well as ferias, the deacon wears over his stole an *orarium*,[30] a large, foot-wide band made of the same material as the stole, and that hardly goes below the waist (PLATE 18). Over this *orarium*, he wears a rather ample chasuble that extends only down to the breast in front, resembling the camail that canons wear during winter. The subdeacon wears a similar chasuble over his alb, and removes it only to read the Epistle. He then puts it back on and does not take it off again. The deacon removes it to read the Gospel, and does not put it back on until after the priest's communion.

A three-hundred-year-old manuscript missal of Angers states that on Sundays of Lent the common Preface *per annum* is said.[31]

Maundy Thursday

On Maundy Thursday, the bishop is not assisted at Mass by the archdeacons, but by two canons chosen by him. When the time comes to bless

---

[30] The *orarium* is known today as the broad stole. Anciently, when deacons and subdeacons wore chasubles they folded them up in front, and between the Gospel and communion, the deacon took it off and tied it lengthwise across his breast, like a stole, in order to free his arms. With time, deacons and subdeacons began to use chasubles that were actually cut at the breast rather than folded, and the former a more ample stole between the Gospel and communion. In the Tridentine rite, the deacon wears the cropped chasuble at the start of Mass and removes it and puts on the broad stole before the Gospel, removing that and putting the chasuble on again after communion. In Angers, the deacon expedited this by wearing the broad stole under the chasuble before Mass.
[31] See, for example, a *Missale Andegavense* (Paris, 1488), 32vb, kept in Angers, Archives diocésaines, Res. 25.

the oils, the archdeacons exit the choir and go in their choir dress to serve and assist the bishop, who performs this blessing outside and in front of the balustrade of the altar. The canons-deacon and -subdeacon remain seated within the enclosure of the sanctuary. When the blessing of the oils begins, the thirteen *cardinaux-curés*[32] of the city approach the altar vested in chasuble, stole, and maniple. They line up on the Gospel side at the foot of the altar; this is their place on the three solemn days when they assist the bishop. These three days used to be Easter, St. Maurice, and Christmas, but at the Synod of 1664 this was changed to the feasts of St. Maurice; St. Maurilius, bishop and patron of Angers; and St. Andrew the Apostle.

On Maundy Thursday after Mass, once the bishop has removed his vestments except for the rochet and pectoral cross and the dean or another assistant his cope and camail, the bursar of the chapter presents each of them a cloth apron which he fastens around them. Thereafter, both go to wash the high altar and only one of the minor altars while the cantors sing the usual antiphons. After this, the bishop and the dean go to the cloister to wash the feet of twelve children of the Hôpital while cantors sing antiphons. The executioner is present and acts as a verger, keeping back the crowd. After the ceremony is done, the bursar washes the hands of the bishop and dean.

At two in the afternoon, once the cathedral clergy of the cathedral has gathered, a deacon accompanied by a subdeacon enters the choir and sings the Gospel *Ante diem festum Paschae*.[33] After this, the dean, or sometimes a junior theologian, delivers a discourse in Latin on the mystery celebrated this day. Following this discourse, the third archdeacon reads in the lesson tone Our Savior's sermon which begins *Amen, amen, dico vobis, non est servus super dominum suum*, and finishes with the words, *Surgite, eamus hinc*.[34] Then everyone in choir rises and goes to the episcopal palace, entering a hall called the Salle du clergé, which is ringed with benches. The bishop, who has been seating towards the front of the room, rises to receive the clergy, who take their seats while the choirboys remain standing in the middle of the room, divided into two rows. Towards the back of the room, a large sideboard is prepared with glasses of white and red wine and water. Towards the middle there is a lectern with a cloth, and towards the front a small table with a cloth, on which is a silver basin and an ewer with a towel on top. Once everyone has taken his place and is seated, the four oldest choirboys make a bow and go to the sideboard. They drape a towel over their arm and each takes two glasses in his hands. The bishop's officers pour white wine into one of them and water into the other, and so all four choirboys present them to the bishop and the

---

[32] On the *cardinaux-curés*, see p. 21, n. 49.
[33] John 13:1–15.
[34] John 13:16–14:31.

entire choir. Each mixes and tempers his wine according to his liking and, once he has finished drinking it, the choirboy goes to the sideboard to wash the glass and brings it to the next cleric, continuing around the table from one corner to the other. After everyone has had white wine, the round is repeated with red wine, and finally a third time with white wine. Each one is free to drink what he likes, or even abstain entirely. Then the bishop rises and a subdeacon places a towel over his arm and hands him the ewer from the small table. This subdeacon takes the basin and both go to wash the hands of the canons and dignitaries, who politely refuse this courtesy. After this, the penitentiary, or sometimes a junior theologian in his place, delivers a discourse in Latin about the institution of the Eucharist. Afterwards they all go back to choir and say Compline in silence, i.e., each one in private. Then they sing Tenebrae. During the above ceremony, the succentor presents the bishop, the dignitaries, and the canons with four pennies each.

Good Friday

If the bishop does not celebrate the Office on this day, the celebrant wears, instead of the alb, a large robe of yellow silk, the bottom of which is adorned at the front and back with embroidery resembling an alb's apparel. He also wears a chasuble in the old style, i.e., wholly conical and closed, made of rich violet fabric.

In this Office, only two prophecies are sung; on the next day, Holy Saturday, four prophecies. The canons who sing them wear, on top of their black capes and camails, similar old-style chasubles in different colors. These are also used on the vigil of Pentecost, on top of the surplice.

The deacon who is at the altar goes to the west end of the choir and sings the narrative part of the Gospel of the Passion. A canon wearing an appareled amice over his head and another large robe of off-yellow silk with a girdle, similar to the one mentioned above, stands at the eagle lectern in the choir and sings the words of Our Lord. A musical ensemble, standing in the rood loft, sings the words of the Jews, such as *Crucifigatur*.

On Good Friday, the minor hours and Vespers are said in choir *sub silentio*.

Holy Saturday

The minor hours are said in choir *sub silentio*. On this day and on the vigil of Pentecost, the Lords Canon of St-Maurice go in procession to bless the font of the parish church, which is located at the right of the entrance to the cathedral. In this procession, two deacons in albs and dalmatics carry the sacred oils in two large vases. Over their heads, they wear a large veil of white silk or transparent gauze that falls over their backs and front, using the ends of these to carry the vases. They walk behind the deacon, who is vested in cope and carries the Paschal candle, which remains lit from the moment it is blessed until after the Benediction of the Blessed Sacrament on Easter day, i.e., until seven in the evening.

On the first three days of Easter, the procession to the font is held after Vespers with the same ceremonies, and the two canons who performed the incensations during the *Magnificat* continually incense the sacred oils as they walk. During this procession, the psalms *Laudate pueri* and *In exitu* are sung, as elsewhere.

Across from the chapel that serves as the parish church, there is a room where the most recent Council of Tours concluded its sessions. The council was transferred to Angers on account of the plague that struck Tours in 1583.

On Holy Saturday before Compline and on Easter Sunday between None and Vespers, the clergy go to the episcopal palace again for a potation similar to the one on Maundy Thursday, except that there are no ceremonies besides the refreshment. On Easter day, the cantor goes there holding his staff with four assistants. The bishop awaits them clad in his pontifical vestments with miter and crosier. On this day, as they go out from the hall where they had their refreshment, the bishop stops by the door, and the clergy likewise stop in the grand hall of the palace and line up in two rows. The two choirboys carrying the candles in front of the bishop sing these first two verses of the hymn:

> Salve festa dies, toto venerabilis aevo,
> Qua Deus infernum vicit, et astra tenet.[35]

The clergy repeat them slowly as they lead the bishop to choir.

On this same day and on Christmas day, at Terce the bishop puts on his pontifical vestments in the parish chapel at the west end of the nave. The entire choir in copes goes to escort him, and they sing the *Salve festa dies* with the same ceremony.

Easter

Towards the evening of Holy Saturday, the enclosure of the high altar is covered above and in front with a great white cloth. It remains covered until the proclamation of the Resurrection, which is done in the following way.

After the third and last responsory of Matins, the two major chaplains of the choir in copes go to the altar with the cantor and hide behind the cloth. Then two *corbeliers* in dalmatic wearing a simple amice on their heads and above it a sort of embroidered skullcap called the *mitella* in Latin, and gloves or mittens on their hands, present themselves at the altar. The major chaplains sing, asking them, *Quem quaeritis?* The *corbeliers*, representing the Marys, say, *Jesum Nazarenum crucifixum*. The major chaplains continue, *Non est hic, surrexit sicut praedixerat; venite, et*

---

[35] Cantus ID a00177.

videte locum ubi positus erat Dominus. The *corbeliers* enter, and the major chaplains continue singing, *Ite, nuntiate discipulis ejus quia surrexit*. As the *corbeliers* go in, they take two ostrich eggs[36] wrapped in a silk cloth, and return to choir singing, *Alleluia, Resurrexit Dominus, resurrexit leo fortis, Christus filius Dei*. The choir replies, *Deo gratias, Alleluia*. This same Office of the Sepulcher or of the Resurrection was performed in Rouen with the same words no more than a hundred or a hundred and fifty years ago, but has since been suppressed there.[37]

The organ begins the *Te Deum*. The two *corbeliers* approach the bishop, the dignitaries, the canons, and all in choir saying into each person's ear, *Resurrexit, alleluia*, to which each replies, *Deo gratias, alleluia*.

St. Mark's Day

The procession on this day is done by the cathedral clergy and the secular chapters mentioned above. The usual litanies are sung, perhaps with minor differences. However, after the six cantors have invoked a saint, the choir replies only *Kyrie eleison, Christe eleison, Kyrie eleison*. The Mass is said in violet vestments at a convent of Benedictine nuns called the abbey of Le Ronceray, of which I will speak hereafter. The clergy enter the nuns' choir.[38]

Rogation Processions

These processions were once made in black winter habits. All the aforementioned secular chapters participate in them together with the cathedral chapter. They carry two banners of the cathedral and two of the royal

---

[36] Ostrich eggs (and those of other birds) were frequently hung in churches in both West and East, as many texts and artistic works from the period attest, but their exact meaning is contested. They are still hung before the iconostasis in many Coptic churches, but Angers seems to be the only example of the use of ostrich eggs to symbolize the Resurrection. Durand points out that their strangeness drew people's attention to God: "In some churches, ostrich eggs and other such things that cause admiration and that are rarely seen, used to be suspended, so that thereby people will be drawn to church and be all the more affected. Again, some say that the ostrich, as a forgetful bird, forgets its eggs in the sand and only when it sees a certain star is reminded and returns to them, and warms them with its gaze. Eggs are therefore hung in churches to signify that man, forsaken by God on account of sin, if eventually, illuminated by divine light, remembers, regrets his sins, and returns to him, is warmed by his merciful gaze. It is in this same way, as is written in Luke, that the Lord looked back at Peter after he had denied Christ. The eggs are also suspended in churches so that each and everyone contemplate that man easily forgets God unless he is illuminated by a star, that is, by the flow of the grace of the Holy Ghost, and remembers to return to him through good works" (Durand, *Rationale* 1.3.43, ed. Davril and Thibodeau, 1:49). On the eggs of Angers, see Louis de Farcy, *L'ancien trésor de la cathédrale d'Angers* (Arras, 1882), 104–6.

[37] On the *Quem quaeritis* drama, which Le Brun des Marettes calls the Office of the Sepulcher, see Hardison, *Christian Rite and Christian Drama*, 178–252. See also p. 217, n. 82.

[38] The nuns of Le Ronceray were not present for this Mass. See Louis de Farcy and Timothée-Louis Houdebine, *Monographie de la cathédrale d'Angers*, vol. 4, *Les évêques—Le chapitre—Institutions diverses—Cérémonies—Anciens usages* (André Bruel, 1926), 185.

chapters, and also a reliquary. The six priests who alternate carrying the reliquary two by two say the confession in the enclosure of the high altar before setting out. The most senior says the *Confiteor* and the others reply *Misereatur*, and then they say the *Confiteor*, and the senior replies *Misereatur* and *Indulgentiam*.

The litany they sing is an extraordinary composition. It is sung on the way back by the last canon and the cathedral succentor, and also by the four canons-cantor of the four collegiate churches.

The procession on Tuesday is quite singular. The people call it *la haie percée* ("the pierced line"), because they stop briefly at several churches to sing a suffrage.[39] The ceremony is based, so they say, on the words *Non habemus hic manentem civitatem*.[40] In the last church, they say the conventual or choir Mass, and no other Masses are said today in the other parishes and collegiate churches that participate in the procession.

The procession on Wednesday is remarkable in that, besides the fact that they again stop at certain churches, on the way back the litany is sung by eight dignitaries or the eldest canons of the cathedral. The dignitaries walk first, followed by the eldest canons, such that the last canon has the place and usual rank of the eldest and most honorable, and is thus closest to the bishop.[41] Entering back into the cathedral, they set the reliquary above the church portal, and all the clergy and people pass under it. The clergy line up in two rows in the nave, and the eight dignitaries or canons singing the litany line up east to west in the nave, and the sacristans vest them in precious green copes. There they resume the litany, facing west toward the relic. At the end of the litany, when they sing *Gloria Patri et Filio*, they turn towards the east and remain facing that direction.

Here follow some other unique aspects of the church of Angers.

Epiphany and Ascension have the same rank as Easter, Pentecost, and Christmas.

They stop singing the alleluia after None on the Saturday before Septuagesima, and at None the alleluia is sung in the short responsory and twice after the *Benedicamus*. This seems to me very sensible.[42]

On Ash Wednesday, after the blessing of the ashes, the clergy process to another church. During the procession, a deacon or other cleric in

---

[39] Namely, at St-Pierre, St-Maurille, St-Mainbœuf, at the door of the church of St-Denis, at St-Julien, and at St-Martin before finally arriving at St-Aubin.
[40] Hebrews 13:14.
[41] I.e., they invert the order from the normal *juniores priores* to *seniores priores*.
[42] This was also once the practice in Rouen, p. 271. Elsewhere, the alleluia was last said at Saturday Vespers, as in the Tridentine rite and Paris after de Harlay's reform (*Breviarium Parisiense, Pars hyemalis* [Paris: 1680], 325); at Saturday Compline, as in Paris before de Harlay's reform (*Breviarium Parisiense, Pars hyemalis* [Paris, 1653], 347); or at Sunday Lauds, as in Lyon (*Breviarium sanctae Lugdunensis ecclesiae, Pars hyemalis* [Lyon, 1693], 456). Angers's custom strikes Le Brun des Marettes as "very sensible" because the alleluia is thereby suppressed before Septuagesima begins at Saturday Vespers rather than on the day itself.

surplice walking immediately after the cross carries the ashes in a basin covered by a violet veil.

On the first Sunday of Lent, they hold a station in the nave after Vespers, at the end of which they veil the great rood, singing the psalm *Miserere mei Deus* with a versicle and an oration of the Holy Cross.

On Good Friday they wear violet.

In the churches of the diocese of Angers, they hold the procession to the font after Vespers not only on the first three days of the Easter octave, as in the cathedral, but also on Easter Wednesday, Thursday, and Friday.

They do not fast on the vigil of Pentecost, in keeping with the spirit of the early Church.

Corpus Christi, usually *la Fête-Dieu* in French, is here called in Latin *Festum Corporis Christi* and *Festum consecrationis Corporis Christi*, and in French *le Sacre*.

On August 6, the feast of the Transfiguration, the celebrant blesses the new grapes after the Epistle at high Mass. They remain upon the altar thereafter in two silver basins, and at the *Agnus Dei* the two major chaplains who are standing with the cantor distribute them to the clergy.

On All Souls day, a quarter of or half an hour before Prime, the major chaplain of the week, vested in black cope with camail and stole, preceded by a verger and a choirboy carrying the holy water stoup, solemnly sprinkles the whole church, the chapels, the portico, the entire cloister, and the cemetery of the parish chapel, saying at each location *Requiescant in pace*.

Abbey of Saint-Nicolas

In the church of St-Nicolas, an abbey of the order of St. Benedict, the Blessed Sacrament is not visible. It is reserved behind the retable of the high altar in the middle of a small aumbry which contains two ciboria, one for the monks and another for the parish, which uses the left aisle of the spacious abbey church. When the parish priest needs the Sacrament, he goes to take it from the aumbry. Above this little cupboard, which is simple and lacking any sort of sculpture, there is a statue of Our Lady flanked by two angels on the retable, with candles on both sides.

Abbey of Le Ronceray

The choir of their church is very large (PLATE 19).[43] One enters by climbing a beautiful stone stairway and going through a large door, which is opened up at the *Sanctus* and the elevations at high Mass every day, and

---

[43] Le Brun des Marettes states further that the choir "is set in the west end of the church," which must be an error, since it was within the apse, above a crypt. A full description of the abbey's structure, as far as can be determined given its ruined state, is found in Eugène Lefèvre-Pontalis, *L'église abbatiale du Ronceray d'Angers. Étude archéologique* (Henri Delesques, 1912).

on Sundays when the priest does the aspersion, and on solemn feasts at the incensations. They are also opened when the canons of Angers process here, for these nuns have not yet adopted strict enclosure.[44] Their consecration to God is performed by the bishop himself on their day of profession, following ancient custom and the pontifical.[45] The late Lord

---

[44] The canons' procession through the monastery was a contentious issue whose history illustrates how dramatic the issue of enclosure could become in the context of overlapping jurisdictions and competing traditions. As Le Brun des Marettes notes above (p. 75), the cathedral canons entered the choir of Le Ronceray and said Mass there on the feast of St. Mark, although the sisters were not present. On Corpus Christi, they crossed the abbey's choir during their procession, while the nuns stood with the people. In 1612, Bishop Charles Miron forbade the nuns from opening the doors of their choir to any procession, and from leaving choir on Corpus Christi, pointing out the danger that someone might enter the regular places and even "go to lunch or dine within the said monastery"! Miron also banned anyone from entering the nuns' choir under pain of excommunication. Although the abbess and most of the community acquiesced, seven recalcitrant religious protested before the royal court, which ordered the ancient custom to be followed on Corpus Christi. For his part, the bishop, confident of the support of the General Assembly of the Clergy, refused to submit to the court's sentence. When, in 1614, the abbess refused to allow the Corpus Christi procession into the abbey church, the lieutenant general and provost, with the agreement of the chapter and governor, summoned carpenters and locksmiths to force the doors open for the canons to enter. The infuriated bishop insulted the canons in the very cathedral church and declared them excommunicate, but he soon abdicated his position and left for Lyon. Miron's successor, Guillaume Fouquet de la Varenne, avoided conflicts with the canons over the procession, but did try to impose strict enclosure upon the nuns of Le Ronceray in 1618. They appealed to the Parlement of Paris, which upheld the bishop's decision, and then to the archbishop of Tours, who did as well. It was never, however, fully implemented. Upon Miron's return as bishop of Angers in 1623, he resumed his attempts to close off the choir of Le Ronceray. The chapter resisted, with the full support of the city's layfolk and of the king of France himself, but Miron remained intransigent, threatening to excommunicate the abbess if she opened the doors, and anyone who might try to force them. Furthermore, he announced he would no longer celebrate Mass in the cathedral, intending to do so henceforth at the collegiate church of St-Pierre instead. On Corpus Christi 1624, the bishop set off on procession alone, while the canons carried another host intending to follow their traditional route. To avoid scandal, the governor obliged them by force to cross the nave of Le Ronceray only. The next year, they contented themselves with crossing a small street next to the abbey church. Finally, the issue was resolved in 1626 when, having been struck with apoplexy, the turbulent bishop sought reconciliation with the chapter, and suggested that the abbess have a tribune built overlooking the choir whither the nuns could retire on Corpus Christi and sing their usual motets without contact with any outsiders. This done, the canons were again able to process through Le Ronceray. See de Farcy and Houdebine, *Monographie*, 202–3, and Henri Labarde, *Le Ronceray. École des gad'z'arts* (Lescher-Moutoué, 1941), 38.

[45] The essential work on the consecration and veiling of virgins is René Metz, *La consécration des vierges dans l'église romaine* (Presses universitaires de France, 1954). The ceremony, already attested in the fourth century and found in the earliest sacramentaries, was extensively elaborated in the Carolingian era. Durand's pontifical codified the rite that was used thenceforth in France and throughout Latin Christendom (1.23; Michel Andrieu, ed., *Le pontifical romain au moyen âge*, vol. 3, *Le pontifical de Guillaume Durand*, Studi e Testi 88 [Biblioteca Apostolica Vaticana, 1940], 411–25). This ceremony, however, fell into desuetude in the late Middle Ages. Nuns of the new mendicant orders did not adopt it, and even among monastic orders consecrations of virgins had become very rare by the fifteenth century. Writing in 1688, the Oratorian

Henri Arnaud blessed more than thirty of them. There are even some nuns here who hold benefices or titular offices,[46] which they can resign *in favorem tertii*.[47] When Fulk, count of Anjou, founded this abbey, he assigned four priests to serve the nuns' church, and in 1028 donated, among other things, slaves of both sexes to serve the monastery.

Collegiate Church of Saint-Julien

In the collegiate church of St-Julien, the holy pyx is suspended above the altar without a canopy. The pyx is dove-shaped, as at St-Maur-des-Fossés near Paris, at St-Liperche in the diocese of Chartres, in St-Paul in Sens, and formerly in the church of Cluny. It is well known that these suspended doves holding the Blessed Sacrament are very ancient in both the Greek and Latin churches. They are mentioned in the fifth general Council of Constantinople;[48] in chapter 6 of the Life of St. Basil the Great usually attributed to Amphilochius;[49] in Epistle 32 of St. Paulinus;[50]

Louis Thomassin exclaimed, "It is astonishing; indeed, how could it have come to pass that a ceremony of such erstwhile holiness and solemnity could have today become so obsolete that only the faintest and fleeting traces thereof remain?" (*Vetus et nova Ecclesiae disciplina* [Paris, 1688], 1:801a). He suggests that the practice was abandoned because the burgeoning number of nuns taxed bishops' ability to consecrate them all and because the emergence of strict enclosure and the rite of profession made consecration appear superfluous (1:803a). Since bishops no longer granted nuns their veil of consecration, abbesses, or priests delegated by them, began to impose a veil of profession (*velum religionis*). Although several Church reformers longed for the restoration of the ancient consecration ceremony, it took the Revolution's destruction of nearly all monastic houses in Christendom to clear the way for Dom Prosper Guéranger, abbot of Solesmes, to consecrate the first nuns of the abbey of Sainte-Cécile in 1868. His example was soon widely imitated; see Metz, *La consécration*, 341–7. See also A. B. Yardley, "The Consecration of Nuns," in *Performing Piety: The New Middle Ages*, ed. Anne Bagnall Yardley (Palgrave Macmillan, 2006).

[46] In the eleventh century, Le Ronceray was granted or founded a number of priories, whose buildings fell into ruin during the Hundred Years' War. However, the abbey kept the revenues attached to these priories separate from the abbey's, and to administer them, nuns continued to be appointed titular prioresses, either by the abbess or by resignation *in favorem tertii*. In 1686, Abbess Charlotte de Grammont tried to suppress the seven titular priories that remained, claiming they were contrary to the Benedictine Rule and to strict observance. The prioresses, however, had recourse to the king's privy council, which upheld their rights, so long as community life was duly observed in the abbey and the prioresses paid an annual pension to the abbess to cover their room and board. See Labarde, *Le Ronceray*, 60–63.

[47] *Resignatio in favorem tertii* was the practice of resigning a benefice on the condition that it be granted to a specific person. Because such a resignation seemed to be a guileful way for a beneficer to appoint his successor, which Church discipline forbids, and moreover was redolent of simony, it could only be approbated by the pope. Hence in French it was often called *resignation en cour de Rome* ("resignation in the Roman Curia"). For more details, see Durand de Mallaine, *Dictionnaire*, 1:207a–217a.

[48] *Concilium Constantinopolitanum...sub Menna...celebratum*, Actio V, in *Sacrosancta concilia*, Philippe Labbe and Gabriel Cossart, eds., (Paris, 1671), 5:159–60.

[49] Pseudo-Amphilochius of Iconium, *Vita et miracula sancti Basilii Magni* 6, ed. François Combefis (Paris, 1644), 176.

[50] St. Paulinus of Nola, *Epistula* 32.7, ed. Le Brun des Marettes, 204; ed. von Hartel, 283. See Jean Mabillon, *De liturgia Gallicana* 1.9.24 (Paris, 1685), 94.

in the testament of Perpetuus, bishop of Tours;[51] and in book 1, chapter 8, and book 2, chapter 30 of the customary of Cluny.[52] A bit lower, set into the wall on the Gospel side, is an aumbry called the *sacraire* or *sacrarium*, where the Body of Christ is still reserved for the parish. The other collegiate churches of Angers keep the same arrangement. Further, all of them have cloisters, a relic of the common and regular life these canons used to lead.

In the cemetery of the church of St-Julien, at the foot of the cross, is a large stone urn which serves as its foot. It is three and a half feet high, square on the bottom and rounded on top, with an opening. It once held the ashes of a pagan lady from antiquity, with an inscription on the west side in large Roman characters four square digits in size:

UXORI OPTIMAE TIT. FLAVIUS AUG. LIB. ASIATICUS.[53]
(See Fig. 6 [PLATE 20].)

This was the wife of Titus Flavius Asiaticus, apparently one of the freedmen of Emperor Vespasian or of his children Titus and Domitian, all three of whom bore the name Titus Flavius, according to M. de Tillemont, who says he has found no further trace of this freedman in the historical record.[54] Therefore this piece must date from the first century. Freedmen normally took the name of those who granted them their freedom.

Collegiate Church of Saint-Maurille

The collegiate church of St-Maurille stands next to a fairly large cemetery. The chant of this church is the finest in all of Angers. The high altar, the porch, and the cloister resemble those in the church of St-Julien, as does the small pyx hanging with no canopy or covering, *sub titulo Crucis*. The baptismal font near the door is made of very large beautiful stone. There is a porch in front of it, as at the other collegiate churches. The exorcisms for baptism are performed on these porches, following ancient custom, and as established by the synodal statutes of Angers.[55] The remainder of the

---

[51] In Luc d'Achery, ed., *Spicilegium* (Paris, 1661), 5:106. This text is a forgery by Jérôme Vignier (1606–1661), a priest of the French Oratory, as demonstrated in Julien Havet, "Questions mérovingiennes, II. Les découvertes de Jérôme Vignier," *Bibliothèque de l'École des chartes* 46 (1885): 205–271.
[52] Ulrich of Zell, *Consuetudines Cluniacenses* 1.8 (PL 149:653C) and 2.30 (PL 149:723A).
[53] "Titus Flavius Augustus Libertus Asiaticus, for his excellent wife."
[54] Louis Sébastien Le Nain de Tillemont (1637–1698) was the author, among other works, of *L'histoire des empereurs et des autres princes qui ont régné durant les six premiers siècles de l'Église*, 6 vols (Paris, 1691–1697). He spent three years in Port-Royal, where he must have made Le Brun des Marettes's acquaintance. He likely transmitted this information about Titus Flavius Asiaticus to Le Brun des Marettes personally, since there is no reference to the figure in *L'histoire des empereurs*.
[55] In France, by the seventeenth century, church porches had begun to be neglected and even destroyed, and the exorcisms before baptism moved into the church, such as in the cathedral of Versailles, where a chapel was specifically designated for this

church is like the other collegiate churches of Angers: they have almost the same layout in every respect, such that if one has seen one of them, one has seen the other six.

Collegiate Church of Saint-Pierre

There is one, however, that deserves to be visited and thoroughly explored. I am referring to the collegiate church of St-Pierre, which is of great antiquity, as we can surmise from the materials with which it is built, by its crypts, and by its ancient sepulchers. The holy pyx hangs above the altar with no canopy but with a tester over it. Behind it rests the reliquary of St. Gohard, in Latin Gohardus or Gunhardus, a bishop of Nantes, between the statues of St. Peter on the Epistle side and of St. Paul on the Gospel side. These two statues are ancient and magnificent, and the drapery is very beautiful, especially from behind. It is visible because the altar is not built against the wall. One can go around it, as in the cathedral, the other collegiate churches which have kept the ancient arrangement, and wherever men are not ignorant of Church discipline.[56] Between the high altar and the choir stands a very large candlestick that holds the Paschal candle all year long. Adjacent to it on the wall *ex parte Evangelii*, a holy ciborium is still kept in an aumbry or *sacrarium* for the use of the parish. Within the choir stands a large brass candlestick with seven branches arranged like so: one row of three branches down the center then two between them on one side, and lastly two more a line parallel to the first, so that this sole candlestick has the shape of the three candlesticks in the choir of the cathedral of St-Maurice. See Fig. 7 (PLATE 20).

In the nave of the church of St-Pierre there are two very old stone sepulchers set into the wall about three feet above the ground. There are also two crypts, which also show signs of great antiquity. In the crypt below the choir one can still see several pulleys—there were once more—used to hold lamps in order to provide light for the faithful that assemble there, for there is no sunlight.

---

ritual; see Jules Corblet, *Histoire dogmatique, liturgique et archéologique du sacrement de baptême* (Paris, 1881–1882), 2:316–17. The 1676 ritual of Angers maintained the old custom, enjoining that the exorcism be performed *ad limen Ecclesiae*, after which the priest was to welcome the infant into the church saying, *N. Ingredere in templum Dei, ut habeas partem cum Christo in vitam aeternam. Amen* ("N., enter God's temple, that thou mayest have part with Christ in life everlasting," *Rituale Andegavense* [Angers, 1676], 13, 20–21). The synodal statutes of Angers insisted that priests follow the prescribed ceremonies for baptism (*Statuts du diocèse d'Angers* [Angers, 1680], 611). The growing disregard for porches, to the point where some were even used as marketplaces, led Jean-Baptiste Thiers to pen a *Dissertation sur les porches des églises* (Orléans, 1679) in their defense.

[56] William Durand's *Pontifical* 2.2.71–74, ed. Andrieu, 470–71, assumes a free-standing altar, since the consecrating bishop is supposed to go around it. A wealth of authorities and rubrics ancient and modern supposing a free-standing altar is assembled by Thiers, "Dissertation sur les principaux autels des églises," 101–23.

DOUÉ

Doué, *Theoduadum* or *Thedoadum* in Latin, and in some old deeds *Doadum*, is an ancient city on the border between Anjou and Poitou.

The Amphitheater of Doué

An amphitheater stands in the outskirts of the city, adjacent to the road, within a walled enclosure. The arena, where animal fights took place, is thirty-three paces across one way and thirty-five the other.[1] Two caverns open onto the arena right next to one another. One, now almost totally blocked, is where the ferocious beasts may have emerged, unless they came through a gate that faces the entry and that has a small turret on each side.

This latter gate leads down to three caves or underground chambers of great size, carved into the rock, with straight and slanting openings or slots to let in the sunlight.

But let us return to the amphitheater (PLATE 21). All around the arena, the central space surrounded by the walls, there are (except at the location of the two doors) twenty-one rows carved into the rock, each one a foot or thirteen inches high and wide, rising like the steps of a staircase. At the top there is a platform or alleyway about nine feet wide that encircles the whole arena, where the seats of highest honor were apparently once placed for noblemen. To enter this platform, there were ten gates at the upper level for entry and exit, and one can still see them, although they are blocked up. To reach the steps of the amphitheater, one must descend and enter a large gate that is now half-blocked. Each row of steps could hold two hundred people, and hence the whole amphitheater could contain between four and five thousand. These rows remain entirely intact, save for some pieces of stone that have become detached. See how the amphitheater was more or less built, as well as I could draw it; see Fig. 8 (PLATE 21).

Inside and around the arena there was a large iron lattice to prevent the wild beasts from jumping onto the spectators, for those of the last bottom row were at ground level, where there is now a vegetable patch.

This is the only fully intact amphitheater that survives in France, besides that of Nîmes in Languedoc, which is also very well preserved. Foreigners who travel to these regions never miss the opportunity to visit them.

The Arena

The central space is called the arena because a bit of sand was scattered upon it to make the ground firmer. It was here that gladiators and wild

---

[1] About twenty-eight and twenty-nine English feet respectively.

beasts engaged in combat, and it was also the site where pagan judges condemned the early Christians to be devoured by these cruel beasts, which had not been fed for one or two days to make them hungrier and more ravenous (PLATE 22). St. Sanctus, a deacon of Vienne; St. Maturus; St. Attalus; St. Alexander; and St. Blandina were among the saints exposed in such an arena in Lyon. Blandina was put in a net: shall we say it was to spare her modesty, or rather the little modesty that remained in those spectators, whose hearts and eyes were no less accustomed to impurity than to cruelty?

To turn early Christians away from both of these vices, the Church took great care to prohibit all these spectacles. Christians only attended to draw inspiration from the martyrs' example, or to carefully collect some of their bones, or to dip their kerchiefs or some cloths in their blood.

FONTEVRAUD

FONTEVRAUD, Fontevrauld, Font-evrault, or Frontevaud, in Latin *Fons Ebraldi*, abbey and motherhouse of the order of Fontevraud, is remarkable for the fact that the abbess is the superior general of not only the nuns, but also the monks of the order.

Here are some interesting points from the ordinary or regulations written under their first abbess, around 1115:[1]

Sick nuns are not to confess on their deathbed, but to be brought to a chapel for confession.

They are to receive Extreme Unction and the Viaticum only in the church, after the priest has incensed the altar and the Blessed Sacrament.

A bell is to be rung for the duration of the reading before Compline.

The nuns who sing the verses of the responsories are to bow in a circle in all directions, *gyrent in circuitu*.[2]

The nuns are to wash their hands and faces before Terce.

At high Mass the Introit was only begun after the priest had said the *Confiteor*, which the nuns repeated, and the *Indulgentiam*.

No mention is made of the elevation of the host nor the chalice, nor of any kneeling.

The Mass concluded with the *Ite, missa est* or *Benedicamus Domino*.

Holy water was blessed every Sunday for sprinkling the nuns and

---

[1] This manuscript has been lost, but a summary of its contents, with some details and quotations Le Brun des Marettes does not include, was made by Honorat Nicquet, *Histoire de l'ordre de Font-Evraud* (Paris, 1642), 299–305.

[2] Ulrich of Zell's *Consuetudines Cluniacenses* (PL 149:702) provide the first description of this monastic bow, which it calls the *ante et retro*, made upon entering the regular places and on several other occasions.

all the regular places in the house during the procession, during which several stations were held, as in the churches of St-Jean in Lyon and St-Lô in Rouen.

There were consecrated nuns, and they received communion for nine days after their consecrations, which time they spent almost entirely in the church in prayer.

A special blessing was said at table when serving fish, first fruits, and new wine.[3]

Readings were held in the cloister several times every day.

In Lent and Advent, the nuns kissed their seat at the *Gloria Patri* after the *Deus in adjutorium* at the beginning of the Offices, and prostrated themselves at the *Kyrie* at the end of each Office. Mass was preceded by a litany sung *in directum*, and they prostrated themselves over the benches from the Preface until the end of the *Pater*.

On the feast of the apostle St. Thomas, the chantress announced the Nativity of Our Lord after the *Benedicamus Domino*.

It seems that Mass finished with the *Agnus Dei*, or that the word *Missa* in these passages refers to the Canon of the Mass.

The nuns confessed even secret sins to their abbess, who then sent them to confess to an elderly priest in front of some altar.

Lessons were practiced before the librarian, and the responsories to be sung in the church before the chantress.

On all feast days of twelve lessons a nun went through all the stalls of the choir during the fourth, eighth, and twelfth lesson holding a dark lantern to check if any nuns had fallen asleep.

The choir responded *Amen* at the end of the Gospel.

On the night of Christmas after the nocturns, immediately before Mass begun, all the nuns and boarders left the church and went to the dorter and cloister to wash. Then they returned to church to sing Mass, beginning the Introit after the priest had said the *Confiteor*, which they repeated, and the *Indulgentiam*. There was both a prophecy and an Epistle in this Mass.

On solemn feasts, the nuns' choir was incensed with two thuribles during the *Benedictus* at Lauds and the *Magnificat* at Vespers, during which two nuns held up two candles at the gate of the high altar. The priest sang the *Pater*, preces, and collect.

The nuns still at this time washed their hands, face, and mouth before going to the Christmas dawn Mass, at which the children and infirm received communion. The abbess and all the nuns received communion at the end of the third Mass celebrated at the high altar, after all the laymen had left and the doors of the church had been closed.

---

[3] See the texts of these blessings in Nicquet, *Histoire*, 300.

On greater feasts the abbess herself served the first course at lunch to the nuns of the right hand side of the refectory, and the deanness to those of the left side.

On Ash Wednesday, they assisted barefoot at the blessing and imposition of ashes and at Mass.

During Lent they prostrated themselves face down on the ground during the two psalms said during the preces at the end of each Office. They went to chapter after Terce.

After Vespers on the first Sunday of Lent, they stripped the altars and removed the crucifixes.

On the first Monday of Lent the officers gave up their offices and duties in chapter by returning the keys.

When the Palm Sunday procession went back into the church the nuns passed under a relic chest.

On Maundy Thursday and the three days following all the nuns were obliged to receive communion: *his quatuor diebus nulla a Communione se subtrahat.*

At several points in the ordinary one finds the phrases *canere sub silentio*, which meant to sing in a moderate tone, as for instance when singing the psalms; and *silenter legere*, which means to read in a lower but still intelligible tone: *lectio mensae silenter legatur, ita tamen ut audiatur.*

After Prime on Good Friday they went barefoot, and in addition to the Office they said the seven penitential psalms and the entire psalter. After Vespers they put their shoes back on and then went to the refectory, where they ate only bread and drank only water.

On Holy Saturday they said None towards the close of day: *advesperascente die dicatur Nona.* The deacon blessed the Paschal candle, to which the Paschal table was attached, as is still done today in Rouen and Reims.[4]

The nuns walked barefoot at the procession on St. Mark's day.

On the feast of the Ascension, they washed after siesta and then went to church to sing None very devoutly, beginning with the hymn *Jesu nostra redemptio*,[5] while the bells were rung and the altars and the entire convent were incensed and perfumed. This was done to honor the hour of None, when Jesus Christ ascended to heaven.

At several points in the ordinary one sees that on fasting days Mass was said after midday and after siesta.

The Epiphany is here called "the Lord's Apparition," and the feast of the Purification of Our Lady is called "the Lord's Presentation": *in Apparitione et Praesentatione Domini.*

At Lauds on the feast of St. Andrew, the *Benedictus* antiphon was

---

[4] See p. 128 and pp. 225–28.
[5] Cantus ID 008331.

triumphed at the four last verses of the canticle, as was also done on the feast of the Circumcision.

Fathers and mothers offered up their daughters to become nuns by presenting them before the high altar and wrapping their right hand in the altar cloth in the presence of the abbess. Thenceforth they were never to renounce either the habit or the monastery.

After the nuns read and signed their profession, it was placed on the altar. It was couched in these terms: *Ego soror ill. promitto stabilitatem meam, et conversionem morum meorum, et obedientiam secundum Regulam S. Benedicti coram Deo et Sanctis ejus, in hoc loco constructo in honore Salvatoris nostri sanctaeque Genetricis Mariae, et in praesentia ill. Abbatissae.*[6] The abbess then covered their faces with a veil that remained until the *Agnus Dei* of the Mass of the third day following.

After a nun died, her body was washed and laid over a haircloth on the bier or coffin. The face was wrapped in a white wimple such that it could not be seen by anyone, and the body was wrapped in a long shroud that was sewn up from the shoulders until the bottom of the feet. Then the abbess took a blessed candle and allowed it to drip in the form of a cross from the head to the navel: *a summo capitis usque ad umbilicum ventris in modum crucis*. This is the origin of the wax cross that is placed over the coffin and pall in Rouen and elsewhere.

---

[6] "I, Sister N., promise stability, and conversion of life, and obedience according to the Rule of St. Benedict before God and his saints in this place built in honor of the Savior of the world and of his holy Mother, Mary, and in the presence of Abbess N."

MARMOUTIER

MARMOUTIER, in Latin *Majus Monasterium*, one of the most famous monasteries of France (PLATE 23), was founded by St. Martin, archbishop of Tours. The altar on which he celebrated Mass is preserved here, set up next to his cell, which can still be seen built into the rock. It is so cramped that a man can barely stand upright or lie down at full length, and it is only wide enough for a pallet or mat. Access to the chapel is gained through a spiral staircase built around a central column that accommodates two flights of stairs, one round and the other square, running side by side. Such a design ensures that two men can ascend or descend simultaneously without encountering each other. A lamp always burns before St. Martin's altar.

An ambulatory runs around the high altar, above which the pyx is suspended. The spacious sanctuary is closed by a marble and jasper balustrade with bronze doors. In front of the Blessed Sacrament there is a candlestick with three lamps, and a beautiful wide rood screen.

TOURS

TOURS, *Turoni* in Latin, situated between the rivers Cher and Loire.

Cathedral of Saint-Gatien

The cathedral of St-Gatien has a very beautiful portal with two splendid towers, with a lovely rose window in between. The church is well proportioned, without a trace of bad taste. It has a single aisle around the nave and choir, which are separated by a rood screen.

There is nothing at all on the high altar. There are some candles on the retable, and the Blessed Sacrament is suspended over the middle under a small canopy at the end of a small brass bracket.

In summer the canons wear the almuce over the arm, as in other cathedrals. The chaplains wear one with a black exterior.

On high feasts, the twelve choirboys, including the candle-bearers, vest in tunicles, and the crucifer in a cope.

When the procession returns to choir, the crucifer enters the sanctuary, places his processional cross on the Gospel side, and the two candle-bearers halt on each side of the sanctuary door. Six paces before reaching the door, the deacon removes the celebrant's cope and gives him the chasuble. Then the priest, standing between the deacon and subdeacon, having reverenced the altar, begins the Mass. The two candle-bearers turn back to take their candles to the middle of the choir, and at the same time three other choirboys come from the sacristy bringing three more candlesticks. One walks alone with a large candle on his candlestick and the two others follow side by side. They place their candles in the middle of the choir, while the two others put them behind next to the eagle. In front of these five silver candlesticks stands another large brass candlestick with three branches upon which three tall candles burn. In front of the high altar, a large hanging brass chandelier holds five lit glass lamps. The altar is majestic, and covered with a large canopy under which the Blessed Sacrament is hung, although according to the second Council of Tours, canon 3, it should be *sub titulo Crucis*.[1] The brass balustrade that encloses the sanctuary is six or seven feet

---

[1] This council was held in November 567, and canon 3 states, "The Lord's Body should be placed on the altar not among the images (*in imaginario ordine*), but under the title of the cross" (Charles de Clercq, ed., *Concilia Galliae (a. 511–a. 695)*, Corpus Christianorum Series Latina 148A [Brepols, 1963], 178). Le Brun des Marettes follows the interpretation of this much debated passage given by Dom Jean Mabillon, who argued that *in imaginario ordine* referred to aumbries on the walls, which were decorated with images; see his *Dissertatio de pane eucharistico, azymo et fermentato* (Paris, 1674), 75–83, and *De liturgia Gallicana* (Paris, 1685), 92–93. Previous authorities had interpreted this canon as referring to the placement of the host upon the altar, or the arrangement of the hosts for the peoples' communion. More recently, Robert Austin Markus has averred

high. The altar has neither candles nor cross, except for the cross placed there just before the Mass, which the priest removes at the end.

After the priest has ascended the altar, the deacon brings the chalice covered only with the pall, with no purificator, to the archbishop in choir, if he is present. The deacon is preceded by two tunicled choirboys, each bearing a large pint-sized silver cruet with the water and wine. These large cruets date from a time when communion was given under two species. Removing the pall, the deacon presents the chalice to the bishop, who takes the cruet of wine, pours some of it in the chalice, and likewise the water, which he blesses. Then all three return in the same order as they came.

There is no incensation of the altar, but only *super oblata*, that is, of the host and chalice, after the offertory.

The crucifer is always on the Gospel side wearing his cope.

At the beginning of the *Gloria in excelsis*, two major acolytes or subdeacons in white copes go with thuribles and very large boats to present the incense to the Lord Archbishop, if he is in choir, and thence they incense the sanctuary with three swings, without entering it. Thereafter they incense the eagle in mid-choir with three swings. Then the thurifer on the Gospel side goes behind the eagle to join the thurifer on the right side, and both incense the Lord Archbishop, each one with three swings. They separate and each one incenses his side of the choir five or six times *in plano*, without going up to the stalls, walking to and fro during the whole *Gloria in excelsis*. They do likewise at the offertory and during the beginning of the Preface, and finally they return to the sacristy, where they take off their copes, put their thuribles down, and return to their places in choir, because there is no incensation or ringing of bells and drums at the elevations of the host and chalice.

They do not sing anything at the elevations, instead adoring Jesus Christ in silence. It was Louis XII who asked that the *O salutaris Hostia* be sung during the elevation of the host at Notre-Dame of Paris.[2]

At the *Praeceptis salutaribus moniti*, the coped crucifer — who had, as I have just said, remained by the altar — goes to take the large washbasin and puts the chalice veil inside. The deacon puts in the paten, covering it with the veil, and then the coped choirboy goes to stand by the large three-branched candlestick and holds this basin up as high as he can. Around the middle of the *Pater* he returns to the altar and presents the basin to the subdeacon, who takes the paten and holds it elevated for some time to be seen by the people, and then gives it to the deacon, who does the same and at the end of the *Pater* goes up to the altar to present it to the celebrant.

---

this canon was intended to prohibit images surrounding the sanctuary in the style of Byzantine iconostases, see *Gregory the Great and His World* (Cambridge University Press, 1997), 176–77.

[2] See p. 44, n. 42.

At the *Agnus Dei*, the deacon takes the paten wrapped in the veil to the archbishop for him to kiss, if he is in choir. As soon as he returns, the two choirboys serving at the altar each take a pax-brede to the celebrant, deacon, and subdeacon to kiss, then to the three coped choirboys, and then to all those in the upper stalls, both canons and laymen.

During the Postcommunion the subdeacon dresses the chalice and places it on the altar *in cornu Evangelii*. This is the reason the book is taken to the right side.

After the celebrant or the bishop, if he is present, gives the final blessing, the celebrant says nothing further.

After Mass, the procession crucifer takes the cross that was by the altar *ex parte Evangelii* and walks four paces in front of the altar. There he is joined by the five candle-bearers, who then go to the sacristy, first one, and then the others two by two. They are followed by the crucifer, then another coped choirboy carrying the cantor's staff, then the other cope-bearers, the subdeacon carrying the chalice, the deacon, and the celebrant, who takes the crucifix that stood on the altar during Mass back to the sacristy. The bishop goes last, preceded by his crucifer.

At the *Te Deum* at Matins on major annual feasts,[3] the Lord Treasurer, wearing a cope, goes to the altar, preceded by nine choirboys each carrying a silver candlestick, and walking four paces apart. When they reach the altar, the treasurer himself places these nine candlesticks on the altar, where they remain during Lauds. Except at this moment on major annuals, candlesticks are never placed upon the altar.

At Mass on major annual feasts, seven candle-bearers enter the choir through the large west door and walk down the middle one by one, six paces apart, followed by four subdeacons and four deacons, and the archbishop or celebrant. When the archbishop celebrates, he gives the solemn blessing before the *Agnus Dei*. If he is absent on a major annual, a canon says the Mass with the same number of deacons, subdeacons, and candle-bearers as the archbishop *propter honorem cathedrae*. He does not, however, give the solemn blessing before the *Agnus Dei*, but the usual common blessing after the *Ite, missa est*.

At Masses on the anniversary of a death, no candles are lit except one held by a choirboy outside of the sanctuary on a silver candlestick two paces from the balustrade while the priest sings the orations. He also holds it in the middle of the choir looking towards the south facing the deacon, who sings the Gospel there facing north.

The deacon and subdeacon always carry their almuce over the left arm during the entire Mass, as in Bourges.

The last Gospel is not said at any sung Mass. Instead, as soon as the priest has given the blessing, he returns to the sacristy with his ministers.

---

[3] The highest-ranking feasts were called "annuals" in many French dioceses.

In this church, new grapes are blessed on the feast of the Transfiguration and St. Sixtus on 6 August. This is the day marked for this blessing in the Sacramentary of St. Gregory.[4]

The library of this church covers the length of one cloister gallery, and is filled with beautiful manuscripts chained to stands in the center and by the wall. These include a thousand-year-old Pentateuch written in uncial letters,[5] and the four Gospels written in Saxon letters, commonly believed to be twelve hundred years old and to have been written by St. Hilary, bishop of Poitiers. This seems to be an error, however, both because of the characters, which are no older than a thousand years, and because of the inscription on the back of the book, written in red Saxon letters: *Ego Holcundus*, which some read as *Ego Hilarius*. What encouraged them to hold this belief, which I hope they have abandoned by now, is the fact that the testament of Perpetuus, archbishop of Tours, includes, among other books he bequeathed, a book of the four Gospels written by St. Hilary of Poitiers.[6]

Saint-Martin of Tours

The church of St-Martin in Tours is very large, but crude and dimly lit. There are three rows of rather small windows, with double aisles around the nave and choir. This church, so illustrious because of the tomb of St. Martin,[7] was first served by monks until the ninth century, and there is

---

[4] This blessing is indeed found among the texts for the feast of St. Sixtus in the original sacramentary sent by Pope Hadrian, *Sacramentarium Gregorianum* 138 (PL 78:129B; ed. Jean Deshusses, *Le sacramentaire grégorien*, Spicilegium Friburgense 16 [Éditions Universitaires Fribourg Suisse, 1992], 1:255).

[5] Known as the Tours Pentateuch or Ashburnham Pentateuch after an eighteenth-century owner, this late sixth-century MS is now in Paris, Bibliothèque nationale, MS. nouv. acq. lat. 2334. Its geographical origin has sparked much scholarly discussion. For a summary, see Dorothy Hoogland Verkerk, "Biblical Manuscripts in Rome 400–700 and the Ashburnham Pentateuch," in *Imagining the Early Medieval Bible*, ed. John Williams (Pennsylvania State University Press, 1999), 102–16.

[6] This Gospel book in insular script, now held by the Bibliothèque Nationale in Paris, MS. nouv. acq. lat. 1587, was written at the end of the eighth century, and came into the possession of the chapter of St-Gatien around the ninth century. See Louis Lemoine, "Maniérisme et Hispérisme en Bretagne. Notes sur quelques colophons (VIIIe-Xe siècles)," *Annales de Bretagne et des pays de l'Ouest* 102, no. 4 (1995): 12–14.

[7] Le Brun des Marettes cites the first Council of Orléans in a footnote here. He might be referring to the statement "The Gallic pilgrimage to venerate the body of the blessed Martin of Tours does not yield to that of Jerusalem or Rome," which the anonymous *Dissertation historique sur les rits et anciens usages de la noble et insigne église de Saint Martin de Tours* (Paris, 1713), 7, attributes to said council. However, it is not actually found among its canons (see de Clercq, *Concilia* 4–19). Aimé-Georges Martimort, *La documentation liturgique de dom Edmond Martène*, Studi e testi 279 (Biblioteca Apostolica Vaticana, 1978), 228, suggests as author of the *Dissertation* one Gatien de Galliczon (1658–1712), who served as a canon and *chevecier* of St-Martin before becoming titular bishop of Agathopolis and coadjutor to the bishop of Babylon. He provided Dom Edmond Martène with liturgical manuscripts from St-Martin. However, a number of the liturgical observations made here by Le Brun des Marettes

still a cloister beside the church. Clerics have been present here since the time of Louis the Pious. In 849, by Charles the Bald's command and the consent of the community, these clerics received the title of canons and their number was set at two hundred. This church still has approximately three hundred prebends, and the clergy consists of fifty canons, fifty vicars perpetual, and fifty chaplains, cantors, and musicians, with ten choirboys. In addition to these ten choirboys, a large number of boys used to be received to be brought up in the spirit of the clergy. These boys, known as choristers (*choristes*), are still received when they ask to assist at the Office, and are installed like the beneficers.

All these clerics were distributed in four rows or stations. The fourth row was composed of clerics and choirboys who stood *in plano*.

In addition to the the *mariliers*[8] and beadles, there is a "pauper of St. Martin" supported by a foundation established by King Louis XI and chosen by the chapter by a plurality of voices. He must not own anything of his own. He is lodged, clothed, fed, and supported in all his needs, in sickness and in health, at the chapter's expense, and cannot be removed from his position except for licentious manners. In solemn processions he walks before the cross with the beadles, and also assists at the Office on solemn days wearing a particolored gown of red and white.[9]

There is nothing on the altar; behind it are twelve candles. The holy pyx is suspended from the end of a crosier-shaped fixture, with no statues on either side. There is a dossal above the altar and riddels on its sides, as well as a six- or seven-foot high balustrade that closes off the sanctuary.

Behind the high altar lies St. Martin's tomb, made of black and white streaked marble, very simple in its design and without an effigy, raised up about three feet from the ground. At all hours of the day, there is a throng of people kissing it in veneration after saying their prayers. The Carolingian kings of France used to pray at St. Martin's tomb before setting out to war, and his cloak was borne at the head of the army. Above the tomb stands St. Martin's altar, accessible by twelve-step staircases on each side, both having a brass railing lest one fall when going up or down. This small altar is very plain, with no images, even of St. Martin himself. It has a frontal and a dossal, a crucifix atop it, and two candlesticks to its sides rather than on it: everything is quite proper.

---

are also found in the *Dissertation*, sometimes with identical wording, which raises the possibility that its author was actually Le Brun des Marettes's correspondent, the subdean Bourrault or Boureau (see p. 101, n. 44).

[8] The four *mariliers*, *marregliers*, or *marguilliers*, in Latin *matricularii*, guarded St. Martin's tomb, said the prayers the pilgrims requested, and received their alms (see Eugène Jarry, "Le chapitre de Saint-Martin aux XVIIe et XVIIIe siècles," *Revue d'histoire de l'église de France* 144 [1961]: 121).

[9] See Louis XI's foundation charter in Pierre Mesnard, "La collégiale de Saint-Martin à l'époque des Valois," *Revue d'histoire de l'église de France* 144 (1961): 99–100.

They use yellow wax in this church, and it has a proper breviary, different from that of Rome and of Tours, like St-Quentin and some other collegiate churches. There are some rather peculiar ceremonies.

I here include a summary of the principal ceremonies of this church, taken from an old ordinary or ceremonial written in 1393.[10]

The officiants for the Divine Office were listed on a wax-coated tablet, as in Rouen.

The *semainiers* begin their week at Sunday Matins.[11]

There was no *Pater* or *Credo* at the beginning of the divine Offices in any of their books before the most recent edition of their breviary in 1635. Even this breviary enjoins it only on those who say the Office in private, because these preparatory prayers are not said in choir, since the *Domine labia mea aperies* and *Deus in adjutorium* themselves serve as such.

From Pentecost until the first Sunday of October, that is, during the summer when the nights are short, the psalms were recited at choir pitch without chant, and the Matins antiphons were omitted to shorten the Office, so that Lauds could be chanted around dawn, its proper time. In winter, when the nights are long, they added the antiphons and sang the psalms in plainchant.[12]

Formerly they said the *Te Deum* at Matins on all Sundays of the year, even during Lent. Only in the latest edition of the breviary, published in 1635, was it suppressed on Sundays of Advent and Lent.

On the day of the Holy Innocents the *Te Deum* is said at Matins and *Gloria in excelsis* at Mass, as in Milan.

The officiant says all the orations of Lauds and Vespers *ad cornu Epistolae in plano Sanctuarii*, and not at the altar, which he kisses at the end of the *Benedictus* and *Magnificat*.

---

[10] This manuscript is now lost (see Martimort, *La documentation liturgique*, 225). It was likely based on the *Consuetudines ecclesiae beati Martini Turonensis* written around 1227 and attributed to the canon Péan Gâtineau, edited by Abbé Fleuret, *Documents et manuscrits. Rituel de Saint-Martin de Tours*, 5 fasc. (Paris, 1899–1901), since Le Brun des Marettes quotes some passages from the 1393 ordinary that are also contained in Gâtineau's, as noted below. However, he also quotes passages from the former that are absent in the latter.

[11] Gâtineau's *Constuetudines* distinguish between the *semainiers* (*septimanarii*) and the hebdomadaries (*ebdomadarii*). There were eight *semainiers* in total, two whereof were assigned to each week. They were responsible for incensing, lighting and extinguishing candles, ringing the bells, and singing certain lessons and chants during the Office and Mass (ed. Fleuret, 112–13). They began their weekly duties only after Sunday Matins, even though the new week was reckoned to start with Sunday Matins for the rest of the community (151). The seven hebdomadaries, on the other hand, took turns leading the Offices for a week starting with Sunday Matins, and had to be priests (116–17). However, the author of the *Dissertation historique* uses the term *semainier* to refer to the hebdomadaries who led the Office. Le Brun des Marettes's use of the term here is unclear.

[12] Gâtineau's *Consuetudines* state that on the first nocturn of Sunday Matins, the twelve psalms are said *submissa voce, sine tono*, whereas the other two nocturns are said *cum antiphonis, alta voce* (ed. Fleuret, 13). There is no indication that the manner of saying Sunday Matins differed between summer and winter.

At the minor hours there are never any antiphons besides the *Alleluia* or *Laus tibi, Domine*, according to the season, as in Vienne and Lyon.

There is no blessing of water or aspersion on Sundays. Instead, the chaplain, who used to ensure the administration of the sacraments to sick pilgrims, was charged with blessing the holy water.[13] He still fulfills this duty every Saturday, filling the large stoup placed at the south gate of the choir, which is in the church's crossing. For the blessing he follows the ritual indicated in the Roman missal, adding nothing further. Every day after Compline the *semainier*, standing facing the altar between the cantor's and schoolmaster's benches, gives holy water to the ten choirboys drawn up in a line in front of him, and to all the beneficers arranged in a semicircle. Thereafter, formerly, everyone went straight to bed.

Every time they leave the church in procession the stoup is always carried in front of the processional cross to sprinkle the places they pass. The six priests-almoner take turns carrying it.

At Mass the celebrant wears the almuce to the altar, taking it off only after intoning the *Gloria in excelsis* and on ferial days before the *Dominus vobiscum*. But the deacon and subdeacon are never without the almuce at the altar.

At high Mass the deacon places the bread and the wine upon the altar on the Epistle side, as in the cathedral of Rouen. It is to make space for him that, at this moment, the missal is taken to the other side of the altar. This church has pint-sized cruets.

At St-Martin of Tours there is a manuscript missal from 1157 in which St. Martin and St. Euphemia are mentioned in the Canon.

The celebrant recites the Gospel of St. John as he goes back to the sacristy and finishes it while he removes his vestments, as an act of thanksgiving. This custom is observed at all sung Masses said in the chapels and at the high altar.

The cope-bearers do not circulate symmetrically, but make stops as needed when someone sings out of tune, too fast, or commits some other fault.[14]

At St-Martin of Tours, *Quoniam in aeternum misericordia ejus* is not repeated at each verse of psalm 135, *Confitemini*, at Thursday Vespers.

The dean or the highest-ranking dignitary present says the *Confiteor*, receives the clergy's confession at Compline, and says the *Misereatur* and *Indulgentiam*, as in the cathedral of Rouen.

---

[13] This chaplain, a dignitary known as the almoner (not to be confused with the six priests-almoner mentioned below), originally oversaw the administration of the two hospices for the reception of pilgrims, but by the seventeenth century they no longer functioned (see Jarry, "Le chapitre," 120).

[14] Choir ceremony included one or more circulators who walked through the choir to ensure no members fell asleep. Precise rubrics regulated in what direction and how many times the circuit was made, depending on the length of the Office. The practice of the cantors walking around the choir is explained on pp. 106, 108, and 113–15.

The Marian antiphons *Salve Regina*, *Regina coeli*, and the rest, are omitted on feasts of Our Lady, because the day's whole Office is about her, and also from the Christmas Vigil to the feast of the Octave of Epiphany, because the Office speaks of her.

In this church there are double feasts of seven, five, and three candles, so called after the number of candles that are carried before the celebrant at high Mass.

On feasts of seven candles the solemnity begins the day before at Terce, right after the feast is announced in chapter after Prime. Likewise the vigil Mass is celebrated with the same ritual as doubles.

On these major feasts the officiant, cantor, schoolmaster, chamberlain,[15] and *chevecier*[16] still wear the ancient choir dress, namely, the amice and alb with cincture under a cope. The surplice, which is simply a shortened form of the alb, came into use long after this church was secularized.

The ornamental hood of their oldest cope, used on Christmas, Easter, and Assumption, is cut like an actual hood and ends in a point.

There are no incensations at Vespers during the *Magnificat*. Instead, at the beginning of the first psalm, the chamberlain and *chevecier*, vested in appareled albs, enter the choir preceded by two beadles and two *mariliers* and take the incense to the officiant to be blessed. Then they kneel between the doors of the sanctuary and incense the Blessed Sacrament with three swings, kissing the altar afterwards. Thence they go, incensing all the way, to the tomb of St. Martin, and after incensing it with three swings, they go to do the same in various places in the church, and finally enter the choir to incense the clergy, each taking one side, and to perfume the church.

At Matins the chamberlain and *chevecier* perform the same incensations during the first psalm of each nocturn, as if they were three different Offices, and indeed, formerly the three nocturns were said separately.[17] At the end of each nocturn the choirboy closes and removes the lectionary and the candle-bearer extinguishes his candle, as if it were time to leave choir.

The hour of Terce is sung solemnly and is begun by the celebrant vested in appareled alb and cope. The cantor, holding his staff, intones the hymn and the psalms. After Terce, they hold a procession with a station in the nave. After the procession the celebrant goes to the sacristy to put on the chasuble.

The celebrant leaves the sacristy preceded by two beadles, seven tunicled candle-bearers, two coped thurifers who incense continuously, seven

---

[15] The *chambrier*, from Latin *camerarius*, was a dignitary in charge of the capitular treasury (see Jarry, "Le chapitre," 120).

[16] The *chefeciers* or *chefciers*, in Latin *capicerii*, guarded the treasury. The chamberlain of St-Martin was a *chevecier*, and there were three others who assisted him, each serving for a week in rotation (see Edgar-Raphaël Vaucelle, *La collégiale de Saint-Martin de Tours des origines à l'avènement des Valois* [Librairie Alphonse Picard et Fils, 1908], 206).

[17] De Vert, *Explication*, 2:248–54, also believes the nocturns used to be said separately, and cites customs of other churches in France that he claims are atavistic remnants of this ancient practice.

tunicled acolytes, two subdeacons, and two deacons. He is followed by a beadle who raises the lower hem of his chasuble, because formerly chasubles were trailing and not clipped, and hence the celebrant, who carries the True Cross,[18] needed this assistance. They all go in this order to the tomb of St. Martin, at the foot of which the celebrant says the confession and the rest in the usual manner. These prayers are said here on account of the words *quorum Reliquiae hic sunt*, "whose relics are here,"[19] for anciently the sacred mysteries were celebrated over the tombs of saints.[20] This was still the practice in the thirteenth century on all Sundays and nine-lesson feasts. Meanwhile, the two subdeacons spread the cloths over the altar.

They go in the same order to the high altar, and having arrived there, the celebrant intones the *Gloria in excelsis*, which is pre-intoned to him, and the choirboys place their candles on the ground, since nothing is set upon the altar except the relics of saints and the book of the holy Gospels.

The celebrant at the altar does not recite what the choir sings, but rather listens respectfully.

After the subdeacon has chanted the Epistle, a deacon and subdeacon enter the choir, ceremoniously carrying the bread and wine as the sacrificial matter. They are preceded by a beadle, two candle-bearers, and two coped thurifers, who continuously incense until they enter the sanctuary.

The celebrant and clergy kneel at *Suscipe deprecationem nostram* during the *Gloria in excelsis* and in the Creed from *Descendit de coelis, et incarnatus est* until *Et resurrexit*, when they rise, because of the words *descendit* and *resurrexit*, and also to adore Jesus Christ's humiliation in his Incarnation and Passion.

When there is a general communion, it takes place after the celebrant's communion, and the clergy in choir remain standing. A deacon holds the paten to catch particles that might fall during the communion, and a subdeacon presents the chalice with wine to the communicants.[21]

The deacon does not turn toward the people when he chants the *Ite, missa est*, because the priest celebrates in view and in the midst of the people, the sanctuary being enclosed only by brass balustrades, and this part of the choir only by an iron grille. Moreover, formerly there was no retable behind the altar.

The celebrant recites the Gospel *In principio* on his way back to the sacristy.

---

[18] St-Martin had two altar crosses, both of which contained fragments of the True Cross (see Achille Dupuoy, *Histoire de saint Martin, évêque de Tours* [Tours, 1858], 478). As in the cathedral of St-Gatien (pp. 88–89), the celebrant at St-Martin placed the cross upon the altar immediately before Mass and removed it thereafter.
[19] From the oration *Oramus te Domine*, which concludes the preparatory prayers.
[20] See de Vert, *Explication*, 2:322, 387, 3:42–44.
[21] The author of the *Dissertation historique*, 22, clarifies that this is not consecrated wine, although he does see this practice as a vestige of the ancient custom of giving communion under both species.

At second Vespers of major feasts, either of seven or five candles, there are no incensations unless the next day is a double feast or a Sunday. The reason is that the feast ended and work recommenced at the end of second Vespers. For the same reason fewer people attended and there was less solemnity. See Rouen.[22]

On Palm Sunday they process to the church of St-Pierre-du-Chardonnet, which was once outside the city, and on their return they chant the *Gloria, laus*[23] in the Chapelle de la Trésorerie, built over the old city gate, apparently because of the words *Hosanna in excelsis* and *Coetus in excelsis*.[24]

On Maundy Thursday after Prime the clergy process to the chapterhouse, where the cellarer and seneschal wash the feet of some paupers, and at two or three in the afternoon the feet of the choirboys, and formerly of all the clergy, as their ancient ritual states.[25]

They recite the psalms of Compline in mid-choir, standing in no particular order. For the next two days the minor hours are recited in the same manner, according to the primitive custom, since formerly this church had no seats.

On Good Friday at Mass, during the prayers for the various estates, after the notice *Oremus*, the deacon said, *Flectamus genua*, "Let us kneel." Then the celebrant and all the clergy and people knelt. Everyone remained kneeling during the prayer, except for the celebrant, who rose and said it standing. At the end of the prayer the deacon said *Levate*, "Rise," immediately before the conclusion *Per Dominum*. Today only the deacon kneels on behalf of the clergy and people, since he is "the public witness and collaborator of the Sacrifice."[26]

As in Chartres, immediately after Good Friday Vespers the altars are stripped and washed for the sake of cleanliness.[27] Elsewhere this is done on Maundy Thursday.

On Holy Saturday, when they reach the words *Propitius esto* in the third litany, a choirboy standing in front of the cantor says *Accendite* three

---

[22] See p. 202.
[23] Cantus ID 008310.
[24] On the old custom of singing of the *Gloria, laus* from an elevated place, see de Vert, *Explication*, 2:90. The same was done in Rouen; see pp. 238–39.
[25] See Gâtineau, *Constuetudines*, ed. Fleuret, 54.
[26] François de Harlay, *La manière de bien entendre la messe de paroisse* (Paris, 1685), 53. The author of the *Dissertation historique* proffers the following allegorical explanation: "The clergy does not kneel during this prayer, and the deacon alone does so in order to signify how few obeyed Jesus Christ's voice. The Jewish people, despite being beloved of God and forewarned, persisted in their blindness, and turned a deaf ear to the voice that called them so repeatedly. Only a small number of faithful men profited from the divine teachings, and this is why the deacon alone kneels. He does not rise until the words *Per Dominum nostrum Jesum Christum* in order to remind us that it is Jesus Christ who earned for us the power to pray and the strength to rise again when we have fallen" (33).
[27] The *Dissertation historique* states that three officers poured water upon them, then wine, and lastly *pigmentum*, "which is a mixture of honey and wine." Then the priest, deacon, and subdeacon scrubbed them with a branch (35).

times, raising his voice each time, and then all the candles are lit.[28] The same ceremony takes place in Rome when the pope officiates. In Angers, on solemn feasts, it is chanted by a small *musique* at the east end of the choir facing the altar before Mass begins.[29]

Since this Mass was said on the most solemn night or eve of the year, and the church was lit by a great number of candles and lamps, no candles were brought to the deacon at the Gospel, because they were entirely useless.[30] Even today in Lyon and Rouen a great number of candles are set on the rood screen on this day.

On Easter Monday morning,[31] the clergy of St-Martin go to hold a station at the abbey of Beaumont, where the clergy is received at the entryway by the abbey's chaplains. The choir grille is open, and the abbess and nuns are gathered there to pay their respects to the founding chapter of their abbey. At noon the clergy of St-Martin go in ceremonial dress to Marmoutier to visit St. Martin's cave. After chanting some antiphons and orations there, they take a light agape in the monastery,[32] and return to Tours to sing None and Vespers at their own church.

On the morning of the next day, Easter Tuesday, the clergy of St-Martin go to hold a station at the monastery of St-Côme, where the main gate is found closed, deliberately, as a sign of honor.[33] There they sing the Resurrection Prose, the religious who are assembled inside under their processional cross respond, and when the clergy repeat it in a higher pitch, the religious open the gates and precede the clergy to the church. After

---

[28] The first litany was sung immediately after the Tract *Sicut cervus* that followed the last lesson, the second on the way to the baptismal font, and the third on the way back (see Gâtineau, *Constuetudines*, ed. Fleuret, 58).

[29] See p. 67. Edmond Martène, *Tractatus de antiqua Ecclesiae disciplina in divinis celebrandis officiis* 24.27 (Lyon, 1706), 416, reports that a choirboy sang the triple *Accendite* in Auxerre, and a deacon in Narbonne and Arles.

[30] De Vert, *Explication*, 4:132 offers the same explanation to account for the ancient custom of not carrying candles at the Gospel at the Easter Vigil Mass.

[31] The morning processions on Easter Monday and Tuesday were held after the morrow Mass, here called the "choirboys' Mass," said every day after Lauds (see *Dissertation historique*, 37, 38).

[32] In keeping with his emphasis on lost rituals of communal life, Le Brun des Marettes is fascinated with what he follows several scholars of his generation in believing to be remnants of the ancient Christian "love feast" or agape mentioned in the New Testament (Jude 1:12; 1 Cor. 11:17–34). For a presentation of contemporary views on the subject, see de Vert, *Dissertation sur les mots*, 119–134. Gâtineau's *Consuetudines* state that only the choirboys ate at Beaumont and at St-Côme the following day, and the bell-ringers who chimed the bells of St-Martin when the procession leaves and returns were given a gallon (*lagena*) of wine, four loaves of bread, and three pence by the abbey of Beaumont and a gallon of wine, twelve loaves, and four pence by the priory of St-Côme (Gâtineau, *Constuetudines*, ed. Fleuret, 62). However, the author of the 1713 *Dissertation historique* confirms that by that time Beaumont and St-Côme offered "some refreshments" for all the clerics of St-Martin, and also connects this with the agapes of the early Christians (38–39).

[33] The author of the *Dissertation historique*, 39, suggests an allegorical reason: the closed gate expresses "the fear of the disciples [whom Jesus visited after his Resurrection], and the state of confusion into which his death had cast them."

chanting a few antiphons and prayers and taking refreshments in the monastery similar to the agape of the early Christians, they make a stop at the tomb of Berengar, erstwhile archdeacon of Angers then schoolmaster of the church of St-Martin, who retired to this place to do penance after abjuring his errors.[34] They recite the psalm *De profundis*, the *Pater*, and the versicles and prayers for the dead over his tomb, then return in the same order they came.

On St. Mark's day the processions of Marmoutier, St-Julien, St-Côme, the abbey of Beaumont, St-Venant, and St-Pierre-Puellier meet at the same hour at the church of St-Martin, entering through seven different doors. There, they meet the chapter's procession on its return from the church of St-Hilaire. Each group takes its designated place and chants the major litany. Those who reach the invocation of St. Martin first wait until the others have done so in order to come together and solemnly chant *Sancte Martine ora pro nobis*, which is repeated three times. Afterwards each choir continues the litany and concludes them simultaneously, with the versicle and oration of St. Martin.[35]

The chapter of St-Venant was a monastery of monks secularized at the same time as the church of St-Martin, its motherhouse. The church of St-Pierre-Puellier was originally a female community which once had St. Monegundis as its superior. It was a guesthouse for lodging noble girls and women who had come on pilgrimage to the tomb of St. Martin. Hence the name St-Pierre-Puellier, *a puellis*.

There are two more guesthouses, one called Hospitale nobilium for lodging noblemen—today the parish of St-Clément—and another for housing poor pilgrims. The grand almoner, one of the dignitaries of the church of St-Martin, was charged with the administration of these three guesthouses with the aid of three alms-clerks.

On 12 May, they hold the feast of the Subvention of St. Martin, in gratitude for Tours's deliverance from a siege by the Normans and Danes in the ninth century. The city was saved through the merits of St. Martin, and the canons of St-Martin went into the woods and caves to find the monks of Marmoutier, who had escaped the fury of these barbarians. They brought them to the cloister of St-Martin, and provided generously for all their needs.

Every year on this day, the monks process to the church of St-Martin with white rods in hand—originally walking sticks—which they leave

---

[34] Berengar of Tours (d. 1088) argued that Christ's presence in the Eucharist was spiritual rather than substantial. His views were repeatedly condemned by several synods and councils.
[35] As the author of the *Dissertation historique* explains, each choir has an assigned place in the large church of St-Martin, and they are arranged such that they "form a sort of cross, of which the Blessed Sacrament is as it were the center" (39). Evidently, each choir sang the litany independently, joining together for the invocation of St. Martin.

at the entrance of the church and reclaim upon their departure. After singing an antiphon, versicle, and oration of St. Martin in the nave, they cross through the choir to the tomb of St. Martin, where they remain for some time in prayer. Four chapter representatives lead them to a place prepared for their welcome, where they are served the refreshments they need. Each monk receives a small cake to take home as a sign of union and confraternity, and to preserve the memory of the hospitality they received at a time of urgent need. The monks sing Terce solemnly, and then Mass with the clergy of St-Martin, which sit on the right side of the choir, while they take the left. Mass is celebrated with the ceremonial of a feast of seven candles.

The cantor of the church of St-Martin begins the Introit, which is continued half by the organ and half by the *musique*. The monks' cantor sings the verse and resumes the Introit, which is taken up by the monks. The church's cantor then sings the *Gloria Patri* and resumes the Introit a third time, which is continued by the *musique*. The rest of the Mass is sung in the same way, in three choirs. After Sext the monks return to their monastery in the same order they came.

On the Sunday within the octave of Corpus Christi, they do not hold a procession, nor do they say the *Confiteor* at St. Martin's tomb, out of respect for the Blessed Sacrament.[36]

On 6 August, the feast of the Transfiguration of Our Lord Jesus Christ, the celebrant at high Mass blesses new grapes after the words *sed veniae, quaesumus, largitor admitte* in the Canon. The grapes are brought up to the altar by the *mariliers*. The prayer of blessing is *Benedic, Domine, et hos novos fructus uvae*, and after having said *in nomine Domini nostri Jesu Christi*, he presses one or two of the grapes and makes their juice flow into the chalice to mix with the Precious Blood as he says *Per quem haec omnia Domine, semper bona creas, sanctificas, vivificas, benedicis, et praestas nobis*. Then the *mariliers* distribute the blessed grapes to everyone in choir.

On the feast of St. Michael, a fire is lit in nine cauldrons set in nine different places in the church, namely, in the four corners of the sanctuary, around the tomb of St. Martin, and around the choir. Incense is added to them at the beginning of the Mass and at the Preface. Some grains are also distributed during the Epistle to all the beneficers, who present them to the celebrant in the offertory procession. All of this is done because of the words of the Offertory chant *Stetit Angelus juxta aram templi...et data sunt ei incensa multa, et ascendit fumus aromatum in conspectu Dei* (see Apocalypse 8:3–4).[37]

---

[36] Because the Blessed Sacrament was exposed during the octave (see *Dissertation historique*, 45).
[37] Cantus ID g00397. A less elaborate dramatization took place at Paris, Reims, and Cluny, where two deacons circled the altar incensing it on Michaelmas during the Offertory *Stetit angelus*, on which see de Vert, *Explication* 1:176.

On the feast of St. Martin, 11 November, from the end of first Vespers until Compline the following day, they hold a *Laus perennis*, as used to be done every day in this church. This is to say, they sing continually from the beginning of first Vespers until Compline of the following day, with different groups of canons and cantors each replacing one another in succession, as noted in the old ordinary: *ita ut a primis Vesperis usque ad vespertinas preces post Completorium diei fit Laus perennis in hac Ecclesia, ut quotidie antiquitus: idciro serotinae preces, scilicet Completorium, non dicuntur post primas Vesperas.* Compline is not said after first Vespers of this feast, nor after first Vespers of the Translation of St. Martin, on account of the Office of Matins that is said afterwards, since Compline is said at bedtime and hence should not be followed by any other Office. Common sense dictates that this Office should be omitted on these days, because Matins are going to be sung and the whole night spent in prayer.[38]

The feast of St. Gregory of Tours is held here on 17 November with a procession and *fête de Chantre*.[39]

Besides the three alms-clerks we have mentioned above, there are six others who must be priests. They were instituted to assist sick beneficers and to help the subdean in the administration of the sacraments. The ordinary states *Sex... Eleemosynarii debent eos inungere*,[40] since at that time,

---

[38] There is no contemporary information about the daily celebration of *Laus perennis* at St-Martin, only later accounts that recall it was once practiced. The canons of St-Martin themselves believed it ceased when their church was secularized, although Vaucelle, *La collégiale*, 356, cites some evidence that suggests it lasted into the seventh century. According to Gâtineau's *Constuetudines*, the canons did not say Matins the three days before the feast of St. Martin, which began at Terce on 10 November. After first Vespers, the canons of St-Martin left choir and those of St-Venant and St-Pierre-Puellier took their place to sing first Matins. Then the canons of St-Martin returned to sing a second Matins, which was much embellished with triumphed antiphons and neums (Gâtineau, *Constuetudines*, 82–83). A fuller description of the unique medieval customs of this second Matins, based on other surviving manuscripts, can be found in Yossi Maurey, *Medieval Music, Legend, and the Cult of St. Martin* (Cambridge University Press, 2014), 168–71. Finally, the monks of St-Julien sang a third Matins (Gâtineau, *Constuetudines*, ed. Fleuret, 145). The *Dissertation historique* adds that Masses were then continually sung until Prime, and the clergy of St-Martin remained occupied with Offices until noon. They had a break until two thirty, when they sang None, followed by second Vespers, Compline, and Benediction of the Blessed Sacrament (42–43). A document preserved among Pierre Le Brun's papers gives more detailed information about how this celebration was carried out at the beginning of the seventeenth century; see a transcription and analysis in Gérard Troupeau, "Une description de l'Office de la Saint-Martin dans la collégiale de Tours au début du XVIIIe siècle," *Bulletin de la Société archéologique de Touraine* 44 (1996): 897–912.

[39] A term for the highest-ranking feasts used in several churches in France, albeit not at St-Martin of Tours, where the feasts were ranked according to the number of candles carried in the procession before Mass, as Le Brun des Marettes notes above (p. 94). In Gâtineau's *Constuetudines*, the feast of St. Gregory of Tours is of merely three candles (Fleuret, 85).

[40] Gâtineau, *Constuetudines*, ed. Fleuret, 130.

as one can see in the old ritual, each of the seven anointings of Extreme Unction was made by each of the assistant priests and by the subdean or the *semainier* in his absence. All this was done in conformity with the text of the Epistle of St. James, chapter 5: *Infirmatur quis in vobis? Inducat* PRESBYTEROS *Ecclesiae, et* ORENT *super eum,* UNGUENTES *eum oleo in nomine Domini.*⁴¹ Today, the duties of these almoners are limited to keeping watch over the bodies of deceased beneficers and carrying the holy water stoup in processions.

These six almoners used to wash and bury the canons and other beneficers upon their deaths, but this is no longer observed at present.

In addition to the four candles that burned around the casket, there were cauldrons filled with fire and incense to dispel foul odors.⁴² At the offertory procession of the high Mass, the dignitaries presented the bread and wine, which young clerics in surplices carried in chalices and patens, and the other canons offered money. *Sex Priores offerunt panem et vinum, quae juvenes in superliciis portant in calicibus et patenis,* states the manuscript.⁴³ The canons of St-Côme, the monks of Marmoutier, and the monks of St-Julien assisted at the funeral, united in fellowship with the canons of St-Martin of Tours, reckoning among them the canons of St-Venant and St-Pierre-Puellier, and after them the nuns of Beaumont, three communities founded by the canons of St-Martin.

They had such great respect for their church that they did not even bury their dean or treasurer within it. They were instead inhumed in the chapterhouse, the six priors or dignitaries in the galleries of the cloister, and the other canons in the cloister.

The *cheveciers* used to take care of the high altar, St. Martin's tomb, and the apse. Today they have endowed four *marilier* priests to carry out these functions on their behalf. The eastern part of the church where the Lady Chapel is built is called *caput Ecclesiae, le chevet de l'Église,* and vulgarly the chapel of Notre-Dame-du-Chevet. The cemetery where the officers of the church and pilgrims used to be buried lies beyond it.

The ordinary and the most beautiful customs of this church were communicated to me by M. Bourrault, the most distinguished subdean of the church of St-Martin of Tours, a man at once learned and pious, zealous for the discipline and rites of the Church.⁴⁴

---

⁴¹ "Is any man sick among you? Let him bring in the priests of the church, and let them pray over him, anointing him with oil in the name of the Lord" (James 5:14).
⁴² In addition to the malodorous explanation, the *Dissertation historique* avers that incense was used "because, according to St. Paul, 'we are the good odor of Christ'" (49, quoting 2 Corinthians 2:15).
⁴³ Gâtineau, *Constuetudines,* ed. Fleuret, 132.
⁴⁴ This canon of St-Martin, who passed away towards the end of 1731, was an opponent of the bull *Unigenitus,* as noted in the obituary on his death published in the Jansenist weekly *Nouvelles ecclésiastiques,* 4 April 1732, 66, which spells his name Boureau.

SAINT-CYRAN

SAINT-CYRAN in the Brenne (Saint-Siran), *S. Sigirannus in Brena*, is an abbey of the order of St. Benedict.[1]

After the *Benedicite* is said in the refectory, the reader immediately goes up the pulpit, without saying *Jube, Domne, benedicere*, because the blessing and permission he received on Sunday after Sext is considered to apply for the entire week. The weekly kitcheners likewise receive no blessing besides that given on Sunday after Lauds for the entire week. Each monk takes his turn for this weekly role.

We shall here relate their customs in winter. Vespers are said at a quarter to five, and after Vespers they go to the calefactory. At six o'clock they have a reading in the common room for an hour, then the bell for Compline rings at seven and they go to choir. The Office is said *recto tono*, beginning with *Deus in adjutorium*, followed by the psalms *Cum invocarem*, *Qui habitat*, and *Ecce nunc*, the hymn, short chapter, versicle, *Kyrie eleison*, *Pater*, oration, and finally *Benedicamus Domino* and *Deo gratias*. Subsequently the superior sprinkles the monks with holy water, and then they make their examination of conscience. At seven thirty, they go to bed in a large common chamber,[2] four or five feet apart from one another, for they have no individual cells. A lamp burns all night in the middle of this dorter. Four leagues from Rouen,[3] one can still see the old dorter of Jumièges.[4] Also still standing is the ancient dorter of the Benedictine nuns that used to be at Sant'Agnese in the outskirts of Rome by the via Nomentana, outside the Porta Pia. There the religious all slept together in a common room, each in his own bed without any division into cells.

At two thirty they say Matins, which lasts beyond five o'clock. They then return all together to the common room, where each reads privately, for they do not return to bed. At a quarter past six, a bell rings for Lauds only once, because all the brethren are already assembled. Lauds are sung in plainchant and lasts an hour or an hour and a quarter. From Lauds until Prime they retire again to the common room to read privately.

Prime is said at daybreak and concludes with the oration *Domine Deus omnipotens* and *Benedicamus Domino*. It is not followed by the reading

---

[1] This abbey is famous in the annals of Jansenism because Cornelius Jansen's friend, Jean Duvergier de Hauranne, who largely introduced his theological ideas into France, was commendatory abbot here between 1620 and his death in 1643. He is hence better known as the Abbé de Saint-Cyran. The abbey fell victim to anti-Jansenist persecution in 1712, when it was suppressed.
[2] Author's note: St. Benedict, *Rule* 22.
[3] About eight imperial miles.
[4] An abbey taken over by the Maurist congregation in 1649, of which Le Brun des Marettes's patron and confidant Cardinal de Coislin was sometime abbot.

from the martyrology, which was not in use at the time of St. Benedict. Instead, they read it in the refectory at the end of meals.

After Prime the monks go back to reading until nine o'clock, when they sing Terce, the bell having rung once. After Terce they go to the calefactory, and while they warm up the superior assigns some work or duty to each. They work until Sext. The bell for Sext is rung at a quarter past eleven between the Exaltation of the Holy Cross until Easter in order to give the brethren enough time to assemble, and the second bell at the half hour. They sing Sext followed by Mass, which during the week begins seven minutes before noon, regardless of whether the Mass is sung or low.

On the Saturday vigils of Easter and Pentecost, when the Mass is extraordinarily long, None begins at half past eleven, and Mass seven minutes before noon, such that it concludes by four in the afternoon. The only reason this Office has been anticipated is to eat earlier, as Hugh of St. Victor attests, saying with respect to Holy Saturday, *Vere antiqui jam fere transacto die Sabbati officium hoc celebrabant; sed modernorum debilitas ad epulas festinans tempus praevenit constitutum.*[5]

After Mass they go back to work until None. The first bell rings at a quarter to one, so that the brethren have time to assemble. Then the second bell rings at two, and all the brethren go to sing None.

After None, there is a short interval of time for each to attend to his needs, and so that the monks who take turns working in the kitchen each week, in accordance with the Rule, have time to prepare and serve. The brethren then go to the refectory, thence to the calefactory, and finally to the conference.

The first bell for Vespers rings at a quarter past four, the second at half past, and the last at a quarter to five. In summer, Vespers are said at five o'clock.

These monks of St. Benedict are not part of a reformed congregation, but one can truly say that they are the most reformed, for they follow the Rule of St. Benedict to the letter, nay, to the last iota. For nearly seven months of the year they have but a single meal, which they take at half past two in the afternoon from 13 September till Lent, and during Lent at half past five in the evening. Are they more robust than we? Have they risen later than we? Let us accuse our own softness.

They sing the entire Office in plainchant all year round, with the exception of Compline. Their chant is most edifying, and they sing almost everything by memory.

This abbey is exceedingly ancient. King Dagobert was the founder and St. Sigirannus, in French Cyran or Siran, was their first abbot. It belongs

---

[5] "Indeed the ancients celebrated this Office after Saturday had passed. However, the weakness of the moderns, hastening to their feasts, has anticipated the established time" (Robert Paululus, *De caeremoniis, sacramentis, officiis, et observationibus ecclesiasticis* 3.21 [PL 117:451D].)

to the diocese of Bourges, under the dependency of the Lord Archbishop, to whom the monks are subject following the spirit of early monasticism.

The church is laid out in the shape of a cross. There are no curtains around the high altar, only an altar frontal and a dossal. Just above the altar there is a reliquary case, above which the Blessed Sacrament is suspended from the end of a crosier-shaped fixture of brass or gilded wood. The small canopy can be easily opened up without touching the holy pyx, since there are only three or four fastening hooks to undo. On the altar, there is only a crucifix and two candlesticks on either side. The church is dim because the window panes are made of thick painted glass. The choir is very large, and the nave is very small, but because women are barred from entering it, as in Carthusian churches, it does not need to be very large.

The monks all work together in the same room, according to the skills they possess. They do everything themselves—shoes, fabrics, habits, bread, and even the harvest, sowing their own wheat and grains, and tending and cultivating their gardens, which furnish them with vegetables and fruits for their sustenance.

BOURGES

BOURGES, in Latin *Bituricae* and *Avaricum Biturigum.*

Cathedral of Saint-Étienne

The cathedral dedicated to St. Stephen is large and beautiful. The main portal is very fine, and is flanked by four smaller ones, all decorated with a number of small figures. A flight of twelve stairs running all along the front leads up to these five doors. Over the last two of these five doors there are two very beautiful towers, not too tall nor perfectly symmetrical.

The high altar is decorated with an altar frontal and a dossal, with nothing else besides the holy pyx, which is suspended in a small round canopy from which a veil falls around it, concealing it from view. Three candles stand on each side of the altar.

The crucifix stands on a small platform in the middle of the altar, which is quite large. The same platform supports the Canon.

At the base of the candle that burns in front of the Blessed Sacrament, there is an iron bar as thick as an arm, which holds a small beam with thirty-two candles that runs across the choir. Between it and the altar there are six large brass candlesticks, each four or five feet tall. There are no riddels or balustrades.

At the end of the choir there is a large seven-branched brass candlestick; see Fig. 2 (PLATE 8).

Right next to this large candlestick there is a small altar table where a Mass is said after Matins nearly every day.

The church's windows are made of very thick and very dark red glass.

In winter, the canons wear a long camail with a four-fingerbreadth fur trim on the hood. On major feasts they wear only the surplice, the almuce over the arm, and on their heads the small furred camail, which they put under the chasuble when saying Mass. In summer they wear the biretta and the almuce over the arm. The cantors dress in the same manner, though with the almuce inside-out,[1] and sit in the upper stalls if they are priests. The deacons and subdeacons sit in the second row of stalls, their almuce also inside-out to distinguish them from the canons, and in the third row the canon-clerks of the lower form with their almuce, as well as the eight choirboys vested in red under their alb. Apart from the Epistle, lessons, and responsories, the latter remain always standing and uncovered during the whole Office, even at the minor hours, at which they assist all the way through.

The deacon and subdeacon wear the almuce on their arm during the high Mass, without ever removing it off. The priest does not wear it. Their albs are not appareled, but only their amices.

At the end of the *Gloria in excelsis*, the two choirboys take the two candlesticks they had placed on the floor at the beginning of the Mass, hold them for a moment behind the subdeacon, then go behind him *in cornu Epistolae* during the collects. When the collects are finished, they put down their candlesticks at the same place. It may be that these two candle-bearers ought to have stood on both sides of the celebrant or slightly behind him. Perhaps the deacon and subdeacon could not tolerate this arrangement, and gradually made them withdraw to the rear, eventually positioning them fully behind. I observed one day, in fact, that these two boys stood at first, very naturally, on both sides of the subdeacon, but he made them move back. What is certain is that they were originally only there to provide light.

We know that the use of candles at Mass, even though it is celebrated in the daytime, has been preserved because formerly in the age of persecutions Mass was said in cellars and other underground places. Furthermore, the majority of churches built since then were so dimly lit that one simply could not do without lights, even during the day.[2] In the cathedral of Chartres and at the Sainte-Chapelle in Paris, lights are sometimes needed even at ten o'clock in the morning during winter.

During the singing of the Gradual, the deacon asks the blessing from the celebrant—who stands at the center of the altar—positioned two steps away *in plano* on the Epistle side without the Gospel book. The Gospel

---

[1] That is, showing the lining of gray fur.
[2] This naturalistic explanation is defended at length by de Vert, *Explication*, 4:132–62, although he acknowledges that the symbolic significance of the use of candles is supported as early as the writings of St. Jerome. De Vert was castigated for his insistence on the primacy of his naturalistic explanation by Le Brun, *Explication*, 1:xxiii–xxv and 66–72.

is chanted in the middle of the rood loft on a bare pulpit. So what is the need for a mystical account of the practice on Good Friday?[3]

Having returned from the rood loft, the candle-bearers go away till the end of the *Pater*, perhaps because the priest originally knew the Canon by heart and thus had no need of light.

At the offertory the celebrant incenses the altar with three swings while kneeling, then is incensed by the deacon, who subsequently goes to incense around the altar and the treasury of relics on the north side, and finally the altar of the Virgin behind the choir.

At the elevation of the host and chalice the two candle-bearers hold their lit torches and the thurifer incenses, but they do not chant either the *O salutaris Hostia* nor anything of the sort. They adore in silence, following the ancient practice of the Church.

At Vespers the two cope-bearers first salute the altar with a profound bow at the front of the choir. Then, having turned around, each greets his side of the choir with a moderate bow, and at the back of the choir they also greet the Lord Dean with a moderate bow; they repeat this at the end of their first circuit in the same manner. All the canons and other clerics likewise salute them as they pass on their way to the back of the choir, as well as when they begin circulating at the first verse of the first psalm of Vespers. They only circulate during the psalms, not during the hymn or *Magnificat*, nor at Mass.[4]

At the end of the last psalm the two choirboys light their candles from the one burning in front of the Blessed Sacrament. They hold them during the short chapter on the Gospel side facing the celebrant who stands on that side. When the hymn begins, they escort him to the sacristy because at the hour when Vespers was formerly said there was need for light to come and go. Once the celebrant has put on a cope in the sacristy, they escort him back to the altar with the thurifer, who always carries the thurible except when the officiant is incensing, during which holds the edge of his cope.

After the *Magnificat* and incensations, the sacristan lights a candle and brings it to the eagle along with the collectary for the oration, which the officiant chants there. This lit candle is a certain indication that Vespers was once said at a late enough hour that light was called for, at least toward the end. Two other choirboys behind the two candle-bearers chant the *Benedicamus Domino*.

In Bourges the response to all the versicles is *eodem tenore*, just as in Orléans.

---

[3] See Durand, *Rationale* 6.77.9, ed. Davril and Thibodeau, 2:372–73, who gives three mystical reasons for reading the Passion on a bare pulpit on Good Friday: to recall that Christ was crucified nude on a bare cross; to show that John, whose Passion is read, left his linen cloth and fled nude from the Jews; and to represent that Christ's secret parts were laid bare just as the innermost parts of the Temple were bared after the veil was split.

[4] On the cope-bearers' circulation around the choir, see p. 93, n. 14.

When the archbishop officiates, the major archdeacon carries and holds his crosier.

On Pentecost at Vespers there is a procession to the font while chanting the psalm *In exitu*[5] and an oration, as on Easter. This practice is eminently sensible, given the solemn baptism held on the vigil of Pentecost, similar to that of the Easter Vigil. There are only three psalms at Vespers on that day and during the whole octave. The psalm *Qui habitat* is not said at Compline,[6] and the hymn is of Pentecost, with the oration *Visita quaesumus*.

The short lesson *Fratres sobrii estote* is not said at Compline at any time in the year. The short responsory *In manus tuas* is said.

After Compline the choirboys go to the steps of the high altar to chant the *O salutaris Hostia* to their own unique melody, with a versicle and oration in adoration of the Blessed Sacrament.

All Sundays of the year are ranked as double majors, and so they always say its Office, at least when it does not coincide with a solemn feast.

On Good Friday they use red vestments, as well as during the whole fifteen days called Passiontide, as in Milan.

At Matins on Ember Wednesday in December a deacon vested in white sings the Gospel solemnly, and a priest sings the homily according to the ancient custom of this church. The *Te Deum* is also said, and the great bell rung.

The Hôtel-Dieu, which is quite beautiful, is located far from the cathedral, near the city gate in the direction of Orléans. The sick hear the Office in the church from the other side of wooden balustrades.

---

[5] Psalm 113.
[6] Durand, *Rationale* 6.89.12, ed. Davril and Thibodeau, 2:468, notes the omission of psalm 90 at Compline during the octave of Easter in certain places. This was maintained by the Dominican use, which also omits this psalm during the octave of Pentecost.

NEVERS

NEVERS, *Nivernum* in Latin, an episcopal city on the river Loire.

Cathedral of Saint-Cyr

The high altar is very beautiful, enriched by two columns of porphyry or red granite stone. It has a large retable with a large crucifix, Our Lady, and St. John in relief. There is nothing above or below the retable; the candles are on the sides.

By the entrance of the church there is a ladder of some nine or ten steps used to go up to an altar located below the organ and which is bereft of any beauty, except that one can go around it in the ancient manner. This is the old apse, for this church used to face west. There are stone benches all around the altar, and, to its side, the old sacristy, which they call the treasury.

The baptismal font is by the entrance of the church, right next to the door.

On semidoubles the Invitatory at Matins is chanted by one semi-prebendary canon in surplice and almuce, and the *Venite* by two cantors at the eagle near the cope-bearers' bench. After the *Venite*, the semi-prebendary in surplice and almuce begins the hymn right beside the cope-bearers' bench; then he circulates bareheaded on his side of choir during the hymn. After he begins the antiphon, one of the cantors on his same side intones the psalm. The semi-prebendary circulates in surplice during the psalms, with the biretta on his head and the almuce over his arm.

From Passion Sunday until Maundy Thursday, they use red vestments in this church.

LIMOGES

LIMOGES, an episcopal city on the river Vienne, *Lemovicum ad Viennam* in Latin. The 1698 ritual of Limoges states, on page 259, that this church still preserves the ancient practice of laying the moribund on a hairshirt or straw and ashes.

MÂCON

MÂCON or Mascon on the river Saône, in Latin *Matisco ad Ararim*, is an old French city in Burgundy. The women in the surrounding countryside wear hats with wide brims and tall, narrow, and pointed crowns, almost like a sugarloaf, which protect them from sun and rain when they go outside or into town. See their shape in Fig. 11 (PLATE 24).

Cathedral of Saint-Vincent

This church's choir is located in the crossing, as in Lyon. The pillars are very refined, and the vault bold. The high altar's retable is in the modern style, full of trifling ornamentation. The rood screen is made of stone. This church has an organ and a *musique*, and there is a cloister on the right side, like in a monastery.

In Mâcon, as in Vienne, when a fasting vigil falls on a feast day, they say the vigil Mass after Prime on a portable table at the east end of the choir. It ought to be celebrated after Sext, however.

The choir's high Mass is said after Terce, and the celebrant, deacon-, and subdeacon-canons, as well as the two cope-bearers if they are canons wear miters. The cantors of the cathedrals of Rodez and Le Puy-en-Velay and of the collegiate church of Brioude also wear them.

At high Mass there are sometimes three deacons and three subdeacons, as in Lyon, and the ceremonies are almost the same.

After the *Agnus Dei*, the celebrant gives the kiss of peace to the deacon, the deacon to the subdeacon, and the subdeacon to all the altar ministers, including the candle-bearers, as well as the two cope-bearers, whom he goes to the choir to kiss. In other words, the kiss is given to all who have some liturgical function, some twelve or fifteen people. The kiss of peace is also practiced in the cathedral of Auch, where it is exchanged not only by the altar ministers, but by everyone in choir.

After the offertory, the thurifer incenses the choir in reverse order, that is, beginning at the east end of the choir by the episcopal throne. This seems the proper way, for those closer to the altar should possess the highest dignity, as is evident from the placement of bishops' thrones.

They sing nothing at the elevations of the host and chalice, adoring Jesus Christ in silence.

The canons of the collegiate church of St-Pierre of Mâcon also wear the miter when they serve at the high altar.

CLUNY

CLUNY or Clugny is a town in Burgundy on the river Grosne, called *Cluniacum ad Graunam* in Latin.

Looking in through the open main portal of the church, one has the impression that this church is the largest in France, so extraordinarily long is the choir. A little westward from the center of the chancel there is a square ambo for the Epistle on one side, and another one on the other side for the Gospel. Each has a stone pulpit facing the opposite side. The thurifer incenses the Gospel book while the deacon reads it, as the Carthusians still do and as used to be done in Rouen.

Three large steeples rise over the choir and crossing of this church, and two square towers over the façade (PLATE 25). They were built by St. Hugh, sixth abbot of Cluny. His tomb is behind the high altar abutting a small altar, where the saint is represented in white marble. The tables of these two altars, as well as that of the original old church of Cluny, which was called St-Pierre-le-Vieux, are of white marble and have surfaces recessed about an inch on top, like the high altars in the churches of St-Maurice and St-Pierre in Vienne, and St-Jean and St-Étienne in Lyon.

The tombs and mausolea of sundry saintly and illustrious abbots rest in the first aisles around the choir on each side. Pope Gelasius II's tomb is on the right side of the choir. The third vault houses several well-kept chapels.

The high altar has a painting and a gilded retable, which is very tall and modern in style.

The parquetry of the flooring in the main sanctuary is very beautiful; all the flooring in the small treasury is parquet as well.

To the left of the high altar stands the small altar, used on Sundays and feasts to give communion under two species to the ministers. After the celebrant has received the host and a portion of the Blood, he gives communion to the ministers from the host, and then they go to the small altar to the side, with the deacon carrying the chalice. There, the deacon, flanked by two candle-bearers, holds the chalice and the silver reed, and the ministers, resting one knee upon a covered prie-dieu, drink the Precious Blood through the reed. This same rite takes place at Saint-Denis-en-France on Sundays and solemn days. The small altar is known as *la Prothèse*.

On great feasts, there are two deacons and two subdeacons. The hebdomadary subdeacon and deacon read the Epistle and Gospel facing the choir on the opposite side.

At the offertory, the celebrant walks down the steps to the foot of the altar, where he receives the hosts from those who are to receive communion. Each puts a host on the paten, kissing its inner edge, since such was the practice in ancient times. For the sake of convenience and decorum, an acolyte stands next to the celebrant holding a box with hosts, and each of those who will receive communion takes one and presents it to the celebrant on the paten. The deacon stands next to the celebrant holding the chalice, and the precentor goes to pour wine into it. Then the priest, deacon, and subdeacon return to the altar and continue the Mass. There are no more peculiar rites except for the communion under two species, which I have described above.

There are six choirboys who are dressed not in the manner of the reformed orders, but like the old ones, in frocks with ample sleeves and hoods, tawny or of natural black, the ancient color of the Benedictine habit, now used only by these boys and by the lay brothers of Cluny, Cîteaux, the Celestines, and a few others.[1] On Sundays and holidays, as well as some other feasts, they wear albs and maniples at high Mass. The same custom is found in the old ordinary of the abbey of St-Benigne in Dijon[2] and in

---

[1] See p. 59.
[2] The surviving thirteenth-century customary ('Statuta seu ordo monasterii Sancti Benigni Divionensis' 4, ed. Louis Chomton, *Histoire de l'église Saint-Bénigne de Dijon* [Dijon, 1900], 354a) as well as the transcriptions made by Hugues Lanthenas (Bibliothèque nationale, MS. Bourgogne 11, fol. 86v) and Edmond Martène (*De antiquis monachorum ritibus* [Lyon, 1690], 1:544) of a lost late eleventh-century customary of St-Benigne of Dijon do mention choirboys wearing albs at Mass on the highest feasts, but do not state they wear maniples. Although St-Benigne was an independent monastery, its customs were heavily influenced by Cluny, where the use of maniples by choirboys is attested as late as the eighteenth century (see *Missale monasticum ad usum sacri ordinis Cluniacensis* [Paris, 1733], xxxvi). De Vert, *Explication*, 2:316–18, agrees with Le Brun des Marettes's

Lanfranc.³ Certain rubricists proffer needless mystical reasons for the use of the maniple when the explanation is simple: because the alb has no opening besides for the head, one has to hold one's kerchief in the hand or on the arm. Eventually, as everyone knows, it evolved into a vestment. See my remarks on the subject in Lyon, page 48.

On great feasts, these choirboys also wear tunicles in the procession and at high Mass.

All Souls' day has second Vespers, as in Vienne, Tours, and Besançon.

Chapel of Saint-Pierre-le-Vieux

At the entrance of the main cloister, which is very large and beautiful, one finds the chapel of St-Pierre-le-Vieux. It used to run down the length of the cloister, and was the first church of Cluny. The altar table is of marble and recessed about an inch or two on top. Behind and adjacent to the altar lies the tomb of Berno, the first abbot of Cluny.

The Lavatory Stone

In the middle of a long and spacious chapel by which one passes from the cloister to the chapterhouse, stands the lavatory stone used to wash the bodies of the dead. It is six or seven feet long, recessed some seven or eight inches, with a stone pillow of one piece with the trough on one end, and a hole at the other, through which the water ran after the body had been washed. See Fig. 12 (PLATE 23).

Today, when a monk dies, he is washed on a table in whatever room he dies in.

The dead used to be thoroughly washed before burial. See Sidonius Apollinaris, book 3, epistle 3.⁴ This practice is very ancient, since it is found in the Acts of the Apostles 9:37. In the cathedrals of Lyon and Rouen, one can still see a trough or washing stone where canons used to be washed after their death, similar to the one represented here. In the hall of the sick poor in the hospital of the town of Cluny, there is a stone on which the dead were washed like the monks. The dead are still washed not only in the monastic orders, such as Cluny, the Carthusians, and the Cistercians, but also by laymen in the Basque Country in the diocese of Bayonne and around Avranches in lower Normandy. This ancient custom might explain

---

practical account for the origin of this custom, against his fellow Cluniac monks who believed it was a privilege of their abbey rather than an atavistic remnant. It does appear that acolytes in Rome wore the maniple from the end of the ninth century until the beginning of the tenth, and across the Alps it was common in monasteries even beyond the Cluniac congregation until around the twelfth century; see Joseph Braun, *Die liturgische Gewandung im Occident und Orient nach Ursprung und Entwicklung, Verwendung und Symbolik* (Herdersche Verlagshandlung, 1907), 522–23.

³ *Epistula* 13 to John of Avranches, in *The Letters of Lanfranc, Archbishop of Canterbury*, ed. Helen Clover and Margaret Gibson (Clarendon Press, 1979), 84–87.

⁴ PL 58:498C.

the superstitious ceremony that survives in country parishes of throwing out all water from a house where someone has just died. It would once have been necessary to throw it out because it had been used to wash a dead body. Throughout the Vivarais the closest relatives of the dead, even children, consider it a pious duty to carry the body of their parents or relatives to the river bank, clad only in a gown, in order to wash them before burial.

Clerics and monks accompanied this ritual with prayers:

> Egressa anima Fratris, incipiat Cantor ℟. Subvenite &c. Kyrie. Collecta *Tibi, Domine, commendamus*. Post istam Collectam deferatur mortuus ad lavandum. Provideat autem Prior a quibus et quomodo abluatur. Interim Fratribus seorsum a defuncto ordinatis circa Abbatem &c. Abbas caeteras quae sequuntur, subsequatur Collectas *Orationes, Deus pietatis. Diri vulneris. Misericordiam tuam, Omnipotens sempiterne Deus. Suscipe Domine. Partem beatae resurrectionis*. Et respondetur a Conventu, *Amen*. Post lavationem corporis, allato corpore, Abbas resumat stolam, si eam deposuit, et aspergens corpus aqua benedicta et thurificans, dicat audientibus omnibus, *Pater noster. A porta inferi. ℣. Nihil proficiat. Dominus vobiscum*. Collecta *Deus cui soli competit*. Tunc efferatur corpus inchoante Cantore ℟. *Libera me Domine*.[5]

One can still see a lavatory stone today in the chapterhouse of the cathedral of Lyon and in the sacristy of the cathedral of Rouen.

The lavatory stone in the middle of this second church of Cluny is used today only to expose the body after it has been dressed until it is taken to the church. This lavatory stone used to be in a recess that is still visible from outside, by the left of the door to the main infirmary.

In the middle of this main infirmary there is still a small recess about six feet long and two and a half or three feet wide, framed by a wooden rod about three inches wide. See Fig. 12bis (PLATE 35). Monks in their last agony used to be laid there on ashes. They are still laid there, but only after their deaths. In many Charterhouses, monks are also placed on ashes before dying, as are the monks of La Trappe. In many ancient rituals, the same ceremony is indicated for laymen. Only our horror of penitence and humiliation has put an end to this holy practice, and yet it was a state very conducive to placating God's justice and obtaining his mercy.

---

[5] "When the brother's soul has departed, the cantor begins ℟. *Subvenite &c. Kyrie*. Collect: *Tibi, Domine, commendamus*. After this collect the body is removed for washing. Let the prior decide how and by whom it is to be washed. The brothers meanwhile stand away from the body around the abbot, etc. Let the abbot say the following collects: *Orationes, Deus pietatis, Diri vulneris, Misericordiam tuam, Omnipotens sempiterne Deus, Suscipe Domine, Partem beatae resurrectionis*. The community responds *Amen*. After the body is washed, it is taken away, and the abbot resumes his stole if he has taken it off, and sprinkling the body with blessed water and incensing it, he says alone: *Pater noster. A porta inferi. ℣. Nihil proficiat. Dominus vobiscum*. Collect *Deus cui soli competit*. Then the body is carried away as the cantor begins ℟. *Libera me Domine*." See Martène, *De antiquis*, 1:776–823.

Behind and beside this ancient infirmary is a cloister where the monks are now buried.

The refectory is vast, with a large and magnificent reader's pulpit in the middle above the abbot's table. The abbot rings a little bell when it is time to conclude the reading and rise from table.

CHALON-SUR-SAÔNE

CHALON on the river Saône, in Latin *Cabilo* or *Cabilonum ad Ararim*, a city in Burgundy.

The Cathedral

In the cathedral, the cope-bearers do not circulate symmetrically. Instead, one walks in the middle of the choir while the other is at the far end, nor are they symmetrical during the hymn and *Magnificat*, when, still in their copes, they lean on their stalls in the middle of the second row.

The high altar is among the simplest, having above it no retable but only a gradine with a cross between two candlesticks. The parish altar is under the rood screen.

The women living in the countryside within three or four leagues[1] of Chalon-sur-Saône wear as headdress a sort of kerchief that covers the shoulders and wraps around like a nun's veil, evoking the modesty of the earliest centuries. This shows that nuns wear this kind of veil simply because all women and girls used to wear them. Similarly, monks or other religious, shunning fashion, have kept the old way of dressing in capes and hoods, even as almost all other men have abandoned such garments, except some like those of Quillebeuf in Normandy, who, instead of a hat, cover their heads with a hood attached to their capes. Similarly, in the Lauragais, peasants wear cowls and pointed hoods like monks. Seeing them thus dressed while working in the fields, one might mistake them for Trappists.

---

[1] Seven and a half to ten English miles.

BESANÇON

BESANÇON, an archiepiscopal city on the river Doux and capital of the Franche-Comté, in Latin *Vesontio ad Dubim fluvium*.

The apse of the cathedral of St-Jean-le-Grand is still visible. The altar is in the middle of the church, which faces west. They generally follow the modern Roman rite.

Among their proper customs: on Holy Wednesday they say all the great intercessions of Good Friday, as in Vienne.

On Easter Sunday and the subsequent week they begin Vespers with a ninefold *Kyrie eleison*.

On the vigil of Pentecost they sing the *Exultet jam Angelica* as on Holy Saturday, adding something about the Holy Ghost to the Preface.[1]

At Mass on All Souls, the canons wear a cope with a train and a black maniple on the left arm, and at the offertory procession all of them carry up the hosts and wine in chalices and patens. This day has second Vespers of the Dead, even though there are also first Vespers of the Dead on All Saints day.

The clergy kneel at the word *supplici* of the Preface, and do not rise until the *Pater*.

The canons wear a purple cassock.

---

[1] The differences between the Pentecost *Exultet* and that of Easter are limited to the Preface section; see *Missale Bisuntinum* (Besançon, 1589), 152–54.

DIJON

DIJON, *Divio* in Latin, located on the rivers Ouche and Suzon, *ad Oscharum et Susonem*, is the capital city and Parlement of the Duchy of Burgundy.

Church of Saint-Étienne

The church of St-Étienne used to be abbatial, but was secularized and is now a collegiate and parish church. It is perfectly beautiful. The high altar stands alone in the middle of the choir, without a retable. Upon it is only a gradine with six candlesticks and a crucifix about eight or ten feet tall. Above, the Blessed Sacrament is suspended on a small structure *sub titulo Crucis*. The chanting is done behind the altar, where the eagle that serves as a lectern stands, as well as about two-thirds of the choir stalls. The remaining third is located west of them, at the place the ancients called the *peribolum*, where the *schola cantorum* used to stand, as in San Clemente in Rome. This church has an abbot with the right to wear a miter and crosier, like St-Pierre in Vienne. His throne is at the back of the apse, flanked by the canons, forming what used to be called the *presbyterium* or *consessus presbyterorum*.

Church of Saint-Michel

St-Michel is a parish church where the cope-bearers circulate not only in the choir but also in part of the nave, as one can also see at St-Herbland in Rouen. They apparently do this to support the chanting and correct those who falter, as well as to quiet those who chatter. Perhaps this is the reason cantors carry staves in hand. For in Le Puy-en-Velay and the church of St-Chaffre (*sancti Theofredi*), a Benedictine abbey in the diocese of Le Puy, the cantor's staff is but a small rod with which the cantors used to hit people who were chattering, immodest, or singing badly or too fast.

The Carthusians

In the Charterhouse of Dijon, the Gospel lectern is a very large brass column topped by a phoenix. Around it are the four animals from Ezechiel's vision, which serve as four pulpits, and it is rotated depending on which Gospel is said. Facing this, on the Epistle side, is an old, large, and magnificently carved seat for the celebrant to sit upon during the Epistle.

Church of Saint-Seine

The abbey church of St-Seine belongs to the order of St. Benedict. There is no retable above the high altar, but only a gradine and six candlesticks. Above them is a crucifix over eight feet tall, beneath which a pyx containing the Blessed Sacrament is suspended. On the sides of the altar are four brass columns and four brass angels holding candlesticks, as well as large curtains. On the left side of the high altar is the mausoleum of William of Vienne, abbot of St-Seine and later archbishop of Rouen. At the east end of the choir there is a large chandelier with seven branches, like that of Bourges.

AUXERRE

AUXERRE is an episcopal city on the river Yonne, *Autissiodorum ad Icaunam* in Latin.

Cathedral of Saint-Étienne

In the cathedral of St-Étienne the *Gloria in excelsis* is sung all the way through by both sides of the choir together, as in Lyon and among the Carthusians. The subdeacon goes behind the altar with the Epistle book, and only leaves to sing the Epistle in the rood loft. Having returned the book to the altar boy accompanying him, he takes the chalice, which is covered only by a pall with no veil, and pours in the wine. He takes it to the side of the altar with the cruet of water, which he pours into the chalice once it has been blessed by the priest. Then he takes the chalice back to the credence and covers it only with the pall.

The Gradual is doubled like the Introit, that is to say, after the verse the first part of the Gradual is repeated. The ancients, therefore, called the Gradual the *Responsorium*.

The deacon always stands at the corner of or to the side of the altar, facing the celebrant in profile, until he has presented the incense and asked for the blessing, whereupon he goes up to the rood loft to read the Gospel. He is preceded by a choirboy carrying a two-and-a-half foot long veil to cover the pulpit upon which the book is placed; by two candle-bearers; and the crucifer. Behind them walk the thurifer, subdeacon, and deacon holding the Gospel book very high. They mount the rood loft in that order and the Gospel is sung near the middle facing north. Everyone else faces the Gospel except at the *Gloria tibi Domine*, when they turn back towards the altar.

When there is no *Credo*, the subdeacon prepares the offertory in advance to save time, as mentioned above, something not written in the *ordo*.

Having presented the Gospel book to the celebrant and deacon to kiss, the subdeacon goes to the credence to fetch the chalice and paten, which are already prepared and covered only with a pall. He holds them raised fairly high, preceded by the two candle-bearers and followed by the thurifer choirboy, who incenses continually. They pass behind the altar from the Epistle side to the Gospel side to the middle of the altar, facing the choir.

After the priest has incensed the altar, the deacon continues the incensation behind the altar. He incenses the choir with three swings and then the two relic chests and sacred vessels in the two aisles, also with three swings.

The deacon and subdeacon close the curtains at the *Pater*, having drawn them open at the *Sanctus*.

After the *Pater*, they sing the psalm *Laetatus sum* or *Ad te levavi oculos meos*,[1] and the celebrant, kneeling with his ministers, says the orations for peace and for the king.

The celebrant does not give a blessing nor read the last Gospel at the altar.

Here are some more practices proper to the church of Auxerre:

They do not veil small crucifixes during Lent.

During Lent, beginning on Ash Wednesday, they say the Preface of Lent *Qui Quadragesimali jejunio* except on Sundays and feasts, when they say the common *per annum* Preface, as was done everywhere not a hundred years ago, and as is still done in Sens.[2]

On Good Friday and Holy Saturday, the minor hours are said privately, and also Vespers of Good Friday: each says them to himself in choir in silence.

On Rogation Monday, if there is no occurring feast, the Mass of the preceding Sunday is said with white vestments before the procession. Then at the station they sing the Mass *Exaudivit* in violet vestments, which makes perfect sense.

---

[1] Psalms 121 and 122 respectively.
[2] See p. 223.

At the end of the first Mass of Christmas, said at night, the deacon sings the antiphon *Ecce completa sunt*[3] instead of *Ite, missa est*, as used to be done in Rouen. At the end of the third Mass, at Low Masses they say the Gospel *Missus est*, as on Ember Wednesday of Advent, instead of *In principio*. At all three Masses of Christmas they still say a prophecy in addition to the Epistle, as used to be done everywhere.

On All Souls, after Lauds, the commemoration of the octave of All Saints is said privately.[4]

The first Council of Auxerre, held in 578, prohibited abbots and monks from being children's godfathers at baptism.[5] It also ordered that women should no longer receive the Holy Eucharist with bare hands, but with hands covered by a veil called the *dominical*.[6] From this practice later arose the use of communion cloths by both sexes.

According to the latest diocesan statutes and the ordinance of the councils of this province, betrothals take place before the publication of marriage banns, as in the diocese of Chartres.

In a four-hundred-year-old manuscript missal of Auxerre, we find that on 6 August there was a blessing for new grapes in the Mass of St. Sixtus. Between the Secret and Postcommunion, as in the new ritual of Reims, p. 446, one finds:

> Uvae a sacerdote benedicendae sunt antequam dicatur *Per quem haec omnia*. Benedictio: *Benedic, Domine, et hos fructus novos uvae, quos tu, Domine, rore coeli et inundantia pluviarum et temporum serenitate atque tranquillitate ad maturitatem perducere dignatus es; et dedisti ea ad usus nostros cum gratiarum actione percipere in nomine Domini Jesu Christi. Per quem haec omnia, etc.*[7]

The same manuscript states that in nuptial Masses, after the priest had said the *Libera nos* and broken the host into three pieces, he covered them with the paten, recited the oration *Propitiare*, and gave the blessing in the form of a Preface. Then it reads: *Per Dominum nostrum Jesum Christum filium tuum. His dictis aspergat eos [sponsum et sponsam] Sacerdos aqua benedicta, et signet eos.* That is, he blessed them by making a sign of the cross over them, as the priest does every day over the people at the end of Mass. *Tunc surgant sponsus et sponsa. Tunc Sacerdos accipiat Eucharistiam, dicat*

---

[3] Cantus ID 002498.
[4] John of Avranches, *Liber de officiis ecclesiasticis*, ed. Le Brun des Marettes (PL 147:41B).
[5] Canon 25, in *Concilia Galliae a. 511–695*, ed. de Clerq, 268.
[6] Canons 36–37, in *Concilia Galliae a. 511–695*, ed. de Clerq, 269.
[7] "The grapes should be blessed by the priest before he says *Per quem haec omnia*. Blessing: Bless too, O Lord, these new fruits of the grape, which thou, O Lord, hast with dew of heaven, deluge of rains, and clement and mild weather deigned to bring to maturity, and given them for us to receive with thanksgiving for our uses, in the name of Our Lord Jesus Christ. *Per quem haec omnia*, etc." See *Missale Antissiodorense* (14 c.), Paris, Bibliothèque nationale, MS lat. 17316, 235rv; and *Missale ad usum Autissiodorensis ecclesiae* (ca. 1250), Auxerre, Bibliothèque Jacques Lacarrière, MS 51, 474v.

alta voce Pax Domini sit semper vobiscum, *etc. usque ad Communionem*.[8]

The manuscript also reports that, in the Litany of the Saints, in place of the *Agnus Dei*, they said three times *Agne Dei qui tollis, etc*. It says too that a choirboy said the *Accendite* three times in mid-choir, raising his voice each time; I mean between each *Agne Dei*, with which the third litany of Holy Saturday and the vigil of Pentecost concluded.[9]

---

[8] "Then let the bridegroom and bride rise. Then let the priest take the Eucharist and say aloud *Pax Domini sit semper vobiscum* and the rest until communion."
[9] On the *Accendite* on the vigils of Easter and Pentecost, see p. 67, n. 17.

SENS

SENS, in Latin *Senonae*, at the confluence of the Vanne and the Yonne, *ad confluentes Vennae et Icaunae*.

Cathedral of Saint-Étienne

In the cathedral of St-Étienne, across from the high altar on the Epistle side, there is a large, long, and very beautiful bench of five seats, each one set lower than the previous. The first, which is the highest, is for the celebrant, and the others for the deacons and subdeacons. Immediately to the west stands the archbishop's throne, which is quite beautiful with well-crafted woodwork.

Above the altar there is a retable usually covered with a dossel matching the antependium; above that, there are two candles and a very large crucifix, below which is a small crosier-shaped fixture with the holy pyx suspended beneath a small canopy. There are four brass columns with angels on top, and large riddels between them.

An eagle stands in the middle of the choir. At the west end is a two-part rood screen, like those in Milan and St-Gervais in Paris,[1] with no loft extending over the great rood gate, which is very wide and allows for a clear view of everything that takes place at the altar and in choir.

Immediately west of the choir is the crossing, with the parish on its right side.

The lower-form canon-clerics wear the almuce as in Rouen (see PLATE 28 for a depiction of an almuce). Under their alb, the eight choirboys wear a red cassock with a four finger-breadth train at the back, and remain bareheaded inside the church and on their way to and from it. The lower-form canons wear a biretta outside the church.

---

[1] On this type of *jubé*, see Jean-Baptiste Thiers, "Dissertation sur les jubés" in *Dissertations ecclésiastiques* (Paris, 1688), 11–12.

Those who sing the lessons at Matins perform the *ante et retro* inclination.² The canons sing the antiphons at Matins, and the choirboys at Lauds.

The hoods of the copes are not round but rather pointed, like most of those in the cathedral of Rouen (see PLATE 26).³

In Sens, the minor hours are not said one after the other, but separated. Prime is said at eight in the morning, Terce at nine before the high Mass, and Sext thereafter, with a quarter of an hour's interval between None and Vespers.

A good number of the canons assist at these minor hours in addition to the major ones.

Of all the minor hours, Prime is always sung best. They have kept the ancient Office of Prime: on Sundays they say *Magna Prima*, or "Long Prime" (*les grands Primes*), which besides the usual psalms also includes the six psalms that were later assigned to Prime of each week day. They also always say the *Quicumque* at Prime, as used to be done in all the churches of France not a hundred years ago.⁴

A deacon and subdeacon prepare the altar immediately before Mass every day, as prescribed in the Cistercian *Liber usuum*.

On Sunday, the water is blessed on the north side, facing east. The aspersion is done in the following way:

After the oration, the celebrant kneels before the high altar and sprinkles it with three strokes. The cantor on semidoubles and the precentor on doubles and above begin the antiphon *Asperges me*, which is taken up by the choir. Following the antiphon two choirs sing psalm 50, *Miserere*, in alternation, according to the mode of the antiphon, as one would do at Lauds. When they reach the verse *Asperges me*, they sing it in plainchant like the antiphon. Meanwhile, the celebrant, having sprinkled and kissed the altar with an inclination, goes behind the altar of St. Peter, above which the relics are reserved, sprinkles it while standing, and kisses it. Then he sprinkles the back of the crucifix of the high altar, which is full of relics. After that, he goes down the three steps of St. Peter's altar, and sprinkles the relics with three strokes. The celebrant then genuflects on one knee on the lowermost step of the sanctuary to sprinkle the processional cross and then, standing, the candle-bearers who have lined up there. Since only archbishops are buried in their choir, he sprinkles the first tomb, then the subdeacon standing at its foot with the Gospel book; then the two other archbishops' tombs up to the eagle, each with a single stroke and a small inclination. After that he sprinkles another tomb to the west of the eagle, the deacon standing at its foot, and the other tombs up to the choir's great gate. Then the eldest member of choir, whether he be a dignitary or canon,

---

² See p. 83, n. 2.
³ On the evolution of copes, see p. 61, n. 3.
⁴ Author's note: This changed with the new breviary of 1702.

presents himself at the west end of the stalls and the celebrant, *in plano*, sprinkles him with three strokes before giving him the aspergill. The elder then sprinkles the celebrant with three strokes; the celebrant bows a little while receiving the holy water. The celebrant thereafter goes to stand at the position of the deacon, who moves a bit to the left and remains there until the end of the aspersion. The elder sprinkles the laymen he sees at the gate on his side of the choir, then goes to sprinkle all the canons in the stalls. The lower-formers turn towards the canons and are all sprinkled by the elder as he walks down the central passage of the stalls. When he arrives at the end of the stalls on the right side, he sprinkles the laymen at the south door with two or three strokes if he sees any there. Then he gives the aspergill to the choirboy carrying the holy water bucket *in plano*, and this choirboy, after the usual reverences, goes to give the aspergill to the elder of the left-hand side, who performs the aspersion just as the elder of the right. After this, a choirboy takes the collectary to the celebrant, who says an oration without a preceding versicle.

During the procession, the subdeacon walks behind the cantors, bareheaded and carrying his book. The deacon, if he is a semi-prebendary, covers his head like the celebrant. These two alone cover themselves; the rest of the clergy remains bareheaded. The celebrant and deacon place themselves in the procession more or less according to their rank in choir.

On annual feasts,[5] when the archbishop does not celebrate, the celebrant named as a substitute by the chapter always goes last in the procession, even if he is among the most junior. The deacon walks to his side holding the end of his cope, even though the celebrant does not do anything that would require it. The precentor never carries a staff at first Vespers or at Matins, but only at high Mass and second Vespers.

The cope-bearers begin the Introit standing behind the eagle, repeating it after the psalm verse and again after the *Gloria Patri* a third time.

Upon returning from the procession to the sacristy with his ministers, the celebrant puts on the chasuble, which has a pointed bottom and a y-orphrey, which seems to form a cross in front whose arms go over the shoulders. The deacon puts on a dalmatic and the subdeacon a tunicle with closed sleeves, and all wear appareled amices of the same color that cover the backs of their heads. When the archbishop is not in choir, they say the *Introibo*, the psalm *Judica me*, the *Confiteor, Miseratur, Indulgentiam*, and the rest in the sacristy. Then they leave, preceded by a surpliced acolyte carrying the processional cross and flanked by two candle-bearers. One of them walks before and the other behind him. The subdeacon carries a cushion on his breast and is followed by the deacon, who carries the holy book of the Gospels closed and elevated but slightly tilted. Then goes the celebrant with his hands joined and without biretta; all are bareheaded.

---

[5] See p. 89, n. 3.

When the subdeacon arrives in the middle of the sanctuary, he makes a profound bow to the altar and turns towards the deacon, who places the Gospel book upon the cushion and immediately presents it to the celebrant for him to kiss. Then, making a profound bow to the altar and a medium bow to the choir, the deacon and subdeacon uncover the altar. Meanwhile, the celebrant, kneeling and inclined over the bottommost step of the altar, says the *Aufer a nobis*. Then he goes up to the altar and kisses it in the middle saying *quorum Reliquiae hic sunt*. The subdeacon places the Gospel book on the Epistle side and then, passing behind the altar, returns to the Gospel side, while the deacon remains at the Epistle side. They are always thus positioned at the corners of the altar, a half a foot or so away from it, facing each other, with hands joined and gaze lowered, except when the priest sings something, in which case they stand behind him, and during the offertory and consecration, when the deacon stands next to the priest.

If the archbishop is in choir, he processes behind the cross accompanied by his chaplains to a spot at some distance from the middle of the altar. The celebrant, deacon, and subdeacon position themselves by the side of the altar, with the subdeacon closest to it, then the deacon, and then the celebrant, who is closest to the archbishop and responds to him. After the archbishop has said the *Introibo*, *Judica*, and *Indulgentiam* until the *Aufer a nobis* exclusive, he goes up to the altar and kisses it. Then he returns to choir to the place near the south door that belongs to the precentor, who steps aside to yield it to him. The deacon always says the *Munda* at the Epistle side, and receives the celebrant's blessing while genuflecting. If the archbishop is in choir, the deacon approaches to receive the blessing from him.

The first chorister or cope-bearer begins the *Kyrie* facing the clergy. If it is an annual, semiannual, or double feast, they add the tropes *Fons bonitatis*, *Pater ingenite*, or *Cunctipotens genitor Deus*, or *Clemens rector*, as is still done in Lyon, Soissons, and elsewhere. These tropes gave rise to the long series of notes that remain in the *Kyrie* today, after the removal of these tropes or sort of poems interspersed between *Kyrie* and *eleison*.

The two choirboys leave their candles five or six feet away from the altar steps and go to their places in choir.

The *Gloria in excelsis* and *Credo* are sung in their entirety by both sides of the choir together, as in Lyon, Bourges, Mâcon, Auxerre, and among the Carthusians, rather than in alternation. Thus both sides form but a single choir, "because," as the ritual of Sens explains, "it is a profession of faith that each must say all the way through."[6] This is also the reason they do not play the organ during the *Credo*.[7]

At the verses *Adoramus te* and *suscipe deprecationem nostram* of the

---

[6] *Rituel du diocèse de Sens* (Sens, 1694), 468.
[7] See also pp. 42–43.

Gloria in excelsis, the celebrant, deacon, and subdeacon kneel, while the clergy remain standing facing the altar.

The choirboys hold their candlesticks up during the orations and the Preface.

When the celebrant sits, he occupies the sedile closest to the altar, the deacon the second closest, and the subdeacon the third, each of them set lower than the previous.

As in Lyon, Proses are said in Sens on annual, semiannual, and double feasts and on privileged Sundays. They used to be said at these same times in Paris and Rouen. But one must not regret their loss too much, since most of them were no more than pitiful patchwork affairs; take, for instance, the one that begins *Alle necnon et perenne coeleste luia*.[8]

The deacon, holding the book slightly tilted and genuflecting on his right knee, says *Jube Domne benedicere* in a clear voice. After the celebrant blesses him, he goes up to the rood loft in procession, where he chants the Gospel standing between the two candle-bearers near the middle of the Epistle-side loft, facing north, with the cross before him.

In the churches of the diocese of Sens that lack a rood loft, the Gospel is sung by the main gate of the choir, so it can be heard by people in both choir and nave.

When the celebrant says *Dominus vobiscum* after the Creed, the deacon, preceded by the two candle-bearers and the subdeacon, proceeds to the small altar behind the high altar. Thence he takes the chalice and paten with the host covered only by the pall, without a veil. As in Auxerre, he goes behind the high altar from the Gospel side to the Epistle side. There, the subdeacon pours the water, blessed by the celebrant, into the chalice. Then the deacon presents the paten with the host upon it to the celebrant, who offers it saying *Suscipe sancte Pater*. He then receives the chalice from the deacon and holds it up while the deacon helps support it, and together they say the *Offerimus tibi, Domine, calicem*. Meanwhile, the two candle-bearers kneel at the foot of the altar holding their candlesticks elevated until the *Sanctus*, when they move them five or six feet away from the altar steps.

At the *Pleni sunt coeli* of the *Sanctus*, the clergy kneel until the *Agnus Dei*. Two thurifers followed by two choirboys carrying torches approach the altar and draw back the riddels on either side. They incense at the three elevations, holding the top of the chains with the left hand, and tossing it up and catching it again with the right. This is their usual manner of incensing, as also practiced in Paris.

After the *Pater*, those in choir sing the psalms *Laetatus sum* and *Deus misereatur nostri*,[9] while the clergy remain kneeling. The deacon and subdeacon kneel on the topmost step of the altar behind the celebrant, who

---

[8] Cantus ID ah53097. Actually *Alle coeleste necnon et perenne luia*.
[9] Psalms 121 and 66 respectively.

kneels on a cushion as in Auxerre. Thus kneeling he says the orations for peace, for the king, for the people, and the rest.

After the choirboys have taken the cruets back behind the altar, they come to hold up their candlesticks during the Postcommunions. When these are over, the celebrant turns with the deacon and subdeacon towards the north while the deacon says *Ite, missa est*. The choir responds *Deo gratias*, and the celebrant, without giving a blessing, makes a profound bow at the bottom of the altar with the deacon and subdeacon. Then, preceded by the cross and candle-bearers, they return to the sacristy in the same order in which they came. The subdeacon carries the missal and its small cushion-rest, and the deacon the chalice and paten covered by the pall. All are bareheaded. If the Lord Archbishop is present, he gives the blessing saying *Adjutorium* and the rest.

The choirboys do not take holy water when they leave the church, but only when they enter, and justly so.[10]

In Sens, there are sixteen parish priests, thirteen of whom are called, as in Angers and Troyes, *presbyteri cardinales* or "cardinal-priests" (*prêtres-cardinaux*), and who assist the bishop at solemn Mass. The late Lord Louis-Henri de Pardaillan de Gondrin, archbishop of Sens,[11] always had them with him at the altar when he celebrated Mass pontifically on major feasts in his cathedral. Today they no longer assist except on the two feasts of St. Stephen, the cathedral's patron; at the Dedication of the cathedral; and on Maundy Thursday for the holy oils. These parish priests are called "cardinals" not without reason. The name comes from the fact that they used to stand by the corners of the altar, as they still do in Sens and Lyon, *ad cardines altaris* or *in cardine altaris*, in French, at the *carnes* of the altar.[12] And so they were "priests of the *carne*" and the bishop the "priest of the middle," *Presbyter de medio*. Similarly, the cardinals of the Roman Church, both priests and deacons, stood at the *carne* when the Pope celebrated Mass solemnly.

On major feasts, when the bishop celebrates first and second Vespers, the two canons who rule the choir together with the cantor and the lower

---

[10] See p. 264–65.
[11] Reigned 1620–1674.
[12] Author's note: "*Carne* is a French word synonymous with 'corner' or 'angle.' M. Châtelain even believes that a hinge is called a *cardo* in Latin because it is at the *carne* of the door." Claude de Vert may have been the first to make this claim about the origin of the term "cardinal," which he discusses in his *Explication*, 1:56–57. The question of this word's etymology was much debated in the sixteenth and seventeenth centuries. For a thorough study of its actual origins, see Stephan Kuttner, "*Cardinalis*: The History of a Canonical Concept," *Traditio* 3 (1945): 129–214. According to Kuttner, the term underwent several semantic shifts since it was originally used by St. Gregory the Great. Outside Rome, it was first applied in the ninth century to distinguish the clergy under the bishop's control, particularly those attached to the cathedral, from the rural clergy under feudal dependance to secular lords. Around the twelfth century, the title began to be restricted to a small number of priests who had certain liturgical privileges that imitated those of the cardinal-priests in Rome (165–70).

choir go to the treasury to escort the bishop in his pontificals. After greeting him, the cantor intones a responsory appropriate for the feast, which is called the *in deductione Episcopi*, and they lead the bishop into choir through the south door. They do the same at second Vespers, except that the precentor also participates and it is he who intones the responsory. When the Lord Archbishop celebrates high Mass pontifically, he gives the solemn blessing before the *Agnus Dei*, and gives no blessing at the end of the Mass. At Vespers those who incensed the choir then go to incense the people and perfume the church.

On Christmas the last bell for Matins rings at midnight. After the ninth responsory they sing the Genealogy[13] and the *Te Deum*. Then the archbishop goes to the Lady Chapel with all the clergy to sing the Mass *ad galli cantum*. Lauds are incorporated into Mass, without the priestly versicle,[14] *Deus in adjutorium*, chapter, or hymn, as is done in Vienne, Paris, Orléans, and elsewhere. Then the clergy goes to another chapel to sing the dawn Mass, which is celebrated by the Lord Dean. All the clergy participate in the offertory procession at the first Mass, which is less solemn than the one after Terce. However, the clergy receive communion at the third Mass, which is also celebrated by the archbishop. Thus, these three Masses are said at three different altars, because in the cathedral of Sens Masses are never said twice in a single day at the high altar, in accordance with the prohibition issued by the council held in Auxerre, a city in the same province, in 578.[15]

On Ash Wednesday, a parish priest from the vicinity used to bring the cilice to the cathedral for the procession of public penitents to the cathedral. Still today, the parish priest of St-Martin, a half-league from Sens, brings the ashes near the preacher's pulpit, where they are blessed. After the sermon, the theologian announces, on the archbishop's behalf, the dispensation to eat milk, butter, and cheese.[16] The ashes are blessed next to the pulpit, and it is there that the theologian distributes them. Thereafter, the entire clergy goes in procession to the church's main door. This is still called the procession of the penitents, a sign that it once involved driving out the public penitents, and perhaps also the imposition of ashes on them. In the collegiate churches of Avallon in the diocese of Autun and Jargeau in the diocese of Orléans, the ashes are distributed at the church door on Ash

---

[13] See also p. 16.
[14] See p. 16.
[15] Canon 10, in *Concilia Galliae a. 511–695*, ed. de Clerq, 266.
[16] The prohibition against consuming milkmeats during Lent began to wane in France during the fifteenth century; in Rouen it was Pope Innocent VIII who granted a dispensation, as Le Brun des Marettes notes on pp. 263–64. In his twentieth letter to Étienne Baluze, dated 30 March 1718, Le Brun des Marettes writes that it was usual for the bishop of Orléans to permit the consumption of eggs during Lent on account of the high cost of fish, but that he had forgone doing so that year, and quips, "This just means that there are more liars [this year], who eat not only eggs but even meat" (Nouaillac, *Lettres inédites*, 30).

Wednesday, and in Avallon they are only given to the public penitents. In Beauvais, the ashes are blessed and distributed not only on Ash Wednesday, but also every Friday in Lent.

In Sens, the common *per annum* Preface is said on Sundays of Lent. The color red is used during the fortnight of Passiontide, and on ferias of Advent and Lent they kneel at the psalm *Venite exultemus* at Matins.

At high Mass on Maundy Thursday, the archbishop is accompanied by two canons in priestly vestments who say everything with him and perform the same ceremonies as he. They even recite the words of consecration with him, over both the bread and the chalice, and make the signs of the cross. Nevertheless, they do not receive communion under both species, but kneeling receive two small hosts, as in priestly ordinations. At the blessing of holy oils, besides the archbishop and these two canons, there are thirteen cardinal-priests who stand at the corners or ends of the altar. There were originally only twelve, as one gathers from this 1517 statute: *Quando Archiepiscopus celebrat in Annualibus, debent assitere sibi duodecim Presbyteri Cardinales induti sacerdotalibus indumentis; ac etiam Feria quinta in Coena Domini, cum duodecim Decanis indutis sacerdotalibus sive infulis.*[17]

On the feast of St. Thomas of Canterbury, they use St. Thomas's old chasuble, which is not clipped but ample and hangs down all around like a mantle.

At the Mass *ex praesanctificatis* on Good Friday, they use an old chasuble that is similarly unclipped. On this day, they show the host immediately before the words *panem nostrum*, and the *Libera nos, quaesumus Domine* is sung aloud, as in Rouen, Rome, and almost everywhere.

At bishops' funerals and on their anniversaries, they place a large long table in choir upon which they set four chalices filled with wine, and on top of them four patens with hosts. At the offertory, the two canons assigned to the treasury present these four chalices with candles to the four chief dignitaries, who bring them to the celebrant at the altar. The celebrant keeps the first chalice and paten prepared with bread and wine for the sacrifice.

The suffragan bishops still swear an oath of obedience to the archbishop of Sens.

The weekly hebdomadary was required to always be in church dress, except for the surplice, and could not leave the cloister, in accordance with the custom and statutes of the chapter of Sens. Hence he never wore a

---

[17] "When the archbishop celebrates on annual feasts, twelve cardinal-priests must assist him dressed in priestly vestments, and likewise on Maundy Thursday, with twelve deans vested in priestly vestments and garb." The eight volumes of cartularies once preserved in the archives of the cathedral chapter of Sens were lost in the Revolution, and the single surviving Sens cartulary kept today in the Bibliothèque national de France dates from 1462. Nevertheless, the *Livre du préchantre de la cathédrale de Sens* (Sens, Bibliothèque municipal, MS. 6), written around 1250, contains a very similar stipulation, except that it reads *duodecim decani induti sacerdotalibus absque infulis*, i.e., the twelve deans wore priestly vestments except for the chasuble (Eugène Chartaire, ed., *Cartulaire du chapitre de Sens* [Duchemin, 1904], 168).

mantle or hat, which were used only to go into town. He performed his weeklong duty in this state of retirement in order to be better united to God, *quia medius est et sequester inter Deum et populum*,[18] as one of the chapter statutes explains.

In the cathedral, they sing several of the most essential phrases in responsories and antiphons very slowly, as for instance the words *Fera pessima devoravit eum*.[19] This custom is expressed in their books in these terms: *cum bona prolatione et mensura*.[20]

Even today, in Sens, the *Quoniam in aeternum misericordia ejus* is not repeated at each verse of psalm 135, *Confitemini*, at Thursday Vespers. It is also omitted in Vienne, St-Martin of Tours, and Cluny, and absent from the breviaries of Lyon, Rouen, Paris, Autun, and Auxerre prior to the last century. It was only added to the breviary of Chartres in 1634 to conform to the Roman breviary. But since the church of Rome has not yet added *laudate et superexaltate eum in saecula* to each verse of the canticle *Benedicite* (Daniel 3) at Sunday Lauds, no church, to my knowledge, has yet thought to include it, so as to remain in conformity with the Roman use, even though the phrase is actually found in the Bible.

The 1694 ritual of Sens prohibits the exorcisms when the ceremonies of baptism are supplied to an infant in danger of death, stating:

> After a name has been given him, the priest shall omit the exorcisms, in conformity with the ancient rituals of this diocese, since it does not appear necessary to expel the devil from the soul of an infant wherein the Holy Ghost dwells, and who has been made a son of God and member of Jesus Christ through spiritual regeneration. The priest shall not, however, omit the renunciations of the devil, since they do not imply that the devil remains in the soul, but simply the resolution not to suffer him there again after he has been expelled. It is also necessary to supply the anointings.[21]

The 1509 ritual of Mechlin, the synodal statutes of the Lord Bishop of Meaux,[22] and those of Angers and Grenoble, similarly order that the exorcisms be omitted when the ceremonies of baptism are supplied to an already-baptized infant.[23] As for the very practice of supplying these

---

[18] "He is the middleman and intermediary between God and people."
[19] "An evil beast hath devoured him" (Genesis 37:20), said in the responsory *Videns Jacob* of the third Sunday of Lent (Cantus ID 007858).
[20] "With proper pronunciation and measure."
[21] *Rituel du diocèse de Sens* (Sens, 1694), 36.
[22] Jacques-Bénigne Bossuet, in the synodal ordinances of 1691, §16, in *Œuvres complètes de Bossuet* (Paris, 1863), 11:605.
[23] The question of whether to perform exorcisms when supplying the ceremonies of baptism arose in the post-Reformation period with regard to the reconciliation of Protestant heretics. One party argued that an exorcism was superfluous for a soul already redeemed from the devil; others, following St. Thomas, insisted that the ceremonies should be supplied in their integrity and were useful for diminishing the devil's power over the will. Although Gregory XIII determined the exorcisms must be supplied, several

ceremonies, it is not found in the Eastern church or even in the Western church, whether in general or local councils, before the end of the twelfth century.

Sacrosancta concilia (Philippe Labbe and Gabriel Cossart, eds. [Paris, 1671]), vol. 10, col. 1802B, constitutions of Odo, bishop of Paris, ch. 3, n. 1: *Doceant frequenter laïcos baptizare pueros in necessitate: et post inundationem, ea facient sacerdotes pueris quae solent fieri* POST *immersionem.*[24]

Sacrosancta concilia, vol. 9, col. 14E, Council of London, held in 1200, ch. 3: *Si vero in necessitate puer baptizetur a laïco; sequentia immersionem, non praecedentia, per sacerdotem expleantur.*[25]

One reads the same in *ibid.*, col. 545C, in the synodal statutes of an anonymous bishop in 1237, and the same in *ibid.*, col. IIIIC, in the Council of Cologne held in 1280, ch. 4: *Item Sacerdos, ad quem infans in necessitate baptizatus deferendus est...faciat ei quae post baptismum fieri consueverunt.*[26]

Ibid., col. 1202C, Synod of Nîmes, held in 1284: *Sacerdos infantem...non rebaptizet, nec faciat catechismum, sed inungat eum in pectore, inter scapulas et in vertice, dicendo orationes quae dicuntur* POST *baptismum.*[27]

Ibid., col. 1266D, Synod of Exeter, held in 1287, ch. 2: *Si postea convaluerit...non ipsa submersio, nec ipsa praecedentia, sed subsequentia duntaxat per sacerdotem, ut convenit, suppleantur.*[28]

Ibid., col. 1450E, Synod of Bayeux, held in 1300, ch. 4: *Suppleatur quod deest...exorcismi tamen non dicantur.*[29]

All of this is in agreement with the ritual of Sens. The same ritual, on p. 158, orders that, in accordance with the ancient custom of the church, the bodies of both clerics and laymen should be buried facing east, with their feet toward the altar.[30]

A bit beyond the abbey of St-Pierre-le-Vif, there is a place called the Arênes, under which there are still caves or underground chambers a bit like those in Doué-en-Anjou.[31]

---

uses still refused to admit them at all, while other ecclesiastical authorities ordered them to be omitted when reconciling heretics in particular. See Corblet, *Histoire dogmatique*, 1:476–78.

[24] "Let [priests] often instruct the laity to baptize their infants in case of emergency, and *after* the pouring of water, priests will perform those things that are usually done after the immersion."

[25] "But if a child is baptized by a layman in an emergency, let the priest supply what follows the immersion, and not what precedes it."

[26] "Likewise the priest to whom the infant who has been baptized in an emergency is to be brought...should perform for him the things that are customarily done after baptism."

[27] "The priest should not rebaptize the infant, nor do the catechism, but anoint him on the breast, between the shoulders, and on the crown of the head, saying those prayers that are said *after* baptism."

[28] "If [the child] should later recover...let the priest not supply the submersion, nor what precedes it, but rather, as is fitting, what follows."

[29] "Let what is lacking be supplied...but the exorcisms not be said."

[30] See also p. 197.

[31] See p. 82.

REIMS

REIMS in Champagne, on the river Vesle, *Remi ad Vidulam* in Latin.

Cathedral of Notre-Dame

The cathedral of Notre-Dame is very large. Its exterior is remarkably beautiful, and its Gothic portal is considered the finest in France. It depicts St. Paul on the right side and St. Peter on the left, which used to be regarded as the place of higher honor. It is in this church that the archbishop of Reims, first duke and peer of France, anoints our kings. One can still see its exceptionally large apse, at the back of which stands the ancient episcopal throne, with seats around the apse for the priests and deacons. The archbishop never sits there today, however. (For the rood screen, see PLATE 27.)

In Reims, feasts are ranked by the number of candlesticks or candles, as in St-Martin of Tours: *Festum III* or *V* or *VII cereorum*.

At solemn Masses in the cathedral, the priest says the psalm *Judica* and the *Confiteor* in the sacristy. Then, when he reaches the large area between choir and the altar, which some call the *solea* and others the *peribolum*, he first makes a reverence to the altar and then turns towards the choir to ask the prayers of those present saying *Orate pro me, fratres, et ego pro vobis. Pax vobis.*[1] Immediately afterwards he goes straight toward the altar and says the prayer *Aufer a nobis* while making a profound bow on the first step. Then he mounts to the altar and kisses it. Thereafter he goes to his chair by the altar where he remains until the offertory, reading everything from the beginning up to the Secret upon a small lectern. As in Laon, he reads the Postcommunion on the same lectern.

The deacons and subdeacons wash their hands during the Preface.

At the end of the Mass, the priest recites the Gospel *In principio* as he returns to the sacristy.

They hold a long reading every day before Compline, like the Benedictines and as used to be done in Rouen and Vienne.

On Holy Saturday, they attach to the Paschal candle a Paschal table similar to the one in Rouen, which we shall describe hereafter.[2]

On Easter day and during the week they begin Vespers with *Kyrie eleïson*.

On Rogation days, they have a dry Mass, that is, a Mass of the Catechumens, at each of the station churches. It consists of an Epistle, Gradual, and Gospel, and nothing further.

On the feast of the Transfiguration, they bless new grapes during the

---

[1] "Pray for me, brethren, and I for you. Peace to you."
[2] See pp. 225–28.

Canon of the Mass immediately before the *Per quem haec omnia*. See our explanation of this practice in the chapter on Orléans.[3]

In an old ritual of Reims, dated 1585, one sees that it was the custom in several parts of the diocese to wrap the priest's stole around the bride and bridegroom on their wedding day as a symbol of their union. This practice was only abrogated with the new ritual of Reims in 1677. The 1687 ritual of Milan states that during the celebration of marriage, after the two parties consent, the parish priest takes the bridegroom's right hand and places it on the bride's right hand as a sign of their marital union and conjugal fidelity. Over their joined hands, he places the two ends of his stole, crossed in the shape of a cross or tie. An old missal of Béziers and one of Narbonne state that, during the blessing prayer over the married couple before the *Agnus Dei*, the priest wrapped his stole around their neck and shoulders, as if to bind them together. And a slightly later ritual of Béziers, dated 1535, indicates that the stole was placed on their heads, a practice that gave rise to the veil placed over the head and shoulders. It must also be noted, however, that this blessing prayer used to be said only after the fraction of the host and immediately before the *Pax Domini sit semper vobiscum*. It appears in this position in the missals of Béziers and Narbonne mentioned above, as well as in a four-hundred-year-old manuscript missal of Auxerre, in the 1519 missal of Vienne, the 1504 missal of Orléans, the 1530 missal of Lyon, the 1530 missal of Autun, and in the 1526 ritual of Paris, the 1581 ritual of Orléans, the 1593 ritual of Autun, the 1604 ritual of Chartres, and the 1694 ritual of Sens. The *Libera nos, quaesumus Domine* is a continuation of the *Pater* and should not be separated from it.

The new ritual of Reims of 1677 ordains that, following ancient custom, priests are to be buried in the same manner as laymen, with their heads towards the door or west end of the church and their feet towards the altar. One can see bishops, abbots, and priests in ancient mausolea and tombs laid out in this manner.

---

[3] See pp. 146–48.

LAON

LAON, in Latin *Laudunum*, and formerly *Lugdunum Clavatum* or sometimes simply *Lugdunum*, a city in Picardy. Its bishop is a duke and peer of France. The cathedral of Notre-Dame is served by eighty-four canons and four dignitaries. Here are the peculiar rites of this church:

The hebdomadaries begin their week with the blessing of holy water, which the priest performs in the middle of the choir facing north, as in Rouen.

In the procession, they carry the holy water stoup before the crucifix, sprinkling everyone they pass in order to purify them, as the ordinary states: *ut ejus aspersione obvius quisque purificetur, dum se per viam supplicantibus voluerit adjungere.*

The Introit is repeated thrice on solemn feasts, as used to be done in Rouen, to provide enough time for the people to enter and assemble in the church, and for the bishop and all his assistants to reach the altar.

The celebrant reads the Epistle, Gradual, Gospel, and Postcommunion in the sanctuary, near to but not at the altar itself.

The Epistle is sung in the middle of the rood loft facing the altar, as in Paris, Rouen, Orléans, and elsewhere.

The Offertory sometimes has several verses, as in Lyon.

After the celebrant incenses the altar, the deacon incenses other places, and the thurifer the choir.

At the elevation of the host, they ring some bells to admonish absent faithful to adore God in spirit and in truth.

The deacon sings the *Ite, missa est* facing north.

When the bishop takes possession of his cathedral, he goes barefoot from the church of St-Michel to the cathedral, accompanied by monks and canons walking before him. When he reaches the cathedral, he is led to the chapterhouse, where he is made to swear an oath to uphold the privileges and exemptions of the chapter. Then he takes his seat in choir.

At high Mass on solemn feasts, there are seven deacons, seven subdeacons, two priests, two thurifers, and two candle-bearers.

The bishop kisses the ministers after the *Confiteor*, as well as the altar and the Gospel book.

The bishop pays those who sing *Christus vincit*, the Gradual, the Epistle, and the Gospel, just after they have sung it.

The bishop gives the solemn blessing between the Gospel and the Creed. It used to be given after the sermon.

It is the acolytes who carry the vials of holy oils on Maundy Thursday. Twelve priests attend the consecration of these oils.

On Thursday in Holy Week, the Maundy is held in the cathedral's chapterhouse. There is a thurifer, candle-bearers, and crucifer, and the deacon incenses the Gospel book as during Mass. After the chanting of the Gospel, the dean or someone else preaches. Meanwhile, the deacon, subdeacon, and other ministers, together with the cross- and candle-bearers, pass through mid-choir to the sacristy to remove their vestments. Then they return to the chapterhouse for the Maundy. It must be noted that during this ceremony they only pour water over the outside of the right hand, which the hebdomadary then dries and kisses, and the parish priest of St-Remi offers each a cup of wine. They then recite the versicle and oration and go to choir to say Compline *submissa voce.*

On Holy Saturday, they read the prophecies at the pulpit. Two acolytes wearing albs and white copes bring up the holy oils covered by a veil hanging from their neck, while two thurifers incense them continually.

Two priests, two deacons, and two subdeacons, all canons, wear copes of the same color. At the litany, one of the priests begins by singing a verse, which each of the six repeats in turn. After all of them have sung it, the choir repeats it once more. Hence this is called the *litania septena*, because each verse is said seven times. Then they sing the *litania quina*, and at the verse *Sancta Dei Genitrix* the procession begins. The bearer of the holy water stoup goes first, followed by two thurifers, two candle-bearers, the crucifer, the two acolytes carrying the vials of oil and chrism, the two deacons, two subdeacons, two cantors, the other members of choir, and finally the celebrant, flanked by two acolytes each carrying a Paschal candle. During the blessing of the font, the celebrant, deacon, subdeacon, and all who carry something face east.

On Easter day, those who put on a cope for the procession do not remove it till after the Gospel.

In the procession to the font at Vespers, held in memory of baptism and the newly-baptized, the celebrant and other ministers face east. As they go they sing the psalm *Laudate pueri Dominum* and *In exitu* on their return.[1]

As used to be done in Orléans, in all the Rogation processions, they carry the two banners that they customarily carry in all processions during Eastertide: one with a dragon and the other with an eagle or cock. They cannot provide an explanation for this. Perhaps the animals are hieroglyphic: the dragon might symbolize the serpent vanquished by Our Lady, patroness of the cathedral, mentioned in Genesis 3:15, *Ipsa conteret caput tuum*,[2] and the cock might represent either some collegiate church dedicated to St. Peter or the entire clergy, whose head is St. Peter. See Orléans.[3] During these processions, stations are held in seven different churches, where they say the seven penitential psalms and the preces, the long series of prayers recited after the Litany of the Saints.

All the priests of the clergy participate in the Corpus Christi procession. They carry torches and flambeaux before the cross, and the confraternity members walk first of all.

At the Candlemas procession, seventeen large feudatory candles are carried before the clergy.[4]

---

[1] Psalms 112 and 113 respectively.
[2] "She shall crush thy head."
[3] See pp. 144–45.
[4] Every year on Candlemas, the chapter's judicial officers summoned the seventeen holders of fiefs from Notre-Dame of Laon to present their candles. Each was obliged to offer one of a specific weight, ranging from the forty-seven-pound candle offered by the chapter for the land of Barenton-Cel to the seventeen-pound candle presented by

At funerals all the clergy accompany the body as it is carried to its grave.

The *Confiteor* at Prime and Compline is said toward the bishop or in his absence toward the dean, or if both are absent toward the celebrant.

Pope Urban IV, who instituted the feast of Corpus Christi, used to be a canon and archdeacon of the cathedral of Laon.

---

the Cistercian abbey of Foigny; the demesne gave a sum of forty-five pounds in place of a candle. If any fief-holder was absent from the roll call, a bailiff cried out *Contumace* and judgment was issued against him. The king of France himself was one of these vassals, holding the county of La Fère, but around 1780 the royal procurator took offense at such irreverence and, when the king's name was called, protested aloud and threatened to appeal for abuse. Thenceforth the king of France ceased being numbered among the seventeen vassals. For more details, see Maximilien Melleville, *Histoire de la ville de Laon et de ses institutions* (Laon, 1846), 1:191–92. A similar custom existed in Orléans; see p. 134.

MEAUX

MEAUX, in Latin *Meldi ad Matronam*, an episcopal city on the river Marne, and capital of the Brie. To my knowledge, they have no peculiar liturgical customs, except that there is an episcopal blessing before the *Agnus Dei* when the bishop celebrates solemn Mass on major feasts.

The two sides of choir sing the Creed together.

The celebrant recites the last Gospel on his way to the sacristy.

SAINT-MAUR-DES-FOSSÉS

ST-MAUR-DES-FOSSÉS, formerly a renowned Benedictine abbey, at present a collegiate church of secular canons situated two leagues from Paris. The Blessed Sacrament is reserved in a hanging golden dove instead of a pyx, as was once the custom at Cluny and several other places. This practice is very ancient.

ÉTAMPES

ÉTAMPES on the river Juine, *Stampae ad Junnam*. At the Franciscan church the holy water font is outside the door, like that of the Dominicans of Le Mans, and not inside the church. The outside is indeed is the proper place for fonts.

ORLÉANS

ORLÉANS, *Aureliani ad Ligerim*, on the river Loire, is a large city built in a semicircle on the slope of a hill, beautifully situated, and enjoying a most wholesome climate.

At the entrance of the bridge, at the base of a cross, one finds three bronze statues, one of the Blessed Virgin holding Christ taken down from the cross, with Charles VII, king of France, on one side, and the Maid of Orléans on the other. Everyone knows this great-spirited girl called Joan of Arc, who forced the English to raise the siege of Orléans in 1428 during the reign of Charles VII, who ennobled her and her whole family. On 8 May of every year, in commemoration of this marvelous deliverance, they hold a general procession of thanksgiving.

Cathedral of Sainte-Croix

The cathedral of Ste-Croix is of exquisite craftsmanship. On the jamb of the clock tower, on the right side of the entrance, at about eight feet above the ground, there is a six-hundred-year-old inscription carved into the stone. It is an act of manumission or enfranchisement of a slave named Letbert by his master Albert, who was a vassal or tenant on a farm belonging to the church of Ste-Croix. Here is the inscription:

> Ex beneficio Sanctae Crucis per Johannem episcopum et per Albertum Sanctae Crucis casatum factus est liber Letbertus, teste hac sancta Ecclesia.

Those who have printed *Lembertus* in several books are mistaken and copied one another.[1]

The holy pyx is kept above the high altar within a small brass tower about three feet tall. There are no riddels around the altar. The sanctuary lamp, silver and composed of two or three crowns, hangs over mid-choir, more than twenty paces from the altar. (See PLATES 29 and 30 for illustrations of some of these features.)

When he makes his first solemn entrance and takes possession of his church, the bishop of Orléans frees all prisoners in the prisons of Orléans, sometimes as many as three or four hundred of them, and even up to nine

---

[1] "By the grace of the Holy Cross, John, bishop, and Albert, tenant of Ste-Croix, have manumitted Letbert in the presence of this holy church." François Le Maire, *Histoire et antiquitez de la ville et duché d'Orléans* (Orléans, 1648), 41, is one of the sources that transcribes the name of the freedman as *Lembertus*. Charles Du Fresne Du Cange, "Manumissio," in *Glossarium mediae et infimae latinitatis* (Frankfurt, 1681), 2:417, gives *Lambertus*. The later *Gallia Christiana* (Paris, 1744), 8:1446C–D, confirms the reading *Letbertus*, but the inscription seems no longer extant.

hundred in 1707. Seated in an armchair on a litter, he is carried on the shoulders of four Lords Baron who are feudal vassals of the bishop, aided by their servants.[2]

As vassals of the Lord Bishop of Orléans, these four barons are still obliged to present him each year with four troughs shaped like biers full of wax during the *Magnificat* of first Vespers of the Invention of the Holy Cross and of the Dedication of this church. I shall not amuse myself by recounting the fabulous tradition the people tell about this practice.[3]

From these first Vespers until the following evening, the *Laus perennis* is held in the church, which is to say that there is singing without interruption. The chapters of various churches and monasteries each sing three-nocturn Matins and Lauds in succession, each at the time assigned to them, namely: the cathedral, the canons of Meung, those of Jargeau, those of St-Samson of Orléans—today the Dominicans take the place of the Jesuits who now own this church and its prebends—and the Feuillants of the abbey of St-Mesmin or Micy, two leagues from Orléans.

On the Invention, on Maundy Thursday, and on the Exaltation of the Holy Cross, twelve parish priests in chasubles together with four deacons and four subdeacons in tunicles assist the bishop at Mass. However, these parish priests stand at the corners or the two ends of the altar, about four or five feet away from it, such that they do not perform any functions. I have trouble believing that it has always been the case, because there must be a reason for their being there. See Sens, Chartres, and Paris.[4]

At high Mass, the officiating bishop gives the solemn blessing before the *Agnus Dei*.

In winter, the choirboys of the cathedral church of Orléans wear a camail that descends no lower than the waist over a violet cassock and alb. On episcopal feasts, the dignitaries wear violet cassocks.

On certain double major feasts, a hearse is placed before the sanctuary called the *râtelier* or *onzaine*, because it holds eleven candles that burn during nocturns and Lauds, but not during the other Offices.

Whenever there is an incensation at Lauds and Vespers, the celebrant, having gone to the sacristy to put on a cope, sings the short chapter at the Epistle corner, facing north, resting the book on the altar. Perhaps it is done this way because formerly he stood in the sanctuary like the parish

---

[2] The barons of Sully (created duke-peer in 1606), Chéray-lès-Meung, Aschères, and Rougemont.
[3] The tale went that four barons from the Orléanais had been imprisoned by the paynim after the Battle of Mansurah in St. Louis's first crusade. They commended themselves to God by the merits of the Holy Cross, and were miraculously transported to the cathedral of Orléans. In thanksgiving, they resolved to offer four *gouttières* of wax yearly to the cathedral. The *gouttières* were long and narrow wooden boxes; only the surface was covered with wax. For a study of this ceremony and the popular mythology surrounding it, see Daniel Polluche, *Dissertation sur l'offrande de cire appellée les goutieres* (Orléans, 1734).
[4] See pp. 123, 169, and 181 respectively.

priests of St-Maclou and of St-Vivien of Rouen, and many rural parish priests, and as the Carmelite ordinary indicates in chapter 29;[5] or perhaps, rather, to be there ready for the incensation that used to be done during the responsory and hymn, or at any rate immediately after the short chapter, as is also marked in the old ordinary of Bayeux. When the *Magnificat* begins, the celebrant, who had been sitting on a bench during the responsory, goes to the middle of the altar, where the thurifer presents him with the boat and the thurible. Having imposed incense, he incenses the altar with three swings, then goes to mid-choir to incense the eagle with three swings, namely one for the book on the eagle, and the others for the cope-bearer on each side. At the east end of the choir, *in plano* on the right side, he is incensed by the thurifer standing across from him on the left side. The thurifer then goes to kiss the hem of the cope where it covers his hand, or rather, to kiss his hand that is covered by the hem of the cope. Thereafter the celebrant salutes the choir profoundly from mid-choir before returning to his place beside the altar. Meanwhile the thurifer incenses the canons on both sides of the high stalls as they do in Paris and Sens: holding the top of the chains with his left hand, he tosses the thurible up with his right and catches it again in the same hand. It is noteworthy that when he gets to the end of the stalls, but before reaching the last canon on each side, he stops and ceases incensing for a moment, then incenses the last canon with three swings, because he is one of the principal dignitaries. That is where the three swings given at the beginning and end of each side come from, but it makes no sense to do so outside of cathedral or collegiate churches. Then the thurifer goes down through the first door on the left side and begins to incense around the cantors who are singing the *Magnificat* in front of the eagle in mid-choir. After making this round, he swings the censer three times toward the eagle from the middle, in order to fully complete his circuit. Finally, he salutes the choir and goes to the sacristy.

Towards the end of the *Magnificat*, the candle-bearers leave their places in choir, go up into the sanctuary, take their candlesticks from the sides of the altar, and come to the center. The celebrant joins them there, and preceded by the beadle they all go to the middle of the choir toward the east end to chant the versicles and orations, during which all stand.

Every day, at the verse *Illuminare his qui in tenebris* of the *Benedictus* at Lauds, and at the verse *Lumen ad revelationem* of the *Nunc dimittis* at Compline, the sacristan brings a lit candle into the middle of the choir to illustrate the words *illuminare* and *lumen*.[6] The sacristan or *marilier* clerk is not always exactly on time,[7] but it was such a constant custom to

---

[5] Sibert of Beka, *Ordinale Ordinis Beatae Mariae de Monte Carmeli*, ed. Benedict Zimmerman, *Ordinaire de l'Ordre de Notre-Dame de Mont-Carmel* (Paris, 1910), 56.
[6] See de Vert, *Explication*, 2:4.
[7] In Orléans, the *marellier* clerks (also *marellier* or *marguillier*) were responsible for guarding the church and taking care of its vestments and sacred vessels. There were

present the candle precisely at the words *illuminare* and *lumen* that the late Lord Jean de Fourcroy, grand vicar of Orléans, emphasized it particularly in a sermon he gave on the Purification of the Blessed Virgin.[8] Near the end of the antiphon, the senior choirboy brings the candle close to the celebrant during the oration, in case he needs light. If he does not need it, the choirboy extinguishes it, and after the Office gives it to the celebrant, who takes it home with him.

Here the Sunday Office is celebrated every Sunday of the year, unless an annual feast occurs, and no octaves are permitted during Advent or Lent. They celebrate no feasts during Lent except for the Annunciation and the principal feast of the principal patron, if it falls during that season. Other feasts are either anticipated before Lent or transferred after the Easter octave, in keeping with the spirit of the early Church, which did not permit fasting on feasts.

On annual feasts, in the procession before high Mass, the scholastic and the schoolmaster walk before the cross and behind the choirboys, wielding staves shaped like those used by pilgrims. When the procession stops for the station before the great rood, a Mamertine canon sprinkles the clergy with holy water.[9]

On his way to the rood loft to chant the Gospel, the deacon is preceded by the thurifer, who incenses continually as he walks, both going to the rood loft and returning to the altar.

Once the deacon has mounted the rood loft, he positions himself on the south side, facing north. He chants the Gospel from the lectern located in the middle of the rood loft, after having incensed the book with three swings while the choir sings *Gloria tibi Domine*.

On solemn feasts, after the *Et incarnatus est* of the Creed, the thurifer incenses the choir while the subdeacon presents the Gospel book to the canons for them to kiss.

Immediately before the subdeacon kneels for the elevation of the host, draws a small black veil to the center of the altar, as in Chartres. The deacon pulls it back to the corner of the altar at the *Per omnia* before the *Pater*. See Chartres.[10]

---

also lay *mariliers* who rang the bells and swept the church, among other similar duties. Until 1508, the *marilier* clerk who presented the candle at the *Magnificat* was required to carry a distaff at the procession on the eve of the Invention of the Cross. After that year, however, he was permitted to bear a white staff instead, or borrow the scholastic's staff. See Amicie de Foulques de Villaret, *Recherches historiques sur l'ancien chapitre de l'église d'Orléans* (Orléans, 1882), 52–53.

[8] Died 1684. He was appointed grand vicar in 1667 by Cardinal Pierre-Armand du Cambout de Coislin, Le Brun des Marettes's patron.

[9] The two Mamertine canons, also called canons of St-Mamert, were so called because they took possession of their benefices at the altar of St. Mamertus. They were very strictly bound to be present at all choir Offices, and considered to act as substitutes for any absent canon. See Foulques de Villaret, *Recherches*, 14–15.

[10] See pp. 165–66.

On Epiphany, which is a major annual, the deacon remains at the rood loft or the pulpit after reading the Gospel and, turning to face the clergy, announces the date of Easter in this manner: *Noverit caritas vestra, fratres carissimi, quod annuente Dei et Domini nostri Jesu Christi misericordia, die N. mensis N. sanctum Pascha Domini celebrabimus.* This is in accordance with canon 1 of the fourth Council of Orléans,[11] and is also done in Paris.

A two-hundred-year-old manuscript ordinary of the church of Orléans states that on Ash Wednesday after Sext the cathedral clergy went in procession to the church of St-Pierre-Lentin,[12] where ashes were distributed: *Die Cinerum fit Processio post Sextam ad Sanctum Petrum Lactentium, et ibi donantur Cineres Canonicis, et illis qui volunt accipere.* Several preces and orations were recited there.

Some vestiges of public penitence can still be seen in this church, although neither the bishop nor the clergy take any part. On Ash Wednesday, the penitentiary preaches in the cathedral, blesses the ashes, and imposes them on the heads of those who present themselves. On Maundy Thursday, after preaching, he goes to his tribune in the chapel of St. John behind the choir, where the penitents stand, some dressed in rags, others in scarves and cloths to cover their faces, although some come barefaced. The penitentiary recites the seven penitential psalms and some other prayers over them, and then they all go in procession two by two on their knees around the outside of the choir. They are preceded by the subpenitentiary and followed by the penitentiary, both of them wearing a stole and reciting the Litany of the Saints. Then they return to the chapel, prostrate themselves at the feet of the penitentiary, and kiss the ground one after another. The penitentiary says the absolution over them, sprinkles them with holy water, and tells them, "Do penance, and sin no more," after which they all retire. There are sometimes thirty or forty penitents, and sometimes as many as fifty. In 1697 there were only seventeen. Mothers whose children suffocated due to their negligence are particularly obliged to go.

Before the last century, they used to sing the three litanies on the Easter and Pentecost vigils, as is still done in Rouen.

They never say the psalm *Judica* at the altar, but do say the *Confiteor*.

On the feast of the Exaltation of the Holy Cross, for a century now they have blessed grapes at high Mass either at the offertory or at the *Per quem haec omnia*, as the celebrant wishes. These grapes are then distributed to the canons, cantors, and choirboys in place of the pax-brede. They are not given to the twelve parish priests, however, even though they are the bishop's assistants. At the offertory of this Mass they hold the adoration

---

[11] *Concilia Galliae a. 511–695*, ed. de Clerq, 132. This council was held in 541.
[12] The church of St-Pierre-Lentin, *Sanctus Petrus Lactentium* (St. Peter of the Unweaned) was apparently so called because children born in the Hôtel-Dieu were taken to this church for baptism. The custom continued until the church was destroyed in the Revolution.

of the cross—as done formerly in the Lavra of St. Sabbas and more or less as it is still done in every church on Good Friday—after the bishop or dean has removed his chasuble and tunicle and all the canons their copes, and all have said the *Confiteor* together in mid-choir.

On simple feasts and ferias there is only one candle-bearer at Mass.

A two-hundred-year-old manuscript ordinary of the cathedral of Orléans states:

There used to be a procession in the nave in front of the crucifix every Saturday of the year after Vespers.

On all Mondays of Lent and every day of the octave of Christmas they held a station at some church in the city. The same is stated in the necrology.[13]

If the St. Mark's day procession fell on the octave of Easter, it was not transferred, but still held on 25 April with abstinence, while the Office of St. Mark was transferred to the Monday after *Quasi modo* Sunday. The same is found in the necrology on 25 April and in the six subsequent articles.

On certain anniversaries of bishops' burials, three canon-dignitaries each took up a chalice to the altar during the offertory procession (see PLATE 31), as is still done in Sens.[14]

There were many obits which stipulated that money be given to the poor by the hebdomadary.

There was a foundation to supply wine for the Masses celebrated at the high altar of the cathedral.

There was a *Laus perennis* with continual singing between five in the morning on 2 May until five in the afternoon on 3 May, the feast of the Invention of the Holy Cross and the Dedication of the cathedral.

The Prose *Laudes Crucis attollamus*,[15] sung on the feast of the Invention of the Holy Cross, was composed by a certain Hugo, scholastic of the cathedral of Orléans. See the necrology on the fifteenth of the kalends of October. This Prose is usually attributed to Adam of St. Victor of Paris.[16]

On the feast of the principal patron of most churches of Orléans, the clergy used to sing Matins of the saint in the churches the evening before, and the high Mass the following morning.

---

[13] On the surviving necrologies from Orléans, see Alexandre Vidier and Léon Mirot, *Obituaires de la province de Sens*, ed. Auguste Longnon, vol. 3, *Diocèses d'Orléans, d'Auxerre et de Nevers* (Imprimerie nationale, 1909), 1–137; and *Répertoire des documents nécrologiques Français*, eds. Pierre Marot and Jean-Loup Lemaître (Imprimerie nationale, 1980), 537–40.
[14] See p. 125.
[15] Cantus ID ah54120.
[16] A thirteenth-century breviary kalendar records the death on the fifteenth of the kalends of October (17 September) of *Hugo Subdiaconus*. The two surviving medieval books of distributions call him *Magister scolarum* and state that he wrote the Prose *Laudes crucis*, in gratitude for which his obit was held on that day, even though it had no foundation. It appears that this *Hugo* was Hugh Primas, a celebrated twelfth-century Latin poet from Orléans. See Nicolas Weisbein, "Le *Laudes crucis attollamus* de Maître Hugues d'Orléans dit Le Primat," *Revue du moyen âge latin* 3 (1947): 5–26, which includes a critical edition of the Prose.

Readers will surely be glad to see what the statutes or ordinances of the chapter of Ste-Croix ordain for the discipline of this illustrious church:[17]

They state that for his insolence, a chaplain was imprisoned for eight days fasting on bread and water, and a cope-bearer was condemned to a day in prison on bread and water for intoning the Introit *Statuit* instead of *Sacerdotes*.

That on 11 September 1287, Giles de Patay, bishop of Orléans, laid the first stone of this beautiful cathedral of Ste-Croix of Orléans in the presence of William, abbot of St-Benoît of Fleury; Laurence, abbot of St-Euverte of Orléans; the abbot of Beaugency; and a great multitude of clerics and laymen. This is also mentioned in the necrology on the third of the nones of September.[18]

That in 1497 or thereabouts the chapter freed a girl who was a slave of the church, together with any children she might later have: *Capitulum manumisit Johannam filiam defuncti Johannis* d'Arboys... *de conditione Ecclesiae existentis, nunc uxorem Johannis* Constant *de Moterello, et a jugo servitutis quo ipsa astringebatur Ecclesiae cum sua posteritate ex nunc et in perpetuum liberavit.*[19]

That in this church—contrary to the use of the metropolitan see, which at that time was Sens—the canons-cleric were not to wear the almuce unless they were dignitaries or *personnats*,[20] nor cover their heads in church, as a means of encouraging them to enter holy orders.

That to earn his chapter bread,[21] a canon had to assist at Mass or at Vespers and one canonical hour, or at the three minor hours, or else be ill, or recently bled, or assigned to some duty by the chapter.

Canons were obliged to sing in choir, and those who fell asleep during the Divine Office or said it privately forfeited the distribution for that Office.

At that time the celebrant incensed not during the *Magnificat* as nowadays, but immediately after the short chapter.

A choirboy, not the celebrant, incensed the cope-bearers, and after incensing the dignitaries he kissed each one's hand out of respect, as well

---

[17] The medieval cartularies of Ste-Croix of Orléans are all now lost. One, dating from the end of the twelfth century, survives in a transcription made by Étienne Baluze in 1667, and another, from the fourteenth or fifteenth century, was partially transcribed by Dom Guillaume Gérou in the eighteenth century. They have been edited in Joseph Thillier and Eugène Jarry, *Cartulaire de Sainte-Croix d'Orléans* (Alphonse Picard et fils, 1906).
[18] 3 September. The surviving medieval books of distributions do indeed give this latter date (Vidier and Mirot, *Obituaires*, 96). Charles de La Saussaye, dean of the cathedral of Orléans, reports that his church's martyrology also states the first stone was laid on 3 September, but transcribes an excerpt from an "old manuscript codex" that gives the date as 11 September instead and reports the presence of the illustrious figures Le Brun des Marettes here mentions (*Annales ecclesiae Aurelianensis* [Paris, 1615], 531–32).
[19] "The chapter manumitted Jane, son of the late John d'Arbois...a dependant of this church, now wife of John Constant of Moterello, and freed her and her descendants from the yoke of servitude by which she was bound to this church, from now and forever."
[20] On *personnats*, see p. 52, n. 75.
[21] I.e., the daily ration of bread distributed to each canon.

as the hand of the celebrant. He still kisses the celebrant's hand today, but through his cope.

The bishop of Orléans used to free all criminals in Orléans during his solemn entry. He proceeds barefoot from the church of St-Euverte to that of St-Aignan, where is shod and borne by four canons-priest of St-Aignan from the choir to the cloister gate, and thence by four barons, vassals of the bishopric, with the help of several others. At the end of this ceremony the bishop celebrates solemn Mass in his cathedral, and they sing the *laudes episcopi*. These praises are the acclamations and wishes expressed in the *Christus vincit, Christus regnat, Christus imperat*:

> Episcopo Aurelianensi et omni clero sibi
>   commisso, pax, vita et salus aeterna.
> Sancte Evurti, tu illum adjuva.
> Christus vincit, etc.
> Sancte Aniane, tu illum adjuva, etc.

These praises or acclamations are still sung in many churches of France, notably in Rouen, between the collect and Epistle when the bishop celebrates pontifically, and that is the place in the books where they are written out in full.[22]

Around 1472 Pope Sixtus IV, at the pressing request of Louis XI, king of France, ordered, under pain of excommunication, that the bells should toll at midday as they did in the evening for the curfew, and granted those who said the *Ave Maria* three times at midday an indulgence of three hundred days, called "the indulgence of peace" (*l'indulgence de paix*).[23]

From 1582 to 1588

It was decided by plurality of voice that, in keeping with the statutes and ancient customs, a nephew of the Lord Bishop of Orléans would not be received as a canon, since he did not have the required age.

It was forbidden to lease houses, granaries, and cellars of the cloister to laymen, and to hold weddings there without the chapter's permission.

All the canons of the chapter were obliged to remain in chapter until the senior choirboy came to say *Ad Missam, Domini mei*.[24]

Leaving Matins to hear Mass was forbidden.

---

[22] On the *laudes*, see p. 18, n. 43.

[23] In 1472, during his war against Charles the Bold, duke of Burgundy, Louis XI instituted the practice of ringing church bells at midday and praying three Hail Marys kneeling "to obtain stable peace for the Kingdom of France." At his request, in 1475 Sixtus IV granted an indulgence of three hundred days to those who observed this custom. The Orléans cartulary containing this information is now lost, but surviving records from Tournai and Beauvais confirm that the indulgence was known as the *Ave Maria pacis*. For further details, and a more general history of the Angelus, see W. Henry, "Angélus," in *Dictionnaire d'archéologie chrétienne et de liturgie*, ed. Fernand Cabrol, vol. 1, part 2 (Letouzey et Ané, 1907), 2068–2078, especially 2075.

[24] "To Mass, my lords."

A canon was declared at fault for having brought a book other than a breviary into choir.

Men received as canons who later married were bound to return the emoluments received while they were canons.

All canons were obliged to reside in the cloister. Those who do not are even today bound to pay seven pounds and ten pence every year *pro domo non habita*.

The penitentiary had the *cura animarum* of the canons' house servants, and administered the sacraments to them.

From 1588 to 1594

It was ordered that theology lessons should be delivered by the theologian in the choir of the church of Ste-Croix, and not elsewhere. They were still held there not sixty years ago.

Rent that a canon earned from the tenants of houses belonging to the chapter beyond what he needed to pay for his own rent was forfeit to the chapter.

No canon should celebrate Mass outside the church of Ste-Croix except for devotional reasons.

That canons-deacon and -subdeacon could enter from the west end of choir to get to their places only if they held the surplice sleeve of a canon-priest.

From 1597 to 1610

All chaplains of the church of Orléans are bound to celebrate the Masses of their chapel in the aforesaid church of Orléans and not elsewhere, and they shall inform the sacristan.

Canons who are assigned Office duties (*ad officium*) shall say the Office in person, under pain of fine and forfeiture of the day's distributions.

From 27 February 1613 to 23 December 1615

The penitentiary is obliged to be present always in the church of Ste-Croix, and he is not allowed to hear confessions outside the said church.

From 1626 to 1629

The Lord Cantor is enjoined to assist and actually to remain in choir until the end of the Office, else he forfeits his distributions.

No canon is to absent himself from the divine service without having requested the chapter's leave.

From 1638 to 1647

Ordered: that canons-scholar studying in Orléans shall be fined a muid of wheat for failing to attend church on feasts and Sundays.[25]

---

[25] An Orléans muid, a measure of dry volume, weighed six hundred pounds; see Jacques Savary des Bruslons, "Muid" in *Dictionnaire universel de commerce* (Geneva, 1742), 2:1455.

From the last Saturday of December 1650

Chapter decision containing the obligations of the cantor and succentor, taken from the martyrology of the church of Orléans ending in the year 1623,[26] and signed by all the chapter canons in said year: *In Festis Annualibus Cantor praecinit in utrisque Vesperis, Matutino et Missa; Succentor vero in Duplicibus; et deesse non possunt Officio nisi de licentia Capituli.*[27] The cantor and succentor swore an oath to obey this order upon their reception.

On 31 October 1697, the general chapter ordered that thenceforth chapter would no longer be held during high Mass or another Divine Office.

Extract of Principal Items Contained in a Three-Hundred-Year-Old Manuscript Breviary of Orléans[28]

It distinguishes the two Sts. Dionysius, the one from Athens being celebrated on the fifth of the nones of October, and the one of Paris with St. Rusticus and Eleutherius on the seventh of the ides of October.[29]

As in Lyon, it contains the major preces on the first Monday of Lent, almost in the same manner as in the new breviary of Orléans of 1693, with the word *terrea* used to signify prostration and *dieta* to indicate that one says the Office of the day, that is to say, of the feria and sometimes of the Sunday.

St. Altinus, formerly considered first bishop of Orléans, is nowhere found, not even in the litany or the kalendar. He is first named in the 1542 breviary, where, in the lessons of Sts. Savinianus and Potentianus, he is described as a priest sent with Eodaldus to preach in Orléans and Chartres. But it says that they then returned by way of Paris to rejoin St. Savinianus, the first archbishop of Sens. Yet St. Altinus is not named in the kalendar nor invoked in the litany in this breviary, nor even that of 1573. He would not have been omitted had it been believed that he was a holy bishop of Orléans, the first one at that.[30]

In this breviary, *Quoniam in aeternum misericordia ejus* is not repeated at the end of each verse of psalm 135, *Confitemini*, nor it is found in the manuscript breviaries and psalters of the churches of the city and diocese of Orléans.

The Office of the vigil of Epiphany was said on Sunday if it fell on that day, just like everywhere else; indeed, Epiphany was celebrated in many churches with even more solemnity than Christmas. See the *Histoire ecclésiastique* of M. de Tillemont, vol. 1, pp. 453–54.[31]

---

[26] Orléans, Médiathèque municipale, MS. 0324.
[27] "On annual feasts the cantor rules at both Vespers, Matins, and Mass; on doubles the succentor; and they cannot be absent from the Office without the chapter's permission."
[28] Orléans, Médiathèque municipale, MS. 0132.
[29] 3 and 9 October respectively.
[30] Le Brun des Marettes duly excised any mention of Sts. Altinus, Savinianus, Potentianus, and Eodaldus in the 1693 breviary of Orléans he helped compose.
[31] Louis Sébastien Le Nain de Tillemont, *Mémoires pour servir a l'histoire ecclésiastique des six premiers siècles* (Paris, 1693).

On Epiphany, mention was made of three mysteries: the adoration of the Magi, the baptism of Jesus Christ, and his first miracle at the wedding feast of Cana. They chanted the Genealogy of Our Lord according to St. Luke after the ninth responsory of Matins.

On Sundays *per annum*, they chanted the hymn *O lux beata Trinitas* at Vespers,[32] as in many other churches.

On Corpus Christi, here called *Solemnitas Eucharistiae Christi*, there are three short proses at Matins, after the third, sixth, and ninth responsories, with a repetition of the response at the end.[33] This was called, unless I am mistaken, *cum fabricis*, from the repetition of a Christmas responsory that ended in *fabricae mundi*.[34] These proses were doubtless meant to allow time for the incensations that took place and still take place at the third, sixth, and ninth responsory on annual feasts.[35]

On Corpus Christi, they sang the *Haec dies* at the minor hours after the antiphon.[36] But they still said the usual hymns, even though they omitted the short chapter and responsory.

The feast of the Holy Trinity was celebrated on the last Sunday after Pentecost.[37]

At first Vespers of feasts with a fasting vigil, the collect was preparatory; I mean it was always or nearly always the collect of the vigil itself. These vigils themselves had a sort of first Vespers, because they said the preces, during which they prostrated, even though the oration was of the preceding Sunday.

At the minor hours on certain feasts there was a versicle, or if you will a second antiphon, after the Lauds antiphon, as is still done today in Orléans at the minor hours of the Invention of the Cross, on Corpus Christi, and as is also done everywhere at the minor hours during the octave of Easter.

On All Souls, at Vespers and Lauds there was a chapter, to which all responded *Deo gratias* as on other days, but no hymns.

At the end of this manuscript breviary is found the *Salve Regina misericordiae*. It is found, with this same text,[38] in the breviaries of Orléans from 1513, 1542, 1573, and 1693. This is how it is still sung today by the churches of Lyon and Orléans, and among the Cluniac, Cistercian, and Carthusian monks. This is the original text, as it was sung everywhere before the last

---

[32] Cantus ID 008358.
[33] *Prophetico plenus spiramine* after the responsory *Respexit Elias* (Cantus ID 601997), *Calix Christi dictus est* after *Accepit Jesus* (600019), and *Ut sit plena* after *Unus panis* (602384), respectively. See Orléans, Médiathèque municipale, MS. 0132, fols. 214r–215v. The proses have not been catalogued by the Cantus index. They were also sung at St-Martin of Tours; see Maurey, *Medieval Music*, table 1.3.
[34] Namely, *Descendit de caelis* (Cantus ID 006411).
[35] On such proses and this (probably false) pragmatic reason for them, see p. 65, n. 14.
[36] Cantus ID a01195.
[37] This was rare but not unknown in other French dioceses. See Peter Browe, "Zur Geschichte des Dreifaltigkeitsfestes," *Archiv für Liturgiewissenschaft* 1 (1950): 74–75.
[38] I.e., without *mater* before *misericordiae*.

century. One day we shall demonstrate this on the basis of more than thirty authorities from various churches and realms. One can see this text embroidered on a green frontal on the high altar of the cathedral of Soissons where the fringe was attached to cover the bar.[39]

On the Thursday nearest 23 October, there is an obit in the church of Ste-Croix for the Messieurs Moreau. At the high Mass, a four-franc loaf of bread is offered and blessed on the high altar and then distributed to the whole clergy. The choirboy, vested in a black cope, says, when presenting it to each, *Requiescant in pace*, and they respond *Amen*.

In this same church, on the Saturday vigils of Easter and Pentecost, the two beneficed priests who carried the vases with the holy oils and chrism at the blessing of the font, upon their return, place these vases on the altar. During Mass, they stand at the corners of the altar facing each other until around the *Agnus Dei*. At that moment they take the two vases into choir, presenting them to the canons only, to kiss in place of the pax-brede. One of the priests says to each canon: *Ecce sanctum Oleum*, and he responds: *Ave sanctum Oleum*. Then the other priest says: *Ecce sanctum Chrisma*, and the canon responds: *Ave sanctum Chrisma*.

On every Monday at the first high Mass, which is of the Dead and celebrated at the high altar for the late Lord François de Brillac,[40] at the *Memento* for the dead the deacon says to the celebrant *Memento Francisci*.

A three-hundred-year old ordinary of the church of Orléans states: The bishop gave the kiss of peace to the canons of the fourth stall at the end of Lauds on Easter Sunday, even in times of interdict.

During Lent, the Preface *Qui corporali jejunio* was said only on ferias, whereas on Sunday they said the common *per annum* Preface, as in Sens and elsewhere.

At the processions on Palm Sunday and the three Rogation days, they carried three banners and a dragon — doubtless a reference to the serpent Moses erected in the desert, which was a figure of Jesus Christ lifted up on the cross, and hence is a reference to the church of Ste-Croix — and a

---

[39] For an overview of the development of the altar cloths and the "fringe," i.e., the *frontellum* or *aurifrisium*, see Joseph Braun, *Die liturgischen Paramente in Gegenwart und Vergangenheit: Ein Handbuch der Paramentik* (Freiburg im Breisgau, 1924), 184–97. De Vert, *Explication*, 2:355, alleges that the literal origin of the "fringe" was as a strip of fabric used to cover the iron bar from which the altar frontal used to be hung: "This frontal or curtain...was attached by rings to an iron bar or rod. For the sake of elegance and propriety, the bar was covered by a sort of garnished band or fringed trim. From there came the fabric called the *frange* or *crépine* that is usually seen above the frontals of altars. So it had the same use as the bands or fabrics we ordinarily use to conceal the rods used for holding the rings of a bed- or window-curtain. When some churches today are content to decorate the altar table with a sculpture or painting without covering it with a curtain or frontal, that is clearly because once one no longer places the bodies of saints under the altar, these curtains or frontals that once served to preserve the cases and protect them from dust were seen to be of no use."

[40] Bishop of Orléans from 1473 until 1502, when he became archbishop of Aix-en-Provence, where he died in 1504.

cock representing St. Peter's denial at cockcrow — in reference to the two collegiate churches of St-Pierre-en-Pont and St-Pierre-Puellier, who assist at these processions along with the cathedral canons.

Tenebrae was said very early in the morning on the last three days of Holy Week. A roughly two-hundred-year-old addition to the manuscript states that no candle was left lit at the end of the third nocturn *ita quod post tertium Nocturnum nullae [candelae] remanent accensae*, and this was because there was no longer any need for candles, since it was already daytime at that point. See Lyon.[41]

On Easter Sunday and during the week, the canons of the altar of St. Mamertus, the chaplains, and the cantors did not sit, but remained standing (*sed erecti*), doubtlessly in order to represent Jesus Christ's resurrected state.

Every time the bishop said Mass pontifically on major feasts, fourteen parish priests of the city assisted him, as on Maundy Thursday, when six canon-priests of the cathedral celebrated and sang the Mass together with the bishop, except that they did not pronounce the words of consecration. The bishop alone consecrated a large host for himself as well as six small ones for the six canons, with which he gave them communion.

A station was held at some church not only on Ash Wednesday and every Monday of Lent, but also on the Rogation days and every day in the octaves of Easter and Christmas.

The bishop used to hold his diocesan synod on Thursday during the octave of Pentecost.

The feast of the Most Holy Trinity was celebrated not on the first but the last Sunday after Pentecost.

The treasury of the cathedral of Ste-Croix has a six-hundred-year-old manuscript Epistle book, which contains a prophecy and Epistle for the Masses of all annual feasts. There, the first Mass of Christmas is entitled *Missa in galli cantu*, and the subsequent day *In commemoratione S. Stephani* rather than *in festo*.

In another Epistle book, some three or four hundred years old, there is likewise a prophecy and Epistle for major feasts, as well as two Masses for the Nativity of St. John the Baptist, in addition to the vigil Mass.

In a six-hundred-year-old pontifical, one finds the solemn blessings that the bishop used to give immediately before the *Agnus Dei* when he celebrated Mass pontifically. Their use, after a period of interruption, was re-established by the late Lord Cardinal de Coislin in 1696, and they are still said at present. One also finds several formulae for the oath of obedience taken to the bishop of Orléans by the abbots and abbesses of the diocese. In this pontifical, it says *pietatis tuae* MORE rather than RORE in the blessing of water.[42]

---

[41] See p. 34.
[42] See pp. 39–40.

In another two- or three-hundred-year-old pontifical containing the rite for Maundy Thursday, the oblation of the host and chalice at the offertory is made *per unum*, that is, under a single formula:

> Tunc elevatur calix duabus manibus cum patena hostia desuper posita, et dicatur haec Oratio: *Suscipe sancta Trinitas hanc oblationem, etc.* (as done today in Lyon). Tunc reponat calicem, et accipiat patenam, et ponat hostiam ante pedes calicis, et cooperiat eum corporalibus. Postea junctis manibus dicat: *Veni sanctificator*.[43]

After the *Simili modo: reponat calicem in loco suo, et cooperiat corporale. Postea extendat brachia in modum crucis.*[44]

After the *Libera nos quaesumus Domine*: *Hic tangat hostiam patena, et tacta hostia, ponat patenam ad os et oculos, et signet se illa dicens, Da propitius pacem*.[45]

The bishop gave his solemn blessing immediately before the *Agnus Dei*.

Finally: *Communicet se, et sumendo Corpus sub specie panis dicat*, Haec perceptio.[46]

Extract of Principal Items in the Ritual of Orléans of 1581

There were three litanies on Holy Saturday, as in the old missals of Orléans.

At the blessing of the font, droplets of wax from the Paschal candle were dropped into the water in the form of a cross. The bells rang at the *Kyrie* on Holy Saturday. Both these things are found in the old missals of Orléans.

New grapes were blessed on 6 August, not at the Mass of the Transfiguration, but of St. Sixtus, because the blessing or prayer used to bless the grapes was attributed to him. This blessing is found not only in this ritual, but also in the sacramentary of St. Gregory the Great on 6 August;[47] in Amalar in the section on the Canon;[48] in a four-hundred-year-old manuscript missal from Auxerre; in the old ordinaries of St-Aignan of Orléans and of St-Vrain of Jargeau, some five hundred years old; in the old customary of Cluny; in the ceremonial of the Congregation of

---

[43] "Then with both hands let him elevate the chalice, with the paten and host placed on top, and say this oration: *Suscipe sancta Trinitas hanc oblationem*. Then let him set down the chalice, take the paten, and place the host before the foot of the chalice, covering it with the corporal. Afterwards, with his hands joined, let him say: *Veni sanctificator*."

[44] "Let him put the chalice down in its place, and cover it with the corporal. Afterwards, let him extends his arms in the shape of a cross."

[45] "At this point, let him touch the host with the paten, and once the host has been touched, let him place the paten to his mouth and eyes, and sign himself with it, saying, *Da propitius pacem*."

[46] "Let him give himself communion, and consuming the Body under the species of bread let him say: *Haec perceptio*."

[47] See p. 90, n. 4.

[48] Amalar of Metz, *Liber officialis* 1.12.7, ed. Hanssens, 2:69.

St-Vanne; in the 1504 missal of Orléans; the 1530 missal of Lyon;[49] the 1607 missal of Amiens; the 1686 missal of Toul; as well as in the pontifical of Arles; the ordinary of St-Vincent of Metz; in the manuscript missal of Montmajour; in an old missal of Moissac; and in the 1519 missal of Vienne.[50] These all distinctly and positively show that the *Infra actionem* and the *Per quem haec omnia* are said for and over the gifts, for in these five latter texts, the blessing of grapes and fruits is entitled *Infra actionem*, and in the lattermost, in the Mass of St. Sixtus, pope and martyr, fol. 231v, one reads:

> *Infra actionem non dicitur nisi in Benedictione Racemorum*, Intra quorum nos consortium, non aestimator meriti, sed veniae quaesumus largitor admitte. Per Christum. *Benedictio uvae*. Benedic, Domine, et hos fructus novos uvae, quos tu Domine rore coeli et inundantia pluviarum et temporum serenitate atque tranquillitate ad maturitatem perducere dignatus es; et dedisti eos ad usus nostros cum gratiarum actione percipere in nomine Domini nostri Jesu Christi, per quem haec omnia Domine semper, *etc.*

And the 1504 missal of Orléans, on 6 August, fol. 23v:

> *Ante* Per quem omnia Domine, *dicatur Benedicto uvae*. Oremus. *Oratio*. Benedic, Domine, et hos fructus novos uvae...percipere in nomine Domini nostri Jesu Christi, Per quem omnia, *etc*.

The blessing of grapes is also mentioned in the *Rationale* of William Durand, bishop of Mende;[51] in the 1692 ritual of Lyon; and even in the most recent missals of Toul and Orléans, with the *In nomine Domini nostri Jesu Christi* at the end. This blessing was and is still said in Reims, St-Martin of Tours,[52] and all Lorraine, immediately before the words of the Canon *per quem haec omnia, Domine, semper bona creas, sanctificas, vivificas, benedicis, et praestas nobis*. These words, just like the signs of the cross, must have referred to the new fruits, grapes, vegetables, bread, and other offerings, and not to Christ, to whom one cannot apply the *creas, sanctificas*, and the rest. This is also sufficiently shown by the Ambrosian

---

[49] *Missale secundum ritum ecclesie Lugdunensis* (Lyon, 1530), fols. 138r–v.

[50] *Missale ad vsum sancte Viennensis ecclesie* (Lyon, 1519), fol. 231v.

[51] Durand, *Rationale* 4.46.8, ed. David and Thibodeau, 1:496; in the chapter on the feast of the Transfiguration, Durand states that "Pope Eutychian established that first fruits and beans be blessed over the altar" (7.22.3, ed. David and Thibodeau, 3:68).

[52] Author's note: It also used to be said in the cathedral of St-Gatien of Tours, as I have indicated on p. 90. I recently learned from an ecclesiastic of Tours, however, that they stopped blessing the grapes at St-Gatien five years ago, because the sacristan was unable to find any ripe grapes that day. I saw it still done in Orléans on this year, 1717, on the feast of the Exaltation of the Holy Cross, immediately before the *Per quem haec omnia* by M. Chereau, a former canon of the cathedral, who is thoroughly knowledgeable about the rites and uses of his church. In Orléans, two ecclesiastics distribute these grapes to the canons and others during the *Agnus Dei*, as in Chartres, Toul, and Angers.

Canon, which adds *largiter*, although the prayer's last two lines refer to the Body and Blood of Jesus Christ. This *per quem haec* is the conclusion of the blessing of fruits that used to be done at this point. The prayer of blessing has been removed, but its conclusion remains. See Auxerre.[53]

In Orléans, two ecclesiastics distribute these grapes to the canons and others during the *Agnus Dei*, as in Chartres, Toul, and Angers.

The exorcisms before baptism used to be done outside the church doors. They were omitted if the infant had been baptized at home. Home baptism was by aspersion, but in the church it seems it was done by immersion. *Dicit Presbyter puero, Et ego baptizo te in nomine Patris, mergat semel, et Filii, mergat secundo, et Spiritus Sancti, Amen, mergat tertio.* The same held for baby girls. Baptism by immersion is still done in the East and in Milan, as one can see on p. 33 of the Ambrosian ritual.[54]

At the Canon of the Mass the priest only extended his hands until the words *diesque nostros in tua pace disponas*, exclusive.

When saying the *Unde et memories*, he extended his arms in the form of a cross, as is still done in many monastic orders.

When he said *Supplices te rogamus*, he bent over the altar with his arms crossed. The same thing is found in a manuscript pontifical and in a 1504 missal of Orléans. There was no blessing or last Gospel.

Nevertheless, I find in the 1504 missal that a blessing was given as most bishops do today: *Erigat se, et cum patena signet se, et benedicat populum dicens, Adjutorium nostrum.* ℞. *Qui fecit. Sit nomen.* ℞. *Ex hoc nunc. Benedicat vos divina majestas, Pater, Filius, et Spiritus sanctus. Amen.* But there is no last Gospel.

These same pontifical and missal also state that the chalice was covered with the corporal, as in Lyon and among the Carthusians, rather than the pall, which is very modern. The priest held the paten slightly raised during the *Libera nos*: *Hic accipiat patenam, et levet eam parum manu dicens, Amen. Libera nos quaesumus Domine.* After the words *cum omnibus sanctis*, the priest touched the host with the paten, and then his mouth and eyes: *hic tangat hostiam patena, et tacta hostia ponat patenam ad os et ad oculos, et signet se illa dicens, Da propitius pacem.*

These same books have the priest say the psalm *Judica* in alb and stole, before putting on the chasuble. They also state that the priest offered the host and chalice *per unum*, that is, together with a single prayer. Ablutions are not mentioned in the 1504 missal nor the 1581 ritual. At the *Quod ore*, it

---

[53] See p. 117. The *Per quem haec omnia* prayer was discussed in the seventeenth century not merely for the (largely) historical curiosity of the blessing of grapes but also because sectarians used the prayer and its signs of the cross as evidence against the doctrine of transubstantiation. Proving that the prayer referred to grapes, rather than to the Body and Blood, was an essential part of Catholic apologetics. For a review of contemporary literature on the *Per quem haec omnia* prayer, including Protestant controversy, see de Vert, *Explication* 4:234–52.

[54] *Rituale sacramentorum ad usum Mediolanensis ecclesiae* (Milan, 1687), 33.

reads: *et corpus et sanguinis Domini nostri Jesu Christi fiat nobis remedium sempiternum in vitam aeternam. Amen.*

The blessing of holy water on Sundays used to be done at the stoup by the church door, as in Lyon and Chartres. This ancient custom is still observed in many churches in the diocese, especially in those of Les Aydes and Fleury, a league from Orléans on the road to Paris.[55]

Royal and Collegiate Church of Saint-Aignan

The royal and collegiate church of St-Aignan used to be a Benedictine abbey, anciently called St-Pierre-aux-Bœufs. It was already so famous in the times of Chlothar II that it was one of the churches where the most important oaths were sworn, as one can see in the chronicle of Fredegarius, who lived in the middle of the eighth century.[56] This church was much enriched by King Robert.

There is an underground church where no Divine Offices are celebrated.

On major feasts, after the celebrant has incensed the altar at the offertory, the deacon incenses him *ex parte Evangelii*, then goes up to the topmost step of the altar, whence he incenses the cantor with three swings. Then he goes to the other side to incense the first coped canon, and returns to the opposite side to incense the other cope-bearer. He thereupon goes down the three steps of the altar and, *in plano Sanctuarii* and *ex parte Evangelii*, incenses with three swings, apparently directed at the entire clergy.

Nothing is sung at the elevations of the host or the chalice.

Here follow some rituals taken from a 450-year-old ordinary of the illustrious church of St-Aignan, which is essentially the cathedral's ordinary, adapted to the customs of the church of St-Aignan.

The choir had four rows of stalls, as in some churches of Flanders, and formerly in Scotland, Ste-Croix of Orléans, and St-Martin of Tours.

At that time, the choirboys of St-Aignan wore surplices, and only used albs during the octave of Easter and when they performed certain duties, such as carrying the thurible, candles, etc.

Every Saturday and Sunday of the year, there was a procession in the nave in front of the great rood, as is still done in Angers.[57]

The hebdomadary priest, after beginning Terce, made an inclination to his neighbor, asking him to finish the Office for him, and then went to the sacristy to vest for Mass. This is still done at present.

The celebrant, deacon, and subdeacon used appareled albs at Mass.

In procession Masses or stations, the deacon sang the Gospel wearing only a stole over his surplice.

---

[55] About 2.4 miles.
[56] See Ps.-Fredegarius, *Chronicarum quae dicuntur Fredegarii scholastici libri IV* 4.54, ed. Bruno Krusch, MGH SS rer. Merov. 2, 147.
[57] See p. 69.

Four hundred years ago, and perhaps more recently, the Offertories contained several additional psalm verses, as in Lyon.[58]

On vigils of feasts, the collect at first Vespers was always that of the vigil, as a preparation for the feast.

On Ember days, Mass was said after None and immediately before Vespers, as during Lent. Hence they broke their fast only after Vespers.

On vigils of major feasts, no commemorations were said at Lauds, *propter Festum Annuale*. After Prime, in the short chapter Office, the schoolmaster (*maître de grammaire*) read the list of those who were to read or sing the following day.

On major feasts of the year when the church was decorated, it was guarded night and day by the lay and clerical *marguilliers*. First Vespers had no commemorations, not even of a double feast. During the responsory at Vespers, two canons—that week's and the previous's hebdomadaries—incensed the altars and the choirboys incensed from the upper stalls, kissing the hand of the cantor,[59] succentor, and *chefcier*.[60] At Matins, the lessons and responsories were chanted in copes, and the *Gloria Patri* and reprise were added to each. The third, sixth, and ninth responsories were repeated after the *Gloria Patri* from the beginning, doubtless in order to give time for the incensation that took place during these three responsories, just as at Vespers.

The procession after Terce comprised three priests, three deacons and three subdeacons, the Gospel book, two processional crosses, two candles, one boat-bearer, and one stoup-bearer.

On annual feasts everyone wore copes at high Mass. At the *Gloria Patri* of the Introit, the celebrant entered with the aforementioned ministers through the west gate and passed through choir. After saying the *Confiteor* before the altar, two assistant priests, two deacons, and two subdeacons went to stand behind the altar. The deacon, preceded by two processional crosses, two candles, and the thurible mounted the rood loft to chant the Gospel.

---

[58] See p. 43.

[59] Author's note: They stopped doing this only a few years ago.

[60] At St-Aignan, the *chefcier* or *chevecier*, in Latin *capicerius*, was in charge of the church lighting. Cf. the role of the *chevecier* at St-Martin of Tours, p. 94, n. 16 and p. 101. The chapter of St-Aignan claimed to enjoy the privilege, from time immemorial, of controlling the production and sale of the candles used in their church, including the numerous candles the faithful lit before the relics of their holy patron, St. Anianus. Hence they asserted their *chefcier* had the right to seize any wax candles sold without their permission: *capicerius a capienda cera*. In the thirteenth century, this claim was contested by the master chandlers of Orléans, who contended they themselves had received the exclusive privilege to work and sell wax candles in the city and bailiwick as a fief from the *chevecier* of the cathedral of Ste-Croix, which itself held it from the bishop, who held it from the king. St-Aignan asked and received confirmation of their right from Rome, but the chandlers appealed to the king. In the end, Ste-Croix's monopoly over the making and selling of candles in Orléans was recognized, except over those candles produced for St-Aignan. For a full account of the affair, see Charles Cuissard, "Étude sur le commerce et l'industrie à Orléans avant 1789," *Memóires de la Société d'agriculture, sciences, belles-lettres et arts d'Orléans* 35 (1897): 149–52.

The *Magnificat* of second Vespers of annual feasts was always triumphed, as is still done in Lyon on certain days. The subdeacon intoned this antiphon and the *Magnificat* antiphon of first Vespers.

On feasts of nine lessons, the hebdomadary priest sang the priestly verse before Lauds, but on feasts of three lessons and ferias it was sung by a choirboy.

It would seem that on Christmas night Matins began after midnight as in Sens, because they began the second Mass immediately after Lauds, which was inserted into the first Mass. It would have been close to dawn, since it is indicated that when the celebrant comes to the Preface, if it is not yet dawn, he should wait until daybreak to sing it. *Finito Offertorio*, says a 450-year old ordinary, *succentor incipit alta voce* Laetemur gaudiis. *Hoc cantato, si dies appareat, incipit canonem sacerdos; sin autem, expectat donec dies appareat. Praefatio et Communicantes ut supra [in I. Missa].* This second Mass was celebrated at the altar behind the high altar to avoid saying two Masses on the same altar. (See what I said about Christmas day in Sens.[61]) The three Masses of Christmas had a prophecy before the Epistle in the ancient Gallican rite.

On Christmas, Easter, Pentecost, and St. Anianus on 17 November, immediately after the collect at Mass, the *Christus vincit* was sung in midchoir by the subdeacon and *chefcier*. The choirboys still sing it almost every day of the year before the high Mass.

In Lent and on other fasting days, the preces at the end of each hour were said prostrate. This prostration was called the *terrea* in the old books of Orléans.

On Ash Wednesday, it is not stated that the priest took or received ashes from anyone, but that he distributed them to all the clergy, while the deacon sprinkled each one after he received ashes. Thereafter, they held the procession with the processional cross, candles, thurible, and holy water, making stations at several chapels. At Mass, there was only one candle, and they never had two except on nine-lesson feasts.

They used black from Septuagesima until Easter.

On Sundays of Lent until Palm Sunday, no cross was carried in the procession. Indeed not carrying it at all has the same effect as veiling it.

On the first Monday of Lent and all the following ferias until Maundy Thursday, everyone kissed his seat upon entering choir. A thick cloth was draped over the top and front of the altar, and all crucifixes and images were veiled. The deacon and subdeacon wore chasubles at Mass. The deacon said both *Levate* and *Flectamus genua*. There was a large veil between the choir and the altar until Holy Wednesday, when it was let fall at these words of the Passion, *Et velum Templi scissum est.*[62]

---

[61] See p. 124.
[62] See de Vert, *Explication*, 2:28.

On Palm Sunday, the palms were blessed behind the high altar. Then the procession was held with four processional crosses preceded by beadles carrying rods or staves in hand to clear the way: *habentes virgas vel baculos in manibus ut praeparent viam Processioni.* This precisely was the purpose of the beadles' rods or staves. After them followed the stoup-bearer in alb, the four processional crosses, the candle-bearers, and the boat-bearers, followed by the whole clergy. The procession followed the same ceremonies as that of the cathedral. The choirboys and their master said the verses of the *Gloria, laus* and *Quis est iste Rex gloriae?* on the tower of the west gate, which was closed with the clergy outside. The cantor sang the *Attollite portas* three times while striking the church door with the processional cross, once the first time, then twice, and finally thrice. Once he began the responsory *Ingrediente*,[63] the procession entered.

At Matins on the last three days of Holy Week, they used twenty-four candles, as in Rouen. At the end of Lauds they sang the *Kyrie eleison*, with no tropes besides *Domine miserere nostri*, as they still do in Angers.[64] At the end they added only *Christus factus est pro nobis obediens usque ad mortem, mortem autem crucis.* Then the *Pater* was said in silence, followed by the psalms *Miserere* and *Domine ne in furore* and the oration *Respice*. Afterwards, the succentor struck three blows with a mallet. Then, after relighting a few candles, they said the seven penitential psalms on their knees, whereafter the hebdomadary priest in stole went to the corner of the altar, said the prayers of absolution, and finally gave the absolution. The minor hours were recited without antiphons or singing, a manner the ordinary calls *dicere psalmos submissa voce sine Antiphona*, that is, in a moderate voice and *recto tono*.

On Maundy Thursday and Holy Saturday at the third nocturn, they read the Gospel and homily as on other days of the year, except without the title *Lectio sancti Evangelii*.

On Maundy Thursday, they consecrated as many hosts as were needed until Saturday. As the ordinary says: *In hac Missa tot Hostiae debent consecrari, quot sufficiant usque in Sabbatum.* The celebrant placed them in a small aumbry during Vespers, which were inserted into the Mass. After Vespers, the altars were stripped and left bare until the following day after the creeping to the cross.

The ceremonies of the Maundy are nearly identical to those we shall describe when we speak of Rouen.[65] There is only this peculiar custom, that after the Gospel, when all the clergy are seated, a sermon was preached, as is still done today in Latin, and a *marguillier* clerk gave the preacher the shaft of the processional cross to lean upon, if he so wished: *et Matricularius*

---

[63] Cantus ID 006961.
[64] See p. 70, n. 28.
[65] See pp. 214–15.

Clericus dat sibi baculum super quem ponitur crux, ut se appodiet super eum si velit. This leads me to believe he preached standing. Afterwards, while the antiphons were sung, all the canons, from the eldest to the youngest, washed the feet of the poor and gave each of them six pence and wine to drink. Finally, all the water that had been used to wash the feet of the poor was taken to be poured over the tomb of the man who established the foundation for the Maundy while the antiphon *Maria ergo ut lavit pedes Jesu*[66] was sung.

On Good Friday, they went about the cloister knocking on the doors with a staff or wooden mallet to announce Matins. The two priest-canons carrying the two processional crosses sang the *Popule meus* and the two deacons who sang the *Agios* wore red copes. The celebrant and these two priests adored the cross, followed by the deacon and subdeacon, and finally the entire clergy in order of seniority. Then the celebrant went, accompanied only by only the deacon and subdeacon and two candle-bearers (without incense) to retrieve the Holy Eucharist that had been reserved the previous day, and took communion after singing the *Pater* in a low voice, without raising the host: *Dicit voce submissa, ita ut possit a circumstantibus audiri, Oremus. Praeceptis salutaribus moniti . . . Pater noster, voce submissa, scilicet sine nota*. This latter expression is noteworthy, since it is the true meaning of *voce submissa*. After Vespers, the celebrant, deacon, and subdeacon removed their chasubles and stoles and washed the two main altars. Then the chaplains brought their altar stones and the celebrant washed them too. During this whole time the responsory *Circumdederunt* was sung.[67] Compline was not said in choir on this day.

On Holy Saturday at the blessing of the Paschal candle, the deacon was vested in an appareled alb, dalmatic, and white chasuble. While the first prophecy was being sung, the celebrant, vested in black chasuble, came to the altar. During the first litany, the celebrant removed his black chasuble and put on a white dalmatic and chasuble. They went to the font singing the second litany, bringing with them a large candle in addition to the blessed candle. The holy chrism was not mixed into the water, unless there was a baby to baptize, etc. They returned to choir singing the third litany. At the end of Mass, the deacon intoned the *Magnificat* antiphon, and concluded Mass and Vespers with *Ite, missa est*. At that point, they took off their winter habit and went to Compline in surplice.

The next day, between Matins and Lauds, they performed the Office of the Sepulcher.[68] Nothing was lacking: they even had soldiers guarding the sepulcher, who concluded the whole ceremony by breaking their lances or pikes on the third stall next to the Lord Cantor, and then went about

---

[66] Perhaps a typographical error for *Maria ergo unxit pedes Jesu* (Cantus ID 003699).
[67] Cantus ID 006287.
[68] See a description of this office on pp. 74–75, and also p. 217.

the whole church with swords drawn. After this, the subdeacon intoned the *Te Deum*. On this day, two crosses were carried in the processions of both Mass and Vespers.

On Easter and Pentecost days, between None and Vespers, the whole clergy processed to escort the Lord Cantor from his house, and he offered them a drink as a mark of gratitude and courtesy, for lack of which the practice was abolished some twenty years ago. Nevertheless, it was a quasi-episcopal honor, one of the most beautiful a dignitary of the chapter could receive.

On each of the Rogation days, they recited fifty psalms, that is, they said the whole psalter over three days. However, they only held a procession on Tuesday, with banners, crosses, candles, holy water, and incense.

On Ascension day, before the high Mass, there was a procession with three crosses, three subdeacons, three deacons, and three priests, all vested.

On Pentecost day, at the second *Alleluia, Veni sancte Spiritus*[69] and during the Prose, they threw fire, tow, flowers, and birds down from the top of the church to the floor. They still do this today.

There is an express indication that when the Purification fell on the Sunday or Monday before Septuagesima, it had an octave that ended on Saturday at None. Note that they had no octaves from Septuagesima until Easter.

If the feast of St. Mark fell on a Sunday after the octave of Easter, they celebrated it on that day, transferring not only the Sunday Office but also the fast and procession to the following Monday: *In ipsa die Dominica fiat de Sancto, et in crastino fiat de Dominica, et fiat ibidem jejunium et Letania*. Today, the practice in the diocese of Orléans is to defer St. Mark's Office to Monday and the procession and abstinence to Friday. It really is not so difficult.

Fasting vigils had a sort of first Vespers, in which they prostrated themselves during the preces, even though the oration of the preceding Sunday was said.

On 6 August, the feast of St. Sixtus, they blessed new grapes at Mass before the words *Per quem haec omnia* in the Canon, as is done today in the whole of Lorraine. This proves that these words referred to fruits, and even the signs of the cross were meant to be made over them.

They began to wear winter habits from first Vespers of All Saints. During this octave, they held no saint's feast, to avoid celebrating both a general feast of saints and a particular saint.

In the procession held on All Souls, they were not content to sprinkle a mere drop of holy water. They did not hold back, as apparent from the fact that two persons carried a large vessel of water on their shoulders for sprinkling over the tombs in the church, cloister, cemetery, and chapterhouse. It is indicated that the water was blessed immediately before the procession.

---

[69] Cantus ID g01092.

Saint-Euverte

St-Euverte is an abbey church of canons regular. The bishops of Orléans used to be buried in this church, as attested by Stephen of Tournai, a canon, cantor, and abbot of this abbey.[70] Today they have no peculiar liturgical customs.

Here are some customs that used to be observed by the canons regular of this house not two or three hundred years ago, as found in a manuscript ritual dating from that time.[71]

In the Sunday procession after the blessing of water, they sprinkled not only the clergy, but also the refectory, kitchen, and dorter, saying a proper oration at each place.

On Ash Wednesday, it seems that they imposed the ashes at the church door. At any rate, it was done in the course of the procession before they re-entered choir.

This manuscript ritual includes blessings of new fire, new fruits, grapes, bread, and wine.

At baptisms[72] the priest did the anointings with his thumb. The priest laid his hand over the head of the child saying *Nec te latet Satana*. The godparents also put their hand over the child's head: *Hic mittat manum super caput pueri, mittant et patrini*. These exorcisms were done in the porch or outside the church, since the ritual reads *deinde intret in monasterium*, "into the minster," that is, into the church. After the usual interrogations, the priest baptized the child by immersion, plunging him in thrice. At the end of the ceremony, the child was brought to the altar and the priest recited Matthew 10:13, *Offerebant Jesu parvulos*, over him. This church has a parish and a baptismal font as the other collegiate churches in Orléans, namely St-Aignan, St-Pierre-en-Pont, and St-Pierre-Puellier.

On sick visits, Extreme Unction preceded communion. At the burial, the body and the open grave were sprinkled and incensed, as is still done in certain churches.

---

[70] Stephen of Tournai, *Epistula* 296 to Hugh de Garlande, bishop of Orléans, ed. Jules Desilve, *Lettres d'Étienne de Tournai* (Valenciennes, 1893), 371–72. Stephen draws a link between the newly-elected bishop's customary pernoctation at St-Euverte before solemnly entering his cathedral city the following day and his eventual burial in that abbey. However, it appears that the belief that the bishops passed the night at St-Euverte because they would eventually be buried there is fanciful, since, according to Bimbenet, only a single bishop (Manasses, Hugh's uncle) was actually buried there; see Eugène Bimbenet, "Justice temporelle de l'évêché d'Orléans à cause de la tour de la Fauconnerie," *Mémoires de la Société archéologique de l'Orléanais* 6 (1863): 66.
[71] This ritual quotes several passages found in the ordinal of the abbey of St-Victor of Paris, which reformed St-Euverte in 1148. An extant late fifteenth-century ordinal of St-Euverte is but a copy, with few variants, of the Victorine ordinal (Bibliothèque nationale, MS. lat. 4384), edited by Luc Jocqué and Ludo Milis, Corpus Christianorum Continuatio Mediaevalis 61 (Brepols, 1984). The manuscript ritual Le Brun des Marettes describes seems to be lost.
[72] Author's note: This abbey has a parish.

At the end of the same manuscript, one finds how Extreme Unction was given to canons in danger of death two hundred years ago. Extreme Unction preceded the Holy Viaticum. The abbot administered it to the sick canon in the presence of the entire community. While he recited the prayers, a canon-priest went to fetch the Holy Viaticum in a chalice or ciborium covered with a large veil: *Exeant duo de Fratribus ad Ecclesiam, videlicet unus Sacerdos qui deferat Communionem cum calice offertorio cooperto.*[73] Another canon went before him carrying a lantern and wine cruet. After the concluding prayers of Extreme Unction, the abbot scrubbed his hands with salt and washed them, and the water was poured into the *piscina*. Finally, the abbot gave the sick canon communion after a series of interrogations.

When the sick canon was on the point of death, a hairshirt was spread on the ground and ashes sprinkled on top in the shape of a cross. The sick canon was laid upon it: *Dum Frater morti penitus appropinquaverit, ad terram cilicium extendatur, et desuper cinis in modum crucis spargatur, ac deinde superponatur.*[74] The entire community was present, as well as the abbot, who, as soon as the sick man had died and the commendations had been said, appointed those who were to wash and bury the body. Then, he put on the stole again and sprinkled the body with holy water and incensed it. It was then taken to the church and laid in choir.

Before burial, the body was sprinkled with holy water and incensed, as was the grave into which the body was lowered after the words *Haec requies mea*, "This is my place of rest."[75] After the burial, the canons returned to the church singing the seven penitential psalms. Once in choir, they prostrated themselves before the steps: *et ingressi medium Chorum prosternantur ante gradus*. The ceremony ended with the orations *Absolve* and *Fidelium*, and then they retired.

Saint-Pierre-en-Pont, Saint-Pierre-Puellier, Saint-Pierre-Lentin, and Saint-Pierre-en-Sentelée

The collegiate, formerly abbatial, church of St-Pierre-en-Pont is called in Latin *S. Petri virorum* or *in puncto*,[76] and the collegiate church of St-Pierre-Puellier is called *S. Petri puellaris* or *puellarum*, perhaps because there were monks in one and nuns in the other, or perhaps for the following reason.

It is said that these two churches were once two baptisteries, one for the catechumen men and boys, and the other for the women and girls. A third parish church, St-Pierre-Lentin, in Latin *S. Petri Lactentium*, was the

---

[73] *Liber ordinis Sancti Victoris Parisiensis* 67, ed. Jocqué and Milis, 259.
[74] *Liber ordinis Sancti Victoris Parisiensis* 68, ed. Jocqué and Milis, 261.
[75] Psalm 131:14. *Liber ordinis Sancti Victoris Parisiensis* 74, ed. Jocqué and Milis, 273
[76] Author's note: That is, *in puncto urbis*, in the middle of the city. This church used to ring the curfew bell that signaled to the entire city it was time to retire.

baptistery for infants, and still today babies born to mothers at the nearby Hôtel-Dieu (which is worth a visit) are baptized here. It is served by six priests who sing the Office every day and administer the sacraments, and by some twenty Augustinian nuns, who take special care of the sick. Near a fountain in the men's infirmary is a stone they call *la pierre des Morts* ("the stone of the dead"), whereon they lay the dead immediately after their passing, before taking them to the place of burial.

We have mentioned the troughs of wax presented to the bishop as payment for feudal dues in Ste-Croix.[77] Feudal payment is also rendered to the dean of St-Pierre-en-Pont, although in very different kind. To this day, every year at the *Magnificat* of first Vespers of the Ascension, the Seigneur of Bapaume of the parish of Ouvrouer-les-Champs is obliged to present to the dean of St-Pierre-en-Pont an old ram with a full coat of wool and gilded horns, to which must be attached two escutcheons bearing the arms of St-Pierre, and a purse hanging from its neck containing five Parisian pounds. It is not presented in the church but in the cloister on the church's left side. When popes and their legates pass through the city, this dean delivers a formal address to them on behalf of the entire clergy of Orléans. At the installation of canons of this church, the cantor makes the new canon touch the antiphonal on the eagle in mid-choir, to signify the obligation of singing.

There is nothing liturgically peculiar in St-Pierre-Puellier, except that in Lent the canons chant Vespers in the afternoon at the same time as the rest of the year. Thus they do not disturb the order of the Office of Vespers.

There still stands in Orléans the church of St-Pierre-en-Sentelée, *in Semita lata*, *lée* meaning "broad," so called because it is near the main road from Orléans to Paris.

On Sundays and major feasts, in the churches of St-Benoît and St-Victor, they sing a psalm in the tone of the Communion antiphon during the people's communion.

There is a certain excellent and praiseworthy custom in Orléans, namely that almost everyone, including the cathedral canons, chooses to be buried in the cemeteries, such that people are rarely buried inside churches. Even at the funerals of commoners there is always a large crowd of people, both relatives and neighbors, accompanying the body not only to the church but all the way to the burial site, together with all the clergy.

At funeral or anniversary Masses, the deceased's wife, or in her absence the closest relative of the deceased, offers a candle, bread, and wine at the offertory procession, both in town and in the countryside. On All Souls, I have seen up to fifty or sixty people in a single parish making this offering, much as is done in Milan by the goodly matrons they call *vetulones*, who bring up bread and wine for the sacrifice at the offertory of the Mass.

---

[77] See p. 134.

Those who receive communion respond *Amen* as a profession of faith after the priest has said *Corpus Domini nostri Jesu Christi*, as in Paris.

In Orléans, they eat meat on the six Saturdays after Christmas.

In the parish church of St-Michel, communion is always given to the people after the priest's communion, at both low and high Masses.

In Orléans, there is a Benedictine monastery known as Notre-Dame-de-Bonne-Nouvelle, to which the late M. Guillaume Prousteau, doctor and professor of law, entrusted his library to be made open to the public. It is quite extensive and full of excellent books. It is open every Monday, Wednesday, and Friday, and is very well frequented. The erudition and courteous manner of its learned librarian, Dom Jacques-Philippe Billouet of Rouen, who has been assigned to the post by the superiors, never fails to attract all the men of letters in Orléans, since he is *paratus ad satisfactionem omni poscenti se.*[78]

---

[78] "Ready to give satisfaction to all who request it of him" (1 Peter 3:15).

JARGEAU

JARGEAU, formerly called *Gargogilum* or *Jargogilum* in Latin, now *Jargolium* or *Gergolium*, is a small city on the Loire four leagues from Orléans. It has a collegiate church of canons.

A manuscript ordinary of the church that is about four hundred years old[1] states that on Ember Wednesday in December, a priest vested in dalmatic and white chasuble read the Gospel and homily in the middle of the choir.

Mass was said after None on the Ember days of Advent and Lent, as well as on the vigil of St. Andrew when it fell during Advent: *propter geminatum jejunium.*[2]

The Genealogy of Our Lord is here called *Generatio*, and the *Kyrie eleison*, the *Kyriela*. There was a prophecy in addition to the Epistle at the three Masses of Christmas.

The *pastourelle* or the Office of the Shepherds was still performed at Lauds on Christmas night.

The deacon did not say *Ite, missa est* at the first Mass, but rather the antiphon *Completa sunt.*[3]

At each suffrage or commemoration made at Lauds and Vespers, they went to each respective altar: the suffrage of the cross was said before the

---

[1] Orléans, Médiathèque municipale, MS. 0143.
[2] "On account of the double fast."
[3] Likely a scribal error for *Ecce completa sunt* (Cantus ID 002498). The deacon actually sung this antiphon after the oration at the end of Lauds, which began immediately after the Communion antiphon of the first Mass. Once the deacon had sung it in full, the choir responded *Deo gratias* and the second Mass began forthwith. At the end of the second Mass the same antiphon was sung: "In place of *Ite, missa est*, the deacon sings this entire antiphon, *Ecce* [sic] *completa sunt*. Choir: *Deo gratias*" (fol. 14v).

great rood, that of the Virgin before her chapel, and so on. In Lyon, they also sing the commemorations of the saints in their chapels.

On Ash Wednesday, after the procession, the ashes were imposed at the church door, and they are still given there at present.

In several places in this ordinary, the church is called *monasterium*, in French *montier* or *moutier*, "minster." This is the origin of that figure of speech *mener la bru au Moutier*, which means to take one's daughter-in-law to the church. The word has been used with this meaning for over eight hundred years.

The lessons of Matins were sometimes chosen at the dean's pleasure. *Per ferias istius hebdomadae leguntur Moralia Job, vel Augustinus super Psalterium, vel Joannes Chrysostomus.*

On Palm Sunday, the antiphon *Occurrunt turbae* was taken as a pretext for everyone to go kiss the cross:[4] *Cantatur ista antiphona* Occurrunt, *et tunc debent omnes occurrere ad adorandam Crucem.*[5] It was also upon reentering the city that they began the responsory *Ingrediente Domino in sanctam civitatem*,[6] in conformity with the literal meaning of the text, even though the church door was not opened until after the *Attollite portas*.

On Maundy Thursday, the sacred host was reserved in the sacristy for the following day, and the antiphon *Hoc Corpus* was sung as it was carried there. In all these cases they act out the words of the chant.[7]

On Good Friday, during the Mass *ex praesanctificatis*, they read the first prophecy behind the altar, and the second in front. Hence at that time the altar had no retable. The priest raised a large cross very high while singing the antiphon *Super omnia*, and then placed it on the altar in a raised place: all gestures and ceremonies that conform to the letter of the sung text. It is all quite natural.[8]

The ordinary explains that the expression *voce submissa* ("in a low voice") means "such that it may be heard by the assistants," *ita ut possit a circumstantibus audiri*. The assistants responded *Amen* to the *Per omnia* in the same tone after the fraction of the host on Good Friday: *Circumstantes voce submissa respondent, Amen.*[9]

On Holy Saturday, the parish priest began the first prophecy at the Mass after the deacon, vested in dalmatic and chasuble, had sung the *Exultet*. At the Mass, in place of the peace they kissed the chrism and oil: *omnes deosculantur Chrisma et Oleum loco pacis.*[10]

---

[4] On the antiphon *Occurrunt turbae* (Cantus ID 004107), see de Vert, *Explication*, 2:22.
[5] Orléans, Médiathèque municipale, MS. 0143, fol. 37r.
[6] Cantus ID 006961.
[7] On the antiphon *Hoc corpus* (Cantus ID g00808) and related ceremonial, see de Vert, *Explication* 1:175–76.
[8] On the antiphon *Super omnia* (Cantus ID 005061) and its ceremonial, see de Vert, *Explication* 1:222.
[9] Orléans, Médiathèque municipale, MS. 0143, fol. 41r.
[10] Orléans, Médiathèque municipale, MS. 0143, fol. 42v.

On Easter day, they performed the Office of the Sepulcher after the third responsory of Matins.[11]

On the three days of Rogations, before the procession, they recited the whole psalter: fifty psalms each day between Terce and Sext. See how they surpassed us!

On Ascension day, two cantors sang the Introit *Viri Galilaei* from behind the altar.[12] The priest intoned the psalm *Omnes gentes*.[13] After the cantors recommenced the *Viri Galilaei*, the rest was continued by the choir.

On the Saturday vigil of Pentecost, there were three litanies, as on the Saturday Easter Vigil.

On 6 August, the feast of St. Sixtus, they blessed new grapes at the Mass immediately before *Per quem haec omnia, Domine, bona*.

On the Exaltation of the Cross, after the Offertory, they adored the cross as on Good Friday.

---

[11] See p. 217, n. 82. [12] Cantus ID g01079. [13] Psalm 46.

ABBEY OF SAINT-MESMIN

ST-MESMIN is a famous abbey (PLATE 32) on the river Loiret near Orléans. It was formerly called Micy; in Latin, *Miciacum* or *S. Maximini ad Ligeritum*. The monastery church has a round holy water stoup with this Greek inscription engraved on the rim of the basin:

ΝΙΨΟΝ ΑΝΟΜΗΜΑΤΑ, ΜΗ ΜΟΝΑΝ ΟΨΙΝ.

The stoup of St-Étienne-des-Grès in Paris, and formerly that of the Hagia Sophia in Constantinople, had the same inscription. The phrase is a palindrome, and may be translated into Latin as follows: *Lava delicta, non solam faciem*, and in English: "Wash your transgressions, not only your face." This abbey has been a nursery of holy abbots and hermits.

CLÉRY

CLÉRY, in Latin *Clariacus*, *Clariacum*, or *Cleriacum*. It has a church with the size and majesty of a cathedral. The altar is very simple, without candles. The Blessed Sacrament is reserved in a large tabernacle of gilded wood behind the altar and above the retable, flanked by two candles.

Louis XI, king of France, ordered this church built. He is buried there, and the white marble mausoleum containing his statue is located on the left side of the nave, between the rood screen and the preacher's pulpit, raised some three or four feet above the floor.

BLOIS

Blois, an episcopal city on the river Loire. There is nothing peculiar besides the bishop's solemn blessing before the *Agnus Dei* when he celebrates Mass on major feasts.

HUISSEAU

In Huisseau, a town in the diocese of Orléans near the abbey of Voisins, only those who intend to communicate join the offertory procession. Everyone rises at *Sursum corda*, a gesture in conformity with the word *sursum*. For the same reason, the priest raises his arms and the chant rises slightly in pitch.[1] The chant rises even higher in Milan, up to the fourth.

[1] For the source of this notion, and a survey of customs of raising the voice, arms, and body at the *Sursum corda*, see de Vert, *Explication*, 1:116–17, 154, 219–22, 3:212–13.

LE MANS

Le Mans on the river Sarthe, *Cenomanni ad Sartam*, is the capital city of Maine.

Cathedral of Saint-Julien

In the cathedral of St-Julien (PLATE 33), there is nothing on the altar except a retable with a dossal, not even a crucifix or candlesticks. Above the retable there is a statue of the Virgin, and higher up a crosier-shaped fixture whence the Blessed Sacrament is suspended under a small brass cross. Close by it are statues of Sts. Gervase and Protase, former patrons of this church, with candles between them.

On Sundays, the celebrant blesses the holy water at the high altar. Making a bow, he sprinkles the altar while kneeling and then the people near him. Afterwards, the dean of the choirboys, carrying the holy water stoup, and the coped crucifer, preceded by two choirboys with candles and followed by the subdeacon and deacon, process with the clergy through the nave. There, the celebrant sprinkles the canons and cantors, and then the stoup-bearer sprinkles the choirboys. Next, they go to several chapels, holding five or six stations, all the while singing responsories as the celebrant sprinkles tombs along the way.

The celebrant carries the Gospel book with him when he goes up to the altar to say Mass. At the foot of the altar, he hands it to the deacon, who then presents it for him to kiss immediately after their genuflection before the altar.

When the bishop is present, he joins the celebrant at the altar as soon as he arrives there and, standing alone before the center of the altar in front of the others, says the *Introibo* with the psalm *Judica* and the rest. Meanwhile, the celebrant and subdeacon stand at the Gospel side and the deacon at the Epistle side, *facie ad invicem conversi*.[1] After the *Confiteor*, the bishop turns towards the clergy and people and says the *Indulgentiam* with the sign of the cross or blessing. Then the priest immediately goes up to the altar by the left side, and the bishop returns to his place.

At the *Lavabo*, the priest washes his hands at the Gospel side.

After the deacon says the *Ite, missa est* and the bishop gives the blessing, the celebrant immediately returns to the sacristy with his ministers.

When the bishop celebrates pontifically, he gives the solemn blessing before the *Agnus Dei*.

Here are some customs of the church of Le Mans:

On the feast of the Circumcision of Our Lord they use red vestments, like the entire Trinitarian order before 1669.

On the vigil and feast of the Epiphany, green vestments.

On the feasts of pontiffs, green, except for the feast of St. Julian, first bishop of Le Mans, when they use red.

On Passion and Palm Sunday and the whole fortnight, they use red vestments, even at the blessing of the new fire, the Paschal candle, and the baptismal font, and at high Mass on Holy Saturday.

They also wear red vestments on Corpus Christi and All Saints.

On all Sundays *per annum*, as well as Sundays in Advent and Lent, they use violet.

On 19 October, they used to say Mass for the anniversary of the consecration of the most recently deceased bishop of Le Mans. The same thing was anciently done by the whole Gallican church.

On Ash Wednesday, the bishop, accompanied by some clerics, expels the public penitents from the church after delivering a short exhortation at the west end of the nave. He reconciles them on Maundy Thursday.

Here are some peculiar practices taken from an old ritual of this church from 1490[2]:

One major feasts that did not fall on Sunday, even though they did not

---

[1] "Facing one another."
[2] Perhaps the same as the ritual of Le Mans mentioned by Dom Edmond Martène that he dates to 1499, as does a catalogue from 1792. All recent attempts at finding this book have failed. The same eighteenth-century catalogue mentions a ritual of Le Mans from 1501, but the earliest printed ritual that has survived was published in Rouen in 1511. See Martimort, *La documentation liturgique*, 237.

bless holy water, they held a procession to sprinkle the people. Instead of the collect *Exaudi nos* said on Sundays, they said *Actiones nostras*.

At baptisms of boys, there were two godfathers and one godmother. At baptisms of girls, there was one godfather and two godmothers.

At betrothals, after the bride and bridegroom plighted their troth in front of the church, they kissed as a sign of their future marriage: *osculentur se in signum matrimonii futuri*.

On the wedding day, the parish priest blessed the nuptial bed at the couple's house, and then some bread and wine, which he gave to the newly-weds to eat and drink.

Marriages were prohibited after None on the Saturday before the first Sunday of Advent until the day after the octave of the Epiphany, and after None on the Saturday before Septuagesima until the day after the octave of Easter, as well as after None on the fifth Sunday after Easter until Trinity Sunday. A 1593 ritual of Autun states the same thing, a sign of the respect they had for fasting days and great feasts. The Council of Trent has reduced prohibition of marriage to Advent and Lent and the octaves of Christmas and Easter.[3]

On Holy Saturday, after the blessing of the new fire and the Paschal candle, the priest, vested in a chasuble, goes to the altar and says the *Confiteor*, after which the prophecies and Tracts are sung. Then the priest removes his chasuble and the first litany is sung in choir, repeating the name of each saint seven times; this is called the *litania septena*. They say the second litany on the way to the font, repeating the name of each saint five times. At the blessing of the font, they usually plunge the candle into the water thrice. After removing the candle, at the end of the sort of brief Preface, the priest allows the candle to drip thrice into the font in the shape of a cross. As is customary elsewhere, after the blessing, the priest sprinkles the altars and the people with holy water that had not been mixed with holy chrism. While processing back to choir, they sing the third litany, repeating each saint's name three times. In the first litany they say *Sancta Maria*, in the second *Sancta Dei genitrix*, and in the third *Sancta virgo virginum*.

At the Lenten absolutions on Ash Wednesday, as the priest and all the people knelt together bareheaded, *crinibus discoopertis*, they said the seven penitential psalms with the greatest possible devotion under the antiphon *Vivo ego, dicit Dominus; nolo mortem peccatoris; sed ut magis convertatur et vivat*.[4] The Litany of the Saints, preces, and orations followed.

I have noticed that this ritual states they gave Extreme Unction to the sick before the Holy Viaticum, as used to be usual everywhere. This is still done in several monasteries.[5]

---

[3] Session 24, *Canones super reformatione circa matrimonium*, ch. 10, eds. Societas Goerresiana, *Concilium Tridentinum diariorum, actorum, epistularum, tractatuum nova collectio*, vol. 9, *Actorum pars sexta* (Herder, 1965), 971.
[4] Cantus ID 005481.
[5] The 1614 Roman ritual foresaw Viaticum being given before Extreme Unction (tit.

At Masses for the Dead, the first verses of the *De profundis* were sung as the Tract if the Mass was said for the soul of a priest,[6] and the first three verses of the psalm *Sicut cervus desiderat* for a layman.[7]

The holy water stoup at the Dominican church is outside the door, in accordance with the ancient placement of stoups after they had replaced fountains. It is indeed the proper place for them.[8]

V, c. 1, §2). Some churches of France, such as Amiens, Avranches, Boulogne, Clermont, Évreux, St-Flour, Laon, Le Mans, and Nantes, did the opposite, and some French bishops sought to restore this order around Le Brun des Marettes's time, including that of Paris, as he notes on p. 185. See François-Aimé Pouget, *Instructions générales en forme de catéchisme* (Lyon, 1730), 442.
[6] Psalm 129; Cantus ID g00634.
[7] Psalm 41; Cantus ID g02374.
[8] See p. 32, n. 1.

LA TRAPPE

La Trappe is an abbey renowned nowadays for the great piety and austere life of its monks, who belong to the order of Cîteaux of the Strict Observance. A statue of the Virgin holds the Eucharist suspended above the high altar (see PLATE 34).[1]

At the *Magnificat* of Vespers in winter, since there is not sufficient light to read, they light several absconces — dark lanterns that give off light only to one side — to sing the antiphons and orations.

At high Mass, the monks exchange a sacred kiss of peace at the *Agnus Dei* and make a prostration before communing.[2]

On Good Friday, they recite the entire psalter barefoot.

---

[1] The Eucharist was originally reserved in a tabernacle upon the altar. During his reform of the La Trappe, Abbot Armand-Jean de Rancé, sometime between 1664 and 1688, replaced this tabernacle "and the indecent statues surrounding it" with a statue of Our Lady holding a suspended pyx with her right hand and the infant Jesus on her left arm, with cherubs at her feet. Some found the new arrangement shocking, and Rancé placed the following inscription below the statue:

> Si quaeras natum cur matris dextera gestat,
>   Sola fuit tanto munere digna parens.
> Non poterat fungi majori munere mater,
>   Non poterat major dextera ferre Deum.

(If thou seekest why the mother's right hand beareth the Son, / She alone was worthy of such a gift. / No greater duty could the mother perform, / No greater right hand could bear God.) The claim by Rancé's defenders that this design was an ancient Cistercian tradition seems unsubstantiated. See Casimir Gaillardin, *Les trappistes* (Paris, 1853), 1:238 and François Macé de Lépinay, "Contribution à l'étude des suspensions eucharistiques au XVIIIe siècle," *Bulletin monumental* 145, n. 3 (1987): 298.
[2] On the rarity of the kiss of peace in Le Brun des Marettes's age, see p. 45, n. 46. Durand claims that monks did not give each other this kiss because it is always omitted in Masses of the Dead, and monks are regarded as being "dead to the world" (*Rationale* 4.53.8, ed. Davril and Thibodeau, 1:546), but de Vert, *Explication* 3:366–67, suggests more literal reasons.

When they are in danger of death, they are given Extreme Unction and then the Holy Viaticum. When *in extremis*, they are placed on straw and ash to die, following the ancient custom of the Church, also maintained by the Carthusians to this day.

CHARTRES

CHARTRES lies on the banks of the river Eure. Its Latin name is *Carnutum* or *Carnotum ad Auduram*.

Notre-Dame of Chartres

The cathedral of Notre-Dame is very beautiful, and the crypt church is richly ornamented and illuminated by many silver lamps. The exterior of this church is impressive, with three spacious porches and two towers above the main entrance visible from four leagues away.[1]

The choir, one of the largest and most magnificent one can find, is filled with a large number of seats arranged in two rows of stalls on each side, and a broad bench for the third row, with a wooden footrest.

The bishop's stall is rather plain, placed on the Epistle side at the end of the canons' seats, as in Paris and Rouen, without a covering. It has only a carpet in front and a faldstool set inside for the bishop, as shown in the illustration (PLATE 35).

The main altar is quite broad. The sanctuary is surrounded not by a balustrade, but by brass columns surmounted by angels. The antependium is attached to the altar cloths a half-foot over the edge of the altar. Its fringe rests on the edge of the altar table itself.[2] The retable has a dossal, above which stands a statue of the Blessed Virgin in gilded silver. Behind her is a brass bar supporting a golden crucifix one and a half feet tall. At its foot, another brass bar protrudes about one or one and a half feet over the altar. On the end of it hangs the holy pyx, as the Council of Tours says, *sub titulo crucis Corpus Domini componatur*.[3]

On major feasts, the Introit of the Mass is sung from the nave as they enter the choir.

Above the corner of the altar a small violet veil about one square foot in size is suspended from a small cord, as in Orléans.[4] Just before

---

[1] About ten English miles.
[2] At some point, before the antependium or frontal became too heavily embroidered, it was often sewn onto the altar cloths. The *aurifrisium* or "fringe" was also, until the fifteenth century, attached to the altar cloth above the frontal. See Braun, *Die liturgischen Paramente*, 194 and p. 61, n. 2 and p. 144, n. 39.
[3] See p. 87, n. 1.
[4] See p. 136.

the consecration, the deacon draws it toward the center of the altar so that, as they explain, the sacred host may be visible to those at the far end of the choir who would otherwise not see it. After the elevation of the chalice, the deacon draws it back to the Gospel corner. They say this small veil has been in use for a very long time in this church. I believe its true purpose was to present the priest with a vivid image of Christ crucified during the consecration. For there is such an image on the veil itself, called the *majestas* or *divina majestas*, as in the rubric *Inclinet ante majestatem*, like the one used in Reims before a crucifix was placed in the middle of the altar.[5]

Side aisles permit one to walk around the choir, but the windows, although very large, are so darkened by the paintings and thickness of the glass that in wintertime those in choir still need candles to say Sext after the conventual Mass at ten thirty in the morning. At that hour, they do not respond *Deo gratias* after the short chapter, nor is there a response to the versicle after the short responsory. The versicle has a melisma as long as that of the versicles of the major hours. Apparently they say the response in a low voice during the melisma.

The oath sworn by the canons when they are received into their office is worth reproducing here:

> Canonicorum Carnotensium juramentum in receptione sua.
>
> *In Capitulo juramentum factum ad caput beatae Annae tale est. Cantor, seu locum ejus tenens, dicit canonizando:* Vos juratis super sacras istas Reliquias quod estis de legitimo matrimonio procreatus; item quod estis liberae conditionis, nec estis colibertus, nec filius coliberti?[6] Item quod pro ista Praebenda, cujus investituram expectatis, non dedistis, nec promisistis, nec alius pro vobis dedit vel promisit vobis scientibus, aurum vel argentum, vel pecuniam aliquam, vel aliud quod per pecuniam aliquam debeat vel valeat comparari: et si promissum fuerit, per vos non solventur? Item juratis quod in

---

[5] Any image of Christ, including the image of Christ crucified on the page of a missal facing the Canon, could be called the *majestas*; see Du Cange, "Majestas," 5:179b. In *Explication* 4:30–40, de Vert traces four stages of evolution in the presentation of this *majestas*. First, there was only the crucifix painted on the *Te igitur* page of the missal. Second, in order for the priest to have before his eyes an image of Christ crucified during the Canon, especially at the consecration, a small veil bearing an image was drawn before his eyes. Third, a crucifix was placed on the altar before Mass, and removed afterwards. Finally, tired of replacing the crucifix after every Mass, the crucifix began to be left as a permanent adornment on the altar. De Vert notes that the veil was still in use in Reims, Orléans, Cambrai, Chartres, and, until recently, in Paris. He also says, however, that the veil at Chartres did not bear any image, and that at Cambrai the common belief about the veil's purpose was that it was to make the host visible. In the later Middle Ages in Germany, devotion to the Holy Face was particularly strong, and many altars bore a painted Veronica at the base of the retable or gradine.

[6] A colibert (Latin *colibertus* or *collibertus*) was a freeman who, although ranking above a serf, was nonetheless still obliged to render some services to his lord.

percipiendis distributionibus fraudem aliquam non facietis? Sic vos Deus adjuvet et haec Sancta.[7]

The blessing of holy water on Sundays is not held after Terce as in most other churches, but at the first Mass, which is said at four or five in the morning. The priest who is to say it vests in an alb and stole and blesses the water in a stoup either at the entrance of the church or in some other place, and then goes to the chapel to sprinkle the people present to hear Mass. Before high Mass, a choirboy brings the holy water stoup (or *orceau*, as it is called in Chartres, from the Latin term *urceus* or *urceolus*) when everyone is ready to hold the stations. The procession goes out from the choir through the rood gate, and without entering the nave proceeds directly to the altar of St. John the Baptist in the left crossing. The priest, deacon, and subdeacon wear albs and hold the almuce over the arm and the biretta in hand; the former two also have stoles. The priest first sprinkles the altar, then the deacon and subdeacon, and finally the entire clergy. After having circled around the entire choir, the procession re-enters through the same gate. The same practice is found in many large churches that I describe in this account, which makes it clear that the purpose of the Sunday procession before Mass was to sprinkle the people and the common places.

At high Mass, the priest, deacon, and subdeacon first reverence the altar, then turn to reverence the choir. Turning back towards the altar, they begin the Mass, and finally go up to the altar. During the *Gloria in excelsis*, the subdeacon proceeds to the rood loft with the Epistle book, while the deacon, having received the Gospel book, retires behind the altar. The priest remains alone at the altar with his assistant priest, who stands at the end of the altar, vested in a surplice, to serve the celebrant. After singing the Epistle, the subdeacon returns to the altar. At that moment, the deacon comes out with the Gospel book and, having received the celebrant's blessing, goes to the rood loft accompanied by the subdeacon, who holds the cushion; the choirboy, who walks in front incensing; and the two candle-bearers. As soon as the deacon leaves the altar, he raises the Gospel book with both hands and, as he passes, the clerics get up and uncover their heads. Once he has sung the Gospel in the rood loft and descended with his ministers, the subdeacon holds the Gospel book on the cushion in front of his stomach. As he passes, the clergy rise. The subdeacon presents

---

[7] "The oaths of the canons of Chartres at their reception. The following is the oath sworn at the chapterhouse before the head of St. Anne. The cantor, or his deputy, says to the incoming canon: Do you swear over these holy relics that you are born of legitimate wedlock, that you are a freeman, that you are not a colibert or the son of a colibert? That you did not give or promise gold or silver or any sort of money or anything that might be bought or changed into money in exchange for the prebend, whose investiture you await, and that no one else gave or promised the same in your name, and that if such was promised, that you will not keep to it? Do you also swear that you shall commit no fraud in receiving your distributions? So help you God and this saint."

the open Gospel book to the celebrant for him to kiss and then to the canons at their places, before returning to the altar.

Once the priest has incensed the altar at the offertory, the deacon takes the thurible from the choirboy, descends the altar steps and, after incensing the altar with three swings, kisses one of its corners. Then he circles it while incensing, giving the two reliquaries three swings each, and returns to his place. Shortly thereafter, the choirboy brings the thurible back to the deacon, who incenses the rest of the altar in the same way, kisses the other corner, and then incenses the priest and subdeacon.

After this, the thurifer receives the thurible from the deacon and incenses him. The deacon holds his biretta in hand during the entire Mass, never putting it down except when taking the Gospel book to the rood loft.

At the *Sursum corda*, the subdeacon receives the paten, which is given to him covered with a veil, and holds it slightly elevated in front of him behind the altar, such that he sees nothing of what takes place there.

All remain standing at the elevation, except at Masses when the *O salutaris Hostia* is said, and then only for its duration.

At the *Pater noster*, the subdeacon goes back in front of the altar and gives the paten, without the veil, to the deacon, who holds it even higher than the subdeacon until the end of the *Pater*, when he puts it back on the altar.[8]

Then the choir sings the psalm *Exaudiat*,[9] during which the celebrant, his ministers, and all the clergy kneel.[10] Then the priest receives communion and the deacon takes the cruets and pours the ablutions: this is the only time the deacon serves the priest. A choirboy holding a basin washes the priest's fingers as at the *Lavabo*, and pours the water out into the piscina, so that the priest is not obliged to drink the rinsings. This was done everywhere in former times, and is still done at Lyon and among the Carthusians, who have remained faithful to ancient customs.

The priest goes to the corner of the altar to say the Postcommunions, and the deacon sings the *Ite, missa est* facing the clergy. Then the celebrant gives the blessing and returns to the sacristy with his ministers in the same order they came in.

When the bishop celebrates pontifically on major feasts, he gives the solemn blessing at the *Agnus Dei* and not at the end of the Mass.

The ceremonies of public penance on Ash Wednesday and Maundy Thursday are more or less the same as those we shall describe for the church of Rouen.[11]

---

[8] On the elevation of the bare paten by the deacon or subdeacon during the *Pater noster*, a practice common throughout northern France (see p. 255) and England and retained by the Premonstratensian use, see de Vert, *Explication*, 3:318n1 and Jungmann, *The Mass*, 2:291. Both explain the gesture as an indication of the imminence of communion.
[9] Psalm 19.
[10] On the medieval addition of prayers after the *Pater noster*, see Jungmann, *The Mass*, 2:292–93. In some places a prostration was expected at this point.
[11] See pp. 234–36.

On Maundy Thursday, six priest-archdeacons celebrate the high Mass conjointly with the bishop, consecrate the holy oils with him, and receive communion under both species from the same host and the same chalice as the bishop. The bishop stands before the middle of the altar, with three priests at his right and three at his left in a single line. All seven sing in unison and perform all the ceremonies of the Mass together. Praiseworthy church, to have so carefully preserved such an august and ancient ceremony that helps us understand why in several churches the bishop is assisted at Mass on major feasts by priests and *curés*![12] At the end of the Mass, the deacon gives a wordless blessing with the sacred host before taking it to the treasury, where it is reserved in a burse for the following day.

The Maundy or washing of the feet was performed on the same day. The altars, however, are not washed until the following day right before the start of the Mass *ex praesanctificatis*. In Milan, at Mass, after the words *emisit spiritum* of the Passion, they remove the altar cloths and simply wipe it.

During Easter week, they hold the procession to the font at Vespers. All the clergy of the cathedral who are neither priests nor deacons, whether or not they are canons, carry a white staff in hand, as does the succentor, who walks at the head of the junior canons. The reason for this custom, they say, is to represent the white habits the newly-baptized used to wear during the octave. On the way to and from the font, they sing the fourth and fifth psalms of the feria.

Although this church fasts on vigils of apostles and observes more fasts than others, it nevertheless does not fast on the vigil of Pentecost, thus following the ancient custom of the Church and of the churches of Angers, Nantes, and Amiens. Indeed, the Fathers testify that there was no fasting during the fifty days of Eastertide, which did not end until the evening of Pentecost Sunday.

On the Ember Wednesday of December, they read the entire Gospel *Missus est*[13] as the first lesson of Matins, as in Sens. Then the choir prostrates and sings the antiphon *Salve Regina*,[14] following which the homily is read as usual.

---

[12] See pp. xxxii–xxxiii.
[13] Luke 1:26–38.
[14] The will of Miles d'Illiers, baron-bishop of Luçon, dated 21 November 1551, describes the ceremony: "During the last psalm of Matins, two canons leave the choir and go to the sacristy together with four choirboys and the cross-bearer, candle-bearers, thurifer, and the subdeacon and deacon wearing white dalmatics. At the middle of the choir, the said deacon is to sing the Gospel *Missus est* until the phrase *Ecce ancilla Domini, fiat mihi*. Thereafter, the priest who begins Matins must kneel, together with the cantor, succentor, and the two cope-bearers at his sides, in front of the eagle. All those in choir prostrate themselves at their stalls and must sing, very calmly and devoutly, the antiphon *Salve Regina*, with its versicles and the oration *Deus qui beatae Mariae Virginis utero*. Then the cantor shall say the *De profundis*, followed by the oration *Deus qui inter*. Then all shall rise and the deacon shall read the explanation of the Gospel" (Armand-Désiré de La Fontenelle de Vaudoré, *Histoire du monastère et des évêques de Luçon* [Paris, 1847], 1:243).

GALLARDON

Gallardon is a small town four leagues[1] from Chartres. One peculiar feature of its parish church is that the altar does not have a frontal, as is customary nearly everywhere, but rather a simple veil of the same fabric as the vestments, in keeping with ancient custom. We know that the relics of the saints used to be kept under the altars, and to prevent dust from damaging the reliquaries a simple covering or veil was placed on the front of the altar. This is why most altar frontals have a fringe on the upper edge to hide the rod, as we saw in Chartres.[2]

---
[1] Ten English miles.
[2] See p. 165.

VAUX-DE-CERNAY

Vaux-de-Cernay, in Latin *Valles Cernaii*, is an abbey of the Cistercian order. The monastery library houses many manuscripts, especially missals and other books of customs. One of these manuscripts states that the hymn *Jesu dulcis memoria*,[1] formerly attributed to St. Bernard, was actually not written by him, but by a pious nun. Another manuscript of the Cistercian *Liber usuum*, more detailed and apparently adapted to the particular use of this monastery, implies that it was sometimes necessary to light a candle in an absconce to provide light for the priest to celebrate Mass after Terce. The deacon and subdeacon washed their hands after the *Orate fratres* and received communion from a fragment of the priest's host and from the chalice. In this manuscript, the large chalice veil is called the *offertorium*. One of the missals, written around 1200, calls *Quasi modo* Sunday *Dominica post albas*. In this same missal and in two other manuscript missals from around 1280, as well as in two other missals of the Cistercian use printed in the last century, *Amen* is said in the Canon only at the end. At the *Memento* for the living, the words *qui tibi offerunt* are not followed by *vel pro quibus tibi offerimus*. On Good Friday, the altar ministers receive communion with the abbot.

The Epistles and Gospels are not written down in any of the manuscript missals, because the priest who celebrated a high Mass did not read them, but rather listened to them like the other assistants. In one manuscript they have been added at the end, and in another in the margins.

---
[1] Cantus ID a07798.

PORT-ROYAL

PORT-ROYAL-DES-CHAMPS is an abbey of Cistercian nuns that lies between Versailles and Chevreuse (see PLATE 36 for three views of the abbey).[1]

The church is quite large, and its simplicity and cleanliness inspire respect and devotion.

The main altar is not attached to the wall, since it has an ample and very neat sacristy behind it. Above the high altar, at the end of a wooden crosier-shaped fixture, hangs the sacred pyx. It is set under a large crucifix above a well-regarded painting of the Last Supper by Philippe de Champaigne.[2]

There is nothing on the altar but a crucifix. The four wooden candlesticks are set on the ground at its sides.

The woodwork of the sanctuary and parquet floor is very clean, as is that of the nuns' choir. Indeed, the stalls are kept in such good condition that one would think they were carved not twenty years ago, when in fact they are over 150 years old.[3]

The church contains some paintings by Champaigne and a very clean holy water stoup to the right of its entry.

Inside the cloister, there are several tombs of abbesses and other nuns.[4] From these tombs one can gather

1. That the first abbesses of the Cistercian order, following the spirit of St. Bernard, did not use crosiers. Even today, the abbess of Port-Royal does not use one.

2. That in this monastery there were nuns consecrated by the bishop.[5] Two of them are represented on the same tomb wearing a sort of maniple (see PLATES 37 and 38).[6] The inscription around the tomb reads:

---

[1] Author's note: This monastery no longer exists.

[2] A noted Baroque painter (1602–1674) who produced a number of works for the abbey of Port-Royal-des-Champs. In 1709, his painting of the Last Supper was taken to the abbey of Port-Royal of Paris, and is now at the Louvre.

[3] Author's note: The altar and choir stalls were purchased by the Cistercian nuns of Paris and placed in their church, where one can see them today.

[4] Mother Angélique de Saint-Jean, who ruled Port-Royal abbey from 1678 until her death in 1684, asked Le Brun des Marettes to transcribe the inscriptions of the tombs in the church and courtyard (Fouré, "Jean-Baptiste Le Brun des Marettes," 74).

[5] On the episcopal consecration and veiling of virgins, see p. 78, n. 45.

[6] Carthusian nuns receive a maniple, which they wear over the right arm, at their consecration and veiling, together with a stole, crown, and ring. They wear these objects again only on the day of religious jubilee and when they are buried; see Archdale King, *Liturgies of the Religious Orders* (Bruce Publishing Co., 1955) 8. De Vert, *Explication*, 2:327, note b, claims that this is not a Carthusian "prerogative or privilege," but the survival of "the ancient practice of similarly vesting other types of nuns at their consecration." However, he provides no further examples of nuns wearing maniples, except for the depiction found on this tomb at Port-Royal (2:315).

> Hic jacent duae sorores germanae, hujus praesentis Abbatiae Moniales Deo sacratae, Adelina et Nicholaa dictae ad Pedem, de Stampis quondam progenitae: quarum animae in pace perpetua requiescant. Amen. Obiit dicta Adelina anno Domini M. C. C. octog. octavo.[7]

There is an old necrology or obituary in this abbey to which is attached the ritual for the consecration or blessing of a nun. It states, among other things, that the bishop celebrated Mass and gave communion to the nun he blessed. To this effect he consecrated a large host, which he broke into eight particles, giving one as communion to the nun. He then placed the seven other particles of his host in her right hand, covered with a *dominical* or small white cloth. During the eight days after her consecration or blessing, she gave herself communion from these particles. Priests also used to give themselves communion like this for forty days after their ordination or consecration.[8]

Under the lamp by the balustrade lies a tomb from 1327, if I remember correctly, which it seems necessary to transcribe here since its most interesting aspect is misreported in the *Gallia Christiana* of the brothers de Sainte-Marthe.[9]

It used to be customary for devout noblewomen to take the veil during their last illness, or at least to be clothed in it after their death. See, for example, the tomb of Queen Blanche, mother of King St. Louis, at Maubuisson Abbey near Pontoise. Here in Port-Royal we find the tomb of one

---

[7] "Here lie two blood-sisters, consecrated nuns of this abbey, called Aline and Nicole, whose family name was once Au-Pied-d'Étampes. May their souls rest in everlasting peace. Amen. Aline died in the year of Our Lord 1288."

[8] The *Ordo Romanus* 34.44, from the middle of the eighth century, attests to the custom of newly-consecrated bishops keeping the host consecrated by the Pope at their ordination Mass and communing from it for forty days (Andrieu, *Les Ordines Romani*, 3:613). This practice made its way into the Romano-Germanic Pontifical (63:58) of the tenth century (Michel Andrieu, ed., *Le Pontifical Romano-Germanique du dixième siècle* [Biblioteca Apostolica Vaticana, 1963], 1:225–226), but by the twelfth century it had fallen into desuetude. The *Ordo Romanus* 39.25, from the end of the eighth century, also mentions that newly-ordained priests kept the host consecrated at their ordination Mass to commune from it for forty days (Andrieu, *Les Ordines Romani*, 4:285), and a letter attributed to Fulbert of Chartres explains the mystical meaning behind this practice, connecting it to the forty days the Resurrected Christ spent with his disciples before they began their mission after his Ascension (numbered 3 in PL 141:192D–195D; it is not included among his authentic works by Frederick Behrends in *Letters and Poems of Fulbert of Chartres* [Clarendon Press, 1976], lxii–lxiii). Later liturgical books repeat this interpretation. In France, a similar practice appeared by the ninth century in the case of newly-consecrated virgins, who would reserve the host and commune from it for eight days, and this custom was also picked up by the Romano-Germanic Pontifical (20.29, in Andrieu, *Le Pontifical*, 1:46). By the thirteenth century, however, this too had become rare. For more details, see Andrieu, *Les Ordines Romani*, 3:586–91.

[9] Among other variants, their transcription has *nomine* where Le Brun des Marettes writes *Nonnae*. See *Gallia Christiana* (Paris, 1656), 4:751. Later editions of the *Gallia Christiana* adopted Le Brun des Marettes's reading of the passage; see 7:912 of the 1744 edition.

Dame Marguerite de Levi—wife of Matthew IV de Marly of the illustrious house of Montmorency, grand chamberlain of France—buried in a nun's habit, with this inscription:

> Hic requievit, ibi post cujus nomen habebis.
> Margareta fuit Matthaei Malliancensis
> Uxor; & hanc genuit generosus Guido Levensis.
> Sex parit ista mares. Vir obit. Petit haec Moniales.
> Intra claustrales elegit esse lares.
> In requie multa sit Nonnae veste sepulta;
> Luceat aeterna sibi lux in pace superna.
> Anno M. C. bis, LX. bis, V. semel, I. bis.[10]

By the church door, in the vestibule, is the tomb of a priest dressed in his vestments. His chasuble is rounded on the sides, not clipped, gathered up over his arms, and falling in points before and behind him. His maniple is not wider at the bottom, and he does not wear his stole crossed over his breast, but straight down like bishops, Carthusians, and the ancient monks of Cluny, who have rejected innovation on this point.[11] His alb has apparels on the bottom matching the vestments: this is what the manuscripts call the *alba parata*. They are still used in cathedrals and ancient abbeys.

Next to the church door and clock tower there is a small cemetery for the domestics, where two epitaphs are worthy of note.

D. O. M.

> Hic jacet EMMANUEL LE CERF, qui cum majorem vitae partem erudiendis populis consumpsisset, vitam evangelicam evangelicae praedicationi anteponendam ratus, ut sibi moreretur, qui aliis tantum vixerat, ad poenitentiam accurrit senex eo festinantius, quo serius; pondusque ipsum senectutis, quo nihil ad patiendum aptius, et varios corporis morbos in remedium animae conversos, tanquam opportunum aeternitatis viaticum amplexus; mortem humilis, nec se jam sacerdotem, sed laïcum gerens, in hoc quietis portu expectavit, quae obtigit fere nonagenario. Obiit 8 Decembris 1674 et in Coemeterio prope Crucem sepeliri voluit. Requiescat in pace.[12]

---

[10] "Here rested she whose name thou shalt have there hereafter. Marguerite was the wife of Matthew de Marly, and daughter of the noble Guy de Levi. She bore six boys. After her husband died, she went to the nuns. Amongst the claustral sisters she chose to make her home. In her long rest, may she be buried in nun's clothing. May eternal light shine upon her in peace everlasting. Year 1327."

[11] De Vert discourses at greater length on the wearing of the stole in *Explication*, 2:328–34.

[12] "To God the Best and Greatest. Here lies Emmanuel Le Cerf, who, after dedicating most of his life to the education of the people, deemed the evangelical life superior to evangelical preaching and, in order that he who had lived only for others should die to himself, embraced a penitential life in his old age as eagerly as he did seriously. He embraced the weight of old age, more conducive to suffering than aught else, and various diseases of the body as remedy for his soul and advantageous provision for the journey to eternity. Humbly he awaited death in this port of rest, living no longer as a priest but as a layman, and attained it nearly ninety years old. He died on 8 December 1674, and

And the other:

> Hic quiescit JOANNES HAMON Medicus, qui adolescentia in studiis litterarum transacta, latine graeceque egregie doctus, cum in Academia Parisiensi eloquentiae laude floreret, et medendi peritia in dies inclaresceret, famae blandientis insidias et superbiam vitae metuens, Spiritus impetu subito percitus, patrimonii pretio in sinum pauperum festinanter effuso, anno aetatis xxxiij in solitudinem hanc, quam diu jam meditabatur, se proripuit. Ubi primum opere rustico exercitus, tum Christi ministris famulatus, mox professioni pristinae redditus, membra Redemptoris infirma curans in pauperibus, inter quos ancillas Christi quasi sponsas Domini sui suspexit; veste vilissima, jejuniis prope quotidianis, cubatione in asseribus, pervigiliis, precatione, et meditatione diu noctuque fere perpetua, lucubrationibus amorem Dei undique spirantibus, cumulavit aerumnas medendi quas toleravit per annos xxxvj quotidiano pedestri xij plus minus milliarum itinere, quod saepissime jejunus conficiebat, villarum obiens aegros, eorumque commodis serviens consilio, manu, medicamentis, alimentis, quibus se defraudabat, pane furfureo et aqua, idque clam et solus, et stando per annos xxij sustentans vitam, quam ut sapienter duxerat, quasi quotidie moriturus, ita inter fratrum preces et lacrymas in alto silentio, misericordias Domini suavissime recolens; atque in Mediatorem Dei et hominum Jesum Christum, oculis, mente, corde defixus, exitu ad votum suum tranquillo laetus, ut aeternum victurus clausit in Domino, annos natus 69 dies 20 viij Kalend. Mart. anni 1687.[13]

In the spirit of St. Bernard, the nuns are subject to the Lord Archbishop of Paris, who is their superior. They also sing the Office according to the

---

wished to be buried in this cemetery near the cross. May he rest in peace."

[13] "Here rests Jean Hamon, doctor, who, having spent his youth in the study of letters, was eminently learned in the Greek and Latin tongues. Seeing that he flourished in the University of Paris by the renown of his eloquence, and that his fame grew daily for his skill of medicine, he feared the lure of flattery and fame and the haughtiness of life. Suddenly stirred by the prompting of the Holy Spirit, he quickly poured out the value of his inheritance into the bosom of the poor and, in the thirty-third year of his age, he dragged himself into this solitude, as he had long pondered doing. First he applied himself to the labor of the fields, then to serving the ministers of Christ, and soon returned to his original profession, healing the wounded members of the Redeemer in the person of the poor, among whom he honored the handmaidens of Christ as the spouses of the Lord. He wore the coarsest garments, fasting nearly every day, slept on a board, spent day and night in nearly perpetual vigils, prayer, and meditation, nocturnal works everywhere breathing the love of God. For thirty-seven years he accumulated the toils of medicine, walking some twelve leagues every day, very often while fasting, to visit the sick in the villages, providing them what they might need, helping them by counsel, by hand, with medicines, with food whereof he deprived himself, living for twenty-two years on bran bread and water, which he ate secretly and alone, while standing up. As wisely as he had lived, considering every day his last, thus he departed this life in the Lord, amidst the prayers and tears of his brethren, in deep silence and sweet meditation of the Lord's mercies, with his eyes, mind, and heart fixed on Jesus Christ, mediator between God and man, rejoicing that he obtained the tranquil death for which he had prayed, that he might gain eternal life, at the age of 69, on 22 February 1687."

use of Paris, except that they sing the ferial psalms every day in order to fulfill the Rule of St. Benedict, which they follow, and which binds them to saying the entire psalter every week. This they do with the approbation of the late Lord Archbishop de Harlay of Paris.

At the blessing and aspersion of holy water on Sundays, the abbess and her nuns come forward to be sprinkled at the grille by the priest.

After the Creed, the priest descends to the bottom of the altar steps and blesses the bread offered by one of the abbey's domestics. He then announces any feasts or fasting days during the coming week, and gives a short exhortation or explanation of the day's Gospel.

At every high Mass of the year, the sacristan or thurifer goes to the nuns' grille at the end of the Creed to receive, through a hatch in the screen, a box from the sister sacristan containing the exact number of hosts needed for the sisters who are to receive communion. He brings them to the altar and gives them to the celebrant.

At high Masses for the Dead, the sacristan goes to the grille to receive the bread, a large host, and the wine in a cruet, and brings them to the altar. He gives the host to the priest on the paten, kissing it on the inside edge, and the cruet of wine to the deacon, who pours the wine into the chalice.

At the *Agnus Dei*, the nuns embrace, giving each other the kiss of peace.

On Sundays and feasts when servile work is forbidden, there is a general communion. At every Mass said in this church at least one of the nuns receives communion.

Devotion for the Blessed Sacrament is so great in this monastery that in addition to engaging in perpetual adoration as part of the Institute of the Blessed Sacrament (it is for this reason that they have exchanged their black scapular for a white one charged with a scarlet cross over the breast, about two fingers in width and a half-foot tall), they also have the custom of prostrating themselves before the Sacrament before going up to receive holy communion.[14]

Nevertheless, the Blessed Sacrament is exposed only during the octave of Corpus Christi, every day *after* high Mass. For here Mass is never said at an altar where the Blessed Sacrament is exposed. We will come back to this point.

The nuns of this monastery observe an exact and rigorous silence. Except in cases of illness, they never eat meat, and fish only rarely, perhaps twelve or fifteen times a year. They drink only water, and observe the great fast of Lent in its full rigor, as in the age of St. Bernard, eating only at five

---

[14] Finding her desires for reform unheeded by the Cistercian order, Mother Angélique Arnaud of Port-Royal formed a new order, the Institute of the Blessed Sacrament in 1633, which, finding little success, became integrated into Port-Royal-des-Champs and her foundation in Paris in 1638. This led both abbeys to adopt perpetual adoration, as well as the change in habit here described. For details, see Ellen Weaver, *The Reform of Port-Royal* (Éditions Beauchesne, 1978).

in the evening after Vespers, which they usually say at four, even though they wake up at night to sing Matins and do manual labor during the day.

After lunch there is a spiritual conference, during which they continue to work and it is not permitted to speak except aloud.

During the summer, the nuns are sometimes allowed to visit the garden after supper, but many refrain from doing so, and those that go do so separately, taking a book to read or some work to do.

Matins are said joined with Lauds at two o'clock, but in winter Lauds are said separately at six, before a low Mass celebrated between Lauds and Prime. During the rest of the year, Prime is said at six, followed by the conventual low Mass. Chapter follows with a reading from the martyrology, the necrology, and the Rule, some chapter of which the abbess explicates once or twice a week. Then they hold the chapter of faults, and appropriate penances are imposed.

Terce is said at eight thirty, followed by high Mass. Sext is at eleven, and on Church fast days at a quarter before twelve, after which they go to dinner, except in Lent when they do not dine, for in the Rule of St. Benedict to dine means not to fast. None is at two in the afternoon in winter and at two thirty in summer.

The first bell for Vespers rings at four and the Office begins some fifteen minutes later. It finishes at five or a quarter past, for they sing very unhurriedly and distinctly. After Vespers in Lent, they sound the refectory bell, and the nuns go there to dine and sup together. One sees nuns following this regime until they are seventy-two or seventy-five or even older. Not too long ago there was a priest who only ate during Lent in the evening, even though he was eighty-seven years old. He lived till he was ninety-two.

On Holy Saturday, they extinguish the lights throughout the entire house, and during the Offices they bring back the newly blessed fire.

The nuns' habits are coarse, and there is neither gold nor silver in their liturgical vestments.

The abbey receives girls without a dowry, and makes neither pacts or conventions for the reception of nuns, following the primitive spirit of their monastery, as is clear from the following acts[15]:

> Noverint universi quod ego Odo de Tiverval miles et Thecla uxor mea dedimus IN PURAM et perpetuam ELEEMOSYNAM, pro remedio animarum nostrarum et antecessorum nostrorum, Ecclesiae beatae Mariae de Portu-Regio et Monialibus ibidem Deo servientibus duos modios bladi, unum scilicet hibernagii, et alterum avenae in decima nostra de Joüy, singulis annis in festo S. Remigii percipiendos. Sciendum vero est quod Abbatissa et ejusdem loci Conventus unam de filiabus nostris in societatem

---

[15] The normal practice among many female orders at this time was to require postulants to bring a dowry, and often a servant, for their own support.

Monialium BENIGNE receperunt. Nos vero ingratudinis vitium incurrere nolentes, praedictos duos modios dictae jam domui de voluntate nostra SINE ALIQUO PACTO eleemosynavimus. Quod ut ratum et immobile perseveret, sigilli nostri munimine fecimus roborari. Actum anno gratiae M. CC. xvj.[16]

Another:

Reginaldus Dei gratia Cartonensis Episcopus, universis primis et posteris praesentem paginam inspecturis salutem in Domino. Notum facimus omnibus tam futuris quam praesentibus quod, quoniam Abbatissa et Conventus Sanctimonialium de Porregio Acelinam filiam Hugonis de Marchesio militis in sororem et sanctimonialiem Dei et caritatis intuitu GRATIS receperant, postmodum dictus miles in nostra constitutus praesentia, ne dictam filiam suam nuptam Christi parte sui patrimonii relinqueret indotatam, Ecclesiae de Porregio et Monialibus ibi Deo servientibus dedit et concessit IN PERPETUAM ELEEMOSYNAM, pro portione dictae filiae suae unum modium bladi annui redditus in granchia sua de Marchesio vel de Lonvilla singulis annis percipiendum ad mensuram Parisiensem de Dordano, et tres modios vini in vinea sua de Marchesio annuatim percipiendos, et decem solidos in censu suo de Marchesio. Ut autem donum ejus ratum et stabile permaneret, ad petitionem ipsius Hugonis praesentes Litteras in testimonium sigillo nostro fecimus roborari. Actum Carnoti anno Dominicae Incarnationis M. CC. septimo decimo, mense Aprili.[17]

---

[16] "Be it known to all men that I, Eudes de Thiverval, knight, and Thècle my wife gave in pure and perpetual alms, for the salvation of our souls and those of our ancestors, two muids of grain—that is, one of winter-crop and the other of oats—from our tithe-district of Jouy-sur-Eure, to the church of Notre-Dame of Port-Royal and the nuns serving God therein, to be collected every day on the feast of St. Remigius. Be it known that the abbess and convent of the said place freely received one of our daughters into their society of nuns. Not wishing to incur the vice of ingratitude, we have given the said two muids of corn in alms to the said house of our own free will and under no obligation. Which, that it may remain ratified and fixed, we have made to be confirmed by the power of our seal. Enacted in the year of grace 1216." For an edition, see Adolphe de Dion, ed., *Cartulaire de l'abbaye de Porrois* [Alphonse Picard et fils, 1903], 1:48).

[17] "Renaud, by the grace of God bishop of Chartres, to all who would earlier or later inspect the present page, in the Lord greeting. We make it known to all future and present that by these presents that the abbess and convent of nuns of Porrois [i.e., Port-Royal] freely received in charity Asceline, daughter of Hugues de Marchais, knight, as a sister and nun of God. Thereafter the said knight, lest he should give away his said daughter to be betrothed to Christ without a dowry from part of his patrimony, standing in our presence did give and grant to the church of Porrois and the nuns serving God therein in perpetual alms for the portion of his said daughter the return of one annual muid of corn, as reckoned in Paris or Dourdan (*vel de Dordan*), from his grange of Marchais or Louville (*Louvilla*) to be collected every year, and three muids of wine from his vineyard of Marchais to be collected yearly, and ten shillings from the rent of Marchais. That his gift may remain ratified and fixed, at the petition of the same Hugues we have made the present letters to be confirmed by our seal in testimony. Enacted at Chartres in the year of the Incarnation of Our Lord 1217, in the month of April" (de Dion, *Cartulaire*, 1:57).

Another:

> Noverint universi quod ego Odelina de Sèvre donavi IN PURAM et perpetuam ELEEMOSYNAM domui Portus-Regis pro anima bonae memoriae Ingeranni quondam mariti mei, et pro salute animae meae, et omnium liberorum et progenitorum meorum; et maxime pro salute et amore Margaretae filiae meae QUAE in eadem domo RELIGIONIS HABITUM ASSUMPSERAT, quatuor arpentos vineae in clauso meo de Sèvre jure perpetuo possidendos. Hanc autem donationem laudaverunt, voluerunt et concesserunt filii mei Gervasius primogenitus, Rogerus et Simon, ad quos eadem donatio jure hereditario pertinebat. Immo et ipsi EANDEM DONATIONEM OBTULIMUS cum libro SUPER ALTARE PORTUS REGIS. In cujus rei testimonium et conformationem perpetuam ego praedicta Odelina, quia praedicti filii mei G. R. et Simon necdum milites erant, et NECDUM SIGILLA HABEBANT de voluntate eorum et assensu praesentem Chartam sigilli mei munimine roboravi. Actum anno Domini M. CC. vigesimo octavo.[18]

---

[18] "Be it known to all them that I, Odeline de Sèvres, gave in pure and perpetual alms to the house of Port-Royal for the soul of my late husband Ingorrent of happy memory, and for the salvation of my soul, and of all my children and ancestors, and especially for the salvation and love of my daughter Marguerite who received the religious habit in the same house, four arpents of my vineyard of Sèvre to be possessed in perpetuity. My sons Gervais the eldest, Roger, and Simon praised, willed, and granted this donation, to whom it belonged by hereditary right. And further we offered the same donation with the book upon the altar of Port-Royal. In testimony and perpetual confirmation whereof, since my said sons Gervais, Roger, and Simon were not yet knighted and did not yet have seals, I the said Odeline confirmed the present charter by the power of my seal with their will and consent. Enacted in the year of Our Lord 1228" (de Dion, *Cartulaire*, 1:107–108).

PARIS

PARIS on the Seine, in Latin *Lutetia Parisiorum ad Sequanam*, the capital of the Kingdom of France, is by all accounts, even those of foreigners, one of the greatest and most beautiful cities in the world. Here, I shall refrain from discussing the Louvre, the palaces, civic buildings, libraries, and other architectural marvels. Others have done so already. Rather, I shall content myself with reporting noteworthy features of its churches.

Notre-Dame of Paris

The church of Notre-Dame of Paris is the greatest and most magnificent cathedral I have seen. It has a double aisle around the choir and nave, and a gallery above with iron balustrades. The choir is large and closed off by a rood screen at the west end. On the east end, beyond the canons' stalls, there are two square pulpits made of wood lined with brass, raised on four or five steps, but without any pediment above. The one on the right side is for the archbishop of Paris, and the left is used for funeral orations and the synodal address.[1]

The high altar is free-standing and roughly octagonal in shape, a very beautiful, rich table of streaked marble, with a fresco representing the burial of Our Lord on the front. On this table is a gradine with six candlesticks and a silver crucifix in the middle, all of extraordinary size. At both cornices of this gradine are two four-foot gilded lead angels, kneeling, with eyes turned toward the altar as if in adoration. Behind this altar, at the back of the apse, there is another one called the morrow altar, also of very precious marble. In a recess there is an elevated cross above which a five-foot gilded lead angel holds the end of the canopy under which the holy pyx is suspended (PLATE 39).

There are very beautiful chapels and many large, exquisite paintings executed by very able artists.

On Major Feasts

An acolyte carrying a thurible goes first before two candle-bearers, followed by the subdeacon between two more vested subdeacons (*induts*), then the deacon between two more vested deacons, and finally the celebrant. He kisses the closed Gospel book presented to him by the major subdeacon and then makes the sign of the cross.

After the *Introibo*, the psalm *Judica*, and the *Confiteor*, the celebrant says the *Aufer a nobis* in its entirety before ascending the altar. Once he has ascended to the altar, but before he approaches it, the subdeacon presents him the True Cross to kiss, bringing it to him from the altar, saying, *Ecce lignum Crucis*. The celebrant says the *Adoramus te Christe et benedicimus* in full, then *Oramus te* while turning back to kiss the altar.

After the incensation of the altar, the deacon kneels and incenses the celebrant with three swings.

While the Gradual is chanted, the bells are rung for the Mass of the Faithful, as they were during Terce for the Mass of the Catechumens.

After saying *Sequentia sancti Evangelii secundum N.*, the thurifer incenses the deacon. The Gospel book is not incensed.

Here, the Creed is sung by both sides of choir together, as in Lyon, Sens, Meaux, and among the Carthusians.

After the choir has sung *Dignum et justum est*, the thurifer goes to incense the cope-bearers and then the higher and lower stalls of both sides.

At the *Sanctus*, the subdeacon ascends to the altar, takes the paten from it, and gives it to be kissed on its outer side to the *spé* or dean of the choirboys. The latter is vested in a *soc* over his alb, and stands at the foot and center of the altar steps holding a large silver basin covered with

---

[1] The synodal address (*sermo synodalis*) was a speech delivered to the diocesan clergy at the yearly synod, held on the Thursday after the first Sunday of July.

a veil. The subdeacon kisses the paten on its inner side and places it in the center of the veil within the basin, which the *spé* then holds aloft a slight distance from the altar (see PLATE 40).[2]

At the start of the *Pater*, the *spé* draws near the altar steps, the subdeacon takes the paten from the basin, and holds it uncovered in his right hand, which is wrapped in the veil. At *Panem nostrum*, the subdeacon gives it to the deacon and hands the veil back to the *spé*. The deacon, kneeling, presents the paten to the celebrant.

When the Lord Archbishop celebrates high Mass on the major feasts of the year, he gives the solemn blessing before the *Agnus Dei*, and when he administers communion to the clergy and people, in place of the second species the deacon gives all the communicants wine from a consecrated chalice.[3]

After the celebrant has said the Postcommunion and the *Dominus vobiscum*, the deacon, standing alone in the middle of the steps, turns toward the people and sings the *Ite, missa est*.

The celebrant blesses the people and, having genuflected before the altar with all his ministers, as they did on entering, he returns with them to the sacristy in the same order they came, reciting the Gospel *In principio* as he goes.

On Christmas night, Lauds are inserted into the Mass, as in Orléans and Vienne.

On Epiphany, the deacon, facing east, announces the date of Easter after the Gospel reading.

In the diocese of Paris, the *prône* is said every Sunday between the Gospel and Creed, as in Rouen, and that is indeed its proper place.[4]

If there should be no subdeacon for the high Mass, the Epistle would be read not by the deacon but by a lector in alb or surplice, if there was one available, as I have done myself many times.

Those who receive communion from the priest respond *Amen*, as in Orléans, after the words *Corpus Domini nostri Jesu Christi*, following the ancient custom of the Greek and Latin churches.

According to chapter eight of the *Rubricae generales* of the missal of Paris, it is permitted on ferias of Lent to say Mass even after noon.[5]

On ferias, there is only one candle-bearer at the high Mass. On ferias

---

[2] On the *soc*, see p. xxxii. On the *spé*, see Joseph Louis Ortigue, *Dictionnaire liturgique, historique et théorique de plain-chant et de musique d'église au Moyen Âge et dans les temps modernes* (Paris, 1853), 1389–90.

[3] De Vert, *Dissertation sur les mots*, 289–94, also argues that the unconsecrated wine the deacon gave the kneeling communicants in certain places was a remnant of the former communion under both species, and not meant for rinsing the mouth. In his *Explication*, 4:278–79, he points out that in Paris, this unconsecrated wine was mixed with water, just like the second species.

[4] The *prône* was a vernacular service for the laity said on holy days of obligation. Usually delivered from the *chaire* or pulpit in the center of the nave, it included announcements — about the feasts and fasts of the week, the reading of marriage banns, excommunications, etc. — as well as vernacular prayers, psalms, and catechetical instruction.

[5] See *Missale Parisiense* (Paris, 1685), 6.

of Advent and Lent and other fasting days, the deacon and subdeacon use chasubles folded across the breast (*utuntur planetis transversis*). The deacon also wears the *orarium* in the shape of the diaconal stole. On Sundays, the deacon and subdeacon wear dalmatic and tunicle.

Red is used in Paris for the feasts of Pentecost, Corpus Christi, and All Saints, as well as on Sundays from Pentecost until Advent. Reddish-yellow (*aurore*), if they have it, can also be used on these feasts, except Pentecost.

On feasts of bishops they use green, and for holy abbots and widows, violet or blue if they have it.

They use ash-colored vestments on the four Sundays of Lent as well as on the ferias, but only beginning on the first Monday of Lent.

During the fortnight of Passiontide, they use black vestments with red orphreys.

On Maundy Thursday, they use red for the Mass. The Lord Archbishop of Paris celebrates the high Mass conjointly with two dignitaries or senior canon-priests. All three wear chasubles and commune under both species.

On Good Friday, at the cathedral, neither the minor hours nor Vespers are said in choir.

During Easter week, the procession to the font takes place after Vespers, more or less as in Rouen.[6]

On the first Sunday of Advent, at the cathedral, St. Jerome's prologue to Isaias is read as the first lesson along with the beginning of that book. One of St. Jerome's prologues is also read on Septuagesima Sunday.[7]

On 14 September, the Exaltation of the Holy Cross, at the offertory of the Mass they say the *Confiteor, Misereatur,* and *Indulgentiam,* and then go to kiss the cross as on Good Friday.

On All Souls, the titles of the Matins lessons are read as on other days.[8] After Terce, they hold the procession to the tombs. They say Sext after the high Mass, but None, which concludes the day's Office, at the usual time. As the brief says: *Officium defunctorum terminatur post Nonam, quae dicitur hora solita paulo ante horam vespertinam.* Empty catafalques are not used.

As in Sens, in the cathedral of Paris the choirboys do not wear the biretta. They go from their house to the church bareheaded and return in the same manner. They take holy water only when entering the church, not when leaving.

The canons who are not yet subdeacons wear the biretta on their way to and from the church, but during the Office they are bareheaded all year, except at Matins, which is said at night. For this illustrious church has the glory of having preserved even to our day the ancient custom of saying

---

[6] See pp. 231–32.
[7] The prologue to the Pentateuch.
[8] The Roman Office of the Dead has no lesson titles, antiphons, or hymns, in imitation of the Offices of the Triduum, and the Parisian breviary of 1680 maintained this custom (*Pars hyemalis,* cxlii). In the Parisian proper Office of All Souls, however, lesson titles were said.

Matins or Nocturns at midnight, at which a large number of canons assist; some particularly distinguished ones are never absent.

Their summer habit consists of a surplice, an almuce over the arm, and a biretta on the head (PLATE 41). In winter, they wear a surplice or rochet, a black cape, and a black *grand camail*[9] of the same fabric (PLATE 42). They switch to the winter habit at Matins the day after the Octave of St. Denis, 17 October, the feast of St. Cerbonius (*Cerbonné*), which the common people call by corruption *St. Serre-bonnet*, since the clerics stow (*serrent*) their birettas. Formerly, they wore this winter habit throughout the whole year at Matins and the other Offices outside Holy Week, except that in place of the surplice they wore an alb. Thus they were received as canons and were buried, as I have learned from an old cartulary of the church of Paris.[10] One notes that the choirboys, who have not changed their ancient rites, have not only retained the use of the alb, but also that the choristers or cope-bearers of this church wear it during the octave of Easter until Vespers of Saturday *in albis depositis* (PLATE 43).[11]

The manner of receiving a canon in this renowned church, taken from an ancient cartulary, as well as the regulation for the Divine Office and the life of the canons, is worth reporting here briefly:

The canon who is to be received enters the chapterhouse and kneels before the deacon, who receives him with these words: *Ecce nos admittimus te in Canonicum et fratrem nostrum*.[12] Then the dean gives him the book of the canons (read every day at the end of Prime after the necrology) saying, *Et tradimus tibi Regularis Observantiae formam in hoc volumine contentam*.[13] The new canon prostrates himself and responds, *Amen*. Then, he kneels and the secretary of the chapter makes him put his hand on the book of the Holy Gospels, upon which he promises obedience to the dean and chapter, as stated more fully in the text of the oath he must take.

After leaving the chapterhouse, he goes to the cloister to put on the canonical habit, which is an ankle-length linen alb, a black cape, and long camail of the same fabric and color. Once dressed, he is led to choir by the cantor. At the entrance of the choir, he makes an inclination toward the east and another toward the west, and then is installed in his place by the cantor, who says the verse *Dominus custodiat introitum tuum et exitum tuum ex hoc nunc et usque in saeculum*.[14] Immediately the new canon prostrates himself to say the *Pater noster*, and remains on the ground during the several versicles

---

[9] A camail with a floppy hood.
[10] See "Ordo ad recipiendum canonicum ex antiquis Chartulariis et Registris Capituli Ecclesiae Parisiensis," in *Dionysii Rikel Carthusiani de vita et moribus canonicorum liber* (Cologne, 1670), 181–90.
[11] They wore appareled and pleated albs instead of their usual copes, in imitation of the newly-baptized.
[12] "Lo, we receive thee as a canon and brother."
[13] "And we hand over to thee the form of regular observance contained in this volume."
[14] "May the Lord keep thy coming in and thy going out, from henceforth now and for ever" (Psalm 120:8).

and one oration the cantor says before the eagle in mid-choir. Rising, the new canon receives a psalter from the cantor and goes on to kiss the dean and all the canons. Then, he returns to his place, unless he has also received a dignity, in which case the dean says to him, *Amice ascende superius*,[15] and then he is assigned the place proper to his dignity.

If this takes place in summer, after the canon has kissed his brethren, at a signal from the cantor he takes off his cape and camail, which an acolyte carries into the sacristy.

We glean from another article of this cartulary that the canons were obliged to chastity, to perpetual residence, and to the psalmody; that clerics at that time were not all destined to become priests, but that even among the canons there were some who were priests, others who remained deacons, and others who stayed subdeacons their whole lives: *aliqui eorum Presbyteri, aliqui Diaconi, aliqui Subdiaconi semper existentes*;[16] that the canons-priest each took their weekly turn to celebrate the Mass; and that the deacons and subdeacons likewise took turns serving weekly.

They chanted Nocturns and Lauds at midnight, as they still do at present.

At sunrise they chanted Prime and then went to the chapterhouse to hear the reading of the martyrology, necrology, and the rule of canons, which they listened to very attentively while seated. After receiving the hebdomadary's blessing, they went to perform any chantry obligations for the day.

They chanted the Office of Terce at its proper time, followed by Mass. At midday, before dinner, they chanted Sext: *In meridie, antequam reficiantur, hymnum Deo persolvunt qui incipit* Rector potens, *cum psalmodia*.[17]

They chanted None at three o'clock: *hora tertia post meridiem*. Around sunset they chanted Vespers more solemnly than the other Offices, lighting a great number of candles and lamps because the people gathered in crowds for the service after finishing their business for the day: *Officium solemnius persolvunt circa occasum solis cum lucernis ac cereis accensis, ad quos fit major concursus fidelium, quia negotia per urbem peracta sunt*.[18] Straightaway after Vespers they went to supper.

Before going to bed each retired to his oratory or to the church to recite Compline. This is why the breviary of Orléans has the orations *Illumina* for the church and *Visita* for the bedchamber.[19] Even today, the Carthusians never sing Compline in the church, but rather recite it in their cells before bed.

These were the hours at which the Church ordained prayer, and so each

---

[15] "Friend, go up higher" (Luke 14:10).
[16] "Ordo ad recipiendum," 184.
[17] "Ordo ad recipiendum," 185.
[18] "Ordo ad recipiendum," 185–86.
[19] That is, the 1693 reformed breviary Le Brun des Marettes helped compose (*Pars hiemalis*, 138). Previously, the oration *Illumina* alone was used in Orléans, except during Eastertide, when it was replaced by *Salva nos* (*Breviarium diocesis Aurelianensis* [Orléans, 1542], fol. 41v).

hour of the Divine Office was sung separately; the idea of joining three or four together was unheard of. Thus prayer took place at intervals, so that the clergy prayed at least seven times each day, as the royal prophet said.[20] Behold the intention of the Church; those who are truly imbued with her spirit may follow it.

They entered and left choir together. If anyone arrived after the first psalm of an Office had been said, he durst not return to his chamber or enter choir, but waited outside. This is still the practice today, for they are not allowed to enter until the short chapter, unless the cantor goes into choir, in which case they enter with him.

God knows how modestly they assisted in choir, and how strictly they observed all its holy practices and ceremonies. No one durst serve at the altar unless he was newly shaven. In processions, they walked two by two at equal distance, with downcast eyes, and they regarded a canon who wandered about the church while his brethren said the Divine Office as a sort of apostate.

They practiced great reserve when they assembled in the chapterhouse or sacristy. Quarrels were never heard, much less injurious language. They covered their heads and sat with great decorum, and after the dean had laid out a matter of business, each one in turn calmly spoke his mind. Once the dean had reached a conclusion following the opinion of the most reasonable part of the chapter, the secretary wrote the outcome in the register, as is still the custom in the chapter Office at present.

On Fridays, they confessed the faults and shortcomings they had committed in choir that week, and were given a suitable penance.

The canons remained inside the cloister and did not dare to spend the night elsewhere without the dean's permission.

If a disagreement arose among the canons, the dean put it right; if between the dean and the chapter, the bishop did so. The dean and the precentor received a double portion,[21] but they were not allowed to be absent from choir: *Qui bene praesunt, duplici honore digni sunt* (1 Timothy 5:17).[22]

Occasional money from bequests, burials, or the sale of timber was not shared amongst the canons but put into the treasury for the maintenance of the fabric and decoration of the church.

The last article of this cartulary gives great glory and honor to both the bishop and the canons, and is too admirable to be omitted here. It shows, on one hand, the obedience the canons rendered to the bishop, and on the other, that their glory was to compose one body with him:

> Super omnia autem discant Canonici magnum honorem se debere Episcopo exhibere, memores se olim, ante separationem fructuum et mensae, ei in omnibus obedivisse, unumque corpus cum illo

---

[20] Psalm 118:164.
[21] That is, double the usual stipend meted out to the canons for attending the Offices.
[22] "Let those that rule well be esteemed worthy of double honor."

> constituere: et ut ipse supereminet omnes; cum est in Choro, nullus praetereat qui non faciat ei profundam reverentiam.[23]

It is any wonder, then, that such great benefits were bestowed upon churches where God was so well served?

In the middle of the choir near the great portal, the illustrious Odo or Eudes of Sully (*Odo de Soliaco*) is buried in a brass tomb. Its inscription testifies that sincerity, purity, sweetness, and charity for the poor were the chief traits of his truly episcopal soul.

He bestowed many great benefits upon both the poor and his church, not the least whereof is that he never had regard either for rank or requests in the distribution of benefices, but only for virtue and learning, as befits a man who truly loves the beauty of God's house.

Two large, tall towers flank the façade of the cathedral, over which there runs a terrace from which one can easily descry the entire city of Paris. The towers house exquisite bells. In front of the great portal there is a square with a fountain in the middle. We shall later explain the purpose of such fountains near churches.[24]

The new 1697 ritual of Paris ordains that both people and clergy should commune during Mass, and that when the Viaticum and Extreme Unction are brought to a sick bed, the latter is to be administered first.[25]

That is how it was in all the ancient rituals of France.[26]

We see from an old 1557 missal of Paris that on Ash Wednesday, after the imposition of ashes on the clergy, there was a procession at the end of which ashes were imposed at the church door: *In reditu Processionis imponuntur cineres ad januam Ecclesiae ab Episcopo*.[27] We find the same thing in the ordinary of the collegiate church of Jargeau in the diocese of Orléans,[28] where it is still done, as well as in the church of the canons of St-Lazare of Avallon, where ashes are not given to everyone, as in the common practice, but only to penitents, and at the door of the church.[29]

---

[23] "Above all let the canons learn that it is their duty to show the bishop great honor, mindful that in former times, before they began to take their payment and victuals separately from him, they obeyed him in all things, and formed one body with him, and that he outranks them all. When he is in choir, let no one pass him without making a profound bow" ("Ordo ad recipiendum," 190).
[24] See p. 32, n. 1.
[25] *Rituale Parisiense* (Paris, 1697), 202.
[26] See p. 163, n. 5.
[27] See *Missale insignis ecclesiae et dioecesis Parisiensis* (Paris, 1557), fol. 28vb.
[28] Orléans, Médiathèque municipale, MS. 0143, fol. 30r.
[29] See de Vert, *Explication*, 2:342–5, who argued that the imposition of ashes was performed at the church door as part of the ancient rites of public penance just before the penitents were expelled from the church for the Lenten season; the custom became generalized to all the faithful and clergy only after the twelfth century when these rites fell into general desuetude. Le Brun des Marettes shares with other reformers and Jansenists of his day a keen interest in the rites of public penance, all the more so because his home city of Rouen had retained them to his day. In the same place, de Vert relates the amusing custom of the church of Autun where a single cleric was chosen to represent

The bishop of Paris expelled the public penitents after a sermon, psalm 50, and a collect: *Tunc ubi Episcopus est, ejiciuntur poenitentes.*

On Sundays of Lent the common Preface *per annum*, not the Lenten Preface, was said. I explain the reasons for this elsewhere.[30]

I also see on folio 162 that one of the ministers always tasted the wine and water before Mass: *Sacerdos exigat a ministro ut gustet tam vinum quam aquam.*[31] In the cathedral of Narbonne, the senior choirboy still tastes the bread, wine, and water at the offertory of Mass every day. At the basilica of St. Peter in the Vatican, a cardinal performs the test of wine and water whenever the pope or his delegate celebrates Mass on major feasts.

At the nuptial Mass, the blessing was given immediately before the *Pax Domini*. At the end of the Mass the priest blessed bread and wine for the agape, which the bride and bridegroom partook of. In the evening, the priest went to bless the nuptial bed as the bride and bridegroom lay or sat upon it.

Saint-Germain-des-Prés

The altar in the abbey church of St-Germain-des-Prés (PLATE 44) is free-standing and located at the crossing near the center of the church. Like the altar of St-Étienne in Dijon, it has no retable. The Merovingian kings of France were buried in St-Germain-des-Prés. The mausolea of Childebert, Chilperic I and his wife Queen Fredegund, his son Clovis I, Clothair II, and Chilperic II lie behind the altar.

There are some very learned monks in this abbey. Everyone knows how obliged the Church is to these erudite religious for having given us such correct editions of the Fathers and so many other fine works of scholarship.[32]

The abbey's large refectory occupies one side of the cloister, while the library occupies the other. The latter is full of excellent books, both printed and manuscript, among which I remember seeing a manuscript missal written some eight or nine hundred years ago that contained only the Mass orations and Prefaces. One can deduce that at that time the priest did not read the Epistle and Gospel at the altar while they were

---

the public penitents. Expelled from the church on Ash Wednesday, he was readmitted on Maundy Thursday.

[30] See p. 223.

[31] According to the Roman *Caeremoniale episcoporum* 1.6.3 and 2.8.62, promulgated in 1600, the sacristan should taste a portion of the bread, wine, and water at the offertory to assure that it had not been poisoned. This "fore-tasting" is called the *praegustatio*.

[32] St-Germain-des-Prés was the main house and scholarly center of the Congregation of St-Maur. Among the many erudite monks of this abbey that participated in what David Knowles calls "the most impressive achievement of cooperative, or at least coordinated, scholarship in the modern world" are Nicolas-Hugues Ménard, Luc d'Achery, Jean Mabillon, Thierry Ruinart, Edmond Martène, and Bernard de Montfaucon. For an accessible précis of the history of the Maurists and their literary endeavors, including portraits of the principal figures, see Knowles, *Great Historical Enterprises* (Thomas Nelson and Sons, 1963), 33–62.

chanted by the subdeacon and deacon, nor indeed anything that was sung by the choir. Rather, he listened. Each minister therefore performed his own function. But when low Masses became more frequent, the low Mass was inserted into the high and the priest was made to say everything. He might as well sing everything and do away with the deacon and subdeacon altogether. This reminds me of something I once read in Navarre: *Praestat sacerdotem missam solemniter celebrantem Epistolam et Evangelium audire, quam interim legere.*[33] What would we say to a man we saw reading the sermon as the preacher delivered it? Surely we would ask, "Why aren't you listening?"[34]

Abbey of Saint-Victor

Many great men are buried in the church and infirmary chapel of the canons regular of St-Victor, bishops as well as abbots and canons regular of this house, which was the nursery of more than thirty houses of canons regular in France. It produced the famous Hugh, Richard, and Adam of Saint Victor, and in our century the illustrious Jean-Baptiste Santeuil, that excellent poet who wrote such admirable hymns to replace the older ones so redolent of the Gothic barbarism of past ages.[35]

Following the ancient practice, these canons regular fast on Wednesdays and Fridays. They wear surplices with closed sleeves and the almuce over the shoulders (PLATE 45), perform the Office according to the use of Paris, and still say Matins at midnight, just as the metropolitan church.

Regarding surplices with closed sleeves, it appears their use was customary in Paris and was preserved by the canons of St-Victor, judging by the first stained glass window in the library of the Collège de Navarre, where a canon is depicted wearing this sort of surplice.

At St-Victor, there is a public library with very good books, both printed and manuscript. It is open every Monday, Wednesday, and Friday from seven to ten in the morning, and from one to five in the afternoon. At times I have seen over two hundred people studying there.

The Carmelites of the Place Maubert

At the church of the Calced Carmelites next to the Place Maubert, the holy water stoup is located outside the church door, not inside. This is the proper place for such fonts.

---

[33] "It is better that the priest who celebrates solemn Mass listen to the Epistle and Gospel, than to read it while it is said."
[34] See p. 36, n. 13.
[35] Jean-Baptiste Santeuil or Santeul (1630–1697) was renowned for his exquisite command of classical Latinity and composed several hymns for the new breviaries of Cluny and Paris, which were adopted by most of the later neo-Gallican uses. He was friends with Nicolas Letourneux and an admirer of Antoine Arnauld, composing some hexameters to adorn the monument at Port-Royal-des-Champs where the latter's heart was interred.

Saint-Étienne-du-Mont

In the most elevated quartier of Paris is the parish church of St-Étienne-du-Mont, where Blaise Pascal, author of the *Pensées sur la religion*, is buried. The main portal of this church is very beautiful, and the preacher's pulpit is considered the finest in Paris. On the feast of the Invention of St. Stephen, 3 August, I saw the abbot of Ste-Geneviève[36] celebrate pontifical Mass with miter and crosier, and I noticed that, as he chanted the collect and read the Epistle and what follows from his seat near the altar, a canon regular of Ste-Geneviève stood next to him holding a small silver candlestick by its handle to give him light.

Sainte-Geneviève

Right next to St-Étienne-du-Mont, to the north, is the renowned church of Ste-Geneviève, patroness of Paris, whose body rests behind the high altar in a reliquary of gilded silver supported by four Ionic columns of extraordinary marble (see PLATE 46). It can be seen from the crypt below.

An ambulatory runs around the high altar as at St-Germain-des-Prés. At the foot of the steps of the high altar is buried St. Clotilde, queen of France,[37] who was the principal cause of the conversation of Clovis I, king of France and founder of the abbey of Ste-Geneviève, who is buried in the middle of the choir.

On the right side of the nave one can see the epitaph of the famous philosopher René Descartes.

From this church one can go visit the library, which has a very large collection, augmented by that of the late Charles-Maurice Le Tellier, archbishop of Reims, the Cabinet des Medailles,[38] and other rare objects.

Val-de-Grâce

The Val-de-Grâce is the most beautiful church in Paris.

The Sorbonne

The church of the Sorbonne is worth a visit, together with its house and library, which is filled with an excellent collection of printed and manuscript books. The lectures on theology are held in the great halls of the new buildings to the left of the Place de Sorbonne.

Collège de Cluny

To the right is the church of the Collège de Cluny. Vespers there are said around six in the evening following ancient custom. I noticed that at

---

[36] The church of St-Étienne-du-Mont belonged to the abbey of Ste-Geneviève. Here, the Congregation of France was founded in 1628 by Cardinal François de La Rochefoucauld and Charles Faure, its first superior general. The canons wore a habit identical to the cathedral canons; see PLATES 42 and 43.
[37] Author's note: Her reliquary of gilded silver is found in her eponymous chapel.
[38] A collection of coins and other antiques founded in the sixteenth century.

the oration at the end of Vespers, one of the two candle-bearers lowered his candle slightly to give light to the officiant, a practice also observed at St-Denis-de-la-Chartre. It is done in nearly the same manner in Lyon.

During Lent the schedule of the canonical hours is not modified. Vespers are at six like the rest of the year, as at St-Denis-de-la-Chartre.

Only monks who are to receive communion participate in the offertory procession, as at St-Martin-des-Champs, which belongs to the same order. In this procession, they present the priest with a host, placing it on the paten. Then the cantor presents the wine and pours it into the chalice held by the deacon.

These ancient Cluniac monks use a new breviary which has set the standard for many others, a work worthy of the learned men who produced it. Their new missal is awaited with much impatience.[39]

Hôtel de Cluny

In the Hôtel de Cluny, on the Rue des Mathurins, one can still see the ruins of the *thermae* or baths of Emperor Julian, and in a house on the Rue de la Harpe, by the sign of the Iron Cross, one sees several old arcades with a sort of vaulted hall of great antiquity, which are supposed to have been a pagan temple or public baths.

Church of the Sépulcre

At the very back of the right aisle of the church of the Sépulcre there is a clothed crucifix,[40] like the one in the church of Santi Cosma e Damiano in Rome, which is dressed in a long robe that reaches down to Christ's heels, and the ones in the churches of Senlis and Casale Monferrato between the choir and nave, which are half-clad with a sort of apron.[41]

Hôpital de la Salpêtrière

The church of the Hôpital de la Salpêtrière is arranged in such a way that the altar is in the intersection of five large aisles, much like the altar that used to be at the tomb of St. Felix on the outskirts of Nola, around which St. Paulinus built five churches. This arrangement is very convenient for hospitals and hospices. At the Hôpital de la Salpêtrière, I saw a practice that struck me as very beautiful and timely in an age that has forgotten the importance of baptismal vows. On Easter Monday, the young girls of the

---

[39] The breviary in question is the *Breviarium monasticum ad usum sacri ordinis Cluniacensis* (1686), the work of Dom Claude de Vert and Dom Paul Rabusson. The missal was published in 1717.
[40] This was a copy of the Holy Face of Lucca, a clothed crucifix housed in the cathedral of Lucca, attributed to Nicodemus, and an object of widespread devotion in the Middle Ages; many churches possessed reproductions. The name St. Voult de Lucques became corrupted in popular speech to St. Vaudelu or Godelu. See Émile Molinier, *Inventaire du trésor de l'église du Saint-Sépulcre à Paris* (Paris, 1883), 3–4, 9.
[41] Jean Mabillon recounts seeing these crucifixes at Santi Cosma e Damiano and in Casale; see *Museum Italicum* (Paris, 1687), 1:133 and 9, respectively.

Hôpital are brought to the procession that takes place after the *Magnificat* to the baptismal font. There, one of the girls, standing on a very high platform by the font, proclaims aloud the renovation of the vows made and the obligations contracted at baptism. Then all the paupers in the Hôpital go up to kiss the font as a mark of respect and gratitude. It would be desirable to see something similar implemented in parish churches, or for parish priests to provide instruction or exhortation to their parishioners on this matter.

There is not much to say with regard to antiquities concerning the many other churches of Paris.

The Palace and the Sainte-Chapelle

One cannot leave Paris without having seen the Parlement—especially the grand-salle and the gilded grand-chambre—as well as Ste-Chapelle, which is adjacent to that august palace where justice is now administered, but which was formerly the usual residence of our kings. St. Louis had this church built next door so as to be able to go to the Office conveniently as devotion moved him. The stained glass windows are highly regarded, but they let in so little light that one sometimes needs a candle at ten in the morning.

The most noteworthy thing is the church treasury, which contains many relics, rare vestments, and other objects. The church is served by canons and vicars perpetual who chant the Divine Office every day.

ABBEY OF SAINT-DENIS

THE road from Paris to St-Denis-en-France is marked by wayside crosses called *montjoies*, spire-shaped objects each including statues of three kings (PLATE 47). They mark the places where the processions bearing the bodies of deceased kings pause on their way to the abbey.

St-Denis-en-France is a town that is home to many parishes and monasteries, above all the famous and wealthy abbey of St-Denis, a large house of Benedictine monks of the Congregation of St-Maur appointed for the burial of France's kings, most of whom are interred here in splendid mausolea, for example Francis I; Louis XII and his wife the queen; Henry II and Catherine de' Medici his wife; Dagobert, the abbey's founder; and Charles II the Bald, who laid down disciplinary rules for the clergy and the manners of Christendom.[1]

Since the days of Louis the Fat, the kings of France have had the Oriflamme, the banner of the church of St-Denis, carried before their armies by the count of the French Vexin, a vassal of this abbey.

---

[1] In a series of capitularies; see *Capitularia regum Francorum*, ed. Alfred Boretius and Victor Krause, MGH Leges 2 (Hanover, 1893), 2:253–328.

I shall not detain the reader with a description of the treasury of St-Denis; one has to see it first hand to properly appreciate it. A monk of the abbey shows it to visitors every day before and after Vespers. I shall rather speak of the church and its peculiar customs. The church is cruciform and its structure is quite beautiful (PLATE 48).

Here they still keep large chasubles in the ancient style. They are ample and closed on all sides, without any clipping.

At high Mass on solemn feasts, one can see the most excellent vestments in all of France; a kerchief on the cantor's staff, which in former times he used to wipe his face; and communion of the altar ministers under both species as at Cluny, both on solemn feasts and on Sundays. On the most solemn days of the year, the whole Mass is sometimes chanted in Greek; on other days, only the Epistle and Gospel are read in both Greek and Latin, as formerly in Rome on all major feasts of the year, because these two languages were both in common use, and there were many Greeks in Italy, especially in Venice, Florence, and Rome. This is still done when the pope celebrates pontifically.[2] The rest is sung in Latin.

Formerly they held *Laus perennis* every day of the year, as at Marmoutier and other places.

---

[2] Author's note: Anselm of Havelberg, *Dialogi* 3.16 (PL 188:1233C–D).

ABBEY OF MAUBUISSON

IN Pontoise stands the abbey of Maubuisson, *Malodunum* in Latin, or, according to M. Châtelain, *Malodumus*. Called Notre-Dame-la-Royale, *Sanctae Mariae Regalis*, it was founded in 1241 by Queen Blanche, mother of St. Louis, who took the habit and veil of these nuns before her death. She was buried in the habit underneath her royal garments, wearing her crown over her veil. Her body rests in mid-choir under a brass tomb. Many princes and princesses are buried between the choir and altar.

CHURCH OF THE DEUX-AMANTS

THE church of the Deux-Amants, dedicated to St. Mary Magdalene at the Foot of the Cross, lies four leagues from Rouen. The church and house is occupied by canons regular from the Congregation of Ste-Geneveìve. Before the arrival of these reformed canons, the original canons wore their round-hooded almuces over their head and shoulders, as in Fig. 15 (PLATE 37).

ROUEN

ROUEN, on the banks of the river Seine (*ad Sequanam*), is the capital city of *Lugdunensis Secunda*, also known as the province of Neustria, called Normandy ever since the Normans made themselves its masters. It is one of the most beautiful cities of the realm. In Latin it is called *Rotomagus*, and by the ancients sometimes *Rotomus* and *Rodomus*.

The city is one of the largest and most populous in the kingdom. Its quay, entirely paved and sloped, is considered the most beautiful in France, and in peacetime one can see it lined with ships. It is a wondrous thing to watch the unloading of merchandise arriving from the foreign countries with which this city has trade, which draws to it people from so many nations.

Rouen has many beautiful squares, among them the Marché aux veaux,[1] where they say Joan of Arc, the Maid of Orléans, was burned. A fountain stands on the spot, and above it a statue of the Maid covered by a turret opened on all sides and held up by three columns.

Clameur de haro

The inhabitants of Rouen and the whole province of Normandy have a lovely privilege we must mention here: the *clameur de haro*,[2] invoked in case of a homicide, theft, or imminent threat of violence to someone. Upon hearing this cry, the criminal or offender is obliged to desist, or else he can be detained until a sergeant or bailiff arrives, and he must present himself before the judge without further delay. All who hear the cry "*Haro!*" must give aid on the spot, being otherwise bound to pay a fine to the prince or feudal lord who has the right of high justice.[3] Under the same privilege, if someone detained as a prisoner cries "*Haro!*" the bailiff or sergeant is obliged to escort him before whatever president or counselor of the Parlement or judge within the bailiwick he chooses. The chosen officer, wherever he might be, even on the road, must promptly order that the man in question be either imprisoned or else set free on bail or under oath, as he deems fit. If the bailiff or sergeant refuses to take him to be heard by the officer of his choosing, he can cry "*Haro!*" a second time to call the townsmen or neighbors to his aid. Fifteen to twenty of them emerge from their homes to force the sergeants and the man they have arrested before the requested judge to determine if the imprisonment is justified.

---

[1] "Calf market." It has been known as Place de la Pucelle since about 1820.
[2] For a brief treatment and bibliography on the *clameur de haro*, see Valérie Toureille, "Cri de peur et cri de haine: haro sur le voleur: Cri et crime en France à la fin du Moyen Âge," in *Haro! Noël! Oyé!: Pratiques du cri au Moyen Âge*, ed. Didier Lett and Nicolas Offenstadt (Éditions de la Sorbonne, 2003), 169–78.
[3] The right to judge all cases and impose all penalties, including death.

Rouen has a Parlement, a Court of Accounts, a Court of Aids, and several other jurisdictions. The Parlement still draws up its chancery acts in the old manner, on scrolls written on a single side and then glued together end to end. These used to be called *volumina*, whence the word "volume."

Cathedral of Notre-Dame

There are in the city and its suburbs thirty-six parish churches and about fifty religious houses of both sexes, and in the diocese twenty-six abbeys and a number of priories, chapels, and sickhouses; ten collegiate churches of canons, and 1,388 parishes distributed under the authority of six archdeacons and twenty-seven rural deans, and the dean of the parish priests of the city and suburbs, who is called the Dean of Christendom (*Doyen de la Chrétienté*), in Latin *Decanus Christianitatis*.[4] He is appointed by the archbishop and must be a parish priest of the city *intra muros*, not from the suburbs. He does not have a seat in choir with the cathedral canons, but does have the right to wear the canonical habit.

The church of Rouen has always enjoyed high distinction. From the fourth century onward it flourished in piety, according to the testimony of St. Paulinus in his letter to St. Victricius, wherein he speaks very highly of the people of Rouen.[5] In the twelfth century it was the most famous church not only in Normandy, but all England and Aquitaine, as Richard II, king of England and duke of Normandy and Aquitaine, attested. Kings of France and England and many prelates referred to it as "holy": *sancta Rotomagensis Ecclesia*.

Archbishop St. Thomas of Canterbury gave another indication of Rouen's impressive piety in the twelfth century when he recommended himself to the prayers, fasts, and good works of its church and people.[6]

The cathedral's nave is large and stately, with galleries running the whole length under stained glass above. Its total length is 408 feet: the nave 210, the choir one 110, and the Lady Chapel eighty-eight feet. The crossing is 164 feet long. The whole church is well-proportioned and paved with large *liais* stones. There is an aisle on either side of the choir and nave, and another one flanking it in the nave housing chapels on both sides. These chapels, very beautiful and well-kept, were decorated and furnished thirty or forty years ago thanks to the generosity of many canons, who also took pains to

---

[4] The area surrounding a cathedral town and subject to its ecclesiastical jurisdiction was called a *plebs* or *christianitas*, or *curia christianitatis*, in which *christianitas* refers specifically to the body of clergy serving the jurisdiction. Each was headed by a dean or archpriest. Because he was an "external" member of the chapter, whose duties were concerned with external, diocesan affairs, he did not sit in choir.
[5] St. Paulinus of Nola, *Epistula* 18.5, ed. Le Brun des Marettes (Paris, 1685), 1:101–2; ed. von Hartel, 132–33.
[6] St. Thomas Becket, *Epistula* 232, ed. and trans. Anne Duggan, *The Correspondence of Thomas Becket, Archbishop of Canterbury, 1162–1170* (Clarendon Press, 2000), 2:1001.

clear up the church significantly.⁷ Currently, the chapels are used for low Masses. Since low Masses were not said in the age when this church was built, these places must have once been used for private prayer and meditation outside the time of the Divine Offices, as well for burying persons distinguished for their piety or rank, as we see in the thirty-second letter of St. Paulinus, who had several churches built in Nola that bear a very close resemblance to our own.⁸ There we see that the high altar was set under a large apse flanked by two smaller apses, one serving as a sacristy, as it still does in the cathedral of Rouen, and the other for keeping the holy books and writings of the Fathers.⁹

In Rouen, this second apse is used not as a library but as a chapel, for it is too small to contain the cathedral library's many books. This library is located at the left end of the crossing. It is reached by ascending a finely crafted staircase that protrudes into the church. Above the stairs are inscribed these two verses of St. Paulinus, which also used to be engraved above the door of the library of the church of St. Felix of Nola:

> Si quem sancta tenet meditandi in Lege voluntas,
> Hic poterit residens sacris intendere Libris.¹⁰

The cathedral canons have opened the library to the public. Outside of Thursdays, Sundays, feasts, and the month of October, from nine in the morning till noon and from two in the afternoon till five, a salaried librarian fetches books for all who ask. Long tables have been arranged in the middle with benches on their sides for readers' comfort. The library hall is quite large and very well lit, and its brass-lined cabinets house a very fine collection. Portraits of donors hang above the cabinets, among them that of Sieur Acarie, who founded the collection with the donation of his personal library. In gratitude to him at the end of the dinner the canons share together in this place on the feast of the Ascension, the canon who says grace says, "Let us pray for the repose of the soul of M. Pierre Acarie, who founded this library."

The flèche or spire is one of the most beautiful pieces of architecture in France, and all who see it marvel. The lantern tower is 152 feet high, and the height of the flèche is 380 feet. It is covered in lead just like the church.

---

⁷ Perhaps referring to the destruction of the tombs, altars, and other devotional elements in the nave. The argument from "clarity" was used to justify clearing away objects that impeded a clear view of the choir and nave, especially the rood screens, since they were thought to disrupt a clear view of the choir and of the geometry of the church. For a learned contemporary objection to this vandalism, see Thiers, "Dissertation sur les jubés," esp. 232–38.
⁸ St. Paulinus of Nola, *Epistula* 32.12, ed. Le Brun des Marettes, 1:206–7; ed. von Hartel, 287–88.
⁹ St. Paulinus of Nola, *Epistula* 32.16, ed. Le Brun des Marettes, 1:209; ed. von Hartel, 291.
¹⁰ "If pondering the Law be your holy pleasure / You may read sacred books here at your leisure."

The choir is closed off with a rood screen with two chapels of very fine and entirely gilded woodwork.

I have already said that the chapels and oratories were built in part to bury people of distinction and piety, as we shall now see.

In the large chapel behind the choir, on the right side, stands the magnificent mausoleum of the two cardinals d'Amboise, an uncle and nephew who were archbishops of Rouen. The white marble figures are depicted kneeling in their cardinalatial habits. A great number of smaller figures in delicate white marble relief are placed in various niches around them. The structure is twenty-one feet high and sixteen feet wide. Carved along the edge of the tomb are these four verses:

> Pastor eram Cleri, populi Pater; aurea se se
> Lilia[11] subdebant, Quercus[12] et ipsa mihi.
> Mortuus en jaceo, morte extinguuntur honores:
> At virtus mortis nescia, morte viret.[13]

The cardinals are buried at the base of this mausoleum in a tomb of black and white marble. The first Georges d'Amboise, for whom the above verses were composed, was not only a cardinal and archbishop, but also a minister of state and intendant of finances under Louis XII, king of France, and legate of the pope in France and Avignon. It was said of him that "he was a minister without pride or avarice, and a cardinal with a single benefice." His nephew Georges II held a council for ecclesiastical discipline in 1522, and nothing is more beautiful than its canons.[14]

Facing this mausoleum on the other side is that of Louis de Brezé, first chamberlain of the king and grand seneschal of Normandy. This structure is no less rich, nor less elevated and large than that of the cardinals d'Amboise.

On the same side lies the tomb of William de Flavacourt, archbishop of Rouen, who founded the Collège du St-Esprit for six chaplains, held several councils whose canons have been preserved, and gave many alms to the poor, especially during a year of scarcity. He died on 6 April 1306.

On the right side of this chapel is the sepulcher of Ralph Roussel, archbishop of Rouen, who showed great zeal for the restoration of ecclesiastical discipline and the correction of abuses that had slipped into this church through false devotion. For these reasons he assembled a council in Rouen in 1445 that produced forty-one canons, which are still preserved and very beautiful.[15] He died in 1452.

---

[11] Referring to the device of the kings of France.
[12] Author's note: An allusion to Pope Julius II of the House of della Rovere, "of the oak".
[13] "I was a pastor to the clergy, a father to the people. / The golden lilies bowed to me, and the oak itself. / Behold me dead; death extinguishes honors, / But virtue, which knows not death, flourishes in death."
[14] Jean-François Pommeraye, *Sanctae Rotomagensis ecclesiae concilia ac synodalia decreta* (Rouen, 1677), 318–25.
[15] Pommeraye, *Concilia*, 304–12.

Nearby is the tomb of the celebrated archbishop Odo Rigaud, who did so much good for the church of Rouen, solicitous for its spiritual as much as its temporal welfare.[16] He reformed the collegiate church of Notre-Dame-de-la-Ronde in 1255 at the entreaty of St. Louis, king of France, establishing its statutes of reform. At the beginning of these acts, he refers to himself as *Frater Odo permissione divina Rotomagensis Ecclesiae minister indignus*. Before his election as archbishop he had been a Franciscan, and out of humility he kept the titles *frater* and *minister indignus* used within that order. He made frequent visitations of his diocese, and took a census of not only the beneficers and parish priests, but even the parishioners of each church. I once saw a list of this peanut gallery (*poulier*) he drew up.

It is worth noting that the crosiers of Rouen's archbishops, like those of all ancient bishops and abbots, did not have a crook, as one can discern on tombs and mausolea that are more than three hundred years old. There was only a sort of pommel on top like one sees on the end of a cane. Then this became more like the curve of a shepherd's staff and finally the end became coiled as it is today.

I would add that kerchiefs used to be hung from the crosiers of bishops and abbots, the staves of cantors, and processional crosses. The cantor's staff in St-Denis and the processional cross of the Dominicans and many country churches still have them. Their purpose was so that those carrying them could wipe and blow their noses, since men used not to have either breeches or pockets. They attached everything to their staves or girdles, to which priests celebrating Mass and some monks still attach their kerchief, monks their rosary and keys, and women their purse and keys. This kerchief was also sometimes attached to the sleeve, and that is the origin of the maniple, which is still attached to the sleeve. Hence the expression *se moucher sur la manche*,[17] as some ill-mannered children still do quite naturally.

In the old chapel of St. Romanus, located on the south side of the nave by the small sacristy, one can see a relief figure of Rollo, first duke of Normandy, halfway up the wall facing the altar.

On the opposite side, in the chapel of St. Anne near the north door, one may see a relief figure of his son William Longsword, who, it is said, provided the canons with their chapter bread,[18] as noted in this verse of his epitaph:

> Panem canonicis in honore Dei Genetricis
> Contulit.[19]

Behind this chapel is the chapterhouse. Archbishop William Bonne-Âme ("Good Soul"), who had it built, is buried in the center. He died in 1110

---

[16] For a recent study in English, see Adam Davis, *The Holy Bureaucrat: Eudes Rigaud and Religious Reform in Thirteenth-Century Normandy* (Cornell University Press, 2006).
[17] "To blow one's nose on one's sleeve."
[18] See p. 139, n. 21.
[19] "He brought the canons bread in honor of the Mother of God."

and was laid in a black marble tomb, with the following epitaph, which is carved on the east-facing wall:

> Relligio tua, larga manus, meditatio sancta,
>   Nos, GUILLELME, tuum flere monent obitum.
> Quod pius Antistes fueris Clerique benignus,
>   Interiora docent, exteriora probant.
> Ecclesiae lumen, decus et defensio Cleri,
>   Circumspectus eras, promptus ad omne bonum.
> Fratribus hanc aedem cum Claustro composuisti,
>   Nec tua pauperibus janua clausa fuit.
> Contulit ad victum tua magnificentia Fratrum,
>   Ecclesias, decimas, rura, tributa, domos;
> Exemploque tuo subjectos dedocuisti
>   Verba pudenda loqui, turpia facta sequi.
> Fine bono felix, biduo ter solveris ante
>   Quam pisces Solis consequerentur iter.[20]

Returning to the church through the chapterhouse door, one can see a sort of large tomb some six feet long, with a cover of blackened wood which looks like black marble from a distance. This is actually the baptismal font. It is quite appropriately just in front of the chapel of St. John the Baptist; it used to be within the chapel of the same saint in Vienne.

In the aisle on the left side of the choir, one sees the chapel of Sts. Peter and Paul under a small dome, where lie two white marble tombs of archbishops represented in pontifical dress. Their identity is unknown, for there is no inscription. All these archbishops look toward the east, as do all those I have seen everywhere in tombs made before the sixteenth century. The modern use of burying priests and bishops facing west is therefore altogether recent.[21] The new rituals of Reims,[22] Sens,[23] and Metz,[24] as well as the Ambrosian,[25] ordain that they should be buried facing east, just like laymen.

In the nave in front of the great rood lies the tomb of St. Maurilius, who died in 1067. Here is his epitaph, composed by a canon named Herluin and engraved on a copper sheet:

---

[20] "Thy piety, generous hand, and holy contemplation, / Admonish us, O William, to beweep thy passing. / That thou wast a pious bishop and kindly clerk, / All things within teach, all things without prove. / O light of the Church, glory and defender of the clergy, / Thou wast circumspect and quick to do good. / For the brethren thou didst build this room with the cloister, / Nor was thy door closed to the poor. / Thy magnificence gathered for the brethren's sustenance / Churches, tithes, fields, tributes, and houses; / And by thine example thou taughtst thy subjects / Not to speak shameful words, nor strive after disgraceful deeds. / Happy in a good death, thou wast released thrice two days before / The Sun's course overtook the Fish."
[21] A position supported by Jean Mabillon, who cites supporting documents in an appendix to his *De cultu sanctorum ignotorum epistola* (Paris, 1705), 99–105.
[22] *Rituel de la province de Reims* (Paris, 1677), 622.
[23] *Rituel du diocèse de Sens* (Sens, 1694), 158.
[24] *Rituale Metense* (Metz, 1713), Pars tertia, 77.
[25] *Instructiones, ritus, et decreta ad funera ducenda* (Milan, 1685), 20, 33, 37.

> Humani cives lachrymam nolite negare
>   Vestro pontifici Maurilio Monacho.
> Hunc Remis genuit, studiorum Legia nutrix
>   Potavit trifido fonte philosophico.
> Vobis hanc aedem coeptam perduxit ad unguem,
>   Laetitia magna fecit et Encaenia.
> Cum tibi, Laurenti, vigilat plebs sobria Christi,
>   Transit, et in coelis laurea festa colit.[26]

He held several councils, finished the construction of the cathedral and dedicated it, and was most zealous for divine worship and the ceremonies of the Church. On certain days, the deacon goes to incense the tomb of this saintly prelate after the offertory.

Under the same tomb was buried the heart of Cardinal Guillaume d'Estouteville, archbishop of Rouen,[27] in accordance with his wishes.

Near the brass eagle in the choir one finds a tomb of black marble that used to be more magnificent before the Huguenot pillage. The heart of Charles V, king of France and benefactor of the cathedral church, is buried under this tomb, under an effigy of the king lying down with his heart in hand.

To the right of the high altar, behind one of the riddels, one sees the tomb that contains the heart of Richard, king of England and duke of Normandy and Aquitaine, called "the Lionheart" on account of his magnanimity. He persevered in this virtue till death, when he ordered the man who had caused his death to be freed from prison, and even granted him a hundred shillings.

On the other side, also behind the riddel, one finds the tomb of his younger brother Henry, son of Henry II, king of England and duke of Normandy.

Every day at high Mass except on simples and ferias, the deacon incenses these three tombs after the offertory, and the celebrant does the same at the *Benedictus* of Lauds and the *Magnificat* of Vespers.

In the middle of the apse behind the high altar, one can still see, as in Lyon and Vienne, the remains of the archbishop's throne, which he used to occupy on solemn feasts. It is a stone seat at the top of eight steps.

Close by and next to this on a pillar there is a wax-coated board, upon which they write with a stylus the names of those who are to perform the offices of hebdomadary, deacon, subdeacon, and cope-bearers. Those named on the board who fail to fulfill their assigned office are punished with a hefty fine that cannot be waived.

---

[26] "O good citizens, do not deny a tear / For your pontiff, the monk Maurilius. / Reims begot him; Liège, his nurse of studies, / Gave him drink from the treble font of philosophy. / For you he perfectly completed this unfinished building, / And with great joy he consecrated it. / When the sober people of Christ hold vigil with thee, O Laurence, / He passed away, and in the heavens he assists at the triumphal feasts."

[27] Died 1483.

If the high altar did not have such an elevated retable, one could say it was the most august in France. It is detached from the wall, as ordained by the ritual of Rouen.[28] The altar table is one of the largest I have ever seen. There is a parament in front and another one above on the retable.

At the same height, there are four large riddels suspended from four well-made brass columns, topped with four angels likewise of brass, carrying candles that are lit on double and triple feasts. There are no candles on the altar or the retable. Above the retable, where the cathedral of Lyon has two crosses, here there are two statues of Our Lady, and between these statues a large, well-regarded painting of the crucifixion, which is said to be in the style of the famous painter Michelangelo.[29] Above this painting protrudes a small triangular platform on which an angel kneels holding the holy pyx *sub titulo Crucis* in his two hands under a small canopy. A large tester above covers the entire altar.

A very old priest has assured me that the Blessed Sacrament did not used to be reserved in the choir for the sick, but only in the parish church of St-Étienne, as in Lyon and Vienne.[30]

In the apse, there are two small altars on either side of the high altar.

There are three silver lamps holding three candles that hang before the altar. The middle candle burns day and night, while the two others are lit during the Divine Offices.

Between these three lamps and the eagle in the east end of the choir, there used to be a large brass chandelier with seven branches before the Huguenot pillage.

At the east end of the canons' stalls on the right side stands the large episcopal throne, used when the archbishop celebrates pontifically. It is considerably more elevated than other thrones I have seen, and very magnificent despite its age, having been built by order of Cardinal d'Estouteville around 1467, like the stalls of the choir, which are quite pretty.

The choirboys wear red under their albs, a zucchetto, and a red biretta. Their heads are shorn.

---

[28] In his 1679 edition of John of Avranches, Le Brun des Marettes refers as his point of reference to a two-volume ritual of Rouen printed in 1651. Since we could not consult a copy, where possible we cite the *Sacerdotale seu Manuale ecclesiae Rothomagensis* (Rouen, 1640).

[29] This image, painted in oil on wood by Michel Du Joncquoy in 1588, was commissioned by a canon of Rouen for the diocese's Charterhouse. Because it was too big for its chapel, however, the cathedral chapter agreed to purchase it, since most of their church's artworks had been destroyed by the Huguenots. When a new high altar was built in 1736–1737, this painting was moved to the chapel of St. Julian, where it remains today. See François Bergot et al., *La peinture d'inspiration religieuse à Rouen au temps de Pierre Corneille (1606–1684)* (Musée des Beaux-Arts, 1984), 69.

[30] Des Marettes has several times mentioned with approbation places where the hosts are not kept in the main sanctuary, e.g., in the abbey of St-Nicolas in Angers (p. 77), and in Lyon (p. 46). He thinks they should be reserved for the Viaticum at some other place. Likewise, those who commune at a Mass should do so from hosts consecrated at that Mass.

In a stained glass window in the chapel of St. Romanus, one can see the form of the ancient birettas of canons and other ecclesiastics, which were almost round.

The canons in the lower form wear the almuce in winter and summer even if not in holy orders, but the chaplains[31] only wear it if they are at least subdeacons. The chaplains' almuce is of a reddish-brown color like that of a hare; that of the canons is of gray squirrel fur as in all cathedrals. In Rouen they wear it over the left arm, as they do almost everywhere else, even when they go to the altar.

On episcopal feasts the dignities and canons who are counselors in Parlement wear a red robe under their surplice.

In winter, all the cantors, chaplains, and choirboys wear a black cape with a long train and a trim of red fabric on the edges in front, and a *grand camail* ending in a point on the back (see PLATE 49).[32] All the canons, both those in holy orders and those who are not, have the same long camail and a cape of black fabric with a train, except that the trim of their cape is of red velvet. Besides this they have, as in Laon, a small fur-lined camail or round-hooded *aumusson* of gray miniver which only covers their head and shoulders,[33] and which they wear over their cape and under their large *grand camail*, whose hood they put down behind their necks. They only put up the hood when it rains or snows in order to avoid damaging the *aumusson*. The eight minor canons of fifteen marks[34] and the chaplains and cantors in holy orders also wear an *aumusson*, but it is reddish-brown like their summer almuce. When they serve as cope-bearers, both take off their black cape and black *grand camail* when they go to put on their copes in the sacristy, and only keep their *aumusson* under the cope, so as to not wear both cape and cope.

The priest, deacon, and subdeacon canons and chaplains wear an *aumusson* or fur-lined camail on top of their chasuble or tunicle, unless the celebrant carries a cross to the altar. In that case, they go to the altar bareheaded, and carry their fur-lined camail in hand. They only place it upon their head going and returning from the altar and when they are seated, as during the *Gloria*, the *Credo*, etc.

In winter, the choirboys who carry the candles and thurible used to remove their capes and camails, and served in albs.

---

[31] There were about 150 chaplains in Rouen. Some had particular roles in the singing of the choir Office, and hence des Marettes calls them "cantors"; others said Mass in an assigned chapel and also participated in the Office. One of them also taught grammar and chant to the choirboys. See Kristiane Lemé, "Les chanoines de la cathédrale de Rouen au XVe siècle," in C. Elaine Block and Frédéric Billiet, eds., *Les stalles de la cathédrale de Rouen* (Presses universitaires de Rouen et du Havre, 2003), 26.
[32] See p. 182, n. 9.
[33] The *aumusson* or *aumuçon* (Latin *almussonum*) was a fur-lined headdress used in winter. According to de Vert, *Explication*, 2:258–60, note a, it gradually became longer and wider, thus evolving into the almuce (see p. 10, n. 14).
[34] See p. 201, n. 35.

Only major canons can serve as subdeacon and deacon and say Mass at the high altar; not even the king's almoner can say a low Mass there in the presence of His Majesty, unless he be a bishop invited by the chapter.

The chapter is composed of ten dignitaries and fifty-one canons counting the archbishop, who is also a canon and in this capacity has a voice in chapter, where he holds the first place and presides. All the canonries and all the dignities of the cathedral are his to nominate, except the high deanery, which is filled by the chapter.

In addition there are eight minor canons of fifteen marks and of fifteen pounds, who have no voice in chapter and sit in the second row of stalls with the chaplains, cantors, and musicians.[35]

There are also four colleges of chaplains and cantors. One of them, called Collège d'Albane, was founded by Peter de Colmieu, cardinal of Albano and whilom archbishop of Rouen, for ten cantors, of which four are priests, three deacons, and three subdeacons, all of whom must live together in the same house or under the same roof and live in community. Not fifty years ago they were still living this way, with readings during meals.[36]

The statutes forbid them

> to haunt taverns, *jeux de paume*,[37] bowls, and other public places, or to play *brelans* or *berlans*;[38] to bring dogs into the church under pain of monetary fine; to rent their college rooms; to carry breviaries or other books to choir or to read during the Office; or to begin a verse before the other side has entirely finished singing its own.[39]

They are obliged to know the psalter and chant by heart, for the chanting is done from memory in this illustrious church, as in Lyon. They have only two books, one for the lessons and another for the short chapters and collects. The major canons, even those who chant four or five responsories on semidouble and greater feasts, and who wear copes on double and triple feasts, are obliged to know by heart everything they chant, and the musicians as well, unless they are singing a Mass *sur le livre*.

---

[35] The four canons of fifteen marks were so called because they were originally supported by fifteen marks of silver taken from the ample revenues of the chapel of Blye in England, donated to the church of Rouen in 1189 by John Lackland, count of Mortain and future king of England, although Rouen lost possession thereof during John's turbulent reign. The canons of fifteen pounds were founded in 1190 by John's brother King Richard the Lionheart, who assigned four clerics that income to offer suffrages for his soul and that of his brother Henry the Young King. For details, see Jean-François Pommeraye, *Histoire de l'église cathédrale de Rouen* (Rouen, 1686), 536–38. The musicians were beneficed clerics who specialized in chant *sur le livre*, an improvisational practice in which one musician sang a pre-existing melody, called the cantus firmus, while one or more musicians sang a countermelody or melodies. They were only grudgingly introduced into the choir of Rouen around the fifteenth century, and had reduced rights; see Pommeraye, *Histoire*, 554–55.
[36] For the foundation charter of this college, see PL 147:211D–216B.
[37] A ball-and-court game, precursor of tennis.
[38] A game where each player received three cards.
[39] Another sign of careful observance, as less-than-enthusiastic communities would have sped through the required psalms.

In the church of Rouen, second Vespers are always less solemn than first Vespers, no matter the feast. Apparently, this is because the solemnity of a feast used to end immediately after second Vespers, and afterward it was permitted to do servile work again. This was still the practice the end of the eleventh century, as I gather from the learned Benedictine Dom Ange Godin, in his notes on a Council of Rouen held in 1072, from the Councils of Compiègne and Lyon, and from the capitularies of Charles the Bald and Louis the Pious, which made it obligatory to stop manual labor beginning with first Vespers in imitation of God's command to the Jews: *A vespera ad vesperam celebrabitis Sabbata vestra*.[40] Although the policy has changed, cessation from manual labor now being obligatory from midnight to midnight, nevertheless the Church has always retained her ancient practice with respect to the celebration of Sundays and feasts, which begin at first Vespers. I do not know precisely when the practice with regard to manual labor changed in Normandy. It could not have been very long ago, because dear old ladies in the Norman countryside still refrain from spinning on Saturday afternoons. Moreover, in the city of Rouen itself the craftsmen of most trades dare not work on the evenings of solemn Vespers after the bell first sounds for first Vespers, according to their statutes. If their guild officers, who purposely make their rounds on those days, find them working, they fine them, as I have observed many times in Rouen. On these principal feasts the city gates are closed except for the small wicket.

Here are some customs and ceremonies taken from the old ordinary and ceremonial of Rouen, which is nearly 650 years old.[41]

The canons of Rouen lived in community at least until the year 1000, and were called brethren. The epitaph of William Bonne-Âme, who died in 1110, shows they had a cloister:

> Fratribus hanc aedem cum claustro composuisti.[42]

They said Vespers at nightfall, *imminente nocte*, as formerly in the church of Paris.[43] Hence this Office is called *Lucernarium* or *Lucernalis*

---

[40] Lev. 23:32. The note in question, and citations of the councils and capitularies, are found in Pommeraye, *Concilia*, 506.
[41] Le Brun des Marettes is referring to John of Avranches, *De officiis ecclesiasticis* (ca. 1060–67), a description of the ritual customs of Rouen which came to form the basis for this liturgical use. The text was first published by a canon of Rouen, Jean Prevost (d. 1648) in Rouen in 1642. Le Brun des Marettes published a corrected edition through the press of his father Bonaventure (Rouen, 1679), along with further excerpts from Rouenais rituals and ordinaries furnished to him by Émery Bigot (as he explains in the volume's preface). Le Brun des Marettes borrowed heavily from these texts and his extensive notes on them when composing this chapter of the *Travels*. However, he also had access to the manuscripts themselves, since he describes customs not covered in the excerpts. Throughout this chapter, where Le Brun des Marettes draws on the 1679 edition, for ease of reference we cite Migne's 1853 reprinting. For a modern edition of John of Avranches's text, see *Le De officiis ecclesiasticis de Jean d'Avranches, archevêque de Rouen (1067–1079)*, ed. René Delamare (Picard, 1923).
[42] "Thou didst build this temple with its cloister for the brethren."
[43] PL 147:29D.

hora, they indeed made use of light to chant the orations. See Bourges and Lyon.[44] For the same reason candles and candlesticks are carried in this Office. After all, it was the time for candles to be lit.

The altar was incensed during the versicle before the *Magnificat*. The versicle *Dirigatur oratio mea sicut incensum* is apparently the literal reason for this,[45] and in fact this versicle is not said on ferial days when there is no incensation. Outside of Sundays and feasts, after the *Magnificat* antiphon, they always said the preces before the oration, as the Carthusians and the illustrious church of Lyon still do. After Vespers they still busied themselves with manual labor.

Before Compline they had a reading from the *Conferences* of Cassian, the *Dialogues* of St. Gregory, or other works containing examples of the saints suitable to encourage one to do good: *In Completorii hora nos contra noctis insidias munientes... quam lectio praecedit de exemplis Sanctorum Patrum excitandas in bono animas fratrum.*[46]

They rose at midnight, as is still done in Paris, to say Vigils or Nocturns, later called Matins. This practice lasted in Rouen until 1325, when Matins began to be said later on account of certain night terrors which troubled them at that time, according to the chronicle of St-Lô.[47] Other handwritten records, however, indicate that in 1324 a statute was enacted in the church of Rouen decreeing that Matins should no longer be said at midnight because a canon on his way to Matins had been killed by a thief.

This Office began with *Domine labia mea aperies*, as seen in the old ordinary of Rouen: *Quia somno dominante hucusque conticuimus, Dominum deprecamur, ut labia nostra ad laudem suam pronuntiandam aperire dignetur.*[48] I also read in Amalar: *Congrue juxta consuetudinem Romanae Ecclesiae, a somno surgentes dicimus primo, Domine labia mea aperies.*[49] Elsewhere this verse is called *Versus apertionis*, because they first opened their mouths to say it immediately after rising to sing God's praises. Properly speaking, the *Domine labia mea aperies* is a preparation for saying the Office. What certain devout people think should be said before this is but a preparation for the preparation, which goes against the axiom of philosophy, *non datur dispositio dispositionis.*[50] Lauds had the same ritual as Vespers.

---

[44] See pp. 203 and 47.
[45] See de Vert, *Explication*, 1:xx.
[46] "At the hour of Compline we fortify ourselves against nighttime snares. [...] It is preceded by a reading from the examples of the Holy Fathers to inspire the souls of the brethren towards good" (PL 147:30C).
[47] Stated under the year 1322 in the edition of the St-Lô chronicle by Adolphe Chéruel, *Normanniae nova chronica* (Caen, 1850), 32.
[48] "Since overbearing sleep still harasses us, we beseech the Lord that he might vouchsafe to open our lips to pronounce his praise."
[49] "It is apt that, following the custom of the Roman Church, after rising from sleep we first say, 'O Lord, thou wilt open my lips'" (*Liber de ordine antiphonarii* 1.2, ed. Hanssens, 3:19).
[50] "There can be no disposing of a disposition." See p. 92.

Every time they chanted the *Gloria Patri*, the canons and other ecclesiastics turned toward the altar and bowed, as the canons of Lyon and choirboys in all cathedrals still do.

The antiphon of Prime was taken from one of the psalms, like that of Compline, no matter what feast day it might be. This changed less than a hundred years ago.

After Prime during the year, and after Terce in Lent, the canons went to the chapterhouse, where they held the reading of the martyrology (they still do this except on solemn feasts), then of the necrology, and finally the rule of canons: *Inde recitetur lectio Regulae Canonicalis. Deinde culpae examinentur, examinatio canonicaliter exerceatur.*[51] They held an examination of faults and punished them as they deserved, as we still find in a 450-year-old ordinary, where it is written: *Post haec solent recitari marantiae et offensae diei et Horarum praecedentium, et ibi puniri.*[52]

The canons did not venture to leave choir without the dean's permission, nor the other ecclesiastics without the permission of the cantor.

At that time in Rouen Mass was said almost exactly as in Lyon. On ferial days there was only one candle-bearer, as in Tours, Orléans, etc. On feasts there were two. The celebrant with his ministers left the sacristy at the *Gloria Patri* of the Introit as in Lyon. After the *Confiteor* the celebrant kissed the deacon and subdeacon. After a prayer the celebrant bowed to the deacon, the deacon to the subdeacon, and the subdeacon to the choir, with reciprocal bows. Then the celebrant went up to the altar together with the deacon who, after kissing the two corners of the altar, presented the Gospel book to the celebrant to be kissed. The celebrant also kissed the middle of the altar. Then the priest went to the right side of the altar followed by the deacon who remained standing until the priest gave the sign to sit, which they did when the *Kyrie eleison* began. Note that the celebrant did not read the Introit or *Kyrie* at the altar.

The candle-bearers, placed at the south side, held up their candles toward the north. At the beginning of the *Kyrie* they put them down in the same place. They held them up in the same spot while the priest chanted the collects, and they were positioned there quite appropriately to give light to the celebrant. Sometimes they added a third candle, apparently on double feasts. On major feasts there were seven candle-bearers. After the collect they placed them down from east to west.

When the deacon was not performing a function at the altar he stayed in choir, as in the church of Lyon.

At the *Gloria in excelsis* the celebrant incensed the altar. Currently he does it during the *Kyrie*, and the acolyte incenses the clergy during the *Gloria in excelsis* and *Credo*.

---

[51] PL 147:32B.
[52] "After these things they usually recite their mistakes and offenses of the day and preceding hours, and are there punished" (see fuller quotation in PL 147:72B–D).

When the subdeacon began the Epistle, the celebrant sat and made the sign to the deacon to sit as well: *Incipiente Subdiacono Epistolam, Sacerdos juxta altare sedeat, et Diacono in loco suo sedere innuat.* From this it is clearly evident that the priest did not read it at the altar, nor elsewhere, since there is no mention of it. The Epistle and Gospel were chanted from the rood screen on feast days, as well as the Gradual and Alleluia, which were chanted *per rotulos* as in Lyon, that is, on ivory tablets. This may be what the old ordinary calls *tabulas osseas quas tenent in manibus*.[53]

When the deacon and subdeacon used folded chasubles, i.e., on Ember Saturdays and throughout Advent and Lent except feast days, the subdeacon took off his chasuble before reading the Epistle and put it on again thereafter. Immediately before reading the Gospel the deacon wrapped his chasuble around over his left shoulder, tying it under his right arm. He wore it this way until communion, when he put it back on as at the beginning of Mass. This practice is still observed today.

When it was time to go up to the rood loft, the celebrant imposed incense in the thurible and censed the altar. Nowadays, he does not incense it at this moment, but when he has ascended to the altar during the *Kyrie*. Then the deacon, having asked and received the priest's blessing, went to the loft carrying the Gospel book resting on his left shoulder, preceded by a subdeacon who held a cushion, the candle-bearers, and the thurifer. The same is done today, except that the subdeacon does not carry a cushion. The deacon, standing in the highest part of the loft between two candles, chanted the Gospel facing north, after having incensed it. They came back down from the loft in the same order they had gone to it.

After the Gospel the candle-bearers extinguished their candles.

The celebrant was incensed after the subdeacon had presented the Gospel book for him to kiss. The deacon kissed it thereafter, and on Sundays and feasts the subdeacon then took it to be kissed by the clergy. This is still done today, except that the deacon does not kiss it. I do not see the reason for this; he does kiss it at other times. The subdeacon kisses it last.

The Offertory antiphon always had verses, as in Lyon, and they are still preserved in some Sunday Masses and especially in Masses of the Dead. A more recent ordinary of the church of Rouen forbade their omission under pain of anathema, unless the priest was about to say the Preface: *Statutum est in ecclesia Rotomagensi per totum annum versus Offerendarum secundum suum ordinem cantare, et sub anathemate jussum ne dimittantur propter Cleri negligentiam, nisi Presbyter fuerit promptus ad* Per omnia.[54] In such cases some were omitted. In Lyon, when this happens the verses are not

---

[53] "Bone tablets which they hold in hand" (PL 147:54A).
[54] Cited also in PL 147:77A,B. In the preface to the 1679 edition of John of Avranches, Le Brun des Marettes indicates that he consulted a two-hundred-year-old ordinary of Rouen cathedral provided him by Bigot.

omitted, but the last ones are sung more quickly, as I have seen done on the Nativity of St. John the Baptist, when there were four Offertory verses with the repetition only of the part of the antiphon after the asterisk, as is done at the Offertory of the Mass for the Dead.

The subdeacon presented the bread and wine to the deacon, and the deacon to the priest, as is still done today. On major feasts the cantor presented the water, covered with a towel, to the deacon, who poured it into the chalice, as the cantor still does in Angers on the most solemn feasts, which they call *jours de fêtage*.[55] On other days it was the acolyte who presented the water, as he still does today.

The chalice was not placed in the middle of the corporal as today, but to the right of the host and on the same line lengthwise. The same arrangement is found in the *Ordo Romanus*,[56] Amalar,[57] the *Micrologus*,[58] and Radulph of Rivo.[59] The chalice was covered not by a pall but by the corporal, just as is done today in Lyon and among the Carthusians, who have made no innovations in this matter.

Next the priest incensed the offerings and handed the thurible to the deacon, who, after incensing around the altar, incensed the celebrant. He then gave the thurible to the acolyte, who proceeded to incense the clergy and the people.

The deacon took the paten from the altar and presented it to the subdeacon, and the subdeacon gave it, wrapped in a veil, to an acolyte if there was one, as in Paris and Tours. Otherwise he held it himself, as is done in Rouen today.

I have said that it was the deacon who took it from the altar, because the subdeacon was not allowed to remove anything sacred from the altar. *Non licet enim*, says the old ordinary, *quidquam sacri ab altari auferre alicui nisi Diacono vel Sacerdoti.*[60] This is still diligently observed in the cathedral, where the subdeacon brings up even the chalice with both hands covered by a veil, and takes it back to the sacristy during the last orations of the Mass in the same way, after the deacon has purified it and helped him place it in the large veil. Thus, the subdeacon never touches it at all, as he was prohibited from doing by canon 21 of the Council of Laodicea.[61]

Everything else until the Canon is unremarkable.

---

[55] This is an ancient aspect of the Roman rite, as old as the *Ordo Romanus* 1.80, in Andrieu, *Les Ordines Romani*, 2:93. See also Pseudo-Alcuin, *De divinis officiis* 39 (PL 101:1246A); Amalar of Metz, *Liber officialis* 3.19.30, ed. Hanssens, 2:320; Honorius Augustodunensis, *Gemma animae* 1.38, ed. Thomas and Eger, 1:76–78.
[56] *Ordo Romanus* 2.9 according to Mabillon (PL 78:973C), numbered 5.55 in Andrieu, 2:220.
[57] Amalar of Metz, *Liber officialis* 3.19.31, ed. Hanssens, 2:321
[58] Bernold of Constance, *Micrologus* 10 (PL 151:983D).
[59] Radulph of Rivo, *De canonum observantia* 23.33.
[60] PL 147:35C.
[61] PL 67:71B, 72B.

During the Canon the deacon, thurifer, and candle-bearers stood bowing behind the celebrant, but the subdeacon bowed in front of the priest, facing him as at Lyon. Note that at that time there was no retable behind the altar, which was a simple table entirely unattached to anything else, without a retable, like the arrangement today in the cathedrals of Lyon, Chalon-sur-Saône, and Blois, and like the morrow Mass altar in Bourges and Mâcon. On solemn feasts with seven subdeacons, they stood in a line behind the altar facing the priest; the seven deacons stood in a line behind the priest.

Neither the old ordinary of Rouen, nor the *Ordo Romanus*, nor any of the ancient commentators on the Divine Offices mention any elevation of the host and chalice separately, but only the single elevation immediately before the *Pater* or during the *Pater*.[62]

The 1516 missal of Rouen states at the prayer *Supplices te rogamus*, the priest bowed profoundly before the altar, his hands not joined like today but crossed right over left until *ex hac altaris participatione*. The same is found in the three missals from England and Scotland before their separation from the Catholic Church, in the missals of Orléans (1504), Vienne (1519), Lyon (1530), and, I believe, in all French missals until the time of Pius V, who established in his missal that the priest should join his hands, a change that has been adopted almost everywhere.[63]

At *Per quem haec omnia, Domine*, the deacon approached the altar and removed the corporal from the chalice, which he uncovered with the priest.

There is a note that the priest touched the four sides of the chalice with the host: *Oblata quatuor partes Calicis tangat*. This is also found in the ancient *Ordo Romanus* and in Ivo of Chartres, Letter 233.[64] The new rubricists insist that the priest must take scrupulous care that the host does not touch the chalice while he makes the sign of the cross at the words *sanctificas* and the rest, doubtlessly because they do not know the real reason for this practice.[65]

The deacon assisted the priest to elevate the chalice over the host, just as he assisted him during the oblation. This was done because the chalice

---

[62] See de Vert, *Explication*, 4:209–30, who argues that the elevation of the species immediately after their consecration was introduced in the thirteenth-century.

[63] On crossing the arms on the breast at the *Supplices* (as some rubrics put it, *cancellatis manibus*), see de Vert, *Explication*, 1:235, who mentions that this custom was also followed by the Dominicans, Carmelites, and Carthusians.

[64] *Ordo Romanus* 2.10 according to Mabillon (PL 78:974B), numbered 5.65 in Andrieu, 2:222. For Ivo's letter, see PL 162:254A–B, but also the semi-critical edition and translation of Ivo's letters by Geneviève Giordanengo, *Lettres d'Yves de Chartres* (2017), which includes valuable discussions of Ivo's sources, accessible here: http://telma-chartes.irht.cnrs.fr/yves-de-chartres.

[65] See de Vert, *Explication*, 4:252–57, who notes that the sign of the cross traced over the chalice results from the original practice of touching the chalice on four sides, described by Ivo of Chartres and others. Modern rubricists (he notes Gavantus by name) counseled against the practice for fear that contact created particles, but thereby removed its literal foundation.

cup used to be larger than it is today on account of the greater quantity of wine that was poured therein for the communion of the faithful, who at that time received this species, as we shall see hereafter.

Just as the deacon helped the priest uncover the chalice, he also helped him cover it with the corporal, which was much larger than it is today. Immediately thereafter, the deacon kissed the altar and then the celebrant's shoulder: *Diaconus altare osculetur, et dextram Sacerdotis scapulam.* This kiss on the shoulder is still in use in the church of Lyon on several occasions.[66]

The old ordinary of Rouen does not say that the priest genuflected in adoration of the sacred host, but only that the deacons and subdeacons remained bowed from the *Te igitur* until the *Sed libera nos a malo*. Three missals from England and Scotland state that the priest should adore the sacred host as he elevates it by an inclination of the head, a use still followed by the Carthusians. The clergy also used to adore the host in this fashion in the church of St-Jean in Lyon, and their 1530 missal does not mention a genuflection. Nor is it indicated in the missals of the church of Scotland before their separation from Rome: *Omnes Clerici post Offertorium stant conversi ad altare quousque completur totum Officium Missae.* It is nowhere stated that they should kneel at the elevation or at any other point in the Mass.[67]

The priest said the Lord's Prayer and finished the office of the consecration with the clergy's response: *Sed libera nos a malo*. The old ordinary reads: *Clero* Sed libera nos a malo *respondente, officium Consecrationis perficiat.*

Then the deacon and subdeacon stopped bowing.

At the *Da propitius pacem*, the acolyte gave the paten to the subdeacon, then the subdeacon to the deacon and the deacon to the celebrant, who broke the host into three, as is still done today.

At the first *Agnus Dei*, the candle-bearers relit their candles. In Advent and Lent, after the choir had sung the second *Agnus Dei*, the deacon put his chasuble back on at the beginning of the Mass. Today he does so after the priest's communion.

During the *Agnus Dei*, a canon approached the altar to receive the kiss of peace from the celebrant, and went on to give it to the most senior canon on each side. Two in the second row received the kiss of peace from two in the top row, and two in the third row received in from two in the second row. All of them gave the kiss such that, without moving from their places, the most junior received the kiss from his neighbor who was more senior than he, each of them bowing to the other.

Through these chaste and holy kisses — *per oscula casta et sancta* — they prepared themselves for communion. Here is how it was carried out:

---

[66] See p. 47.
[67] See de Vert, *Explication*, 1:249–62, who defends the more ancient custom of remaining standing during the Canon, even during the elevations.

After breaking the host into three parts, the priest put the smallest particle into the chalice and the two others on the paten, as still done today. He, the deacon, and the subdeacon received communion from the larger of the two particles, while the other was reserved for the Viaticum of the dying: *tertia, Viaticum morientis*. If there was no need because a particle was already reserved, the priest or one of the ministers consumed it. The people as well as the priest, deacon, and subdeacon communicated from the same large particle of the host: *per comestam a Sacerdote vel a populo*, as the old ordinary says. The priest made no fuss about sharing his host with the people, who, having offered it with him, had a right to it.[68] The priest and ministers of the altar received communion under the two species separately. The priest received as priests do today. The deacon and subdeacon received the priest's kiss and then kissed his hand when he presented them with a particle of the sacred host, placing it in their mouths. Then the priest consumed with the small particle of the host some of the Precious Blood, giving the rest to the deacon and subdeacon to drink, as done today at Cluny and St-Denis. If there was too much Blood for the ministers to consume entirely, the celebrant dipped the people's hosts in it. This much I have learned from the ancient 640-year-old ordinary of Rouen, and the practice may well have continued for centuries; there is no evidence to the contrary.

After communion the priest did not consume an ablution. Rather, while the ministers received communion from the chalice, an acolyte brought another vessel to wash the priest's hands—as observed today in Lyon, Chartres, and among the Carthusians, and as they still did in Rouen before the last century—so that the priest would not obliged to drink the rinsings of his fingers.

The subdeacon assisted the deacon in purifying the chalice and paten. Today, in the cathedrals of Rouen and Lyon, the deacon does this alone, while the subdeacon carries the book to the other side of the altar. An acolyte received the chalice and paten wrapped in a large veil.

The ordinary does not say that the priest read the Communion antiphon, but only the oration preceded and followed by *Dominus vobiscum*, and then the *Ite, missa est* or *Benedicamus Domino* chanted by the deacon: *Clero respondente* Deo gratias, *Officium finiat*. The Mass and all the Divine Offices used to end in this way. What has been added afterwards is very modern, only around a century or century and a half ago, as one can see in the old books. The people of Rouen are not even accustomed to it yet. As soon as the priest has given the blessing, all depart. And if Sext is to be said, the choir begins the *Deus in adjutorium* immediately without any regard for the priest reciting the last Gospel.[69] We have already seen

---

[68] See de Vert, *Explication*, 3:374, on the former sharing of communion between priest, ministers, and laity.

[69] De Vert, *Explication*, 1:137–43, 3:424–25, argues that the prayer *Placeat* and following blessing was not considered part of the Mass proper, but the priest's private thanksgiving,

that the celebrant still does not recite it at high Masses in most churches.

Our old ordinary states that Mass was rarely said before nine in the morning nor after three in the afternoon, unless there was some necessity. On fast days, it was only said around two or three in the afternoon, since the fast extended that long.

From Advent to Christmas, and from Septuagesima to Easter, if a feast fell on a Sunday, it was transferred to the next day.

On solemn feasts, at the first ringing for first Vespers all the bells were rung, as still done today, and the altar was incensed at each nocturn, as is still practiced in Paris, Orléans, and Angers. The altar was also incensed at the *Te Deum*. Today, it is incensed on all triple feasts, on which the *Magnificat* and *Benedictus* antiphons are said thrice. The altar was and is still incensed during these canticles with two thuribles, except at second Vespers of triples of the second class when only one is used.

On Christmas night, the first stroke of Matins sounded at ten in the evening, *prima noctis vigilia*. The three Gospels of the third nocturn were chanted with incense and candles, as still at present. The principal priest of the church, *major Ecclesiae Sacerdos*, vested in dalmatic and chasuble, solemnly read the Genealogy of Jesus Christ. Today a priest still chants it on Christmas and Epiphany to a very beautiful melody and wearing a very old unclipped chasuble, but without dalmatic; instead there is a subdeacon vested in tunicle.

Immediately after the *Te Deum*, the clergy and people left to wash themselves at the fountain before the start of Mass, as we also find in the customaries of Cluny and Fontevraud.[70]

The three Masses of Christmas were celebrated by three different priests, as in Lyon and among the Carthusians.

The second Mass used to be sung just before dawn, *incipiente diluculo*, according to the ordinary, and this is still the case today in the parish churches. In the cathedral, however, it is sung immediately after Lauds, which indeed ought to be sung just before dawn like the second Mass. Therefore they assembled in church three times on that day to celebrate three Masses: as many assemblies as Masses.

Once low Masses were introduced, simple priests thought they had just as much right to say three Masses as did parish priests. This is why most individual priests now say three Masses.

On solemn feasts a procession was held before the high Mass, and all the clergy remained in copes for the Mass.

I pass over a number of things in the old ordinary that are neither beautiful nor useful.

---

until the missal of Pius V, and discusses the various customs regarding the Gospel *In principio*. See also p. 224.
[70] See Ulrich of Zell, *Consuetudines Cluniacenses* 1.46 (PL 149:692D) and, on Fontevraud, p. 84.

On page 176, I note that the word "to dine" (*dîner*) means "not to fast." One therefore sees that fasting meant not having dinner, for on fasting days they only had supper, which was at five or six in the evening in Lent and at about three in the afternoon on other fasting days. We mentioned this practice previously with regard to the abbey of St-Cyran.[71] Some further very convincing evidence of this fact is that, in all breviaries, the blessing for the evening meal is said at the repast usually taken at midday on fasting days.

On Epiphany, three Gospels and a Genealogy were said at Matins, just like at Christmas and with the same ceremonies. The antiphons and responsories of the third nocturn were about Jesus Christ's baptism.

On the Purification, the blessing of the candles was done at a different church or chapel. Today in the cathedral it is performed at the chapel of the Cross or of St. Cecily.

On Ash Wednesday, the ordinary does not mention the archbishop either receiving ashes or imposing them upon himself. Formerly this was also the case in Vienne and Orléans.

On that day and throughout all of Lent, Prime was sung once the sun was up. Chapter was held after Terce, and the morrow Mass was said thereafter, followed by Sext. This is still observed.

It is clear from the ordinary that at that time they avoided saying the minor hours one immediately after the other, so that there was a space of time between Sext and None. This is still the case in Lyon, Vienne, and Sens, and the ritual of Rouen exhorts clerics to keep this practice. There was also a prohibition on anticipating None before the hour at which it ought to be said: *Nona hora sua dicatur, quam Missa diei sequatur*, states the ordinary with respect to Lent. After None, the Mass of the day was said at three in the afternoon. After Mass, Vespers of the Dead was said, and then Vespers of the day. Today, Vespers of Our Lady is said in addition to that of the Dead. One sees therefore that they did not eat until five or six in the evening, and Vespers are truly thus said before eating: *Vesperae ante comestionem*. We have seen many monasteries of both sexes that still strictly observe this today, for they act with simplicity of heart, and have not grown too delicate. Everywhere else they have had the ingenuity to anticipate Vespers in order to anticipate the meal, and in most churches it is said at ten or eleven in the morning. This is truly absurd, and it must be said, to the praise of the cathedral of Rouen, that of all the churches in France it is the one that has anticipated Vespers the least, and there this hour sometimes ends at one in the afternoon. I have seen this happen many times on semidouble feasts in Lent, and if the three Vespers had not been sung hastily, then surely they would have left choir around two.

After Vespers they went to take their repast. Before Compline, at the sounding of a bell all the clergy assembled and sang the Vigils of the Dead.

---

[71] See p. 103.

Then they held a conference where they usually read the *Dialogues* of St. Gregory the Great, as was still being done less than a hundred years ago. Then the bell rang again for Compline.

Although the conference reading is no longer done—and which, according to the Rule of St. Benedict and the custom of some monasteries of his order, lasted an hour—at least they still ring the bell on ferias before Compline for two hours. As I understand it, this represents the ringing during the hour or so that the reading lasted, and the ringing for an hour during the Vigils of the Dead. If someone disagrees, I would ask that he explain why this bell rings, for after it has stopped, another larger bell rings for Compline, and my explanation fits what the old ordinary says. Thus God has allowed that the bell continue to be rung, even though the reading is no longer done, perhaps as a sign that someday will serve for its restoration.

After each hour of the Office, a Gradual psalm was added for the brethren—*pro fratribus*—and then the psalm *De profundis* was said for the departed, together with certain oration, as is still done in Lyon today on ferias, together with psalm 50, *Miserere mei Deus*, which was still said less than a hundred years ago in Rouen at all the minor hours as well as Vespers and Lauds.

After Lauds and Vespers in Lent, there was a suffrage for the remission of sins; it was still said less than a hundred years ago.

No feasts were celebrated in Lent. Instead, a commemoration was done of those saints whose feasts had fallen during the course of the week at Saturday Vespers and Sunday Lauds and Mass. The old ordinary reads:

> In Vesperis et Matutinis nulla Sanctorum commemoratio fiat, nisi tantum in Vesperis Sabbati et Matutinis vel Missa Dominicae diei, in quibus est Sanctorum agenda memoria, quorum Festa in praeterita evenerint hebdomada, secundum Laodicensis Concilii Decreta, quae cum aliis quamplurimis statuunt aliter in Quadragesima nullius Sancti recolere Festa.[72]

On Ash Wednesday after None the clergy and people made their confession before the altar. After receiving penance, they prostrated themselves and received the absolution of the archbishop or the principal priest of the church. He imposed ashes on each and sprinkled them with holy water. Then he expelled the public penitents and put them out of the church. We will discuss this day's ceremonies as they are performed today below.

After the expulsion of the public penitents there was a procession to a church or chapel. When they had arrived and the antiphons were finished,

---

[72] "At Vespers and Matins [i.e., Lauds], let no saints' commemoration be said, except at Vespers of Saturday and Matins and Mass of Sunday, on which days a commemoration is to be said of those saints whose feast fell during the preceding week, in accordance with to the decrees of the Council of Laodicea, which with several others set down that during Lent no saint's feast is to be kept" (PL 147:46D).

everyone prostrated himself on the ground and said the Lord's Prayer. In this humble posture they said psalm 50, *Miserere mei Deus*, along with the preces and the oration. Then two choirboys rose and chanted the litany, which they continued as they made their way back to choir. Then Mass was celebrated. This procession was and is still done on all Wednesdays and Fridays of Lent. It is a vestige of the processions that were formerly performed every day to the stational churches where they went to say Mass.

On Wednesday of the fourth week in Lent something peculiar took place. A prophecy and Gradual were added to the Mass in view of the scrutiny of the catechumens, which are still done today in Vienne. In the scrutiny, the catechumens were instructed, interrogated about faith and morals, and taught the Lord's Prayer and the Creed, which they were obliged to learn by heart and recite on Holy Saturday before being baptized: *Quod in Sabbato sancto debent reddere.*[73]

Vespers of Holy Wednesday were sounded with all the bells. On Thursday and the following days at Matins a large candle-stand or hearse with twenty-four candles was put behind the altar; note that at that time there was no retable. Since there is one now with a large painting, this twenty-four-candle hearse is placed in the center before the altar. One candle is extinguished at each psalm and lesson. In parishes and monasteries there are only thirteen or fifteen candles, which are extinguished at the end of each psalm. However, these parish and monastic churches—indeed, nearly all the churches in France—during these days, rather than extinguish candles after beginning Matins around four in the afternoon, should rather light them as evening approaches, since light is more needed then than at four in the afternoon. This was not taken into account when this Office stopped being said near the end of night. Doubtless certain mystics who are ignorant of the true reasons for the institution of ceremonies will find some mystical interpretations for those of these three days, as if they were somehow different from those that used to be done every day. Once, when I was at Matins in the illustrious church of St-Jean in Lyon, I saw them extinguish many candles during the last psalms of Lauds, and this was on Corpus Christi. I challenge anyone to devise a mystical explanation beyond the fact that, as the day grew brighter, there was less need for light. But in any case, our cathedral church of Rouen does nothing against sound reason when it extinguishes candles one by one on these three days, since it enjoys the honor of never having ceased to say this Office at night during those days. On Good Friday, the Office takes place at four in the morning and on Thursday and Saturday at five. Daughters should imitate their mothers.

As still today, they did not chant the *Gloria Patri* on these three days, because originally in the Church responsories and psalms were sung without

---

[73] PL 147:47D.

the *Gloria Patri*,[74] and because it is not fitting to add it during these three days, just as it is not suited to the Office of the Dead.

At the end of Lauds they extinguished even the last candle, because it was then daytime and they had no more need of it. But since they needed to light candles for the Office of the Mass, they lit them from new blessed fire, and this is still done on these three days in the cathedral, no longer in the porch but in the parish church of St-Étienne, the large church close to the west portal on the right side. All parishes do this on Holy Saturday, quite nonsensically in my opinion, since they already have lit candles in chapels or the lamp hanging before the Blessed Sacrament. But the ceremony has become necessary due to the edifying interpretations the mystics have given it.[75]

On Maundy Thursday the people assembled at midday. All the clergy went to the porch for the blessing of the new fire. The bishop convoked the public penitents there and finally let them into the church and reconciled them by giving absolution. This is still done today in Rouen, and I will describe the ceremony below.

Finally the bishop consecrated the chrism and oil of the catechumens at the Mass, at which the *Gloria in excelsis* was said if the bishop was present. The Mass was sung under semidouble rite and the deacon and subdeacon wore dalmatic and tunicle. The peace was not given.

When the celebrant held the chalice to receive the Blood of Jesus Christ, he sang the antiphon *Calicem salutaris* for the psalms of Vespers. Then all the bells were rung, after which they remained silent until the *Gloria in excelsis* of Holy Saturday. Still today in the cathedral the bells for Vespers are rung at the *Agnus Dei* of the Mass, but in parishes bells are not rung after the *Gloria in excelsis*. During the two remaining days, instead of bells they use certain tablets which the common people call *tartevelles*. It must be noted here that although the bells for Vespers in the cathedral are usually rung on that day before noon, the great bell still strikes twelve at noon like on other days of the year. This is doubtlessly a sign that this church has never lost sight of the fact that Vespers always belongs to the afternoon, and that the midday bell is supposed to precede it. The altar is incensed at the *Magnificat* and Vespers concludes with the Postcommunion.

The clergy and people communicated with the hosts that were just consecrated, half of which were reserved on an altar in carefully folded corporals for communion on Good Friday, for not only were both the clergy and the people permitted to receive communion on Good Friday, but it seems it was even some sort of obligation for the clergy. This custom

---

[74] Author's note: Amalar, *De ordine antiphonarii* 1.13, ed. Hanssens, 3:21.
[75] For de Vert's notion that the ancient *Lucernarium* was a solemn blessing of fire at the end of each day, subsequently restricted to the Holy Triduum — as in Reims, Rouen, and Cluny in his day — or to Holy Saturday, see *Explication*, 2:352–54.

ceased less than a hundred years ago, as one can see in all the old missals of Rouen and other churches of France.[76]

A candle burned before these sacred hosts until the end of Lauds, when it was extinguished.

On Good Friday, Mass and communion were *ex praesanctificatis*, as on all Fridays of Lent in Milan.

Our ordinary states that the sacrifice of the Eucharist was not celebrated on Good Friday and Holy Saturday: *Isto biduo non celebratur sacrificium*. This is even clearer in the rubrics for Maundy Thursday: *Ab ipsa die ad Missam noctis Dominicae non fit Sacramentorum consecratio*.

After Vespers on Maundy Thursday, they went to eat. After the meal, they assembled in church and stripped the altars while singing a responsory. The altars were cleaned with wine and holy water, and the walls and floor of the church were washed with water only. Then they went into a large room to hold the Maundy, that is to say, the archbishop and the most senior canons washed and dried the feet of the poor and then those of the canons and other clerics. During this ceremony, the proper antiphons were sung, and at the end the deacon, vested in an alb and dalmatic as at Mass, with lit candles and incense, sang the Gospel *Ante diem festum Paschae* in the lesson tone. Thereafter, they went as if in procession to the refectory, where the deacon continued to read the Gospel from the point where he had stopped until the Passion. The archbishop or dean presented a glass or cup of wine to each of the clergy; this, as we will see, is still in use in the other churches of Rouen: *Unicuique fratrum vel Episcopus vel Decanus phialam vini exhibeat*. Then the archbishop, the deacon, and the others who had served as ministers sat down, and Compline was said in silence.

On Good Friday, besides Matins which was sung, all the hours were said in silence, and Vespers and Compline in private. After Matins of Good Friday, the entire clergy went to the cloister to say the psalter. Thereafter, they returned to the church, where they sat and prayed in silence until None, when they blessed the new fire at the door of the church like yesterday. This is still done on these three days in the cathedrals of Rouen and Reims. After that they went back into choir and began the Office of the Mass with a lesson taken from Exodus and then one from Osee, with two Tracts. Then the Passion according to St. John was read in the lesson tone, except the proper words of our Savior, which were sung in the Gospel tone. Then, the main priest of the church said the bidding prayers and the rest as is still done today.

The *Populus meus* and *Ecce lignum Crucis* were sung. As soon as the priest uncovered the cross, all the clergy prostrated themselves. Then the

---

[76] See de Vert, *Explication* 3:352, 4:286–87, on the distribution of the chalice on Good Friday. He asserts that it was the ancient custom of all French churches and of the religious orders, and still practiced in certain French dioceses (such as Verdun and Clermont) in his day. He blames the Tridentine reform for restricting communion to the priest alone.

priest and his ministers went to adore the crucifix, followed by the entire clergy and the people, lying flat on the ground, which according to St. Augustine is the state of the greatest adoration. *Adoratio omnium ita fiat*, says the ordinary, *ut uniuscujusque venter in terra haereat: dum enim (juxta Augustinum in Psalmo XLIII) genuflectitur, adhuc restat quod humilietur: qui autem sic humiliatur, ut totus in terra haereat, nihil in eo amplius humilitatis restat.*[77] I have seen this still practiced in Rouen by well-instructed people. The two canons who sang *Popule meus* lay prostrate during the adoration of the cross, as the Carthusians do before celebrating Mass. After this ceremony, the crucifix was washed with water and wine, which the clergy and the people drank after communion.

The two priests in chasuble who had borne the cross retrieved the sacred hosts that had been reserved the preceding day. They brought them to the high altar, where the celebrant incensed them and sang only *Praeceptis salutaribus moniti* until *Sed libera nos a malo*. Then all received communion from the eldest to the youngest: *postea a majore ad minorem omnes communicentur*.[78] We will see elsewhere that it was not permitted to forgo communion without the superior's permission.

Then the tablets were sounded, and each said Vespers in silence by himself. Thereafter, they went to the refectory to take their meal of bread and water: *ad refectionem panis et aquae pergant*. Thus did the canons observe Good Friday six hundred years ago. And we shall see that over two hundred years later the same practices continued, or that at most they added a few raw herbs.

They went back to the church to say Compline in silence by themselves.

On Holy Saturday they sang Matins and said the minor hours in silence as on the preceding day.

In those days it was not permitted for the Mass of Holy Saturday to begin before the evening, as can be seen in a council held in Rouen in 1072, because this Mass is proper to the night of the Resurrection of Our Lord: *ad noctem enim Dominicae Resurrectionis respicit*.[79] And indeed the blessing of the Paschal candle and the Preface of the Mass show and presuppose that it is nighttime. I have already explained on page 103 the reasons why this Mass came to be anticipated. A canon from the aforementioned council states that "he who eats before three or four in the afternoon in Lent does not fast."[80]

On Holy Saturday, then, around three in the afternoon, at the sound

---

[77] "Let the adoration of all be done such that each one's belly clings to the ground, for, following Augustine in psalm 43, when one kneels, there still remains something to be humbled, but for him who humiliates himself such that he entirely clings to the ground, nothing further remains to be humbled" (PL 147:51D).
[78] PL 147:52A.
[79] Canon 22 (PL 147:272A).
[80] Canon 21 (PL 147:272A).

of the tablet the people assembled in the church. The clergy went in procession to the door of the church to light and bless the new fire. This fire was taken to the homes of the Christians, who had previously extinguished their hearth fires. This still takes place even today at about ten in the morning in the cathedral and the better-run parishes, where the fire is given to the people who are duly instructed. From this new fire, they lit a candle in the church placed atop a long stick, at the top of which was the figure of a serpent. The archbishop or officiant held it at the bottom and the deacon at the middle, and they went back to the choir singing the psalm *Dominus illuminatio mea*.[81] All of this is still practiced in Rouen both in the cathedral as well as the other well-run churches, except that there is no longer a serpent at the top of the stick.

It is truly unfortunate that one or two leaves are missing here in the manuscript of the old ordinary, which might have apprised us of beautiful things about the blessing of the candle, the prophecies, Tracts, bidding prayers, the three litanies, the blessing of the font, and the baptism of the catechumens and children. It picks up again to say that the neophytes were clad in albs or white habits, and each of them was given a candle to hold, that they wore these white habits during eight days, and took them off on the Saturday called *in albis depositis*, which was elsewhere dubbed *la Desauberie*.

The entire Mass and Vespers of Holy Saturday was celebrated in Rouen as it is today, and as everywhere else, except that the altar was not incensed until the *Gloria in excelsis*, that the clergy and people received communion (*communicato Clero et populo*), and that the altar was incensed at the *Magnificat*.

After the meal they went back to say Compline.

At ten at night they rang all the bells and they said Matins. After the third responsory they celebrated the Office of the Sepulcher, more or less as it is said today at Angers. Such spectacles have been wisely abolished, for they are not to the taste of our century.[82]

Already at that time the *Benedictus* antiphon was repeated thrice, as well as that of the *Magnificat*, as is still done today on all triple feasts.

After a procession held after None on Easter day and the five days thereafter in the nave before the great rood, they held a procession to the font after Vespers, as they still do today.

The last day of the octave of Easter was celebrated solemnly like the first day, as did the Jews following the command God had given them. (See Leviticus 23:35–36.)

---

[81] Psalm 26.
[82] Le Brun des Marettes was the first to transcribe the music for the *Officium stellae* and *Visitatio sepulchri* in Rouen from a manuscript in Émery Bigot's library (see PL 147:135D–142A). For an introduction to the early study of liturgical drama, including a discussion of Le Brun des Marettes's role in the early study of the *Officium stellae* and the *Visitatio sepulchri*, see Michael Norton, *Liturgical Drama and the Reimagining of Medieval Theater* (Medieval Institute Publications, 2017), 19–53, esp. notes 18 and 30.

On the Sundays after Easter they said three nocturns with nine lessons.

They held a procession or station before the great rood on Saturdays after Vespers and on Sundays after Lauds until Christmas. From Easter to Pentecost they sang a responsory of the Resurrection, and from Pentecost to Christmas of the Cross. On Sundays between Easter and Ascension the morrow Mass was of the Sunday and the high Mass of the Resurrection, *Resurrexi*, as on Easter day. This is the case in many missals from the past century, and was changed only a hundred years ago to conform to the Roman missal.

If a feast fell on one of the Sundays in Eastertide, as well as those of Advent and Lent, it was transferred to the following day: *Si in Dominicis hujus temporis [Paschalis] festivitas evenerit, in crastino celebranda reservetur*. Indeed, the holy season of Easter should not yield in any way to those of Advent and Lent. In Orléans and Châlons-en-Champagne, ferias in Eastertide are commemorated like those of Advent and Lent, and feasts are never celebrated on Sundays, except for annual feasts like Christmas, All Saints, etc., since Sundays are particularly consecrated to the Lord and the memory of his Resurrection.

If the Major Litany, on 25 April, fell during the octave of Easter or on one of the Sundays after Easter, they observed no fasting or abstinence, and made no commemorations except for a procession that was appropriately festal —*nisi Festiva tantum Processio*—, where they sung nothing sad or redolent of penance. This is still observed in Rouen, for in these cases they go to the nearest church singing the responsory *Christus resurgens*. Inside the stational church they sing a responsory or antiphon of the holy patron, with its versicle and oration. Then they return to their own church singing the Litany of the Saints, and after they have entered the church they sing an antiphon, versicle, and oration of the patron saint, and that is all. This procession for the fruits of the earth is always held on 25 April. In former times, on the same date, the pagans similarly prayed to their gods for their earthly goods, as M. Châtelain has discovered.[83]

But "if it should fall at any other time," says the old ordinary, "let all fast, except little children and the infirm." In those days, not more than a hundred years ago, all who had passed their seventh or eighth year were obliged to fast in the province of Normandy. I have learned this from two breviaries, one of Rouen from 1578, and the other of Avranches from 1592, at the beginning of which, before the kalendar, I find the following instruction: *Sacerdotes ecclesiarum praecipiant* OMNIBUS AETATEM ADULTAM HABENTIBUS *instituta jejunia observari, ut jejunium Quadragesimae &c. et omnia praedicta prohibeant expresse et sub poena peccati mortalis.*[84]

---

[83] On Châtelain, see p. 56, n. 82.
[84] "Let the priests of the churches command all those who have reached adulthood to observe the established fasts, such as that of Lent and the rest, and let them expressly prohibit all the aforementioned under penalty of mortal sin."

This fast on St. Mark's day was later changed to abstinence in order to avoid fasting in Eastertide, in accordance with the spirit of the early Church. There are still families in Normandy that have observed from time immemorial and still today observe the great fast of Lent, that is, eating only one meal a day. In the diocese of Autun there are parishes where twelve or even up to sixty plowmen or threshers work from daybreak, and by seven in the evening have still not taken any food, as one of their parish priests has assured me.[85] God is pleased to preserve this spirit of fervor in certain families and persons in order to confound the laxity of others. Thus one can see that such a fast is not impossible, and one should be convinced thereof by everything that we have reported about different places in this entire account. One shall be fully persuaded when told that in Ireland they do not eat during Lent until evening, and that in Rouen a certain major canon and a chaplain are still fasting at four or five in the evening on the vigil of the Assumption, when the weather is much hotter than during Lent, and so such a long abstinence must be even more unbearable.

Since on ordinary fasting days during the year they did not eat until after None, the old ordinary states that on St. Mark's day the procession from the cathedral to St-Ouen began at noon. The priest, deacon, and subdeacon wore albs, stoles, and maniples, as still observed at present in the cathedral and other well-run churches. Neither the old ordinary nor the more recent one state that one should kneel during the prayers in the stational church; the more recent one says that the Mass *Exaudivit* should be said there. The two state that, after returning from the procession, they said None around two in the afternoon, and then went to their meal. The same thing was practiced on the three minor Rogation days.

Ascension day was solemn like Easter. There were nine lessons on that day, as on Sundays of Eastertide.

The Acts of the Apostles were read in the church of Rouen from Ascension until the first Sunday after Pentecost. That is truly the proper season, since this history begins at that point, and most of what it contains occurred during those days.

On Pentecost day they sang hymns. At Terce they lit all the candles. The hymn was intoned by three coped canons, who incensed the altar as it was sung. We shall see hereafter how this celebration became even more solemn.

The last day of the octave of Pentecost was solemn like the first, and like Easter. The ordinary says: *Dies octavus ut primus celeberrime agatur.*

The Ember days were celebrated like the season of Lent, as in Orléans. On Ember Saturday, when holy orders were conferred, the cantor ruled

---

[85] Author's note: The learned M. Bocquillot, currently a canon of Avalon, and author of the excellent *Traité historique de la liturgie* (Paris, 1701).

the choir at Mass, which did not end until the night of Sunday, for the Mass of priestly ordinations began in the evening at the hour for Vespers, which belongs to the Sunday, says the ordinary of Rouen. This is the reason why the Gospel of the Sunday is read at the Mass of Ember Saturday, a use that has remained unto the present day. *In Missa vespertinali quidem hora, quae pars est Dominicae Resurrectionis, a B. Leone summo Pontifice caeterisque sanctis Patribus Ordinum consecratio fieri consituitur, quae jejunis a jejunantibus conferatur.*[86] These last three words explain why the Mass has now been anticipated so much. Nevertheless, the ordinary continues, *Ante Nonam fieri sacra auctoritate prohibetur.*[87]

The consecration of bishops was always held on Sundays. We see in an old manuscript pontifical from the cathedral of Rouen, some seven hundred years old, how a bishop was consecrated.[88] It states that the dean, the major archdeacon, the cantor, and the chancellor chose those that should serve as ministers for the bishop, just like they did on major feasts: *sicut in majoribus mos est festivitatibus*, says the ordinary. There were two acolytes with two thuribles, seven acolytes who each carried a candlestick and candle, seven subdeacons with the Gospel books, seven deacons who carried relics of the saints, and twelve priests wearing chasubles.

It cannot be doubted that this pontifical is belongs to the church of Rouen, for it contains these words:

> *Interrogatio:* Vis sancta Rotomagensi Ecclesiae mihique et successoribus meis obediens esse et subditus? ℟. Volo.
>
> *Interrogatio:* Vis mihi et Ecclesiae meae professionem facere, sicut mos ANTIQUITUS constitutus obtinuit? ℟. Volo, et paratus sum in omnibus obedire.[89]

This ancient custom is still observed in the present day in the cathedral of Rouen. There it is considered that this church has a right to receive an oath of allegiance from the suffragan bishops of the province, because it is the metropolitan and primatial church of Normandy. The right is confirmed by most ancient possession, as seen in the old pontifical mentioned above, which even states that it is "anciently established custom"; in papal bulls; and in rulings from the court of Parlement. The suffragan bishops must make this oath in the hands of the Lord Archbishop, if he

---

[86] "The Supreme Pontiff Blessed Leo and the other holy Fathers established that the consecration of orders should be done at Mass in the evening hour, which is part of Resurrection Sunday, by those fasting upon those fasting."
[87] "Holy authority prohibits its celebration before None."
[88] See PL 147:141B–144D.
[89] "Question: Doest thou will to be obedient and subject to the church of Rouen and to me and to my successors? Response: I will.
   Question: Doest thou will to make profession to me and my church, as ordained by anciently established custom? Response: I will, and am prepared to obey in all things" (PL 147:142D).

is present; if he is absent, in the hands of the celebrant at the moment when he has gone up to the altar before reading the Introit. Even if the day is a feria, Mass is said under double rite, with the *Gloria in excelsis* and the *Credo*, and the cantor ruling choir, which he only does on doubles and triples.

Here is the formula for the oath the suffragan bishop swears on the Gospel book:

> Ego N. Episcopus (Lexovinensis) Venerabili Ecclesiae Rotomagensi ac Reverendissimo Patri Domino N. Archiepiscopo et suis successoribus canonice intrantibus reverentiam et obedientiam me perpetuo exhibiturum promitto, et manu mea confirmo.[90]

And he signs his name on an ivory-covered manuscript kept in the cathedral sacristy. This manuscript contains a number of signatures made by suffragan bishops and abbots and abbesses of the diocese of Rouen.[91]

At the first solemn Mass which Monseigneur Colbert,[92] archbishop of Rouen, sang in his cathedral after receiving the pallium, two suffragan bishops swore their oath of obedience before the reading of the Introit. Without swearing this oath the suffragan bishops are not recognized in the metropolitan church, are not admitted into the provincial assemblies, and are not allowed to be provincial deputies to the Assemblies of the Clergy. Not only must they swear the oath of obedience, but provide dinner for the lords of the chapter, in lieu of which they usually offered a hundred crowns. This is apparently what is called the *droit de past* or right of repast, *jus pastus* in Latin.[93]

On Pentecost day 1694, the new abbess of the Benedictine monastery of St-Amand in Rouen swore the same oath of obedience with much solemnity at high Mass. This abbess came accompanied by twelve of her nuns, who took their places in the second row of the stalls of the chaplains, while the abbess took hers in the upper row, the same place as a suffragan bishop when he is present at the Office or for a similar ceremony. At first she simply had a foot mat. During the *Kyrie*, the Lord Archbishop's faldstool was placed at the bottom altar step. With his back to the altar, he received in his hands the kneeling abbess's oath of allegiance. She was led to the altar by the dean, the cantor, the treasurer, and the major archdeacon,

---

[90] "I, Bishop N. (of Lisieux), promise that I shall always show reverence and obedience to the venerable church of Rouen and to the Most Reverend Father, Lord N., Archbishop, and to his canonically instituted successors, and I confirm this with my hand."
[91] Now in Rouen, Bibliothèque patrimoniale Villon, MS 1405/Y27, 193–230.
[92] Jacques-Nicolas Colbert (r. 1691–1707).
[93] According to François Pommeraye, this custom arose because "the clergy suffered much fatigue during the long and arduous ceremonies" in the cathedral, and, taking pity on their lot, the new suffragan bishops invited them to a meal. This practice eventually became mandatory, but when "the delicacy and luxury of the times" made a suitable banquet more difficult to arrange, it was agreed to turn replace it with a sum of money for the chapter (*Histoire*, 483).

who are the first four dignitaries, and likewise escorted back by them to her place in choir, where she found a cushion a verger had placed there immediately after she swore the oath. From that spot the abbess heard Mass with her twelve nuns.

Let us return to our old ordinary of Rouen. There remains the treatise *de festivitatibus Sanctorum*. It does not favor an excessive number of feasts, lest they become wearisome and distasteful, nor does it call for all to be removed, but for a reasonable balance. Apart from the feasts of Our Lord and the Purification, Annunciation, Assumption, and Nativity of Our Lady, there are very few of them, and two hundred years ago fewer still. Here is how this section begins, and this is its most salient part: *Oportet nos festivitates Sanctorum discernere qualiter celebrentur, ne sint nobis fastidiosae si superflue agimus: aut si nimis reticemus, eorum juvamine careamus.*[94] It prescribes a fast for the vigil of the Assumption, and states that the feast itself should be of a superior rank to the other feasts of Our Lady, so that the others might be lesser. I do not know in what sense they are to be lesser, for it goes on to say that the feasts of the Annunciation, Purification, Nativity of Our Lady, and All Saints should be of the same solemnity. Perhaps it means that these feasts are not to have vigils or octaves. It was Sixtus IV that granted the latter an octave in 1480, and there are churches that still do not observe one.

On the day of the Commemoration of all the Faithful Departed, they said the Office of the day in addition to that of the Dead, something still observed in the Roman breviary and some others. The Office of the Dead had no hymns nor invitatories. It seems that it had second Vespers; there are a few missing words in the manuscripts that could hardly indicate anything else. What confirms my conjecture is that second Compline is marked in full like the other hours of this Office. Second Vespers are still said not only in Cluny, but also in the illustrious churches of Vienne, Tours, and Besançon.

On semidouble feasts Matins of the feria was said rather than Matins of the feast.

Now we will present several practices and ceremonies drawn from an ordinary of the church of Rouen and from some other documents about two hundred years old, all of which are still observed, except some I will make sure to point out.

Before and after chanting a lesson or responsory from the rood loft, a bow with a half-turn (*semigyrus*) is made at the eagle.

On Sundays of Advent and Lent the deacon wears a broad stole (*orarium*) in addition to a folded chasuble.

---

[94] "It behooves us to discern how saints' feasts should be celebrated, lest they be tedious to us if we observe them excessively, or, if we omit too many, we be left bereft of their help" (PL 147:59D).

According to this ordinary, on all ferias of Lent until Maundy Thursday, the canons, chaplains, and choirboys make the sign of the cross over their seat and kiss it at the beginning of an Office. They also do this if they enter choir after the Office has begun.

Also on the ferias of Lent, a large violet veil is stretched all across the east end of the choir during the entire ferial Office from Monday of the first week of Lent until the reading of the Passion on Holy Wednesday, when it is split in two at the moment the deacon says the words *et velum Templi scissum est*. The veil is only lifted during the Gospel and from the *Sanctus* until the elevation of the chalice.

Less than a hundred and fifty years ago, a minor canon read from the *Collations* before Compline in Lent. The same was done at Bayeux, Vienne, and Salisbury in England, and this extensive reading is still done in the church of Reims and nearly its entire province. It lent its name to the small evening meal of Lent. At Compline, if the dean is present he says his *Confiteor*, hears the clergy's, says the *Indulgentiam*, and, at the end of Compline, sprinkles the clergy, except on Sundays. If he is not present, the *journeyeur*[95] does so.

The Preface *Qui corporali jejunio* was only used on ferias before the last century, as is apparent in all the ancient missals of Rouen, Orléans, and elsewhere. On Sundays in Lent they said the common *per annum* Preface, as still done today in Sens, Auxerre, and elsewhere, because Lenten Sundays are not fasting days, and in the early twelfth century they even ate meat on those days. See the Life of St. Godfrey, a bishop of Amiens who died in 1118, written by Nicholas, a monk of St-Crépin in Soissons, who was a contemporary of the bishop's, and edited by Surius in volume 6 under 8 November, book 3, chapter 12.[96]

All the missals of Rouen printed in the last century have, at the *Quod ore sumpsimus*, the reading *de corpore et sanguine Domini nostri Jesu Christi* instead of *munere temporali*[97] There was only one ablution with wine, as in Lyon and among the Carthusians.

---

[95] See below, p. 233.
[96] Laurentius Surius, ed., *De probatis Sanctorum historiis* (Cologne, 1575), 6:207–208, wherein it is related that on Ash Wednesday St. Godfrey prohibited his flock from eating fleshmeat until Easter Sunday. Many, however, refused to abstain therefrom on the first Sunday of Lent, "saying that the bishop was making up and advancing harsh and unheard of things from his own imagination, that they did not and could not give up their customs, and that it was fitting not only to use food, but even to abuse it, and spend their days indulging in sweet delights." St. Godfrey duly chastised them during his sermon on Maundy Thursday, imposing upon them as penance that they should abstain from receiving the Eucharist until Easter Monday. One man, spurning the bishop's sentence, decided to disguise himself in women's clothes, and thus presented himself for communion on Easter Sunday. As soon as he had received the Eucharist, he was seized with stomach pains and, spewing bloody froth, he regurgitated the holy Sacrament. His deception uncovered, all the people were horrified at his crime, and praised Christ's judgments as expressed through St. Godfrey, whom they promised to obey diligently thenceforth.
[97] See, e.g., *Missale [...] iuxta institutum Rothomagensis episcopatus* (Rouen, 1585), fol. 103r.

The final ablution with water and wine did not exist at that time, and the priest was not obliged to drink the rinsings from his fingers. He went to wash his hands in the washbowl or laver near the altar: *Sacerdos vadat ad lavatorium.* The same thing is noted in the Carmelite missal of 1574. The ritual of Rouen states that there should be such a washbowl near all altars, as found in the church of St-Étienne-des-Tonneliers in Rouen.[98] *Reversus ad Altare dicat Communionem et Postcommunionem; deinde se vertat ad populum, dicens:* Dominus vobiscum, *et* Ite, missa est. Then the priest gave the blessing, with which the Mass ended. *Et benedictione accepta recedatur,* read the old sixteenth-century missals of Rouen. This remains the practice today in Rouen, where the people depart after the blessing has been given, and quite properly, since the priest or deacon has dismissed them with the *Ite, missa est.* In 1576, the last Gospel according to St. John was still not said in Rouen. It was only introduced in the missal of 1604, but even then the priest only said it when removing his chasuble. This missal states: *Vertit se ad populum et ei benedicit manu: interim exuitur casula, dicendo,* Dominus vobiscum, *et Evangelium secundum Joannem.* We have already seen that in most of the churches whereof I have spoken, the last Gospel is still not said at high Masses.

During the fifteen days of Passiontide the psalm *Judica me* is not said at the beginning of Mass, because until relatively recently it was not said at the foot of the altar. It is still never said in Milan, Sens, nor among the Carthusians, Carmelites, and Dominicans. The psalm *Judica* that begins the Mass of Passion Sunday prevented the psalm from being added, in order to avoid repetition.

About two hundred years ago, they stopped extinguishing the last candle at the end of Lauds of Holy Thursday, Good Friday, and Holy Saturday in Rouen. It is instead hidden until the officiant has said the oration. Formerly, he knocked thrice to indicate the candle should be relit, according to the Carmelite ordinary: *Expleta Oratione, qui facit Officium, sonitum trina percussione faciat in signum ut lumen extinctum reaccendatur.*[99] In conventual churches, they perform the discipline immediately afterwards: *Perlato autem lumine a Sacrista, recipiantur disciplinae.* In some churches each person knocks several times.

This ordinary's section on Maundy Thursday Mass shows that the archbishop of Rouen's pontifical throne was still behind the altar, like in Vienne and Lyon.

On Good Friday, they say the four minor hours—Prime, Terce, Sext, and None—at the four corners of the choir, that is, one hour at each corner. Vespers are said in a ring around the inside of the sanctuary, and Compline in the middle of the choir around the tomb of Charles V, king of France, in a low voice.

---

[98] This church was destroyed by the Allied bombing of Rouen in 1944.
[99] Sibert of Beka, *Ordinale,* ed. Zimmerman, 163.

Before the Office of Good Friday, they place a large cloth upon the altar that extends beyond its edges and covers it on top and on all sides. This used to be done every day, for cloths were placed on the altar only just before Mass was said. I have already made note of this above, in the chapter on Angers,[100] and this is still practiced in the many monasteries of the order of Cluny, where frontals are not attached to altars because they were not used in the early centuries of the Church. They are also still not used in the cathedral of Angers. One can be sure that almost every peculiar usage during Holy Triduum is of the greatest and purest antiquity. The Blessed Sacrament for the sick is not reserved at the altar in those days, because in former days it was never kept there, but somewhere else, as we shall see was the case throughout the year in many churches of Rouen. Likewise, during these three days neither *Deus in adjutorium*, nor *Gloria Patri*, nor the short chapter, nor hymns are not said in the Office, because they were not said in the early centuries of the Church. They were added later, and they have still not been inserted into the Office of the Triduum, nor to the Office of the Dead. To call the faithful to the Divine Office in the cathedral, they use wooden mallets to strike the doors of the church. In the other parishes they use tablets or *tartevelles*, because these were used in former days before bells were invented. Finally, on Good Friday and Holy Saturday, Mass begins with the prophecies, since in the first centuries of the Church Mass began with a reading from the Old Testament. This practice has also been retained on the Saturday vigil of Pentecost.

There is a very ancient practice in Rouen, which we would doubtless have discovered in the old 640-year-old ordinary had not several pages been torn out at this point. It is the inscription of the Paschal table, written on a beautiful vellum attached at eye level to a large wax column some twenty-five feet tall, on top of which the Paschal candle is placed, between the tomb of Charles V and the three silver lamps. This table was, I imagine, once read out loud by the deacon after he had chanted the *Paschale praeconium*, of which the table was apparently a part. At any rate, it was and still is displayed to everyone's view from Easter until Pentecost inclusive. It is mentioned in book 6, chapter 29 of Abbot Rupert's *De divinis officiis*;[101] chapter 102 of the treatise *De antiquo ritu Missae* of Honorius of Autun's *Gemma animae*;[102] book 6, chapter 80 of William Durand's *Rationale*;[103] and chapter 108 of John Beleth's book on the Divine Offices[104] in these terms: *Annotatur quidem in Cereo Paschali annus ab Incarnatione Domini:*

---

[100] See p. 61.
[101] Rupert of Deutz, *Liber de diuinis officiis* 6.29, ed. Rhaban Haacke, Corpus Christianorum Continuatio Mediaeualis 7 (Brepols, 1967), 211–13.
[102] Honorius Augustodunensis, *Gemma animae* 3.102, ed. Thomas and Eger, 160.
[103] Durand, *Rationale* 6.80, ed. Davril and Thibodeau, 2:392–98.
[104] John Beleth, *Summa de ecclesiasticis officiis* 108, ed. Heribert Douteil, Corpus Christianorum Continuatio Mediaeualis 41A (Brepols, 1976), 200–1.

inscribuntur quoque Cereo Paschali Indictio vel Aera, atque Epacta.[105] I would fail to do it justice if I were merely to say that it recorded the year and epact, the movable feasts, the number of years since the foundation of the church of Rouen, who its first bishop was, how many years since it was dedicated, the regnal year of the pope, of the archbishop of Rouen, and of the king; I must reproduce it here as it appeared in 1697:

PASCHAL TABLE

Year of Our Lord 1697	
Year since the creation of the world	5697.
Year since the universal Deluge	4052.
Year since the Incarnation of Our Lord	1697.
Year since the his Passion	1664.
Year since the Nativity of Our Lady	1711.
Year since her Assumption	1647.
Year of indiction	5.
Year of the solar cycle	29.
Year of the lunar cycle	7.
The current year from the preceding Easter until the following Easter is common abundant.[106]	
Epact	7.[107]
Golden number	7.[108]
Dominical Letter	F.[109]
Letter of the Martyrology	G.[110]
Term of Easter	14 April.
Moon of the same	16 April.
Annotine Easter	22 April.[111]
Rogation days	13 May.
Ascension day	16 May.
Pentecost day	26 May.
Corpus Christi	6 June.
Sundays from Pentecost until Advent	26.

---

[105] "The year from the Lord's Incarnation is noted in the Paschal candle; the indiction or era and the epact are also inscribed on the Paschal candle." See PL 202:111D.

[106] The Hebrew year can be common ordinary (*communis ordinarius*) with 354 days, common lacking (*communis deficiens*) with 353 days, common abundant (*communis abundans*) with 355 days, or, if a leap month is added, embolismic ordinary (*embolismaeus ordinarius*) with 384 days, embolismic lacking (*embolismaeus deficiens*) with 383 days, or embolismic abundant (*embolismaeus abundans*) with 385 days.

[107] The number of days since the new moon at the beginning of the kalendar year, used to compute the date of Easter.

[108] The number showing a year's place in the Metonic lunar cycle, used to compute the date of Easter.

[109] Indicates which days of the month are Sundays.

[110] Used to determine the lunar day, which is announced at the beginning of the martyrology after Prime.

[111] The date of the previous year's Easter Sunday, which was celebrated as a feast in many places when it fell after the present year's Easter Sunday, because it was the anniversary of baptism for those who had received it the previous year. As baptisms on Easter became less common, the feast fell into desuetude, but still appears in the 1585 Rouen missal (fol. 110v); it is absent from the 1668 missal.

First Sunday of Advent	1 December.
Dominical Letter of the following year	E.
The following year is 1698, common ordinary.	
Letter of the Martyrology of the following year	t.
Sundays from the Nativity of the Lord until Septuagesima of the following year: 4.	
Term of Septuagesima of the following year[112]	26 January.
Septuagesima Sunday of the following year	26 January.
First Sunday of Lent of the following year	16 February.
Easter Day of the following year	20 March.
Year since the consecration of St. Mellonius	1437.
Year since the passing of the same	1388.
Year since the consecration of St. Romanus	1066.
Year since the passing of the same	1053.
Year since the consecration of St. Audoin	1051.
Year since the passing of the same	1008.
Year since the Dedication of this metropolitan church	633.
Year since the proclamation of Rollo as first duke of Normandy	785.
Year since the passing of the same	779.
Year since the coronation of William, first duke of Normandy, in the Kingdom of England:	623.
Year since the death of the same	609.
Year since the restoration of the Duchy of Normandy to Philip II, king of France:	493.
Year since the second restoration of the Duchy of Normandy to Charles VII, king of France:	247.
Year of the Pontificate of Our Most Holy Father and Lord Pope Innocent XII:	5.
Year since the consecration of Our Reverend Father and Lord Jacques-Nicolas, archbishop of Rouen and primate of Normandy:	7.
Year since the birth of the Most Christian Prince Louis XIV, king of France and Navarre:	59.
Year of the reign of the same:	54.

This candle has been consecrated in honor of the Immaculate Lamb and in honor of his Mother, the glorious Virgin Mary.

It was very appropriate for this table to be published on Easter night, because for many centuries this was considered the first day of the year. Only in 1565, by an edict of Charles IX, king of France, did the first day of January come to be reckoned as the first day of the year. This table was a sort of ecclesiastical kalendar. The Lord Chancellor of the cathedral of Rouen is tasked with writing it, or having it written at his own expense.

---

[112] The *terminus* was a date that helped determine that of Easter and other movable feasts linked to it. It was calculated by taking a fixed date (*loci* or *sedes clavium*) for each variable feast (7 January for Septuagesima, 28 January for the first Sunday of Lent, etc.) and adding a certain number of days (the *claves terminorum*) linked to a year's golden number. The Sunday after the *terminus* was the date of the respective feast. . For an explanation of this system, see Natalia Turkiewicz, "The Durand *Computus* in Book VIII *Rationale divinorum officiorum*," *Archiwa, Biblioteki i Muzea Kościelne* 120 (2023): 489–508. These calculations, however, do not work with the Rouen table as described here.

These tables were not only used in this church; there is every reason to believe they were put up in collegiate churches, or at least in abbatial ones, such as that of Bec, as one sees in the statutes issued by its prior, Blessed Lanfranc, to be observed in the monasteries of the order of St. Benedict, and also in the customary of Cluny and the *Liber usuum* of Cîteaux.

There are similar wax columns with the Paschal candle but without the Paschal table in the churches of St-Ouen, Notre-Dame-de-la-Ronde, and St-Sauveur, all in Rouen.

From the moment the Paschal candle is lit on Holy Saturday, it burns continuously day and night until the evening of Easter day, following the literal sense of Scripture: *ad noctis hujus caliginem destruendam indeficiens perseveret...flammas ejus lucifer matutinus inveniat.*[113] It also burns during Mass and Vespers throughout the octave and double feasts in Eastertide until the Ascension, during the entire Office of triple feasts in Eastertide until the Ascension, and from the procession and blessing of the font on the Saturday vigil of Pentecost until the evening of Pentecost day, which is properly speaking the end of the fifty days of Eastertide, or "holy Quadragesima," as the Fathers call it.

As far as I can tell, at that time the psalm *Judica me* at the foot of the altar was not yet said. This is what the new ordinary's section on Holy Saturday states: *Archiepiscopus vel Sacerdos cum Diacono et Subdiacono, candelabris et thuribulis veniat, et confessione humiliter dicta, alte incipiat Gloria in excelsis Deo absque tropis; et prosternat se omnis Chorus.*[114] It adds, *Et interim omnes campanae pulsentur, et dehinc per omnes Abbatias et Parochias totius civitatis.*[115] The ritual indicates the same thing, and it seems customary for the principal church to be the first to toll. However, due to lack of enforcement, there are parish and monastic churches that ring the bell over an hour before the cathedral.

Here is one of the most beautiful practices one could witness, which was still done in Rouen less than 150 years ago: On Easter day, at the procession after Lauds in the nave in front of the great rood, the archbishop kissed all the canons while saying to each, *Resurrexit Dominus*. The same thing is still practiced not only in the cathedral of Vienne and the collegiate church of St-Vulfran in Abbeville, but also throughout the East, when both the clergy and people greet each other by saying Χριστός ἀνέστη, "Jesus Christ is risen."

At that time, the archbishop still gave the solemn blessing before the *Agnus Dei* at the Mass of Easter day, as bishops still do today in several

---

[113] "May it continue [to burn] unfailingly to dissipate the darkness of this night...may the day-star find it aflame" (from the blessing of the Paschal candle).
[114] "Let the archbishop or priest with the deacon and subdeacon go forth with candles and thuribles, and having humbly said the confession, let him intone aloud the *Gloria in excelsis* without tropes, and the entire choir prostrates itself" (see PL 147:103B, note 214).
[115] "And during it let all the bells ring, and thereafter throughout all the abbeys and parish churches of the entire city."

churches of France. We can hope that the zeal of the Lord Archbishop of Rouen shall restore it, as the Lord Bishop of Orléans has recently done.[116]

At this Mass and that of solemn feasts, tropes and *laudes* or praises, were sung: *cum tropis et laudibus*. I believe I have already said that tropes were stanzas or words mixed into the *Kyrie eleison*, such as *Kyrie orbis factor* or *Fons bonitatis*, which are still sung at Lyon, Sens, and elsewhere. The words were eliminated, but the notes were kept, and this is the reason why today there are so many notes over a single syllable in the *Kyrie*. The *laudes* or praises are acclamations that begin *Christus vincit, Christus regnat*, etc. *Ludovico Regi Francorum pax, salus et victoria*, etc., which are sung at Rouen between the collect and the Epistle every time the Lord Archbishop celebrates pontifical Mass on triple feasts of the first class. Perhaps this term also refers to an antiphon that began *Hunc diem*, and which was once sung immediately after the Communion in the church of Vienne.[117]

Here is the *Christus vincit* as it is sung on all solemn feasts when the Lord Archbishop celebrates pontifical Mass.

From the middle of the choir, two major canons sing:

Christus vincit, Christus regnat, Christus imperat.	Christ conquereth, Christ reigneth, Christ commandeth.
℟. Christus vincit, Christus regnat, Christus imperat.	℟. Christ conquereth, Christ reigneth, Christ commandeth.
℣. Exaudi Christe. ℟. Christus vincit, etc.	℣. Hearken, O Christ. ℟. Christus conquereth, etc.
℣. N. Summo Pontifici et universali Papae vitae et salus perpetua.	℣. To N., Supreme Pontiff and universal pope, life and everlasting salvation.
℟. Christus vincit, Christus regnat, Christus imperat.	℟. Christ conquereth, Christ reigneth, Christ commandeth.
℣. Salvator mundi. ℟. Tu illum adjuva.	℣. Savior of the world. ℟. Help thou him.
℣. Christus vincit, etc. ℟. Christus vincit, etc.	℣. Christ conquereth, etc. ℟. Christ conquereth, etc.
℣. Exaudi Christe. ℟. Christus vincit, etc.	℣. Hearken, O Christ. ℟. Christ conquereth, etc.
℣. N. Rotomagensi Archiepiscopo, et omni Clero sibi commisso, pax, vita et salus aeterna.	℣. To N., archbishop of Rouen, and all the clergy entrusted to him, peace, life, and eternal salvation.
℟. Christus vincit, Christus regnat, Christus imperat.	℟. Christ conquereth, Christ reigneth, Christ commandeth.
℣. Sancta Maria. ℟. Tu illum adjuva.	℣. Saint Mary. ℟. Help thou him.
℣. Sancte Romane. ℟. Tu illum adjuva.	℣. Saint Romanus. ℟. Help thou him.
℣. Christus vincit, &c. ℟. Christus vincit, etc.	℣. Christ conquereth, etc. ℟. Christ conquereth, etc.

---

[116] See p. 145.
[117] See p. 18.

℣. Exaudi Christe. ℟. Christus vincit, etc.

℣. N. Regi Francorum, pax, salus et victoria.

℟. Christus vincit, Christus regnat, Christus imperat.

℣. Redemptor mundi. ℟. Tu illum adjuva.

℣. Sancte Dionysi. ℟. Tu illum adjuva.

℣. Christus vincit, &c. ℟. Christus vincit, etc.

℣. Exaudi Christe. ℟. Christus vincit, etc.

℣. Episcopis, et abbatibus sibi commissis, pax, salus, et vera concordia.

℟. Christus vincit, Christus regnat, Christus imperat.

℣. Sancte Martine. ℟. Tu illos adjuva.

℣. Sancte Augustine. ℟. Tu illos adjuva.

℣. Sancte Benedicte. ℟. Tu illos adjuva.

℣. Christus vincit, &c. ℟. Christus vincit, etc.

℣. Exaudi Christe. ℟. Christus vincit, etc.

℣. Cunctis principibus, et omni exercitui Christianorum, pax, salus et victoria.

℟. Christus vincit, Christus regnat, Christus imperat.

℣. Sancte Maurici. ℟. Tu illos adjuva.

℣. Sancte Georgi. ℟. Tu illos adjuva.

℣. Christus vincit, &c. ℟. Christus vincit, etc.

℣. Tempora bona veniant, pax Christi veniat, regnum Christi veniat.

℟. Christus vincit, Christus regnat, Christus imperat.

℣. Ipsi soli laus et jubilatio per infinita saecula saeculorum. Amen.

℟. Ipsi soli laus et jubilatio &c.

℣. Ipsi soli laus et imperium, gloria et potestas per immortalia saecula saeculorum. Amen.

℟. Ipsi soli laus et jubilatio per infinita saecula saeculorum. Amen.

℣. Hearken, O Christ. ℟. Christ conquereth, etc.

℣. To N., king of the Franks, peace, salvation, and victory.

℟. Christ conquereth, Christ reigneth, Christ commandeth.

℣. Redeemer of the world. ℟. Help thou him.

℣. Saint Denis. ℟. Help thou him.

℣. Christ conquereth, etc. ℟. Christ conquereth, etc.

℣. Hearken, O Christ. ℟. Christus conquereth, etc.

℣. To the bishops and abbots entrusted to him, peace, salvation, and true concord.

℟. Christ conquereth, Christ reigneth, Christ commandeth.

℣. Saint Martin. ℟. Help thou them.

℣. Saint Augustine. ℟. Help thou them.

℣. Saint Benedict. ℟. Help thou them.

℣. Christ conquereth, etc. ℟. Christ conquereth, etc.

℣. Hearken, O Christ. ℟. Christ conquereth, etc.

℣. To all princes, and the entire Christian host, peace, salvation, and victory.

℟. Christ conquereth, Christ reigneth, Christ commandeth.

℣. Saint Maurice. ℟. Help thou them.

℣. Saint George. ℟. Help thou them.

℣. Christ conquereth, etc. ℟. Christ conquereth, etc.

℣. Let good times come, let Christ's peace come, let Christ's kingdom come.

℟. Christ conquereth, Christ reigneth, Christ commandeth.

℣. To him alone praise and jubilation for endless ages of ages. Amen.

℟. To him alone praise and jubilation, etc.

℣. To him alone praise and authority, glory and power for undying ages of ages. Amen.

℟. To him alone praise and jubilation for endless ages of ages. Amen.

Less than a hundred years ago, on Easter day and the ensuing week Vespers still began with *Kyrie eleêson*, in accordance with the ancient Roman order, the ancient and new ordinaries of Rouen, the book on the Divine Offices attributed to Alcuin, those by Rupert, Honorius of Autun, and William Durand, an old Dominican breviary, the Carmelite ordinary, and the breviaries of Rouen of 1491 and 1578. This is still done in the churches and dioceses of Besançon, Châlons-sur-Marne, Cambrai, the province of Reims, and among the Carmelites of the Ancient Observance and Premonstratensians.[118] I write *eleêson* following the breviary of Cluny, since that is how it is sung by the musicians of the cathedral of Rouen and in all the churches of the Low Countries, and that is how it ought to be pronounced.

On that day, Vespers was said as it is still said today in Rouen and nearly everywhere else, with three psalms and alleluia antiphons, the Gradual *Haec dies*, and the *Alleluia* with its verse and without a Prose.

After the *Magnificat*, the oration, and the *Benedicamus*, they hold the procession to the font. Two priests in albs carry the vials containing the sacred oils and the holy chrism. Each has upon his neck a large veil, and they use the ends thereof to carry the vials. Between them, a deacon in alb and dalmatic carries the blessed candle. All three walk together along the same line, their heads covered with birettas, even though everyone else is bareheaded. I think this is because when they leave the sacristy, their heads are covered, for nothing requires them to bare them then, and, since their hands are occupied holding the vials with the sacred oils and the candle, they cannot uncover them any more. We have similarly seen that in Lyon the subdeacon who carries the cross in procession wears his miter even in the presence of the Blessed Sacrament. The rest of the clergy, with the deacon and subdeacon, follow, and then the celebrant. While processing towards the font, they sing the psalm *Laudate pueri*[119] with the alleluia antiphon, and once around them the versicle *Laudate pueri Dominum, laudate nomen Domini*. The officiant says the oration *ad Fontes* for the newly baptized. Then they sing the psalm *In exitu Israel de Aegypto*,[120] which, like the psalm *Laudate pueri*, is triumphed. The procession proceeds through the church aisle to the west door, finishing the psalm as they return to the nave, where they hold a station. Thereafter the procession goes back into the choir singing the antiphon *Lux perpetua lucebit sanctis tuis Domine* in fauxbourdon,[121] with its versicle and oration. The choirboys conclude *Benedicamus Domino, alleluia, alleluia*.

---

[118] Author's note: On *Quasimodo* Sunday and the rest of the year one says *Deus in adjutorium*, which is how the ancient hermits began the Office, for *meum* is in the singular. The clergy, which always sang together, commenced by saying *Kyrie eleêson hemas*, since *hemas* is in the plural. This is what M. Châtelain has written to me about the matter.
[119] Psalm 112.
[120] Psalm 113.
[121] Cantus ID 003653.

This procession is still done properly today in the cathedral and the better-run parish churches. In the others they do not carry the sacred oils, but only the Paschal candle, without a deacon or subdeacon. This procession is very well-suited to remind Christians of their baptismal vows. I discussed this above when describing the Hôpital de la Salpêtrière in Paris.[122] This procession used to be held in Rome, since it is indicated in the ancient *Ordo Romanus*,[123] in the book about the Divine Offices usually attributed to Alcuin,[124] in William Durand's *Rationale*,[125] in an old ordinary from Rouen written over 640 years ago, in another written four hundred years ago, in one written two hundred years ago, and in the old breviaries of Rouen published in 1491 and 1578, as well as in most of the churches I discuss in this account. It is a very ancient and praiseworthy practice.

Every Saturday from Easter to Ascension, they used to and still hold a station after Vespers. It is done in the nave before the great rood, which is incensed with three strokes by the coped celebrant while the responsory *Dignus est Domine Deus noster accipere* is sung.[126] No processional cross is borne during this station, apparently because it always remains in front of the great rood, but the thurifer and two candle-bearers are present.

Every Sunday from Easter to Ascension, they hold a similar procession or station before the great rood after Lauds. It is done with the cross, banner, and candles, but without incense, and in addition to the usual procession held before high Mass.

At Terce on Pentecost Sunday, seven canon-priests wearing chasubles over their surplices, the canon-deacon and canon-subdeacon vested in dalmatic and tunicle respectively, and the two candle-bearers go to the bottom altar step in the sanctuary. The priest in the middle sings the *Deus in adjutorium* and kneeling all together they sing the first stanza of the hymn *Veni Creator Spiritus*, during which they incense with thuribles. The choir sings the second stanza, the seven priests the third, and so on in alternation. After the hymn, the seven priests turn towards the clergy and incense them while they sing an entire antiphon. The clergy and people have remained kneeling from the beginning of the *Veni Creator* until the end of this antiphon. Then the cantor begins the psalm *Legem pone*. The seven priests, the deacon, and the subdeacon recite Terce together in the sanctuary, and thereafter return to the sacristy. This is also done in well-run parish churches.

At Terce during the octave of Pentecost, the priest who sings the high Mass, the deacon, and the subdeacon vested as for Mass, except for the

---

[122] See pp. 189–90.
[123] *Ordo Romanus* 1.12–18 according to Jean Mabillon (PL 78:965A–968C), numbered 27.67–94 in Andrieu, 3:362–72.
[124] Pseudo-Alcuin, *De divinis officiis* 20 (PL 1222C–1223A).
[125] Durand, *Rationale* 6.89.9–11, ed. Davril and Thibodeau, 2:465–67.
[126] Cantus ID 201244.

chasuble and tunicles, go with the two candle-bearers to the west end of the choir by the stalls, and the officiating priest begins the *Deus in adjutorium* for Terce. He and the deacon each take a thurible, and, kneeling with the subdeacon, they begin the hymn *Veni Creator*, and continue this first stanza together with the left side of the choir, incensing all the while. The right side of the choir sings the following stanza, and so on in alternation. This is the order throughout the week, during which the leading side of the choir otherwise changes every day, just as during the octaves of Christmas and Easter, because at these times the Office is not led by the hebdomadary but by the *journeyeur*, who is called in Latin *dietarius*. The cantor intones the psalm *Legem pone* after the antiphon *Repleti sunt*.[127] Meanwhile, celebrant sits with his ministers on the stalls, and after the psalms and antiphon, he stands and sings the short chapter, the oration after the short responsory, and concludes Terce with the *Benedicamus Domino*. Then immediately the cantor begins the Introit of the Mass.

On the feasts of Easter, Pentecost, the Assumption, the Dedication of the Church, and St. Romanus, all the clergy wore copes during the procession, and remained thus vested at high Mass, during which nine of them stood in a line in the middle of the choir. Today only five do so.

Public Penance Observed in Rouen

There is perhaps no church in France where public penance is observed with more exactitude and ceremony than in the church of Rouen. This remnant of ancient discipline is too beautiful to overlook here. Here follows an account of how it is practiced in this church.

Extract from a memorandum by M. François de la Fosse, Grand Penitentiary of the Church of Rouen, 1673

We subject all sorts of persons to public penance here: men, women, and youths. This year I have already obliged two young men aged twenty or twenty-five to undergo this penance for having uttered blasphemies in the presence of several people of their parish with whom they were working.

The offenses for which public penance is usually imposed are: the smothering, drowning, or burning of children as a result of their parents' grave negligence; public concubinage; horrible blasphemies that cause scandal, etc. I have received report from several places in this diocese about the satisfactions performed by gentlemen who fought inside a church.

The way in which this penance or public satisfaction is done varies, because I usually require it to be performed at the location where the fault was committed, in addition to the appearance the penitents are obliged to make at the cathedral on Ash Wednesday and Maundy Thursday of

---

[127] Cantus ID 004613.

the following Lent. Since they are sent to me by their parish priests to be absolved in reserved cases, I order them to hear their parish Mass from the porch or portal of their church for one or more Sundays and feasts before receiving absolution. I make this referral through a note written in the following manner:

> Lator praesentium, vel praesens mulier genuflexa orabit ad fores Ecclesiae proximis tribus diebus Dominicis dum Missa Parochialis celebrabitur; deinde Feriis 4 Cinerum et 5 in Coena Domini proximae Quadragesimae hora octava matutina conveniet ad praesentem Cathedralem Ecclesiam: quorum executio venerabili D. Parocho commendatur. Datum, etc. *Signed* N. Poenitentiarius Rotomagi.[128]

They never fail to show up in my chapel on the appointed day and time. Those who come from farthest away arrive the day before at Vespers, usually carrying letters from their parish priests that attest to their fulfillment of what was prescribed to them.

In the case of penitents from the city, I usually make them hear their parish Mass *ad fores interiores Ecclesiae*,[129] since the church portals open onto the streets. This, however, still makes them quite noticeable, when one sees ladies in silk coifs or scarves leave their pews to hear Mass or the Divine Office at the church door.

Ash Wednesday Ceremony for the Imposition of Public Penance

On Wednesday morning, the archbishop delivers his sermon from the pulpit at the east end of the nave, very close to the door of the choir. Subsequently, this same pulpit is moved, with a particular ceremony, to an arcade near the main portal, so that the penitents who cannot enter the church with the others to assist at the divine mysteries may still at least hear the word of God during Lent. And so on Ash Wednesday the archbishop, in pontifical vestments, or in his absence the head of the chapter, goes into the choir to bless the ashes and impose them on the clergy. After this the clergy go in procession into the nave with the cross, candles, and a hairshirt carried like a banner by the canon-deacon. When all are in their places, the canon-deacon reads a long lesson addressed to the penitents containing the reasons why the Church imposes this penance upon them and how they must carry it out. Below is a summary of this Latin exhortation:

> The voice of your brethren, whom you have killed, cries out before God. Holy Church is in mourning and sadness for the loss of her

---

[128] "The bearer of these presents, or this woman, shall pray kneeling at the doors of the church on the next three Sundays while the parish Mass is celebrated. Then, on Ash Wednesday and Maundy Thursday of the next Lent he shall come at eight in the morning to this cathedral church. The execution whereof is entrusted to the venerable Lord *Curé*. Given, etc. Signed N., Penitentiary of Rouen."

[129] "At the inner doors of the church."

children, but she suffers even more for the loss of your souls. This is what obliges her to cast you out today from her bosom, and to deliver your bodies to the devil, so that your souls may be saved on the day of Our Lord Jesus Christ. I urge you to apply yourselves with much ardor and vigilance to expiate and repair the crimes you have committed, so that being delivered from the power of the devil, you may re-enter under the protection of your Holy Mother the Church.[130]

Then, after citing the words of St. Leo to show them the horrible state to which sin has reduced them, where they are separated from the sacraments and communion of the Church, and the obligation they have to perform their penance with fervor and fidelity, lest it be necessary to extend it, he tells them what they must do:

During the entire time of your penance, you must wear the hairshirt, eat no meat, fast on bread and water, abstain according to the orders of your parish priest from riding on horseback and going to war, from baths, from shaving, and from the company of your wives as much as they allow. For the sole recourse for one who has become a criminal by using what was forbidden to him is to abstain from what is permitted. Be assured that we can offer you no indulgence, nor relax any of these acts of penance, unless you redeem them with long and fervent prayers, by feeding the poor, and by other good works.[131]

After this lesson, or rather exhortation, is read, the archbishop or officiant sits on a faldstool prepared for him at the head of the clergy, on the right side. Then one of the beadles comes into my chapel,[132] where the penitents are waiting, each holding a lit candle. He leads them, still holding their candles, through the multitudes of the people assembled for the ceremony. They pass through all the clergy to prostrate themselves on their knees before the seated officiant, who blows out their candles. Then they proceed in the same order to the main door of the church, which is ajar, and leave one by one. I accompany the archbishop or officiant to close the door with him once the last penitent has left. Then we rejoin the clergy, where I take my place according to my rank and return in procession to choir, where Mass is celebrated.

---

[130] Vox sanguinis fratrum vestorum quos interficistis clamat ad Dominum, sancta Ecclesia de amissione filiorum constristatur; sed acrius dolet de animarum vestrarum interitu. Unde oportet vos ab ejus communione projicere, et corpora vestra juxta Apostolum tradi satanae, ut salvi sint spiritus in die Domini. Inde vos moneo ut absque tepore et torpore, quae prave commisistis, summa vigilantia emendare studeatis, quatenus a potestate satanae erepti, sub tutelam matris vestrae sciliter sanctae Ecclesiae redite valeatis, &c.

[131] Modum itaque satisfactionis, ut a sanctis Patribus definitus est, accipite. Tempore poenitentiae vestrae cilicio uti debetis, a carne abstinere, in pane et aqua jejunare. Secundum judicium et institutionem Sacerdotum vestrorum, ab equitatu, a militia, a balneis et tonsura, et ab uxorum vestrarum cohabitatione, quandum quidem ipsae permiserint, coërcere vos oportet. Restat enim, testante sacra Scriptura, ut qui illicita perpetrat, a licitis se abstineat. Nec in his, pro certo teneatis, vobis indulgere possumus; nisi orationis assiduitate, pauperum sustentatione, aut aliis bonis operibus redimantur.

[132] Author's note: i.e., St. John the Baptist.

The Public Reconciliation Ceremony on Absolution Thursday

The penitents of Ash Wednesday and others who have been sent away during Lent, report on Absolution Thursday around eight in the morning to the penitentiary's chapel in the cathedral. They come with their candles that had been extinguished on Ash Wednesday.

After the celebration of None, the clergy go into the nave in procession, led by the Lord Archbishop in pontifical vestments or in his absence by the head of the choir, who assumes this role on this properly archiepiscopal day as on Ash Wednesday. The deacon reads the lesson that begins *Adest, venerabilis Pontifex*, which appropriately contains a request the deacon addresses to the bishop in the name of all the faithful and the whole Church to reconcile the penitents and grant them the grace of absolution that the Church asks for them with humility, and of which they have made themselves worthy by their continual tears and groans, their fasts, and other exercises of penance.

While this lesson is chanted, the beadle leads the penitents outside the church to stand before the main door through which they had been expelled on Ash Wednesday. The Lord Archbishop or officiant begins to say *Venite*, which the clergy repeat three times in alternation, and he concludes saying *Venite filii, audite me, timorem Domini docebo vos*. Then the main door is opened to the penitents, who prostrate themselves one after the other before the Lord Archbishop or the officiant, who gives them the kiss of peace. Meanwhile, the deacon and subdeacon take the penitents' extinguished candles of the penitents, light them from those carried by the acolytes, and return back to the penitents. They then proceed in single file through the clergy to a designated area in front of the pulpit at the east end of the nave, as on Ash Wednesday. There, they hear a sermon delivered by the penitentiary or someone he has appointed The clergy and a large number of people assist at this ceremony, and are greatly edified by it.

After the sermon, which the penitents hear kneeling, lit candles in hand, the cantor begins the *Domine ne in furore* and the clergy present continue the seven penitential psalms in alternation, after which the Lord Archbishop or officiant, preceded by two acolytes with lit candles, mounts the pulpit to grant the general absolution as prescribed in the Manual.[133] Then the penitents return to the chapel of the penitentiary, who sends them away in peace after a word of exhortation.

As for the number of penitents, I remember that I presented about forty of them to our Lord the Archbishop last year.

Rouen, 6 February 1673
Signed,
De la Fosse
Canon, Theologian, and Penitentiary of Rouen

---

[133] *Sacerdotale seu Manuale ecclesiae Rothomagensis* (Rouen, 1640), 293.

In 1697, the cathedral of Rouen had thirty-eight public penitents.

Processions in Rouen

Here I give, in brief, what is most noteworthy about the year's major processions, taken from the nearly two-hundred-year-old ordinary.[134] They are all still performed today, except for some small details which I will be sure to point out.

On all Wednesdays and Fridays of Lent, after None, the clergy process to a stational chapel with subdeacon, deacon, and priest in albs, maniples, and stoles, while chanting the Litany of the Saints to a rather sorrowful melody. Once they arrive, they stop the litany to say the preces and suffrages. In former times they lay fully prostrate during these preces. Today they still lie prostrate, but in a less humiliating way: there are several facing benches over which the clergy bend as they kneel during the preces. We will see this elsewhere too; it is called *prostratio super formas* or *se incurvare super formas* (PLATE 50). It is very similar to the ancient prostration. When the preces and orations are finished, the two chaplains resume the litany where they left off and continue it until everyone has retaken his place in choir, at which point they finish it and immediately begin Mass. These two stational days were devoted to longer prayers and more austere fasts.

Processions in Rouen are carried out with great gravity and ceremony. Five or six of them are so beautiful we must mention them here.

On Palm Sunday they hold a rather singular procession called the Procession of the Holy Body (*la procession du Corps saint*).[135] The ritual is as follows: Between three and four in the morning the cathedral's sacristan lets down the suspended pyx and places the sacred ciborium in a sort of tabernacle or bipartite lantern of wood and glass that is attached to a litter. He sets this near the south door of the choir upon a table decorated with a carpet and two chandeliers with lit candles. The Sacrament is exposed there for the veneration of the faithful who come from all parts of the city to accompany the sacred Body of Jesus Christ in procession. Meanwhile, Matins are said, and toward the end of Lauds, at around five thirty, when the great bell rings in peal, two chaplains of the commune vested in albs carry this litter on their shoulders, surrounded by twelve large torches provided at the Lord Archbishop's expense and bearing the prelate's coat of arms. An unbelievable number of people attend, but none of the clergy besides these two chaplains, because the lords of the chapter, so zealous for ancient custom, have even refused the offer of a foundation to accompany the procession with a number of their clergy. The procession wends its

---

[134] For Le Brun des Marettes's transcriptions from this manuscript ordinary — which belonged to Émery Bigot and is now in Paris, Bibliothèque nationale, MS. lat. 1213 — relating to these processions, see PL 147:117A–124B.
[135] In the manuscript ordinary, PL 147:117A–119C.

way by the broad Rue des Carmes to the church of St-Godard, which is adorned with the most beautiful tapestries in the city. They put down the litter in the middle of the choir on a rich dais, where it rests until nine in the morning. Around seven thirty, in the cathedral, after Terce and the sprinkling with holy water, the celebrant, deacon, and subdeacon, vested without chasuble or tunicle, preceded by an uncovered cross and lit candles, go down into the nave with the clergy, who line up in two lines in front of the great rood while the celebrant and his ministers ascend to the altar of the Holy Cross (better known as the altar of St. Cecily)[136] and bless the palms for all the canons, who each get one, and branches for the cantors, chaplains, and choirboys. For this blessing a dry Mass is said, composed of an antiphon; oration; Epistle chanted at the rood loft by the subdeacon in tunicle and facing the people; Gradual; the Gospel *Cum appropinquasset*,[137] also chanted at the loft by the deacon in a dalmatic; an oration; a Preface; three orations; and finally two antiphons and one oration.

After two priests in surplices distribute the branches, all process with palms or branches in hand to the church of St-Godard (*ad sanctum Gildardum*) chanting responsories and antiphons. Once they arrive, a sermon is delivered, today in the neighboring church of St-Laurent, but formerly in a large cemetery between the two churches. In this cemetery, by the Rue de l'École, they used to construct a large wooden platform of at least twenty square feet for the preacher to stand on in the midst of such large crowds of people. I have seen it several times, and it has been less than forty years since the custom ceased, both because of the unpredictability of the weather and because the preacher almost always had a cold or was otherwise inconvenienced. As a result the sermon is now held in the nearby church of St-Laurent. After the sermon, the clergy of the cathedral return to St-Godard, where five chaplains stand before the small chest containing the Blessed Sacrament and sing a few versicles or antiphons to which the ministers and the choir respond in alternation. The celebrant kneels with his ministers and incenses the Blessed Sacrament.

After the antiphon *Hosanna filio David*, the cantor begins the antiphon *Coeperunt omnes turbae*, and the procession returns in very pompous array, passing down roads strewn with tapestries. The most prominent burghers of the city and a crowd of people follow the procession, and the *cinquanteniers*[138] and one hundred arquebusiers line the procession to prevent disturbances. When they arrive where the old city gate once stood, the Gate of St. Apollonia, patroness of the nearby Carmelite church, sometimes also called the Porte du grand pont ("Gate of the Great Bridge"), they hold a station at an altar of repose. The choirboys and musicians go up to a nearby

---

[136] In the rood loft.
[137] Matthew 21:1–9.
[138] Commanders of units of fifty men in an urban militia.

room and sing the verses of the *Gloria, laus, et honor*. They used to ascend to the gate's actual tower: *cum Processio ad portam civitatis ornatam venerit, sex pueri turrim ascendant*.[139] While the Lord Archbishop sings the *Gloria, laus* with the cantor, the vested ministers, and the choir, he continually incenses the Blessed Sacrament on the altar of repose. Once the verses are finished, the cantor begins the responsory *Ingrediente Domino in sanctam civitatem*, and the procession enters the city, as the ordinary puts it; in other words, it passes into the limits of the old city walls. When they enter the cathedral's parvis, the cantor begins the responsory *Collegerunt Pontifices*. Four priests in black copes (formerly red and green) sing the verse *Unus autem ex ipsis* before the church door. Finally, the two vested priest-chaplains carry the litter upon which the Body of Our Lord rests inside the lantern across the door, and hold it firmly, such that all the clergy and people enter the church passing under the Blessed Sacrament.

Immediately thereafter, they uncover the great rood and the archbishop, the cantor, the deacon, and the subdeacon kneel and sing *Ave Rex noster*, which the choir repeats. Finally they enter the choir and, if the archbishop is present, he blesses the people. The Blessed Sacrament is again reserved, and Mass begins.

The ordinary says that on Rogation Monday after Sext, they prepare for the procession, which the clergy and the people of the city are obliged to attend, and they do so carrying their reliquaries, crosses, and banners.[140] They assemble at the metropolitan mother church: *ad metropolitanam et matrem Ecclesiam convenire tenentur*. While the processions from the other churches are making their way thither, the reliquaries of the saints are taken from the church treasury and placed on the high altar one after the other by two chaplains of the commune vested in albs. The relics are escorted to the sanctuary enclosure by two choirboys carrying candles, the deacon and subdeacon with their usual vestments except the tunicle, and the officiating hebdomadary or *journeyeur* also in an alb, stole, and purple maniple, who incenses each reliquary from the treasury until the entrance to the choir, while the cantors sing an antiphon proper to the saint whose relics are borne. When the antiphon is finished, the officiant and his minister halt and he sings the versicle and oration proper to the saint whose reliquary is being placed on the high altar. When all the reliquaries have been brought to the altar, and the clergy of the city is assembled, the procession departs from the cathedral at about nine thirty in the morning, that is to say after the Office of Sext. They are not so delicate as to fear the blazing sun, as in other places where to avoid it they begin the procession at seven in the morning, interpreting the rubric *post Sextam* as meaning after six in the morning.

First, led by their banners, go the reliquaries of three or four parishes

---

[139] A similar custom existed in St-Martin of Tours, see p. 96.
[140] In the manuscript ordinary, PL 147:120A–121C.

with their clergy, and three or four reliquaries of the cathedral each flanked by two torches. Then follow all the crosses and banners of all the other parishes. Led by the cross and banner of the church of St-Maclou, the biggest parish in the city, walk all the numerous clergy of all the parish churches of Rouen in a straight line, in two rows, with the city's parish priests bringing up the rear.

After them walk the canons regular of the churches of La Madeleine and St-Lô, who had taken their place on one side of the choir with the cathedral canons. Then go the Benedictines, both the Cistercians and those of the Royal Abbey of St-Ouen. They had also taken their place in choir with the cathedral canons, on the side opposite the canons regular. These churches have a common association, as I will explain later.

After them goes a beadle of the chapter carrying the great banner of the cathedral, and he is followed by an acolyte bearing the processional cross with a small banner attached. Then walk all the clergy of the cathedral, composed of the choirboys, a great number of chaplains, and the cantors or choristers who are also chaplains.

According to the ordinary, between the cantors walked the Lord Cantor, preceded by the two parish priests of the churches of St-Denis and St-Vigor, who held white staves to keep the procession of the chaplains in good order both going and returning. Then go the canons, with the deacon and the celebrant bringing up the rear. After them go two large dragons the common folk call "gargoyles" (*gargouilles*: see PLATE 51); similar ones are carried in other churches of France, such as Paris, Lyon, etc. They are followed by the reliquaries — or "feretories" (*fiertes*), from the Latin *feretrum* — of Our Lady and St. Romanus, amid the harmonies of various musical instruments. Then go the richest merchants of the city and the people. When the procession passes by the door of a church, and the door of the stational church, the clergy is incensed by the parish priest or the vicar.

The staves the two parish priests of the churches of St-Denis and St-Vigor used to carry to keep order in the procession were not unique to the church of Rouen. We have also seen them in Lyon *ad defendendam* or *custodiendam Processionem*, that is, to protect the path of the procession, to alert the populace to make way, and to prevent confusion. The other parish priests of the city and many other clerics have them too, and the dignitaries and elder canons as well. But, since all things degenerate with time, they were later shortened to two feet or two and a half feet. Finally it was found embarrassing to carry them bare, so flowers were added to the top of the staff, and eventually to the middle as well.

Formerly, the Benedictines of Bec carried staves or canes on their way to these three Rogation processions, either for support or to clear obstacles from their path, since these processions used to be done barefoot, as one can see in the *Ordo Romanus* and as I have observed in Lyon. Since the abbey of Bec is in the diocese of Rouen, is not very far from the city, and followed a good part of the rites of Rouen, it is possible that the staves carried today by some of the clergy—all the ones that receive or buy them—used to be longer and thicker and served a similar purpose. The monks of St-Martin-des-Champs of the Congregation of Cluny in Paris still carry a staff during the Rogation processions, and likewise those of St-Benigne in Dijon, Lisieux, and the entire order of Cluny. This helps confirm my theory. Further evidence is the fact that in Rouen on Rogation Tuesday they process to the church of St-Gervais outside the city, and must go uphill. The same used to be the case on Rogation Wednesday, when they went to the abbey church of Ste-Catherine-du-Mont, which sits atop a very high mountain, very tough and painstaking to climb. Staves or canes would have been very helpful for the ascent and descent. But I leave the final judgment to those learned in the rubrics.

Let us resume the course of our Monday procession. It holds a station at the parish church of St-Eloi. After the procession enters the church, a sermon is delivered, which apparently used to take place after the Gospel of a dry Mass celebrated there, perhaps like in Metz in Lorraine, for there the subdeacon, deacon, and celebrant go on the procession vested as for as ferial Mass, except for the chasuble, and in Vienne the celebrant walks vested even with the chasuble. After the sermon, the preces are said kneeling (formerly everyone prostrated) in front of the altar. Then, three chaplains sing the Litany of the Saints on their way back to the choir of the cathedral, where it is concluded.

The ordinary of the cathedral adds:

> Nota quod qualibet die trium dierum Processionis Religiosi S. Audoëni tenentur mittere per suos servitores ad domum Cantoris Ecclesiae Rotomagensis vel ejus locum tenentis, hora prandii unum panem magnum, unum galonem boni vini, honestum ferculum piscium, et unum magnum flaconem de pinguedine lactis, sicque in duobus diebus reportantur vasa, et in teria die dimittuntur, et pertinent Cantori.[141]

On Rogation Tuesday the procession goes to the church of St-Gervais with the same ceremonies as the day before.[142] There is a sermon, and when it is over, they say the preces kneeling (formerly all prostrated in front of the altar). Then they sing the responsory O *constantia Martyrum*. When it is finished, three canons sing the litany that begins *Humili prece et sincera devotione ad te clamantes Christe exaudi nos*,[143] which the choir repeats

---

[141] "Note that on all three Procession days, the religious of St-Ouen must send their servants at lunch time to the house of the cantor of the church of Rouen or his representative bearing a large loaf of bread, a gallon of good wine, a large helping of fish, and a large flagon of cream. On two days the dishes are carried back, and on the third day they are left there, and belong to the cantor" (PL 147:121C).

[142] In the manuscript ordinary, PL 147:119C–122A.

[143] Cantus ID a01386. This litany, known technically as a *versus*, was written by Hartmann

after each couplet, each of which is composed of a verse in hexameter and one in pentameter containing the names of the saints in order. The quality of the text is as pitiful as the chant is charming.

The procession goes alongside some ditches in which there are towers with listening posts or vaults that echo this beautiful chant and its cadences. Nothing could be more pleasing or charming to the ear. The cantors continue the litany until they enter the choir of the cathedral, where they finish it with two final stanzas, the last of which is in Greek.

On Rogation Wednesday they go in procession to the church of St-Nicaise (formerly to the abbey church of Ste-Catherine-du-Mont before it was destroyed) at the same time and with the same ceremonies as on Monday, and also with a sermon.[144] On their way back three cantors begin the litany *Ardua spes mundi*,[145] which is repeated after a stanza composed of a verse in hexameter and one in pentameter containing the names of the saints in order. The text is not beautiful, and neither is the chant. But when they reach a certain crossroad, three priest-chaplains begin another litany with a more beautiful chant, which produces quite a beautiful effect with its refrains. This is its order: the three priest-chaplains sing *Rex Kyrie, Kyrie eleïson, Christe audi nos*. The choir repeats the same. Then the three priest-chaplains in the middle of the procession sing *Sancta Maria ora pro nobis*. After that, three deacon-chaplains sing *Rex virginum Deus immortalis*. Three subdeacon-chaplains add, *Servis tuis semper miserere*. The choir sings, *Rex Kyrie, Kyrie eleïson, Christe audi nos*.[146] And thus all of them continue the litany along the way until they reach the choir, where they finish. Upon their return they say None, and then go to dinner, for it is well past midday.

Procession for the Release of a Prisoner on the Day of Our Lord's Ascension

One of the most beautiful rights of the church of Rouen is her power to free a criminal and all his accomplices every year on Ascension day.[147] The ceremony draws a large number of spectators to the city. To fully satisfy their curiosity, they have to go at nine or ten o'clock in the morning to the Great Hall of Parlement by the grand stairway in the Palace Court. At the end of this hall they will see a small and very well kept chapel where the parish priest of St-Lô celebrates a solemn Mass with the organ and *musique* of the cathedral and with the twelve choirboys. The lords president and counselors of Parlement all assist in red robes, and make certain notable

---

of St-Gall (d. 884), and can be found in St. Gall Cod. 381, 29–35, and in a thirteenth-century gradual of Rouen, Paris, BnF, lat. 904, f. 129v–132r.

[144] In the manuscript ordinary, PL 147:122B–C.

[145] This *versus* was written by Ratpert of St-Gall (d. 884). It is also contained in St. Gall Cod. 381, and appears with musical notation in BnF, lat. 904, f. 136r–37v.

[146] Cantus ID a02289

[147] In the manuscript ordinary, PL 147:122D–123A.

reverences in the offertory procession. After Mass they go to the grand gilded chamber, where they are served a magnificent dinner around midday.

After their dinner, at around two o'clock in the afternoon, the chaplain of the Confraternity of St-Romain goes in surplice, almuce, and biretta to the grand chamber to present a warrant on behalf of the members of the chapter of the cathedral indicating which prisoner they have chosen. (They may not choose someone guilty of lese-majesty or willful murder). The warrant is examined, the prisoner is given a hearing and interrogated, his trial is carried out and reported, and he is condemned to the punishment that his crime deserves. Then, in virtue of the privilege given in consideration of St. Romanus,[148] he is pardoned by his grace and released into the hands of the said chaplain, who leads the bareheaded criminal to the Place de la Vieille Tour. Once the procession has arrived there, the archbishop, assisted by the celebrant, deacon, subdeacon and several canons, goes up to the platform on top with them and the two priests who carry the feretory or reliquary of St. Romanus, which they place under the arcade on a decently dressed table. Then the archbishop or in his absence the officiant canon delivers an exhortation to the criminal who kneels bareheaded, telling him about the horror of his crime and his obligation to God and St. Romanus, by whose merits he is delivered. Then he orders the criminal to say the *Confiteor*, places his hand on his head and says the *Misereatur* and *Indulgentiam*. He makes him put his shoulders under one end of the reliquary and orders him, still on his knees, to raise it slightly. Immediately a crown of white flowers is placed on his head. Then the procession returns to the church of Notre-Dame in the same order it came, the prisoner holding the front part of the reliquary. Once the procession has entered the church and the criminal has placed the reliquary on the high altar, they say the high Mass, however late it may be, sometimes five or six in the evening. The archbishop delivers another short exhortation to the criminal and he is led before the dignitaries to the chapterhouse, where he is given another exhortation before being led to the chapel of St. Romanus, where he hears Mass. Then he is taken to the Viscounty of the Water,[149] where he is given a light meal, and thence to the Master of the Confraternity of St. Romanus, where he sups and lodges. The next day at eight o'clock in the morning the criminal is led by the chaplain into the chapterhouse, where the penitentiary or another canon gives him another exhortation and hears his confession. He is made to take an oath on the

---

[148] The legend of St. Romanus, bishop of Rouen (seventh century), holds that a certain man condemned to death was the only one willing to help this holy bishop slay a dragon (called the *gargouille*) who was ravaging the left bank of the Seine. Hence the custom arose of freeing a prisoner in the saint's honor.

[149] A judicial district where Rouen was located, and by extension the headquarters thereof. See François Farin and Ignace Du Souillet, "Vicomté de l'Eau," in *Histoire de la ville de Rouen* (Rouen, 1731), 142–46.

book of the Gospels to lend his arms to the lords of the chapter whenever required, and then he is set free.

Procession on the Day of Corpus Christi

Before the beginning of Terce, the sacristan brings down the suspended pyx and takes from it a large host, which he puts into the monstrance.[150] The celebrant immediately begins to sing the *O salutaris Hostia* while incensing the Blessed Sacrament. Then they say Terce, everyone bareheaded and standing without leaning on his stall. This demonstrates the profound respect that the canons of Rouen have for Jesus Christ, as they rightly should. Indeed, if one stands before the king, with all the more reason one ought to stand in the presence of the King of kings.

After Terce, they hold the procession. All the clergy are in copes and the choirboys in tunicles. They go out through the south door and return through the main west door. Two canons vested in white chasubles carry the Blessed Sacrament on a litter under a rich canopy borne by four minor canons. At their sides are two acolytes carrying lit torches, in front of them two choirboys incensing the Blessed Sacrament, and behind them two other choirboys incense it as well. When the procession returns, they hold a station in the middle of the nave. The Blessed Sacrament is placed there on the litter held crosswise atop two high trestles. All the clergy and people pass under the Blessed Sacrament while the antiphon *O quam suavis est Domine* is sung for the entry into choir.[151] Once the antiphon is finished, the archbishop, if present, gives the blessing. Then they reserve the Blessed Sacrament and begin Mass, since in this church they are very attached to the preservation of the ancient discipline.[152]

That very evening they have Benediction, a foundation for which was established about forty years ago. About thirty years ago they began to hold two other Benedictions on the Sunday and Thursday within the octave in the evening, from the foundation of two canons. The entire church is illuminated with a great number of candles. A procession is held within and all round the church. The celebrant in cope carries the Blessed Sacrament under a canopy with two torches at the sides, and four choirboys incense it as in the morning procession. After a few prayers the celebrant gives the blessing with the Blessed Sacrament without saying anything, unless the archbishop does so.

On the same day each parish has a procession in the morning on its territory, since the clergy of Rouen is very numerous: four parish churches in Rouen have nearly a hundred clerics each, and the others forty, thirty, fifteen, or twenty.

---

[150] In the manuscript ordinary, PL 147:123A–124A.
[151] Cantus ID 203554.
[152] That is, the discipline of not celebrating Mass with the Sacrament exposed.

Exposition of the Blessed Sacrament for the King

Besides the occasions I have mentioned above, the Blessed Sacrament is never exposed in the cathedral except in cases of grave necessity, such as when the life of the king is at risk on account of war or sickness. Then the Blessed Sacrament is exposed in the following manner and circumstances:

On the preceding Sunday, during the *prône* in the parish churches a notice is put out that on such and such a day the Forty Hours prayers will begin with exposition of the Blessed Sacrament for the preservation of the king's sacred person.

On the eve of the Forty Hours, at eight o'clock in the evening, the two largest bells of the cathedral (except Georges d'Amboise) ring in peal for about a quarter of an hour to give notice.

The nave is strewn with the most beautiful tapestries in the city. The altar of the chapel of Our Lady of Vows, near the rood screen under the great rood, is dressed with the finest ornaments and entirely covered with silver-gilt candlesticks, with a very rich canopy on top. Here the Blessed Sacrament is exposed. This arrangement ensures that nothing is disturbed and that the ritual of the Office, always said in choir, remains unchanged. No Mass is celebrated in the presence of the Blessed Sacrament, and God is no less adored for it. On the contrary, it is to give him greater adoration and respect that the lords of the chapter do things thus. Of course, they do not leave the Blessed Sacrament alone there. From the altar enclosure to the pillar of the lantern, large barricades are placed on each side to prevent the crowds from entering the square space this barrier forms. A large Turkish carpet covers this large space, where there are two prie-dieux covered with two rugs for two canons. Behind them is a bench similarly covered with a rug to mark the place for four chaplains, and behind them a smaller bench to mark the place for two choirboys. All eight of them kneel there bareheaded praying and adoring the Blessed Sacrament in silence for an hour, after which eight others take their places and so on, hour after hour, from morning to evening. There are always large crowds of people coming in to offer their prayers and adorations.

In the morning, as the Blessed Sacrament is being exposed they only chant the *Ave verum*, and in the evening, without procession, they chant at Benediction the *Ave verum* or *Pange lingua* with the *Exaudiat* and some prayers for the king. Then the celebrant gives the blessing without saying anything, unless he be the archbishop. On that day, even if it is Sunday, there is never a sermon. And this is sensible and in conformity with what God demands on these occasions: *Sileat omnis caro a facie Domini, quia consurrexit de habitaculo sancto suo*: "Let all flesh be silent at the presence of the Lord, for he is risen up out of his holy habitation" (Zacharias 2:13). Thus silent adoration is what best befits Jesus Christ exposed on our altars. This has always been the ancient custom of the Church and it is still observed in many churches, as I have remarked in several sections of this account.

General Procession after Vespers on Assumption Day, 15 August

This is surely the most frequented and most beautiful of all the general processions in Rouen. Everyone knows that it is held in fulfillment of the vow of King Louis XIII and in thanksgiving for the felicitous birth of the Most Christian King Louis XIV.[153]

First go the two convents of Capuchins, two convents of calced and discalced Augustinians, the Recollects, the Franciscan Tertiaries,[154] the Minims, the Franciscans in great number, the Carmelites, and the Dominicans, all without regard to rank.

Then follow all the crosses and the numerous clergy of the city parishes. After them go the canons regular of La Madeleine and of St-Lô and the Benedictines of St-Ouen. Finally go the clergy of the cathedral with the Lord Archbishop, who gives his blessing to the innumerable crowd of people who line the main streets through which the procession passes.

Outsiders who wish to see all the clergy of the city, the beautiful ornaments, and the splendid ceremonies of the cathedral ought to choose this day above any other. One might also recommend Ascension day, but there is more confusion and less devotion. Easter day, Corpus Christi, and the feast of the Dedication of the Church on 1 October are also days when one can see the rich ornaments, the beautiful ceremonies, and the great number of candles of this church, which illumine the night as if it were day.

There is perhaps no church in France more magnificently lit than the cathedral of Rouen. They use brand-new yellow wax which gives off a very pleasant scent, and which is truly virgin wax, having not been bleached. On the day of the Purification, three large blessed candles are carried in the procession before the cross. One of these is provided by the abbess of Fontaine-Guérard, of the Cistercian order.

On 14 September, the feast of the Exaltation of the Holy Cross, they hold a procession before high Mass in the cathedral nave, where at the altar of the Cross the celebrant blesses the new wine in a large silver basin. After the blessing they fill the wine cruet for the sacrifice of the high Mass, and the sacristan distributes the remainder with a silver ladle to those who want it.

On the feast of the Dedication, on 1 October, before the high Mass there is a procession in copes around the nave inside the church, not outside; this is quite sensible.

---

[153] Louis XIII made several acts of devotion to Our Lady in propitiation for an heir. After twenty-three years of childlessness, his wife Queen Anne gave birth to Louis XIV, and Louis XIII consecrated France to Our Lady. He ordered a procession to be held in her honor after Vespers on the feast of the Assumption.
[154] Formally the Brethren of Penance, known as Picpus Penitents in France after the location of their monastery in Paris.

Sermons in the Cathedral

All sermons delivered in the cathedral draw large crowds, even though only two are announced with bells, namely the one given at the synod and on the feast of St. Severus, bishop of Avranches, celebrated on 1 February. The sermon is given by a canon as assigned by the board, unless he finds someone else to take his place. The sermon on the feast of St. Severus is done in a quite extraordinary manner. The preacher climbs up to the pulpit in the rood loft and positions himself under the small wooden arcade that supports the great rood. He wears an alb, stole, cope, and biretta, whether he is secular or a regular, even a Capuchin or Recollect. Next to him in the loft, the saint's relics are exposed beside lamps. They are carried below after the sermon to be venerated by the crowds of people who attend the ceremony. In the time of St. Augustine, the relics of St. Stephen Protomartyr were exposed in the rood loft of the church of Uzalis in Africa, as one can see in the appendix to the seventh volume of St. Augustine, in column 27 of the new edition, in chapter 3 of *De miraculis S. Stephani*.[155] So it is to the credit of the lords of the chapter that they preserve a custom founded on such firm ancient authority.

Archiepiscopal Sermons

Archiepiscopal sermons, so called because they are given by the archbishop or someone he delegates, are delivered on the first and fourth Sundays of Advent, Septuagesima Sunday, Ash Wednesday, and the first and fourth Sundays of Lent. They take place during the pre-Mass procession at the station held in the nave before the clergy enter the choir, from about a quarter past nine until a quarter past ten, or half past ten. During this hour it is forbidden to say Masses or any other divine service in the parish churches, so that the people are not prevented from going to hear the voice of their bishop. And there is no point in trying to find a Mass during that time, whether in the cathedral or in the parishes.

Reception of the Archbishop of Rouen, Primate of Normandy, Upon His First Entrance or Taking Possession

The new archbishop takes possession of his church barefoot, regardless of the cold. He processes from the parish church of St-Herbland, where the sacristan removes his shoes. From there the archbishop walks barefoot along the goldsmiths' shops, treading on a bit of straw strewn on the road to spare him the mud. The cathedral clergy, lined up in two lines in the

---

[155] *De miraculis Sancti Stephani* 1.2–3, in Congregation of St-Maur, eds., *Sancti Aurelii Augustini Hipponensis Episcopi operum*, vol. 7 (Paris, 1685), Appendix, 27D–E (reprinted in PL 41:833). Le Brun des Marettes abuses his source here in order to justify the contemporary custom of Rouen: in the account he cites, the relics are reserved in the apse, not in the rood loft. In the cited account, a commendation of St. Stephen's virtues is indeed delivered from the rood loft (*de pulpito...recitata est*), but his relics are reserved in the apse (*in loco absidae super cathedram velatam*).

churchyard or parvis, welcome him after the dean has given him the book of the holy Gospels to kiss and the archbishop has taken the usual oath, with his hands on the book, in these terms:

> I, N., pastor of this church of Rouen by God's sufferance, swear on these holy Gospels that I will protect it with courage and defend it against any who attack or oppress its dependent persons or properties, and that I will faithfully safeguard the rights of this same church, its franchises, privileges, statutes, and approved customs, and that I will not alienate any of its properties nor permit them to be alienated. On the contrary, if any have been alienated, I will do my utmost to recover them. So help me God and these holy Gospels.

Notwithstanding the chapter's bull of exemption, the archbishop has the right to visit the chapter of his cathedral church once, just as he can visit the other churches of his diocese. He may even initiate a second visitation to the chapter, but only after he has visited his whole diocese and the six others of the province.

Dignitaries of the Chapter of Rouen

The Lord High Dean is the first dignitary of the chapter after the archbishop, and when he is present at Prime and Compline he says and hears the *Confiteor*, and in Lent sprinkles the holy water at the end of Compline.

At high Masses of triple and double feasts and at solemn obits, the Lord Cantor officiates in cope holding his staff. He is in charge of making sure no one talks in choir, and has the right of light correction over the clergy, which means he can give at most one blow. He had the right to hold or oversee chant schools.

The chancellor is the intendant or master of schools. In other churches he is therefore called the *capiscol, ecolâtre,* or *scholastique*. He is in charge of making the chronological table that is fixed on the Paschal candle, and of keeping the *matricule*,[156] or assigning someone else to do so in his place. He must also assign the Matins lessons to the choirboys and other clergy and even to the three subdeacon-canons who sing the lessons of the first nocturn at Matins on major feasts, and he must listen to all of them when requested.

The penitentiary delivers the sermon on Maundy Thursday and is responsible for the reconciliation of the public penitents.

Unlike other churches, this illustrious church does not have vicars perpetual, semi-prebendaries, or canon-serfs[157] to perform hebdomadary

---

[156] The register of clerics, based on which he assigns a duty to each.
[157] There was a distinction within many French cathedral chapters between "free" canons (*chanoines francs*) and "serf" canons. The former, usually drawn from the nobility or high bourgeoisie, had more freedom to be absent from their choir duties than the latter, who were strictly obliged to be present, and thus bore the larger part of the burden of

duties for the others. The worthy canons of Rouen conduct themselves with such honor that not for anything in the world would they permit a subdeacon, deacon, or priest who is not a major canon to celebrate or serve Mass at the high altar. They would rather do without a deacon or subdeacon altogether.

The hebdomadary is so respected in the cathedral of Rouen that when a canon performs his role in turn, no other canon passing through the stalls or choir dares to pass in front of him, taking another way to his place instead. This distinction is not given to any other canon. I have been assured that formerly, during the week of his service, the hebdomadary lived and slept in a room next to the sacristy — today called the sacristan's chamber — separated from the society of men so as to be more united to God, and to be in a better state to offer his prayers and sacrifices for the people.

There is one more thing. On Saturday after None, in accordance with a very ancient practice, the hebdomadary was obliged to lie prostrate in the middle of the choir, humbly give thanks to God, and ask forgiveness for any omissions and faults he may have committed in his duties that week. Sixtus IV made this prostration obligatory under pain of excommunication if the hebdomadary refused to do it, but the chapter could absolve him after he had made satisfaction.[158] In 1489, the dean and chapter wrote to Pope Innocent VIII to modify this practice. They argued that this prostration did not simply consist in a genuflection and profound bow, but in lying down flat on the pavement in the middle of the choir, which at that time was not covered during winter, contending that this custom was very harsh, difficult, and dangerous for the elderly and the infirm. Instead, they proposed that this sort of prostration be done before the high altar instead of in mid-choir,[159] as is the current practice. After None, as they begin Saturday Vespers, the hebdomadary leaves his place in choir and approaches the high altar, and kneels and prays, slightly bowed, on the predella, during the first psalm. When he finishes his prayer he kisses the altar and returns to his place.

Only the hebdomadary has a candle in choir in the winter, in a dark lantern, in order to read the absolutions and benedictions at Matins, and the chapter and oration at Lauds.

Besides this dark lantern there is another very large silver lantern, with a candle that is kept lit in winter and summer during the three nocturns. At

---

the Office, yet had no voice in chapter. On the social tensions within chapters, mirroring those of the Ancien Régime in general, see p. 353.

[158] By a bull dated 27 March 1481, Pope Sixtus IV decreed that anyone who violated the chapter's statutes which he had approbated was excommunicated *latae sententiae*. See Armand Collette, *Histoire du bréviaire de Rouen* (L. Mégard, 1902), 75.

[159] By a bull dated 5 January 1489, Pope Innocent VIII allowed the canons of Rouen to modify their usages and customs, including this prostration. For French translation thereof, see François Pommeraye, *Histoire*, 605–607. Cf. *Sacerdotale seu Manuale ecclesiae Rothomagensis* (Rouen, 1640), xliiii.

the first or second psalm of Matins, a major choirboy holds it up high in the middle of the choir or in the rood loft before an acolyte- or subdeacon-cantor, who carries the great lectionary. The fact that this lantern is used in both summer and winter to read the lessons, and even on the vigil of the Assumption, the only day of the year when Matins are said after Vespers, is a sign that the canons of Rouen have never lost sight of the fact that Matins should be said at night.

Ceremonies Observed During the Offices

We must here indicate the order and ceremonial of Matins and the other Offices.

On triple feasts, there are two coped canons who begin the psalms. Four others, who chant the responsory at both first and second Vespers, also coped, remain in choir until the end of Vespers, whereas the two others move behind them during the short chapter and return to the sacristy when the four begin the responsory. At Matins, four canons sing the Invitatory and the psalm *Venite*, and remain until the end of Lauds. Two of them intone the psalms at Matins and the two others the psalms at Lauds.

On doubles, two coped canons rule the choir at Matins and Vespers.

On semidoubles, two minor canons or chaplains go to the sacristy to put on copes to sing the responsory at first Vespers, and remain until the end of Vespers. They also wear copes at Matins and at high Mass, but not at second Vespers. The succentor intones the psalms, the hymn, and the *Magnificat* from his place.

At Matins on semidoubles, the succentor gives the cope-bearers the incipit of the antiphon and the psalm tone. Hence each cope-bearer goes before him a bit before the end of the psalm and bows. Then the succentor rises and says, for instance, *Respice, de octavo*; or *Impleat, de quarto*; where *tono* is understood. Then, at the end of the psalm, this cope-bearer preintones the antiphon for him who must intone it, and himself intones the psalm thereafter. When intoning it, he turns to face his side of the choir; it is perfectly reasonable that he should face those to whom he is intoning the psalm.

When the choirboys sing the versicles in mid-choir, they not only bow to the east and west, which is called *ante et retro*, but also to the south and north, which is called *in ambitu*, "in a circle."

In Rouen, on triple feasts there used to be an incensation at each nocturn. Today, they only use candles and incense at the first Gospel, that is, at the seventh lesson, except on Christmas night, when they use candles and incense at the three last lessons, because all of them begin with an excerpt from the Gospel.

On triple feasts, the celebrant still incenses the altar during the *Te Deum*. Two ministers incense the altar and choir during the *Benedictus* at Lauds and the *Magnificat* at first and second Vespers, except that at second Vespers of triples of the second class only the celebrant incenses. The minister who incenses with the celebrant remains at his side until they return to the sacristy with all the cope-bearers.

At Lauds, Vespers, and high Mass, a choirboy incenses the upper stalls on both sides, holding the thurible by the top of the chains with both hands. He must handle it adroitly so as to avoid hitting his knees, but nevertheless swings it quite high.

High Mass

On triple feasts, the cantor wears a cope and rules the choir with his staff. He intones the *Gloria in excelsis* and *Credo* for the celebrant. During the *Gloria in excelsis*, he chooses two chaplains to sing the Gradual in the rood loft. After singing, they descend and go to the sacristy. Four coped canons sing the Alleluia from the loft and accompany the cantor in choir during the rest of the Mass until the communion. The reverences they make near the bench when going to and from the offertory procession are worth observing, for they are not usual (PLATE 52).

The ceremony for Masses on double feasts is the same, except that only two coped canons sing the Alleluia, and there is no offertory procession.[160]

On semidoubles, two minor canons of fifteen marks or two coped chaplains rule the choir. Two choirboys sing the Gradual in the rood loft and two coped canons the Alleluia from the same place. Both pairs leave the loft after the Gospel is sung. On certain privileged Sundays two chaplains in albs sing the Gradual. On Sundays of Lent, when the Tract is very long, it is chanted between the lamps and Charles V's tomb by four coped canons. They sing the first and last verses together, alternating the rest in pairs. They stay in place during the Gospel, and then go to the sacristy.

On simple feasts and ferias, one coped chaplain rules the choir at Mass, which is sung from the eastern end of the choir on the Epistle side, which is more or less the place where the *schola cantorum* stood in the *Ordo Romanus*. Choirboys sing the Gradual, Alleluia, or Tract from memory at the eagle, each of them singing his verse solo.

Before Terce on Sundays (or after Terce on triples), the blessing of water and aspersion is done at the corner of Charles V's tomb near the eagle by the celebrant of the Mass, who is vested in alb, stole, and maniple in the color of the day, facing north. Near the end of the blessing, the cross-bearer (who, according to the ritual of Rouen, should be a subdeacon) and the two candle-bearers leave the sacristy, followed by the subdeacon in tunicle carrying the Gospel book upon his breast, and the deacon in dalmatic.

They arrange themselves near the choir lamps. The celebrant sprinkles the high altar, then the processional cross, the deacon, subdeacon, the tombs of the kings of France and England, and finally the entire choir.

---

[160] See p. 254, n. 162.

The major choirboy accompanies him carrying the stoup. The celebrant then goes behind the deacon at the foot of Charles V's tomb and faces the altar to say the versicle and oration, at the end of which the sacristan helps him put on the cope which has been placed folded at the foot of the tomb. The ceremony is done this way so that one never has to wait for the celebrant or any of the ministers. If anyone delays or neglects any ceremony he is fined. As a result, everything in this church is done very punctually and with great exactitude.

The procession follows. Whether it is done inside or outside the church, the major beadle always walks before the cross with the dean of the choirboys, who continually sprinkles the places and people he meets on his way, both within and without the church. Note that the purpose of the procession is to sprinkle the people and places. In well-run parishes, the acolyte who walks before the cross sprinkles not only the people he finds on the way, but also the entire cemetery where the faithful are buried. They hold a station in the nave before the great rood, singing a responsory whose verse is sung from the rood loft by two or four canons or chaplains facing the clergy or the main west door. After the responsory, the cantor intones an antiphon or a responsory without verse, which is sung while the procession makes its way into choir.

During the procession, or during Terce if there is no procession, the bell for the Mass of the Catechumens is rung. On fasting days and during Advent, this bell is rung during Sext, and in Lent during None.

Unless the celebrant carries a cross to the altar, the subdeacon, deacon, and celebrant, all three of whom are always major canons, wear the almuce over their left arm and cover their head with the biretta during summer; in winter they wear the *aumusson*, which covers their head and shoulders, over the chasuble or tunicle. When they arrive at the foot of the altar, however, they remove their almuces, birettas, and *aumussons*, regardless of the season.

The choirboys kneel with their candles until the priest goes up to the altar. At that point they immediately go fetch the Epistle and Gospel books, which have silver covers, and take them to the two corners of the altar. The Gospel book is placed on the left side, which used to be considered more noble but is today called the Epistle side; the Epistle book is placed on the right side, which today we call the Gospel side.

The priest incenses the altar during the *Kyrie*, and the thurifer incenses the choir during the *Gloria in excelsis* and *Credo*.

During the *Gloria in excelsis* and *Credo*, the celebrant and deacon sit and don birettas or almuces, as does the subdeacon when he is present. As in Auxerre and Lisieux, everyone kneels at *suscipe deprecationem nostram*, including the celebrant, deacon, and subdeacon if they are at the altar. If they are sitting, however, they only uncover their heads and bow as these three words are sung.

Until the last century they had proper Epistles and Gospels for every Wednesday and Friday.

The choirboys hold their candles up during the collects. Then they put them down, make a reverence to the altar, and stand by Charles V's tomb during the Epistle—whether it is sung at the rood loft or the eagle—without going down the step, waiting for the subdeacon. At the end of the Epistle, he gives one of the two choirboys the Epistle book to take to the sacristy, and accompanies them thither.

The choirboys take the cruets, the large silver basin, and the large towel from the sacristy and take them to the altar followed by the subdeacon carrying the chalice and paten in both hands covered by a large veil placed over his shoulders such that he touches neither the chalice nor the paten, even if he is an ordained priest. Meanwhile, the deacon moves the book from the left or south side of the altar to the other side to make room for the chalice. It is noteworthy that in the cathedral the chalice is placed in the same place where the book stood, rather than on the credence, which only holds the cruets, washbasin, and towel. This is the literal reason for moving the missal, as well as the fact that placing it on the south side of the altar is more comfortable for the celebrant (*Micrologus* 9).

The deacon then immediately presents the incense for the celebrant to bless, says the *Munda*, and asks the celebrant for the blessing while resting the book against his head. Thereupon he goes to the rood loft with the Gospel book resting on his left shoulder, preceded by the thurifer, the two candle-bearers, and the subdeacon who does not carry anything. As they pass, all the canons and the rest of the clergy rise to honor and salute the book of the holy Gospels. The deacon climbs to an elevated place in the loft, incenses the book with three swings, and sings the Gospel facing north flanked by the two candle-bearers. All the clergy remain standing facing the deacon. After the reading, they all return in the same order, and as they pass, the entire clergy salute them in the same manner, except that this time the subdeacon carries the Gospel book and presents it open to the priest to kiss. Whenever the Creed is said, he then presents the book closed to the coped cantors on the right side and in the upper stalls of that side, and then to the coped cantors on the left side and in the upper stalls of that side.

Just before as well as during the reading of the Gospel, they ring the bells for the Mass of the Faithful.

On simple feasts and even ferias, the deacon incenses the Gospel book before reading it, and the priest incenses the *oblata* in accordance with the first canon of an ancient Council of Rouen held in the ninth century, which states: *Ut tempore quo Evangelium legitur, finitoque Offertorio, super oblationem incensum ponatur, decrevimus.*[161] I think that *tempore quo Evangelium legitur* means during the entire time the Gospel is read. This is

---

[161] Pommeraye, *Concilia*, 33.

what the Carthusians and some other churches do, always or nearly always incensing the Gospel book during the entire time the deacon chants from it.

On major feasts, the celebrant, deacon, and subdeacon descend the altar steps and present the paten to be kissed by the offerers.[162] The subdeacon receives the offerings and takes them to the altar, just as in parish churches. In some churches they are placed beside the corporal.

The two candle-bearers present the wine to the deacon and the water to the subdeacon: according to the ritual of Rouen, enough water is to be poured so that the resulting mixture is two-thirds wine. Some scrupulous men count the drops of water, and grow quite vexed if they pour in more than two or three. The ritual of Rouen relieves us of such a scruple. The deacon presents the chalice to the priest, kissing the pommel in the middle. Still today he holds the priest's arm with one hand and the foot of the chalice with the other, since, as we learn from St. Gregory the Great's letters, chalices used to be very large and heavy, containing a good deal of wine, because after the consecration it was consumed by all the clergy and people as well as the priest. The cruets used to be similarly large; consider those of Tours above.[163] Hence one can see that there was good reason to help the priest hold the chalice. This ritual has remained so that we can understand what used to be done before and what led to it. After the deacon covers the chalice with the pall, the priest blesses the incense, and incenses the *oblata*, the cross, and the entire altar. There is a similar explanation for why the deacon and subdeacon hold the edge of his chasuble. The priest's chasuble used to be entirely round and not clipped, but ample like a large cloak. It had a single opening on top for the head, and covered his whole body, including his arms and hands. Chasubles of this sort are still found in the cathedral of Rouen and elsewhere. Hence the deacon and subdeacon were obliged to lift the sides of the celebrant's chasuble at certain moments in order to help him perform his functions. Even though most chasubles today are clipped and have openings for the arms, the ancient custom of lifting and holding the sides of the priest's chasuble during the elevation of the host and chalice has persisted. It actually helps the priest in the cathedral church, where the chasubles cover the entire arms.

After incensing the altar, the celebrant gives the thurible to the deacon, who incenses him, then around the whole altar from behind, and finally the kings' tombs. Meanwhile, a minor choirboy holds over his head with two

---

[162] On Sundays and triple feasts, after the priest read the Offertory, there was a general offertory procession in which the people brought their offerings, usually monetary, and kissed a pax-brede. Here it does not take place on double feasts. Though forbidden by Pius V (in a letter to the archbishop of Tarragona, cited in Bartholomew Gavantus, *Thesaurus sacrorum rituum* 2.10.8, note c [Antwerp, 1634], 1:170) and regional councils, the cathedral of Rouen kept this ancient practice of offering the paten to the offerers to kiss, as seen in PLATE 56.

[163] See p. 88.

hands a large silver basin, while the thurifer pours water over the priest's hands and the other minor choirboy holds the large towel all outspread. Everything here is done gravely and with a sense of the grandeur of the holy repast that will take place at the Lord's table. After the thurifer washes the priest's hands, he goes to join the deacon, who gives him the thurible after the incensations. Then the deacon puts the paten into the subdeacon's veil, and he holds it covered until the *Pater*.

At the Preface and the *Pater* the acolytes hold their candles up.

At the *Sanctus*, the deacon opens the riddels to allow the host and chalice to be seen and adored at the elevations, during which two acolytes hold lit torches, the candle-bearers hold their candles up, and the thurifer incenses. Meanwhile, many large bells are rung to alert the absent faithful who, due to sickness or some other cause, were not able to come to church, to adore the Body and Blood of Jesus Christ in spirit in their homes.

The host and chalice are elevated together at *Omnis honor et gloria*, while the choir kneels, the deacon lifts the chasuble, the acolytes hold their candles up, and the thurifer incenses as at the two previous elevations.

At the beginning of the *Pater* the subdeacon holds the uncovered paten with the humeral veil, and in the middle of the *Pater* he gives it to the deacon, who holds it up quite high without the veil to display it to all those assisting. This is a sign that communion is near, showing them that there is nothing on the vessel, that their offerings are on the altar. He thus indicates to them that they should prepare to receive the Body of Christ, provided they have no impediment. The people respond to the last verse of the Lord's Prayer, which shows that they have a place in all the prayers said by the priest. The deacon closes the riddels once more.

In Rouen, the *Libera nos quaesumus Domine* is said in a low voice, except on Good Friday when it is said out loud: note, in line with what I said above, that formerly it was said out loud every day, as still today in Lyon and Milan. So our rubricists' keenness to find mystical reasons here is in vain.[164] Those of Lyon will never succeed, as hard as they might try. And to be honest, there is nothing mystical here, this diversity of practice having arisen only since the proliferation of the low Mass, from which many customs have been introduced into the high Mass.[165]

At the *Agnus Dei* they still ring many church bells, and the ringing is called the *Boutte-hors*, "which is the bell for Sext," as we read in a large notice from 1476 displayed on the wall of the chapterhouse.[166]

---

[164] The usual mystical explanation — transmitted by Durand (*Rationale* 4.49.3, ed. Davril and Thibodeau, 1:520) and Gavantus (*Thesaurus sacrorum rituum* 4.9.17, 1:260) — was that the *Libera nos* was said aloud on Good Friday to signify Christ's harrowing of hell.
[165] For this account of the *Libera nos* said in a low voice, see de Vert, *Explication*, 1:312–13, 394–95, 3:320. But see Pierre Le Brun's refutation of arguments for an audible embolism in his *Explication*, 4:343.
[166] Cf. de Vert, *Explication*, 1:46, note c.

We saw above that in Rouen, as elsewhere, they went to communion only after exchanging a kiss of peace. Neither the kiss nor the pax-brede are used today.

The ritual of Rouen, after marking triple feasts of the first class as communion days for young ecclesiastics, adds:

> It would be desirable for the deacons and subdeacons to receive communion on all the other triple feasts as well, and on all Sundays, at least when they serve at the altar; and newly-ordained priests even more often, in order to become familiar with the holy mysteries, in imitation of the ancients[167] who took communion from the host they received at their ordination for the subsequent forty days.

The choirboys depart directly after the Communion antiphon. Formerly the Mass concluded with this antiphon, as evidenced by the Mass of Good Friday, which has no Postcommunion.

The deacon pours the wine for the purification and the ablution, while the subdeacon pours the water. After the celebrant has drunk the ablution, in the cathedral church, the deacon purifies the chalice and places it in the subdeacon's veiled hands, such that the subdeacon never touches the holy vessels, even if he be a priest.

The deacon turns towards the people, dismisses them with the *Ite, missa est*, and everybody departs after receiving the priest's blessing. The priest recites the Prologue to the Gospel of St. John at the altar, with only the cantors remaining in choir to sing Sext.

Since we have been speaking about the priest, deacon, and subdeacon, we must note here that the clergy of Rouen used to be divided into three groups: priests, deacons, and subdeacons, not counting the minor clerics. I see this division in the charter for the translation of the body of St. Romanus to a very costly relic case. The church of Rouen had sold the original case, which was made of fine gold, in order to provide urgently needed help to the poor who were dying of hunger. In this they followed St. Ambrose, who stated, *Aurum Ecclesiae habet non ut servet, sed ut eroget, et subveniat in necessitatibus.*[168] But as I was saying, this charter, dated 1179, states that there were twenty-nine canons present at this translation together with the dean, the cantor, and four archdeacons. Of these canons, seven were priests, seven deacons, and fifteen subdeacons. We have previously seen this same custom in many other churches. But today everyone flocks to the priesthood, because there are greater revenues attached to it.

There is nothing remarkable in the reception of the canons of Rouen,

---

[167] Pseudo-Fulbert of Chartres, *Epistula* 2 (to Einhard). Numbered 3 in PL 141:193B. Judged spurious by Frederick Behrends, ed. and trans., *The Letters and Poems of Fulbert of Chartres* (Clarendon Press, 1976), lxii.

[168] "The Church has gold not to keep it, but to distribute it, and help those in need" (*De officiis* 2.28).

which is done by touching the book of the holy Gospels for the spiritual and bread for the temporal. It remains only to note that this church has always observed and still observes today as an inviolable rule that no bastard is to be admitted as a canon, whatever his qualities. Even Richard I, duke of Normandy, had to marry Gunnor and legitimize his natural son Robert in order to allow him to become a canon and later archbishop. The chapter was vigorously opposed to this, and has resisted it since on other occasions.

The canons obtain their daily chapter bread by assisting at the *Venite* of Matins, and this is a remnant of the common life they used to lead.

General Chapter of the Cathedral

The general chapter of the cathedral of Rouen begins every year on the day after the Assumption. During the first four days, which are solemn, the place where the chapter is held is covered with tapestries. The High Dean, or in his absence the eldest canon, presides and opens the chapter. All the officers and servants appointed yearly by the chapter relinquish their charges to the community, giving up the keys, seals, and other insignia of their offices. On the sixth day after the Assumption, they read the ancient statutes in the presence of the canons, cantors, chaplains, *habitués*, and choirboys, who are all obliged to be present. He who presides over the chapter delivers an address about observance of the statutes and chastises those who have broken them. One may say that this chapter is one of the most rigorous in France, after Lyon, in punishing the faults of its members, both small and great. When someone has committed a considerable fault, he loses his right to the almuce, even if he be a priest, and during the Office he must stand bareheaded with the lower-formers for fifteen days and usually on a major feast. He receives no distribution during these days. I have seen this happen myself several times.

Here follow some disciplinary rules of the chapter of Rouen.

At the chapter of 1548, the statute that "all must shave their beards on the established days under penalty of a fine" was renewed, as well as the "prohibition against wearing shirts with fringes or lace at the collar and sleeves, and against wearing open-toed shoes decorated with velvet, or velvet shoes."

At the chapter of 1596, it was

> ordered that both canons and chaplains who are found wearing short cloaks or unworthy dress shall forfeit ten shillings to the fabric, under the charge of the Lord *Promoteur* who is responsible for exacting the said fine.

Renewing the ancient statutes of the chapter, chaplains were once again forbidden to wear short cloaks and to walk around the church during the divine service. Rather, they were required to wear becoming clothes worthy of their priestly dignity. The Lords Canon are forbidden to wear red robes of silk camlet, Ypres silk-rash, or any other sort of silk over their surplice. Rather, they shall only wear a robe of cloth or serge, under penalty of what punishment or fine soever the lords of the chapter should wish to impose.

The prebends of this church are not all the same. Most of them are noble fiefs[169] and the canons have the right of *Committimus* to the Chambre des Requêtes.[170] Many charters record donations made to this church of *hommes de corps* ("villains"), serfs of both sexes, franchises, immunities, *sauvegardes*, and protections, and the church of Rouen has taken great care to uphold these rights whenever occasion has warranted. Another of its rights is to administer the sacraments to all the canons, choristers, and servants of the chapter, in whatever part of town they might be, and to remove their bodies after death to prepare them for burial.[171]

Funerals, Obits, and the Thirty Canonesses of the Church of Rouen

We have spoken enough about the canons, their rights, and their offices; it is time to say a few words about their funerals. It usually takes place at four in the afternoon, when the clock sounds. The celebrant and deacon always wear alb, stole, and maniple, and the subdeacon alb and maniple. In summer, they cover their heads with birettas and wear the almuce over their arm; in winter, they cover their heads with the *aumusson* or fur-lined camail. All the cathedral clergy walk behind the processional cross and candle-bearers to escort the body from whatever part of the city it might be. The body is carried by four or six chaplains wearing albs and stoles on their necks if they are priests, while four canons hold the four corners of the funeral shroud or pall. The body is laid down in choir surrounded by silver candlesticks set with candles and large torches. They sing the three nocturns and Lauds of the Office of the Dead, then bury the body to the chanting of psalms and the other prayers and ceremonies prescribed by the ritual. The fact that the celebrant, deacon, and subdeacon wear alb, stole, and maniple is a sign that funerals were never conducted without the Sacrifice being offered in presence of the body. See what I have written with respect to Clermont on page 58 above.

There remains only to say a word about the obits. There are solemn obits with five copes, and lesser obits with three or two copes. Among the many solemn obits, I shall discuss only two that are noteworthy.

On the twenty-fifth day of each month, at the sound of the large Georges d'Amboise bell, they hold a solemn obit for this cardinal-archbishop of Rouen. What is noteworthy is that on the following day at Mass, at the *Memento* for the dead, the deacon says to the celebrant: *Memento*

---

[169] A fief that carried with it the right to administer high justice.
[170] The right to raise one's case in the first instance before the Chambre des Requêtes of Parlement, without needing to pass through the lower courts.
[171] In other words, the canons and their dependents were considered to belong legally to the cathedral parish, even when residing within the boundaries of one of the city parishes.

Cardinalis Georgii de Ambasia. This practice appears to be founded upon a statement made in the Apostolic Constitutions—which may date to the fourth century—in the forty-seventh chapter of book 8: *Postquam Diaconus absolvit orationem sic dixit: Pro quiescentibus in Christo fratribus nostris rogemus,*[172] as well as upon the ancient custom of reciting the diptychs in both the Greek and Latin churches.

There are three obits—on the feast of St. Maurus (15 January), the vigil of St. John the Baptist (23 June), and the Translation of St. Benedict (11 July)—that are attended by "thirty canonnesses" who participate in the offertory procession. This is the name given to thirty maidens or widows who possess prebends called the "thirty prebends of St. Romanus." It is believed that they used to wash and bleach the church cloths, and that the revenue of the prebends used to be greater. Today the revenue is not very sizable, and so the duties are not great either, consisting solely in assisting at these three obits. Their assistance begins in the evening at Vigils, and continues on the next day at high Mass, where they all join the offertory procession. The lords of the chapter give six pounds to those present, and the Lord Archbishop pays them the *gros* of their prebend. They receive their prebend from him, and are free to relinquish it to someone else. What makes their prebends more valuable is that, by virtue of the privileges of the lords of the chapter, in which they participate on this head, they have the right of *Committimus*, i.e., to have their cases taken up by the Chambre des Requêtes. Hence their prebends are sought after even by well-off persons more on account of this privilege than for the revenue, which is only a hundred shillings or six francs each.[173]

Archbishops of Rouen and Illustrious Persons

This renowned church has counted a number of illustrious personages in its ranks, including:

Three popes, namely Martin IV, Clement VI, and Gregory XI;

Twenty-seven cardinals, among them Jean Cholet, founder of the Collège des Cholets at Paris; the pious and learned Pierre d'Ailly, one of the foremost men of his age, chancellor of the University, grand almoner, confessor of King Charles VI of France, and lastly archbishop of Cambrai; Gilles Descamps, who was cardinal and bishop of Coutances; Prospero Colonna, who, after being named archdeacon of the Roman church, had the honor of crowning three popes; the two Cardinals Georges d'Amboise, archbishops of Rouen; François de Tournon, later archbishop of Lyon and lastly dean of the college of cardinals; and Antoine Sanguin Cardinal de Meudon, grand almoner of France, bishop of Orléans, and lastly archbishop of Toulouse;

---

[172] "After the deacon finished the prayer he said: 'Let us pray for our departed brothers in Christ.'"
[173] This paragraph is taken, at times word for word, from Pommeraye, *Histoire*, 561–62.

Around twenty-five archbishops or bishops, of which I shall omit the names of many quite famous ones, to mention only that the church of Rouen had as a canon Peter of Blois, who was quite well-known for his works. I have several proofs that he was a canon of Rouen among my papers, but it suffices to point out his Epistle 151 to Archbishop Walter, and his signature at the bottom of a written copy of a verbal process for a translation of the relics of St. Romanus that took place in 1179, where he signs with the deacons.

In the last century there have been many canons of this church illustrious for their piety and doctrine, among whom we must name M. Jean Le Prévost, treasurer of the cathedral of Rouen, whose services to the church of Rouen are too great for his name to be forgotten by posterity. Even today there are many who honor this church with their doctrine and piety. Their modesty prevents me from naming them here.

Few churches have maintained ecclesiastical discipline with as much vigor as the church of Rouen through its councils and synodal statutes, which are numerous and which have been collected in a volume *in quarto*.[174] Rouen has also been governed by very learned and illustrious prelates, among them twelve saints. The most well known are St. Mellonius, the apostle and first bishop of Rouen; St. Victricius, who raised the church of Rouen to a very high degree of piety; St. Romanus, patron of the city and the entire diocese; St. Audoen; St. Ansbert, who held a national council in 693 whose acts were written by a lector named Ragnomir; St. Remigius; St. Wenilo; St. Maurilius, who held many councils, finished the the cathedral of Rouen, and dedicated it; John of Bayeux, better known as John of Avranches, who dedicated his book on the Divine Offices[175] to his predecessor St. Maurilius and organized many important councils; William, dubbed Bonne-Âme, who held many councils and built the chapterhouse where he is buried at his own expense; Rothrod, who made peace between Archbishop St. Thomas of Canterbury and King Henry II of England; Walter; Robert Poulain; Maurice; Peter de Colmieu, who wrote so many beautiful synodal statutes and who founded the Collège d'Albane for ten cantors in the cathedral of Rouen; Odo Clement; Odo Rigaud, a Franciscan who did much to exalt the church of Rouen temporally and spiritually; William I of Flavacourt, who held many beautiful councils and did much good for the poor and for his church, establishing a foundation for the six cantors of the Collège du St-Esprit; Giles Aycelin, who instituted the feast of Corpus Christi in Rouen in 1317; Peter Roger, who later became pope Clement VI and who founded in Rouen the Collège des Clementins for sixteen cantors;[176] Raoul or Radulph Roussel, who held a famous council

---

[174] Pommeraye, *Concilia*.
[175] John of Avranches, *De officiis ecclesiasticis* (PL 147:27–116).
[176] For the papal bull establishing this college, see PL 147:215C–220C.

in 1445 that issued forty-one canons; Guillaume d'Estouteville and Georges I d'Amboise, who did much good for the church of Rouen and donated to it one of the largest church bells in France; and Georges II d'Amboise and Charles I de Bourbon who gave to the church of Rouen several vestments and two beautiful councils.

The Cathedral Sacristy, Fountain, and Hebdomadary's Chamber

In the sacristy on the right side the choir, one can see the reliquaries of the saints, which used to be far more numerous before the Huguenot pillaging, as well as pontifical and priestly vestments, notably the ones donated by William, king of England and duke of Normandy, and by Cardinal Georges d'Amboise. There are miters of great price adorned with gold, diamonds, and precious pearls; a crucifix and two silver-gilt chandeliers *en ovale*, some of the most beautiful in the world; and a trove of rich ancient vestments in every style, among them two old unclipped chasubles entirely rounded at the bottom and with a single opening at the top for the head. A white one is still used twice a year for chanting the Genealogies of Christmas and Epiphany; the other, violet, is used by the celebrant on the Saturdays of Easter and Pentecost during the prophecies, Tracts, and orations. All the other chasubles, even the modern ones, are very ample and cover the priest's arms entirely.

The ritual of Rouen orders the following concerning them:

> Sacrarum vestium ea forma servetur quam Patrum institutio et Cathedralis Ecclesiae veneranda praescribit antiquitas, videlicet ut casulae seu planetae in tantam hinc inde amplitudinem extendantur, ut brachia tota saltem obtegant; ideoque ex commoda et plicabili materia fiant, ut facile per fimbrias levari possint, nec celebrantem impediant.[177]

The tunicles are likewise sewn on the sides up to the waist, and under the arms to the wrists, like the costume of the burghers and gentry around Pau in the Béarn, and have embroidered bands or orphreys. There are also two old red copes with pointed hoods, which are used at first Vespers, Matins, and Mass of semidouble feasts of martyrs, as well as at the procession on solemn feasts before the high Mass. We know that this hood was once worn over the head.

Next to the sacristy, under the dome there is a fountain that supplies the water necessary for Masses and holy water, for hand washing before Mass, and for the use of the hebdomadary, who did not go out in public during

---

[177] *Sacerdotale seu Manuale ecclesiae Rothomagensis* (1640), xxxiii: "Sacred vestments should retain the form that our fathers' custom and the venerable antiquity of the cathedral church prescribe, namely the chasubles or *planetae* should be of such an amplitude all around that they cover at least the whole of the arms; and they should be of made of a material soft and flexible enough that they can be raised by the hem and not impede the celebrant."

his week, but, apart from the hours of the Office, remained in retreat day and night in a chamber which is to the right of this fountain, and which is today called the Cirerie. The chamber is linked to the common spaces now used for the necessities of nature, but used to be for his exclusive use, so that he could satisfy all his needs during his retreat. He was supplied with drink and food at the chapter's expense, but today he is given a cash payment of twenty-two pounds in addition to what he usually earns. There is a lavatory stone shaped like a trough with a hole on one side, where the corpses of the canons used to be washed, as in Lyon.

The Belfry, Great Portal, Towers, Parvis, and Fountain of Rouen Cathedral

Next one must go see the church's ten or twelve beautiful bells, so harmonious and so in tune, including the famous bell in the south tower called Georges d'Amboise, which can be heard eight leagues down the river. Outsiders who come to Rouen never miss a visit to it. It weighs between thirty-six to forty thousand pounds.

Curfew is sounded at half past three in the evening on Saturdays and Sundays, on public holidays, and the evenings prior. They ring a triple stroke three times for a total of nine rings and then a full peal for the space of a *Miserere*. On certain major feasts they play a very harmonious carillon. On the vigil of Epiphany between five and six in the evening they ring seventeen kinds of carillons. On other days only one bell is rung, larger or smaller depending on the rank of the feast being celebrated, with one exception: when the archbishop returns to Rouen after a period of absence, a bell larger than the feast requires is rung as a signal of his arrival.

In the chapterhouse of the cathedral is a large placard entitled *Déclaration de la Sonnerie ordinaire de l'Église de Notre-Dame de Rouen, ordonnée en Chapitre général l'an 1476* ("Declaration of the usual ringing of bells in the church of Notre-Dame of Rouen, established in the general chapter of 1476"), which contains two or three articles I think worthy of note, and that might help clarify some things that are no longer understood at present:

"On triple feasts the bell is not rung for the hour of Compline." Was it because it was not said on these days, as in Lyon? Or was it because the solemnity of the Office and sermon delayed Vespers on those days until around the hour for Compline, which was said immediately afterwards? One of the canons might tell us. If the latter explanation is the case, this is what led Compline and Vespers to be joined on all days of the year, for it is plain that in 1476 Compline was said separately from Vespers. The placard states:

> On every other feast, whether of three or nine lessons, or *per ferias*, between five and six in the evening a ringing called Complie is made, which must have forty strokes. It has two peals. The first, whether on a feria or feast of three or nine lessons, is played on

three bells: Marie, Robin de l'Huys, and one of the Saints Benoîts. The second peal plays immediately after the first without interval. If it is not a double feast, this peal is made with a single bell called Complie. If it is a double feast, one of the Saints Benoîts is rung together with Complie.

The ringing at half past six or seven in the evening we mentioned above was actually done closer to eight at that time, and still today the bells of Rouen are rung at eight on the evening before the Forty Hours devotion. The placard states: "The last ringing of the day is called the Curfew Ring (in Latin *Ignitegium*), and it is done at between seven and eight in the evening with only one bell, if there is no carillon, and must have six score strokes." This last ringing signaled the time for prayer and retiring, or ultimately the curfew to go to bed, such that no one was allowed to leave his house after this bell. I have learned this from canon 2 of an old council of the province of Normandy held in Caen in 1061: *Ut quotidie sero per signi pulsum ad preces Deo fundendas quisque invitaretur, atque occlusis foribus domorum ultra vagari amplius vetitum admoneretur.*[178] Indeed, it is not seemly for a true Christian to go out late into the street.

Inside the cathedral church of Rouen, near the west portal there is the parish church known as St-Étienne-la-Grand'Église, whose baptismal font is outside in the tower itself.[179]

Exterior of Rouen Cathedral

It is time to leave the cathedral and observe its exterior. First, there is the Gothic main portal on the west end, flanked by two smaller portals on its sides. All solemn entrances pass through the main portal, as well as the entrance of the public penitents on Maundy Thursday. It is not easy to describe this portal. The good number of statues that adorn it bear the hideous marks of the Calvinists' fury. Above it is a communicating gallery with a sort of balustrade and openwork parapet. Two canons in albs used to sing the responsory *Viri Galilaei, quid admiramini aspicientes in coelum* on Ascension day from this gallery when the solemn procession held at noon for the release of a prisoner, made its way back.[180] To this day a very old banner representing the release of the prisoner is suspended from this gallery on the three Rogation days and on Ascension. The passage between the towers goes through this gallery.

To the right of the main portal there is a very beautiful pierced steeple standing 230 feet high with a belfry that holds the famous Georges d'Amboise bell. This tower is called the Tour de beurre ("butter tower"), like

---

[178] "Let one and all be called to offer prayers to God every evening by the strike of a bell, and let the doors of their homes be closed and let them be advised that further wandering outside is prohibited."
[179] The Tour de beurre (see below).
[180] Cantus ID 007904.

in Bourges, because it was built with the tithes paid by the faithful for permission to consume butter and milk during Lent, which was granted by Pope Innocent VIII at the earnest pleas of the archbishop of Rouen, Cardinal Guillaume d'Estouteville, on the condition that the faithful give alms to the cathedral of Rouen. Hence butter and milk have been consumed during Lent in Rouen only in the past two hundred years. Today they are consumed by virtue of this same dispensation—which is announced during the *prône* at parish Masses—on the condition that each head of family donate five pennies to the cathedral fabric. The archbishop adds to this dispensation the permission to eat cheese, and both dispensations are announced on Quinquagesima Sunday. I remember that about thirty years ago the Lord Archbishop forgot to issue the dispensation for cheese on time, and no one dared to eat it during the first four days of Lent until the first Sunday, when it was finally announced. After these relaxations of the ancient severity of the Church's discipline, it is very wrong to complain about the rigors of Lent.

In front of the main portal there is a large nearly-square plaza called the Parvis or Aître de Notre-Dame, from the Latin word *atrium*. It is paved and enclosed by elbow-high walls, with two large stone crosses on both sides at the entrance and barriers at the four corners of the parvis to prevent carts or horses from entering. In the middle of this large square there is a beautiful fountain shaped like a tower, which spouts water from four sides through four pipes, filling up a very large stone basin, which is octagonal, if I remember correctly. These kinds of fountains were meant for washing one's hands and even rinsing one's mouth before going into the church, as we find in the works of St. Paulinus, St. John Chrysostom, Eusebius of Caesarea, and Baronius. I have even seen very well-dressed persons, both men and women, washing their hands and faces at this fountain before attending Matins at the cathedral on feast days. One can find such fountains with basins on the parvis and near the doors of most of France's old churches. There are many of them in Rouen near churches, and I have seen all of them in the past, noticing that men have preferred to let them fall into complete ruin rather than to repair them. Men used to wash their hands and faces or at least rinse their mouths at them, because one receives the Body of Jesus Christ through the mouth. Pagans themselves always took care to purify themselves before approaching their gods. It is said that this fountain used to be closer to the main portal. The holy water stoup that one finds today at church doors (and which should be outside the church, as in the Franciscan church in Étampes and the Dominican one in Le Mans) has replaced the use of these fountains. All that has remained of the ancient custom of washing one's hands and face is the practice of dipping a part of the hand in the stoup and thus washing a part of the right hand and the main parts of the face, such as the forehead and mouth. This is properly done when entering the church, but most men also have the habit of dipping in their hands when leaving, being struck more by the sight of the stoop itself rather than by the reasons for its use, which they often do not know, because the *curés* rarely take the trouble to instruct them.

From under the fountain, one must look up and see the beautiful 380-feet spire that rises over the cathedral.

In front of the south portal there is a square called the Place de la Calende or Calendre, which used to be a place of judicial immunity and asylum, which an old chapter register from 1504 calls *locus immunitatis ex antiquo*. It is marked by a large cross.

Hôtel-Dieu of Rouen

Next to this square stands the Hôtel-Dieu, whose church is under the patronage of St. Mary Magdalene. It is a regular priory with members appointed by the king, which has parish rights over certain houses, appointing ten or twelve *curés*, as well as high, middling, and low justice over about a hundred parishes. This priory has a double convent: one of fifteen to twenty canons regular who celebrate the divine service in the church and administer the sacrament of the sick, and the other of about thirty canonesses regular who minister to the sick. The kings of France and England have been very generous to this Hôtel-Dieu, having granted it 365 cartloads of wood to be taken from nearby forests, a complete exemption from levies on imported beverages and other taxes and contributions, and a hogshead of salt. King Charles V of France in particular did much good for this institution, and in thanksgiving every day at six in the evening, as soon as Compline is over, the celebrant says out loud: "Pious souls, pray to God for Charles V, king of France, and for our other benefactors." One of the cannonesses says the same words in the sick ward.

Saint-Ouen

The abbey church of St-Ouen is one of the largest and most beautiful in France. One cannot help admiring the craftsmanship and magnificence of the structure. It is 416 feet long counting the Lady Chapel. It is not as wide as one would like, only seventy-eight feet, including the two aisles, all paved with *liais* stone. It is one of the best lit churches in France, with three rows of large windows and three beautiful rose windows, one at the main west door and the two others at the sides of the crossing, which is 130 feet long. Above it stands the steeple, which is of very delicate craftsmanship. A gallery runs all around the interior of the church, with a beautiful elbow-high balustrade. A very beautiful stone screen closes off the choir, where there are two rows of stalls of beautiful woodwork. The main altar is quite simple, separated from the wall, with riddels on each side, a wooden balustrade, and four pillars surmounted by four angels, as in the cathedral. Above the retable there is the suspension for the holy pyx at the foot of the cross and two statues of Sts. Peter and Paul, the abbey's principal patrons, flanked by two or three candles on each side. In front of the main altar there are three lamps with three candles, as in the cathedral, and a large wax column in front of them where the Paschal candle is placed.

Before it was taken over by the reformed Congregation of St-Maur, the original monks here chanted the entire Office from memory as in the cathedral. A century or two ago these monks started to wear a biretta under the hood or cowl of their habit. This hat evolved from the ancient zucchetto.

To see the full beauty of the church's interior, one has to stand under the organ at the west portal; and to observe all the beauty of its exterior, one must view the portal and vestibule at the end of the south crossing, and then enter the cloister, which is very large: from here one can see the church in all its splendor.

In the aisle of the cloister next to the church are two rows of desks,[181] one of wood and the other of stone desks, built into the columns that support the vault. This is where the monks came together to study, read, and copy books. From here came the manuscripts found in the abbey libraries. There is still a large cupboard built into the wall to store the books under lock and key. The abbot did not dispense himself from these literary tasks. At the base of the stairway from the church to the cloister, one can still see his bench and wooden desk, which has a pediment or capital of sculpted wood.

The learned Émery Bigot de Sommesnil, whose friendship I have the honor of enjoying, tells me that he once saw in this monastery's archive a handwritten letter from St. Gregory the Great addressed "to the canons of St-Pierre of Rouen." Hence we must conclude that this church was first occupied by canons; or, if it was initially occupied by monks (a claim for which I believe there is no evidence), it was occupied, since the time of St. Gregory the Great — that is to say around sixty years after its foundation — by canons who replaced the original monks. The first hypothesis, however, seems to me the more probable, and is supported by the author of the Life of St. Clotilde, at the end of *Acta sanctorum Ordinis sancti Benedicti*, vol. 1, no. 13: *Ibi adgregavit non modicam congregationem Clericorum Deo servientium*.[182] Similar changes occurred at the abbeys of St-Saëns and of Fécamp, and others.

Next to the monastery gate is the abbatial palace which Antoine Bohier, abbot of St-Ouen and cardinal-archbishop of Bourges, built of ashlar and bricks.[183] It is here that kings, queens, princes, and princesses of the blood lodge when they come to Rouen.

---

[181] Author's note: These pulpits were removed several years ago.
[182] "Vita S. Chrothildis reginae Francorum" 13, in *Acta sanctorum Ordinis sancti Benedicti*, ed. Jean Mabillon (Paris, 1668), 1:102.
[183] Antoine Bohier (c. 1460–1519).

Saint-Amand

The abbey of St-Amand of Rouen (PLATE 53) belongs to the Benedictine order. The nuns, sometimes called *les Amies-Dieu de S. Leonard,* used to be consecrated by the bishop. Not a hundred years ago they still emerged from their cloister to participate in the Rogation processions with the entire clergy, as did the nuns of Vienne and elsewhere. They also came out on the feast of St. Leonard to sing the Office of his feast in a chapel near their monastery that belonged to them. Likewise, they went out for the burials of the abbots and priors of St-Ouen, Ste-Catherine-du-Mont, and later of St-Julien and St-Lô—all monasteries with which they were associated—and there sang the first nocturn of the Dead. Even today, upon the death of the abbess of St-Amand, the monks of the above-mentioned monasteries have the custom of going to the nunnery to each sing a nocturn of the Office of the Dead. The nuns then sing Lauds. They used to sing all the chants of Matins in full every day at two in the morning and fasted throughout the year, keeping that most rigorous silence which one might call the guardian of monastic discipline.

This monastery used to have deannesses (*doyennes* or *dixenières*) in accordance with the Rule of St. Benedict, but they were not called by that name. The first in rank was simply dubbed prioress and the others second- or perhaps sub-prioress, third-, and fourth-prioress. These last three were ranked only by the date of their reception.

Saint-Lô

St-Lô (*S. Laudus*) is a community of canons regular of the Augustinian order. The canons secular who used to minister to this church were replaced by canons regular in 1144. The canons here today belong to the Congregation of Ste-Geneviève, whose manner of life is so well known there is no need to discuss it here.

The former canons who preceded them wore an almuce of violet cloth lined with white fur over the arm during the summer, and in winter donned a long violet camail pointed at the bottom over their violet capes. They wore appareled albs at the altar.

I do not know when they began to use birettas and almuces. They are not mentioned in the ritual on the manner of receiving a novice written 180 years ago, which states rather that they wore a cassock, surplice, and cape or camail: *postea induatur cappa sive caputium* (PLATE 54).[184] In any case, there is proof their cape was black and not violet four hundred years ago. Novices wore secular clothing during their novitiate. The day they took the habit was also the day of their profession, and one ceremony followed the

---

[184] Le Brun des Marettes included an edition of this *Vetus ordo ad instituendum canonicum regularem in ecclesia S. Laudi Rotomagensis* in his edition of John of Avranches's *Liber de officiis ecclesiasticis;* see PL 147:153D–156D, at 155B.

other, or rather both were done in a single ceremony. They did not then wander from house to house, but promised stability in St-Lô, as is evident in the wording of their vows: *Ego frater N. offerens trado meipsum divinae pietati in Ecclesia beati Laudi serviturum secundum Regulam S. Augustini, et promitto obedientiam Domno N. Priori praefatae Ecclesiae, et successoribus ejus canonice intrantibus.*[185] This used to be the case almost everywhere.[186]

After an antiphon and an oration were said, the novice was admitted into the common society of the brethren and received the kiss of peace from each of them, beginning with the prior. Finally, after another oration the prior had them swear an oath to keep the rights of the church, the statutes of the order, and the secret of the chapter. Thus ended the whole ceremony.

These canons regular celebrated the Office of Rouen in conformity with the discipline of the Church set down by so many conciliar canons,[187] which ordered all the churches throughout a diocese, and even throughout a province to use the same books, the same chant, and the same ceremonies as the metropolitan church. I have therefore concluded we can shed some light on the rites of the church of Rouen from an old ordinary of the church of St-Lô.[188] It is four hundred years old, and so comes between the two I have mentioned above when discussing the cathedral of Rouen.

Here are the most salient points:

On the first Sunday of Advent, the cantor chanted St. Jerome's prologue to Isaias with the first lesson of Matins.

Before Terce on Sundays the hebdomadary priest blessed water; the celebrant sprinkled the altars and choir. Thereafter the procession went from the church into the cloister and held a station there while the celebrant accompanied by the stoup-bearer went to sprinkle all the rooms of the house with holy water, first the chapterhouse and then the dorter and the other regular places, as is more amply stated in their collectary: *Moveat Processio, et dicatur haec Antiphona,* Missus est. *Tunc eat Sacerdos cum bajulo aquae benedictae qui aspergat aquam per officinas, primo in Capitulo ubi dicat Orationem* Absolve quaesumus Domine, *deinde in*

---

[185] "I, Brother N., offer and entrust myself to divine piety in the church of St-Lô, to serve according to the Rule of St. Augustine, and promise obedience to the Lord N., prior of the aforesaid church, and to his canonically appointed successors." (PL 147:156A)

[186] By the eighteenth century many monastic and collegiate houses belonged to congregations. Members' vows of stability were made to the congregation rather than to an individual house. This arrangement, encouraged by the Councils of Basel and Constance as a response to the abuses of commendatory abbots, allowed religious to move among the houses of a congregation ruled by one abbot and a general chapter.

[187] Author's note: Concilium Venetense an. 465, can. 15; Epaonense an. 517, c. 27; Gerundense an. 517, c. 1; Bracarense II an. 563, c. 1; Toletanum IV an. 633, c. 2; Toletanum XI c. 3; Rotomagense an. 1189, c. 1.

[188] *Ordinarium canonicorum regularium S. Laudi Rotomagensis,* edited by Le Brun des Marettes in his edition of John of Avranches (PL 147:157A–192D). Aimé-Georges Martimort was unable to find any trace of the original manuscript (*La documentation liturgique,* 198).

Dormitorio &c. sicut in Collectario habentur. In statione Claustri &c.[189] When considering this together with the holy water aspersion as it is done on Sundays in the cathedrals of Lyon, Vienne, Le Mans, Chartres, and Rouen, one immediately realizes that the motive for the Sunday procession was to sprinkle the altar, regular places, and people, that the station was meant to give enough time for the celebrant to finish the aspersions, and that the responsory was sung to occupy the choir in the meantime, as I believe I have already said above.

The procession finished with a versicle and oration said at the steps of the sanctuary. From that same place the celebrant began Terce, and then he said Mass, which concluded with *Benedicamus Domino*. The table reader then immediately went up to the steps of the sanctuary to ask for his blessing with the same prayers recited by the order of St. Benedict.

During Advent, the deacon and subdeacon wore folded chasubles on ferias and Sundays. They removed and put them on at the same times and in the same manner as in the cathedral.

During the entirety of Advent they abstained from meat and animal fat, and also fasted until None, only eating once a day: *Per totum Adventum singulis diebus jejunamus, bis in omnibus Dominicis solummodo comedentes.*[190] They were allowed to eat eggs and cheese, although it seems this was merely a concession: *caseus et ova conceduntur.*[191] Below we shall see that these ancient canons performed even greater mortifications.

As in the cathedral, they had a wax-coated board upon which they wrote with a stylus the names of those who had to perform an office or function. Although the names were written down there and placed in a prominent spot, they were also read out at the end of chapter after the short lesson. Thereafter they read out the names of those who had died on that day, if there were any, and then said *Benedicite* and discussed the affairs of the order.

On the vigil of Christmas, they adorned the chapterhouse and assembled there after Prime. When the reader of the martyrology said the words *In Bethleem Judae Jesus Christus Filius Dei nascitur*, they prostrated themselves on the ground and each said a short private prayer of personal devotion. At the prior's signal, they got up and the reader continued. This custom is still kept in several monasteries. They then designated the celebrants for the three Masses of Christmas, which were each to be said by different priests. Each had a prophecy before the Epistle. They anticipated the Matins lessons and those who were to chant them were made to memorize

---

[189] "Let the procession set out, and this antiphon be said: *Missus est*. Then let the priest go with the holy-water bearer and sprinkle water throughout the rooms, first in the chapterhouse, where he shall say the oration *Absolve quaesumus Domine*, then in the dorter, and the rest as is stated in the collectary. At the station in the cloister, etc." (PL 147:158D).
[190] "We fast every day during all of Advent, only eating twice every Sunday" (PL 147:183C).
[191] PL 147:159B.

them, as in the cathedral, a practice we shall also see elsewhere: *Ut statim spatiatim et diligenter cuncta compleantur, statim post Capitulum Lectiones audiantur.*[192] The ritual of Rouen is clear, but who observes it?

Midnight Mass was sung at a lower tone than the Mass after Terce: *Ad hanc Missam submissius quam in crastino cantatur.*[193] It is evident that it was less solemn in its entirety, as I have noted above. All the candles in the church were lit on this day: the seven on the large seven-branched chandelier by the choir steps, the seven lamps between the choir and the altar, three candles in basins near the high altar, four candles near the crucifix, and one at each altar. The entire Office was said as in the cathedral, with the same prayers and the same rites, for these canons were too regular to disobey the discipline the Church set down in so many councils. They would have thought themselves quite irregular if they had done differently.

When the prior incensed the altars, chanted the Gospel and homily,[194] the short chapter, and the oration at major feasts, he was always flanked by two candle-bearers giving him light. The cantor presented him with the collectary or held it for him: *Cantore sibi de libro ministrante.*[195]

On major feasts there was a neum at all the antiphons,[196] the Introit was sung three times at the Mass,[197] and the body of the Gradual was repeated after the verse, as was done in Rouen not more than a century ago, and as is still done today in Lyon, Auxerre, in the Congregation of Cluny, and elsewhere; and the *Kyrie* with tropes. During the Creed, the subdeacon carried the Gospel book to be kissed by the clergy, the thurifer incensing it immediately before, and this remains the custom in Rouen today.

After Christmas Lauds they lit the lanterns and went to lie down in the dorter, if they wished, fully dressed. This was the only time they were allowed to go back to sleep after Lauds.

At the first glow of dawn, *summo diluculo*,[198] they rose to say the dawn Mass. Thereafter they went into the cloister, washed their hands, then each took a book and sat down to read. Meanwhile, those who were priests said their low or private Masses.

After Prime they held chapter, where they spoke of nothing but the love of God and the solemnity of the feast.

When this or another solemn feast fell on a Sunday, the hebdomadary blessed the holy water and began Terce. While this Office was chanted he went to sprinkle with holy water the rooms of the house in the customary

---

[192] "That everything might be done spaciously and diligently, let the lessons be heard immediately after Chapter" (PL 147:160B).
[193] PL 147:160B. Le Brun des Marettes incorrectly writes *Messe de la nuit*, whereas the passage refers to the Mass of the vigil of Christmas.
[194] The homily at the third nocturn.
[195] PL 147:161A.
[196] A melisma added at the end of the antiphon.
[197] That is, before and after the verse, and a final time after the *Gloria Patri*.
[198] PL 147:162B.

manner, then returned to choir to finish the Office of Terce. They all received communion at the Mass—as they did every Sunday—save those who abstained for some reasonable cause after having consulted the superior. When these solemn feasts fell on Sunday, the table-reader asked the blessing at the end of the morrow Mass.

They fasted on all Fridays of the year, but from Christmas to the Purification they ate twice a day, even on Fridays: *Per idem tempus quotidie bis comeditur, etiam Feria sexta de consuetudine approbata.*[199]

They ended the alleluia after None and did not sing it at Vespers of the Saturday before Septuagesima, as is still the custom in Angers, and this seems reasonable to me. For the first lesson of Matins on Septuagesima Sunday they read the Prologue of St. Jerome along with the beginning of Genesis, as they still do today in Paris.

Formerly they also held a procession every Wednesday and Friday of Lent, and on those days they kept silence in the cloister.

On Ash Wednesday after None they removed their shoes in choir, unless the prior dispensed them from doing so when the cold was too severe. Similarly, we read that St. Godfrey,[200] bishop of Amiens, always assisted at this ceremony in bare feet and dressed in a hairshirt. They all prostrated themselves during the seven penitential psalms. Then the prior, standing before the altar and having put on a stole, gave absolution. Thereafter the sacristan brought him ashes he had made from the previous year's branches, which he blessed and sprinkled. Then he gave his stole to the subprior, and received ashes and holy water from him: then he donned the stole once more, and imposed ashes on the subprior and all the others, whom the subprior sprinkled with holy water one by one after receiving ashes from the prior, as was done in the cathedral of Rouen and elsewhere.

On Ash Wednesday and during all of Lent on both Sundays and ferias, the deacon and subdeacon used folded chasubles. During the Epistle the canons put on their shoes. When the previous day was not a solemn feast or a Sunday, the celebrant began Vespers at the altar at the end of Mass. A short while after Vespers, the refectory bell was rung and they went to sup. *Post Vesperas facto brevi intervallo pulsetur cymbalum, et* EANT COENATUM. Note that it says "to sup" and not "to dine," since there was no dinner on fast days.

On the first Sunday of Lent after Compline the sacristan set up a large veil between the altar and the choir and covered the images. The same is noted in Lanfranc's statutes for the order of St. Benedict,[201] and in a 150-year-old Carmelite ordinary.

---

[199] PL 147:165B.
[200] "Vita S. Godefridi episcopi Ambianensis" 12, in Surius, ed., *De probatis Sanctorum historiis*, 6:207.
[201] Lanfranc, *Consuetudines* 20–22 (ed. and trans. David Knowles, *The Monastic Constitutions of Lanfranc* [Clarendon Press, 2002], 28–29).

Starting on the first Monday of Lent, at the beginning of the major hours each kissed his seat. They did the same at all the hours, both minor and major, on Holy Thursday, Good Friday, and Holy Saturday, and on all ferias of Lent during the Canon they lay prostrate or bent over their desks, *prostrati super formas.*

On Palm Sunday, because of the burden of the Office, and from Easter until the first day of October, they slept at midday after dinner, except on fasting days when they did not eat or sleep until after None. Upon rising they washed their hands in the lavatory that was in the cloister. During these six months whenever they sat in the cloister they were obliged to observe silence.

On Maundy Thursday and the following two days a hearse with twenty-four candles was placed before the altar. On these three days they observed an even stricter silence than usual.

On Maundy Thursday at noon the almoner led the paupers whose feet were to be washed into the cloister, and at the end of Sext the prior and all the canons took off their woolen capes and went into the cloister to wash the feet of the paupers. The prior washed the feet of four men and each of the other canons one, from which one can see that their number was not then fixed at twelve. After having washed their feet, they dried them with linen cloths and kissed them. Then they likewise poured water over their hands, and dried them with linens presented by the chamberlain. After they dried their own hands, the almoner gave each of them two coins for each pauper, and to the prior four for each of his four paupers. Both he and the other canons presented them to the paupers, kissing their hands. Then they went to the lavatory to wash their hands and don their capes once more. The paupers were led to the almonry, where each was given his prebend, which is to say a portion of food, and they were free to eat it there or to take it home. *Pauperes ducantur in Eleemosynariam, ubi data unicuique* PRAEBENDA, *in eorum arbitrio relinquitur vel ibi comedere, vel secum deportare.*[202]

After None the canons of St-Lô went to receive absolution from the archbishop or the bishop who officiated that day in his place. Note that they were subject to the archbishop. If neither one was present, the prior of St-Lô gave it to his religious at his residence after reciting the seven penitential psalms. Finally the bell was rung for Mass, which the prior celebrated. The deacon took care to put out as many hosts as needed for a general communion on that day and on Good Friday. I have already said above that the clergy and people of Rouen still received communion on Maundy Thursday not more than one hundred years ago. This practice was not only set down in the old 630-year-old ordinary of Rouen and in the ordinary we have been discussing here, but also in Beleth, chapter 99,[203]

---

[202] PL 147:170D.
[203] PL 202:103C, ed. Douteil, 182.

and in the capitularies of Bishop Theodulf of Orléans, who lived in the ninth century, chapter 41.[204]

No dispensations were granted from this general communion, at least for ecclesiastics and regulars. Besides what Beleth says in the chapter cited, the ordinary of our canons regular of St-Lô is quite explicit: *His quatuor diebus nullus se, nisi rationabili causa, a Communione debet subtrahere.*[205] We read the same in the statutes of Lanfranc for the order of St. Benedict.[206] The purpose is better to proclaim the death of Our Lord on the day it happened.

After Mass the celebrant gave the deacon the sacred hosts reserved for the next day wrapped in corporals atop the chalice for him to carry to the place prepared for them, and the prior incensed the tabernacle before and after putting them in. Then they returned to the altar to finish Vespers with the Postcommunion prayer, and the deacon said *Benedicamus Domino*, and not *Ite, missa est*, because as soon as the celebrant put aside his vestments, the altars were first washed with water, then wine was poured over them in the shape of a cross.

A little later the subprior struck the board at the door of the refectory to announce the meal. After grace, while the domestic and refectory servants ate, everything necessary to wash the feet of the canons was prepared in the chapterhouse. When the servants had gotten up from table, the cantor struck the board and all assembled in the chapterhouse. The prior took off his camail and cape, girded himself with an apron or (as the commoners say) a *devanteau*; poured water in a basin, and washed the feet of all the canons, drying and kissing them, as he had done with the paupers. Once all the religious had their feet washed, they prostrated and humbly kissed the ground. The subprior then washed the feet of the prior, and another senior canon washed the feet of the hebdomadary who had assisted the prior. After that the prior took the basin and poured water over everyone's hands, and the hebdomadary offered them a hand towel, and the prior kissed their hand. Then the subprior and his assistant did the same for the prior and the hebdomadary. After chanting the antiphon *Dominus Jesus*,[207] the versicle, and the oration, the deacon, vested in dalmatic, went back to the chapterhouse from the sacristy accompanied by the subdeacon in tunicle and two candle-bearers. As soon as he entered the whole community rose. Then the deacon, after having the incense blessed by the prior and received his blessing, went to the lectern and read in the lesson tone the Gospel *Ante diem festum Paschae*, that is, the discourse Our Lord made to his disciples at the Last Supper. When he came to the words *Surgite, eamus*

---

[204] Theodulf of Orléans, *Capitula* 41 (PL 105:204D).
[205] PL 147:170D.
[206] Lanfranc, *Consuetudines* 28–31, ed. and trans. Knowles, 46–47.
[207] Cantus ID 002413.

hinc, everyone rose and went two by two to the refectory. Once there the prior gave the signal and they said *Benedicite*, and the prior said: POTUM CARITATIS *benedicat dextera Dei Patris*.[208] Then the deacon began, *Ego sum vitis vera* and the rest, until the prior gave the sign for him to stop. Meanwhile, the prior gave each of the canons a cup to drink and kissed their hand, assisted by the refectorian, who poured wine into the cups: *Singulis manus osculans, potum caritatis offerat*. Then the subprior presented the cup to the prior, who finally gave the signal and said the versicle *Benedictus Deus in donis suis*. At that point, everyone returned to church and said Compline, while the deacon and his ministers went to the sacristy to fold their vestments and have a drink, after which they said Compline. After Compline, the canons were sprinkled with holy water and then went to bed.

On Good Friday Matins was said like the day previous, and they went back to bed after it. After getting up in the morning, they remained barefoot until all the hours of the Office had been said, that is, until around four or five in the afternoon. When the cold was too severe, the prior partially dispensed them, so that they only had to be barefoot during the Offices. On this day they recited the entire psalter in the cloister.

The hours of Terce, Sext, and None were not said one after another but separately as on the previous days: *Non continuatim, sed ut pridie divisim dicantur*.[209] I would add that the ritual of Rouen states that "in order to conform to the spirit and the intention of the Church, one must never say more than one canonical hour at a time, and each should be said at the time prescribed by the Church, or close to it."

After None, the prior, wearing an alb and purple chasuble, went barefoot with the deacon and subdeacon, both in albs, to the altar. There he said the *Pater* with the sign of the cross and went to sit while the lector began the first lesson or prophecy: *Praelatus casula purpurea induatur; qui cum Diacono et Subdiacono... nudis pedibus ad altare venit... dicto tamen Pater noster, et signans se, mox lectore incipiente primam lectionem, sessum eat*.[210] I cannot find at this point or anywhere else in the ordinary anything that obliges the celebrant to read the prophecy, Epistle, or Gospel at high Masses; he merely listened like everyone else. Almost all the ceremonies of the Mass and the adoration of the cross were done as in the cathedral. After the prior put on the shoes and chasuble he had removed for the adoration of the cross, he went with the deacon and subdeacon wearing albs, stole, and maniples, and preceded by the candle-bearers and thurifer to the place where they had put Our Lord's Body the day before. The prior incensed it and then gave it to the deacon for him to carry to the high altar, where he presented it to the celebrant. The deacon, meanwhile, put wine and water

---

[208] "May the right hand of God the Father bless the drink of charity."
[209] PL 147:173B.
[210] PL 147:173B,C.

into the chalice, and after the celebrant incensed it and washed his hands, he said the *Confiteor* with his ministers, followed by the *Pater noster* and *Libera nos quaesumus Domine*. Then he took a fragment of the host and put it into the chalice. He and the others received communion in silence. The ordinary reads: *Sumat de Sancto et ponat in calice, nihil dicens, sicque se et caeteros cum silentio communicet; sanctificatur enim vinum non consecratum per Corpus Domini immissum.*[211]

After Mass they said Vespers, then went to wash their feet and warm themselves. Within a short space of time the tablet was sounded for supper. They went to the refectory and ate bread and raw herbs and drank water: *In mensa nonnisi panis et aqua, et herbae crudae apponantur.*[212] We have seen above that the cathedral canons were even more austere two hundred years earlier, for on that day their meal consisted of bread and water only: *ad refectorium panis et aquae pergant*. The usual meals of the canons of St-Lô were still prepared and cooked on that day, but they were taken from the kitchen to the almonry, where they were given to the poor with their usual drink.

Because the Office of the following day, Holy Saturday, was said later than usual — as in the cathedral, as I have mentioned above — and that led to fatigue, on Friday evening they were allowed to have a drink in the refectory: *Quia vero officium in crastino die solito tardius agendum est, propter laborem post collationem in refectorio* POTUM CARITATIS *omnes accipiant.*[213] M. de Vert explains the meaning of these two words in his treatise on the words "Mass" and "communion."[214] Compline was said just as on the preceding day.

On Holy Saturday, the entire night Office was done as on the previous two days. Immediately after chapter they went to be shaved, *et in lectis interim singulorum munda et nova mutatoria ponantur a Camerario.*[215] The entire church was adorned. After Sext they anticipated the lessons, to avoid making mistakes, and covered the altars. After None they removed their capes and put on white surplices, with a hood, if needed. The prior, wearing a silk cope, blessed the new fire in the usual place, sprinkling it with holy water. Then they filled up the thurible with coals from the new fire. The sacristan lit the candle atop the reed he carried with the new fire as well as a candle placed inside a lantern, so as to be able to relight the candle on the reed if it went out. Fires had already been extinguished in all the rooms of the house, and they were relit with the new fire: *in omnibus quoque officinis, extincto veteri igne, novus ab aliquibus deportetur.*[216] Finally, when the procession re-entered the choir, the celebrant blessed the incense. The prior, who was the celebrant, went to his place in choir while the

---

[211] PL 147:175A.
[212] PL 147:175C.
[213] PL 147:175C.
[214] See de Vert, *Dissertation sur les mots*, 123–24.
[215] "And meanwhile the chamberlain puts out clean new clothes for each" (PL 147:175D).
[216] PL 147:176B.

subdeacon went to the last place in choir, and meanwhile the deacon sang the *Exultet* for the blessing of the Paschal candle, on which the sacristan had placed the five grains of incense before the Office began.

After the blessing of the candle, the celebrant, wearing a less distinguished chasuble, went up to the altar with the deacon and subdeacon and, having said the *Pater noster* and kissed the altar, returned to his seat. In the meantime the prophecies were read: *Statim prima Lectio incipiatur,* In principio fecit Deus: *tunc et Praelatus indutus una de mediocribus planetis cum Diacono et Subdiacono ad Altare procedens, praemisso* Pater noster, *et osculato Altari, cum suis ministris sedeat.*[217] Thus it is clear that he sat like everyone else and did not read the choir's part at the altar. Finally, the three litanies were said and the font was blessed as in the cathedral. The deacon carried the holy chrism to the font. Before pouring the holy chrism into the baptismal font, they removed some holy water for the aspersions of the altars, the clergy, and the rooms of the house the next day, as well as to allow the faithful to carry some to their homes, both to sprinkle them and to use in case of extreme necessity to baptize some new-born infant, whether in the house or on the way to the church. This is the water that people ought to carry to church in an ewer for the baptism ceremonies, or at least natural water, not rose water, which cannot be used to baptize the infant on the way in case of necessity because it is distilled and not natural.[218] I thought it necessary to mention this in passing, seeing that few parish priests instruct their parishioners on the matter.

Lastly, the baptismal font was covered with a white linen cloth shaped like a canopy, and this is still done in several of our country parishes. At the end of the third litany the sacristan lit all the candles in the church from the new fire, *quia omnis anterior ignis debet esse extinctus.*[219]

At Mass, the cantor intoned the *Gloria in excelsis* for the prior, and while it was sung all the bells were rung. Everyone received communion at this Mass.

At the *Sanctus*, they rang the bell for Vespers. Mass and Vespers ended with the *Ite, missa est: Dicto* Ite, missa est *a Diacono, Missa et Vesperae pariter finiantur. Post haec egressus de Ecclesia.*[220] That is, they left the church as soon as the *Ite, missa est* was said. They did not read the Gospel *In principio*.

Following a short space of time, they rang the refectory bell.

After Compline, the canons were sprinkled with holy water and went to bed. The custom of saying Matins right before bed had not yet arisen; the day concluded with Compline, hence its name. These are the proper prayers for bedtime, as anyone who knows Latin can easily see.

All the Easter Offices were done as in the cathedral.

---

[217] PL 147:176C,D.
[218] As mentioned in the *Rituel de la province de Reims* (Paris, 1677), 9.
[219] "because all earlier fire should be extinguished" (PL 147:177B,C).
[220] PL 147:177D.

The Sunday we call *in albis*—with *depositis* understood—is here called *Dominica post albas*,[221] just as in the *Ordo Romanus* and by the aforementioned Alcuin.[222] This is its more proper name.

On the Rogation days, they all wore their black wool capes for the procession, except those who carried something. After Sext, the prior sprinkled the high altar and the entire clergy before the procession. This procession went to the cathedral, where the canons sat on the left side of the choir, as they still do today.

On the day before the Ascension, Pentecost, the Annunciation, and the feasts of their patrons St. Augustine and St. Laud, they said Vespers with the ferial psalms. This was also the case in Rouen and nearly everywhere else 120 years ago.

The ordinary does not mention Corpus Christi, because it had not yet been instituted when it was written.

They never fasted on feast days except during Advent and Lent. When the feast of St. Laud (kept on the same day as the feast of St. Matthew) fell on Ember Wednesday, Friday, or Saturday, they did not fast, on account of the feast, but rather anticipated these three fasting days in the preceding week. The ordinary states: *Notandum si Festum sancti Laudi Feria IV vel V vel Sabbato venerit, fiat jejunium Quatuor temporum in hebdomada praecedenti.*[223] These men knew that the Church's discipline could not countenance fasting on feast days. The reformed canons currently in St-Lô still do not fast on holy days of obligation that fall on a Friday, moving the fast to the following day. In the same spirit, the inhabitants of the town of St-Quentin in Vermandois do not fast on the feast of their patron St. Quentin, held the day before All Saints, but instead anticipate the fast by one day, on which they fast for the vigils of both their patron and all the saints. This is done with the approbation of the Holy See.

Notre-Dame-de-la-Ronde

The church of Notre-Dame-de-la-Ronde, *Sanctae Mariae de Rotunda*, belongs to canons whose dean is the head of the chapter and *curé* of the parish. On major feasts and certain privileged Sundays the dean celebrates a single high Mass for both the parishioners and lords of the chapters who assist. On Sundays and feasts, ten or twelve priests of the parish also join the canons in singing the Office. In the middle of their choir, there is a brass angel as tall as a man, of the finest craftsmanship one can see, and whose front and back serve as a double lectern. It is worth seeing, as is the statue of the Virgin at the church's main portal; it is well-regarded by sculptors

---

[221] PL 147:179B.
[222] Pseudo-Alcuin, *De divinis officiis* 20, 21 (PL 101:1223A, 1224D). It is not so called in the *ordines*.
[223] PL 147:188D.

who never fail to show it to sculptors visiting from foreign lands, both because of its beauty and because of the size of the stone, which forms one body with the pillar.

The layout of this church has changed at least three or four times, both with respect to the body of the nave and with respect to the high altar. I am disinclined to amuse myself by explaining these changes, but will only say that originally the Blessed Sacrament was reserved for the Viaticum of the dying in a small aumbry built into a pillar on the Gospel side under a statute of the Virgin, just as it is today in the church of St-Candé-le-Vieux. At Notre-Dame-de-la-Ronde, the Sacrament is still kept there on Maundy Thursday and Good Friday, because it was once kept there all year round. Later, the Sacrament was placed above the retable in a glass lantern adorned with gilded woodwork. Finally, when all taste for antiquity was gone, it was placed in a tabernacle on the altar.

On Maundy Thursday afternoon, the canons and other clerics hold an agape in one of the chapels, and their drinks are served in old silver cups. In Lent, a large violet curtain is stretched across the choir, and on Easter they put up a large wax Paschal candle, as in the cathedral.

On major feasts they put the processional cross on the altar when the procession returned, as written in the eleventh *Ordo Romanus*.[224] This is the origin of the custom found in many churches of placing it next to the altar.

There is a unique and very ancient custom in this church, namely that at funeral Masses a large round white bread is brought up in the offertory procession in a large silver basin, together with wine in a silver vase. These are placed on the sides of the altar[225] because they used to be used as the matter for the sacrifice. They ought to use this wine, as is done elsewhere.

Saint-Georges

In the collegiate church of St-Georges there are only four canons who pay wages to four chaplains to sing the Office. There is nothing worth noting except that during Lent they say Vespers in the afternoon at the same time as in other parts of the year, not altering their schedule. At least they make only one major fault, not two.

The Filles-Dieu

The Filles-Dieu ("daughters of God") who today are canonesses regular of St. Augustine used to be simply women who lived off the work of their hands, observing a few modest rules they prescribed for themselves. On Sundays and feasts they went to the high Mass celebrated at their parish church of St-Eloi, receiving the sacraments from the hands of their *curé* just

---

[224] Le Brun des Marettes cites Mabillon's note to *Ordo Romanus* 11.10 (PL 74:1030C).
[225] Author's note: I saw this done myself, but I have recently learned they stopped doing it a few years ago.

like the other parishioners. Their way of life was such that in 1345 Clement VI allowed them to take the veil under the rule of St. Augustine. The grand vicar of Rouen granted them a white habit and black veil (PLATE 55). Some sixty years ago they placed themselves under the direction of certain Benedictine monks, and so abandoned their white habit for the black one they still wear today. Above it they don a long black mantle bordered with ermine. Although they have abandoned their original habit, they have not forsaken their original spirit. They have always kept the custom of singing the Divine Office in their parish according to the use of Rouen, which they followed from the very beginning, and so these religious use the same books as the other ecclesiastics of the diocese.

Saint-Vincent

In my youth, I saw the Blessed Sacrament reserved for the sick in the church of St-Vincent in an aumbry built into a pillar on the Gospel side, just as mentioned above. Later they abandoned this ancient practice and, following the modern fashion, placed it in a tabernacle on the altar. At funeral Masses they put the large white bread and the wine brought up in the offertory procession onto the altar on each side.

Saint-André

A bit beyond stands the parish church of St-André, where on Easter day the holy table, which is as wide as the choir, is entirely covered by a white tester of the same length, as I have also seen in some country parishes in Normandy. Moreover, an acolyte, when there is no deacon, holds a cup filled with wine and walks immediately behind the priest as he gives out communion, presenting the wine to each communicant after they receive the host, apparently in place of the species of the Blood. See what M. de Vert writes on the words "Mass" and "communion," on page 292 of his treatise. This is still observed at ordination Masses and at pontifical Masses in the cathedral parish for the clergy and people who receive communion. In this church of St-André in Rouen, at funeral Masses they take the wine that is brought up during the offertory in an ewer, and pour it into the chalice.[226] This makes good sense, since that is the reason it is offered.

Saint-Étienne-des-Tonneliers

The parish church of St-Étienne-des-Tonneliers ("of the coopers") is one of the best-kept in town, and has five altars with *piscinae* beside them. The Divine Office is celebrated very well here. I have never seen a more disinterested clergy: they never demand any money for funerals or for the administration of the sacraments. For thirty years now I have seen the poor buried here just like the rich, with the processional cross, candles, and silver

---

[226] Author's note: This practice has fallen into neglect in the last few years.

holy water stoup, copes, with the three nocturns and Lauds of the Office of the Dead sung in plainchant, and with a high Mass for the Dead that the *curé* celebrated gratis, even when the deceased was a stranger or passer-by.

At funeral Masses, although they do not leave the bread and wine on the altar after the offertory procession, they do at least leave them on the balusters of the altar until after communion, and I have seen them sometimes use the wine presented in the offertory procession, pouring it into the chalice for the sacrifice. There are a good number of endowed chantries in this church, at which following a venerable devotion they still distribute twenty, thirty, or forty shillings' worth of bread to the poor of the parish, who assist at the obit kneeling on the deceased man's tomb, praying to God for him. In an old chantry foundation of this church dating from 1374, I find that a certain Peronelle, widow of the late Mahieu Cherisier, donated twenty-two shillings[227] of land rent "to have a share in the prayers of the Church." Thus were all the ancient chantry foundations performed. We shall see this again elsewhere.

In this church the subdeacon puts the tray with the offertory money next to the corporal. They do not sing anything at the elevations of the host and chalice, adoring Jesus Christ in silence, following the Church's ancient practice. During the people's communion, which takes place immediately after the priest's, they sing a psalm verse after the Communion antiphon on major feasts when the communicants are more numerous. This was the custom in the church of Africa according to St. Augustine in book 2, chapter 11 of his *Retractationes*. Apparently it was also done in the Gallican church; at least St. Aurelianus, bishop of Arles, ordains it at the end of his rule.[228]

At the sides of the high altar there are two large riddels as in the cathedral. In Lent, a large violet veil the width of the choir is stretched between the choir and altar. The chasubles they use for Mass at the high altar are the most ample in all Rouen, after those of the cathedral. The interior of the lid of the baptismal font is one of the most delicate works of sculpture one can find. During the octave of Easter, it remains open. On the vault above the baptistry there is a depiction of the baptism of Emperor Constantine. One must not forget that here the Blessed Sacrament used to be reserved for the sick not at the altar, but in a small aumbry on the Gospel side near a statue of St. Stephen, where one can still see its hinges.

Saint-Candé-le-Vieux

In the collegiate and parish church of St-Candé-le-Vieux there are only four canons who are *curés*, performing their duties in alternation, each one taking a week, assisted by ten or twelve *prêtres habitués*. These four

---

[227] Author's note: A very large sum at the time.
[228] St. Aurelianus of Arles, *Regula ad monachos*, "Ordo etiam quo psallere debeatis" (PL 68:396B).

canons used to be the chaplains of the duke of Normandy, who entered this church, which was his chapel, from his Palais de la Vieille Tour through a gallery that crossed the road. The gallery was destroyed in 1508 by order of the exchequer. These four canons-*curé* have the honor of having as their perpetual dean the bishop of Lisieux, who has the right of exemption over this parish and four others, three of them between a half league to a league from the city on the opposite side of the river. The investigation of the crime of heresy in these parishes is reserved to him, as well as the reception of the oaths of obedience of the abbots and abbesses, who by law are under the jurisdiction of the archbishop of Rouen. One peculiar thing about this church is that the Blessed Sacrament,[229] following the ancient custom, is not at the high altar but off to the side in an aumbry built into a pillar on the Gospel side. This shows that these lords have affection and love for the ancient discipline of the Church, and they shall be always commendable for holding out alone against modern custom. In Rome the Blessed Sacrament is not at the altar either. Recall that in the seven collegiate churches of Angers the Blessed Sacrament for the use of the sick and the parishioners is also kept in an aumbry (which they call *le Sacraire*) built into the wall on the Gospel side. It is reserved in the same place in many churches of the East, as we learn from several accounts. The fact that it is so reserved also in the cathedral of Rouen, in the churches of Notre-Dame-de-la-Ronde, St-Vincent, and St-Étienne-des-Tonneliers, as well as here, makes me think that this was formerly the general practice of the Church.

The Vieille Tour where the Prisoner Lifts the Feretory

From this church, passing through the Harangerie where the salted fish merchants are, one passes under an arcade amidst the Halles,[230] which are all open on Friday. Near the Halles, in the so-called Place de la Vieille Tour, is a sort of square pierced tower atop an elevated platform, where on Ascension day a prisoner lifts the feretory of St. Romanus and receives absolution for his crimes. This ceremony can be seen from a very large square ringed by the Halles. The Halles used to be the large halls and other rooms of the palace of the dukes of Normandy. In the middle of this Place de la Vieille Tour there is a fountain which shoots water through three spouts into a stone basin in the shape of an equilateral triangle. The fountain, also in the shape of a pyramid, has a statue of Alexander the Great on top in all his accouterments.

Saint-Maclou

The parish church of St-Maclou is so beautifully built both inside and outside that foreigners have had it portrayed in intaglio prints sold in Rome.

---

[229] Author's note: According to the Carmelite ordinary it must be incensed before the high altar.
[230] A large emporium of shops.

The nave is seventy feet long, the choir forty feet, and the Lady Chapel thirty feet. Thus the church itself is 140 feet long and sixty-five feet wide. The height of the lantern tower above the great rood is 124 feet. Still fifteen feet higher are the eight bells, which are the most tuneful in Rouen: on solemn feasts, at the first ring for the main Offices plays the entire hymn that is to be sung in that Office. The rest of the bell tower, which ends in a spire, is some hundred feet higher, for a total height of 240 feet. It is so artfully crafted that one can go up to the cross from the outside without the use of ladders or scaffolding. There are galleries all around the nave and the choir, which is enclosed by a rood screen and a high balustrade.

This parish is very large and densely populated, counting some 18,000 communicants. The *curé* has his seat in the sanctuary, as in St-Vivien. There is also a vicar and four sub-vicars, each having a quartier where he administers the sacraments. In addition, there are almost a hundred clerics. There used to be a *musique* not long ago, as in two other parishes of this city. The church of St-Maclou leads the city's parish clergy in general processions. It also keeps the holy oils, which it distributes to all the other parishes of the diocese. They say that this is the reason why on both sides of the cross that crowns its main portal there are two vases supported by two iron bars. The doors of this church are masterpieces of architecture and sculpture, bearing representations of various mysteries of our religion. The main portal has a very beautiful porch. This church has two foundations which are quite remarkable and which, having certain peculiarities, deserve to be mentioned here. One is a donation of a house "to have a share in the prayers of the Church." See the similar foundation in the church of St-Étienne-des-Tonneliers above. The second foundation is for the bread and wine needed for the celebration of all future Masses said in this church of St-Maclou. For this purpose Jean Donchin and his wife Agnès donated a house which hangs the sign of the Cup on the Rue des Savetiers. The renters of this house furnish the bread and wine every day, and pay in addition a sum to the treasurers of St. Maclou. There is yet a third chantry with something worth mentioning: it is a chapel dedicated to St. John the Baptist in 1248 by the knight François Montauberger in thanksgiving for having been baptized there.

Saint-Godard

The church of St-Godard, whose clergy is made up of about a hundred clerics, is more or less as large as that of St-Maclou. It was formerly outside the city and was called Notre-Dame. But after Archbishop St. Godard of Rouen, in Latin *S. Gildardus*, was buried and performed many miracles there, the church was named after this holy prelate. Archbishop St. Romanus of Rouen, patron of the city and the diocese, was also buried in this church in a subterranean crypt found in the left aisle beside the choir. His body was transferred there towards the end of the eleventh century, but his tomb remained, and by a singular felicity it escaped the fury of the Calvinists when they pillaged our churches. It is made of a single jasper stone seven and a half feet long (as a priest-sacristan of this church assures me), two feet and two inches wide, and ten feet and four inches long. It is placed on two stones that raise it two feet from the ground. It is in this church that they hold the procession of the Holy Body on Palm Sunday, whereof I have spoken above.

Its stained glass windows are held in high regard for their craftmanship and colors, which are exceedingly lively and dazzling. Skillful painters say that the first window in the chapel of St. Nicholas, donated by Richard Le Caron, Sieur de Fossey, is the most beautiful in Rouen.

Within the territory of this parish, near the Jesuit College, stands the Seminaire de Joyeuse founded by Cardinal de Joyeuse, archbishop of Rouen, for thirty poor scholar-clerks who wear violet cassocks because at the time of its foundation clerics wore violet.

Saint-Laurent

Exiting by the south door and crossing the cemetery, one enters the church of St-Laurent. The learned Émery Bigot is buried in the left side of the choir at the foot of the sanctuary baluster in front of the chapel of the Lord Jean Bigot, president of the Parlement of Rouen.

Saint-Gervais

The parish church of St-Gervais stands outside the Porte Cauchoise. In front of its great rood one descends a staircase to enter into a crypt where St. Mellonius, the first archbishop of Rouen, is buried. This was formerly a cemetery on which the church was later built, and this should not be surprising, for the Roman laws which governed Rouen at the time did not allow burials within city limits. Besides the constant tradition that the city's ancient communal cemetery was located here, when excavations were made behind this church on the mountainside in order to build a wall to enclose the cemetery on that side, entire vaults and cellars were found. And when graves were being dug to bury the dead some thirty-five or forty years ago, three very ancient stone sarcophagi were discovered which I have seen myself. One of them had an inscription of four or five Latin words in uncial script and was of about the same size as the urns in the cemetery of St-Julien in Angers. Finally, it is located beside two important roads, like all ancient cemeteries.

Saint-Sauveur

In the parish church of St-Sauveur, a large violet curtain is hung across the choir near the balusters of the altar during Lent, and on Easter a large wax Paschal candle is put up as in the cathedral. On Good Friday during the Passion reading, a small *chœur de musique* sings the words of the Jews, as in the cathedral of Angers.

Saint-Herbland

In the parish church of St-Herbland, near the parvis of the cathedral, on solemn feasts the cope-bearers not only circulate around in the choir but also in the nave,to direct and support the chant as well as to quiet any chatterers. There I have also seen all the people incensed, as well as the clergy, which is to say that the entire church was perfumed.

The Prône *and Administration of Baptism*

In the whole diocese of Rouen the *prône*, the Gospel reading in French, and its explication are done immediately after the deacon has chanted the Gospel, which is the natural place for it. In the *prône* the *curé* commends all the needs of the Church to the parishioners. They are urged to pray for men in all stations, for the pope, for the diocesan bishop, for the king, for the royal house, for all members of the parish, and finally for all orthodox Christians both living and deceased. To that end two psalms and a few prayers are said in the *prône*. It was not always done this way. These same intentions were indeed commended, but they were prayed for in the Canon of the Mass at the *Te igitur* and the two *Memento* prayers, and that is their natural place, where the priest and deacon still say them today. A very old priest of Rouen has also assured me that he has seen some very old rituals where the *prône* did not include prayers. I have two old rituals where all these things are found in the *Memento*.

The ritual of Rouen recommends that except in danger of death infants should wait for baptism until Holy Week, in order to be solemnly baptized on Holy Saturday immediately after the blessing of the font. I have seen it done several times in Orléans, as ordered in that church's ritual.

As soon as the baptismal ceremonies are complete the infants are brought to the high altar because they used to receive the Eucharist there,[231] and only one or two centuries ago they still received a few drops of blessed wine in many dioceses. Then the priest says the Gospel *In principio erat Verbum*. One thing that might confirm what I have just said is that the present ritual of Rouen states after the baptism of adults, that if the Lord Archbishop is present, the neophyte is to be confirmed right away, and that if thereafter it is time to say Mass, the neophyte shall be present and receive communion.[232] Consult what I said on this subject above in Vienne, pp. 23–24.

---

[231] Le Brun des Marettes cites St. Ambrose, *De mysteriis* 8 (PL 16:403B), ed. Otto Faller, Corpus Scriptorum Ecclesiasticorum Latinorum 73 (Hoelder-Pichler-Tempsky, 1955), 107, and St. Paulinus of Nola, *Epistula* 32.5, ed. Le Brun des Marettes, 1:202; ed. von Hartel, 280.
[232] See *Sacerdotale seu Manuale ecclesiae Rothomagensis* (Rouen, 1640), 52.

Marriage and Agapes in the Churches of Rouen

At the end of the nuptial Mass, the priest—following the prescriptions of the missal and ritual of Rouen—delivers an exhortation to the newly-weds on the fidelity they owe to one another and on the continence they must observe on days of prayer and fasting and on major feasts. That is why marriages are not celebrated during Lent or Advent, which was formerly a season of fasting, nor on the feasts of Christmas, Epiphany, or Easter, nor even from the fifth Sunday after Easter until after the Octave of Pentecost in some dioceses, as can be seen in several rituals. This is in conformity with what St. Paul says in chapter seven of his First Epistle to the Corinthians. This is not particular to the church of Rouen: I have seen many missals and rituals from different churches, including from Rome, both from the past century and the present, and this rule is contained in all of them.

In Rouen and in the diocese, after this exhortation the priest blesses a loaf of white bread and wine. Then he presents (or has the priest-sacristan present) to the newly-wedded husband and wife some bread dipped in wine as a sign of their union, and as a symbol love and of conjugal life: *conjugalis convictus symbolum sponso et sponsae panem distribuat vino intinctum*, says the ritual of Rouen.[233] After this, the parents and especially the children also eat some of this blessed bread dipped in wine, which is a remnant of the agapes of charity and unity.

It is also a pious custom in this diocese to bless the bridal bed in the afternoon or evening in the presence of the newly-weds. The priest, vested in surplice and stole and accompanied by his sacristan, sprinkles holy water upon the bridal bed and the newly-weds saying *Asperges me* and then the oration *Visitet Dominus habitationem istam* from Compline, albeit in the third person; psalm 127 *Beati omnes qui timent Dominum*, which is so fitting for this ceremony; then *Kyrie eleison* and *Pater* with two orations, the latter of which is:

> Benedicat Deus corpora vestra et animas vestras, et det super vos benedictionem suam, sicut benedixit Abraham, Isaac et Jacob: manus Domini sancta sit super vos, mittatque Angelum suum qui custodiat vos omnibus diebus vitae vestrae. Per Christum Dominum nostrum. ℟. Amen.[234]

Then he blesses bread and wine and offers the newly-weds some bread dipped in wine, as at the end of the nuptial Mass.

In all the parishes of Rouen on Easter day, after Mass, in the middle or towards the back of the church's nave an agape of large wafers about

---

[233] *Sacerdotale seu Manuale ecclesiae Rothomagensis* (Rouen, 1640), 136.
[234] "May God bless your bodies and souls, and give his blessing over you, like he blessed Abraham, Isaac, and Jacob; may the Lord's holy hand be over you, and may he send his angel to guard you all the days of your life. Through Christ Our Lord. ℟. Amen" (*Sacerdotale seu Manuale ecclesiae Rothomagensis* [Rouen, 1640]), 138.

the size of both hands and as thick as a farthing is distributed to the faithful, along with a cup of wine and a napkin to wipe the mouth after drinking. But since people in Rouen are not accustomed to drinking wine, few actually consume it. This agape that has been preserved on Easter day used to be practiced on all major feasts, as we read in the Life of St. Ansbert, archbishop of Rouen, who "gave the people an agape in his church after communion on solemn days and served at the table himself, particularly the poor."[235] Since the obligation to receive communion has been reduced to Easter day alone, the agapes have been retained only on that day. This is apparently what John Beleth calls the *parvum prandiolum*, a small luncheon before the meal or main dinner.[236]

In Rouen, the six Saturdays after Christmas are flesh days, which is a survival of the ancient custom of this province of eating meat on Saturdays.[237] It is well known that in Spain they eat trotters and offal on all Saturdays of the year. The Rule of the Venerable Peter de Honestis states that Saturdays in Eastertide are flesh days,[238] and the same was the case in Metz in the eighth century, according to M. Châtelain.

Some Practices of the Church of Rouen

The missal of Rouen also orders (p. 109) that the aspersion of the people with holy water should take place at the Sunday procession, both in the nave and around the church, by one or two acolytes walking immediately in front of the processional cross: *Sacerdos celebraturus aspergit in Choro tantum, deinde unus vel duo Acolythi praecedentes Crucem processionalem, hinc inde aspergunt populum in navi et per circuitum Ecclesiae.* Note that this procession's purpose is to make the aspersion.

On Sundays in Rouen, blessed bread is eaten in the church as a supplement to communion, and some small pieces are taken home as a eulogia for those who could not attend Mass. The ritual and missal prescribe that

---

[235] Ansgrad, "Vita S. Ansberti episcopi Rotomagensis" 24, ed. Mabillon, *Acta sanctorum Ordinis sancti Benedicti* (Paris, 1669), 2:1055–56; numbered 16 in Bruno Krusch and Wilhelm Levison, eds., MGH SS. rer. Merov. 5, 629–30.

[236] Beleth, *Summa*, 119, ed. Douteil, 221. Cf. the remarks of Jean Mabillon, "Traité de la Messe," in *Ouvrages posthumes de D. Jean Mabillon et de D. Thierri Ruinart* (Paris, 1725), 2:284.

[237] Abstinence on Saturday, recommended in antiquity, was made obligatory by St. Gregory VII in the 1078 canon *Quia dies* (*De cons.* D. 5 c. 31, in Friedberg, *Corpus*, 1:1420). In France in the seventeenth century those found eating meat on that day were punished by the civil authorities. The practice gradually faded out of use in the eighteenth and nineteenth centuries. A tendentious contemporary history, written by an "old theologian" who, like Le Brun des Marettes, had doubts abouts its antiquity, can be found in *De l'abstinence du samedi* (Brussels, 1844).

[238] Peter de Honestis, *Regula clericorum* 2.2 (PL 163:721B–C) actually states that during Eastertide meat is not to be eaten on ferial Wednesdays, Fridays, and Saturdays, although it allows the use of blood on Wednesdays and Saturdays; chapter 2.10 (PL 163:723A) does allow the consumption of meat on Mondays, Wednesdays, and Saturdays of Eastertide if there is a nine-lesson feast or day within an octave.

the blessed bread should be distributed only by clerics, not by laymen, and certainly not by women.

When priests fall ill, they receive the whole of their usual distributions as if they continued to say Mass and as if they were present at the Divine Offices. The same is the case for the canons and other beneficers. Although they do not offer the sacrifice of the Mass, they do offer God their sufferings as a sacrifice, and this is acceptable to God who has willed their condition. And it is a wholly praiseworthy thing to give them their share of the distributions. Otherwise the fate of Our Lord's anointed would be worse than the lot of valets, who are ordinarily cared for and given all they need in their illness by men of the world. Without their distribution they would be reduced, after long serving the Church, to end their days in a hospice alongside the poor. Prelates who love the honor of the church and the clergy cannot allow them to suffer this.

Extreme Unction. Bread and Silver Distributed at Funerals

The custom is still kept at Rouen, during the administration of the sacrament of Extreme Unction, of putting ashes in the form of a cross upon the breast of the sick person before the anointings with the holy oils, according to the previous ritual of Rouen of 1640: *Deinde Sacerdos faciat crucem ex cinere in pectore infirmi, dicendo*: Memento homo quia pulvis es †, et in pulverem reverteris.[239]

There is another practice at Rouen that is as ancient as it is praiseworthy, because it was already in use since the fourth century at least, judging from St. Paulinus's Letter 13 to Pammachius.[240] At funerals, a large loaf of white bread, weighing eight, ten, or twelve pounds, is given to each of the poor of the Hôpital général—both boys and girls—who assist, numbering thirty, forty, sixty, or one hundred twenty, according to the wishes of the deceased's relatives. This concerns the poor of the Hôpital général. As for those from the parish and the neighboring parishes, they gather before the door of the house of the deceased and are given money, as was done in the time of St. Augustine, as one can see in his Letter 22 to Aurelius.[241] It is to be hoped that such good and ancient customs, which are, as these two saints say, both useful to the deceased and advantageous to the poor, are not neglected.

The 1586 ritual of Rouen contains the absolution for the deceased after his burial, which I have seen done in Paris. The clergy sang the same four psalms said today as they accompanied the body to the tomb, and returned to the church chanting psalm 50, *Miserere*, with the oration *Fidelium*.[242]

---

[239] *Sacerdotale seu Manuale ecclesiae Rothomagensis* (Rouen, 1640), 163.
[240] St. Paulinus of Nola, *Epistula* 13.11-14, ed. Le Brun des Marettes, 73–75; ed. von Hartel, 92–96.
[241] St. Augustine, *Epistula* 22.6 (PL 33:92), ed. Klaus-Detlef Daur, Corpus Christianorum Series Latina 31 (Brepols, 2004), 55.
[242] CO 2684b.

Finally, burials are not performed in Rouen on the principal feasts of the year,[243] nor on Good Friday, even after the service. On other feasts and Sundays, burials are permitted after the Office. If the body cannot be kept so long and must be buried in the morning, the ritual orders that a time be chosen such that the parish Mass is neither anticipated or delayed and the solemnity of Our Lord's Resurrection is not disturbed: *Ne symbolica Dominicae Resurrectionis aut aeternae festivitatis gloriae solemnitas, et ordo canonici Officii perturbetur.*[244]

I close this account of my *Travels*, as you see, with death, which is a passage to that great and final voyage to Eternity that we all must make, and that surely merits our thoughts and attention.

THE END

---

[243] Namely Christmas, Easter, Pentecost, All Saints, the patronal or titular feast of the particular church, and the feast of the Dedication of the churches of the diocese. See *Sacerdotale seu Manuale ecclesiae Rothomagensis* (Rouen, 1640), 193.

[244] *Sacerdotale seu Manuale ecclesiae Rothomagensis* (Rouen, 1640), 193.

PLATES

PLATE 1. Depiction of the choir of Notre-Dame of Paris in the High Middle Ages. Eugène Viollet-le-Duc, *Dictionnaire raisonné de l'architecture française du XIe au XVIe siècle*, vol. 3 (Paris, 1859).

PLATE 2. Frontispiece of Pierre Le Brun's *Explication littérale, historique et dogmatique des prières et cérémonies de la Messe* (Paris, 1716). Note, at the center, a cleric wearing the *soc*, according to the use of Paris.

PLATE 3. The Tour de Pilate. Engraving by Josef Resch, *Illustrierte Zeitung* 48 (1867): 266.

PLATE 4: Examples of two surviving marble altars with recessed tables. *Above*, a twelfth-century altar from the Comminges, perhaps originally from the abbey of Bonnefont, today in the Musée de Cluny, Cl. 22392 (photograph © RMN-GP/cliché Jean-Gilles Berizzi). *Below*, the eleventh-century high altar of the basilica of St-Sernin in Toulouse, consecrated by Pope Urban II in 1096 (photograph by Gerhard Eger).

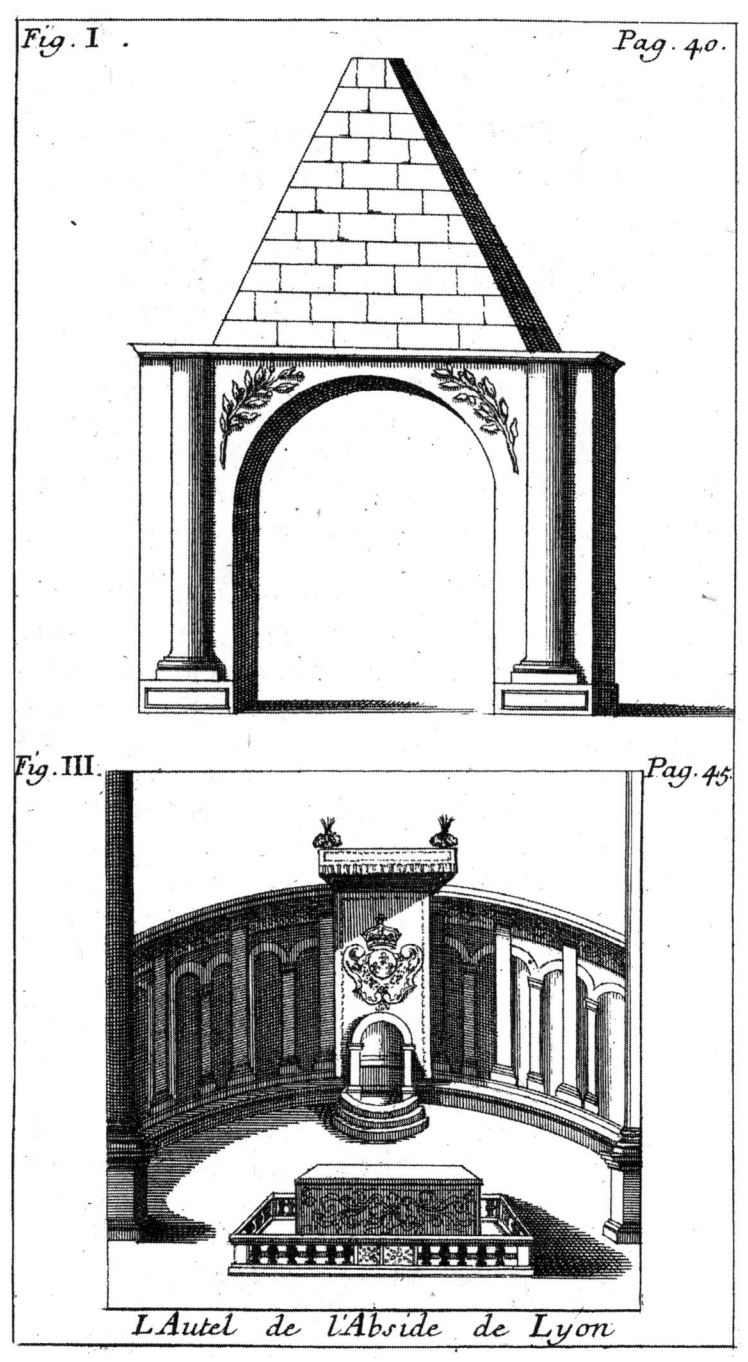

PLATE 5. Fig. 1, the Pyramide near the Porte d'Avignon. Fig. 3, the altar in the apse of St-Jean of Lyon (Le Brun des Marettes, *Voyages liturgiques*).

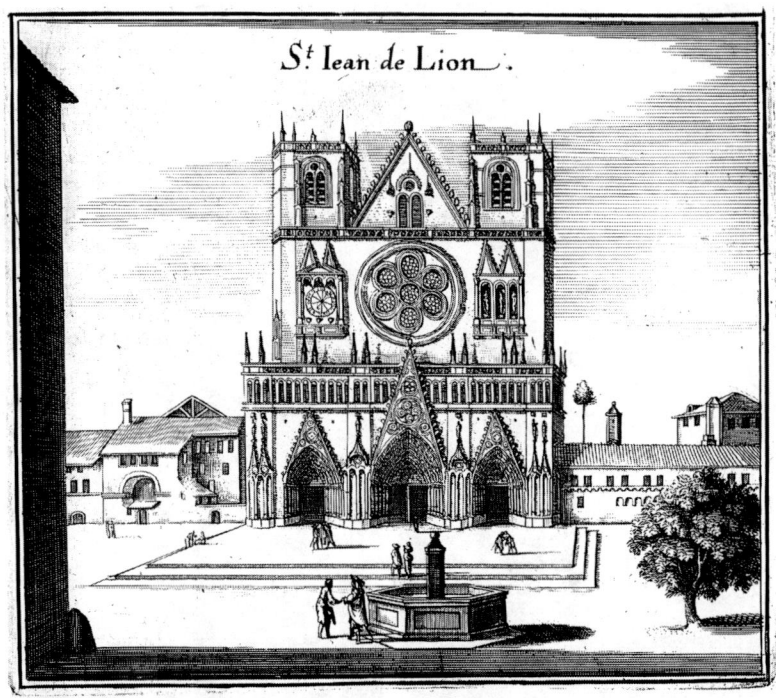

PLATE 6. View of the cathedral of St-Jean of Lyon. Printed in Frankfurt by Caspar Merian in 1657, www.vintage-maps.com/en/.

PLATE 7. The astronomical clock of St-Jean of Lyon. Engraving by Guillaume Nourrisson, 1660.

296　*Liturgical Travels Through France*

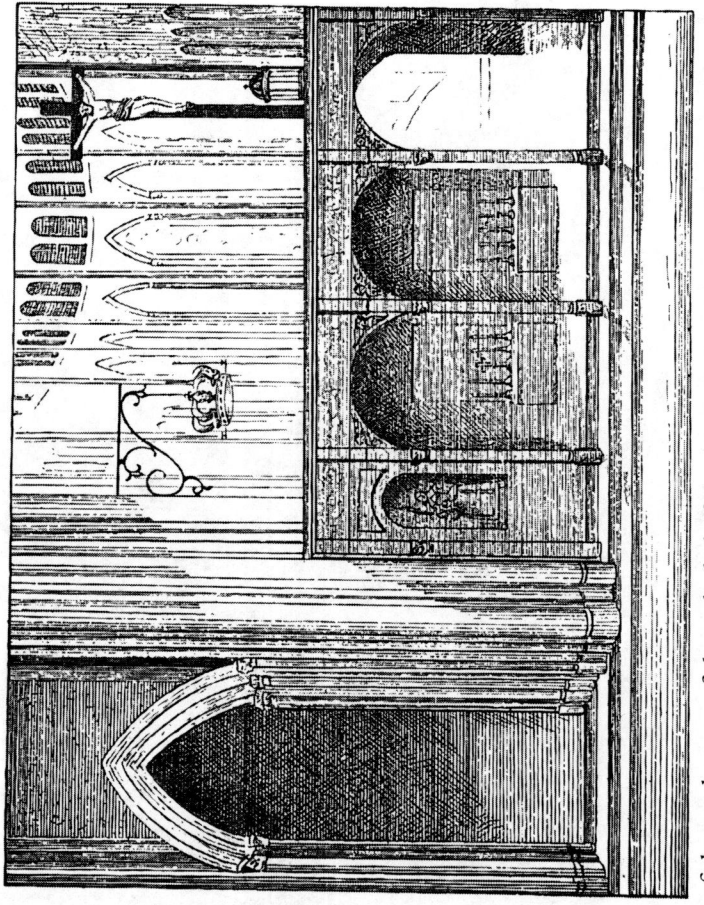

PLATE 8. Part of the rood screen of the cathedral of Lyon, rebuilt in 1582–1585 after the older screen was destroyed by the Huguenots. Reproduced in Alphonse Sachet, *Le grande jubilé séculaire de Saint-Jean-de-Lyon* (Lyon, 1886).

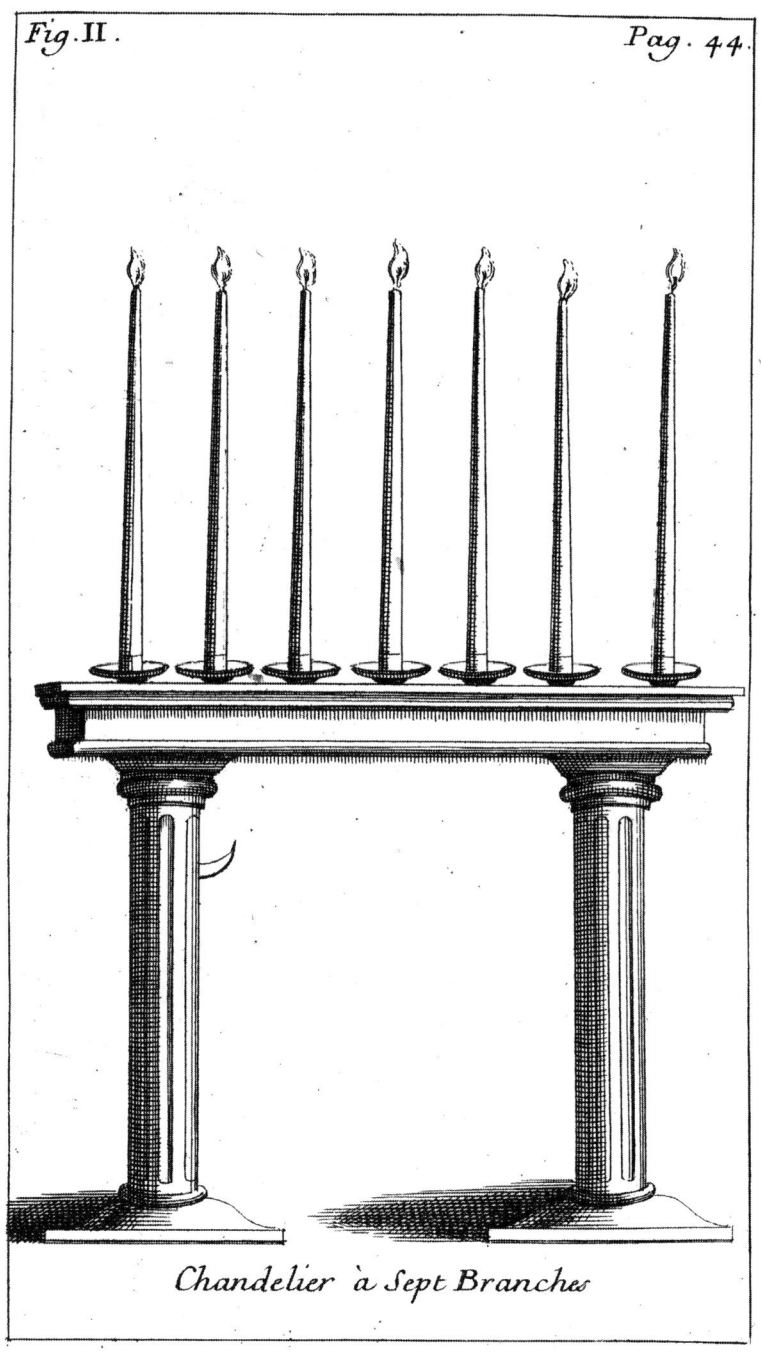

PLATE 9. Fig. 2, the *râtelier* or seven-branched candlestick. It was removed by order of the chapter in 1749 (Le Brun des Marettes, *Voyages liturgiques*).

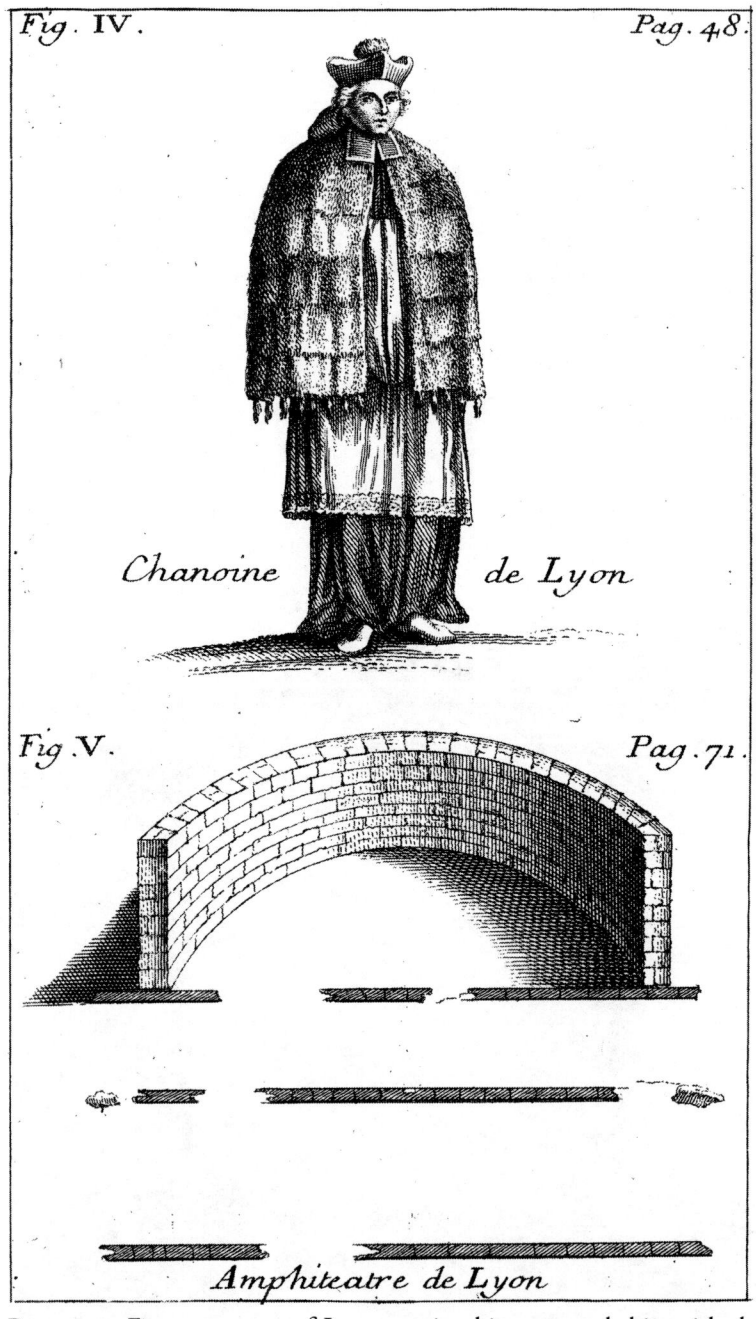

PLATE 10. Fig. 4, a canon of Lyon wearing his summer habit, with the almuce over his shoulders. Fig. 5, the amphitheater of Lyon (Le Brun des Marettes, *Voyages liturgiques*).

PLATE 11. Types of surplices. Fig. 1, An alb. Fig. 2, an alb shortened and reduced to a rochet. Fig. 3, a rochet made into a surplice by elongating the body and sleeves. Fig. 4, a surplice with long, open, trailing sleeves. Fig. 5, sleeveless surplice or rochet. Fig. 6, the same surplice or rochet, reduced to a piece in front and back, in the form of a short scapular. Fig. 7, reduced to a simple band (de Vert, *Explication*, vol. 2).

PLATE 12. A canon of Lyon in winter habit, showing the cape or *domino*: "not very graceful, but comfortable" (reproduced in Sachet, *Le grande jubilé*).

PLATE 13. Pontifical Mass in St-Jean of Lyon, initial prayers and Confiteor (reproduced in Sachet, *Le grande jubilé*).

PLATE 14. View of the apse during the Creed at a pontifical Mass in St-Jean of Lyon. Drawing by Ferdinand-Sigismond Delamonce and engraving by Jean-Louis Daudet, 1737. Used as the frontispiece of the *Missale sanctae Lugdunensis ecclesiae* (Lyon, 1737).

PLATE 15. View of the main entrance of St-Maurice of Angers. Engraving by Louis Boudan, 1699. Bibliothèque nationale, Estampes et photographie, EST VA-49 (5).

PLATE 16. Choir and altar of the cathedral of Angers before the 1699 reforms. Engraving by Louis Boudan, 1699. Bibliothèque nationale, Estampes et photographie, EST VA-49 (5).

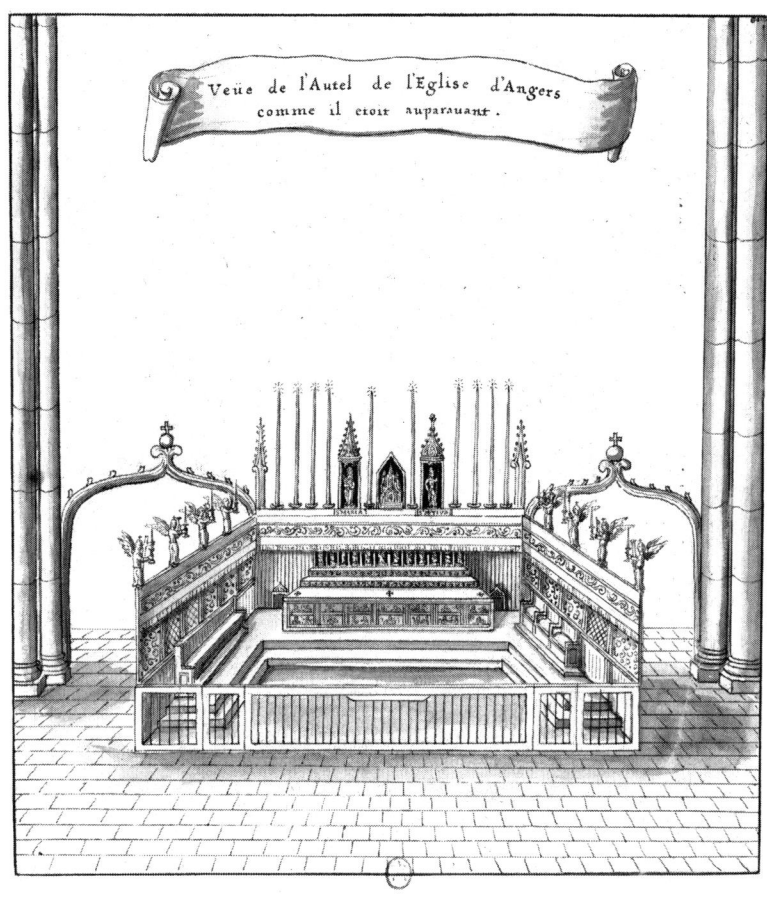

PLATE 17. View of the altar of the cathedral of Angers before the 1699 reforms. Engraving by Louis Boudan, 1699. Bibliothèque nationale, Estampes et photographie, EST VA-49 (5).

PLATE 18. Fig. 1, a sailor's cape and hood. Fig. 2, A cleric with a Franciscan tonsure, wearing a red robe and an almuce over his shoulders. Fig. 3, a deacon's chasuble, rolled up and tied in the shape of a band or scarf passing across the shoulders. Fig. 4, a linen kerchief or napkin with an embroidered hem, worn on the left arm and known as a maniple. Fig. 5, a linen kerchief or maniple, tied to the little finger of the right hand, as is the custom in the church of Reims (de Vert, *Explication*, vol. 2).

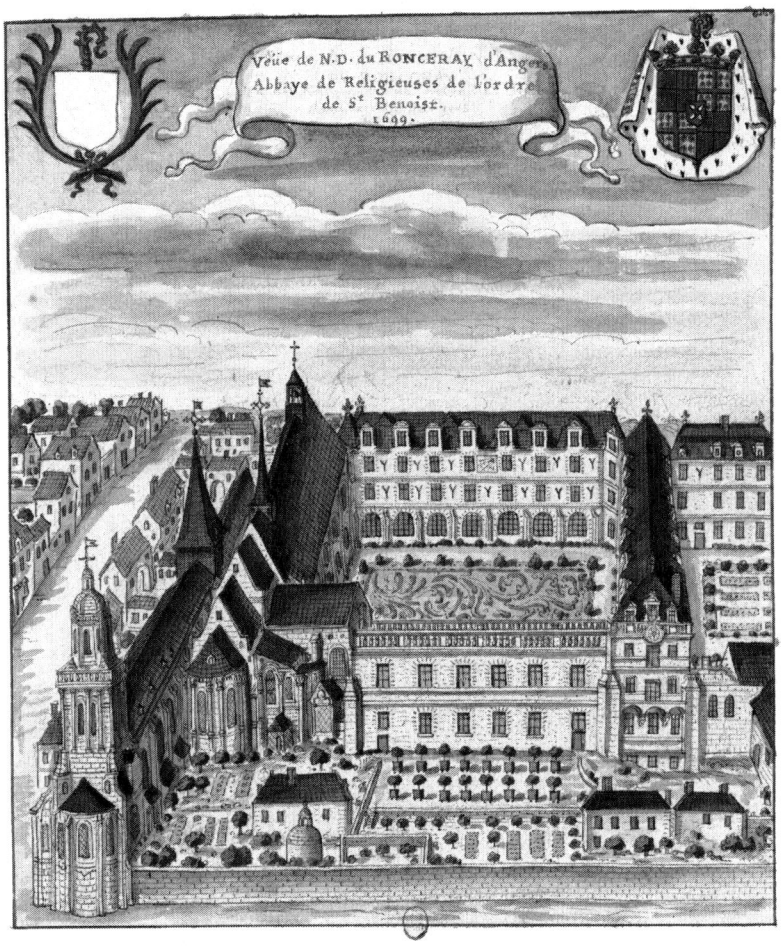

PLATE 19. View of Notre-Dame of Le Ronceray. Engraving by Louis Boudan, 1699. Bibliothèque nationale, Estampes et photographie, EST VA-49 (5).

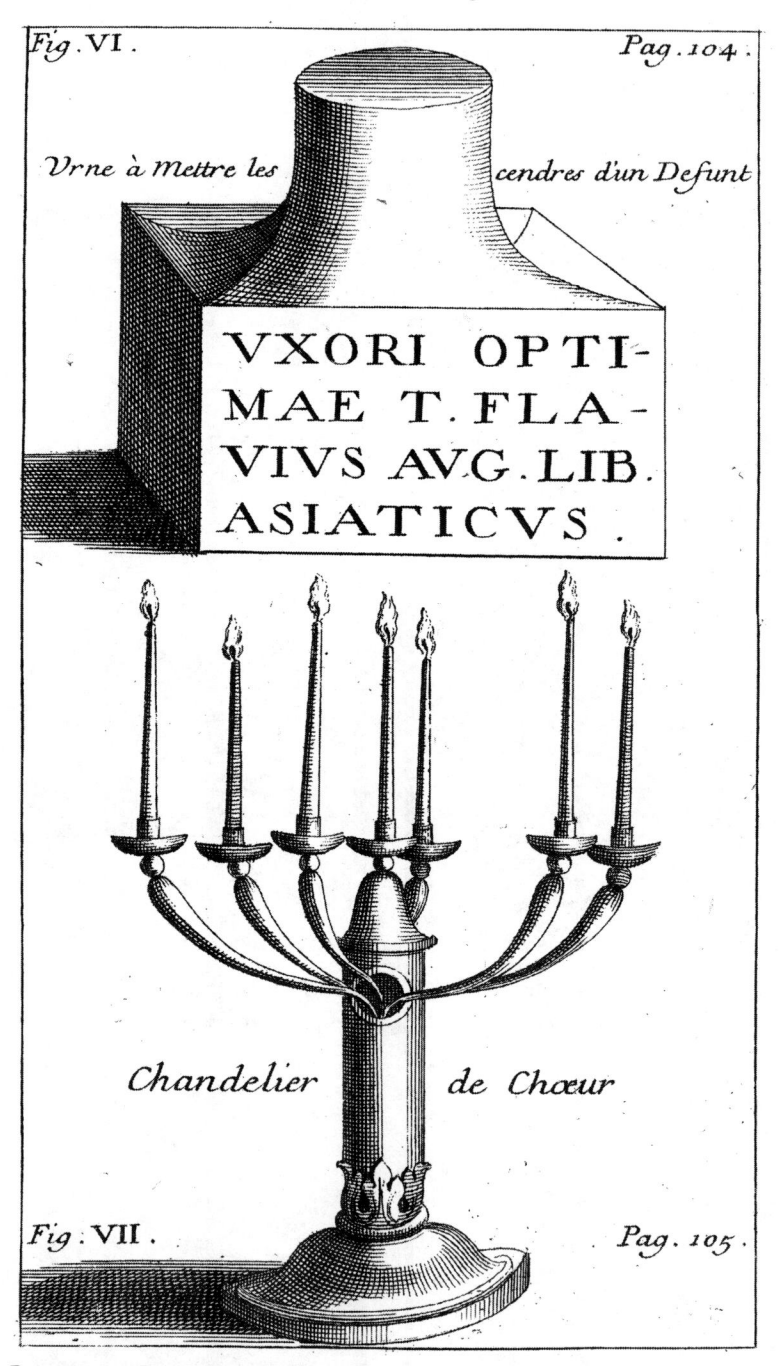

PLATE 20. Fig. 6, an ash urn. Fig 7, a choir chandelier (Le Brun des Marettes, *Voyages liturgiques*).

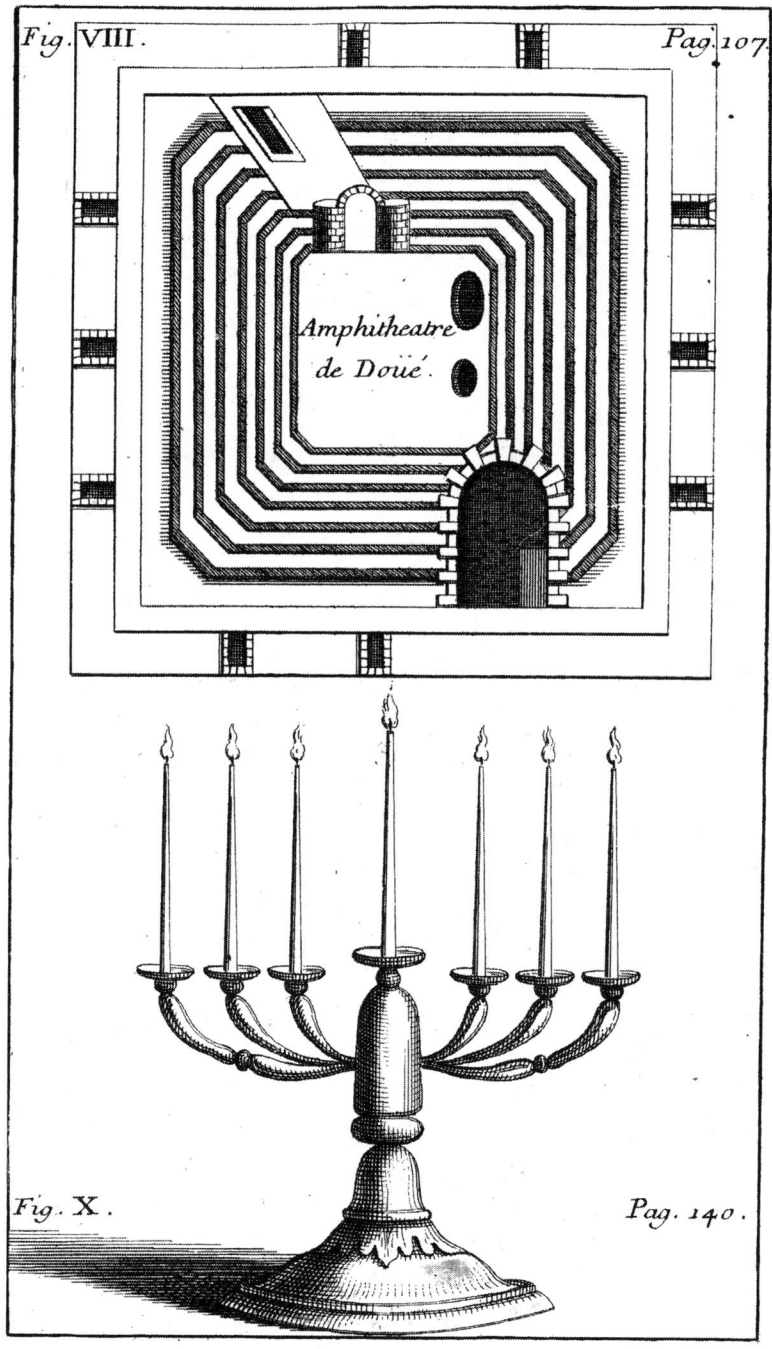

PLATE 21. Fig. 8, the amphitheater of Doué. Fig. 10, a choir chandelier (Le Brun des Marettes, *Voyages liturgiques*).

PLATE 22. Fig. 9, the arena, with gladiators and athletes (Le Brun des Marettes, *Voyages liturgiques*).

PLATE 23. View of the abbey of Marmoutier. Engraving perhaps by Louis Boudan, seventeenth century. Bibliothèque nationale, Estampes et photographie, EST VA-407.

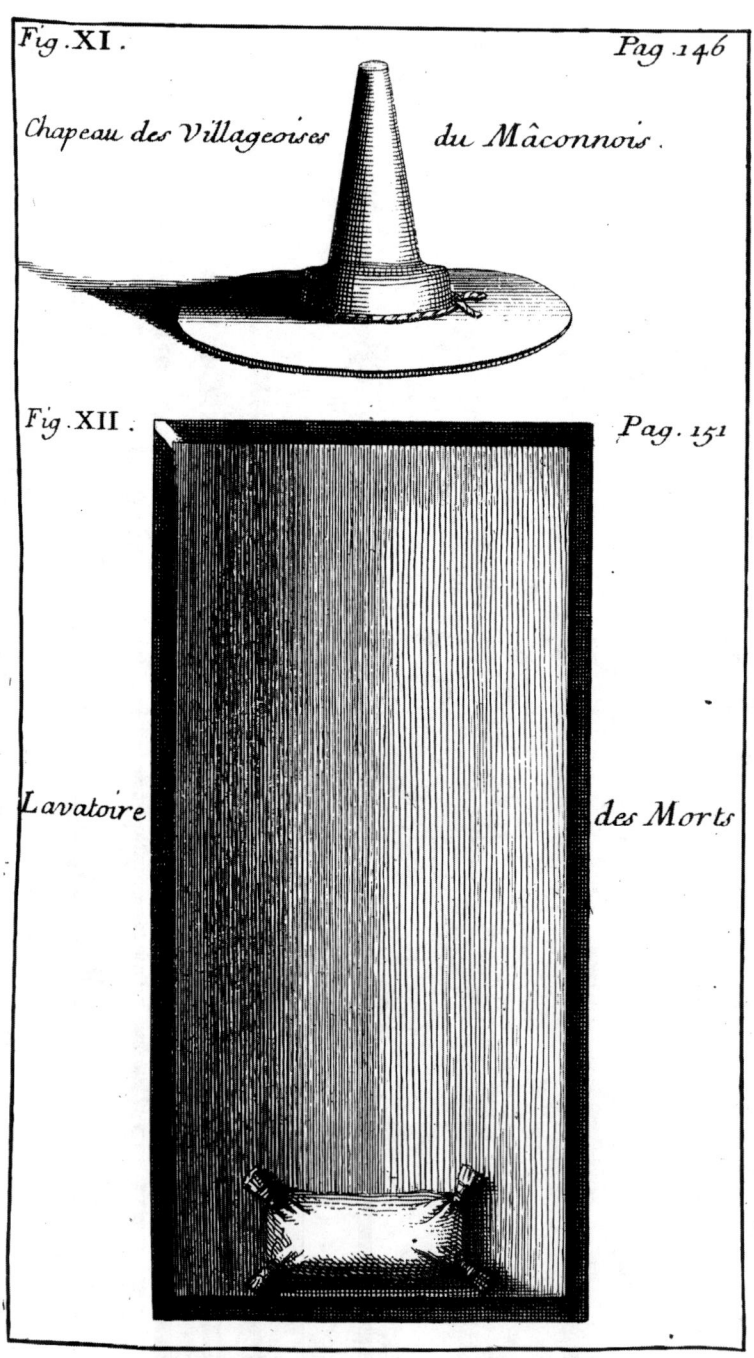

PLATE 24. Fig. 11, hat of the country women of the Mâconnais. Fig. 12, a lavatory stone for the dead (Le Brun des Marettes, *Voyages liturgiques*).

PLATE 25. Exterior view of the chevet of the abbey of Cluny in the sixteenth century. The abbey was destroyed in the Revolution. Engraving by Émile Sagot. Bibliothèque nationale, Estampes et photographie, EF-355-FOL.

PLATE 26. A miniature depicting a clerical choir, from a sixteenth-century French breviary. New York, Morgan Library, MS M. 8 fol. 189r.

PLATE 27. The fifteenth-century rood screen of the cathedral of Reims, demolished in 1744. Louis Paris, *Le jubé et le labyrinthe de la cathédrale de Reims* (Paris, 1885).

PLATE 28. St. Gregory's Mass. Engraving in the 1519 *Missale ad usum et consuetudinem ecclesie Aurelianensis* (fol. 1r). Note the almuce worn over the arm.

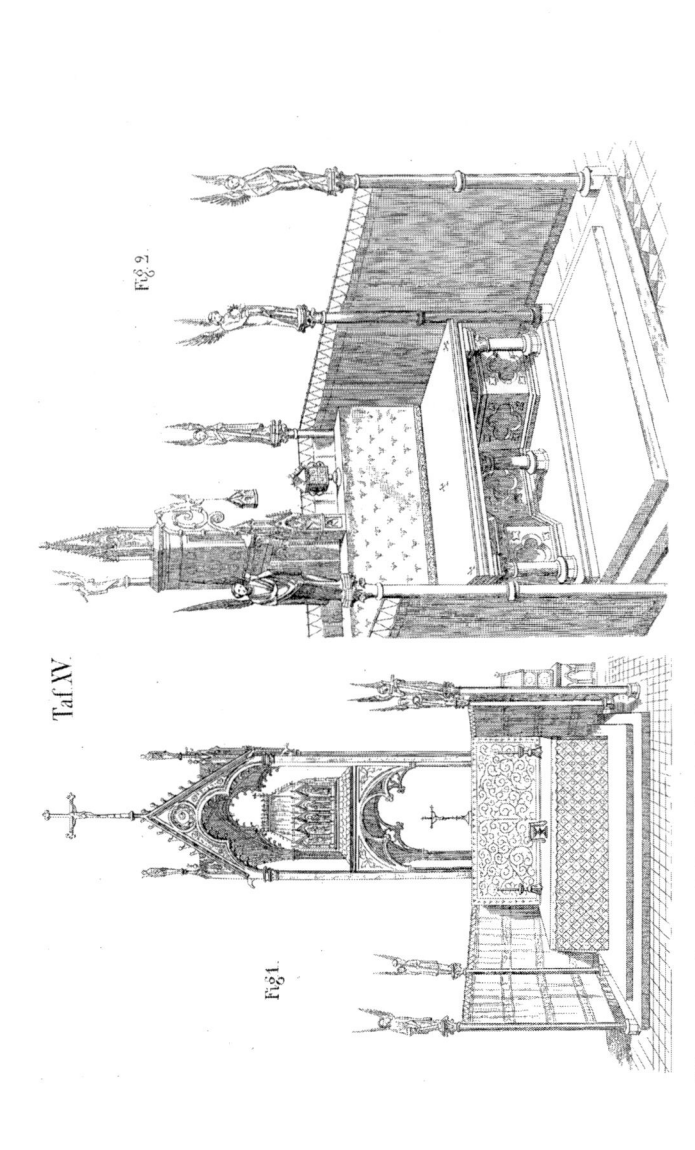

PLATE 29. The main altars of the cathedral of Paris (Fig. 1) and Arras (Fig. 2) in the Middle Ages. Note the altar curtains or riddels around both altars, and the suspended pyx and dossal in the latter figure. Franz Bock, *Geschichte der liturgischen Gewänder des Mittelalters*, vol. 3, *Die Paramentik des Altares und des Chores im Mittelalter* (Bonn, 1871).

Suspended Pyxes

Suspended Dove

Dove — Host inside

Suspended Dove with veil

Suspended Pyx with Veil and Canopy

Triple Crown Suspended Pyx

Renaissance Suspended Pyx.

'Sacrament Tower'

Early Box-Tabernacle (enamelled)

PLATE 30. Forms of medieval suspended pyxes. Peter F. Anson, *Churches: Their Plan and Furnishing* (Bruce Publishing Company, 1948; reprinted by Romanitas Press), 87.

PLATE 31. An offertory procession in the cathedral of Auxerre. The sacrament is reserved above the altar under a trumpet-shaped canopy. From the frontispiece of the 1738 *Missale sanctae Autissiodorensis ecclesiae*.

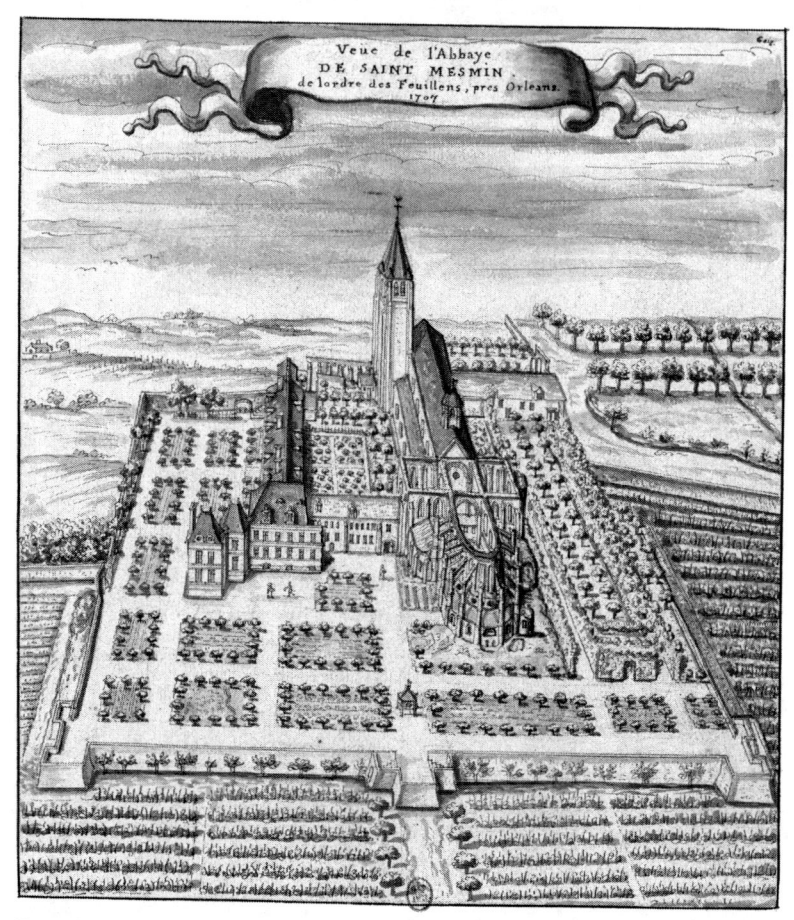

PLATE 32. View of the Cistercian (Feuillant) abbey of St-Mesmin near Orléans; destroyed in 1790. Engraving by Louis Boudan, 1707. Bibliothèque nationale, Estampes et photographie, EST VA-45 (1).

PLATE 33. The cathedral of St-Julien of Le Mans. Engraving by Louis Boudan, 1697. Bibliothèque nationale, Estampes et photographie, EST VA-72 (3).

PLATE 34. The choir of the abbey of La Trappe. Note the suspended pyx hanging from the right hand of the statue of Our Lady. Printed by Daumont in Paris, seventeenth century. Bibliothèque nationale, Estampes et photographie, Reserve QB-201 (74)-FOL.

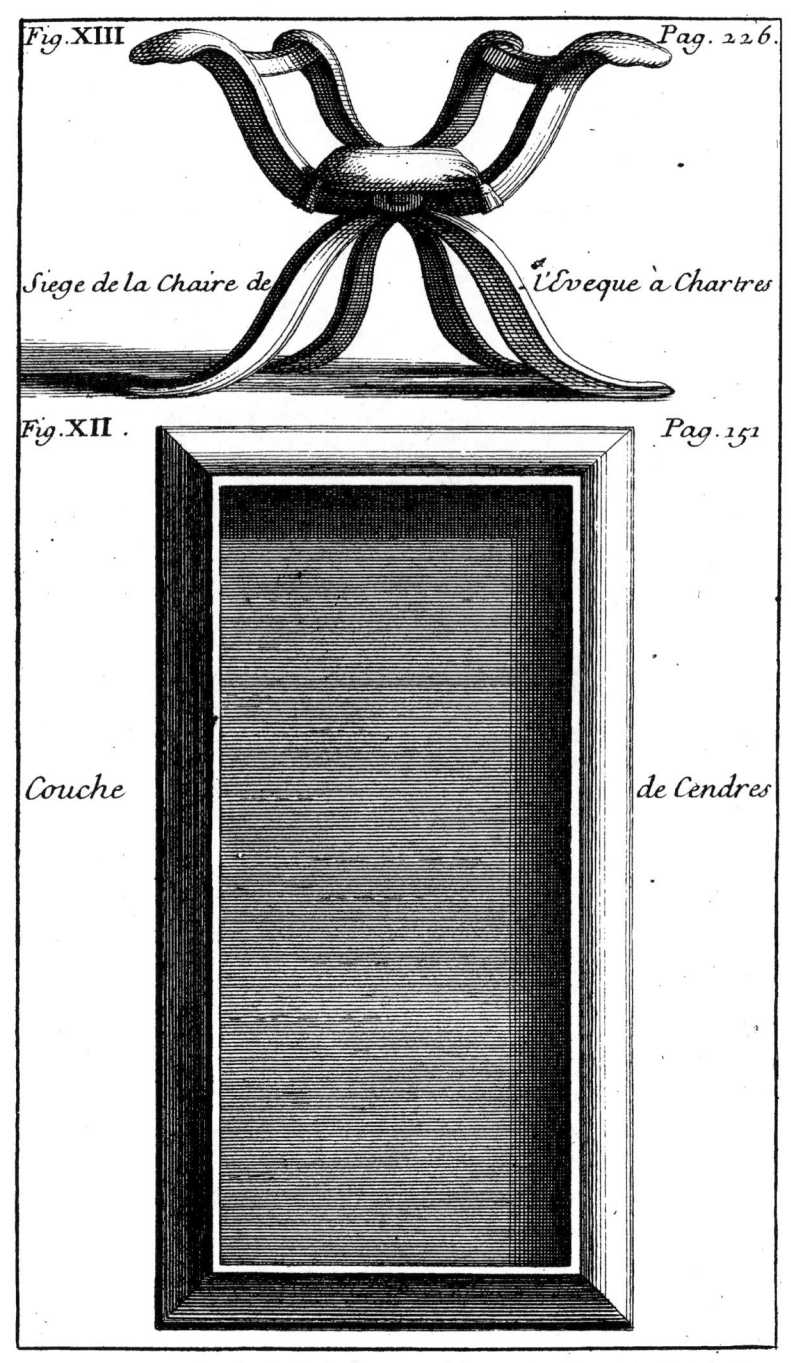

PLATE 35. Fig. 12bis, bed of ashes. Fig. 13, faldstool in the stall of the bishop of Chartres (Le Brun des Marettes, *Voyages liturgiques*).

PLATE 36. Three views of the abbey of Port-Royal-des-Champs. *Top*, the screen closing off the nuns' choir at the west end, with two altars attached to it. *Middle*, the sanctuary and high altar. The nuns' choir was closed off at the east end as well. *Bottom*, Corpus Christi procession in the cloister. The clergy's surplices are split, as was the custom in the diocese of Paris. Gouaches preserved in the Musée de Port-Royal-des-Champs (© RMN-GP / Gérard Blot).

PLATE 37. Fig. 14, a nun with a maniple. Fig. 15, a canon regular of Deux-Amants (Le Brun des Marettes, *Voyages liturgiques*).

Religieuse Chartreuse en habit de Ceremonie le jour de sa Consecration

PLATE 38. Carthusian nun in ceremonial habit on the day of her consecration. Hippolyte Hélyot and Maximilien Bullot, *Histoire des ordres monastiques, religieux et militaires et des congrégations séculières*, vol. 7 (Paris, 1714–1721).

PLATE 39. The high altar of Notre-Dame of Paris before the completion of Louis XIV's renovations, depicted in the 1703 *Caeremoniale Parisiense*. The numbers indicate the order of incensation.

PLATE 40. The elevation at pontifical Mass in Notre-Dame of Paris. Note the *spé* wearing a *soc* at the center, holding the veiled basin. The depiction of the sanctuary reflects its arrangement after 1723. Engraving by Bernard Picart, *Cérémonies et coutumes religieuses de tous les peuples du monde*, vol. 1 (Amsterdam, 1728).

Chanoine Régulier de la Congrégation de France,
en habit de Chœur, l'Été.

PLATE 41. The canons regular of the Congregation of France, whose motherhouse was Ste-Geneviève in Paris, wore the same habit as the cathedral canons. Here, a canon in summer dress. Note the almuce over the arm and open surplice sleeves (Hélyot and Bullot, *Histoire*, vol. 2).

Chanoine Régulier de la Congrégation de France,
en habit de Chœur l'hyver.

PLATE 42. A canon regular of the Congregation of France in winter habit, showing the *grand camail* the cathedral canons also wore (Hélyot and Bullot, *Histoire*, vol. 2).

PLATE 43. *The Mass of Canon Antoine de La Porte*, by Jean-France de Jouvenet, 1708–1710. Louvre, Département des Peintures, INV 5502. The painting shows this revered member of the chapter of Notre-Dame of Paris giving the last blessing at the cathedral's high altar. Note the choirboys' shorn heads and albs, and the split sleeves of the clerics' surplices. The view of the sanctuary is imagined, since it was then undergoing the renovations ordered by King Louis XIV and partly financed by La Porte himself; the statuary of the descent from the cross would only be installed in 1723. The large monstrance the artist has taken the liberty to include was donated to the cathedral by La Porte in 1708.

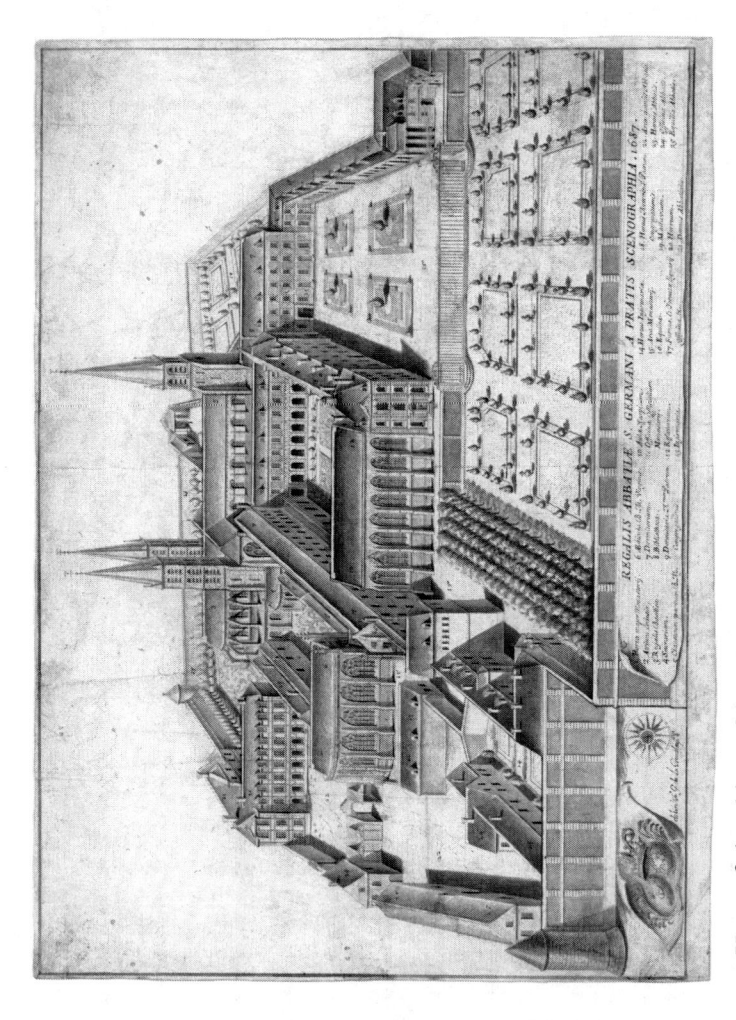

PLATE 44. View of the abbey of St-Germain-des-Prés, largely destroyed in the Revolution. Engraving by Guillaume de la Tremblaye, 1687. Bibliothèque nationale, Estampes et photographie, Reserve B-II (A,13)-(FT 4).

Chanoine Régulier de S. Victor, en habit de Chœur l'Été.

PLATE 45. The summer habit of the canons of St-Victor, showing the surplice with closed sleeves and almuce worn over the shoulders (Hélyot and Bullot, *Histoire*, vol. 2).

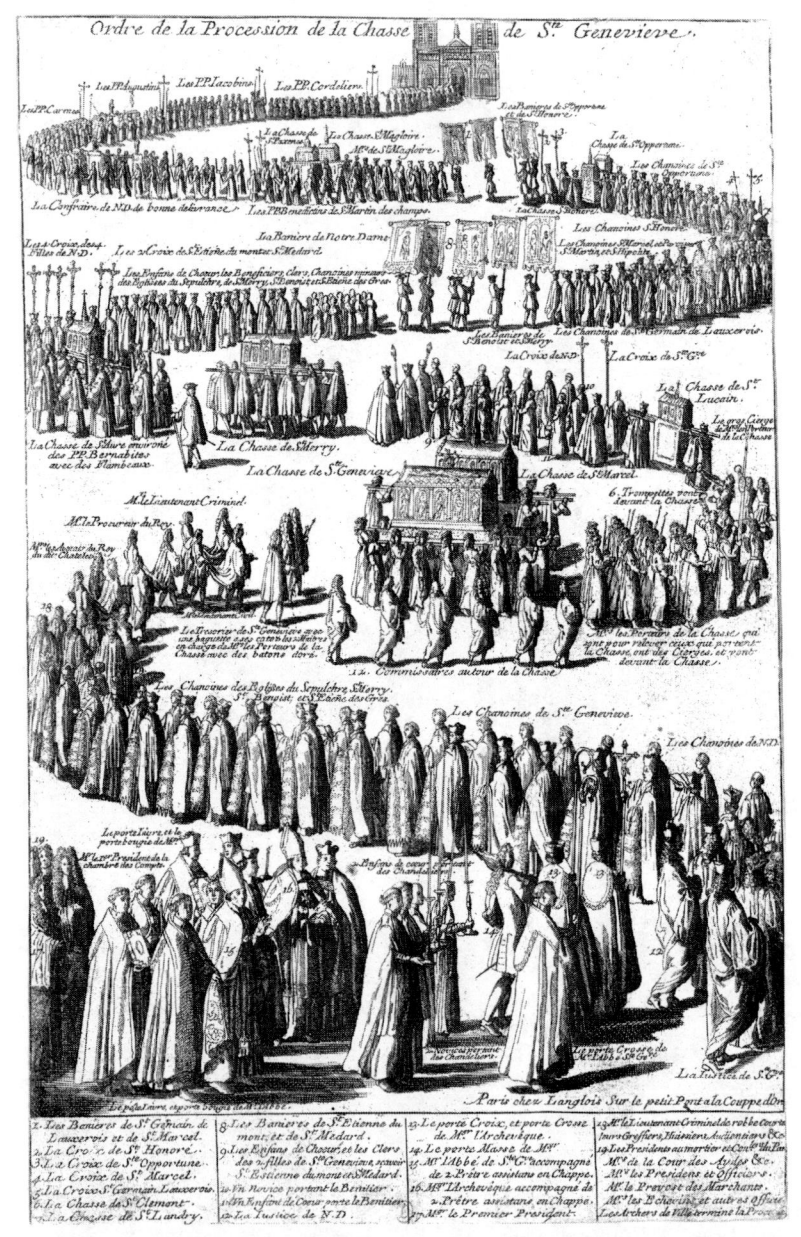

PLATE 46. Order of procession with the relics of St. Genevieve, engraving by Nicholas Cochin, ca. 1675. Paris, Bibliothèque de l'Institut national d'histoire de l'art, collections Jacques Doucet, OC 54.

PLATE 47. Three of the seven *montjoies* on the road from Paris to St-Denis before their destruction during the French Revolution. Engraving by Guillaumot, nineteenth century. Archives municipales de Saint-Denis, 69 S 30.

PLATE 48. Depiction of the choir of the abbey of St-Denis in the High Middle Ages. Viollet-le-Duc, *Dictionnaire raisonné*, vol. 3.

PLATE 49. Fig. 1, a fur-lined *aumusson* that solely covers the head, worn under the winter *grand camail*. Fig. 2, a longer and larger *aumusson*, or almuce with a rounded hood covering the head. Fig. 3, a mantle worn over the head, with tufts of untreated wool. Fig. 4, an almuce with a square hood over the head. Fig. 5, an almuce pulled down over the neck. Fig. 6, a mantle, also pulled down over the neck. Fig. 7, an almuce shaped like a short mantle, with the hood folded back. Fig. 8, an almuce worn over the left arm, with a breviary inside its hood. Fig. 9, a mantle, also worn over the left arm (de Vert, *Explication*, vol. 2).

PLATE 50: Dominicans performing the *prostratio super formas* at a French Dominican house in the 1950s.

PLATE 51. The procession of the gargoyles (*gargouilles*) in Rouen. Painting by Clement Boulanger, 1837.

PLATE 52. An offertory procession (*offrande*), as shown in an illumination in the *Chronique de Normandie*, ca. 1460. Paris, Bibliothèque nationale, MS. fr. 2623, fol. 40v.

PLATE 53. View of the entrance of the Benedictine abbey of St-Amand. It was nationalized and demolished after the Revolution, except for a single tower. Engraving by Louis Boudan, 1702. Paris, Bibliothèque nationale, Estampes et photographie, EST VA-76 (18).

Ancien Chanoine Régulier de S.t Lô, à Rouen

PLATE 54. The former habit of the canons regular of St-Lô (Hélyot and Bullot, *Histoire*, vol. 2).

Fille-Dieu de Rouen.

PLATE 55. A Fille-Dieu of Rouen (Hélyot and Bullot, *Histoire*, vol. 2).

APPENDIX I

A Short Presentation
of the
Cathedral Chapters
of the Ancien Régime

François Hou

THE diverse customs Le Brun des Marettes describes in the *Liturgical Travels Through France* arose from the accumulated traditions of the ancient cathedral and collegiate chapters. Indeed, canons and the dignitaries or officers of the choir are omnipresent in the ceremonies the Lord of Moléon so punctiliously describes. Bernard Plongeron has referred to these chapters as "citadels of the past."[1] Swept away by the French Revolution, the capitular life of the Ancien Régime seems from our temporal remove like a bygone world. From an American perspective, they might appear especially alien, since the dioceses of the United States have never established canonical traditions. As Robert Trisco has pointed out, the absence of cathedral chapters has long been an "American anomaly."[2]

A chapter might be defined as a college of clerics — the canons — attached to the choir of a church for the solemn celebration of the Divine Office. Under the Ancien Régime, both cathedral and collegiate churches stood out for the fervor of their liturgical life. At the cathedral of Clermont, for example, the chapter rose to chant Matins at 3:00 a.m. for most of the liturgical year, and at 1:30 a.m. during Advent and Lent; it was followed by the little Office of Our Lady and Lauds of the Office of the Dead. During the short break that followed, canons could celebrate their private Mass before reconvening in choir to sing Prime and the Mass of Our Lady,

---

[1] Bernard Plongeron, *La vie quotidienne du clergé au XVIIIe siècle* (Hachette, 1974), 113. On the French chapters under the Ancien Régime, see especially Olivier Charles, *Chanoines de Bretagne. Carrières et cultures d'une élite cléricale au siècle des Lumières* (Presses universitaires de Rennes, 2004); Philippe Loupès, *Chapitres et chanoines en Guyenne aux XVIIe et XVIIIe siècles* (Éditions de l'École des hautes études en sciences sociales, 1985); John McManners, *French Ecclesiastical Society under the Ancien Régime: A Study of Angers in the Eighteenth Century* (Manchester University Press, 1960); Anne Massoni, ed., *Collégiales et chanoines dans le centre de la France du Moyen Âge à la Révolution* (Presses universitaires de Limoges, 2010).
[2] Robert F. Trisco, "An American Anomaly: Bishops without Canons," *Chicago Studies* 9, no. 2 (Summer 1970): 143–57.

which lasted an hour and a quarter. The chapter then honored the obits, i.e., Masses for anniversaries of the dead, directly followed by Terce and a procession with the singing of the litany, culminating with the celebration of the day's high Mass, which was followed by Sext. Offices, therefore, encompassed almost the entire morning. In the afternoon, as the clock struck three, the liturgical proceedings resumed with None, Vespers of the Dead, solemn Vespers of the day, and Compline.[3] The members of the chapter, as well as the general populace of the city, took great pride in the punctuality and reverence wherewith the canonical hours were celebrated. As Pierre Audiger, a canon of Clermont and local historian, boasted early in the eighteenth century, "There is no cathedral where the ceremonies are conducted with more majesty, or where the Divine Office is chanted with more modesty and a more edifying piety."[4]

While the activities of collegiate chapters centered primarily around public prayer, cathedral chapters played an important role in church government. As heirs of the ancient *presbyterium*, they historically formed the senate of the diocesan church and the bishop's council. Unlike the former, which were generally founded by medieval endowments, the latter could lay claim not only to an ancient origin but also to a role in church government. This is why the revolutionary National Constituent Assembly, when plotting ecclesiastical "reform," hesitated to suppress cathedral chapters, even as it condemned collegiate ones with hasty abandon.[5] Nevertheless, in actual fact, by the time Le Brun des Marettes was writing the *Liturgical Travels Through France*, chapters had lost the right to participate in diocesan governance as a body, even if individual canons continued to serve as fiscal promoters, officials, and vicars general in most dioceses.[6] The chapters had retained their essential function in one respect, namely the election of capitular vicars general during the vacancy of the episcopal see, ensuring the continuity of spiritual jurisdiction. And yet the cathedral chapter remained, in fact, the custodian of the local church's tradition, and, as such, the bishop was obliged to consult it and obtain its consent, for example, to alienate church property, but also and above all for any decision related to the liturgy. The maintenance of ancient practices and the drafting or adoption of new liturgical books thus fell under the chapter's competence. In Chartres in 1781, for example, the chapter played a decisive role in the adoption of a new breviary derived from that of Paris.

---

[3] Louise Welter, "Le chapitre cathédral de Clermont. Sa constitution, ses privilèges," *Revue d'histoire de l'Église de France* 41, no. 136 (1955): 21–22.

[4] Cited by Nathalie Da Silva, "Être maître de musique à la cathédrale de Clermont au XVIIe et XVIIIe siècles," in *Les bas-chœurs d'Auvergne et du Velay*, ed. Bernard Dompnier (Presses universitaires Blaise-Pascal, 2010), 135.

[5] François Hou, *Chapitres et société en Révolution. Les chanoines en France de l'Ancien Régime à la monarchie de Juillet* (Presses universitaires de Rennes, 2023), 59–70.

[6] François Ducasse, *Traité des droits et des obligations des chapitres des églises cathédrales* (Toulouse, 1706).

The breviary was composed by commissioners appointed by the chapter, which later voted upon it.[7]

If the chapters as we have described them appear foreign to contemporary sensibilities, it might be largely because, by the seventeenth century, they had become a body of secular clergy without care of souls. This was the consummation of a process that had begun in the Middle Ages and was largely complete by the seventeenth century. Although in the following century some canons of Jansenist leanings continued to entertain the idea of an urban parish ministry collectively exercised by the chapter,[8] by then it was more of a dream colored by antiquarianism than the reality of capitular institutions, in general entirely disengaged from direct pastoral responsibilities. Most cathedral churches were not parishes. In the few cases when a cathedral did host a parish, it was modest in size, clearly distinct from the chapter, and had to use a secondary altar, since the high altar was reserved for the bishop and his chapter.[9] Relations between parish and chapter were not always peaceful, as in St-Brieuc, where the canons, claiming that parish services disrupted the canonical hours, transferred the parish to a simple neighborhood chapel served by a vicar perpetual appointed by the chapter.[10] In fact, it was rare for a cathedral's parish priest to be a canon. A figure like Jean Darralde, who was both parish priest and a canon of the cathedral of Ste-Marie of Bayonne at the end of the Ancien Régime, was altogether exceptional.[11] The presence of a parish priest in a collegiate church, however, was more frequent, and there it was also less unusual for a canon to shoulder pastoral duties. For instance, the dean of Notre-Dame-des-Vignes in Soissons was also *ex officio* the parish priest.

On the eve of the Revolution, the Kingdom of France had between ten and fifteen thousand canons, resident in hundreds of chapters remarkable for their diversity. First, they differed in size. For instance, the powerful cathedral chapter of Chartres boasted seventy-six canons and seventeen dignitaries, while the chapter of Gap counted only four dignitaries and twelve prebendaries. In general, the large cathedral chapters of the north of the realm were financially better off and able to support a larger number of canons, while the communities of the south, where the ecclesiastical map

---

[7] Archives départementales de l'Eure-et-Loir, G333, Actes capitulaires de la cathédrale de Chartres, deliberation on 20 May 1781.
[8] Edme Moreau, *Fonctions et droits du clergé des églises cathédrales* (Amsterdam, 1784), 10.
[9] As was the case in Vienne (p. 12) and Chalon-sur-Saône (p. 114).
[10] Bruno Restif, "Les paroisses desservies dans les églises cathédrales et collégiales. Enjeux, concurrence et conflits (XVIe-XVIIIe siècle)," in *La paroisse urbaine du moyen âge à nos jours*, ed. Anne Bonzon, Philippe Guignet, and Marc Venard (Cerf, 2014), 187.
[11] Archives départementales des Pyrénées Atlantiques, G46/1, Registre des insinuations ecclésiastiques du diocèse de Bayonne, 18 January 1779. This worthy priest had already had cure of souls as parish priest of St-Jean-Pied-de-Port before assuming the same post in the parish of the cathedral of Bayonne in 1778. He was named canon in 1781, but fled to Tudela in Spain after the Revolution. After his return to France, he became parish priest of Navarrenx, where he died in 1811.

was divided up into numerous dioceses, were much smaller. Indeed, the number of canons in a chapter was closely tied to its financial prosperity. The decline in the cathedral chapter of Soissons's fortunes, for example, led to a reduction of prebendaries from fifty-four to forty-five in 1743. Collegiate chapters, though generally smaller than cathedral chapters, still showed considerable variation in size. St-Martin of Tours, the largest collegiate church in France, housed fifty-one canons,[12] surpassing the majority of cathedrals, while the small collegiate church of Lamballe in the diocese of St-Brieuc had only six canons.[13]

Becoming a Canon

In contrast to the uniformity imposed on capitular organization after the Revolution, the chapters of the Ancien Régime exhibited wide diversity in terms of their statutes. Forty-two chapters held the privilege of nomination, granting them the ability to elect their own members.[14] In chapters like those of Angoulême or Clermont, when a canonry became vacant, the chapter convened to elect a new canon. Such a manner of nomination often favored the nearly exclusive selection of members of prominent local families. On the other hand, in other chapters, such as that of Metz, canons named by the chapter were appointed by the *tournaire*, that is, the canon whose turn it was the week the vacancy took place. Meanwhile, in fifty-eight cathedrals, including most large chapters like those of Paris and Chartres, bishops retained the right to nominate canons in accordance with the common law of the Church. In such cases, bishops often tended to appoint clergy from outside the diocese to reduce the influence of local elites. Finally, in thirty cathedrals, mostly in the south of the kingdom, bishops and canons jointly participated in the appointment of new members. This collaboration could take various forms. In Toulouse, the nomination of the twelve canonries of the right side of the choir belonged to the bishop, while the chapter's *tournaire* appointed the twelve canonries of the left side. In Bayonne, by contrast, the chapter as a whole chose the new canon, but the canonical collation of the benefice was reserved to the bishop.

In practice, these differences were blurred by the fact that, no matter his chapter's method of nomination, a canon could opt to resign his position *in favorem tertii*, that is, to relinquish his benefice in favor of an ecclesiastic of his choice.[15] This practice could lead to the formation of veritable canonical

---

[12] Eugène Jarry, "Le chapitre de Saint-Martin aux XVIIe et XVIIIe siècles," *Revue d'histoire de l'Église de France* 47, no. 144, (1961), 120.

[13] Olivier Charles, "Les *chanoines-chapelains* d'une petite collégiale bretonne," *Les Amis de Lamballe et du Penthièvre* 32 (2005): 81–106.

[14] These numbers were obtained from data furnished by Henri-Gabriel Duchesne, *La France ecclésiastique pour l'année 1788* (Paris, 1787).

[15] See p. 79, n. 46.

dynasties. Thus, in Angoulême, cathedral canonries were passed down in the families Thinon and Sauvo from uncle to nephew uninterruptedly from the early eighteenth century until the Revolution. Moreover, since the Pragmatic Sanction of Bourges of 1438, confirmed by the Concordat of Bologna of 1516, the months of January, April, July, and October were reserved for the so-called "expectant" graduates: a canonry that became vacant during these months was granted to the most senior member of choir who had become associated with the chapter after obtaining his university degree. This path to obtaining a canonry sometimes required patience, especially since the statutes and privileges of a chapter could greatly reduce the number of months reserved for graduates. For instance, a bachelor of theology named Jean Garat became attached to the chapter of Bayonne in 1767, but was not admitted to a canonry until 1788.[16]

Finally, a number of canonries were filled by the temporal authority. At the start of his reign, a new monarch could bestow a *brevet de joyeux avènement* on an ecclesiastic of his choice, granting him the right to expect the next vacant benefice in whatever chapter the king desired. By virtue of the *droit de régale*, the king also filled canonries that became vacant when the episcopal see was also unoccupied. In addition to the royal *brevets*, there were the indults of the Parlement of Paris, by which the president and counselors could, once in their lifetime, obtain from the king letters patent to name an ecclesiastic to a benefice. The kingdom's diversity further complicated the system of appointing canons. In the dioceses where the German Concordat of 1448 applied, the king's right of nomination was even more extensive. In Metz, for instance, the king named canons for six months of the year. In practice, canonries filled by royal nomination were generally given to ecclesiastics recommended by the bishop.

After being accepted into the chapter and swearing an oath to uphold its constitution and privileges, the new canon was bound to undergo the *rigoureuse*, a probationary period of ranging from only a few months to a year. During this time, he was not entitled to receive the *gros fruits* of his prebend and had to attend the Offices and become acquainted with the customs of the choir. Upon completing the *rigoureuse*, he gained a voice in chapter and could receive the distributions, undertake missions on behalf of his community, and receive a canonical residence. The canon took his seat in the higher stalls or upper form of the choir, his position determined by his seniority within the chapter.

Some chapters had semi-prebendary canonries. At Clermont, for instance, the six prebends known as "priestly" — because since the Middle Ages they had been reserved for priests strictly bound to the duties of the Office — were in 1623 divided into twelve semi-prebends. Often recruited amongst former

---

[16] Archives départementales des Pyrénées Atlantiques, G47, Registre des insinuations ecclésiastiques du diocèse de Bayonne, 16 January 1788.

choir-boys or the cathedral's *prêtres habitués*, semi-prebendary canons had no voice in chapter and formed an intermediate group between canons and the choir priests, beneficers, and *prêtres habitués* of the lower form.[17] The size of the latter depended on the chapter's importance and resources. In Arras, at the end of the eighteenth century, the cathedral had ten beneficed vicars, a beneficed music master, a beneficed sub-treasurer, and a beneficer assigned to two chantries.[18] On ordinary days, priests of the lower form were employed as cope-bearers, deacons, subdeacons, or even choristers. The lower form's purpose, therefore, was to elevate the solemnity of the Offices and to bolster the often less-than-satisfactory chant of the canons. Guillaume André René Baston, a canon of Rouen at the twilight of the Ancien Régime, noted that often the lower form's "melodious voices drowned out" those of the members of the chapter,[19] while a critic of the canons of Metz reproached them for having become "idle spectators of high-pitched and droning voices."[20]

Moreover, chapters also included a number of lay employees. In the moderately-sized cathedral chapter of Angoulême, the *musique du chœur* before the Revolution consisted of a master assisted by an under-master, six choir-boys dedicated solely to singing, two *hautes-contre*, four *basses-contre*, two tenors, two basses, and two serpents or bassoons, joined on solemnities by a small orchestra of amateur violinists.[21] Although it was generally rare for instruments to accompany the singing, wealthier chapters maintained true orchestras for the performance of instrumental concert pieces. This was notably the case in Reims and Notre-Dame in Paris, whose instrumental ensembles stood out for their remarkably modern configuration.[22] Chapters with sufficient resources appeared to attach great significance to the *musique*, as evidenced by the regular increase in the allocated funds for the music school (*psallette*) in certain communities throughout the eighteenth century.[23]

---

[17] A choir priest was one employed to sing in choir, a beneficer a cleric who held a benefice belonging to the chapter, and a *prêtre habitué* a priest who was attached to a chapter but not prebended or semi-prebended. They all sat in the lower form of the choir.
[18] Archives départementales du Pas-de-Calais, 2L1/172, Noms des hauts et petits vicaires, musiciens, bénéficiers et autres attachés à l'église d'Arras, around 1790.
[19] Guillaume André René Baston, *Mémoires de l'abbé Baston, chanoine de Rouen*, ed. Julien Loth and Charles Verger, vol. 5, *1741–1792* (Paris, 1899), 270.
[20] *Quelques réflexions d'un Patriote sur une Brochure ayant pour titre: Mémoire du Chapitre de la Cathédrale de Metz, au Roi* (Metz, 1789), 16.
[21] Archives de l'évêché d'Angoulême, Renseignement sur l'état actuel de la liturgie, de la musique et du chant ecclésiastique, 14 November 1812. On these professional musicians, see Bernard Dompnier, *Maîtrises et chapelles aux XVIIe et XVIIIe siècles. Des institutions musicales au service de Dieu* (Presses universitaires Blaise-Pascal, 2003), and Bernard Dompnier and Jean Duron, eds., *Le Métier du maître de musique d'Église (XVIIe–XVIIIe siècles). Activités, sociologie, carrières* (Brepols, 2020).
[22] See John McManners, *Church and Society in Eighteenth Century France* (Clarendon Press, 1998), 1:458.
[23] Da Silva, "La maîtrise," 43–45.

Dignities and Offices

Each chapter comprised a number of dignities, that is, benefices which gave their holders rank and privileges, especially preeminence in choir.[24] The term can refer both to the benefice and its holder. Their number varied considerably. The cathedral chapter of Chartres had seventeen dignitaries, while the smallest communities might have only one or two. In cases where the dignities were attached to canonries, the dignitaries are referred to as canons. However, a dignitary could also be held by an ecclesiastic bereft of a canonry. In Rouen, for example, the four archdeacons held rank in the metropolitan chapter without being prebendaries.[25] In Clermont, a dignity could be bestowed upon an ecclesiastic from outside the chapter, but subsequently the first vacant canonical prebend was always given to him.[26]

In most cathedrals the archdeacon, whom the Council of Trent called the *oculus episcopi* (bishop's eye),[27] held the highest dignity by right. His duties, however, could vary greatly. The canonist Pierre-Toussaint Durand de Maillane puts it succinctly: "One sees therefore that in certain dioceses archdeacons wield extensive episcopal rights, while in others their authority is almost entirely titular."[28] The provost or dean usually acted as head of the chapter and officiated on greater feasts in the bishop's absence. The major cantor, or precentor, was responsible for the chant sung in the choir, which he conducted personally on the most solemn feasts. In the cathedral of Angoulême, for instance, there were thirteen "cantor's feasts" a year,[29] during which two canons acted as cope-bearers and two others as deacon and subdeacon. On other days, the cantor delegated his responsibilities to one or more succentors, but still maintained his authority in the choir, where canons and members of the lower form owed him obedience. In some chapters, a treasurer watched over the church's relic collection. Some dignities did not have any real function. Thus, the cathedral of Metz's first dignitary was a prince with mostly honorary duties, while at Clermont the chapter's "abbot" harked back to the time before the chapter's secularization, when the community of canons lived under the authority of an abbot. Indeed, many dignities were vestiges of the medieval past. Many chapters, for instance, retained the dignity of the canon *écolâtre* or *scolastique*, a legacy of the ancient cathedral schools that had largely lost its practical role by

---

[24] Pierre-Toussaint Durand de Maillane, *Dictionnaire de droit canonique et de pratique bénéficiale conféré avec les maximes et la jurisprudence de France* (Paris, 1761), 1:523.
[25] Pierre Langlois, *Essai historique sur le chapitre de Rouen pendant la Révolution (1789–1802)* (Rouen, 1856), 6.
[26] Welter, "Le chapitre cathédral," 7.
[27] Council of Trent, Session 24, chap. 12 *De reformatione*, in *Canons and Decrees of the Council of Trent*, ed. H. J. Schroeder (B. Herder Book Co., 1950), 201, 470.
[28] Durand de Maillaine, *Dictionnaire*, 1:118.
[29] Archives départementales de la Charente, 2V12, Individus de l'ancien chapitre d'Angoulême, around 1805.

the eighteenth century. Nevertheless in Soissons, to take one example, this dignitary continued to play a role inspecting the college and the primary schools and was responsible for overseeing the chanting of the Matins lessons by the clerics of the lower form.[30] In most communities, the chapter elected the dignitaries, with the exception of the archdeacons.

Besides dignities, there were offices attached to specific functions. The Council of Trent had ordered each cathedral chapter to maintain a canon theologian and a canon penitentiary. The former was required to teach Scripture to the canons and clerics who served the chapter, as well as to preach a certain number of sermons in the cathedral each year. So Le Brun des Marettes reports that the theologian of the cathedral of Angers gave a sermon on every first Sunday of the month before the general procession.[31] He had to be a theology graduate and was strictly bound to residence. As for the penitentiary, he was the general confessor of the diocese, with faculties from the bishop to hear confessions in the entire diocese and to absolve reserved cases.

Canonical Prebends

The canonry was composed of two elements: the canonicate, which is the spiritual role of the canon, and the prebend, the right to certain revenues in a cathedral or collegiate church. These revenues consist of the *gros*, which forms the major portion and is derived from the chapter's income or attached to a parish's tithes, and the distributions tied to a canon's regularity of attendance at the Offices, verified by the *pointeur* placed at the entrance of choir. The size of the prebend varied significantly from one chapter to another. On the eve of the Revolution, at Clermont a typical canonical prebend was worth a little over 1,100 pounds, whereas at Angoulême it reached 2,000 pounds, exceeded 4,000 pounds at Metz, and rose as high as 7,000 pounds in Paris. Furthermore, within the same community there could be substantial disparities of income, especially where substantial prebends were attached to the dignities. For instance, during the same time period, the canon who held the archdeaconry of Arras received 2,000 pounds more than the usual income, while the princely dignity of Metz brought in over 5,400 pounds, and the deanery over 9,000 pounds. While the remuneration of cathedral canons far exceeded that of the parish clergy, the incomes of canons in small collegiate churches were sometimes very modest to the point of insignificance as is the case of Lamballe, where the prebend only yielded 50 pounds to its holder, who could therefore had to acquire multiple benefices to sustain himself.

---

[30] Pierre Houllier, *État ecclésiastique du diocèse de Soissons* (Compiègne, 1783), 442. According to des Marettes, the *capiscol* in Vienne (see p. 11, n. 16) still had a liturgical role, and that of Rouen (p. 248) still assigned the Matins lessons.
[31] See p. 70.

Throughout the eighteenth century, these significant disparities and, in particular, the growing difficulties faced by low-born ecclesiastics aspiring to become canons in important chapters bred resentment and conflicts which challenged the very existence of chapters. The Jansenist and Richerist canonist Gabriel-Nicolas Maultrot defended the chapter's rights and mission as a counterbalance to episcopal despotism, but his position became increasingly isolated.[32] The exemptions from episcopal jurisdiction enjoyed by most cathedral chapters were the object of nearly unanimous disapproval, and many parish priests openly questioned the usefulness of these institutions and denied their antiquity. "Even if there were no more canons at all in the diocese of Auxerre, or even in the entire Church of God," cried Claude Salomon, a parish priest in Auxerre, "the Church would still be the mystical Body of Jesus Christ, and one cannot see what the faithful would thereby lose that could hinder them from working towards their salvation."[33] For his part, Henri Reymond, a radical advocate of the rights of parish priests, asked, "If an entire collegiate church [...] should come to perish in an accident, with all its members, it would indubitably be a dreadful tragedy. [...] But would they leave any orphans behind?"[34] Although not aligned with theological Jansenism, Reymond nevertheless embraced the Jansenist call for a more collegial form of Church government and deplored the competition between capitular and parish services in cities. The only capitular function that escaped his radical criticism was the jurisdiction they held during *sede vacante*, but he called on them to incorporate pastors of lesser rank. In many dioceses, parish priests also demanded that certain canonries be reserved for elder members of the parochial clergy. "It would undoubtedly be appropriate,"

---

[32] Edmond Richer (1560–1631) was a prominent Gallicanist theologian who defended the collegiate forms of government at all levels of the Church. Thus, he believed the pope's power should be tempered by that of the assembly of bishops, the bishops' power by the assembly of parish priests, and that of parish priests by the assembly of the faithful. His ideas enjoyed much currency among the Jansenists, and significantly influenced the discussions about the reorganization of the Gallican church in the Revolutionary National Constituent Assembly.

[33] Claude Salomon, *Lettres d'un Auxerrois à M. Frappier, Chanoine de l'Église Cathédrale d'Auxerre, et Agent des Réparations du Chapitre* (n.p., 1779), 42.

[34] Henry Reymond, *Droits des curés et des paroisses, considérés sous leur double rapport spirituel et temporel* (Paris, 1780), 27. This parish priest of Vienne (1737–1820) drew significantly from Richerism in his arguments that parish priests, the direct successors of Christ's seventy-two disciples, were, together with the pope and bishops, ministers of divine institution, unlike monks and canons, and therefore ought to have ordinary jurisdiction in their parishes, like bishops in their dioceses. He led illegal associations of parish priests to call for increases in their salaries, and his turbulent activities led his bishop to dub him the Don Quixote of parish priests. After the Revolution, he signed the Civil Constitution of the Clergy and became bishop of Isère, but after the Concordat of 1801 he signed a formula of retraction and was named bishop of Dijon with papal approval. For a discussion of his career, see Timothy Tackett, *Priest and Parish in Eighteenth-Century France: A Social and Political Study of the Curés in a Diocese of Dauphiné, 1750–1791* (Princeton University Press, 1977), 241–8.

wrote a parish priest of the diocese of Clermont on the eve of the Revolution, "to allocate a certain number of prebends, either in the cathedral or the collegiate churches, for parish priests, professors, and vicars bound to retire and to give up their noble functions."[35] Such demands collided with the unyielding conservatism of the majority of the canons of the larger chapters up to the Revolution.

In the eighteenth century, therefore, the *ordo canonicus* in France was a complex and hierarchical universe that mirrored the society of the Ancient Régime. In addition to the hierarchy of metropolitan, cathedral, and collegiate chapters, there were internal hierarchies among the dignitaries, full canons, semi-prebendaries, and the lower-formers, i.e., clergy or laymen at the service of the chapter. Largely disconnected from parish life and attached to their own peculiar traditions and privileges, canons in cathedrals and large collegiate churches shared an *esprit de corps*, and formed an intermediary ecclesiastical élite linked by birth and interests to the nobility of the gown. For that reason the *ordo canonicus* and the ancient system of benefices that maintained it were destined to be swept away by the French Revolution along with the whole network of orders and corporations of the Ancien Régime. When the cathedral chapters were refounded after 1802, they retained many of the essential functions of canons—celebrating the Office, supplying officials for the diocese, etc.—and attempted as best they could to revive some ancient customs. But the new structure imposed upon them by the Concordat emphasized uniformity and subordination to episcopal authority, in contrast to the relative independence and remarkable diversity of the pre-Revolutionary capitular world.[36]

---

[35] *Catéchisme des curés auvergnats amis de leur patrie, de leur roi et de leurs frères* (n.p., 1789), 67–68.
[36] For a recent discussion of the transformations of canonical life under the concordat and the modern Code of Canon Law, see Jerome Bertram, *Vita Communis: The Common Life of the Secular Clergy* (Gracewing Publishing, 2009), 250–90.

APPENDIX 2

A Brief History
of
Christian Altars and Sanctuaries

Shawn Tribe

IN the course of the *Liturgical Travels Through France*, Jean-Baptiste Le Brun des Marettes describes the sanctuaries in dozens of cathedrals, monasteries, and parishes. French churches in his day boasted features from many ages: elements from the paleo-Christian period, as well as the Middle Ages, the Renaissance, and the Baroque. While the architectural and art-historical elements of these churches would have been familiar to his readers, many are unfamiliar to readers today. The following brief history orients readers in these sanctuaries in order to help them visualize some of the objects and ornaments found there. It also touches on the disputes that were waged in the early modern period over the arrangement and decoration of these sanctuaries.

I. HISTORY AND FORMS OF THE CHRISTIAN ALTAR

Altars are the architectural and liturgical focal points of the interior of Catholic churches. Given their evident importance, it should come as no surprise that there have been different approaches and even disagreement about the ideal form of the altar and the proper arrangement of the sanctuaries built around. To understand those debates, one needs to know how the altar and sanctuary have been arranged at different periods of church history.

Early Christian Antiquity

Early Christian antiquity was the age of the house churches and catacomb churches. The altars of the house churches were, according to Stefan Heid, likely in the form of the Roman *mensa* or "sacred table."[1] As for the catacomb churches, they present a case of the Christian community coming to the site of the tomb of a martyr to celebrate the Eucharistic liturgy. It is believed that the tombs of the martyrs themselves may have served as altars. Evidently, however, much about this period remains necessarily speculative and interpretive.

---

[1] Stefan Heid, *Altar and Church: Principles of Liturgy from Early Christianity* (Catholic University of America Press, 2023), 21–22.

Late Antiquity and the Age of the Roman Basilicas

Wooden altars were used into the Middle Ages, but stone altars gradually came to be preferred. The *Catholic Encyclopedia* suggests:

> The idea of the stone altar, the use of which afterwards became universal in the West, is evidently derived from the custom of celebrating the anniversaries and other feasts in honor of those who died for the Faith. Probably, the custom itself was suggested by the message in the Apocalypse (6:9): "I saw under the altar the souls of them that were slain for the word of God." With the age of peace, and especially under the pontificate of Pope Damasus (366–384), basilicas and chapels were erected in Rome and elsewhere in honour of the most famous martyrs, and the altars, when at all possible, were located directly above their tombs. The *Liber Pontificalis* attributes to Pope Felix I (269–274) a decree to the effect that Mass should be celebrated on the tombs of the martyrs. However this may be, it is clear from the testimony of this authority that the custom alluded to was regarded at the beginning of the sixth century as very ancient.... The great veneration in which the martyrs were held from the fourth century had considerable influence in effecting two changes of importance with regard to altars. The stone slab enclosing the martyr's grave suggested the stone altar, and the presence of the martyr's relics beneath the altar was responsible for the tomblike under-structure known as the *confessio*. The use of stone altars in the East in the fourth century is attested by St. Gregory of Nyssa and St. John Chrysostom; and in the West, from the sixth century, the sentiment in favor of their exclusive use is indicated by [a] decree of the Council of Epaon.... Yet even in the West wooden altars existed as late as the reign of Charlemagne, as we infer from a capitulary of this emperor forbidding the celebration of Mass except on stone tables consecrated by the bishop. From the ninth century, however, few traces of the use of wooden altars are found in the domain of Latin Christianity.[2]

In this early period, great care was taken not to disturb the remains of the martyrs. Rather than relocating the martyrs to pre-existing churches and altars, these were effectively brought to the martyrs' resting places. An example of this *confessio* arrangement can be seen in the basilica of San Lorenzo fuori le mura in Rome, where the sanctuary is raised above the nave level, allowing the altar to be built directly over the tomb while leaving it undisturbed.

The fourth century saw the advent of the *ciborium magnum*. This was a fixed canopy built over the altar, set on four pillars. It became one of the most significant and distinctive features of the Christian altar. This

---

[2] Maurice Hassett, "Altar, History of the Christian," in *The Catholic Encyclopedia*, ed. Charles George Herbermann (Robert Appleton Company, 1907), 1:362–63.

particular feature gave what were otherwise smaller and simpler altars a certain architectural and symbolic prominence. Some suggest it was meant as a visual echo of coverings placed over certain martyrs' tombs, such as those of St. Peter and St. Paul.

The following description, taken from the *Liber Pontificalis*, of the great ciborium that originally stood in the Lateran basilica gives some idea of the grandeur of these structures in late antiquity:

> The interior of the Lateran ciborium was covered with gold, and from the centre hung a chandelier (*farus*) "of purest gold, with fifty dolphins of purest gold weighing fifty pounds, with chains weighing twenty-five pounds." Suspended from the arches of the ciborium, or in close proximity to the altar, were "four crowns of purest gold, with twenty dolphins, each fifteen pounds, and before the altar was a chandelier of gold, with eighty dolphins, in which pure nard was burned."[3]

These ciboria also had veils or curtains suspended around it that, it is thought, could be closed or opened at particular points within the liturgy. The liturgical scholar Cyril Pocknee notes the accounts of various veils donated by popes for this very purpose.[4] Further, the rods and other mechanisms used for suspending these veils are in a number of cases still in evidence on these ciboria.

While the altars of today tend to be longer, rectangular structures, altars in the first millennium were rather more cube-like in construction.[5] An example of this can be seen in the "Miracle of the Sea of Azov" fresco, located in the lower basilica of San Clemente in Rome. In addition to the smaller size of the altars of this period, it should additionally be noted that, unlike in later centuries, nothing was placed on the *mensa* (i.e., table-top) of the altar itself other than what was strictly needed for the Eucharistic sacrifice—a practice which may help to explain their smaller proportions.

Geoffrey Webb notes that the early altars of this period were also draped with fine silk or linen, but no candlesticks were placed upon the altar itself (see PLATES 17, 26, 27, 29, 36, 39, 48). Rather, "any lights used were also hung from [the ciborium], or stood on the steps, or on the podium—that is, the screen of open columns between the altar and nave, which may still be seen in the Church of Santa Maria in Cosmedin in Rome" (see PLATES 13, 31).[6] By "podium" Webb refers to the chancel screen that separated the sanctuary from the nave. These screens would sometimes have candles placed along its top (see PLATES 13, 48), a feature that can still be seen on the great screen of

---

[3] Hasset, "Altar, History of the Christian," 1:364.
[4] Cyril Pocknee, *The Christian Altar: In History and Today* (A. R. Mowbray, 1963), 59–63.
[5] PLATE 4 shows two examples of altars from the eleventh and twelfth centuries that retain the primitive small cubic shape. Both have a recessed top, a feature of earlier altars Le Brun des Marettes is careful to note in the *Travels*.
[6] Geoffrey Webb, *The Liturgical Altar* (The Newman Press, 1949), 27.

the Sistine Chapel. In general, hanging lamps and great standing candlesticks and candelabra were a common practice in ancient churches of both East and West, whether in the form of large *candelabra magna* placed near the altar, or other candelabra placed in and around the sanctuary, chancel, and nave (see PLATES 1, 20, 48).

In the Lyonese and Dominican rites (as well as other medieval rites), remnants of this type of usage can be seen in the manner by which the candle-bearers place their candles on the ground near the altar (see PLATES 31, 43). This practice was further developed in the primatial cathedral of Lyon where, prior to 1748, a great fixed candelabrum of seven candles known as the *râtelier* stood before the high altar. This structure held seven candles, one of which burned continuously (see PLATE 9). Later, the *râtelier* was replaced by seven standalone, moveable candlesticks that were set on the ground before the high altar within the chancel (see PLATE 13).

Finally, where the Sacrament was reserved at the altar, no tabernacle was placed atop it. Instead, a hanging pyx, frequently in the form of a dove, was used; this too would have been suspended from the ciborium (see PLATE 30).

The Medieval Period (ca. 800–1400) and the Age of Relics

The eighth and ninth century was the great age of the relics. In this turbulent period, many of the Roman martyrs' relics were brought out of the catacombs into the city and its churches—in part to keep them safe during those chaotic times. These relics were eventually displayed on the altars as well as behind them and above them in various sorts of relic shrines. As a result, the shape of the altar began to expand to accommodate these devotional relic displays. Relatedly, on some great feasts, moveable decorations—a painting, a textile, or a decorative piece of metalwork—could be placed behind the altar to add an additional layer of symbolism, solemnity, and festivity to the occasion (see PLATE 29). During the later Middle Ages, this screen developed into the retable, an ornamental piece placed behind or on the back side of the altar.

As relics were transferred to new locations, the practice of building altars over them (i.e., the *confessio* model) faded. Similarly, as altars grew in size and relic shrines began to be placed on or behind them, the *ciborium magnum* itself gradually disappeared to make room. The use of retables and the ever-increasing size of the altars during this period made the tomb form the most practical choice, as it could best support the weight of this new arrangement.

Concurrent with their increasing size, altars also began to be placed further back within the sanctuary (see PLATE 1). This not only further contributed to the gradual disappearance of the *ciborium magnum*, but also led to the introduction of elements intended to compensate for that loss, such as the "tester," i.e., a canopy suspended from the ceiling (see PLATES 13, 26, 56). Furthermore, what had been the four columns of the ciborium would become, in some places, riddel posts located on or near the four corners of the altar. From these, curtains were suspended and some have proposed that these curtains may well have been derived from the curtains that once hung from the *ciborium magnum* (see PLATES 16, 29, 31).

Candlesticks were placed on the altar itself by the eleventh century — at first only during the liturgy proper, but eventually as permanent fixtures as we are most familiar with today. At the time of the writing of the *Travels*, however, Le Brun des Marettes was still able to find a number of altars that did not have candles permanently placed upon them. Eventually an altar cross also came to occupy a place upon the altar (see PLATES 2, 8, 29, 34, 43), whereas until then the cross was either suspended from the ciborium or simply stood near the altar, whether it was a processional cross or not (see PLATES 31, 40).

During this period, tabernacles were not placed directly on the altar. Instead, the Sacrament was typically reserved elsewhere, such as in an aumbry built into the church wall, a Sacrament tower, or, from about the eleventh century, in a hanging pyx that was generally covered with a veil (see PLATES 26, 29, 30, 31, 34, 39).

The number of candlesticks found on the altar was also not universal at this time; it too varied according to place and custom. Historical records mention various numbers — including five, seven, nine, and sometimes even more — but most medieval illuminations depict the use of two candlesticks, one at either end of the altar (see PLATES 28, 29, 56).

Finally, it is worth noting that the *predella* (i.e., the raised platform upon which the altar itself was set), a feature common from about the fourth century onward, continued to be maintained during this period. It was most frequently in the form of a single step or platform, but by the fifteenth century, it had grown to consist of three steps, and sometimes even more (cf. PLATES 1, 17, 28, 31, 34, 36, 39, 48, 56).

The Renaissance to the Eighteenth Century and Beyond: Eucharistic Piety and Baroque Drama

While the age of relics encouraged the development of larger and more embellished altars, it was the Eucharistic piety of the late medieval and Counter-Reformation periods that fully pushed them into the form that we now consider the classic Latin or Tridentine Catholic altar. What had been relatively modest retables, relic shrines, or temporary decorative images placed behind the altar, grew in size and ornamentation, turning into what we now tend to call a reredos in English, i.e a great ornamental screen directly behind the altar. The reredos developed throughout the Renaissance and Baroque periods in a way that was consonant with the more elaborate ornamentation and larger scale of churches (see PLATES 16, 17, 28, 31, 36, 48, 56 for various types of altarpieces).[7]

By the sixteenth century, gradines—small, raised shelves that sit adjacent to the *mensa* of the altar—grew in size and number, and the tabernacle came to take its now familiar place on the center of a church's high altar, reflecting the Eucharistic piety of the time as well as the post-Tridentine emphasis on the doctrine of the Real Presence. It was also during this period that candlesticks and crosses became permanent fixtures on the altar (or on the gradines, if present), and the number of candles became standardized. As the decades and centuries passed and Eucharistic exposition became an ever more popular expression of Latin Catholic piety, permanent exposition thrones attached to altars were introduced, becoming especially popular in the late eighteenth and nineteenth century. This development led to a larger and more ornamental form of the tabernacle.

There were regional variations in style during these centuries. In the central and northern parts of Europe, for example, emphasis was placed on the use of elaborate reredoses. In the south, by comparison, the tendency was toward altars with large gradines and tabernacles. The same patterns are observable in France, with the more northerly portions of the country tending more toward the former, while those parts closer to the Mediterranean and Italy saw a greater tendency toward the latter. Suffice it to say, exceptions can always be found and it is impossible to make absolutes of these matters, but there were certainly observable regional tendencies and trends, and those trends often informed some of the controversies around the altar and its arrangement.

II. HISTORICAL MODES OF EUCHARISTIC RESERVATION

In the history of the Church, there have been different approaches to the reservation of the Holy Eucharist. In early times, Eucharistic reservation was primarily a practical consideration rather than a devotional one, done mainly for the sake of timely administration of Viaticum to the sick and dying. As the centuries passed, a deeper devotion to the Eucharistic Sacrament arose, and with it a concurrent desire to give it a more prominent and visible placement. This resulted in developments in the place and manner in which Eucharist was to be reserved.

Four main types can be identified, most of which appear in the *Travels*:

The Aumbry

An aumbry is a small recessed space set into the wall, be it in the apse, in the sacristy, or sometimes even the altar itself. Wherever it was located,

---

[7] Editors' note: Other languages do not draw a distinction between a retable and a reredos, and our translation of the *Liturgical Travels* follows the French original in using the single term "retable" to refer to the structure behind an altar.

it was enclosed by a door and within the Eucharist was reserved. This was a common method for Eucharistic reservation during the Middle Ages.

The Hanging Pyx

The hanging pyx was another and more elaborate method of Eucharistic reservation. As the name suggests, it is a form of suspended tabernacle for the Blessed Sacrament (see PLATE 30). Archdale King suggests that this was a "very general," albeit not universal, form of Eucharistic reservation throughout England, Scotland and France during the Middle Ages. In France, it seems to have continued even later still. Of its characteristics, ornamentation and function, King writes:

> The usual method for fixing the pyx was for a crane or pulley to be so arranged over the altar as to permit of the ready raising or lowering of the pyx, which was suspended by a cord or chain attached to a ring on its top. Above the pyx was hung the canopy, a circular tent-like construction formed of some costly fabric, which was generally attached to a ring and ornamental crown of metal. The pyx itself was veiled in a pyx cloth, which often had the form of a square napkin, with a hole in the middle, through which the suspending cord passed, and weighted tassels at the four corners which kept it down close by the pyx.[8]

The circular tent-like canopy sometimes placed above the pyx can be seen in various medieval manuscripts and illustrations (see PLATES 26, 29, 30, 31, 34, 39). In France, pyxes were often suspended from a structure that looked like a large crosier. This rose up from behind the center of the altar like a large staff, curving at the top like a crosier; from this the pyx was suspended (see PLATES 29, 30, 39). An example of this crosier-suspension can still be seen today in the Cistercian abbey church in Valloires, France.

The Sacrament Tower

Another, even more elaborate form of Eucharistic reservation was the so-called "Sacrament house" or "Sacrament tower." This was a large architectural structure typically positioned within the presbytery or near the sanctuary, typically off to one side. Within that tower-like structure was a door, behind which the Eucharist was reserved. This method of reservation was effectively an aumbry, but with a much more elaborate, prominent and decorative structure surrounding it to give it greater visibility and prominence.

The Tabernacle

Finally, there is the tabernacle, the most familiar and modern method of reservation, having dominated the Catholic world since the

---

[8] Archdale King, *Eucharistic Reservation in the Western Church* (A.W. Mowbray & Co., 1965), 83.

Counter-Reformation. There are two primary types. The first is akin to a smaller Sacrament tower, typically cylindrical or rectangular in shape and covered by a silk veil in the liturgical color of the day or season. The second is more similar to an aumbry, but one set within the gradines or embedded within the reredos. Regardless of which of these two forms the tabernacle takes, it is, unlike a Sacrament tower or aumbry, usually attached to the center of the church's main altar. In the case of cathedrals, however, the tabernacle was typically placed on a separate altar within a designated chapel due to the ceremonial requirements of the pontifical liturgy.

In his *Travels*, des Marettes expresses hostility to Counter-Reformation era developments that saw tabernacles placed on the main altar, seeing this as contrary to earlier historical approaches to Eucharistic reservation. While this was a debate Le Brun des Marettes was destined to ultimately lose, it is one that was picked up again in the twentieth century when some figures within the Liturgical Movement advocated for what they saw as more primitive arrangements of the altar and presbytery.

III. THE ANTEPENDIUM, PALLIUM ALTARIS, OR ALTAR FRONTAL

The Historical Development of the Antependium

The Catholic Encyclopedia suggests that the origins of the antependium may be found in the metallic coverings or silk veils that were hung before the *confessio* where the relics of some venerated martyr were deposited.[9] Obviously this is somewhat speculative but certainly in paleo-Christian times veils were also hung from the balustrades (i.e., chancel screens) that surrounded the altar itself, as well as being also hung from the ciborium over the altar. As far as its specific form is concerned, Cyril Pocknee notes:

> Even in the primitive period not only was the altar covered with a linen cloth or pall for the celebration of the Eucharist; but also the [altar] was vested with silk cloths.... Palladius, writing about 421, mentions some Roman ladies who, renouncing the world, bequeathed their silks to make coverings for the altar.... The *Liber Pontificalis* testifies that during the eighth and ninth centuries coverings for the altar made of gold thread and decorated with jewels and pearls and embroidered with figures of Our Lord, the Blessed Virgin Mary and the apostles were given to the great Roman basilicas by succeeding popes.[10]

Pocknee further speaks to the development of its form as follows:

> While the altar remained cubical in form, the "throw-over" type of pall continued in use.... This linen cloth, known as the

---

[9] Augustin Joseph Schulte, "Altar," in *The Catholic Encyclopedia*, 1:353.
[10] Pocknee, *Christian Altar*, 45–46.

palla corporalis, was thrown over the altar, much as an ordinary table-cloth is spread today, by the deacons, and it fell down around all sides of the table. But in the Gothic period, when the altar tended to be lengthened, two things happened: (a) the linen pall became divided into two parts, one part being a long strip which covered the top of the altar and fell down over each end of the *mensa*, while the other part became the "corporal" which covered the elements; (b) the silk pall becomes the antependium or frontal covering the front elevation of the altar only when it stood close to a wall or screen. But it should be noted that where the longer type of altar was free-standing a "frontal" was provided for both back and front.[11]

J. B. O'Connell comments that the earliest frontals were "often made in purple and gold and ornamented with jewels, or with beautiful embroideries,"[12] something Pocknee mentions as well.[13] An illumination found in the benedictional of St. Ethelwold seems to show this form.[14]

Two further developments were the metallic altar frontal and color schemes. Specific schemes for liturgical colors began to be formalized in the later Middle Ages, leading to the current practice of vesting the altar in the color of the liturgical day or season.

The Symbolism of Antependia in Relation to the Altar

Traditionally the altar is understood as a symbol of Christ. It is in view of this that the antependium takes on its own symbolic aspect as a kind of clothing or even vesture for the altar. This is why Geoffrey Webb refers to the antependium as a "a covering of honor"[15] and "robes of majesty."[16] Likewise, Peter Anson speaks in similar terms of the altar being "clothed in precious vestments" on account of the altar's dignity as a Christological symbol.[17]

As Webb notes, this usage furnishes the liturgy with powerful symbolism at times like the liturgy of Holy Thursday when the altar is ceremonially stripped: "... when the Robes of Majesty are all removed on Holy Thursday, more is indicated than the removal of His garments. His faithful, His costly garments, His disciples, are all stripped from Him; and His desolation is made all the more evident by this complete annihilation of color."[18]

---

[11] Pocknee, *Christian Altar*, 46.
[12] J. B. O'Connell, *Church Building and Furnishing: The Church's Way* (University of Notre Dame Press, 1995), 193.
[13] Pocknee, *Christian Altar*, 45–46.
[14] London, British Library, MS. add. 49598, fol. 118v.
[15] Webb, *Liturgical Altar*, 63.
[16] Webb, *Liturgical Altar*, 65.
[17] Peter Anson, *Churches: Their Plan and Furnishing* (The Bruce Publishing Company, 1948), 117.
[18] Webb, *Liturgical Altar*, 65.

The antependium also has a practical dimension insofar as it furnishes the altar with, as Webb says, an "architectural prominence which its central position in the liturgy requires."[19]

IV. THE ARRANGEMENT OF SANCTUARIES IN THE *LITURGICAL TRAVELS*

This edition of the *Liturgical Travels Through France* is enriched with several illustrations of early-modern French sanctuaries as they would have appeared to Le Brun des Marettes during his visits. The liturgies he describes, whether contemporary or late-medieval, took place in church settings such as these. A brief description therefore seems warranted.

The larger churches, monasteries and cathedrals of France still often preserved arrangements from the medieval and Renaissance periods. The altar and chancel were separated from the nave of the church by some form of barrier, which could be a full-fledged chancel or rood screen, or be a smaller barrier with a separate rood beam located above.

Within the chancel, also referred to as the choir—the space immediately beyond the chancel barrier—seating was built in a choral arrangement, where the seats faced one another, which is to say, perpendicular to the altar. Here, the canons and other clerics not formally engaged as liturgical ministers participated in the Mass and Divine Office (see PLATES 1, 13, 26, 34, 50). Sometimes a lectern was placed in the middle of the chancel, often shaped like an eagle, and a form or bench from which the coped cantors led the liturgical chants proper to a given service (see cover and PLATES 26, 34).

In some instances, the aforementioned chancel screens might also have secondary side altars attached to them, located on the nave side of the screen on either side of the central door (see PLATES 1, 8, 16, 36, 48). These altars were used for smaller scale low Masses. If the church hosted a parish, its Masses took place at one of these altars outside the screen (see PLATES 1, 8, 48), or at an altar located in the transept or a side aisle of the church. The laity assisted at ceremonies from the nave, though certain important laymen—such as nobles or important patrons—could be allowed in choir as well, or even have their own stalls. The rood screen's doors were usually closed during services to allow for the free movement of the clergy, but circulation in the choir was often permitted at other times.[20]

Past the chancel is the part of the sanctuary where the altar is located, frequently enclosed by a balustrade akin to an altar rail (see PLATES 1, 5, 13, 14, 16, 17, 36, 48). In Le Brun des Marettes's day, the altar was often still in

---

[19] Webb, *Liturgical Altar*, 67.
[20] For documentation, see Jacqueline E. Jung, *The Gothic Screen: Space, Sculpture, and Community in the Cathedrals of France and Germany, ca. 1200–1400* (Cambridge University Press, 2013), 68–69.

the form inherited from the later Middle Ages and Renaissance, with the altar surrounded on three sides by curtains hung from riddel posts (see PLATES 1, 16, 17, 26, 28, 29, 31, 34, 39, 48).

The eighteenth century would, however, see many of these sanctuaries converted into the Baroque style, and they further began adopting the liturgical ordering that became normative during the Counter-Reformation following the Council of Trent. During this period, there was a strong impulse to make the liturgical rites and ceremonies more visible to the laity. As a result, chancel screens were frequently removed and replaced by low altar rails, and the use of riddel posts and curtains around the altar was abandoned. The end result was an unobstructed view of the altar from the nave (see PLATES 2, 40, 43). Additionally, tabernacles were frequently placed on the main altar (with the exception of cathedrals) and reredoses grew ever more monumental in size. These developments were not without some measure of opposition and controversy and some sought to preserve the earlier Medieval and Renaissance orderings, as can be observed in Le Brun des Marettes' own text. It is, in fact, a point of debate that has continued into contemporary times, particularly as a result of the nineteenth and twentieth century Gothic revival movement, which sought to restore anything and everything "medieval."

BIBLIOGRAPHY

"4 Avril 1732." *Nouvelles ecclésiastiques* (1732): 65–68

De l'abstinence du samedi. Brussels, 1844.

Ado of Vienne, *Chronicon sive Breviarium de sex mundi aetatibus ab Adamo usque ad annum 869*. PL 123:23–143.

Allmer, Augustine and Alfred de Terrebasse, eds. *Inscriptions antiques et du moyen âge de Vienne en Dauphiné*. 6 vols. Vienne, 1875–1876.

Amalar of Metz. *On the Liturgy*. Edited and translated by Eric Knibbs. 2 vols. Dumbarton Oaks Medieval Library 35 and 36. Harvard University Press, 2014.

———. *Amalarii Episcopi opera liturgica omnia*. Edited by Jean Michel Hanssens. 3 vols. Studi e testi 138–140. Biblioteca Apostolica Vaticana, 1948–1950.

Ambrose, St. *De mysteriis*. Edited by Otto Faller. Corpus Scriptorum Ecclesiasticorum Latinorum 73. Hoelder-Pichler-Tempsky, 1955.

Amiet, Robert, ed. *Missels et bréviaires imprimés*. Éditions du Centre national de la recherche scientifique, 1990.

Andrieu, Michel, ed. *Les Ordines Romani du haut moyen âge*. 5 vols. Spicilegium sacrum Lovaniense, 1948.

Ansgrad. *Vita S. Ansberti episcopi Rotomagensis*. In *Acta sanctorum Ordinis sancti Benedicti*, edited by Jean Mabillon. Vol. 2, 1055–56. Paris, 1669.

Anson, Peter F. *Churches: Their Plan and Furnishing*. Bruce Publishing Company, 1948.

Arnauld, Antoine. *Défense des versions de l'Écriture sainte, des offices de l'Église, et des ouvrages des Pères*. Cologne, 1688.

"Article I." *L'Europe savante* 5, no. 2 (October 1718): 163–200.

The Assisi Papers: Proceedings of the First International Congress of Pastoral Liturgy, Assisi-Rome, September 18–22, 1956. Liturgical Press, 1957.

Augustine, St. *Contra duas epistulas Pelagianorum*. Edited by Karl F. Urba and Joseph Zycha. Corpus scriptorum ecclesiasticorum Latinorum 60. Hoelder-Pichler-Tempsky, 1913.

———. *Epistulae*. Edited by Alois Goldbacher. 4 vols. Corpus Scriptorum Ecclesiasticorum Latinorum 34, 44, 57, 58. F. Tempsky, 1894–1923.

Aurelianus of Arles, St. *Regula ad monachos*. PL 68:385D–94B.

Avril, Joseph, ed. *Les conciles de la province de Tours*. Éditions du Centre national de la recherche scientifique, 1987.

Barthe, Claude. *A Forest of Symbols: The Traditional Mass and Its Meaning*. Translated by David J. Critchley. Angelico Press, 2023.

Baston, Guillaume André René. *Mémoires de l'abbé Baston, chanoine de Rouen*. Vol. 5, *1741–1792*, edited by Julien Loth and Charles Verger. Paris, 1899.

Beauduin, Lambert. "Messe basse ou messe solennelle?" *Les questions liturgiques et paroissiales* 5 (1919–1920): 90–97.

Becket, St. Thomas. *Epistula* 232. In *The Correspondence of Thomas Becket, Archbishop of Canterbury, 1162–1170*, edited and translated by Anne Duggan. Vol. 2. Clarendon Press, 2000.

Beleth, John. *Summa de ecclesiasticis officiis*. Edited by Heribert Douteil. Corpus Christianorum Continuatio Mediaeualis 41A. Brepols, 1976.

Bennett, Peter. *Music and Power in the Court of Louis XIII: Sounding the Liturgy in Early Modern France*. Cambridge University Press, 2021.

Bergot, François et al. *La peinture d'inspiration religieuse à Rouen au temps de Pierre Corneille (1606–1684)*. Musée des Beaux-Arts, 1984.

Bernard, Philippe. "Liturgies chrétiennes en Occident (de l'Antiquité tardive à l'époque moderne)." *Annuaire de l'École pratique des hautes études (EPHE), Section des sciences religieuses* 131 (2024): 187–192.

Bernold of Constance. *Micrologus*. PL 151:977C–1022B.

Bertram, Jerome. *Vita Communis: The Common Life of the Secular Clergy*. Gracewing Publishing, 2009.

Bérulle, Pierre de. *L'office de Jésus*. Paris, 1673.

Beyssac, Jean. "Les grands prêtres de l'église de Lyon." In *Mémoires de la Société littéraire, historique et archéologique de Lyon, années 1898 à 1902*, 137–56. Louis Brun, 1903.

Bimbenet, Eugène. "Justice temporelle de l'évêché d'Orléans à cause de la tour de la Fauconnerie." *Mémoires de la Société archéologique de l'Orléanais* 6 (1863): 1–109.

Bisaro, Xavier. *Chanter toujours. Plain-chant et religion villageoise dans la France moderne (XVIe-XIXe siècle)*. Presses universitaires de Rennes, 2020.

———. *Le passé présent. Une enquête liturgique dans la France du début du XVIIIe siècle*. Histoire religieuse de la France 38. Cerf, 2012.

Blanchard, Shaun. *The Synod of Pistoia and Vatican II: Jansenism and the Struggle for Catholic Reform*. Oxford University Press, 2019.

Blanchard, Shaun and Richard T. Yoder, eds. *Jansenism: An International Anthology*. Catholic University of America Press, 2024.

Bock, Franz. *Geschichte der liturgischen Gewänder des Mittelalters*. Vol. 3, *Die Paramentik des Altares und des Chores im Mittelalter*. Bonn, 1871.

Bocquillot, Lazare-André. *Traité historique de la liturgie*. Paris, 1701.

Bona, Giovanni. *Rerum liturgicarum libri duo*. 2 vols. Rome, 1671.

Bossuet, Jacques-Bénigne. *Œuvres complètes de Bossuet*. Vol. 11, *Œuvres diverses*. Paris, 1863.

Braun, Joseph. *Die liturgische Gewandung im Occident und Orient nach Ursprung und Entwicklung, Verwendung und Symbolik*. Herdersche Verlagshandlung, 1907.

———. *Die liturgischen Paramente in Gegenwart und Vergangenheit*. Herder, 1924.

Bresc-Bautier, Geneviève. "Les imitations du Saint-Sépulcre de Jérusalem (IXe–XVe siècles). Archéologie d'une dévotion." *Revue d'histoire de la spiritualité* 50 (1974): 319–42.

Bricout, Hélène and Gilles Drouin, "Liturgie in Frankreich in der nachtridentinischen Epoche," in *Geschichte der Liturgie in den Kirchen des Westens: Rituelle Entwicklungen, theologische Konzepte und kulturelle Kontexte*, edited by Jürgen Bärsch and Benedikt Kranemann, vol. 2, *Moderne und Gegenwart*, 7–50. Aschendorff, 2018.

Browe, Peter. "Zur Geschichte des Dreifaltigkeitsfestes." *Archiv für Liturgiewissenschaft* 1 (1950): 65–81.

———. *Die Verehrung der Eucharistie im Mittelalter*. Herder, 1967.

Bruslons, Jacques Savary des. "Muid." *Dictionnaire universel de commerce*. Vol. 3. Geneva, 1742, 1454–55.

Buenner, Denys. *L'ancienne liturgie romaine. Le rite lyonnais*. Emmanuel Vitte, 1934.

Bugnini, Annibale. "Le 'Variationes' ad alcuni testi della Settimana Santa." *L'Osservatore Romano*, 10 March 1965.

Capitularia regum Francorum. Edited by Alfred Boretius and Victor Krause. MGH Leges 2. Hanover, 1893, 253–328.

Charles, Olivier. "Les *chanoines-chapelains* d'une petite collégiale bretonne." *Les Amis de Lamballe et du Penthièvre* 32 (2005): 81–106.

———. *Chanoines de Bretagne. Carrières et cultures d'une élite cléricale au siècle des Lumières*. Presses universitaires de Rennes, 2004.

Chartaire, Eugène, ed. *Cartulaire du chapitre de Sens*. Duchemin, 1904.

Chédozeau, Bernard. "Les grandes étapes de la publication de la Bible catholique en français du concile de Trente au XVIIIe siècle." In *Le Grand Siècle et la Bible*, edited by Jean-Robert Armogathe, Bible de tous les temps 6, 341–60. Beauchesne, 1989.

Chéruel, Adolphe, ed. *Normanniae nova chronica*. Caen, 1850.

Chevalier, Ulysse. *Étude historique sur la constitution de l'église métropolitaine et primatiale de Vienne*. 2 vols. H. Martin, 1922.

Chorier, Nicolas. *Histoire sur les antiquitez de la ville de Vienne*. 2nd ed. Vienne, 1673.

Clercq, Charles de, ed. *Concilia Galliae (a. 511–a. 695)*, Corpus Christianorum Series Latina 148A. Brepols, 1963.

Cognet, Louis. "Spirituality in Seventeenth-Century France: Christian Life," in *The History of the Church*, vol. 6, *The Church in the Age of Absolutism and Enlightenment*, edited by Hubert Jedin and John Dolan, translated by Gunther J. Holst, 84–88. Crossroad, 1981.

Colonia, Dominique de. *Bibliothèque Janseniste*. Vol. 1. Brussels, 1739.

———. *Histoire littéraire de la ville de Lyon*. 2 vols. Lyon, 1730.

Corblet, Jules. *Histoire dogmatique, liturgique et archéologique du sacrement du baptême*. 2 vols. Paris, 1881–1882.

Collette, Armand. *Histoire du bréviaire de Rouen*. L. Mégard, 1902.

Collomb, Pascal. "L'ordinaire liturgique perdu de la collégiale Saint-Paul de Lyon (fin XIVe siècle)." L'Institut de recherche et d'histoire des textes. Last modified 24 September 2015. https://irht.hypotheses.org/650.

Concilium Constantinopolitanum...sub Menna...celebratum, Actio V. In *Sacrosancta concilia*, edited by Philippe Labbe and Gabriel Cossart. Vol. 5, 1A–276B. Paris, 1671.

Concilium Tridentinum diariorum, actorum, epistularum, tractatuum nova collectio. Edited by Societas Goerresiana. 13 vols. Herder, 1901–2001.

Corpus des inscriptions de la France médiévale. Edited by Robert Favreau et al. 26 vols. CNRS Éditions, 1974–2020.

"Copia cujusdam Epistolae a venerabili Facultate theologiae studii Parisiensis." PL 207:1169C–1176C.

Cuissard, Charles. "Étude sur le commerce et l'industrie à Orléans avant 1789." *Memóires de la Société d'agriculture, sciences, belles-lettres et arts d'Orléans* 35 (1897): 149–52.

Cyprian, St. *De lapsis*. Edited by Maurice Bénevot. Corpus Christianorum Series Latina 3, 217–42. Brepols, 1972.

d'Achery, Luc, ed. *Spicilegium sive collectio veterum aliquot scriptorum qui in Galliae bibliothecis delituerant*. Vol. 5. Paris, 1661.

Da Silva, Nathalie. "Être maître de musique à la cathédrale de Clermont au XVIIe et XVIIIe siècles." In *Les bas-chœurs d'Auvergne et du Velay*, edited by Bernard Dompnier, 135–53. Presses universitaires Blaise-Pascal, 2010.

Davis, Adam. *The Holy Bureaucrat: Eudes Rigaud and Religious Reform in Thirteenth-Century Normandy*. Cornell University Press, 2006.

Davy-Rigaux, Cécile, Bernard Dompnier, and Daniel-Odon Hurel, eds. *Les cérémoniaux catholiques en France à l'époque moderne. Une littérature de codification des rites liturgiques*. Brepols, 2009.

Davy-Rigaux, Cécile. "La Fête de Noël dans le diocèse de Paris au XVIIème siècle," *Siècles* 21 (2005): 27–39.

de Harlay, François. *La manière de bien entendre la messe de paroisse*. Paris, 1685.

Delamare, René, ed. *Le De officiis ecclesiasticis de Jean d'Avranches, archevêque de Rouen (1067–1079)*. Picard, 1923.

De miraculis Sancti Stephani. In *Sancti Aurelii Augustini Hipponensis Episcopi operum*, edited by the Congregation of St-Maur. Vol. 7, Appendix, 25–32 (Paris, 1685).

Desgraves, Louis et al., eds. *Répertoire bibliographique des livres imprimés en France au XVIIe siècle*. 32 vols. V. Koerner, 1968–2017.

de Vert, Claude. *Dissertation sur les mots de Messe et de Communion*. Paris, 1694.

——. *Explication simple, littérale et historique des cérémonies de l'Église pour les nouveaux convertis*. 4 vols. Paris, 1709–1713.

Diefendorf, Barbara B. *Planting the Cross: Catholic Reform and Renewal in Sixteenth- and Seventeenth-Century France*. Oxford University Press, 2019.

Dion, Adolphe de, ed. *Cartulaire de l'abbaye de Porrois*. Vol. 1, *1204–1280*. Alphonse Picard et fils, 1903.

Dissertation historique sur les rits et anciens usages de la noble et insigne église de Saint Martin de Tours. Paris, 1713.

Dompnier, Bernard, ed. *Les cérémonies extraordinaires du catholicisme baroque*. Presses universitaires Blaise-Pascal, 2009.

——. "Les 'petites farces ou comédies spirituelles' de Noël. Des traditions liturgiques contestées entre XVIIe et XVIIIe siècle." *Siècles* 21 (2005): 55–72.

——, ed. *Maîtrises et chapelles aux XVIIe et XVIIIe siècles. Des institutions musicales au service de Dieu*. Presses universitaires Blaise-Pascal, 2003.

—— and Jean Duron, eds. *Le Métier du maître de musique d'Église (XVIIe–XVIIIe siècles). Activités, sociologie, carrières*. Brepols, 2020.

Dubois, Alice. *Le chapitre cathédral de Saint-Lambert à Liège au XVIIe siècle*. Faculté de philosophie et lettres de Liège, 1949.

Doucette, Leonard E. *Émery Bigot: Seventeenth-Century French Humanist*. University of Toronto Press, 1970.

Ducasse, François. *Traité des droits et des obligations des chapitres des églises cathédrales*. Toulouse, 1706.

Du Cange, Charles Du Fresne, Sieur, et al., *Glossarium mediae et infimae latinitatis*. Edited by Léopold Favre. 10 vols. Niort, 1883–87. Accessed 26 January, 2025. http://ducange.enc.sorbonne.fr/

Du Lac, Melchior. *La liturgie Romaine et les liturgies françaises*. Le Mans, 1849.

Du Mont, Henri. *Cinq masses en plain-chant*. Paris, 1669.

Dupuoy, Achille. *Histoire de saint Martin, évêque de Tours*. Tours, 1858.

Durand, William. *Rationale diuinorum officiorum*. Edited by Anselme Davril and Timothy Thibodeau. 3 vols. Corpus Christianorum Continuatio Mediaeualis 140. Brepols, 1995–2000.

Durand de Maillane, Pierre-Toussaint. *Dictionnaire de droit canonique et de pratique bénéficiale conféré avec les maximes et la jurisprudence de France.* Vol. 1. Paris, 1761.

Duchesne, Henri-Gabriel. *La France ecclésiastique pour l'année 1788*. Paris, 1787.

Eusebius of Caesarea. *Ecclesiastical History*. Edited by Gustave Bardy, *Histoire ecclésiastique*. Vol. 2, *Livres V–VII*. Sources chrétiennes 41. Cerf, 1955.

Farcy, Louis de. *L'ancien trésor de la cathédrale d'Angers*. Arras, 1882.

Farcy, Louis de and Timothée-Louis Houdebine. *Monographie de la cathédrale d'Angers*. Vol. 4, *Les évêques — Le chapitre — Institutions diverses — Cérémonies — Anciens usages*. André Bruel, 1926.

Farin, François and Ignace Du Souillet. "Vicomté de l'Eau." In *Histoire de la ville de Rouen*, edited by François Farin. Vol. 2, 142–46. Rouen, 1731.

Fayolle, Léo. "L'aube était-elle portée par les moniales de Sainte-Croix au XIIIe siècle?" *Bulletins de la Société des antiquaires de l'Ouest* 9, series 3 (1933): 672–75.

Fiedrowicz, Michael. *The Traditional Mass: History, Form, and Theology of the Classical Roman Rite*. Angelico Press, 2020.

Friedberg, Emil, ed. *Corpus iuris canonici*. 2 vols. Akademische Druck- und Verlagsanstalt, 1959.

Földváry, Miklós István. "Continuity and Discontinuity in Local Liturgical Uses." *Ephemerides Liturgicae* 137 (2023): 23–26.

———. *USUARIUM: A Guide to the Study of Latin Liturgical Uses in the Middle Ages and the Early Modern Period*. 2023; privately published study.

Forest, Jean-Marie H. *L'école cathédrale de Lyon*. Paris, 1885.

Foulques de Villaret, Amicie. *Recherches historiques sur l'ancien chapitre de l'église d'Orléans*. Orléans, 1882.

Fouré, André. "Jean-Baptiste Le Brun des Marettes. Visiteur janséniste de la Cathédrale de Rouen à la fin du XVIIe siècle." *Précis analytique des travaux de l'Académie des sciences, belles-lettres et arts de Rouen* (1967): 71–97.

Fulbert of Chartres. *Epistulae*. PL 141:189A–264C.

———. *Epistulae*. Edited and translated by Frederick Behrends, *Letters and Poems of Fulbert of Chartres*. Clarendon Press, 1976.

Gavantus, Bartholomew. *Thesaurus sacrorum rituum*. Vol. 1. Antwerp, 1634.

Gaillardin, Casimir. *Les trappistes*. 2 vols. Paris, 1853.

Gâtineau, Péan. *Consuetudines ecclesiae beati Martini Turonensis*. In *Documents et manuscrits*. Vol. 1, *Rituel de Saint-Martin de Tours*, edited by Abbé Fleuret. Paris, 1899.

Girard, Bernard. "Conflits, violences et transgressions dans les trois psallettes de la France de l'Ouest aux XVIIe et XVIIIe siècles." In *Maîtrises et chapelles aux XVIIe et XVIIIe siècles*, edited by Bernard Dompnier, 83–96. Presses universitaires Blaise-Pascal, 2003.

Gomis, Stéphane. *Les "enfants prêtres" des paroisses d'Auvergne, XVIe-XVIIIe siècles*. Presses universitaires Blaise-Pascal, 2006.

Goujet, Claude-Pierre . *Supplément au grand dictionnaire historique, généalogique, &c., de M. Louis Moréri*. Vol. 1. Paris, 1735.

Grand, Antoine. "Notice historique et descriptive sur l'horloge astronomique de la cathédrale de Lyon." In *Mémoires de la Société littéraire, historique et archéologique de Lyon, années 1898 à 1902*, 81–98. Louis Brun, 1903.

Guilbert, Pierre. *Mémoires historiques et chronologiques sur l'Abbaye de Port-Royal des Champs*. Vol. 7, *Depuis de la paix de l'Église en 1668, jusqu'à la mort des dernières Religieuses et Amis de ce Monastère*. Utrecht, 1756.

Hardison, O. B. *Christian Rite and Christian Drama in the Middle Ages: Essays in the Origin and Early History of Modern Drama*. Johns Hopkins University Press, 1965. Reprint, 2019.

Hassett, Maurice. "Altar, History of the Christian." In *The Catholic Encyclopedia*, ed. Charles George Herbermann. Vol. 1, 362–67. Robert Appleton Company, 1907.

Havet, Julien. "Questions mérovingiennes, II. Les découvertes de Jérôme Vignier." *Bibliothèque de l'École des chartes* 46 (1885): 205–271.

Heid, Stefan. *Altar and Church: Principles of Liturgy from Early Christianity*. Catholic University of America Press, 2023.

Hélyot, Hippolyte, and Maximilien Bullot, *Histoire des ordres monastiques, religieux et militaires et des congrégations séculières*. 8 vols. Paris, 1714–1721

Henry, W. "Angélus." *Dictionnaire d'archéologie chrétienne et de liturgie*, edited by Fernand Cabrol. Vol. 1, part 2, 2068–2078. Letouzey et Ané, 1907.

Hiley, David. *Western Plainchant: A Handbook*. Oxford University Press, 1993.

Holy Office. "Dubium de valida concelebratione." 23 May 1957. *Acta Apostolicae Sedis* 49, 370.

Honestis, Peter de. *Regula clericorum*. PL 163:691A–748D.

Honorius Augustodunensis. *Gemma animae*. Edited and translated by Zachary Thomas and Gerhard Eger, *Jewel of the Soul*. Dumbarton Oaks Medieval Library 79–80. Harvard University Press, 2023.

Hou, François. *Chapitres et société en Révolution. Les chanoines en France de l'Ancien Régime à la monarchie de Juillet*. Presses universitaires de Rennes, 2023.

Houllier, Pierre. *État ecclésiastique du diocèse de Soissons*. Compiègne, 1783.

Huglo, Michel. "Du répons de l'Office avec prosule au répons organisé." In *Altes im Neuen. Festschrift Theodor Göllner zum 65. Geburtstag*, edited by Bernd Edelmann and Manfred Schmid, 25–36. Hans Schneider, 1995.

Hurel, Daniel-Odon. "Le *Voyage littéraire* de dom Edmond Martène et de dom Ursin Durand (Paris, 1717 et 1724), édition critique. Érudition mauriste et regard sur la vie religieuse en France aux Pays-Bas et en Allemagne au début du XVIIIe siècle." PhD diss. University of Tours, 1991.

Irving, Andrew J. M. "On the Counting of Mass Books." *Archiv für Liturgiewissenschaft* 57 (2015): 24–48.

Isidore, St. *Sententiae*. Edited by Pierre Cazier. Corpus Christianorum Series Latina III. Brepols, 1998.

Ivo of Chartres. *Epistulae*. Edited by Geneviève Giordanengo, *Lettres d'Yves de Chartres*. Institut de Recherche et d'Histoire des Textes, 2017. Accessed 26 January, 2025. http://telma-chartres.irht.cnrs.fr/yves-de-chartres.

Jarry, Eugène. "Le chapitre de Saint-Martin aux XVIIe et XVIIIe siècles." *Revue d'histoire de l'église de France* 144 (1961): 117–49.

John of Avranches. *Liber de officiis ecclesiasticis*. Edited by Jean-Baptiste Le Brun des Marettes. PL 147:27B–116D.

Jung, Jacqueline E. *The Gothic Screen: Space, Sculpture, and Community in the Cathedrals of France and Germany, ca. 1200–1400*. Cambridge University Press, 2013.

Jungmann, Joseph. *The Mass of the Roman Rite*. Translated by Francis Brunner. 2 vols. Benziger, 1951/1955. Originally published as *Missarum sollemnia*, 2 vols. Herder, 1949.

Kantorowicz, Ernst. *Laudes Regiae: A Study in Liturgical Acclamations and Mediaeval Ruler Worship*. University of California Publications in History 33. University of California Press, 1946. Reprint, 1958.

Kelly, Thomas Forrest. "Modal Neums at Sens." In *Western Plainchant in the First Millenium: Studies in the Medieval Liturgy and its Music*, edited by Sean Gallagher et al. Routledge, 2003.

King, Archdale. *Eucharistic Reservation in the Western Church*. A. W. Mowbray & Co., 1965.

Knowles, David. *Great Historical Enterprises*. Thomas Nelson and Sons, 1963.

King, Archdale. *Liturgies of the Primatial Sees*. Longmans, Green and Co., 1957.

King, Archdale. *Liturgies of the Religious Orders*. Bruce Publishing Co., 1955.

Kuttner, Stephan. "*Cardinalis*: The History of a Canonical Concept." *Traditio* 3 (1945): 129–214.

Labarde, Henri. *Le Ronceray*. École des gad'z'arts. Lescher-Moutoué, 1941.

La Fontenelle de Vaudoré, Armand-Désiré de. *Histoire du monastère et des évêques de Luçon*. 2 vols. Paris, 1847.

La Saussaye, Charles de. *Annales ecclesiae Aurelianensis*. Paris, 1615.

Lanfranc. *Consuetudines*. Edited and translated by David Knowles and C. N. L. Brooke, *The Monastic Constitutions of Lanfranc*. Clarendon Press, 2002.

Lanfranc, *Epistulae*. Edited by Helen Clover and Margaret Gibson, *The Letters of Lanfranc, Archbishop of Canterbury*. Clarendon Press, 1979.

Lang, Uwe Michael. *The Roman Mass: From Early Christian Origins to Tridentine Reform*. Cambridge University Press, 2022.

Langlois, Pierre. *Essai historique sur le chapitre de Rouen pendant la Révolution (1789–1802)*. Rouen, 1856.

Le Brun, Pierre. *Explication littérale, historique et dogmatique des prières et cérémonies de la Messe*. Paris, 1716.

Le Brun des Marettes, Jean-Baptiste. *Lettres inédites de Lebrun Desmarettes à Baluze*. Edited by Joseph Nouaillac. Crauffon, 1905.

Leclercq, Henri. "Liturgies néo-gallicanes." In *Dictionnaire d'archéologie chrétienne et de liturgie*, edited by Ferdinand Cabrol and Henri Leclercq, vol. 9.2, 1636–729. Letouzey et Ané, 1907.

Lefèvre-Pontalis, Eugène. *L'église abbatiale du Ronceray d'Angers. Étude archéologique*. Henri Delesques, 1912.
Le Maire, François. *Histoire et antiquitez de la ville et duché d'Orléans*. Orléans, 1648.
Lehner, Ulrich. *The Catholic Enlightenment*. Oxford University Press, 2016.
Lemaître, Jean-Loup. *Répertoire des documents nécrologiques Français*. 2 vols. Recueil des Historiens de la France publié par l'Académie des Inscriptions et Belles Lettres, série obituaires 7–8. Imprimerie nationale, 1980.
Lemoine, Louis. "Maniérisme et Hispérisme en Bretagne. Notes sur quelques colophons (VIIIe-Xe siècles)." *Annales de Bretagne et des pays de l'Ouest* 102, no. 4 (1995): 7–16.
Lemé, Kristiane. "Les chanoines de la cathédrale de Rouen au XVe siècle." In *Les stalles de la cathédrale de Rouen*. Edited by C. Elaine Block and Frédéric Billiet, 19–32. Presses universitaires de Rouen et du Havre, 2003.
Lépinay, François Macé de. "Contribution à l'étude des suspensions eucharistiques au XVIIIe siècle." *Bulletin monumental* 145, no. 3 (1987): 291–305.
Lett, Didier and Nicolas Offenstadt. "Les pratiques du cri au Moyen Âge." In *Haro! Noël! Oyé! Pratiques du cri au Moyen Âge*, edited by Didier Lett and Nicolas Offenstadt, 5–41. Éditions de la Sorbonne, 2003.
Loupès, Philippe. *Chapitres et chanoines en Guyenne aux XVIIe et XVIIIe siècles*. Éditions de l'École des hautes études en sciences sociales, 1985.
Lours, Mathieu. *L'autre temps des cathédrales. Du concile de Trente à la Révolution française*. Picard, 2010.
Mabillon, Jean. *De cultu sanctorum ignotorum epistola*. Paris, 1705.
———. *De liturgia Gallicana*. Lyon, 1685.
———. *Dissertatio de pane stico, azymo et fermentato*. Paris, 1674.
———. *Museum Italicum*. 2 vols. Paris, 1687.
———. *Traité de la Messe*. In *Ouvrages posthumes de D. Jean Mabillon et de D. Thierri Ruinart*, edited by Vincent Thuillier. Vol. 2, 272–310. Paris, 1725.
Magnin, Charles. Review of *Drames liturgiques du moyen âge*, by M. E. de Coussemaker. *Journal des savants* (1860): 309–19, 521–40; (1861): 481–503.
Maillard, Christophe. "Les chanoines et la défense des traditions cérémonielles au XVIIIe siècle." In *Les langages du culte aux XVIIe et XVIIIe siècles*, edited by Bernard Dompnier, 97–109. Presses universitaires Blaise-Pascal, 2020.
———. "La fête de Saint-Martin d'hiver à Saint-Martin de Tours au XVIIIe siècle Le maintien d'une liturgie particulière dans le plus illustre chapitre collégial de France." In *Les cérémonies extraordinaires du catholicisme baroque*, edited by Bernard Dompnier, 525–44. Presses universitaires Blaise-Pascal, 2009.
Maral, Alexandre. *La chapelle royale de Versailles sous Louis XIV. Cérémonial, liturgie et musique*. Éditions Mardaga, 2010.
Markus, Robert Austin. *Gregory the Great and His World*. Cambridge University Press, 1997.
Mesnard, Pierre. "La collégiale de Saint-Martin à l'époque des Valois," *Revue d'histoire de l'église de France* 144 (1961): 89–100.
Martène, Edmond. *De antiquis monachorum ritibus*. 2 vols. Lyon, 1690.
———. *Tractatus de antiqua Ecclesiae disciplina*. Lyon, 1706.

Martimort, Aimé-Georges. *La documentation liturgique de dom Edmond Martène*. Studi e testi 279. Biblioteca Apostolica Vaticana, 1978.
Massoni, Anne, ed. *Collégiales et chanoines dans le centre de la France du Moyen Âge à la Révolution*. Presses universitaires de Limoges, 2010.
Mathias, Antoine. *Catéchisme des curés auvergnats amis de leur patrie, de leur roi et de leurs frères*. n.p., 1789.
Maurey, Yossi. *Medieval Music, Legend, and the Cult of St. Martin*. Cambridge University Press, 2014.
McManners, John. *Church and Society in Eighteenth Century France*. 2 vols. Clarendon Press, 1998.
———. *French Ecclesiastical Society under the Ancien Régime: A Study of Angers in the Eighteenth Century*. Manchester University Press, 1960.
Melleville, Maximilien. *Histoire de la ville de Laon et de ses institutions*. 2 vols. Laon, 1846.
Metz, René. *La consécration des vierges dans l'église romaine*. Presses universitaires de France, 1954.
Migne, Jacques-Paul. *Troisième et dernière encyclopédie théologique*. Vol. 15. Paris, 1856.
Mocquereau, André, ed. *Le codex 903 de la Bibliothèque nationale de Paris (XIe siècle). Graduel de Saint-Yrieix*. Paléographie musicale 13. Société Saint Jean Évangeliste, 1925.
Moeller, Edmond, ed. *Corpus benedictionum pontificalium*. 3 vols. Corpus Christianorum Series Latina 162. Brepols, 1971–1973.
Molin, Jean-Baptiste and Annik Aussedat-Minvielle, eds. *Répertoire des rituels et processionnaux imprimés conservés en France*. Éditions du Centre national de la recherche scientifique, 1984.
Molinier, Émile. *Inventaire du trésor de l'église du Saint-Sépulcre à Paris*. Paris, 1883.
Monsabert, Pierre de. "Documents inédits pour servir à l'histoire de l'abbaye de Sainte-Croix de Poitiers." *Revue Mabillon* 9 (1913–1914): 373–95.
Moreau, Edme. *Fonctions et droits du clergé des églises cathédrales*. Amsterdam, 1784.
Moreau, Édouard de. "Récitation du canon de la messe à voix basse. Étude historique." *Nouvelle revue théologique* 51, no. 2 (1924): 65–94.
Morel de Voleine, Louis. "Du costume des chanoines de Lyon." *Revue du Lyonnais* 3 (1877): 233–34.
Munier, Charles, ed. *Concilia Galliae (a. 314–a. 506)*. Corpus Christianorum Series Latina 148. Brepols, 1963.
Neveu, Bruno. *Érudition et religion aux XVIIe et XVIIIe siècles*. Bibliothèque Albin Michel, 1994.
Nicole, Pierre. *Traité de l'oraison*. Paris, 1679.
Nicquet, Honorat. *Histoire de l'ordre de Font-Evraud*. Paris, 1642.
Norton, Michael. *Liturgical Drama and the Reimagining of Medieval Theater*. Medieval Institute Publications, 2017.
Nourrigeon, Paul. "Voiler l'autel." In *Le rideau, le voile et le dévoilement du Proche-Orient ancien à l'Occident médiéval*, edited by Lucien-Jean Bord, Vincent Debiais, and Éric Palazzo, 91–100. Geuthner, 2019.

Oakley, Francis. *The Conciliarist Tradition: Constitutionalism in the Catholic Church 1300–1870*. Oxford University Press, 2003.
Olier, Jean-Jacques. *The Mystical Meaning of the Ceremonies of the Mass*. Translated by David J. Critchley. Angelico Press, 2024.
O'Malley, John. *Trent and All That*. Oxford, Oxford University Press, 2009.
———. *Vatican I: The Council and the Making of the Ultramontane Church*. Belknap Press of Harvard University Press, 2018.
Ordinarium canonicorum regularium S. Laudi Rotomagensis. Edited by Le Brun des Marettes. PL 147:157A–192D.
Ordo ad recipiendum canonicum ex antiquis Chartulariis et Registris Capituli Ecclesiae Parisiensis. In *Dionysii Rikel Carthusiani de vita et moribus canonicorum liber*, 181–90. Cologne, 1670.
"Ordo Romanus antiquus." In *De divinis catholicae Ecclesiae officiis et mysteriis*, edited by Melchior Hittorp. Paris, 1624.
"D'Orléans, le 4 avril." *Nouvelles ecclésiastiques*, 17 April 1731, 79.
Ortigue, Joseph Louis. *Dictionnaire liturgique, historique et théorique de plainchant et de musique d'église au Moyen Âge et dans les temps modernes*. Paris, 1853.
Ousterhout, Robert. "*Loca Sancta* and the architectural response to pilgrimage." In *The Blessings of Pilgrimage*, edited by Robert Ousterhout, 108–24. University of Illinois Press, 1990.
Pasqualigo, Zaccaria. *De sacrificio nouae legis quaestiones theologicae morales juridicae*. Lyon, 1662.
Paris, Louis. *Le jubé et le labyrinthe de la cathédrale de Reims*. Paris, 1885.
Paulinus of Nola, St. *Epistulae*. In *Sancti Pontii Meropii Paulini Nolani episcopi opera*. Edited by Jean-Baptiste Le Brun des Marettes. 2 vols. Paris, 1685.
Paulinus of Nola, St. *Epistulae*. Edited by Wilhelm von Hartel. Corpus scriptorum ecclesiasticorum Latinorum 29. Vienna, 1894.
Pecklers, Keith. "The Jansenist Critique and the Liturgical Reforms of the Seventeenth and Eighteenth Centuries." *Ecclesia orans* 20 (2003): 325–39
Petit, Vincent. *Église et nation. La question liturgique en France au XIXe siècle*. Presses universitaires de Rennes, 2010.
Pettegree, Andrew and Malcolm Walsby, eds. *French Books III & IV*. 2 vols. Brill, 2012.
Picart, Bernard. *Cérémonies et coutumes religieuses de tous les peuples du monde*. Vol. 1. Amsterdam, 1728.
Pinault, Olivier. *Histoire abrégé de la dernière persécution de Port-Royal*. n. p., 1750.
Plongeron, Bernard. *La vie quotidienne du clergé au XVIIIe siècle*. Hachette, 1974.
Pocknee, Cyril. *The Christian Altar: In History and Today*. A. R. Mowbray, 1963.
Poirier, Jean. *La maîtrise de la cathédrale d'Angers. Six cents ans d'histoire*. Self-pub., 1983.
Polluche, Daniel. *Dissertation sur l'offrande de cire appellée les goutieres*. Orléans, 1734.
Pommeraye, Jean-François. *Histoire de l'église cathédrale de Rouen*. Rouen, 1686.
———, ed. *Sanctae Rotomagensis ecclesiae concilia ac synodalia decreta*. Rouen, 1677.
Pouget, François-Aimé. *Instructions générales en forme de catéchisme*. Lyon, 1730.

Pristas, Lauren. *Collects of the Roman Missals: A Comparative Study of the Sundays in Proper Seasons Before and after the Second Vatican Council*. Bloomsbury, 2013.

Prost de Royer, Antoine-François, and Jean-François-Armand Riolz. "A-priva." *Dictionnaire de jurisprudence et des arrêts*. Vol. 5, 777–78. Lyon, 1786.

Pseudo-Alcuin. *De divinis officiis*. PL 101:1174B–1286D.

Pseudo-Amphilochius of Iconium. *Vita et miracula sancti Basilii Magni*. In *SS. Patrum Amphilochii Iconiensis, Methodii Patarensis, et Andreae Cretensis Opera Omnia*, edited by François Combefis, 159–227. Paris, 1644.

Pseudo-Fredegarius. *Chronicarum quae dicuntur Fredegarii scholastici libri IV*. In *Fredegarii et aliorum Chronica. Vitae sanctorum*, edited by Bruno Krusch, MGH SS rer. Merov. 2, 1–193. Hanover, 1888.

Quelques réflexions d'un Patriote sur une Brochure ayant pour titre: Mémoire du Chapitre de la Cathédrale de Metz, au Roi. Metz, 1789.

Quoëx, Franck. *Liturgical Theology in Thomas Aquinas: Sacrifice and Salvation History*. Translated by Zachary Thomas. Catholic University of America Press, 2024.

Radulph of Rivo. *De canonum observantia*. Edited and translated by Gerhard Eger and Zachary Thomas, *On the Observance of Canons*. Brepols Library of Christian Sources 16. Brepols, 2025.

Reymond, Henri. *Droits des curés et des paroisses, considérés sous leur double rapport spirituel et temporel*. Paris, 1780.

Reynolds, Roger. "Liturgy, Treatises on." *Dictionary of the Middle Ages*, edited by Joseph R. Strayer. Vol. 7, 624–33. Charles Scribner's Sons, 1986.

Restif, Bruno. "Les paroisses desservies dans les églises cathédrales et collégiales. Enjeux, concurrence et conflits (XVIe–XVIIIe siècle)." In *La paroisse urbaine du moyen âge à nos jours*, edited by Anne Bonzon, Philippe Guignet, and Marc Venard, 183–98. Cerf, 2014.

Robertson, Anne Walters. "From Office to Mass: The Antiphons of Vespers and Lauds and the Antiphons before the Gospel in Northern France." In *The Divine Office in the Latin Middle Ages: Methodology and Source Studies, Regional Developments, Hagiography*, edited by Rebecca A. Baltzer and Margot E. Fassler, 300–23. Oxford University Press, 2000.

Robert Paululus. *De caeremoniis, sacramentis, officiis, et observationibus ecclesiasticis*. PL 177:381A–456C.

Rocha, Pedro Romano. "Les 'tropes' ou versets de l'ancien office de Ténèbres." In *Mens concordet voci: pour Mgr A. G. Martimort à l'occasion de ses quarante années d'enseignement et des vingt ans de la Constitution 'Sacrosanctum Concilium'*, edited by Jacques Dutheil and Claude Dagens, 691–702. Desclée, 1983.

Rosweyde, Heribert, ed. *Divi Paulini episcopi Nolani Opera*. Antwerp, 1622.

Roux, Joseph. *La liturgie de la Sainte Église de Lyon d'après les monuments*. Lyon, 1864.

Rupert of Deutz. *Liber de diuinis officiis*. Edited by Rhaban Haacke. Corpus Christianorum Continuatio Mediaeualis 7. Brepols, 1967.

Sachet, Alphonse. *Le grande jubilé séculaire de Saint-Jean-de-Lyon*. Lyon, 1886.

Sacramentarium Gregorianum. Edited by Jean Deshusses, *Le sacramentaire grégorien*, Spicilegium Friburgense 16. Éditions Universitaires Fribourg Suisse, 1992.

Saint-Crépin, Nicholas de. *Vita S. Godefridi episcopi Ambianensis*. Edited by Laurentius Surius, in *De probatis Sanctorum historiis*. Vol. 6, 179–214. Cologne, 1575.

Sainte-Marie, Joseph de. *The Holy Eucharist—The World's Salvation: Studies on the Holy Sacrifice of the Mass, its Celebration, and its Concelebration*. Gracewing, 2015.

Sainte-Marthe, Gaucher and Louis de, eds. *Gallia Christiana*. 4 vols. Paris, 1656.

Saint-Marc, Charles-Hugues Le Febvre de, and Claude-Pierre Goujet, *Supplément au nécrologe de l'abbaïe de Notre-Dame de Port-Royal des Champs*. Vol. 1. n.p., 1735.

Salomon, Claude. *Lettres d'un Auxerrois à M. Frappier, Chanoine de l'Église Cathédrale d'Auxerre, et Agent des Réparations du Chapitre*. n.p., 1779.

Schaefer, Mary M. "Latin Mass Commentaries from the Ninth through the Twelfth Centuries: Chronology and Theology." In *Fountain of Life*, edited by Gerard Austin, 35–49. The Pastoral Press, 1991.

Schulte, Augustin Joseph. "Altar." In *The Catholic Encyclopedia*, ed. Charles George Herbermann. Vol. 1, 346–59. Robert Appleton Company, 1907.

Seeck, Otto, ed. *Notitia dignitatum. Accedunt Notitia urbis Constantinopolitanae et Laterculi provinciarum*. Berlin, 1876.

Sommar, Mary E. *The Slaves of the Churches: A History*. Oxford University Press, 2020.

Sonnet, Martin. *Directorium chori Parisiensis*. Paris, 1656.

"Statuta seu constitutiones ecclesiae Lugdunensis." Edited by Luc d'Achery, *Spicilegium*. Vol. 1, 718–19. Paris, 1723.

"Statuta seu ordo monasterii Sancti Benigni Divionensis." In *Histoire de l'église Saint-Bénigne de Dijon*, edited by Louis Chomton, 351–441. Dijon, 1900.

Stephen of Tournai. *Epistulae*. Edited by Jules Desilve, *Lettres d'Étienne de Tournai*. Valenciennes, 1893.

Statuts du diocèse d'Angers. Angers, 1680.

Tackett, Timothy. *Priest and Parish in Eighteenth-Century France: A Social and Political Study of the Curés in a Diocese of Dauphiné, 1750–1791*. Princeton University Press, 1977.

Theodulf of Orléans. *Capitula ad presbyteros parochiae suae*. PL 105:191C–208D.

Thiers, Jean-Baptiste. "Dissertation des jubés des églises." In *Dissertations ecclésiastiques*. Paris, 1688.

———. *Dissertation sur les porches des églises*. Orléans, 1679.

———. "Dissertation sur les principaux autels des églises." In *Dissertations ecclésiastiques*. Paris, 1688.

Thillier, Joseph and Eugène Jarry. *Cartulaire de Sainte-Croix d'Orléans*. Alphonse Picard et fils, 1906.

Thomassin, Louis. *Vetus et nova Ecclesiae disciplina*. 3 vols. Paris, 1688.

Thorode, Louis Michel. *Notice de la ville d'Angers*. Angers, 1897.

Tillemont, Louis Sébastien Le Nain de. *L'histoire des empereurs et des autres princes qui ont régné durant les six premiers siècles de l'Église*. 6 vols. Paris, 1691–1697.

———. *Mémoires pour servir a l'histoire ecclésiastique des six premiers siècles*. 16 vols. Paris, 1693–1712.

Toureille, Valérie. "Cri de peur et cri de haine: haro sur le voleur: Cri et crime en France à la fin du Moyen Âge." In *Haro! Noël! Oyé!: Pratiques du cri au Moyen Âge*, edited by Didier Lett and Nicolas Offenstadt, 169–78. Éditions de la Sorbonne, 2003.

Travers, Nicolas. *Histoire civile, politique et religieuse de la ville et du comté de Nantes*. Vol. 3. Nantes, 1841.

Trisco, Robert F. "An American Anomaly: Bishops without Canons." *Chicago Studies* 9, no. 2 (1970): 143–57.

Troupeau, Gérard. "Une description de l'Office de la Saint-Martin dans la collégiale de Tours au début du XVIIIe siècle." *Bulletin de la Société archéologique de Touraine* 44 (1996): 897–912.

Turkiewicz, Natalia. "The Durand *Computus* in Book VIII *Rationale divinorum officiorum*." *Archiwa, Biblioteki i Muzea Kościelne* 120 (2023): 489–508.

Ulrich of Zell. *Consuetudines antiquiores Cluniacenses*. PL 149:643–779.

Vaucelle, Edgar-Raphaël. *La collégiale de Saint-Martin de Tours des origines à l'avènement des Valois*. Librairie Alphonse Picard et Fils, 1908.

Verkerk, Dorothy Hoogland. "Biblical Manuscripts in Rome 400–700 and the Ashburnham Pentateuch." In *Imagining the Early Medieval Bible*, edited by John Williams, 97–120. Pennsylvania State University Press, 1999.

Vidier, Alexandre and Léon Mirot. *Obituaires de la province de Sens*. Vol. 3, *Diocèses d'Orléans, d'Auxerre, et de Nevers*. Imprimerie nationale, 1909.

Vildera, Anna. "Formulari processionali per il canto del vangelo *Liber generationis*." *De musica disserenda* 9, no. 1–2 (2013): 139–55.

"Vita S. Chrothildis reginae Francorum." In *Acta sanctorum Ordinis sancti Benedicti*, edited by Jean Mabillon. Vol. 1, *Saeculum I quod est ab anno Christi D ad DC*. Paris, 1668.

Weaver, Ellen. *The Inner History of a Reformation That Failed: The Monastery of Port-Royal (1647–1684)*. Princeton University Press, 1973.

———. "Liturgy for the Laity: The Jansenist Case for Popular Participation in Worship in the Seventeenth and Eighteenth Centuries." *Studia liturgica* 19 (1989), 47–59.

———. "The Neo-Gallican Liturgies Revisited." *Studia liturgica* 16, no. 3–4 (1986): 54–72.

———. *The Reform of Port-Royal*. Éditions Beauchesne, 1978.

Webb, Geoffrey. *The Liturgical Altar*. The Newman Press, 1949.

Weisbein, Nicolas. "Le *Laudes crucis attollamus* de Maître Hugues d'Orléans dit Le Primat." *Revue du moyen âge latin* 3 (1947): 5–26.

Welter, Louise. "Le chapitre cathédral de Clermont. Sa constitution, ses privilèges." *Revue d'histoire de l'Église de France* 41, no. 136 (1955): 5–42.

White, James F. *Roman Catholic Worship: Trent to Today*. Liturgical Press, 2003.

Xibaut, Bernard. "La concélébration dans le Mouvement liturgique et dans l'œuvre du Concile." *La Maison-Dieu* 224 (2000): 7–27.

Yardley, A. B. "The Consecration of Nuns." In *Performing Piety: The New Middle Ages*, edited by Anne Bagnall Yardley. Palgrave Macmillan, 2006.

Zachary, Pope. *Epistula* 13. MGH Epp. 3:369–72.

LITURGICAL BOOKS

Breviarium Aurelianense (Orléans, Médiathèque municipale, MS. 0132).
Breviarium Aurelianense. Orléans, 1693.
Breviarium diocesis Aurelianensis. Orléans, 1542.
Breviarium insignis ecclesiae Nivernensis. Orléans, 1727.
Breviarium monasticum ad usum sacri ordinis Cluniacensis. Paris, 1686.
Breviarium Parisiense, Pars hyemalis. Paris, 1680.
Breviarium Parisiense, Pars hyemalis. Paris, 1653.
Breviarium sanctae Lugdunensis ecclesiae, Pars hyemalis. Lyon, 1693.
Breviarium sanctae Lugdunensis ecclesiae, Pars verna. Lyon, 1693.
Breviarium sanctae Viennensis ecclesiae. Paris, 1678.
Caeremoniale episcoporum. Rome. 1600.
Caeremoniale Parisiense ad usum omnium ecclesiarum collegiatarum, parochialium et aliarum urbis et dioecesis Parisiensis. Paris, 1662.
Cérémonial de l'église d'Angers. Angers, n.d.
Graduale iuxta Missale Parisiense. Paris, 1662.
Instructiones, ritus, et decreta ad funera ducenda. Milan, 1685.
Liber ordinis Sancti Victoris Parisiensis. Edited by Luc Jocqué and Ludo Milis. Corpus Christianorum Continuatio Mediaeualis 61. Brepols, 1984.
Livre du préchantre de la cathédrale de Sens (Sens, Bibliothèque municipale, MS. 6).
Manuale continens modum sacramenta ecclesiastica secundum usum insignis ecclesie Aurelianensis. Paris, 1581.
Missale ad usum et consuetudinem ecclesie Aurelianensis. Paris, 1519.
Missale ad usum provinciae Viennensis. Grenoble, 1784.
Missale ad vsum sancte Viennensis ecclesie. Lyon, 1519.
Missale Ambrosianum. Milan, 1669.
Missale Andegavense. Paris, 1488.
Missale Andegavense. Paris, 1489.
Missale Andegavense. Paris, 1717.
Missale Autissiodorense (Bibliothèque nationale, Paris, MS. lat. 17316).
Missale ad usum Autissiodorensis ecclesiae (Auxerre, Bibliothèque Jacques Lacarrière, MS. 5).
Missale Bisuntinum. Besançon, 1589.
Missale insignis ecclesiae et dioecesis Parisiensis. Paris, 1557.
Missale...iuxta institutum Rothomagensis episcopatus. Rouen, 1585.
Missale monasticum ad usum sacri ordinis Cluniacensis. Paris, 1733.
Missale Parisiense. Paris, 1685.
Missale sanctae Autissiodorensis ecclesiae. Troyes, 1738.
Missale secundum ritum ecclesie Lugdunensis. Lyon, 1530.
Missale secundum ritum ecclesie Lugdunensis. Lyon, 1530.
Ordinaire de l'église cathédrale de Vienne. Edited by Ulysse Chevalier. A. Picard, 1923.
Ordinarius ecclesie beati Verani de Jargolio (Orléans, Médiathèque municipale, MS. 0143).

Ordinarium Cartusiense. Lyon, 1641.
Ordinale Ordinis Beatae Mariae de Monte Carmeli. Edited by Benedict Zimmerman, *Ordinaire de l'Ordre de Notre-Dame de Mont-Carmel.* Paris, 1910.
Processional de Sens. Sens, 1756.
Rituale ad usum dioeceseos Claromontensis. Clermont, 1656.
Rituale Andegavense. Angers, 1676.
Rituel de la province de Reims. Paris, 1677.
Rituel du diocèse de Sens. Sens, 1694.
Rituale Metense. Pars tertia. Metz, 1713.
Rituale Parisiense. Paris, 1697.
Rituale Romanum. Rome, 1614.
Rituale sacramentorum ad usum Mediolanensis ecclesiae. Milan, 1687.
Sacerdotale seu Manuale ecclesiae Rothomagensis. Rouen, 1640.
Sonnet, Martin. *Caeremoniale Parisiense ad usum omnium ecclesiarum collegiatarum, parochialium et aliarum urbis et dioecesis Parisiensis.* Paris, 1662.
Supplementum Missalis Romani ad usum ecclesiarum dioecesis Viennensis. Lyon, 1680.

INDICES

SUBJECTS AND PROPER NAMES

abbesses, xxvii, 4, 78n44, 83–86, 97, 145, 171, 175–77, 221–22, 246, 267, 281
   hearing confessions, 84
   See also under oaths
ablutions
   no final ablution, 148, 224
   only with wine, 223
   priest does not drink, 168, 209, 224
abstinence from meat
   during Advent, 269
   during public penance, 235
   on Monday and Tuesday of Quinquagesima, 29
   on Saturdays, xlvi, 158, 286
   on St. Mark's and the Rogation days, 60, 138, 154, 218–19
   on Sundays of Lent, 223
   perpetual, 175
Accendite (acclamation), 23, 27, 52, 67, 96–97, 118
acolytes or candle-bearers
   in tunicles, xxiv, xxix, 94–95
   nuns acting as, xxx, 59
   seven at Mass on major feasts, xxx, xxxiii, 14, 17, 25, 35, 37, 55, 89, 94–95, 204, 220
Adam of St. Victor, 138, 187
Ado, St., 7, 10, 31
adoration
   of the Blessed Sacrament, xlvi, 175, 245, 360
   of the cross
      on Good Friday, 153, 159, 215–16, 274
      on the feast of the Exaltation, 137–38, 160, 181
agapes, xlviii–xlix, 186, 278, 285–86
Agde, Council of, 48
Agnus Dei
   marking the conclusion of Mass, 84
   said only once at Mass, 48–49
   solemn episcopal blessing before (*see under* blessings)
albs
   appareled, 28, 48n50, 67, 94, 105, 149, 153, 182n111, 267
   as ancient choir habit, 94, 182
   worn by choirboys, 13, 37, 40, 105, 110, 118, 131, 134, 149, 182, 199–200, 331
   worn by nuns, xxx, 59
Alcimus Avitus, St., 31
Alcuin, 40n34, 231–32, 277
Alexander, St., 54, 83
Alexander VII, xlii
alleluia
   after *Deus in adjutorium* serving as an antiphon for the little hours, 13, 50, 93
   chanted formerly even on the first Sunday of Lent, 51
   chanted until the end of Lauds of Septuagesima, 50–51
   ending after None on the Saturday before Septuagesima, 76, 271
All Saints, xxx, 14n29, 50, 114, 117, 154, 162, 181, 218, 222, 277, 288n243
All Souls, 10, 14, 77, 111, 114, 117, 143, 154, 157, 181
alms, 9, 91n8, 177–78, 195, 264
almuces
   hood, 10n14, 37
   inside-out, 105
   on the head, xlvii, 3, 10n14, 12, 37–38, 191, 337
   on the shoulders, 12, 37, 38, 187, 191, 298, 306, 333, 337
   originally a head-covering, xlvii
   over the arm, 10n14, 12, 38, 63, 87, 89, 105, 108, 167, 182, 252, 258, 267, 298, 316, 329, 337
   over the chasuble, 10
   over the surplice, 37, 187, 243
altars
   dressed only just before Mass, xxx, xlv, 62, 91, 95n18, 119, 161, 166n5, 225, 359
   free-standing, 81, 179, 199, 265, 363
   with recessed table, 9, 31, 34–35, 46, 109, 111, 292, 357n5
Altinus, St., 142
Amalar of Metz, xxv, 146, 203, 206, 214n74
Ambrose, St., 24, 256, 284n231
Ambrosian rite. *See* Milan

Amen
    after the Gospel, 84
    after the words of consecration, xxviii
    when receiving communion, 158, 180
amices
    appareled, 67, 73, 105, 120,
    as choir dress, 94
    worn over the head at Mass, 67, 73–74
amphitheaters, 7, 32, 54, 82, 298, 309
Anastasia, St., 17
Anianus, St., 150n60, 151
Angelus. *See* indulgence of peace
Ansbert, St., 260, 286
ante et retro (bow), 83n2, 119, 250
Ante Evangelium (antiphon), 68
antependia, 35, 61–62, 118, 165, 362–64
anticipation
    of feasts, 136, 277
    of hours, xlvii, 103, 211, 269
    of Mass, 216, 220, 288
antiphons
    O, 15, 50, 55, 69
    of Lauds and the minor hours with verses, 143
    of Prime taken from a psalm, 204
    omitted at Matins, 92
    omitted at minor hours, 50, 152
    triumphed, 15, 50, 55, 85–86, 100n38, 151, 210, 217, 231
    with neum, 270
à privat (Lyon), 53. *See also under* chant
aqueducts, 4, 7, 32, 54
archdeacons, xxxviii n10, xliii n33, 16–17, 21–22, 26, 72, 98, 107, 132, 220–21, 259, 351
Arnaud, Henri, 79
Arnauld, Antoine, xxxix n15, l, 187n35
ashes
    at the church door, 155, 159, 185, 214–25
    bodies of the moribund laid on, 4, 108, 112, 156, 165, 323
    celebrant did not receive, 19, 151, 211
    imposed during Extreme Unction, 287
    imposed every Friday in Lent, 125
    imposed for the Rogation processions, 26, 56
    imposition on Ash Wednesday, 19, 85, 124–25, 137, 212, 234, 271
Ash Wednesday, 4, 19, 29, 51, 76–77, 85, 116, 124–25, 137, 145, 151, 155, 159, 162, 163, 168, 185, 211–212, 223n96, 234–36, 247, 271. *See also* ashes *and* bare feet

aspersion
    after Compline, 71, 102, 223, 248, 274, 276
    of nuns on Sunday, 83, 175
    of the clergy and people on Sunday, xlviii, 4, 24–25, 39, 119–20, 130, 162–63, 167, 251–52
    of the clergy on Sunday, 66, 69, 136, 161, 268
    of the common places on Sunday, xlviii, lii, 4, 14–15, 19, 39, 83–84, 93, 155, 167, 251–52, 268–69, 270–71
    of the dead, 156
    on All Souls, 77, 154
    on Ash Wednesday, 151, 212, 271
    on Holy Saturday, 163
    on major feasts, 66, 136
    on the Rogation days, 26, 277
astronomical clock (Lyon), 33, 295
asylums, 8, 57, 265
Attalus, St., 83
Attollite portas, 20, 152, 159
Auch, 109
Augustine, St., 24, 45n44, 216, 247, 277, 280, 287
Augustinians, 70, 157, 246, 267–68, 278–79
aumbries, 77, 80–81, 152, 278–81, 359–62
aumussons, liv, 3, 200, 252, 258, 337
Auvray, Jacques-Accurse, xlii, 2
Avallon, xxiv, 124–25, 185

Baluze, Étienne, xxxix, xl, 124n16, 139n17
banners, 26, 48n50, 52, 56, 190, 232, 234, 240, 263
baptism
    at the vigil of Easter, lii, 21–23, 213, 217, 284
    at the vigil of Pentecost, 27, 107
    cannot be done with rose water, 276
    followed by Confirmation (*see under* Confirmation)
    supplied or conditional, xlvi, 126–27
    vows, xlvi, 189–90, 232
baptismal fonts
    blessing of (*see under* blessings)
    placement near the door, 80, 108, 263
    procession to during the octave of Easter, 25–26, 56, 74, 77, 131, 169, 181, 189–90, 217, 231
    procession to during the octave of Pentecost, 27, 56, 107
bare feet
    at Mass on Ash Wednesday, 85, 271

Subjects and Proper Names

in processions, 4, 26, 52, 56, 85, 130, 140, 240, 247
on Good Friday, 21, 85, 164, 274
Baronius, Caesar, 264
baths, liii, 4, 7, 32, 189, 235. *See also* washing before Mass
Bayeux, Synod of, 127
Beauvais (Picardy), 24, 60, 125, 140n3
Beleth, John, 225, 272, 286
bells
    at the elevation, 130, 255
    rung for the Mass of the faithful, 57, 88, 179, 253
Benedictines, xxiii, xxv, xxvii, xlix, 20, 59, 75, 102–104, 109–13, 115, 128, 132, 149, 158, 190–91, 202, 221, 240, 246, 267, 279, 341
Benediction of the Bl. Sacrament, 47–48, 74, 100n38, 244–45
Berengar of Tours, 98
Berno of Cluny, 111
Bérulle, Cardinal Pierre de, xix, xxiv
Bigot, Émery, xxxviii–xxxix, 202n41, 205n54, 237n134, 266, 283
Billouet, Jacques-Philippe, 158
birettas, 38–39, 68, 118, 120, 168, 181, 267
    formerly round, 3, 200
    origin, xlvii, 10n14, 39, 266–67
    worn by choirboys, 63, 199
    worn under hood or cowl, 266
Bissy, Cardinal de, xx
Blanche, Queen, 172, 191
Blandina, St., 8, 28, 83
blessed bread (*eulogia*), xlviii, 186, 285–87
blessings
    final at Mass, 14, 69, 89, 123, 148, 162, 168, 180, 186, 209, 224, 256, 331
    not said, 116, 123, 148
    of ashes, 19, 56, 76, 85, 124–25, 137, 234, 271
    of bread, 144, 175
    of bread and wine, 21, 39, 147, 155, 163, 186, 285
    of candles, 28, 60, 211
    of food, 27, 84, 211
    of fruits, 84, 147–48, 154–55
    of grapes, xlviii, 77, 90, 99, 117, 128–29, 137, 146–48, 154–55, 160
    of holy chrism and oils of the catechumens and of the sick, xxxii, 20, 71–72, 125,
    of holy water, xlviii, 14–15, 24–25, 39–40, 69, 83, 93, 119, 129, 145–46, 149, 154–55, 161, 167, 175, 251, 268, 270
    of new fire, 22, 155, 162–63, 214–15, 217, 275
    of nuts, 29
    of palms, 20, 152, 238
    of the baptismal font, 22, 40, 73–74, 97n28, 131, 144, 146, 153, 162, 217, 228, 276, 284
    of the nuptial bed, xlvi, 163, 186, 285
    of the Paschal candle, 21–22, 74, 85, 153, 162–63, 216–17, 276
    of wine, 84, 246
    solemn episcopal at Mass, xlviii, 45, 58, 69, 89, 124, 130, 132, 134, 145–46, 161–62, 168, 180, 228–29
Bocquillot, André, xxiv–xxv, 219n85
Bohier, Antoine, 266
Bona, Cardinal Giovanni, xxxvi, 23
Bossuet, Jacques-Bénigne, xx, xxvi, 126n22
Bourrault, subdean of St-Martin of Tours, xl, 91n7, 101
boy bishops, 27
Brézé, Louis de, 195
Burchard, Bl., 31
burial
    of priests facing west or east, xlvii, 127, 129, 197
    only after a Mass, xlvii, 58

camails, 38–39, 61n3, 66, 71–72, 77, 105, 134, 182–83, 200, 258, 267, 273
Cambrai, xxv, 166n5, 231, 259
candle-bearers. *See under* acolytes
Candlemas. *See* Purification of Our Lady
Canon
    recited by concelebrants, 18
    recited out loud, xx–xxi, xxviii, xliv, l
canons
    attendance requirements, 349, 352
    canon serfs, 248
    common life, xlix, li, 10, 52, 80, 184–85, 257
    payment, 46, 69n21, 130, 139, 184–85, 196, 257, 259, 262, 278, 349, 352
    residence requirements, 46, 52, 141, 183, 349, 352
    semi-prebended, 36, 40n36, 53, 108, 120, 248, 349–50, 354
cantores et baudes (feast rank), 14
capiscols, 11, 21, 30, 248, 352n30
Carmelites, 34n7, 43, 60, 70, 135, 187, 207n63, 224, 231, 238, 246, 271, 281n229
Carthusians, 34n7, 42–44, 57, 109, 111, 115, 121, 148, 165, 168, 173, 179, 183, 203, 206–10, 216, 223–24, 254

cassocks
    black, 12
    purple, 63, 114
    red, 37, 118
    tawny, 59
    violet, 134, 283
    white, 63
catechumens, 3, 11, 21–22, 27, 156, 213, 217
Celestines, 110
cemeteries, xlvii, 4, 10, 29, 54, 77, 80, 101, 154, 173, 238, 252, 282
Châlons-en-Champagne (Châlons-sur-Marne), 231
Champaigne, Philippe de, xxix, 171
chant
    measured plainchant, 43
    sung by memory, xlix, 12, 34, 36n14, 103, 106, 201, 251, 266
    sung in a low tone or voice, 25, 40, 51, 53, 224, 270
    sur le livre, 201
Chapelle tabernière (Vienne), 9
chaplains to the bishop, 16, 19, 35, 37, 121
chapter of faults, 64, 176, 184, 204, 249
chapter Office, 85, 94, 150, 176, 183, 184, 204, 211, 270
Charlemagne, 356
Charles I de Bourbon, 261
Charles II the Bald, 190
Charles V, 198, 224–25, 265
Charles IX, 227
Charlier, John. *See* Gerson, John
chasubles
    ample, xlvii, 61, 71, 73, 95, 125, 173, 191, 210, 254, 261, 280
    folded, 51, 71, 181, 205, 222, 269, 271, 306
    worn by deacons and subdeacons, 51, 71, 153, 159, 181, 200, 205, 208, 222, 252, 271, 306
    worn in processions, 26, 244
Châtelain, Claude, xxxix, xlii, 2, 56, 123n12, 191, 218, 231n118, 286
chevecier or *chefcier*, 90n7, 94, 150–51
Chlothar II, 149
choirboys
    bareheaded, 38, 48, 63, 118, 181
    choir schools, 64n11, 248, 350, 351–52
    raised *in gremio Ecclesiae*, 29
    shorn heads of, xlix, 37, 63, 199, 331
    See also under acolytes, birettas, cassocks, clergeons
choristes (choristers), 91

Christe qui lux es et dies, 15
Christus vincit. See Laudes regiae
Cistercians, 34n7, 110–11, 119, 132n4, 143, 164–65, 170–78, 228, 240, 246, 320, 361
clameur de haro, 192
Clement VI, 259–60, 279
Clement XI, xlii
clergeons, 11nn16–17, 12–13, 17–18, 26, 38, 44, 47
Clotilde, St., 188, 266
Clovis I, 186, 188
Colbert, Jacques-Nicolas, xvi, xli–xlii, 16n35, 221
Colmieu, Peter de, 201, 260
colors, liturgical, xxx, 19–21, 24, 28, 30, 73, 75–77, 107–108, 116, 125, 151, 153, 162, 181, 239, 261
Committimus, 258–59
communion
    general, 48, 51, 55, 84, 95, 175, 216–17, 271–73, 276
    of baptized infants, xlvi, 3, 24, 284
    of new priests for forty days after ordination, 3, 172
    of nuns, 84–85, 172, 175
    of the deacon and subdeacon at Mass, xlvi, 110, 170, 191, 209, 256
    on Good Friday (*see under* Good Friday)
    under two species, xxx, xxxiii, xlvi, li, 3, 24, 88, 95n21, 110, 125, 169, 180n3, 181, 191, 208, 209
    See also under Amen
Communion verses, 45
concessus. See synthronos
Concordat of Bologna, 349
Confirmation
    of adults after baptism, 284
    of infants after baptism, xlvi, 3, 23
Confiteor
    at Mass, xxx, 13, 17, 41, 137, 150, 162, 179, 204, 301
    at Prime and/or Compline, 71, 93, 132, 223, 248
    before adoring the cross, 137, 181
    before Easter Matins, 24
    before the Rogation procession, 76
    not said, 99, 228
    on Good Friday, 21, 275
    said after the blessing of the Paschal candle, 163
    said at St. Martin's tomb, 95
    said by a pardoned criminal, 242

said by nuns at high Mass, 83, 84
said in the sacristy, 21, 120, 128
See also kisses
Congregation of St-Maur. See Maur, St-
Conrad, king of Burgundy and Arles, 8, 11
consecration of virgins, xlix, 3, 78, 84, 171–72, 267, 326
Constantinople, fifth general Council of, 79
corbeliers, 64, 66–67, 71
Corpus Christi, xxx, 14–15, 46, 48, 56, 77, 78n44, 99, 131–32, 143, 162, 175, 181, 213, 244, 246, 260, 277, 324
crosiers
    development of shape, 196
    use by abbots and abbesses, 114, 171, 196
curés- or *prêtres-cardinaux*, xlviii, 3, 72, 123
curfew, 140, 156n76, 262–63

d'Achéry, Luc, xxxix, 186n32
Dagobert, 103, 190
d'Ailly, Pierre, 259
Darralde, Jean, 347
de Harlay, François, xxxviii
de Harlay de Champvallon, François, xxxix, 56n82, 75n42, 96n26, 175
Descartes, René, 188
de Vert, Claude, xxvi–xxvii, xl–xli, l–liii, 2, 59, 275, 279, and in the footnotes *passim*
Dialogues (St. Gregory), 19–20, 203, 212
Dionysius, St., 142
Dominicans, 43, 70, 132, 134, 196, 207n62, 224, 246, 338, 358
domino (winter cape, Lyon), 38n26, 300
Domninus, St., 31
dossals, 35, 91, 104, 161, 165, 317
doubled readings and propers at Mass, xliv n35, xlviii, 57, 170, 186, 204–205, 276
Doyen de la Chrétienté, 193
dragons, 131, 144, 243n148
Du Cambout de Coislin, Pierre-Armand, xvi, xli–xlii, 102n4, 136n8, 145
Dupanloup, Félix, xxiii
Durand, Ursin, xxvii
Durand, William, 51, 147, 225, 231–32, and in the footnotes passim

ecolâtres, 248, 351
eggs
    during Lent or Advent, 124n16, 269
    ostrich, 75

elevation (major)
    posture, 44, 136, 168, 208, 328
    music or silence during, xlvi, 44, 70n24, 88, 106, 109, 130, 149, 168, 255, 280
    not performed, 83, 207
elevation (minor), 44, 207, 255
Elvira, Council of, 48
Enlightenment, xxi, xxxvi, lii
Epagathus, St., 8
Epipodius, St., 54
Ermengarda, Queen, 11
Estouteville, Guillaume d', 198–99, 261, 264
Esztergom, xxiv
eulogia. See blessed bread
Euphemia, St., 93
Eusebius of Caesarea, 7–8, 28, 264
Exeter, Synod of, 127
exorcisms for baptism, 21, 81n55, 126n23
    omitted when ceremonies of baptism supplied, xlvi, 126–27, 148, 155
    performed outside, 80–81, 148, 155
exposition of the Blessed Sacrament, xlvi, 175, 245, 360
expulsion of penitents. See public penance
Extreme Unction, xlvi, 83, 101, 155–56, 163, 165, 185, 287
Exultet, 114, 159, 276

Faber, or Le Fèvre, Jean, 8
fabrics
    furs, 10n14, 37, 105, 200, 258, 267, 337
    lace, 12, 257
    linen, 182, 272, 276, 306, 357, 362–63
    silk, 17, 19–21, 67, 73, 75, 234, 257–58, 275, 357, 362–63
    velvet, 200, 257
    wool, 157, 272, 277, 337
fasting, xxi, xlvi, liii, 4, 12n23, 31n87, 154, 174n13, 175, 211, 216, 218–19, 222, 237, 267, 271, 277
    in Advent, 269, 277, 285
    lasting until evening, 56, 150, 175, 211, 216, 271
    not permitted on feasts or Eastertide, xlix, 60, 77, 136, 169, 219, 277
    on Holy Innocents, 28
    on Fridays throughout the year, 271
    on the Rogation days, 31, 218–19
    on Wednesdays and Fridays, 187
Fénelon, François, xxvi
feretories (*feretra*), 240, 243, 281

fêtage, 66–69, 206
Fête des Miracles. *See* Blandina, St.
feudal payments, 134, 157
Filles-Dieu of Rouen, 278–79
Flavacourt, William de, 195, 260
Forty Hours, 245, 263
Fosse, François de la, 233–36
Franciscans, xvii n10, 36n13, 70, 132, 196, 246, 260, 264, 306
　Tertiaries, 246
frocs, 37–39
Fourcroy, Jean de, 136
Fulk III of Anjou, 79

Gallia Christiana, xxvii, 63, 133n1, 172
gargoyles, 240, 339
Gavantus, Bartholomew, xl, 207n65, 254n162, 255n164
Gelasius II, Pope, 109
Genealogy of Our Lord, 16, 58, 59n1, 143, 158, 210–11
Geneviève, Congregation of Ste-, 38, 267
Gerson, John, 57
Gloria laus, 96, 152, 239
Godfrey, St., 223, 271
Godin, Ange, 202
Gohard, St., 81
Good Friday
　adoration of the cross, 153, 159, 215–16, 274
　communion on, xlvi, 170, 214–16, 272
　fasting on bread and water, 216
　Mass *ex praesanctificatis*, 55–56, 125, 159, 215
　offices said barefoot, 21, 85, 164, 274
Grancolas, Jean, xxv
grands camails, 200, 330, 337
Greek
　inscriptions, 7–8, 160
　in the Rogation litany, 242
　Mass, xxxi, 191
Gregory XI, 259
Gregory of Tours, St., 28, 100
Gregory the Great, St., lii, 123n12, 146, 212, 266
Grenoble, xxxii, 126
Guéranger, Prosper, xix n15, xxiii, l, 79n45

haie percée, la, 76
Hamon, Jean, 174
Hesychius, St., 31
Hilary, St., 90

Honorius of Autun, 49n57, 225, 231
Hôpital de la Salpêtrière, xlvi, 189–90, 232
Hospitale nobilium (Tours), 98
Hotel de Cluny, 189
Hôtel-Dieu (Rouen), 265
hours
　said privately or *sub silentio* on major feast days, 47, 73, 100, 116, 153, 181
　said separately, xlvii, 50, 119, 176, 183–84, 262, 274
Hugh of Cluny, St., 109
Hugh of St. Victor, 23, 103

incensations
　after the short chapter at Vespers, 139
　at Matins, 16, 65–66, 94, 143, 150, 210, 250
　at the beginning of Mass, 17, 29, 179, 205, 252
　at the third elevation of Mass, 122, 255
　before and after the Gospel at Mass, 42–43, 68, 136, 205, 253
　before the *Magnificat* at Vespers, 94, 139, 150, 203
　during the *Benedictus* at Lauds, 65–66, 84, 198, 210, 250–51
　during the *Credo* at Mass, 136, 204, 252, 270
　during the *Gloria* at Mass, 88, 204, 217
　during the *Gospel* at Mass, 109, 253–54
　during the hymn at Terce, 219, 232–33
　during the *Magnificat* at Vespers, 47, 65–66, 84, 106, 124, 135, 198, 210, 214, 217, 250–51
　during the offertory at Mass, 13, 149, 168, 43–44, 68–69, 88, 106, 109, 116, 130, 149, 168, 179, 198, 206, 254–255
　extraordinary at Mass on Michaelmas, 99
　none at second Vespers, 96
　of the clergy during the *Gloria* at Mass, 88, 204, 252
　of the dead and graves, 155–56
indulgence of peace, 140
induts, xxxi–xxxii, 179
Innocent VIII, Pope, 124n16, 249, 264
Innocents, feast of the Holy, 28, 92
Institute of the Bl. Sacrament, 175
Irenaeus, St., 54
Ivo of Chartres, 207

Jansen, Cornelius, xv n5, l, 102n1
Jerome, St., xlii, 105n2, 271
Jesu dulcis memoria, 170

Joan of Arc, St., 133, 192
John of Avranches, xvi, xlii, 202n41, 260
John the Baptist, feast of the Nativity of St., 28, 41, 46, 48, 145
Josephinism, xxi
journeyeurs, 223, 233, 239
Jubé, Jacques, xliv n35, l
Judica me, xxx
    never said before the altar, 137, 224, 228
    not said, 224, 228
    said before the altar, 121, 162, 179, 301
    said in the sacristy, 120–121, 148
Jurieu, Pierre, xl
jus pastus, 221

kisses
    after the *Confiteor*, 130, 204
    a seat, 19, 84, 151, 223, 272
    by the bishop of public penitents, 236
    of peace at Mass, xxxi, xlviii, 17–18, 45, 55, 109, 144, 164, 175, 208, 256
    of the paten, 89, 110, 175, 179–80, 254
    of the pax-brede, xlviii, 45, 89, 254n162, 256
    on the shoulder, xxx, 46–47, 208
    passed to all altar ministers and servers, or to the whole choir, 45, 89, 109
    the baptismal font, 190
    the ground, 19, 137, 273
Kyrie eleison
    at Easter Vespers, 114, 128
    pronunciation, 231
    troped at Mass, 17, 121, 229
    troped at Tenebrae, 70, 152
    why ninefold at Mass, 22
Kyriela, 158

Lady Chapel, 16, 124, 193, 265, 282
Lamentations, 48
Lanfranc, statutes of, 111, 228, 271, 273
Languet de Gergy, Jean-Joseph, xxvii
La Poype de Vertrieu, Jean-Claude de, xl, 51n69
last Gospel, xlviii, 46, 69, 89, 116, 132, 148, 209, 224
Laudes Crucis attollamus, 138
Laudes regiae, 18, 130, 140, 151, 229
Laus perennis, 100, 134, 138, 191
lavatory stones, 46, 111–12, 262, 312
Le Brun, Pierre, xxvii–xxviii, xxxii
Le Cerf, Emmanuel, 173

Lent
    beginning on the Monday after Quinquagesima, 29
    customs that begin on the first Monday of, 19, 50–51, 85, 142, 151, 181, 272
    Preface *per annum* on Lenten Sundays, xlix, 116, 125, 144, 186, 223
    See also under ashes, Ash Wednesday, bare feet, eggs, fasting, milkmeats, stations, veiling, Vespers
Leonianus, St., 31
Le Prévost, Jean, xxxviii 260
Le Tellier, Charles-Maurice, 188
Letourneux, Nicolas, xvi, xxviii n42, xxxix, l, liii, 187n35
Levi, Marguerite de, 173
Liber pontificalis, 356–57, 362
Libera nos (embolism), 44, 117, 125, 129, 146, 148, 255, 275
libraries
    of Émery Bigot, xxxviii, 217n82
    of Notre-Dame-de-Bonne-Nouvelle (Orléans), 158
    of Rouen, xxxviii, 194
    of the Collège de Navarre, 187
    of the Sorbonne, 188
    of St-Gatien (Tours), 90
    of Ste-Geneviève, 188
    of St-Germain-des-Prés, 186
    of St-Ouen, 265
    of St-Victor (Paris), 187
    of Vaux-de-Cernay, 170
Lisieux, 221, 241, 252, 281
Liturgical Movement, xxi–xxii, xlv, l–lii, 362
London, Council of, 127
Louis XI, 91, 140, 160
Louis XII, 44n42, 88, 190, 195
Louis XIV, xxxvi, 227, 246, 331

Mabillon, Jean, xxv, xxxvi, liii, 87n1, 186n32, 189n41, 197n21
maître de grammaire (schoolmaster), 94, 98, 136, 150
majestas, 166
Mamertus, St., 28n78, 31, 136n9, 145
Mangeant, Luc-Urbain, xvi
maniples
    always used when wearing an alb, 69
    origin, xlvii, 48, 111, 196, 306
    worn by choirboys, xxx, 110–11
    worn by nuns, xxx, 59, 171, 325

marantiae, 204
mariliers or *marguiliers*, 101, 135
Mark, feast of St., 28, 52, 60, 75, 78n44, 85, 98, 138, 154, 218–19
Martène, Edmond, xxxvi, 90n7, 97n29, 110n2, 162n2, 186n32
Martin IV, 259
Martin of Tours, St.
  altar and cave of, 86, 97
  feasts of, 98, 100
  mentioned in the Canon, 93
  tomb of, xxx, 90–91, 94–95, 98–99, 101
martyrology
  read at the Chapter Office, 204
  read solemnly on the vigil of Christmas, 269
Mass
  dry, xxxi–xxxii, 4, 58, 128, 238, 241
  ex praesanctificatis (*see under* Good Friday)
  morrow, 62, 97n31, 207, 211, 218, 271
  nuptial, 117, 186, 285
Matilda, Queen, 11
matricule, 248
Maturus, St., 83
Maultrot, Gabriel-Nicolas, 353
Maundy, 21, 72, 96, 130, 152–53, 169, 215, 272
Maur, Congregation of St-, xxv, xxvii, 186n32, 190, 266
Maurice, St., feast of, 14n29, 15, 29, 72
Maurilius of Angers, St., 62, 72
Maurilius of Rouen, St., 197–98, 260
Mellonius, St., 227, 260, 283
Michael, feast of St., 38, 99
Micrologus, 49n57, 206, 253
Milan, 26, 40, 44, 49–50, 56, 92, 107, 118–19, 148, 157, 161, 169, 215
milkmeats in Lent and Advent, xlvi, 124, 263–64
Minims, 54, 246
mitella or *mitelle*, 65, 74
mitered canons, xxx, 3, 13, 17, 25, 36, 39–41, 48, 108–109, 231
Monegundis, St., 98
Montiou, Bernard de, 38
montjoies, 190, 335
musiques (musicians' choirs), 39, 64, 70n27, 97, 99, 108, 242, 282, 284, 350

Nantes, Edict of, xvii, xxi, xxvi, xxxvi
Nîmes, Synod of, 127

nocturns originally said separately, xlvii, 13, 94
Norbertines. *See* Premonstratensians

O antiphons. *See under* antiphons
oaths, 149, 192, 243–44
  of abbots and abbesses, 4, 145, 221–22, 281
  of bishops, 4, 35n12, 125, 130, 220–21, 248
  of canons, 166–67, 182, 349
  of cantors, 142
  of novices, 268
obedientiae, 53
obelisks, 32
obits, 10, 138, 144, 248, 258–59, 280, 346
Odo or Eudes of Sully, 185
offertorium (chalice veil), 170
offertory processions (*offrandes*), lii n47, 48, 68, 99, 101, 114, 124, 138, 157, 161, 189, 243, 251, 254n162, 259, 278–80, 319, 340
Offertory verses, 18, 27, 43, 130, 150, 205–6
Office of Our Lady, 345
Office of the Dead, 19, 181n8, 214, 222, 225, 258, 267, 280, 345
Office of the Sepulcher, 27, 75, 153, 160, 217
O lux beata Trinitas, 143
O Noël, 69
onzaine, 134
orarium, 71, 181, 222
Ordines Romani, xxx, xxxiii n54, 23–24, 36n13, 69n22, 172n8, 206–207, 232, 240, 251, 277–78
organs, 39, 65n13, 67–68, 75, 99, 107–108, 121, 242, 266
Oriflamme, 190
O salutaris Hostia, 44, 88, 106–107, 168, 244

Palaiseau (Île-de-France), 58
Pardaillan de Gondrin, Louis-Henri de, 123
Parlement, 220, 258n170
  of Burgundy, 114
  of Paris, 53n76, 78n44, 190, 349
  of Rouen, 192–93, 200, 242–43, 283
Pascal, Blaise, 188
Paschal table, xlii, 85, 128, 225–28, 248
Passion (liturgical reading), 21, 48, 51, 73, 106n3, 151, 169, 215, 223, 284
pastourelle, 57, 58n87, 70, 158
Pater and *Credo* before an Office, 92, 203
Pau (Béarn), 261
Paulinus of Nola, St., xvi, 24, 79, 189, 193, 194, 264, 284n231, 287

paupers
   buried in the cathedral cloister, 29
   kiss baptismal font, 190
   of St. Martin, 91
   See also Maundy
pax-bredes, xlviii, 45, 62, 89, 137, 144, 254n162, 256
Perpetuus of Tours, St., 80, 90
Per quem haec omnia, 20, 29, 99, 117, 129, 137, 147–48, 154, 160, 207
per rotulos, 18, 42, 205
personnats, 52, 139
Peter de Honestis, Ven., 286
Peter of Blois, 260
Philip II, duke of Orléans, xvi, xliii
pietatis tuae more or *rore*, 39, 145
Pistoia, Synod of, xxi–xxii, xxxvi, li–lii
Pius VII, xxii
Pius X, St., xxiii n29
Pontius Pilate, 7, 291
potus caritatis, xlix, 20, 274
praegustatio, 186
Pragmatic Sanction of Bourges, 349
prayers at the foot of the altar. See *Confiteor* and *Judica me*
prebends, 46n49, 166, 259, 272, 349, 351–52
Prémery, Charles Fontaine des Montées de, xli
Premonstratensians, 58, 168n8, 231
prêtres habitués, 257, 280, 350
priestly versicles, 16, 124
procession. *See* offertory procession *and under* aspersion, Corpus Christi, Rogations
prône, 180, 245, 264, 284
Proses, 28–29, 36, 42, 57–58, 97, 138, 154, 231
   at Matins, 65, 143
prostrations, xlix, 70–71, 142, 151, 164, 168n10, 237, 249
   prostratio super formas, 70n29, 237, 338
Prothèse, la, 110
Prousteau, Guillaume, 158
psallettes (music school), 64n11, 350
psalteurs, 64n9, 65, 67, 69
public penance, xlvi, 4, 168, 185n29, 233–36
   expulsion, xlvi, 51, 212, 236
   reconciliation, xlvi, 20, 236, 248
Purification of Our Lady, feast of the, 28, 60, 89, 85, 131, 136, 154, 211, 222, 246, 271

Quem creditis, 26
Quem quaeritis, xlvii, 25, 67n17, 74–75
Quicumque, 119
Quillebeuf (Normandy), 113
Quoniam in aeternum misericordia ejus
   not repeated in psalm 135, 13, 93, 126, 142

Racine, Jean, xv
râtelier, 18, 34, 36, 41–43, 47, 134, 297, 358
Recollects, 246
reconciliation of penitents. *See* public penance
recordations, 12
Remigius, St., 46, 177, 260
retables, xxi, xlv, 9, 35, 62, 77, 87, 95, 107–108, 110, 113–15, 118, 159–61, 165–66, 186, 199, 207, 213, 278, 358, 360n7
Reymond, Henri, 353
Richard II of England, 193
Richerism, 353
riddel curtains or posts, xix, xxx, 62, 91, 104, 115, 118, 122, 133, 198–99, 255, 265, 280, 317, 359, 365
Rigaud, Odo, 196, 260
Rogations, 8, 26, 28n78, 42n38, 52, 56, 75–76, 116, 128, 131, 144–45, 154, 219, 239–42, 263, 267–77
Rollo of Normandy, 196, 227
Romanus, St., 196, 200, 227, 240, 243, 256, 259–60, 281–82
Romêtang or Romestang (Vienne), 32
Rothrod, 260
rotuli (choir rolls), 42n38
Roussel, Ralph, 195, 260
rubricists, xl, 51, 111, 207, 255
Rule
   of St. Augustine, 268, 279
   of St. Aurelianus, 280
   of St. Benedict, 50, 79n46, 86, 102n2, 103, 175–76, 212, 267
   of Ven. Peter de Honestis, 286

sacrament towers, 133, 359–62
Saint-Cyran, Abbé de (Jean Duvergier de Hauranne), xv n5, 102n1
Salle des Clementines (Vienne), 30
Salve festa dies, 74
Salve Regina, 94, 143, 169
Sanctus, St., 83
Santeuil, Jean-Baptiste, xl–xli, 187
Sarum use, xxiv

Savinianus and Potentianus, Sts., 142
schola cantorum, 114, 251
scrutinies, 3, 20, 29, 213
Sidonius Apollinaris, St. 111
Sigirannus, St., 103
Sixtus IV, 140, 222, 249
slaves or slavery, 4, 11, 79, 133, 139
soc, xxxii, 179, 290, 328
solea, 128
spé, xxxii, 179–80, 328
Speratus, St., 36, 46
stations, xlix, lii, 15–17, 34, 47, 66–68, 77, 94, 238, 244
　at the great rood, 69, 136, 218
　during Easter week, 26, 97–98, 231–32
　during the Sunday procession, 15, 39, 84, 161, 167, 268–69
　Lenten, 19, 70, 138, 145, 151, 212–13, 237, 247, 252
　See also under baptismal fonts
staves and batons, xxx, xlvii 11, 52, 136, 152–53, 169, 196
　of cantors, xxx, xlvii, 25, 42, 65, 67, 74, 89, 94, 115, 120, 169, 191, 196, 248, 251
　used to clear the way, 56, 152, 240–41
Stephen of Tournai, 155
strict enclosure of nuns, 78–79
stripping of the altars, 85, 152, 215, 363
submissa voce, xlviii, 25, 50, 92n12, 130, 152–53, 159
sub silentio, 55, 73, 85
surplices
　books in sleeves, 34, 39
　closed sleeves, 12, 37, 187, 333
　origin, 94, 299
　split trailing sleeves, 63, 299, 324, 329, 331
suspension of the Bl. Sacrament: xxiv, xxix, xlv, 79, 86–87, 91, 104, 114–15, 118, 161, 164–65, 179, 237, 244, 317–18, 322, 358, 361
symmuses or *symmistae*, 37
synthronos, 35

tabernacle, xxix, xlv, 160, 164n1, 237, 273, 278–79, 358, 360–62
tartevelles, 214, 225
Te Deum, 14n29, 16, 20, 28, 50–51, 65, 71, 75, 89, 107, 124, 154, 210, 250
Tenebrae, xlvii, 48, 56, 70, 73, 145
terrea, 142, 151

thrones, episcopal
　in the apse, xlv, 14, 17, 29, 35, 114, 128, 198, 224
　on the east side of the stalls, 12, 34, 109, 118, 199
Tillemont, Louis Sébastien Le Nain de, xl, 80, 142
Tomasi, Giuseppe Maria, xxxvi
tonsure, 12, 19, 306
Tours
　second Council of, 87, 165
　third Council of, 48–49
　twelfth Council of, 74
Transitorium. See Venite populi
Trappists, 113
Trent, Council of, xvii–xxv, xxxv–xxxvi, 70n26, 163, 351–52, 365
Trinitarians, 162
triumphed antiphons. *See under* antiphons
tropes, xlviii, 17, 66n14, 67n17, 70, 121, 152, 228–29, 270

Ulger of Angers, 62–63
Urban IV, 132
Ut queant laxis, 33

Van der Burch, François, xxv
Vatican II, xxi–xxii, li–lii
veiling or veils
　elevation, 136, 165–66
　Lenten, xxix, 116, 151, 223, 271, 278, 280, 283
　marriage, 129
　of dying devout noblewomen, 172–73 191
　of nuns, xlix, 3, 79n45, 86, 113, 279
　of the altar (*see* riddel curtains)
　of the chalice, 46, 88, 170, 206, 209, 253
　of the ciborium, xxix, 357, 359
　of the holy oils, 73, 131, 231
　of the paten, xxxii, 89, 168, 180, 206, 255
　of the pyx, 104, 359, 361
Venite populi, xxxi, 18, 25, 27, 48–49, 55
versicles
　after antiphons at Lauds and the minor hours on certain feasts (*see under* antiphons)
　priestly (*see under* priestly versicle)
Vespers
　at Pentecost, 27, 277 (*see also under* baptismal fonts)
　during Lent, xlvii, 51, 77, 85, 157, 175–76, 189, 211, 271, 278

during the Easter octave, 26, 114, 128, 182, 228, 231 (*see also under* baptismal fonts)
during the Holy Triduum, 20–21, 51, 56, 73, 96, 116, 152–54, 181, 214–17, 224, 273, 275–76
of All Souls, 111, 114, 143
Viaticum, xlvi, 83, 156, 163, 165, 185, 199n30, 209, 278, 360
Victricius, St., 193, 260
Vienne, Council of, 30
vigils
of Assumption, 219, 222, 250
of Christmas, 30, 269
of Epiphany, 142, 262
of Pentecost, xlix, 27, 40, 60, 73, 77, 107, 114, 118, 160, 169, 225, 228
of St. Andrew, 158
of St. John the Baptist, 259

Villette, Claude, xxv
Vivarais, 112

washing
before Mass or entering church, xlv, 32n1, 83–84, 160, 210, 261, 264–65, 270
bodies for burial, xlvii, 4, 46, 101, 111–12, 156, 262
hands during the Preface, 128
of the altars and church on Maundy Thursday or Good Friday, 72, 96, 153, 215, 273
of the crucifix on Good Friday, 216
See also Maundy
Wenilo, St., 260
Willa, 31
William Longsword, 196
William of Vienne, 115

LITURGICAL BOOKS

BREVIARIES
Avranches (1592), 218
Chartres (1634), 126
*Chartres (1781), 346–47
Clermont (?), 58
Cluny (1686), xxxix, 189
Dominican ("old"), 231
Lyon (1693), 50, 76n42
Martin of Tours, St- (1635), xxii, 92
*Nevers (1727), xxi, xli
Orléans (13th cent.), 142–44
Orléans (1513), 143
Orléans (1542), 142–43, 183n19
Orléans (1573), 142
Orléans (1693), xxi, xli, 142–43, 183
*Paris (1680), xxxix, 76n42, 181n8
*Paris (1738), xxxiv
Rome (1568), xviii, xxxix, 126, 222
Rouen (1491), 231–32
Rouen (1578), 218, 231–32
Sens (1702), 119n4
Vienne (1678), 12

CEREMONIALS
Martin of Tours, St- (1393), 92
*Paris (1662), 15n30, 56n80
Paris (1703), xliii, 57, 327
*Rome (1600), xviii, 186n31
Vanne, Congregation of St- (1695), 146–47

CUSTOMARIES
Cîteaux, *Liber usuum* (12th cent.), 119, 170, 228
Cluny (1079–1082), 80, 146, 228
Fontevraud (?), 210
St-Benigne ("old"), 110

EPISTLE BOOKS
Croix, Ste-, Orléans (11th cent.), 145
Croix, Ste-, Orléans (14th cent.), 145
Maurice, St-, Angers (undated), 61

GOSPEL BOOKS
St-Maurice, Angers (undated), 62

GRADUALS
*Paris (1662), 44n42
*Rouen (13th cent.), 242n143

MISSALS
Amiens (1607), 147
Angers (15th cent.), 71
*Angers (1488), 71n31
*Angers (1489), 68n19
*Angers (1717), 68n18
Autun (1530), 129
*Auxerre (14th cent.), 117n7
*Auxerre (ca. 1250), 117n7
Auxerre (14th cent.), 117–18, 129, 146
*Besançon (1589), 114n1
Béziers ("old"), 129
Carmelite (1574), 224
Cistercian (16th cent.), 170
*Cluny (1717), 189n39
*Cluny (1733), 110n2
England and Scotland (undated), 49, 207–208
*Laon (1702), 40n34
Lyon (1530), 39, 49, 52, 129, 147, 207–208
Martin of Tours, St- (1157)
*Meaux (1709), xx, xliv n35, 40n34
Milan (1669), 49
Moissac ("old"), 147
Montmajour ("manuscript"), 147
Narbonne ("old"), 129
Orléans (1504), 40, 43, 129, 147–49, 207
Orléans (1696), 147
Paris (1557), 40, 185
Paris (1685), 180
*Paris (1736), xxxiv
Rome (1570), xviii, 60, 93, 207, 218
Rouen (1516), 40, 207
Rouen (1576), 224
Rouen (1585), 223, 226n111
Rouen (1604), 224
*Rouen (1668), 226n111
St-Germain-des-Prés (9th cent.), 186
St-Martin of Tours (1157), 93
Toul (1686), 147
*Troyes (1736), xx, 36n13
Vaux-de-Cernay (ca. 1200), 170

Vaux-de-Cernay (ca. 1280), 170
Vienne (1519), 21–22, 40, 129, 147, 207
*Vienne (1784), 16n36

ORDINARIES

Aignan of Orléans, St- (13th cent.), 146, 149–156
Bayeux ("old"), 135
Carmelite (14th cent.), 135, 224, 231, 281n229
Carmelite (16th cent.), 271
Fontevraud (ca. 1115), 83–86
Martin of Tours, St- (1393), 92–93
Orléans (15th cent.), 144–45
Orléans (16th cent.), 137–38
Paul of Lyon, St- (14th cent.), 45
Rouen (11th cent.), 202–20, 222–25, 232, 272
Rouen (13th cent.), 204
Rouen (16th cent.), 205n54, 237–42
Rouen ("new"), 228
St-Lô of Rouen, St- (14th cent.), 267–77
Vienne (ca. 1240), 8, 11, 14–29
Vienne (1524), 18
Vincent of Metz, St- (undated), 147
Vrain of Jargeau, St- (13th cent.), 146

PONTIFICALS

Arles (undated), 147
Orléans (11th cent.), 145
Orléans (15th cent.), 146
*Rome (1595), xviii
Rouen (11th cent.), 220–21

RITUALS

*Alet (1664), l
*Angers (1676), 81n55
Autun (1593), 129, 163
Béziers (1535), 129
Chartres (1604), 40, 129
*Clermont (1656), 58n92
Euverte, St- (15th cent.), 155–56
Le Mans (1490), 162–64
Limoges (1698), 108
Lyon (1692), 147
Mechlin (1509), 126
Metz (1713), 197
Milan (1687), 40, 129, 148
Orléans (1581), 129, 146–49
Paris (1526), 40, 129
Paris (1697), 185
Reims (1585), 129
Reims (1677), 129, 197, 276n218
*Rome (1614), xviii, xlv–xlvi, 58n92, 163n5
Rouen (1586), 287
Rouen (1640), 199n28, 236, 249n159, 261, 284, 285, 287–88
Sens (1694), 121, 126, 129, 197

CATHEDRALS, CHURCHES, AND MONASTERIES

Agnese, Sant' (Rome), 102
Aignan, St- (Orléans), 140, 149–55
Amand, St- (Rouen), 221, 267, 341
André, St- (Rouen), 279
André-le-Haut, St- (Vienne), 26, 28, 31
André-le-Bas, St- (Vienne), 8, 26, 29
*Aubin, St- (Angers), 76n39
Aydes, Les, 149

Beaugency, 139
Beaumont (Tours), 97–98, 101
Bec, 26, 56, 228, 240–41
Benoît, St- (Fleury). *See* Fleury
Blandine, Ste- (Vienne), 28
*Brieuc, St-, 347–48
Brioude, 58, 109

Candé-le-Vieux, St- (Rouen), 278, 280–81
Carmel of the Place Maubert (Paris), 187
Catherine-du-Mont, Ste- (Rouen), 242, 267
Chaffre, St-, 115
Chapelle, Ste- (Paris), 105, 190
Charterhouse of Dijon, 115
Clément, St- (Tours), 98
Clemente, San (Rome), 114, 357
Cluny, xxix, xxx, xlvii, 48, 59, 79–80, 99n37, 109–113, 126, 132, 173, 191, 209–210, 214n75, 222, 225, 228, 231, 241, 270, 313
Collège de Cluny, church of the (Paris), 13, 188–89
Colombe, Ste- (Vienne), 8, 26
Côme, St- (Tours), 97–98, 101
Cosma e Damiano, Santi (Rome), 189
Crépin, St- (Soissons), 223
Croix, Ste- (Lyon), 46, 48, 56
Croix, Ste- (Orléans), xxxii, xxxiii, 133–49, 150n60, 157
Croix, Ste- (Poitiers), xxx, 59
Croix-de-la-Bretonnerie, Ste- (Paris), 58
Cyr, St- (Nevers), 107–108
Cyran-en-Brenne, St-, xv n5, xxix, xliv, xlix, 102–104, 211
Denis, St- (Angers), 76n39

Denis, St- (Rouen), 240
Denis, St- (St-Denis-en-France), xxxi, 110, 190–91, 196, 209, 336
Denis-de-la-Chartre, St- (Paris), 189
Deux-Amants, 38, 191, 325
Dominican church of Le Mans (Église des Jacobins), 132, 264

Eloi, St- (Rouen), 241, 278
Étienne, St- (Auxerre), 115–18
Étienne, St- (Bourges), xxvi n37, 104–107, 207
Étienne, St- (Dijon), 114–15, 186
Étienne, St- (Lyon), 31, 46, 109
Étienne, St- (Meaux), 132
Étienne, St- (Sens), xxxii, 118–27
Étienne, St- (Toul), xxxii, 148
Étienne-des-Grès, St- (Paris), 160
Étienne-des-Tonneliers, St- (Rouen), 224, 279–80, 281, 282
Étienne-du-Mont (Paris), 188
Étienne-la-Grand'Église, St- (Rouen), 199, 214, 263
Euverte, St- (Orléans), 139, 140, 155–56

Fécamp, 266
Fleury, 139, 149, 157
*Foigny, 131n4
Fontevraud, 83–86, 210
Franciscan church of Étampes (Église des Cordeliers), 132, 264

Gatien, St- (Tours), 87–90, 95n18, 147n52
Geneviève, Ste- (Paris), 188, 329
Georges, St- (Rouen), 278
Germain-des-Prés, St- (Paris), xxv, 186–87, 188, 332
Gervais, St- (Paris), 118,
Gervais, St- (Rouen), 241, 283
Godard, St- (Rouen), 238, 282–83

Hagia Sophia (Constantinople), 160
Herbland, St- (Rouen), 114, 247, 284
Hilaire, St- (Poitiers), 59
Hilaire, St- (Tours), 98

Cathedrals, Churches, and Monasteries 395

Irenée, St- (Lyon), 54

Jean, St- (Lyon), xxx, xxxii, xxxiii, 18n42, 31, 32–54, 55–56, 63, 84, 109, 207–208, 213, 293–98, 300–302
Jean-le-Grand, St- (Besançon), 113–14
Julien, St- (Angers), 76n39, 79–80, 283
Julien, St- (Le Mans), 161–64, 321
Julien, St- (Rouen), 267
Julien, St- (Tours), 99, 100n38, 101
Just, St- (Lyon), 39n27, 45n46, 46, 54

Lamballe, 348
Laurent, St- (Lyon), 56–57
Laurent, St- (Rouen), 238, 283
Lazare, St- (Avallon), 124–25, 185
Liperche, St- (Chartres), 79
Lô, St- (Rouen), 84, 240, 242, 246, 267–77, 342

Maclou, St- (Rouen), 135, 240, 281–82
Madeleine, La (Rouen), 240, 246
*Mainbœuf, St- (Angers), 76n39
*Marie, Ste- (Bayonne), 347
Marmoutier, xxix, 86, 97–98, 101, 191, 311
*Martin, St- (Angers), 76n39
Martin, St- (near Sens), 124
Martin, St- (Tours), 34n7, 90–101, 126, 128, 143n33, 147, 149, 348
Martin-des-Champs, St- (Paris), 189, 241
Maubuisson, 172, 191
Maur-des-Fossés, St- 79, 132
Maurice, St- (Angers), xxxiii, 61–77, 81, 303
Maurice, St- (Vienne), xxxi, xxxiii, 8–30, 31, 109
Maurille, St- (Angers), 76n39, 80–81
Mesmin, St-, 134, 160, 320
Meung, 134
Michel, St- (Dijon), 114–15
Michel, St- (Laon), 130
Michel, St- (Orléans), 158
Micy. See Mesmin, St-

Nicaise, St- (Rouen), 242
Nicolas, St- (Angers), 77
Nicolas, St- (Nantes), 60
Nizier, St- (Lyon), 47
Notre-Dame (Chartres), xxxii, 165–69
Notre-Dame (Cléry), 160
Notre-Dame (Laon), 129–32
Notre-Dame (Le Ronceray). See Ronceray, Le

Notre-Dame (Paris), xxxii, 88, 178–86, 289, 327–28, 331, 350
Notre-Dame (Port-Royal). See Port-Royal-des-Champs
Notre-Dame (Reims), xxxii, 128–29
Notre-Dame (Rodez), 109
Notre-Dame (Rouen), 193–265
Notre-Dame-de-Bonne-Nouvelle (Orléans), 158
Notre-Dame-de-la-Ronde (Rouen), 277–78, 281
*Notre-Dame-des-Vignes (Soissons), 347
Notre-Dame-la-Royale. See Maubuisson
Notre-Dame-de-la-Vie (Vienne), 8
Notre-Dame-du-Puy (Le Puy-en-Velay), xxx, 109, 115

Ouen, St- (Rouen), 219, 228, 240–41, 246, 265–67
Ouvrouer-les-Champs (Orléans), 157

Paul, St- (Lyon), 45–46, 55–56
*Paul, St- (Marseille), 62n4
Paul, St- (Sens), 79
Peter, St. (Rome), 186
Pierre, St- (Angers), 76n39, 78n44, 81
Pierre, St- (Lyon), 55
Pierre, St- (Mâcon), 109
Pierre, St- (Nantes), 60
Pierre, St- (Poitiers), 59
Pierre, St- (Troyes), xxxiii, 21n49, 22, 36n13, 123
Pierre, St- (Vienne), 19–20, 26, 28–31, 109, 114
Pierre-aux-Bœufs, St-. See Aignan, St-
Pierre-du-Chardonnet, St- (Tours), 96
Pierre-en-Pont, St- (Orléans), 145, 155–57
Pierre-en-Sentelée, St- (Orléans), 157
Pierre-Lentin, St- (Orléans), 137, 156–57
Pierre-le-Vieux, St- (Cluny), 109, 111
Pierre-le-Vif, St- (Sens), 127
Pierre-Puellier, St- (Orléans), 98, 100n38, 101, 145, 155–57
Port-Royal-des-Champs, xv, xvi, xxxvi, xxxix–xliv, li, liii, 80n54, 171–78, 187n35, 324

Quentin, St- (St-Quentin), 92

Remi, St- (Laon), 130
Ronceray, Le (Angers), 75, 77–79, 307

Saëns, St-, 266
Samson, St- (Orléans), 134
Sauveur, St- (Rouen), 228, 283–84
Savigny, 59
Seine, St- (Dijon), 115
Seine, St- (Huisseau), 161
Sépulcre (Paris), 189
Sévère, St- (Vienne), 7–8, 26, 28–29
Solenne, St- (Blois), xxxii, 161, 207
Sorbonne, the (Paris), 188

Trappe, La, 112, 164–65, 322

Val-de-Grâce (Paris), 188

Vaux-de-Cernay, 170
Venant, St- (Tours), 98, 100n38, 101
Victor, St- (Orléans), 157
Victor, St- (Paris), xl, 155n71, 187, 333
Vigor, St- (Rouen), 240
Vincent, St- (Chalon-sur-Saône), 113–14, 207
Vincent, St- (Mâcon), 108–109, 207
Vincent, St- (Metz), 147
Vincent, St- (Rouen), 279, 281
Vivien, St- (Rouen), 135, 282
Voisins, 161
Vrain, St- (Jargeau), 146, 158–60
Vulfran, St- (Abbeville), 24, 228

Made in United States
Cleveland, OH
04 August 2025